The Making of
Psychological
Anthropology

The Making of

edited by George D. Spindler

Contributions by
John and Beatrice Whiting
Victor Barnouw
Margaret Mead
Francis L. K. Hsu
Louise Spindler
Anthony F. C. Wallace
George DeVos
Weston La Barre
John J. Honigmann
Melford E. Spiro

Psychological Anthropology

George Devereux
Theodore Schwartz
Robert B. Edgerton
Erika Bourguignon
Theodore D. Graves
Nancy B. Graves
Victor Turner
Douglass Price-Williams
Michael Cole

UNIVERSITY OF CALIFORNIA PRESS
BERKELEY   LOS ANGELES   LONDON

This volume is dedicated to
A. Irving ("Pete") Hallowell,
whose influence on the making
of psychological anthropology
is pervasive and profound, and to
Maude Hallowell,
without whom this influence
would have been much diminished.

University of California Press, Berkeley and Los Angeles, California
University of California Press, Ltd., London, England
Copyright © 1978 by The Regents of the University of California
ISBN 0-520-03320-5
Library of Congress Catalog Card Number: 76-24597
Printed in the United States of America

1 2 3 4 5 6 7 8 9 0

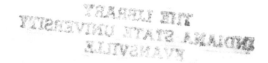

Contents

Preface

This volume includes critical reviews of their own work by twenty of the people who have contributed significantly to the development of that subdiscipline known today as psychological anthropology. These reviews, in their totality, interact with nearly every currently important part of psychological anthropology. Some authors have emphasized selected themes of their work, casting back into their past and bringing the evolutionary process up to date. A few have elected to discuss a problem that has recently emerged in their studies, but that has roots in the past. Some focus almost entirely upon current work. Whatever strategies are employed, these scrutinies of one's work are particularly telling because they are *scrutinies by the worker himself or herself* with the virtues of hindsight. This volume provides an inside view of the making of psychological anthropology.

The volume was conceived after Louise Spindler reviewed her and George Spindler's work on the psychology of cultural change for the Ninth International Congress of Anthropological and Ethnological Sciences held in 1973.* Several colleagues read it and talked about it with her. It suddenly seemed quite clear others should do the same thing. *The Making of Psychological Anthropology* was underway. The idea was circulated to colleagues in a series of memos and letters. Their responses were enthusiastic and many discussions followed. The initial focus was upon veterans who had labored for several decades in this particular vineyard. Many of them were founders of the culture and personality movement as well as contributors to psychological anthropology. Certain relative newcomers were invited to contribute so that the profile of the field could be brought into focus in all of its dimensions. A few potential contributors declined the invitation to participate due to serious illness or preoccupation with ongoing work. Not everyone is represented who should be, of course. There are more makers than twenty and some very significant ones.

The Making of Psychological Anthropology is therefore both a historical document and a rather special kind of contribution to the sociology of knowledge. Self-analysis always reveals more than the

*Published in *Psychological Anthropology,* edited by Thomas R. Williams, Mouton & Co., The Hague & Paris, 1975, and substantially revised for this volume.

analyst knows. This volume is also a statement of current concerns. All the contributors are still very active in the field; some have the larger part of their careers before them. A book of this kind is not only a report of the evolution of a field of knowledge and a statement of its present condition; it helps determine the future course of its development. Many different strands are being woven together—from the older culture and personality, from cognitive psychology, psychoanalysis, behaviorism, ethnoscience, biology, and symbolic anthropology. It is not surprising it lacks sharp boundaries and profiles. This book cannot, therefore, furnish final judgments. It can make important contributions to character definition. It is a substantial sample of what is going on in minds that have created theories, devised methods, produced descriptions and interpretations of ways of life now gone or much changed, all of which are part of the foundations of an emerging field as well as its history. It is worthy of serious study by anyone who is interested in culture and personality, psychological anthropology, cross-cultural psychology, social psychiatry, social psychology, or allied fields. It is not intended as a text for an introductory course in culture and personality, though students in such a course can read most of the chapters with profit.

George Spindler claims the editorship of this volume, though it might well carry the joint editorship of George and Louise, for the latter contributed to the development of it from the very start. As the book took shape it seemed more efficient for one to take primary responsibility for the editorial work and the other to do the review and critique of their contributions to the field, as Louise Spindler has done in her chapter.

As editor I want to extend my heartfelt gratitude to all of the contributors to this book. They have been extraordinarily diligent, resourceful, and patient. Many colleagues contributed heavily to the evolution of this project and they shall go unnamed but for Thomas R. Williams, Paul Bohannan, Pertti Pelto, Henry Selby, Lois Floyd, Bertha Quintana and David P. Boynton, who read the manuscript and made cogent suggestions for its improvement. We all owe Julia Kringel, Lillian Shapro, Marion Wachtel, Wini McCaffrey and Nancy Ortiz special thanks for help on preparation of the manuscript and circulation of memos and letters and related support activities.

The chapters in this book were written by people who are enthusiastic about their work and its potential for a better understanding of human affairs. It is all too easy to become jaded with the practical exigencies of funding, administration, and academic politics and the smallness and myopia endemic in academia, and to become disillusioned with our discipline in the modern context of rejection and criticism that so often appear to be more politically than substantively motivated. This book renews one's idealism. The high level of personal commitment as well as the honest scholarship of the contributors are apparent to anyone who cares to read carefully. The problems dealt with in these chapters are variegated, real, and exciting, and they are treated with enthusiasm. As teacher as well as researcher and editor I am motivated to share the experience of this volume with others.

GEORGE D. SPINDLER

Stanford University
February 28, 1977

The Editor

GEORGE DEARBORN SPINDLER, born in Wisconsin in 1920, is Professor of Anthropology and Education at Stanford University. His publications range over cultural transmission and cultural change in United States and German communities and schools as well as in the North American Indian communities in which he and Louise Spindler have studied, the psychology of acculturation and urbanization, changing American character and values, formal organizations including school systems and the military, and research methods. With Louise Spindler he is editor of four series published by Holt, Rinehart and Winston, including *Case Studies in Cultural Anthropology, Case Studies in Education and Culture, Studies in Anthropological Method,* and *Basic Anthropology Units.* He and L. Spindler served as editors of the *American Anthropologist* (1962–1966). He was Executive Head of the Department of Anthropology at Stanford during the same period. He says of himself:

My remote intellectual ancestors are Max Weber, Vincento Pareto, William James, Freud, Franz Boas, Edward Sapir, and less so Karl Marx. My more immediate ancestors are talented teachers and vigorous intellectuals like Howard Becker, Hans Gerth, C. W. M. Hart, and Scudder Mekeel at Wisconsin, where I did three years of graduate work after World War II; and Walter Goldschmidt, Philip Selznick, and Bruno Klopfer, at U.C.L.A., where I acquired the Ph.D. in 1952 in anthropology, sociology, and psychology. I have learned much through personal contact with senior colleagues like Alfred Kroeber, A. Irving Hallowell, Margaret Mead, and Cora DuBois. Some of my most influential teachers have been people like Napone Perrote, Munroe and Jennie Wesoe, Johnson Awanahopy and Helen Wynoss among the Menomini, Ben Calf Robe, Percy Two-Gun, Allan and Gerald Tailfeathers among the Blood, and Herr Burgemeister Hermann Plessing, Herr Oberlehrer Fritz Hochmut, Frau Oberlehrerin Sophie Weissharr, and many others in Burgbach and Schönhausen, Germany. My most influential teacher was my father, Frank Nicholas Spindler, a student of William James.

I share with many of the authors of this volume the "somewhat inchoate" model to which Melford Spiro refers in his chapter, compounded out of neo-Freudianism, Gestalt and field theory, behaviorism, learning theory, and structural-functionalism. I have moved somewhat toward symbolic interaction-ism and cognitive models recently, but I am grateful for the flexibility the "inchoate" model has given me. The sociological influence has also been very strong in my case, and helped early to rescue me from accepting whole-heartedly a culturally over-deterministic model. Contact with Norman Cam-eron at Wisconsin, and a practicum in social psychiatry at Madison General Hospital had a profound influence on me as well and convinced me that one of the main roots of psychological theory must be clinical. Three semesters with Bruno Klopfer's projective techniques seminar at U.C.L.A. reinforced this conviction.

I have provided this much detail, and have encouraged others contribut-ing to this volume to do the same, because I feel that such information helps to put one's work and one's biases in useful perspective.

GEORGE D. SPINDLER

General Introduction

The eighteen chapters contained in this volume represent current psychological anthropology in light of its recent past and in anticipation of its future. They were written in response to the editor's invitation to review and critique one's own work in the context of current and recent concerns in psychologized anthropology.* There were diverse responses to this request. The authors of these chapters are not only diversified in experience and training, but are highly individualistic as persons. They represent a subdiscipline that has been growing in many directions since its beginnings as "culture and personality" in the 1930s. It is apparent that diversity of formulations, canons of credibility, and interests should be a keynote of this volume.

At the same time there is unity, though the specific dimensions of this unity do not cut equally across all eighteen chapters. There is a search for universal processes of cognition, motivation, perception, and adaptation—for the key features of human nature. There is fatigue with an over-deterministic model of culture and its influence on personality. There are struggles with emic versus etic strategies, sometimes explicit, more often implicit. There is a growing concern with individuation and diversity and less with norms and modalities. There is a movement away from tests and experiments as sources of credible data, but the movement is not toward an unbridled humanism. Rather it is toward a mix of techniques and strategies employing virtually every style of elicitation and observation. There is strong interest in the accurate recording of relevant or potentially relevant data, oriented, but not confined by explicit theoretical models. There is no tendency to throw out insight and little tendency to overembrace quantitative methods and controls. Rather, the contributions that a wide variety of research stances can make are acknowledged.

The age range of the contributors is from the thirties to the seventies. The period of professional activity ranges from a little over a decade to half a century. The authors included in Part I are veterans who have

---

*The term "psychologized anthropology" is used to cover both the former culture and personality and present psychological anthropology where it is relevant to conceive of these two intergraded areas as engaged with some of the same problems and when their continuity is more important to the point than their difference.

1

worked in various subfields of psychological anthropology for three decades or more—a combined total of 390 years. If there is a conceptual structure common to them, it is one derived from neo-Freudianism, Gestalt, and social learning theory and given special impetus by the Kardiner-Linton seminars at Columbia University in the 1930s. Though the individuals so influenced have gone far beyond this original model the influence of the earlier model is acknowledged and must be seen as a major part of the evolution of the field.

The authors included in Part II have contributed to psychological anthropology for a shorter time period. Most have the greater part of their active careers before them. Some relative veterans are included among them because their topics—symbolic anthropology, altered states of consciousness and cognitive anthropology—have only recently emerged as primary concerns of psychological anthropology. The diversity characteristic of the field is apparent in Part II. The feature held in common is that these workers have turned to relatively more limited definitions of problems. Global constructs like ''culture'' and ''personality'' are hardly present.

Most of the contributors to this volume are anthropologists who have done field research requiring prolonged residence in a non-Western community of some sort. Even though three of the contributors received their Ph.D.s in psychology they too have experienced this *sine qua non* of the anthropologist—prolonged, intimate field work in a community with a human group whose culture is very different from one's own. No one can live as an observing, interacting, questioning stranger in another culture for a substantial period of time without profound changes in personal outlook and intellectual strategy. These influences give the chapters of this book a certain unity of character that transcends differences in problem, methodology, or theory.

Though all of the chapters in this book are clearly written, they have complex ideas to communicate. The authors are often dealing with concepts, systems of thought, and with evidence, that are currently evolving very rapidly. This book requires, and is worthy of, serious study. It is a statement of the ongoing, creative process of development that has characterized the field, both in its early conception as culture and personality and in its recent development as psychological anthropology. It is not a historical statement abstracted from personal experiences and personalities. It is an intensely personal book. It is full of self-revelation. The authors speak of *themselves,* of *their* work. Some, of course, reveal themselves more than others.

The psychologizing of anthropology has suffered many vicissitudes. It began with a great flourish in the late 1930s, prospered through the 1940s, and came under severe fire by the 1950s. It was declared dead during the 1960s. Anthropologists, having only recently stabilized some crucial thinking about culture and social structure, were threatened by the reductionism to a psychological level that was implicit in personality and culture formulations. It was also true that some of the issues addressed were unresolvable using the tools on hand at the time. Ambiguity, redundancy, seemingly atrocious hypotheses, circularity of argument and evidence, and grand theories, were all present at times as this work proceeded. And the acceptance of a Freudian or neo-Freudian model seemed personally unforgiveable to many anthropologists. Some of the rejection of early culture and personality work, as well as today's psychoanalytically oriented interpretations seem to have more than pure intellectual motivation. For these and other reasons a whole generation of young anthropologists has come to think of "culture and personality" as a weak sister in the siblingship of anthropology, with a pervasive prejudice against and various misconceptions of its aims and methods. Nevertheless, culture and personality workers had addressed themselves to problems that were real and persist, often rephrased, into the present. And the productivity of a psychologized anthropology never abated, despite premature obituaries.

New problems, definitions of problems, and approaches to them have appeared, representing significant departures from established ones, and yet there is much continuity. The contributors to Parts I and II overlap in their current interests, concepts and methods. Modern psychological anthropology incorporates some of the strategies of the older culture and personality but has many dimensions, focii, strategies, and concerns that were not clearly anticipated in the older frame of reference. This volume encompasses this whole panorama.

It seems appropriate to refer to the present developments in psychological anthropology as a kind of revitalization. This volume ties the revitalization and its antecedents together. It is scarcely a neat joining, but rather a complex of intellectual knots of various kinds.

This is not an easy book to read, but it is rewarding to study. Some chapters will require several readings, depending upon the sophistication of the reader in the matters taken up, but none of them is opaque. All of them can be understood, with profit, by any literate reader, and some are gems of clarity. As an aid to study they have been arranged in an order beginning with chapters by veteran contributors reporting well-known projects and studies, proceeds through chapters that are more querulous than reportorial, and ends with chapters on topics that are only recently of direct concern to psychological anthropology. This arrangement is most decisively reflected in the division into two parts, each with its separate introduction. There is no implication of greater or less difficulty, worth, or relevance in this ordering. Rather its framework is one of unfolding comprehension, a kind of sociology of knowledge. As a further aid to study, the editor has described certain salient features of each chapter to help focus the reader's attention on critical issues and contributions and has provided biographical information about each author to aid in understanding the relation between the person and the contribution. The introductions to Parts I and II are intended to provide a degree of unity to the volume and to engage with broad background problems and developments extending beyond the individual papers.

Part I

John and Beatrice Whiting
Victor Barnouw
Margaret Mead
Francis L. K. Hsu
Louise S. Spindler
Anthony F. C. Wallace
George DeVos
Weston La Barre
John J. Honigmann
Melford E. Spiro
George Devereux

Introduction to Part I

GEORGE SPINDLER

DISMAL DIAGNOSES AND OBITUARIES

In his presidential address to the Royal Anthropological Institute of Great Britain in 1923, C. G. Seligman stated:

Brought up in the main in the Tylorian school of anthropology, having thereafter gained some knowledge of and made use of the historical school of Rivers and of late years watched the development of the functional method, the writer has become convinced that the most fruitful development—perhaps the only process that can bring social anthropology to its rightful status as a branch of science and at the same time give it the full weight in human affairs to which it is entitled—is the increased elucidation in the field and integration into anthropology of psychological knowledge. (Quoted in Hallowell 1953, p. 598)

Seligman's call for the psychologizing of anthropology went largely unheeded by British anthropology. In American anthropology it found a supportive climate. By the mid-thirties the personality and culture movement was well underway in the United States, and it continued in full force until approximately the mid-fifties. By then a critical barrage had been mounted against it that would cause many personality and culture workers to turn to less troublesome problems. Critics pointed to inadequate sampling, lack of controls, outrageous hypotheses, circularity of argument, psychological reductionism, misplaced causation, and inadequate caution in applying psychological interpretations cross-culturally. Many of the strongest attacks were leveled at the national character studies that received so much impetus from the work in psychological warfare during World War II, but they were directed at all parts of the field and affected all of the workers in them. As John Honigman says, in the beginning of his chapter in this volume on the personal approach in culture and personality research:

The loss of confidence in culture and personality resulting from the critical barrage directed against it after its heyday came about simultaneously with the

7

beginning of my professional career. It disturbed me, but I did not attempt much explicit rebuttal of the attacks. Still, the problem was always with me.

By the time the first review in the field appeared, in 1959, in the *Biennial Reviews of Anthropology* edited by Bernard Siegel under the title "Psychocultural Studies," Honigmann, the reviewer, stated that "the area of culture and personality, in America at least, is supposed to be dead" (Honigmann 1959, p. 67). Honigmann himself was skeptical of this diagnosis, and indeed, he reviewed a "plethora of works," 407 to be exact, published between 1955 and 1957. Nevertheless, the fact that he did report this as a widely held opinion in the major review of the field at that time, tells us much about the situation. Three biennial reviews later, Jack Fischer had to cut his long list of relevant works for review by one-half, there were so many (Fischer 1965). And four biennial reviews later, Pertti Pelto noted that "previous studies of psychologically-oriented research have noted the continuing disenchantment with culture and personality studies." (Pelto 1967, p. 141.) But, like Honigmann in 1959, Pelto devoted to the review of the field some fifty pages of text citing 385 references published over a two-year period. In the next Review the editor stated that "we have correspondingly omitted from review some of the more conventional fields (for example, psychological anthropology) that have developed little . . ." (Siegel 1969, p. v). However, in that same year, George DeVos and Arthur Hippler published a massive review of the field in *The Handbook of Social Psychology* (DeVos and Hippler 1969), and Alex Inkeles and Daniel Levinson published a very substantial review of the closely related area "Modal Personality and Sociocultural Systems" (Inkeles and Levinson 1969). Together these two reviews covered over 700 articles and books.

Dismal diagnoses continued to be sounded. In the November 1974 issue of *Reviews in Anthropology,* edited by the Peltos, Pertti Pelto, in reviewing Robert Levine's *Culture, Behavior, and Personality: An Introduction to the Comparative Study of Psycho-Social Adaptation* (1973), said, "Culture and personality study or psychological anthropology as some of us prefer to call it, has been suffering from serious psychiatric breakdown for a long time. . . . In recent years the prognosis has been so bleak that no one even bothered to suggest new courses of therapy . . ." (Pelto 1974, p. 509). I hasten to add that Pelto lauded Levine's book as what the doctor ordered (with some reservations). In the same issue John Bennett ascribes a "death-wish" to cultural anthropology in general and cites as partial support the "discarding of culture and personality as one of the more promising viewpoints permitting engagement with larger and more accessible social systems'' (Bennett 1974, p. 569).

VITAL SIGNS

Despite dismal diagnoses and premature obituaries, psychologized anthropology continued to show positive vital signs. Two heavily revised textbooks appeared in 1972 and 1973 (Hsu 1972; Barnouw 1973), and Robert Levine's text and its accompanying reader appeared also in 1973. The massive volume *Psychological Anthropology,* edited by Thomas R. Williams (1975), includes twentyseven papers from the Ninth International Congress of Anthropological and Ethnological Sciences ranging over an extraordinary wide spectrum—a species-specific framework of man and evolution, projective doll play, dreams, dominance, aggression, native therapy, ritual process and healing, role failure, and many others. This volume also includes a review of the field by John Honigmann (1975). Other recent reviews providing useful coverage in the field in its current dimensions in light of its past include Bourgignon (1973), Malefijt (1974), coverage interspersed in a very substantial review of ethnology by Voget (1975), and the forceful interpretation of developments in culture and personality by Marvin Harris (1968).

Our field also continues to show vitality as a part of the curriculum. As most everyone knows who teaches anthropology in almost any institution of higher learning in North America, courses labeled ''Culture and Personality,'' ''The Individual and Culture,'' or ''Psychological Anthropology'' are very popular with students. Psychologized anthropology has brought home to them many of the basic lessons about cultural differences and commonalities, human nature and thought, identities, values, and ethics that anthropology has the potential to teach.

The contributors to Part I of this volume have survived the vicissitudes of faddism, attack, dismal diagnoses, psychiatric breakdown, and death wishes. All of them have experienced the major phases of the life span of the field. Some of them were there at parturition. All have self doubts. All have been on the defensive and have responded to the threat and to their own defensive feelings. Unlike scores of other workers who left for greener grass and more trouble-free skies, they hung on, doing their work, criticizing themselves and being criticized, improving and changing, adapting to the times and to new criteria of credibility. Their productivity never slackened. They all are prolific writers and all have continued to do field research. If anyone can speak to the hazards and rewards of psychologizing anthropology, they can.

Unless we assume that the critics of psychologized anthropology were simply pervasively hostile (perhaps because their defenses were aroused by some of the implications of psychologized, particularly psychoanalytic interpretations), or that the research in this field was nearly all bad and that its major protagonists (most of whom are represented in this book) were at least careless and at worst stupid, we must look to the circumstances of the emergence of the field, to its challenges to other parts of anthropology, to its boundary definitions and to its strengths and weaknesses in concept and method, for an explanation of the critical barrage mounted against it. We can start with the problem of defining boundaries. What does psychological anthropology include? Or perhaps the right question is: What does it exclude?

WHERE ARE THE BOUNDARIES?

It is difficult to draw boundaries around the territory "psychological anthropology." It is in fact possible that there is no field, or subdiscipline in the usual sense of the word. There is an implicit if not explicit psychological element or process in almost every formulation or treatment of ostensibly social or cultural process. Even most widely accepted definitions of culture are heavily psychological. Tylor's classic definition of culture, "that complex whole which includes knowledge, beliefs . . . and any other capabilities and habits acquired by man as a member of society" (Taylor 1871, p. 1), clearly draws one to psychological processes. In fact, it is a psychological definition of culture. This is apparent in nearly every other well-known definition: Robert Lowie (1937, p. 3), "the sum total of what an individual acquires from his society—those beliefs, customs, artistic norms, food habits, and crafts which come to him not by his own creative activity but as a legacy from the past, conveyed by formal or informal education."; Ralph Linton (1945, p. 32) "the configuration of learned behavior and results of behavior whose component elements are shared and transmitted by the members of a particular society."; Alfred Kroeber (1948b, p. 253), "culture consists of conditioned or learned activities (plus the manufactured results of these) . . ."; Kluckhohn and Kelley (1945, p. 98), "historically derived system of explicit and implicit designs for living, which tends to be shared by all or specially designated members of a group."; and Kroeber and Kluckhohn (1952, p. 181), with a definition resulting from their exhaustive analysis of the culture concept and purported, by them, to represent the concensus of "most social scientists, . . . patterns, explicit and implicit, of and for behavior acquired and transmitted by symbols, constituting the distinctive achievement of human groups, including their embodiments in artifacts; the essential core of culture consists of traditional (i.e. historically derived and selected) ideas and especially their attached values. . . ." There are many other more recent working definitions of culture by prominent contributors such as R. Keesing, Goodenough, and Geertz, who are not psychological anthropologists, that are essentially psychological.

The tendency to psychologize goes well beyond definitions of culture. As Hallowell said (1953, p. 179), "The interest in personality and culture is by no means unique. It represents a more explicit articulation of the kind of psychological problem that is inherent in anthropological data." Marvin Harris has also recognized this explicitly, "The most obvious diagnostic of commonality . . . is the occurrence in the average ethnographic monograph of numerous terms and concepts which are derived from the vernacular of scientific lexicons devoted to expressing the mental and emotional condition of the individual human actors." Further, "psychologizing is a deeply rooted habit among cultural anthropologists" (Harris 1968, pp. 395, 397).

In a comprehensive review of culture change and acculturation literature published in 1963, George and Louise Spindler found that of ninety-four such articles and books published from 1929 to 1952, twenty percent used psychological concepts with explicit citations, twenty-three percent used them without citation, and another thirty percent did not use psychological concepts but should have done so, given the definition of the problem. Reification, anthropomorphization, substitution of values for motivations, and taking psychological processes as given were used as criteria to define the latter category. The percentage using psychological concepts, with or without citation, dropped off during the later period covered by the review (1952-62), reflecting the disengagement between psychology and anthropology that occurred during the mid-fifties. Judging from the continuing reification etc., the need for psychological concepts and data did not, however, diminish.

The tendency to incorporate a psychological dimension in analyses that are not frankly psychologically oriented continues today. As Honigmann points out, "At the present time almost every other article in a journal of anthropology refers to psychological dynamics operative in culture, to the repercussions of culture on the individual, or to the role of individuals in the cultural process" (Honigmann 1975, p. 602). It appears that the psychologizing of anthropology, which surfaces most explicitly in contributions labelled "culture and personality" or "psychological anthropology," has diffused the boundaries between what is and what is not psychological anthropology to the point where they are not recognizable. Much of this tendency, as Hallowell, Harris and Honigmann pointed out, is inherent in anthropological data and interpretation. There is a potentially threatening and confusing situation here. By trying to make explicit what was implicit and taken for granted by others, we have made ourselves targets for attack. We challenged the comfortable, everyday psychologizing our colleagues were doing and made it seem complicated—which it was.

IDENTITY PROBLEMS

There were other consequences. Psychological anthropology suffers identity problems and presents a confused image to outside viewers, whether friendly or hostile. The diffuse quality of psychological concerns and the difficulty of drawing boundaries around the subdiscipline militates against the development of a secure self-image and made the identity of the field ambiguous to others. The peculiar relationships between explicitly psychologized anthropology and the rest of the discipline not only affected images and identity but also character structure. As Voget (1975) pointed out, in order for there to be a discipline, there must be a special subject matter, a special theory of reality and of causal explanation, a distinctive methodology, and a special set of factual materials. Culture and personality—psychological anthropology —could regard all of social and cultural anthropology as potentially overlapping in subject matter and its factual materials could include any culturally influenced behavior (and some behaviors that presumably were not). Psychologized anthropology had the beginnings of a special theory, or theories, but many of the sources for this theory lay outside of anthropology, and worst of all, with clinicians, psychiatrists, psychoanalysts, projectivists, and the like, and much less so with respectable academic psychology. Our subdiscipline, it appears, had to rest its case on its distinctive methodology, but here we were in even worse trouble. Anthropologists in general were not strong on method. "Just give us a pencil and a pad of notepaper," said one prominent anthropologist at an interdisciplinary meeting in the 1950s to consider methods in the social sciences. Our psychologizing colleagues had to invent methodologies for studying complex and subtle relationships in alien cultural settings that were not being studied any too successfully by psychologists and psychiatrists in hospitals, clinics, and laboratories in a familiar cultural setting. They drew methods and techniques from their psychological and psychiatric colleagues and combined them, often without modification, with standard anthropological procedures. This contributed to the weak development of character structure and furthered the ambiguous image presented to non-psychological colleagues.

We must grant that the problems of territorial and self-definition were acute for the subdiscipline as it emerged and that they persist into the present. Now we should turn to another cause of trouble.

THE THREAT OF REDUCTIONISM

"Is anthropology to sell its culturologial birthright for a mess of psychiatric pottage?" agonized Leslie White (with humor as well as agony), well known for his relentless antagonism toward psychologizing (White 1946, p. 85).

The context for this remark was a review of Kroeber's *Configurations of Cultural Growth* (Kroeber 1944), which White welcomed as a rarity for it was a study of culture, not the study of personality or reactions of the human organism. He went on to say that, "The movement away from culturology to psychology, which we are witnessing today in American anthropology, is definitely a regression from a higher to a lower level in the developmental series of strata achieved by science" (ibid., p. 85). He, like many other social scientists, rejected "psychological reductionism" and accepted a Comtian notion of "levels" of phenomena, of which the social and the cultural were the highest, the most explanatory, when it came to human affairs.

Clyde Kluckhohn, reviewing the same book, felt that Kroeber's concept of superorganic culture (1946) was misunderstood, but was made "uncomfortable" by phrases like "it is entirely possible for a culture not to seize upon its finest patterned potentialities; to be lacking in ability to select and concentrate, and, instead, to dissipate its energies in random or conflicting endeavors at expression" (Kroeber 1944, p. 796). Kluckhohn went on to say that Kroeber's refusal to deal with the agents of change (people) in psychological terms made it impossible for him (Kroeber) to develop a satisfying theory of culture change.

The opposing positions taken by White and Kluckhohn are diagnostic of the persisting conflict between those who want to deal with culture as a thing in itself, with its own dynamic—culture *sui generis*— abstracted from social and psychological processes (and yet dependent upon those processes) and those who find it necessary to incorporate these dimensions in their theoretical constructs and interpretations of data. Many of our ancestors contributed to this argument and it is a continuing concern. Voget (1975) devotes a forty-page chapter to "Establishing the Autonomy of Culture," and this and other related concerns are the subject of a recent compilation of ideas about culture edited by Frederick Gamst and Edward Norbeck (1976).

Reduction of the level of explanation through the hierarchy from cultural, to social, to psychological, and finally to biological was, and probably still is, regarded negatively by many anthropologists. White states the case succinctly: "culture has in a very real sense, an extra-somatic character. Although made possible only by the organisms of human beings, once in existence and under way it has a life of its own. Its behavior is determined by its own laws, not explained by the laws of human organisms. The culture process is to be explained in terms of the science of culture and culturology, not in terms of psychology" (White 1949, p. 140). Culture determines behavior. Everything that people do, as human beings, and everything that they think or feel, is culturally determined. Some people loathe milk, pork, or human flesh. Some sanction premarital intercourse, others demand chastity tests at marriage, some lend their wives, others jealously guard their wives' sexuality. All these and other behaviors are explained by culture (White 1947, p. 690).

This view is a product of Western intellectual history, but most directly, in anthropology, reflects the struggle of anthropologists to disengage from the bio-racist determinism that ignored the observations about cross-cultural diversity that anthropologists were beginning to assemble by the turn of the century. Alfred Kroeber's "The Super-organic" (Kroeber 1917) is usually considered to be the definitive early statement of this position. Though widely cited as the starting point of a culture *sui generis* view, it was mainly directed at the disengagement of what he then called "the social" (later he specified cultural) level of process and determination from the biological. It was not intended as a prolegemon for a completely self-sufficient culture construct, though Kroeber had tendencies in this direction. Paradoxically, both he and White granted that the ultimate reality of culture was in the "psyche" or in social psychological processes, but one could best act as an anthropologist as if culture had a life of its own and as if human beings did not exist (White 1947; Kroeber 1948a, 1949). (See also Murdock 1932 for a related statement.)

Kroeber, it should be said, modified his view during his long meditation on the problem of the reality of culture (Kroeber 1952; Kroeber and Kluckhohn 1952). Nevertheless, after this long meditation and after the exhaustive analysis, with Kluckhohn, of nearly every definition and idea about the culture concept written by almost anyone, he (with Kluckhohn) concluded that, "The best hope in the foreseeable future for parsimonious description and 'explanation' of cultural phenomena seems to rest in the study of cultural forms and processes as such, largely—for these purposes—abstracted from individuals and personalities" (Kroeber and Kluckhohn 1952, p. 167). There is food for thought in this statement by a very influential figure in anthropology who had once been a lay analyst, and particularly because it is a joint statement with Clyde Kluckhohn, one of the major contributors to the early phases of development of the culture and personality movement.

Edward Sapir, "Do We Need a Superorganic?" (1917) and Alexander Goldenweiser, "The Autonomy of the Social" (1917) attacked Kroeber's concept of the superorganic in the next issue of the *American Anthropologist*. They made what are by now familiar charges: the individual as an idiosyncratic and biographical entity has to be taken into account; culture, as transmissible and accumulative, is based upon psychic or psychological processes that depend upon a self-awareness seemingly unique to humans; and the "social" or "cultural" is philosophically an arbitrary selection out of a total mass of phenomena and it is consequently not correct to imply it has a force or a life of its own. They agreed, however, on the necessity of separating the cultural from the biological.

Starting with Sapir and Goldenweiser, continuing through Benedict and Mead (with Boas as instigator) up to the present, explicitly psychologized anthropology has challenged the culture *sui generis* position head-on. This subfield has been a persistent threat to those committed to this position (and to a greater or lesser degree this includes the majority of anthropologists) of reductionism to a "lower order" or explanation. This is clear in the very nature of psychological anthropology and is explicit in statements such as the following by Hallowell:

A living functioning culture is not, existentially, dependent upon a group of interacting human beings, abstractly considered, but upon the manner in which such individuals are psychologically structured. A culture may be said to be just as much the expression of their mode of human psycho-dynamic adjustment as it is a condition of the grooming of successive generations of individuals in this mode. (Hallowell 1953, p. 911)

One of the authors included in Part II of this volume, Theodore Schwartz, carries this thinking even further when he says that psychological processes define "not merely the possibility but the content of culture,'' though this statement must be understood in the context of his discussion of the distributive locus of culture.

A DOUBLE JEOPARDY

In emerging as it did and continuing to the present to challenge culture *sui generis* and threaten reductionism, psychologized anthropology has suffered a double jeopardy. It threatened to bring the abstracted culture construct down to a grubby level of individual motivation, thinking, and emotion. But it was unable to offer viable alternative causal linkages between culture and its psychological processing on the one hand and biological or techno-environmental factors on the other. By challenging the culture *sui generis* position and at the same time the biologism of Freud and other universalists the emerging subfield launched itself in a sea of non-causality, charting an uncertain course between the Scylla of cultural determinism and the Charybdis of bio-racism.

Psychologized anthropology offered an alternative analytical approach, called attention to the mediating and expressive role of individuals, and offered new models for the integration of cultural systems, as in the Kardiner-Linton schema. These were considerable accomplishments, but they left psychologized anthropology in an equivocal position, for this sector of our discipline was under the heavy hand of its own kind of cultural determinism.

It is probably correct to say that most of us represented in Part I have done our work under the thumb of cultural over-determinism. While challenging culture *sui generis* and insisting on psychologizing, we have accepted the determinism of culture as paramount. The very challenge—that culture was mediated, reinterpreted, individualized, projected in social institutions, only to be recycled through child training (varying from culture to culture of course) to adult personality and belief systems, in an infinite regression of personality upon culture and culture upon personality—is a complex but not too subtle acknowledgement of the primary determinism of culture, largely free of material or biological input. Whatever the process, culture was considered to be prior in time to the individual and superordinate in causality, and until quite recently, unrelated to a biological or techno-environmental base. The struggle with cultural over-determinism (as we refer to the excesses of a cultural position) is an implicit or explicit theme in most of the chapters in both Part I and Part II. I will leave to the reader the identification of the problem and the responses to it in these papers.

CONTINUING PROBLEMS

The revolt against bio-racist determinism led by our ancestors and the struggle for a distinctive disciplinary definition for anthropology led to the abstraction and reification of the culture construct—to culture *sui generis*. The revolt against this particular form of cultural reification and determinism led to the concept of personality in interaction with culture and the mediation of cultural forms by psychological processes. The whole culture and personality movement contributed to this development and we cannot trace it further in this short statement. It was anticipated in Edward Sapir's early statement already cited, "Culture . . .as transmissible and accumulative is based upon the psychic processes depending on self-awareness seemingly unique to humans" (1917, p. 447).

In a much later paper (1934), Sapir refined ideas that by that time had begun to become a part of the emerging framework of culture and personality. He pointed out that the "purely formalized and logically developed schemes" we call ethnographies do not explain behavior until "the threads of symbolism and implication" that "connect patterns or parts of patterns with others of an entirely different formal aspect" are discovered. Without this discovery, the impersonalized "culture" of the anthropologist can really be little more than "an assembly" of "loosely overlapping ideas and action systems, which through verbal habit, can be made to assume the appearance of a closed system of behavior" (Sapir 1934, p. 411).

Attention to psychological process provided a way of going beyond this formal statement of culture toward understanding the interconnections within behavioral systems. As work and time went on these interconnections were summed up by the concept personality, and particularly basic, or modal personality. Like culture, however, "personality," particularly when regarded as a collective or even centrally distributed phenomenon, has the potential for reification and abstraction. The very term "personality and culture," a "false dichotomy" as Spiro (1951) aptly termed it, implies two reified abstractions confronting each other over the prostrate corpse of humanity.

Sapir raised two other points that have not been responded to adequately by most of us who explicitly psychologize.

In spite of the oft-asserted impersonality of culture, a humble truth remains that vast reaches of culture, far from being "carried" by a group or community . . . , are discoverable only as the peculiar property of certain individuals, who cannot but give these cultural goods the impress of their own personality. (ibid., p. 412)

And further:

The common acceptance of the idea that culture is *given* to each individual is false: *it is never given,* it is "gropingly discovered." Some parts of it are never acquired by some individuals, and biographical idiosyncracies . . . of the "culture givers" will affect this "discovery." (ibid., p. 112)

Sapir was anticipating the problem of the distributive locus of culture dealt with in T. Schwartz' paper in Part II, and by Anthony Wallace in his arguments that cultural systems are characterized by an "organization of diversity" and not a "replication of uniformity," as the modal or basic personality constructs infer (Wallace 1970). There is an implication in the attention to the "patterns" of child rearing as determinants of adult personality that psychocultural systems are a kind of replication of uniformity. In the Kardinerian scheme this was carried to a logical extreme. "Primary" institutions, mediated through basic personality structure, determine "secondary" institutions, such as religious belief and concepts of illness (Kardiner 1939, 1945). A uniformitarian view is a logical outcome of cultural determinism. The problem of the distribution of culture within a given population and the implications of this for a concept of personality and culture relations are considered explicitly by Schwartz in Part II, but are also present in various guises in other papers, particularly Whiting's, Spiro's, Edgerton's, L. Spindler's, the Graves', and DeVos's. None of the papers project a firmly uniformitarian viewpoint, but the Whitings in their summary of their hologeistic research position and Barnouw in his attention to the basic personality scheme, touch upon some of its assumptions.

Another point raised by Sapir is less attended to but no less critical. In fact, it may be considered pivotal in the development of a psychological anthropology and another of the reasons why this development has never followed a smooth course and has been greeted with less than universal enthusiasm by fellow workers.

The study of culture as such, which may be called sociology or anthropology, has a deep and unacknowledged root in the desire to lose one's self safely in the historically determined patterns of behavior. The motive for the study of personality . . . proceeds from the necessity which the ego feels to assert itself significantly. (Sapir 1934, p. 410)

This problem is treated, in diverse ways, in the papers by Honigmann, La Barre, Spiro, and Devereux. Its implications are difficult to assess accurately, for by its very nature the problem tends to be submerged in rationalization, ignored, or defended against. At the very least, it implies that the motivations for doing research and communicating it to others could be very different for those interested in psychologized anthropology and for those interested solely in the formal treatment of observed behavior. It seems to imply that the world views and even personality structures of the members of these two interest groups might be quite different. As a psychological anthropologist, one often has the sense, in arguing cases with colleagues who are not so oriented, that the differences go very deep and are irreconcilable. It seems reasonable to infer, in any event, that whatever the magnitude of differences in motivation, outlook, and personality there may be between those attracted to psychocultural problems and interpretations and those who are not, these differences have contributed, and will continue to contribute, to a failure in complete and sympathetic interpretation. These differences may also help account for the barrage of criticism so quickly mounted and the many scathing attacks on psychologized anthropology.

Devereux brings another dimension to our discussion with the review, in his paper, of his book *From Anxiety to Method in the Behavioral Sciences*. His argument is that the scientific study of man is impeded by the anxiety aroused by the overlapping between subject and observer and that the disturbances ensuing in communication result in compensation that distorts the perception and interpretation of data and produces resistances that masquerade as methodology, causing further distortions, *ad infinitum*. The reader will have to study Devereux's statement in his paper, or better yet, read the book, to appreciate the full complexity of the argument and its implications.

Devereux's argument applies to all of the social sciences but it is clearly particularly acute in psychologized anthropology, where the researcher is presumably working through these very relationships and paradoxes. Most of us know what Devereux means when he says that we must avoid the temptation to compensate for the *completeness* of communication between subject and observer on the *unconscious* level, and that this arouses anxiety and countertransference reactions. We have experienced it. But it is sobering to think that much of our methodology may be a kind of compensation produced by this dynamic process and its further dialectics. John Honigmann's discussion of the "personal approach" to culture and personality research tackles the same problem area that Devereux discusses but with quite different starting paradigms.

In any event, the process described by Devereux accounts for some of the noise in and around the methodology of psychological anthropology. When rigorous (compensatory?) methodologies are not developed, the research can be attacked for lack of rigor. When such methodologies are developed, the research may be attacked for lack of qualitative analysis, irrelevance, or statistical ineptness. In either case the observer-interpreter is anxious and this may be reflected either in the methodology, or the lack of it. This is a bit of overstatement, but there is enough truth in it to make it worth saying.

We see, then, that psychologized anthropological theory and research emerged as a way of reducing culture as an abstraction to an interpretative level where psychological interconnections between different sectors of culturally influenced behavior could be analyzed. This raised further questions about causality and determinism, and the distributive locus of culture and personality. We are left with a rather different but related problem to solve—the relationships between observer and subject and the consequences in interpretation and methodology.

SO FAR

In this introduction I have tried so far to set the stage for the papers to follow with very broad and rather crude strokes. This introduction has not provided a history of psychologized anthropology; the overviews cited at the beginning of this piece will be of use to the reader unfamiliar with this history.

The points that I hope are clear by now are:

1. The psychologizing of anthropology started off with great expectations.
2. It came under very vigorous, at times strident, attack shortly after it got seriously started.
3. Obituaries were read over it, and still are, but the outpouring of psychocultural anthropology has continued unabated.
4. One of the reasons why this kind of anthropology continues, despite attack and discouragement, is that psychologizing is central to cultural anthropology, even to anthropologists who are not explicitly psychologically oriented.
5. This is also one of the reasons for the rejection of psychologizing.
6. The threat of reductionism posed by psychological anthropology is also a reason for its rejection by some anthropologists.
7. Psychological anthropology has suffered identity problems due to a lack of boundaries and extensive borrowing from outsiders.
8. Culture *sui generis* was an answer to bio-racist formulations.

9. Though psychologically oriented anthropologists may have successfully challenged the kind of cultural determinism that is explicit in the culture *sui generis* concept, they have not been so successful in escaping their own forms of cultural determinism, thus contributing further to the ambiguity of their position.

10. Sapir anticipated what proved to be persisting concerns on the part of psychological anthropologists.

    a. He challenged the utility of ethnographies without psychologizing to tie the idea and action systems together. Most of us have been working on this.

    b. He raised questions about the distribution of culture within any given culture system, questions which have been considered from time to time by psychologizing anthropologists but not approached too seriously until recently. Our cultural determinism made a uniformitarian orientation more compatible than a distributive construct.

    c. He raised a question that remains a basic challenge to the credibility of our enterprise—how the personal relationship to the study of behavior may affect interpretation.

11. George Devereux has taken this last matter further and differently. His analysis is not heartening, for the complexities of the relationships involved seem beyond control, but he urges us to take heart, for in them lie data that should be at the core of psychological anthropology.

We are left with four major problem indices. Keeping them in mind will be helpful as the chapters in this book are read. They are:

1. Culture *sui generis* and reductionism.
2. Cultural overdeterminism.
3. The distributive locus of culture and personality.
4. The personal relationship of investigator to subject.

I will conclude this introduction by direct attention to the papers included in Part I. I have provided an editorial introduction to each paper under the heading "This Chapter"; these are limited to considerations directly relevant to the chapters themselves. In the continuing discussion in the introduction to Part I, I will use the papers as points of departure for brief sallies into background history and theory and will connect, where relevant, the papers to the points made in the discussion so far. The chapters represent a wide range of both theory and history, and I do not presume to be able to treat this range adequately in this introduction. Such treatment would require seminars.

THE CHAPTERS IN PART I

The first chapter, by John and Beatrice Whiting, sums up a strategy of research that has been pursued consistently over more than thirty years. This is rare in psychological anthropology, as Honigmann has pointed out (1975) and has allowed for an accumulation of wisdom and a consistent improvement of methodology. The payoff has been substantial. The research methodology is cross-cultural, nomothetic, and statistical—what is called hologeistic. This alone distinguishes it from the rest of the papers in this volume, with the exception of Bourgignon's. The theory guiding the generation of hypotheses is a combination of neo-Freudianism resembling the Kardinerian model, and Hullian learning theory.

Both the theoretical system and the methodology and its use of the Human Relations Area Files have been widely criticized as well as praised. Harris (1968, pp. 450–56) is one of the most supportive reviewers in a reference book easily available to most readers, and Victor Barnouw, one of the more critical (1973, pp. 184-90).

The distribution of culture is a problem for the Whiting strategy. If culture is distributed unequally and unevenly it is probable that child training patterns are not uniform within any single cultural system. Considerable uniformity is required to make hypotheses based on the effect of child training upon personality work. When ethnographic reporting is used as a source for rating cases that then go into a statistical matrix, there may be over-concretization of cultural patterning. This is a characteristic form of cultural overdeterminism in culture and personality.

In this way, and also in the sense that culture is both prior to child training and consequent to personality, the Whitings have not escaped the trap of cultural determinism. They have, however, made serious attempts to identify possible techno-environmental variables, such as climate, protein deficiency, and house structures as affected by availability of building materials, which in turn influence such primary variables as sleeping arrangements and therefore child training.

Chapter 2 by Victor Barnouw describes research inspired by the Kardiner-Linton Seminar at Columbia University. This is the seminar that generated two basic books for culture and personality, *The Individual and Society* (1939) and *The Psychological Frontiers of Society* (1945), with Kardiner, Ralph Linton, E. Sapir, R. Benedict, Ruth Bunzel, Cora DuBois and Carl Withers participating. The seminar started in 1936 and moved to Columbia in 1937, when Linton, DuBois, and Carl Withers joined it. They submitted ethnographic data that served as the cultural content for the psychocultural analysis. As a leading neo-Freudian, Kardiner had discarded phylogenetic memory, the primal scene, the classical model of the Oedipus complex and the rigid three-stage development of sexuality. His style of analysis, and the kinds of psychological mechanisms employed in interpretation remained Freudian.

The Kardiner-Linton model of relationships, comprised of primary institutions, basic personality, projective systems, and secondary institutions linked together in a positive chain, was supremely culture-deterministic. The neo-Freudian revolt against the biological determinism of Freud was in part a result of anthropological influence, as anthropologists attacked this aspect of psychoanalytic theory. In this way the Kardiner-Linton seminar, influential for a whole generation of workers including all of us represented in Part I, invented its own ''superorganic'' culture, together with the others who revolted against Freud's biological determinism. Once culture was underway psychological analysis helped to explain it and how personality both determined and was determined by culture, but psychological analysis could not explain how the chain of interacting determinisms got started, or how personality could be anything but a cultural product. Nevertheless, this model was a major breakthrough in the attempt to integrate psychocultural systems with one explanatory model. It promised to bring it all together. It is impossible now to recapture the great excitement that this grand model generated. I returned to graduate school in September, 1945, after three years of World War II, and my first seminar in culture and personality under Scudder Mekeel focused on the two Kardiner volumes. We internalized the whole structure. It was a daring conception and we have not seen its like since. Today this model is still somewhere in the thinking of most of us. It is a central pivot in the Whiting scheme, though the thinking of the Whitings and their associates was formed from several influences and makes important innovations not anticipated by the Kardiner-Linton model, particularly in the more explicit incorporation of learning theory and the fact that it makes a place for cultural materialism in its schema.

Margaret Mead's paper is true to form. Without doubt, she has challenged more ethnocentric shibboleths and firm scientific generalizations based on samples unleavened by attention to cross-cultural variability than any other anthropologist. *Coming of Age in Samoa* challenged established ideas about the universality of emotional disturbance during adolescence. *Sex and Temperament* challenged ideas about univeral sex linked characteristics. *Growing Up in New Guinea* challenged ideas about fixed stages of maturation, particularly the concept of children as animistic, "primitive" thinkers. She is the one anthropologist most frequently quoted by psychologists writing general textbooks.

The success of her challenges contributed to the development of cultural overdeterminism in culture and personality theory. She showed there are critical differences between cultures, and these differences made suspect any generalizations based upon presumably universal, pan-human features.

In her paper for this volume she deals with animistic thinking, challenging Piaget's conclusion that young children pass through a stage where their relationships with the physical world are characterized by "animism," the tendency to regard objects as living and endowed with will. Gustav Jahoda (1958) reviews cross-cultural evidence accumulated between 1945 and 1958 on the occurrence of animism among children. He finds that of eight major studies in non-Western settings, only Mead's found no evidence of "the occurrence of animistic thought, which she therefore regards as wholly culturally determined" (ibid., p. 202). Jahoda goes on to discuss the evidence, methodology, and logic of Mead's findings. He regards as "the crux of the matter" Mead's definition of animism, "that a child spontaneously attributed personality phenomena to animals, or inanimate objects, or created nonexistent personal beings" (Mead 1932, p. 181). He points out that this "goes far beyond Piaget's conception of animism, which requires merely the attribution of certain characteristics of living beings to inert objects" (Jahoda 1958, p. 207). He concludes that Mead's negative findings cannot be regarded as conclusive evidence against the assumption of universality implicit in Piaget's theory.

Readers can judge for themselves what Margaret Mead intended to study and how she went about it. The methodology itself is fascinating and in the best tradition of anthropological holism and innovative flexibility. The results obtained show there is substantial *patterned* evidence the Manus children do not think animistically. This situation illustrates two problems that are a part of the culture and personality profile: (1) How does one set up the equivalent to controlled experimentation, or even observation, in the field in another culture? (2) How does one communicate findings so that their whole character is understood? I do not intend to take sides on the question of universality of child animism. The problems of methodology and communication have dogged culture and personality *cum* psychological anthropology since the beginning.

Francis Hsu's chapter approaches the study of complex national wholes. It therefore sets as a task the same one that students of national character set, however differently. There is no part of psychologizing anthropology that has been more severely criticized than the national character studies. Assumptions about toilet training as explanations for Japanese "compulsivity" and about swaddling for some aspects of Russian character, when there were no reliable data on these primary variables, were enough to get this approach into trouble. Apparently these excesses were a by-product of the necessity for studying culture "at a distance" during World War II. It is easy to dismiss the whole national character approach as invalid, even ridiculous, but as a graduate student of mine, set to studying the whole literature, remarked, "At first I thought you must hate me for suggesting all this stuff, but now I really am beginning to think there is something to it. They seemed to have arrived at a lot of the right conclusions for the wrong reasons."

"Wrong reasons" (methodologically and in respect to assumptions) are partly at fault but this work may simply have bitten off a piece of reality too big to chew. The "macro approach" in some degree seems to have characterized much of our work in psychologized anthropology. If problems of the distribution of culture and of cultural overdeterminism dogged other concerns and styles of research, the national character studies must be considered hag-ridden. What remains impressive, however, as one reads studies by historians and social philosophers that are essentially national character studies, is that anthropologists tripped themselves up by trying to be scientific. They tried to isolate variables and develop logical causal chains. This is another problem in psychologized anthropology. We use science, or pseudo-science, when literary humanism would do—but then we would probably not have a very large anthropological audience. Hsu's paper escapes many of these problems and he develops certain models that appear to make crosscultural comparison possible. Hsu also addresses the problem of personal relationship to the field study and the resulting bias. This will remain a basic concern for psychological anthropologists.

Chapter 5 by Louise Spindler, reporting on the evolution of work by both Spindlers, centers on the use of projective techniques and related methodology in the study of psychological process in culture change. I will focus on the projective techniques in these introductory comments, since the change aspect is explicitly treated in the chapter and it is also a major focus in Barnouw's chapter, and the Graves' paper in Part II. It is difficult for our current generation of anthropologists to appreciate the promise that these techniques seemed to hold for the resolution of certain basic problems in psychological anthropology. The most important promise was close to the logic of our discussion—an escape from cultural over-determinism. Most of us working with projective techniques were looking for a way of eliciting a response that was culturally influenced but not culturally predetermined. We were not, as many colleagues seem to assume, primarily interested in uncovering hidden depths in the psyches of our subjects. Ink blots, cloud tests, mosaics, and so forth, were culturally ambiguous. The "projection" by the respondent was presumably formed out of the experience of an individual within a cultural field, but the processing of that experience by the individual was what produced the perceptual-cognitive structure that was "projected"—along with defenses, anxieties, fixations, and so on. Therefore, it seemed we had a way of getting away from linear cultural determinism and also a way of getting at the distribution of culture and personality within our target population. Even now it is difficult to fault the logic of this attempt. The problem seemed to lie, as it so often does in our field, with interpretative procedures and validity. What scoring system should we use? How do we handle the cross-cultural problems posed by interpretative guidelines developed in single-culture, Western contexts? How do we get around the demonstrated investigator effect syndrome? The fluctuation of scores? And worst of all, it seemed at times, how could we deal with the horrendous statistical problems involved when one deals with interdependent "scores" as though they were independent, and with statements of central tendency when standard deviations have little or no meaning? Here we see the Devereux effect working. Some of us offered elaborate rigorous, statistical, index-defining procedures to compensate for what we consciously regarded as ambiguities and uncertainties in basic assumptions and interpretative procedures. Perhaps we also intuitively recognized the "complete communication" between ourselves and our respondents that the Rorschach or projective contexts made all the more painful. But could we have done otherwise? The statistical treatments and "experimental designs" we attempted within the limits of rigor as we understood it at the time, have made it possible to look back upon this research with a certainty that is usually lacking. We know what it is we thought we knew and much of it still seems right. But the costs were substantial. In our own case we intuited and surmised much more than we could ever allow ourselves to print. Our commitment to methodological rigor made it quite impossible to do otherwise. It is relevant here that Louise Spindler was able to move further in these directions, with concepts like "latescence" as a characteristic feature of social interaction among Menominee women, than George Spindler could. This seems to have something to do with what Jessie Bernard calls the *"machismo* element in a research" (Bernard 1974, p. 23), and what Rae Carlson (1971) terms "agentic" as against "communion" types of research. The former pursues mastery, separation, and ego enhancement—the creation of a controlled reality. The latter disavows control, for control "spoils the results." Women more frequently prefer the latter, according to Carlson's studies of psychologists. However that may be, anthropology is traditionally more communion than agentic oriented. Attempts at rigor and control, as exemplified in works by the Spindlers, DeVos, Gladwin, and others, with extensive, statistically treated samples and research designs, may also, in this context, be seen as compensations for tendencies toward communion-oriented approaches heuristic to a psychocultural approach—particularly where projective techniques are used.

Nearly all of the authors in Part I have used projective techniques during their long careers. Most have not used them for years. There is some evidence there is a reawakening of interest in such procedures (Bates 1976; Bushnell 1974). They were applied to problems that still seem very real. Perhaps with a lowering of expectations and with more attention to the interpretation of results in the context of more limited problems the projective techniques still have a future in anthropological research.

Chapter 6, by Anthony Wallace, is the only one in this volume to give primary attention to biological and chemical determinants of human behavior, though it is a part of the scenario in others. He focuses on what appears to be a functional mental illness, a form of hysterical behavior, in the Arctic—*piblokto*—that is prototypical for certain other syndromes that are culture-area specific. Various psychocultural explanations have been advanced for piblokto, involving such factors as culturally patterned dependency needs and psychological insecurity in combination with threats of deprivation in a harsh environment. Workers pursuing Wallace's hypothesis—that a condition resembling hysteria might be caused by calcium deficiency—found that in ten cases of *piblokto* examined with appropriate techniques, all exhibited abnormally low calcium serum due to a calcium-poor diet and to disturbance of circadian rhythms in the human body because of the absence of regular night and day alterations during much of the arctic year.

Whether it eventually turns out that such factors as these are specifically accountable for the *piblokto* syndrome is unimportant in the context of our discussion. What is important to us is that certain aspects of what we have conceptualized as personality-in-culture or psychological expressions of culture may turn out to be biogenic in origin. Our strong commitment to cultural determinism has made us slow to recognize this possibility. And at this moment biogenic explanations are not politically popular. (Perhaps some of the unpopularity is due to a confusion of genetic with biogenic.) However, since biology as well as culture is adaptive, and the two interact in any human adaptive process, there is no ultimate reason for a political rejection of the implications of a biogenic view. There has recently been a turn toward biological process in explanations of what has seemed to be until now entirely cultural behavior. John Whiting was one of the first to seriously acknowledge such factors in culture and personality research, with attention to *kwashiorkor,* a disease associated with protein deficiency during infancy which is in turn related to post-partum sex taboos, making a second wife essential and therefore affecting parent-child relationships, and so on (Whiting 1964). A. I. Hallowell was a pioneer in his concern with the evolution of human nature, beginning with his 1959 essay on behavioral evolution and the emergence of the self, but anticipated by other essays contained in his volume of collected works up to 1955 (G. and L. Spindler 1975). Most dramatic in its implications is the recent attention to biocultural evolution by ethologists, population geneticists, and a growing number of anthropologists. In political science a new field, biopolitics, has emerged, stimulated by the biology of aggression, dominance, and related ethological hypotheses. The mathematical geneticists talk about "species personality," characteristics such as altruism, coyness, jealousy, greediness, with the explicit assumption that there are specific genes determining these traits. This is much further than most of us are willing to go. E. O. Wilson (1975) surveys most of these trends in what Donald T. Campbell, in his presidential address at the meeting of the American Psychological Association in Chicago in August 1975, termed "a magnificent volume that every psychologist should own" (Campbell 1975, p. 1110), and that Elliott D. Chapple characterizes as a bad book to which he reacted with "extreme annoyance and bursts of uncontrolled laughter at its stupidity, its arrogance, and its pretentiousness." (Chapple 1976, p. 108). It has been reviewed in a more temperate mood by other anthropologists (Smith, Munroe, and Washburn 1976).

Although we can be sure biogenic explanations of human behavior are not going to be greeted with universal enthusiasm, we might remember that "learned habits, attitudes, thoughts, and values must have an anatomical and physiological embodiment just as full and complete as do unlearned behavioral tendencies'' (Campbell 1975, p. 1110). We may even find ourselves dealing with hypotheses such as that advanced by C. H. Waddington some time ago (1960) that biological evolution has predisposed children at the pre-adolescent period to be eager orthodoxy seekers, when we want to talk about initiation ceremonies or their functional equivalents. We may have to consider seriously the possibility that conformity to social pressure, suggestibility to prestige figures, need for moral norms, bravery, and any other tendencies of this kind are a part of human nature and a product of biocultural evolution. Such attributes of human nature, if they can ever be established, will provide us with yardsticks to measure the adequacy of cultural systems, thus removing us from the petard of cultural relativism.

We are a long way from anything resembling a coherent integration of biosociocultural evolution and we are in a no man's land when it comes to making direct application of what we do know about human biology to the analysis of cultural forms and personality and culture relationships. But if we are to escape the double bind of our cultural overdeterminism we are going to have to go beyond culture and even ecology, to biochemistry, to physiology and neurology, to genetics—to biology in the broadest sense of the term. It is improbable many of us can do this ourselves, but we can use our sociocultural and psychocultural knowledge and sensitivities to interact with others (or their ideas and data) who have the skills and knowledge we need and vice versa. Of course it is important for us to remember that however significant biological and other factors may seem, our level of specificity will always require an ethnographic interpretation beyond biology and we will do well to remember that culture is the major human adaptive mechanism. Any given culture will always be a finite working out of basic human nature and a product of learning. Every culture always has been, but our cultural overdeterminism and our extreme relativism, both, paradoxically, the products of revolts against biological determinism, have prevented us from acting as if this were so.

"The Japanese Adapt to Change," Chapter 7 by George DeVos, brings the issue of appropriate theory to the fore, though this is not what the chapter is explicitly about. John Bennett reviews *Socialization for Achievement: Essays on the Cultural Psychology of the Japanese* (1973), by DeVos with contributions by Hiroshi Wagatsuma, William Caudill, and Keiichi Mizushima in *Reviews in Anthropology* (Bennett 1974) as having a "problem of basic theory" (ibid., p. 482). The same may be said about DeVos's chapter in this volume, though there is *more* theory than in most. No one reading terms like "submerged active suppression," "passive dependency," "sado-masochistic orientation," "object cathexis," "sense of guilt," "internalized negative attitudes towards self," and "unconsciousness and suppressed negative self image," should have the slightest doubt as to the origin of the basic theory. Within the framework of generalized psychodynamic theory, DeVos's chapter seems to be internally consistent. His application of concepts seems appropriate, and the insights so derived seem significant. He also appeals to concepts of achievement motivation, to role expectations, and particularly to Durkheimian anomie for further theoretical models useful in explaining Japanese adaptation. The problem seems to be that the psychodynamic model is taken for granted and that moves toward other models are partial. There is therefore a quality of expedient foraging for theory from a neo-Freudian base camp. This is worth saying because it is about what most of us in Part I have done. We have rarely examined the roots of our theory and have not worried enough about the integration of concepts from non-psychodynamic sources in our generalized and sometimes quite diffuse psychodynamicism.

In the same issue of *Reviews in Anthropology*, Pertti Pelto reviews Robert LeVine's (1973) *Culture, Behavior, and Personality: An Introduction to the Comparative Study of Psychosocial Adaptation* (Pelto 1974). In the framework of a thoughtful, critical, but on the whole favorable review Pelto expresses shock at LeVine's choice of "psychoanalytic ethnography" as the method and theory that will implement his application of a Darwinian variation-selection model to the processes of socialization and the institutionalization of cultural behavior (ibid., p. 513). Pelto regards "depth probes and the whole psychoanalytic framework" as "theoretically bankrupt." Though I find myself, in company with some, but not all, of the contributors to this volume, in sharp disagreement with this estimate, this disagreement is not the point. The point is that when we use psychodynamic, neo-Freudian concepts and interpretative principles, we place our work and our reputation in some jeopardy, for such theory is unpopular with many anthropologists (and psychologists). A careful appraisal and clear theoretical statement of sources and reasons for using concepts and principles are in order whenever we launch research projects or interpret the results.

Again, I am not really criticizing DeVos. His methods and theory are productive. And his efforts, together with those of his Japanese colleagues (and he is a model for the rest of us in his early and consistent collaboration with indigenous colleagues) are, as I see it, not far from what LeVine advocates as "therapy for an ailing discipline" (to use Pelto's phrasing). And there are clear indications in DeVos's work that he is somewhat less subject to errors of cultural over-determinism and uniformitarianism than most of us.

Weston La Barre's paper raises many issues about method and stance in the behavioral sciences in general and anthropology in particular. Like Devereux, he sees the relationship of the scientists to the field in which he is immersed as of paramount importance. Experimental psychologists, for example, he terms "honest compulsives, they obscurely suspect that the truth is not in them so they armor themselves more and more with protective method," and "academic psychology becomes a kind of institutionalized compulsion neurosis." Anthropology he characterizes as a reaction to the intellectual crises posed by the Renaissance. Faced with the fact of bewildering cultural diversity, Western intellectuals attempted to create "some nomothetic Rock of Ages amongst a sea of ideographic relativism" and "the relativist flounders, but every would-be nomothete distorts and transforms" as anthropologists attempt to interpret this diversity. He goes on to say that the "nomothetic aspect of any culture as a postulational system is a psychic defense mechanism."

Many of the papers in Part I explicitly try to cope with the nomothetic-idiographic problem, and all are products of one compromise or another with the anthropological necessity to be both. Ethnography is idiographic until it is used for nomothetic purposes, but the idiography of ethnography may be distorted by the nomothetic orientation of the ethnographer. The polarity of nomothetic and idiographic was first given currency in psychology by Gordon Alpert (1937) and is only occasionally explicitly cited in anthropology. Neither Voget's encyclopedic history of ethnology (1975) or Harris's treatment of anthropological theory (1968) carries either as entries in the index. The distinction in anthropology is overshadowed by emic and etic, but there are some differences that it is useful to keep in mind. An idiographic psychology would seek to describe the personality of each individual in terms of its own unique organization and an idiographic anthropology the unique organization of each culture, according to Brewster Smith (1954, pp. 45-46). Nomothetic refers to the search for general laws by successive approximation without pretending to capture the unique. Cross-cultural research in the Whiting mode is obviously nomothetic, as is the Spindlers when searching for regularities exhibited by different groups within a single community. Idiographic procedures may not, however, as is often thought, be opposed to the development of laws.

The idiographicist searches for general principles that appear in the study of single cases. The principles appear as cases are compared, but these principles are derived from relationships that remain imbedded in each case. At some point an idiographic approach may transform into a nomothetic form, as hypotheses developed out of idiographic research are tested nomothetically. Behavioral scientists may be temperamentally inclined toward one or the other approach, with, as Brewster Smith points out, "the tender-minded and intuitive aligned on one side with a nurturant, appreciative attitude toward the data, as against the tough-minded and conceptual who have no hesitation in rending apart the presenting phenomena in order to abstract regularities" (ibid., pp. 45-46). If there are such temperamental preferences operating they help to account both within anthropology and between anthropology and other disciplines for some of the redundant noise in criticism.

Emic and etic are not the same thing as idiographic and nomothetic, though they are intergraded concepts. Kenneth Pike, the first to use "emic" and "etic" defined them: "Descriptions of analyses from the etic standpoint are 'alien,' with criteria external to the system. Emic descriptions provide an internal view, with criteria chosen from within the system. They represent to us the view of one familiar with this system and who knows how to function within it himself" (Pike 1954, p. 8). Phenomenal distinctions thus derived are regarded as appropriate by the actors themselves. Many colleagues regard extremes of emicism and idiographicism as barriers to the development of anthropology as a generalizing science. On the other hand, probably many of us included in Part I regard wholehearted etic and nomothetic approaches as violations of cultural reality and barriers to understanding that reality—even though some of us do that kind of research. Readers should be aware of this ambivalence in anthropology and within anthropologists and ask themselves how this may have affected the work and points discussed in the papers of both Part I and Part II.

John Honigmann's distinction (chapter 9) between the "objective" and "personal" approach is not isomorphic with idiographic/nomothetic or emic/etic distinctions. The personal approach "assumes that a qualified investigator possessing a unique combination of interests, values, aptitudes, and sensibilities will in a largely unrepeatable manner reach significant conclusions about a culture that others can accept as credible." The objective approach "suppresses the element of personalization as much as possible. . . . It assumes that a degree of independence exists between knowledge and the particular individual who produces it.'' The personal approach may tend to be idiographic in that the unique culture and the unique interpreter-observer produce a unique ethnography, but surely the personal approach might be applied to cross-cultural evidence and comparative materials in the sense that a single investigator applies his or her genius to the understanding of implications without primary dependence upon rigorous, consistent ''automated'' methodology. Further, a personal approach is not necessarily sympathetic to ethnoscience or other emic approaches. Indeed, the ''unique combination of interests'' etc. brought by the investigator to the field and into the interpretation of observations is, by definition, external to the culture and alien to the native actor. These interests may not, however, be etic. They may not ''depend upon phenomenal distinctions judged appropriate by the community of scientific observers'' (Harris 1968, p. 575). They may be idiosyncratic with the investigator, but they probably have an undefined etic character.

Honigmann places the personal approach in the context of holism. Controversies of elementarism versus holism have been a part of the evolution of social science since the beginning. In both psychology and anthropology the initial period of elementarism (as in culture trait analysis) gave way to a period of holism (as in configurationalism). At present, anticipating the character of many of the papers in Part II, there is a tendency towards a new kind of elementarism, in that highly specific variables, or factors, are isolated as relevant to a specific problem. It may be said that holism is only possible with the personal approach, for reality (as in a single cultural system) is too complex to treat excepting by a selective, synthetic translation through the genius of an individual mind.

There are many queries the reader should be able to address to every one of the papers in this volume, keeping in mind the problems and definitions just discussed. For those who wish to pursue matters further, relevant sections of Voget (1975), Harris (1968), and Gillin (1954), will be useful. These problems are not merely questions about how many angels can dance on the head of a pin. They are central to the character and purposes, and to the history, of psychological anthropology.

Melford Spiro (chapter 10) in his paper has such a clear message, and it has been so influential in the thinking of this editor during the course of preparing this editorial overview, that it would be redundant to comment on it extensively. He attacks cultural over-determinism and with it many of the assumptions with which we have all worked. He

concludes that many motivational dispositions and cognitive orientations are culturally invariant and that this invariance stems from pan-
human biological and cultural constants, and that they "comprise
that universe of human nature which, together with received anthropological opinion, I had formerly rejected as yet another ethnocentric
bias." But having arrived at this point, he introduces important qualifications that the reader avoids at his or her own peril. The clue lies in this
statement, "it may be said that since his culture and culturally derived
psychological characteristics are man's species specific characteristics,
they are the uniquely *human* part of his nature." I will not spoil the
reader's enjoyment of discovery by finishing the argument in capsule
form, but will only say one of our problems is that we swing from one
extreme in anthropology to another in the rejection or enthusiastic
support of ideas. This swinging is a part of the sociology of knowledge of
all fields, but seems more acute in the social than the natural sciences,
and in anthropology more than in the sibling disciplines. This is probably a reflection of the degrees of ambiguity and uncertainty with which
we must cope—the more uncertainty, the more desperate the search
for guiding norms and heroes (see what Weston La Barre has to say
about this!). In teaching introductory anthropology each year Louise
Spindler and I are reminded how important cultural relativism, holism,
and cultural determinism are as ways of attacking the ethnocentrism and
narrow understanding of human adaptability characteristic of students
raised in our North American culture—despite the seeming openness
and variety of contemporary youth culture (it is more apparent than
real). Perhaps we anthropologists were like ethnocentric youth. We had
to subject ourselves to the culture shock treatment before we could face
the ultimate issues. Perhaps it is a problem of the limits of diversity and
difference—when is a cultural difference merely a variation on a basic
theme and when does it push human adaptibility to the outer limits?
When is a cognitive structure and process so different that *for some
purposes* it is unique? Process will always be less different than structure.
For some purposes it is most important to recognize the unity of human
nature. For other purposes it is most important to recognize the diversity
of cultures.

Like Spiro's chapter, the paper by George Devereux, has been
influential in the formation of this editorial overview. It has been mentioned in several contexts. Attention to the inside/outside, observer/
subject relationship is one of Devereux's big concerns. He states that no
device can filter out the observer's distortions. If this is true, we have no
alternative but to exploit the self-scrutiny of the observer to obtain

insight into his or her manner of distorting the phenomena observed. The methods for doing this are by no means clear, and in our attempts to apply Devereux's insight we may find ourselves in another infinite regression—this time of attempts to exploit self-scrutiny, as observer observes observer—now subject. And yet we cannot afford to ignore the effect with which Devereux is concerned. Perhaps this attention itself and the self-awareness of the phenomenon may act as an input into a partially self-correcting feedback. In any event, we have not taken this seriously enough in our research training. The highly subtle and complex communication between anthropologist and informant calls for training sessions in psychiatric interviewing. Sensitivity can be taught. One can learn to hear with the "inner ear." We can also learn to observe with the "third eye" after having been exposed, for example, to filmed sequences of interviewing with interpretative sessions on interaction synchrony and dissynchrony, following ethnomethodological and symbolic interactionist persuasions.

I leave this introductory overview without a conclusion. Indeed there can be no conclusion, for it is an introduction to a process of learning that I hope the reader will now enter into with questions rather than with answers.

REFERENCES CITED

Barnouw, V.
  1973   *Culture and Personality*. Homewood, Illinois: The Dorsey Press.
Bates, M.
  1977   Measuring Peasant Attitudes to Modernization. *Current Anthropology,* 17: 641-666.
Bennett, J. W.
  1974   The Japanese Character. *Reviews in Anthropology* 1:469–488.
Bernard, J.
  1974   My Four Revolutions: An Autobiographical History of the ASA. *American Journal of Sociology* 78:11–29.
Bourguignon, E.
  1973   Psychological Anthropology. In *Handbook of Social and Cultural Anthropology,* ed. J. Honigmann, pp. 1073–1118. Chicago: Rand-McNally.
Bushnell, J. and Bushnell, D.
  1975   Projective Doll Play Reconsidered: The Use of a Group Technique with Rural Mexican Children. In *Psychological Anthropology,* ed. T. R. Williams, pp. 163–220. The Hague: Mouton Publishers.

Campbell, D. T.
  1975   On the Conflicts Between Biological and Social Evolution and Between Psychology and Moral Tradition. *American Psychologist* 30:1103–1126.
Carlson, R.
  1971   Sex Differences in Ego Functioning: Exploratory Studies of Agency and Communion. *Journal of Consulting and Clinical Psychology* 37:267–76.
Chapple, E. D.
  1976   The Emperor Has No Clothes! Wilson, Sociobiology: The New Synthesis. *Reviews in Anthropology* 3:108–114.
DeVos, G. and Hippler, A.
  1969   Cultural Psychology: Comparative Studies of Human Behavior. In *The Handbook of Social Psychology,* eds. G. Lindzey and E. Aronson, pp. 323–418. 2nd ed., vol. 4. New York: Addison-Wesley Publishing Co.
Fischer, J.
  1965   Psychology and Anthropology. *Biennial Reviews in Anthropology,* ed. B. Siegel, pp. 211–61. Stanford: Stanford University Press.
Gamst, F. and Norbeck, E., eds.
  1976   *Ideas of Culture: Sources and Uses.* New York: Holt, Rinehart and Winston.
Goldenweiser, A.
  1917   The Autonomy of the Social. *American Anthropolgist* 19:447–49.
Hallowell, A. I.
  1953   Culture, Personality and Society. In *Anthropology Today: An Encyclopedic Inventory,* ed. A. Kroeber, pp. 597–620. Chicago: University of Chicago Press.
  1954   Psychology and Anthropology. In *For A Science of Social Man,* ed. J. Gillin, pp. 160–226. New York: The MacMillan Co.
Harris, M.
  1968   *The Rise of Anthropological Theory.* New York: Thomas Y. Crowell Co.
Honigman, J.
  1959   Psychocultural Studies. In *Biennial Reviews of Anthropology,* ed. B. Siegel, pp. 67–106. Stanford: Stanford University Press.
  1975   Psychological Anthropology: Trends, Accomplishments, and Future Tasks. In *Psychological Anthropology,* ed. T. R. Williams, pp. 601–626.
Hsu, Francis L. K., ed.
  1972   *Psychological Anthropology.* Cambridge, Mass.: Schenkman Publishing Co.
Inkeles, A. and Levinson, D.
  1969   Modal Personality and Sociocultural systems. In *The Handbook of Socail Psychology,* eds. G. Lindzey and E. Aronson, pp. 418–506. 2nd ed., vol. 4.
Jahoda, G.
  1958*a* Child Animism: I. A Critical Survey of Cross-Cultural Research. *Journal of Social Psychology* 47:197–212.
  1958*b* Child Animism: II. A Study in West Africa. *Journal of Social Psychology* 47:213–22.
Kardiner, A.
  1939   *The Individual and His Society.* New York: Columbia University Press.

Kardiner, A., Linton, R., DuBois, C., and West, J.
    1945   *The Psychological Frontiers of Scoeity.* New York: Columbia University Press.

Kluckhohn, C.
    1946   Review of Configurations of Cultural Growth, by A. L. Kroeber. *American Journal of Sociology* 51:336–41.

Kluckhohn, C. and Kelly, W. H.
    1945   The Concept of Culture. In *The Science of Man in the World Crisis,* ed. R. Linton, pp. 78–106. New York: Columbia University Press.

Kroeber, A. L.
    1917   The Superorganic. *American Anthropologist* 19:208–16.
    1944   *Configurations of Cultural Growth.* Berkeley: University of California Press.
    1948*a* White's View of Culture. *American Anthropolgist* 50:3.
    1948*b* *Anthropology.* New York: Harcourt, Brace and Jovanovich.
    1949   The Concept of Culture in Science. *Journal of General Education* 3:182–88.
    1952   *The Nature of Culture.* Chicago: University of Chicago Press.

Kroeber, A. L. and Kluckhohn, C.
    1952   *Culture: A Critical Review of Concepts and Definitions.* Papers of the Peabody Museum of American Archaeology and Ethnology, Harvard University. XLVII No. 1 Cambridge, Mass.

LeVine, R.
    1973   *Culture, Behavior and Personality: An Introduction to the Comparative Study of Psychosocial Adaptation.* Chicago: Aldine.

Linton, R.
    1945   *The Cultural Background of Personality.* New York: Appleton-Century-Crofts, Inc.

Lowie, R.
    1937   *The History of Ethnological Theory.* New York: Henry Holt and Co.

Malefijt, A. D. W.
    1974   *Images of Man: A History of Anthropological Thought.* New York: Alfred A. Knopf.

Mead, M.
    1928   *Coming of Age in Samoa.* New York: William Morrow and Co., Inc.
    1930   *Growing Up in New Guinea.* New York: William Morrow and Co., Inc.
    1935   *Sex and Temperament in Three Primitive Societies.* New York: William Morrow and Co., Inc.

Murdock, G. P.
    1932   The Science of Culture. *American Anthropologist* 2:200–15.

Pelto, P. J.
    1967   Psychology and Anthropology. *Biennial Reviews in Anthropology,* ed. B. Siegel. Stanford: Stanford University Press.
    1974   Therapy for an Ailing Subdiscipline. *Reviews in Anthropology* 1:509–15.

Pike, K.
    1954   *Language in Relation to a Unified Theory of the Structure of Human Behavior,* vol. 1. Glendale: Summer Institute of Linguistics.

Sapir, E.
  1917   Do we need a Superorganic? *American Anthropologist* 19:441–47.
  1934   Emergence of a Concept of Personality in a Study of Cultures. *Journal of Social Psychology* 5:410–16.

Siegel, B., ed.
  1969   *Biennial Reviews in Anthropology.* Stanford: Stanford University Press.

Smith, A. S., R. L. and R. H. Monroe, S. L. Washburn
  1976   Sociobiology Revisited. *Reviews in Anthropology* 3(5):544–60.

Smith, M. B.
  1954   Anthropology and Psychology. In *For A Science of Social Man,* ed. J. Gillin, pp. 32–36. New York: MacMillan.

Spindler, G. and Spindler, L.
  1963   Psychology in Anthropology: Applications to Culture Change. In *Psychology: A Study of a Science,* ed. B. Koch, pp. 510–51. New York: McGraw-Hill Book Co., Inc.
  1975   A Man and A Book: Hallowell's Culture and Experience. *Reviews in Anthropology* 2(2):144–56.

Spiro, E.
  1951   Culture and Personality: The Natural History of a False Dichotomy. *Psychiatry* 14:19–46.

Taylor, E. B.
  1871   *Primitive Culture: Researches into the Development of Mythology, Philosophy, Religion, Art and Custom.* London: John Murray (Publishers) Ltd.

Voget, F. W.
  1975   *A History of Ethnology.* New York: Holt, Rinehart and Winston.

Waddington, C. H.
  1960   *The Ethical Animal.* London: Allen and Unwin.

Wallace, A. F. C.
  1970   *Culture and Personality,* 1st revised edition. New York: Random House.

White, L. A.
  1946   Review of Kroeber's Culture Configurations. *American Anthropolgist* 48: 78–93.
  1947   Culturological Versus Psychological Interpretations of Human Behavior. *American Sociological Review* 12:686–98.
  1949   *The Science of Culture: A Study of Man and Civilization.* New York: Grove Press, Inc.

Williams, T. R., ed.
  1975   *Psychological Anthropology.* The Hague, Paris: Mouton Publishers.

Wilson, E. O.
  1975   *Sociobiology: The New Synthesis.* Cambridge, Mass.: Harvard University Press.

The Authors

JOHN W. N. WHITING, born in Martha's Vineyard, is a professor of social anthropology at Harvard University. He received his B.S. from Yale University in 1931 and his Ph.D. from the same university in 1938. He was associated with the Laboratory of Human Development in the Graduate School of Education between the years 1949 and 1963, becoming director in 1955. In 1963 he left the Laboratory and joined the Social Anthropology Department.

BEATRICE BLYTH WHITING, born in New York City, is a professor of education and anthropology in the Harvard Graduate School of Education. She received her B.A. in history from Bryn Mawr College in 1935, and her Ph.D. from Yale University in 1943. She was a research associate in the Laboratory of Human Development between 1952 and 1963 and a Lecturer in Social Anthropology between 1963 and 1969 when she rejoined the Laboratory of Human Development. From 1968 to 1973 the Whitings directed the Childhood Development research unit in the Department of Education of the University of Nairobi, Kenya.

This Chapter

The Whitings begin their chapter by naming their totemic ancestors. They are deviant from any other contributors to this volume in that they prefer a materialist, evolutionary, and cross-cultural approach. They also prefer Pavlov to Piaget. They have, however, neatly combined in their basic working model attention to materialist variables in the environment and maintenance systems and to nonmaterialist expressive-projective systems such as religion, beliefs, and ritual. Their model and their method, focusing attention on relationships between childhood training and later consequences, have produced for them a series of hypotheses that they have tested both macro-culturally and micro-culturally. Their macro-cross-cultural studies utilizing worldwide samples are famous and represent the antithesis of the idiographic and emic approaches that are implicit in much psychological anthropology. Their micro approach, however, involves detailed studies of type cases such as those represented in the six cultures study or in their current research in Kenya.

John Whiting's first major cross-cultural research related child training processes to theories of disease and sorcery (Whiting and Child 1953). Since then he and Beatrice Whiting have placed more and more emphasis on antecedent material conditions in the formation of their hypotheses. Sleeping arrangements, household structures, the effect of climate on physical contact with the mother, even the structure of houses as affected by the availability of large timbers, all have proven useful as base lines for the erection of hypotheses related to such factors as identification, conflicts in sex identity, styles of communication, severity of initiation ceremonies, and many others.

G.D.S.

1 A Strategy for Psychocultural Research

JOHN AND BEATRICE WHITING

Our approach to psychological anthropology can best be introduced by using a genealogical metaphor. Our totemic ancestors are William Graham Sumner, Sigmund Freud, Bronislaw Malinowski, Ivan Petrovich Pavlov and Franz Boaz.

The Sumner lineage provided us with a number of basic notions, the most important of which is that culture has evolved by a process of trial and error rather than by a rational plan. As Sumner puts it in the opening paragraph of his *Folkways* (1906), "Men begin with acts, not with thoughts. Every moment brings necessities which must be satisfied at once. Need was the first experience, and it was followed at once by a blundering effort to satisfy it." This materialist approach lead us in the development of our theory to start with the environment and history and to end with magic, art and religion. It led us to prefer Marx to Weber and Pavlov to Piaget. "The maintenance mores are basic" is the phrase we learned to express our commitment to a materialist theory of social change.

Sumner went on to say in his "charter" statement (*Folkways,* p. 3): "From recurrent needs arise habits for the individual and customs for the group." The assumption of the equivalence between custom and habit made it possible for us to use theories of learning, developed by psychologists to explain individual behavior, to interpret the customary behavior of a group (Whiting and Child 1953).

G. P. Murdock was a member of the Sumner lineage of our parental generation—he was a teacher and thesis director for both of us. From him we learned many things but perhaps the most important was the cross-cultural method. Starting with Sumner's voluminous notes on the peoples of the world, Murdock developed the Human Relations Area

41

Files, set standards for proper use of ethnographic materials to test hypotheses on world wide samples, and published in the Ethnographic Atlas (*Ethnology*, 1962–1966) coded materials on over one thousand societies describing such items as subsistence patterns, social organization, settlement pattern, division of labor, political organization and religious beliefs. Many of the studies that we will describe below made use of coded material from the Ethnographic Atlas, drew on the Human Relations Area files to make judgments of our own, and used the cross cultural method to test our hypotheses.

The materialist, evolutionary and cross-cultural approach of Sumner and Murdock was strongly opposed by the American Historical School whose leading figure was Franz Boaz and whose student, Leslie Spier, was one of our teachers. He imbued in us the importance of careful fieldwork and of historical processes, such as diffusion and borrowing, migration, and invention as principles by which the beliefs, values and techniques of a particular culture can be explained. He was critical of "grand theories" which include British evolutionists such as Tylor and Frazer and particularly critical of the French "sociological" school as represented by Durkheim. Perhaps the most important lesson that we learned from him was that, if you describe something about a culture, you must be sure that you know how it works. We spent one summer together while Bea was working with the Paiute gathering material for her thesis and John was coding ethnographies for the cross-cultural material files and editing some of Bea's field notes on material culture. One of these concerned a deadfall rabbit trap. John had read the description and approved it but when Leslie read it he called Bea in to ask her to please explain how it could possibly work. Bea passed the buck to John and we both had to agree that any Paiute who made a trap as we described it would probably go hungry. This lesson has stood us in good stead. Child rearing practices and women's daily routines must be described so that they will "catch the rabbit."

Bronislaw Malinowski was another teacher who had a strong influence on our thinking. A British functionalist, he emphasized the importance of explaining customs in terms of individual and social needs. Malinowski came to Yale the year John came back from New Guinea and was writing his thesis on the Kwoma. We were asked to his house one evening so John could read a draft of one of his chapters out loud. He had asked a group of his non-anthropological friends to listen and criticize. Their criticisms were devastating—almost as traumatic as when Murdock told each of us in turn that the first drafts of our theses were excruciatingly bad, or when Spier told us our rabbit trap wouldn't work.

The Institute of Human Relations which flowered during our careers as graduate students and with which we were both affiliated brought us in contact with learning and behavior theory through Clark Hull, Neal Miller, Don Marquis, Hobart Mowrer and Bob Sears. The assumption of this school that drive reduction was a necessary condition for learning was quite compatible with the materialism of Sumner and Murdock, the practicality of Spier, and the functional approach of Malinowski. But more important than this particular theory of learning and behavior, we learned from them how to formulate and test hypotheses, the meaning of probability statistics, and the value of the experimental method. We spent one summer running white rats through a maze for a study of "habit progression and regression" that we carried out with Hobart Mowrer (1943). From Hull in particular we learned the importance of distinguishing between coherence and correspondence truth and, hence, the difference between proving a hypotheses and testing it. Like a theorem in geometry, the proof of a hypothesis consists of showing that it logically follows from and does not contradict other assumptions in the theory. The *test* consists of observing whether empirical reality does or does not correspond to that which is stated in the hypothesis. From Hull we also learned that science progresses from the creative acts that follow when a hypothesis is disconfirmed in such a way that theory must be revised. To jeopardize assumptions that are taken for granted is more productive and exciting than to illustrate them.

The Freudian lineage, as well as the Pavlovian, was strongly represented at the Institute of Human Relations. We learned psychoanalytic theory from John Dollard through lectures, seminars and informal discussions. The most important learning experience came from our personal analyses. We both received fellowships for this purpose. Our analyst was Earl Zinn. We discovered that the meaning of unconscious motivation and the way in which one can delude oneself by various defensive maneuvers could be more profoundly understood when they were illustrated from one's own life than from a text book case.

The psychoanalytic assumption that early experience had a determining effect on the development of personality was responsible for our interest in child rearing. A concerted effort was being made at the Institute to redefine the basic concepts of Freudian theory in such a way that they could be subjected to empirical test. This was done by integrating them with the concepts and principles of both learning and behavior theory and those of cultural anthropology. The Freudian principle of displacement was described as a special case of stimulus generalization as defined by Pavlov. Identification, a psychoanalytic concept, was related to imitation, a concept from the field of learning. The magico-religious beliefs reported by anthropologists were interpreted as manifestations of various mechanisms of defense proposed by Freud. Both of us participated in this enterprise.

The lineages we have mentioned thus far represent the materialistic, practical, functional and scientific hypothesis testing approaches to psychological anthropology. It was Edward Sapir who represented for us the more subtle and humanistic point of view. He stressed the importance of knowing the native language for understanding culture. His stress on the importance of metaphor anticipates the position of the present symbolic school. His explication of the phonemic analysis of language was a model for the emic approach developed in ethnoscience. He also speculated on the relationship between culture and personality and made suggestions that were much more subtle and persuasive than the ethnologically naive approach of Freud in his attempt to explain *Totem and Taboo* (1938). Although others soon followed his lead, Sapir inspired us to isolate the expressive-projective domain of magic, religion and art as a potential index of the modal personality of a culture.

The influence of our various intellectual forebears guided our subsequent research and eventually lead us to formulate the model presented in Figure 1. This model serves as a guide for our thinking. It enables us to relate the various studies that we undertake and have undertaken so their results are more cumulative than might otherwise be the case. It also enables us to relate our research to those of others in the field of psychological anthropology. It is for us a cognitive map for psychocultural research.

Over the years we have elaborated this model and the variables whose interrelationship forms the basis for our theories and governs our research. Figure 1 is its most recent form. The arrows should not be interpreted as irreversible indicators of causal relations. They represent assumptions about the direction of causality but they do *not* imply that in some, if not many, instances the true direction of causation is the reverse, or that there are not feedback loops or that steps in the assumed sequence may not be skipped. On the basis of this model we have formulated hypotheses which we have attempted to test using published ethnographic descriptions of societies and data from field work which we have designed in collaboration with our colleagues and students. Our pleasure comes from testing these hypotheses, finding them probable or improbable, revising them and repeating the process. We are most satisfied when one of our projects follows logically from the preceding ones and when our hypotheses are interrelated in a coherent manner.

Figure 1

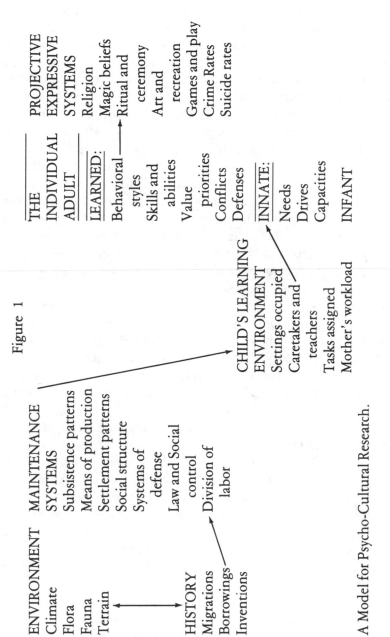

A Model for Psycho-Cultural Research.

Reproduced from *Children of Six Cultures: A Psychocultural Analysis.*

We have attempted to test hypotheses both across and within societies. In the former case we have treated societies as units of analysis, have rated them on sets of variables and made tests of association between the variables. In many instances there are the same variations within as across societies thus enabling us to replicate our findings by case studies. As an example, cultures can be characterized as either monogamous or polygynous but there are no so-called polygynous societies in which monogamous families cannot be found. All of our findings are of necessity based on correlational studies. Since when one is working with human beings it is difficult to devise appropriate experiments, one is forced to search in his own and other societies for naturally occurring variations in the life experiences of individuals and attempt to assess their influence on behavior and related aspects of culture. We have found it wise, whenever possible, to pretest all of our hypotheses on published ethnographic data. If hypothesized associations look promising we try to turn to the detailed analysis of type cases and to testing the hypotheses in societies which are particularly suited because of variation in the predictor variables.

To illustrate this method let us take one of our current hypotheses: children brought up by mothers who make a substantial contribution to the subsistence of the family will be more concerned with the welfare of others than children brought up by mothers who do not make such a contribution. To test this theory across cultures on the basis of published data two sets of judges are needed. One set reads the ethnographies of a sample of societies distributed around the world and rates the mothers' reported contribution to the subsistence economy; the other set reads the same sources and rates the children on their tendency to help others and take responsibility for the welfare of others. Neither set of judges should know the hypothesis to be tested. If this evidence supports the hypothesis, a field study can be designed to investigate the relation of these variables within a society. The field study can identify a sample of women, estimate their contribution to subsistence, and record the rate of helpful and responsible behavior observed in their children. If the hypothesis holds up within this society we have further evidence for its validity.

Few of our studies encompass the entire model. Most of them have focused on a segment. In this chapter we will give examples of some of the studies, attempting at the same time to indicate how they are related historically. The original version of the model appeared in *Child Training and Personality,* the collaborative work of John Whiting and Irvin Child (1953, p. 310). This cross-cultural study explored the relation between a child's learning environment as measured by reported child training practices and one of the projective systems, theories of disease. The hypotheses relating these two sets of variables were derived from psychoanalytic and learning theories. The ethnographic accounts of seventy-five societies were read, analyzed and rated as to the parental treatment of critical issues during the Freudian stages of psychosexual development (oral, anal, and phallic) and parental behavior concerning two other problems which seemed of universal concern, training for independence and the management of aggression. Raters made judgments of the socialization practices surrounding these issues. They included assessments of (1) the initial indulgence or permissiveness associated with the behavior system; (2) the age at the onset of socialization; (3) the severity of socialization; and (4) the technique of punishment characteristically used by parents and other socializing agents. Two other raters made judgments of the society's most common explanations for illness, classifying them according to their relevance to these five behavior systems. For example the belief in magical poisoning was classified as an oral theory of disease.

Although the main thrust of this study was the relationship between an aspect of a child's learning environment and one type of projective system, the chapter on guilt considered the relation of social structure to child training practices and initiated another chain of studies. In the discussion of the possible origins of guilt, residence rules (whether a newly married couple set up residence independently of either set of parents, i.e., neolocal; or with the husband's family, i.e., patrilocal; or the wife's family, i.e., matrilocal) and forms of marriage (sororal polygyny, polygyny, monogamy) were explored as index measures of the relative role of parents, relatives and nonrelatives in the training of children (ibid., pp. 250–55. See also "Sorcery, Sin and the Superego: A Cross-Cultural Study of Some Mechanisms of Social Control," J. Whiting 1959). The cross-cultural work of George Peter Murdock on social structure (Murdock 1949) gave impetus to the analysis of the effect of these variables on a child's learning environment. Further exploration of the relation of social structure to child training practices was presented in 1951 by Murdock and Whiting at a conference on the problems of infancy and childhood (Murdock and Whiting 1951). The most interesting finding concerned the relative severity of parental training in the five areas of socialization rated in the Whiting and Child study. Societies with sororal polygyny were judged to be less severe in their training than societies with non-sororal polygyny or monogamy. This was interpreted as reflecting the cooperation of the cowives (who are sisters) in the first type of household. These women, because they had worked out their interpersonal relations and rivalries in childhood, were able to help each other and share the care of each other's children and hence could give them more attention and postpone socialization. Since they could share their workload, these women seemed to be under less pressure than women in monogamous households where there were no other adult females or in non-sororal polygynous families where the women were rivalrous and had no long established pattern for working out these rivalries.

These findings in turn led to the expansion of the model and to the exploration of the influence of the maintenance systems, particularly economic and social structure variables on child training practices.

Two important decisions about our future research in culture and personality were the result of Irvin Child and John Whiting's collaboration in writing *Child Training and Personality*. In the first place the issues centering around the Freudian concept of psychosexual development appeared to be of less universal concern than others which could be identified: toilet training was seldom mentioned in the literature as being any problem at all. Weaning from the breast was usually not nearly so important as weaning from the back or training for independence. The socialization of sex turned out to be dealt with by rules governing premarital sex behavior in late childhood and adolescence rather than during early childhood. Training for aggression was, as expected, a universal problem, as was training for independence. Parents in most cultures were more concerned with interpersonal relations than with body functions. It was clear that a different set of variables was needed to describe the most important feature of the child's learning environment.

Irvin Child, together with Margaret Bacon and Herbert Barry set out to work on a new analytic framework for analyzing child training practices using a combination of Henry Murray's theory of personality (1938) and the theory of learning of Hull (1943) and Miller and Dollard (1941). They developed the well known "Barry, Bacon and Child code" (1967). In this code infant indulgence was reanalyzed but, more importantly, independence training was broken down into six categories: responsibility, nurturance, self-reliance, achievement, obedience, and general independence.

Second, as a result of combing the ethnographic sources, John Whiting and Irvin Child were convinced that the accounts of child life and socialization were inadequate and that special field work should be undertaken by researchers who were particularly interested in children and were willing to attempt to collect comparable data on a sample of societies which represented the variety of cultures existing in the world. With the help of Professor Robert Sears, the Social Science Research Council, and the Ford Foundation a field study was planned with a goal of studying the child's learning environment and the socialization practices in six societies. The field teams were committed to collecting data according to an agreed upon design developed by Irvin Child, William Lambert and John Whiting in collaboration with a group of consultants (see *Field Guide for the Study of Socialization,* Whiting et al. 1966). This field work was carried out from 1954 to 1956 in six societies and has been reported in a series of monographs (B. Whiting 1963; Minturn and Lambert 1964; Whiting and Whiting 1975). Some of the results will be discussed later.

Returning to our model, the next important analysis of the relation of child training to the maintenance systems appeared in Bacon, Barry and Child's paper on the relation of subsistence economy to their new ratings (1959). They reported that in societies with a high accumulation of property children were pressured to be responsible, obedient and nurturant while in socieities with low accumulation of property pressure was exerted on children to be self-reliant and achievement oriented. Our most recent publication on the six culture study has included a follow up on the paper (Whiting and Whiting 1975). The hypotheses concerning the relation of a mother's workload to children's responsibility and nurturance suggested at the beginning of this chapter was tested with positive results.

The revision of the Bacon, Barry and Child hypothesis focused on the workload of the mother rather than on the accumulation of property as the more important predictor variable. In fact, in what might be considered the most complex and highly accumulating society in our sample, Orchard Town, New England, U.S.A., children scored comparatively low on nurturance and responsibility as measured by our code. The mothers of Orchard Town were also judged to have the lightest workload.

The extensive study of type cases has been invaluable in revising this theory and identifying new predictor variables. In the Bacon, Barry and Child sample societies which scored highest in pressure toward responsibility and nurturance were the subsaharan African groups who combined agriculture and herding (Barry, Child and Bacon 1959; Whiting and Whiting 1971). Since one of our societies in the six culture study, the Gusii of Kenya (LeVine and LeVine 1966) fit this description, we were able to analyze in detail the learning environment and the training children received. We were able to assess the mother's workload and the animal husbandry, farm work, child care and housework expected of children between the ages of three and eleven.

However, our sample of families in Gusii was not large enough to test many of our hypotheses on the basis of within culture differences and we could only compare Gusii as a unit with the other five cultures. In order to carry out a within culture test we are now engaged in a field study of a Kikuyu village in Kenya where we are able to assess the differences in the workload of various mothers in the village, the work required of their children, and compare the children's responsibility as observed in social interaction in naturally occurring situations.

In the Barry, Bacon and Child sample the hunter and gathering societies ranked comparatively low in reported socialization pressure toward nurturance and responsibility and high in pressure toward self reliance and achievement (1959). As in the case of the Gusii we have been able to profit by analyzing detailed data from one of these societies, the !Kung Bushmen of The Kalahari Desert in South Africa. Patricia Draper, who had previously worked with us on a cross-cultural study of children's chores, spent eighteen months living with the Bushmen observing parental and child behavior. It is clear from her data that the workload of these women is far lighter than that of the agriculturalists and the children are not expected to do any real work until their teens (Draper 1972). The nature of the settlement camp and the spacing of children makes the use of child nurses to help busy mothers less important. The children spend time playing and practicing skills and are not overtly supervised or directed in their activities. These are the practices which have contributed to their high score in pressure toward self-reliance and achievement.

In our present work in Kenya we hope to be able to continue our comparative study of the influence of the economy on a child's learning environment, not only by comparing the herding cultures (Masai and Samburu) with the groups who combine herding and agriculture (Kipsigis, Luo, and Gusii) and with the more intensive agriculturalists (Kikuyu and Luhyua) but also with groups who are moving into a wage earning economy and successful white collar workers who are urban dwellers.

The progression of our research in this area best exemplifies the strategy which we try to follow, namely, working back and forth between the macro cross-cultural level and the micro level, the detailed study of type cases, if possible making comparisons within a geographic area, and finally the study of individual differences within a society. We have attempted to replicate the associations we find between custom complexes on each of these levels. We favor beginning on the macro level, if possible, using the extensive cross cultural ratings which have grown out of the library research of George Peter Murdock and his followers (see *Ethnology* 1962–1966). If our hypotheses seem to work on this macro level, wherever possible we turn to the analysis of the best field research type cases or best of all organize the field work ourselves. Finally, we attempt to do a test of the hypothesis within a culture if there is sufficient individual variation in the independent variables. Obviously such strategy requires team work, and the more collaboration among researchers in exploring similar hypotheses the more fruitful the results.

Returning to our model, we have developed another promising set of hypotheses about the relation of family structure variables to characteristics of the child's learning environment and a child's behavior. As mentioned above, the first findings in this area were reported by Murdock and Whiting in 1951. Following these leads, John Whiting with his interest in the origins of guilt and self-control began exploring the effect of family form, household structure and mother-father-child sleeping arrangements on the development of identification and conflicts in sex identity. This research spans the entire model. Temperature and diet, *environment,* are hypothesized as being associated with household type and sleeping arrangements, *maintenance systems* (J. Whiting, 1964), the degree of salience of the father during infancy and childhood, *child's learning environment* (Burton and Whiting 1961), sex identity conflict and behavior styles, *the individual adult* (Carlsmith 1964, 1973), and magical beliefs as exemplified in theories of disease, ritual as exemplified by initiation ceremonies (Whiting, Kluckhohn and Anthony 1958), and the practice of couvade (Munroe, Munroe and Whiting 1973) and crime rates (B. Whiting 1965), *the projective-expressive systems.* It is impossible here to discuss these theories in detail or to describe the type of field work and the collaboration which is involved in this series of hypotheses. It has been recently summarized by one of the authors (J. Whiting 1973). Again, this research follows not only the model presented in Figure 1 but our research strategy. The original research relating child training practices to theories of disease and sorcery was cross-cultural (Whiting and Child 1953). Similarly the early research on the relation of climate, diet and social structure and household type was cross-cultural followed by field work by the staff of the Laboratory of Human Development at Palfrey House, Harvard, among a group of Barbadians in Central Square, Cambridge (D'Andrade 1962, 1973; Longabaugh 1962, 1973; Tancock 1961), followed by John Herzog's field work in the Barbados (1968) and the Munroe's field work among the Black Carib in British Honduras (Munroe and Munroe 1971, 1973) and other couvade practicing males, in this case a sample of fathers in the Boston area (Munroe and Munroe 1973). This field work was followed by new cross-cultural research, followed by extensive field work in Kenya, the analysis of which is still in process (Daniels 1970; Herzog 1973).

It should be noted again that research of this type involves team work and in the present world is greatly aided by the help of local students and scholars in any of the host countries which offer settings suited for testing the hypotheses. It should also be stressed that ideally the selection of field sites should be based on the presence and/or absence of important variables which are components of one's hypotheses. Thus if one has theories about the custom complexes associated with the practice of circumcision rites at puberty, male bonding and sex identity conflict, a field site such as Kenya which has groups of people some of whom have all the associated characteristics, some of whom have some but not all and some of whom have none, is an ideal place. The value of collaborative work in the field with Kenyan students and colleagues has been well documented by our research in this host country.[1]

It will be noted that in the studies of sex identity conflict environmental factors including climate and flora and fauna appear for the first time as predictor variables. Two particular studies have focused on their effect on social structure and settlement patterns and hence on a child's learning environment, particularly on the relative salience of the father in infancy and early and late childhood (*Ethos* 1 (4) Winter 1973 passim). Children in divergent cultures grow up in houses which include a variety of human beings. As infants and young children they are in intimate contact with different categories of people. Since both psychoanalytic and behavioral psychology postulate different outcomes as a result of these experiences, some of our studies have focused upon the amount of contact between various categories of people. Among the most intimate relations are those between persons who sleep together. Investigation of sleeping arrangements in various parts of the world indicate that there were four main types which occurred with frequency

---

1. This research has been conducted under the auspices of the Child Development Research Unit in the Department of Education in the University of Nairobi, financed by a grant from the Carnegie Corporation.

in a world sample of societies; husband and wife might share a bed and the infant sleep in a crib or cradle, the wife and baby might sleep together and the husband sleep in a separate bed in the same room, in a different room, or in a different house, the husband and wife and baby could all share the same bed, or all three could sleep in separate beds. Analysis of the distribution of these sleeping arrangements indicated that they were associated with climate and that temperature appeared to be the predictor variable (J. Whiting 1964, p. 514). When the winter temperature falls below freezing husband and wife most frequently sleep together and the baby is wrapped well and put in a separate cradle or crib. In societies where the winter temperature does not fall below 68°F the mother and baby most frequently share a bed and the father sleeps alone. When the mother and infant share a bed it is possible for the baby to have access to his mother's breast with little effort. If on the other hand he is in a separate bed he has to cry in order to summon his mother, and if the bed is in a separate room his crying might need to be loud and prolonged. The body contact with the mother and easy access to her breast most frequently terminates when the mother becomes pregnant with a new child or when the new child is born.

Recent changes in our own society suggest that invention and the borrowing of technology can change existing patterns. Although psychoanalysts' warnings about the Oedipal complex and pediatricians warning about smothering the child or disturbing his sleep have in the past discouraged mothers from taking their babies into bed with them, there are indications of changing patterns among U. S. middle-class mothers. Many of these mothers who are breast feeding find it most convenient not to have to get up during the night, and hence they allow the infant to sleep in the parental bed. Associated with this change is the improvement of our modern heating facilities so that the temperature of the sleeping room may be kept warm enough during the winter months for the infant to be comfortable in the parental bed without extensive swaddling or close wrapping. Of equal importance for this culture change may be the invention of leakproof rubber pants which make the infant's presence less irritating to both mother and father (B. Whiting 1973).

Temperature not only effects body contact during the night but also during the day. A search of the ethnographic literature on over two hundred societies indicated that in about sixty judges could rate the amount of physical contact between a baby and its mother or surrogate caretaker during the day (J. Whiting 1971). In some societies the baby was carried or propped up in a cradleboard or wrapped in thick clothing or placed in some other type of container; in others it had more physical contact with the mother during the day; and in still others he was judged to be in direct physical contact most of the day, carried by his mother or surrogate mother with no clothing or only light clothing separating him from his caretaker's skin. With few notable exceptions, the Eskimo and the Yahgan of Patagonia, this latter type of close physical contact again is associated with climate. Forty of the forty-eight societies lying in the tropics between latitude 20 degrees north and 20 degrees south were reported to have close and frequent contact between mother and infant, whereas twenty-nine out of thirty-seven societies situated in the temperate and frigid zones used heavy swaddling or strapped the baby into cradleboards or crib-like containers. It is our hypothesis that close physical contact may have lasting effects on reactions to physical stress, physical growth (Landauer and Whiting 1964; Gunders and Whiting 1968; Whiting, Landauer and Jones 1968) and on styles of communication (J. Whiting 1971).

For the infant and young child who is dependent on caretakers and stays near home, the structure of the house determines the persons who are around during the day and night which in turn is associated with the size of the dwelling in which his mother lives. In areas of the world lacking large timber, before the importation or manufacture of building materials it was difficult to build large houses (Whiting and Ayres 1968). Families either lived in close intimate contact within one small structure or built separate huts which served as separate bedrooms or living quarters. In sub-Saharan agricultural areas of East Africa, for example, the husband often had a hut of his own in which he might sleep and eat with his elder sons. Furthermore, if he was polygynously married each wife had a hut of her own. As a consequence of this arrangement the younger children were not in intimate contact with their fathers. Our recent research in a Kikuyu village in Kenya suggests how new technology can effect this pattern. One of the traditional Kikuyu's woman's most time consuming burdensome chores was providing water for her family, often walking for over a mile twice a day and carrying five to eight gallons of water on her back. With the importation of metal roofing and barrels, it was possible to rig up a system whereby rain which fell on a metal roof could be collected in rain barrels. Traditional Kikuyu houses were circular in floor plan with mud and wattle walls and thatched roofs. Circular tin roofs were impractical and hence when families could afford the metal the house plan became rectangular. This made it possible to include more rooms under the same roof. As a result the husband often abandoned his separate hut and moved into a room in the new house. In some cases he even put his polygynous wives under one roof since it was cheaper to build one metal-roofed house than two (B. Whiting 1974).

In our research in the Kikuyu village over the last six years we have monitored changes in house types and sleeping arrangements. We have discovered that with the introduction of the rectangular house and tin roofs there is also an increase in use of the master bedroom reserved for the father, mother and infant—older children being relegated to another bedroom. The new house often also houses the kitchen and a livingroom for receiving guests. These shifts in architecture have the effect of increasing the contact between the father and his young children, a variable which we postulate has important effects on the child's learning environment.

The effect of environment and history is obvious on a more macro level and has been documented by anthropologists for many years. Agriculture cannot easily exist in desert land, nor can industry exist where there is no source of power. People cannot live in large aggregations unless there is enough water and food. If large numbers of people live together there must be formalized ways of solving conflict (B. Whiting 1950). The larger the aggregate of people, the more complex the social and political structure, the more specialized the status and roles (Murdock 1949). Thus economy, settlement pattern, social and political structure, and the legal system are all directly influenced by climate, terrain, flora, fauna and technological knowledge.

For psychological anthropology the importance of these environmental factors stems primarily from their effect on the maintenance systems, the economy, settlement pattern and social structure factors which determine the division of labor, and the status and role of the adults. These are the variables which influence parental behavior and are so often overlooked in the study of child development because there is comparatively little variation in Western societies where most of our psychological theories have been developed. One of the important functions of psychological anthropology is to identify these hidden variables which have been obscured because there is a cultural blindness (J. Whiting 1954; B. Whiting 1973). Although child psychologists have paid lip service to social structure and economic variables they have summarized them in the concept of SES (social economic class) and have spent too little time exploring the independent effect of the elements hidden in this concept (B. Whiting 1973).

In conclusion we would like to describe one of our most promising present research projects which represents our effort to develop better instruments for evaluating personality. In the six culture study we decided to use observed behavior as our dependent variable. (Whiting and Whiting 1975). Our decision in 1955 to invest the innumerable man hours required to observe, record, code, and analyze samples of individual children's behavior as it occurred in natural settings, grew out of a dissatisfaction with projective tests. As mentioned earlier one of the great problems in the study of the effect of culture on personality has been the problem of measurement. How does one assess and compare personality types? In the six culture study, although we attempted to study and describe the projective-expressive systems of each society, we did not attempt to collect data on an individual's perceptions of these systems and hence had no measures for "modal personality." The samples of behavior collected by the field teams on twenty-four children, age three to eleven, in each of the societies were analyzed in terms of the nine behavior systems which were selected for attention by Irvin Child, William Lambert and John Whiting (Whiting and Whiting 1975). All of the behavior was recorded and coded in terms of interacts—exchanges between individuals, which could be considered to be oriented toward helping, being responsible, hurting, roughhousing, seeking help and physical contact, seeking competition and dominance, and seeking friendly interaction. Comparisons between children were made both within societies and across the six. We were interested in exploring the degree to which the behavior of children brought up in diverse cultures was similar or different. We explored for universals which could be explained by sex, age, sibling order and culture type. In our attempt to assess the particular role of culture in influencing children's behavior, we turned to our model exploring economic factors, the division of labor, settlement patterns, social structure, the settings occupied by children, the persons responsible for their training, the tasks assigned to children, and the child training practices observed and reported by mothers.

Although the culture of the society in which one grew up had a significant effect on behavior, we found there were indeed universals. There were similar differences between boys and girls in all six cultures, most of which seem to be attributable to the similarity of the role of adult woman in all cultures (Whiting and Edwards 1973; Whiting and Whiting 1975). We found consistent changes in behavior with age: we found the youngest children in all six societies shared behavioral characteristics; and we found one of the most important predictors of a child's behavior was the status and age of the person with whom he interacted.

Thus, in all cultures children tend to offer help, support, and entertainment to infants, they tend to seek help, information, physical proximity and friendly interaction and support from adults. Aggressive behavior was most frequent between peers. If one interprets personality to be the tendency to behave in certain ways regardless of the specific setting, it seems reasonable to suppose that habits associated with the settings one occupies most frequently will influence one's "personality." Thus we would predict from our findings that one of the important effects of culture is in determining the type of settings an individual is most apt to frequent. A child growing up in an isolated nuclear family with one or two other siblings is high on seeking behavior and sociability as his interaction with adults is frequent; he will be comparatively low on nurturant behavior since the chances are that when he is at an age when in other societies he would be expected to help care for an infant sibling, there will not be any infants in his family. Children growing up in families where there are infant siblings and where their mothers are busy and need help, will be more apt to offer help and support to others because of the habits established in their role as child nurses. They will have less experience in exclusive face to face interaction with adults (Whiting and Whiting 1975), and fewer seeking behaviors focused on them.

One aspect of our present work in Kenya is a follow up on these findings focused on further exploration of the effect of setting on the behavior of parents and children, where setting is conceived as including the physical space in which customary behavior takes place, the cast of characters with whom one frequently interacts and the activities one customarily performs. Again Kenya offers unusual opportunities for research. Thomas Weisner and the authors have identified a group of mothers and children who spend some time in both the country and the city (Weisner 1973; B. Whiting 1969) and we are able to train Kenyan students to observe these adults and children as they interact in both settings. With modernization, family and household structure are in rapid transition so that it is possible in various communities in Kenya to contrast children who are growing up in divergent settings but who are not, as is so often the case when we work in our own society, members of a depressed minority. Observational studies are facilitated by the fact that much of the daily living in Kenya occurs outside the house and hence observers are less obtrusive than in U. S. society.

We would like to stress the need for cooperation in this type of exploration of the relation of culture and personality. If we are to make headway in understanding the interaction, we need the collaboration of anthropologists, ethologists, psychologists and other behavioral scientists. We need the assistance of students and scholars in host countries, and we need to be willing to collect data for each other and replicate each other's findings. If we are to develop theories which are valid they must stand up to repeated tests on many samples of individuals in various parts of the world.

All our work has been directed toward developing and testing general principles that apply across cultures and/or across individuals within a culture. Because of this preoccupation we have been accused of neglecting the unique and idiosyncratic. There are many who prefer a more humanistic approach to psychological anthropology. Their goal is to discover and portray the subtleties of metaphor, the complexities of structure and ritual, and the unique "emic" meanings of each culture. To these individuals the fact that snowflakes are octagonal and will melt if the temperature rises above freezing is of little interest compared to the beauty and uniqueness of each flake. Although we are committed to the hypothesis jeopardizing, snowflake melting approach, we depend on the careful and insightful descriptions of cultures and peoples by those ethnographers with a more humanistic orientation. Likewise, it is true they often use the findings of science to interpret the individual case.

We remain dedicated to developing and testing hypotheses designed to be true for all peoples at all times. We are also interested in explaining the individual, culture, and the interaction between them. And we remain convinced that child rearing involves more than the simple and intentional transmission of culture.

Unless otherwise noted, all the research reported in this paper has been financed by a grant from United States Public Health MH 01096–19.

REFERENCES CITED

Barry, H. III, Child, I. L., and Bacon, M. K.
    1959   Relation of Child Training to Subsistence Economy. *American Anthropologist* 61:51–63.
    1967   Code. In *Cross-Cultural approaches,* ed. C. S. Ford, pp. 293–331. New Haven.

Burton, R. R. V. and Whiting, J. W. M.
   1961   The Absent Father and Cross-Sex Identity. *Merrill-Palmer Quarterly of Behavior and Development* 7(2):85–95.

Carlsmith, L.
   1964   Effect of Early Father Absence on Scholastic Aptitude. *Harvard Educational Review* 34:3–21.
   1973   Some Personality Characteristics of Boys Separated from their Fathers During World War II. *Ethos* 1(4):466–77.

D'Andrade, R. G.
   1962   Father Absence and Cross-Sex Identification. Ph.D. dissertation, Harvard University.
   1973   Father Absence, Identification and Identity. *Ethos* 1(4):440–55.

Daniels, R. E.
   1970   By Rites a Man: A Study of the Societal and Individual Foundations of Tribal Identity among the Kipsigis of Kenya. Ph.D. dissertation, University of Chicago.

Draper, P.
   1972   !Kung Childhood. Ph.D. dissertation, Harvard University. Social and Economic Constraints on !Kung Childhood. In *Kalahari Hunter Gatherers,* eds. R. B. Lee and I. DeVore. Cambridge, Mass.: Harvard University Press, in press.

Freud, S.
   1938   Totem and Taboo, *Basic Writings of Sigmund Freud.* Translated by A. A. Brill. New York: Modern Library.

Gunders, S. M. and Whiting, J. W. M.
   1968   Mother-Infant Separation and Physical Growth. *Ethnology* 7:196–206.

Herzog, J. D.
   1968   Household Composition and Boys' School Performance in Barbados, W. I. Ph.D. dissertation, Harvard University.
   1973   Initiation and High School in the Development of a Kikuyu Youths' Self-Concept. *Ethos* 1(4):478–89.

Hull, C. L.
   1943   *Principles of Behavior.* New York: Appleton-Century-Crofts.

Landauer, T. K. and Whiting, J. W. M.
   1964   Infantile Stimulation and Adult Stature of Human Males. *American Anthropologist* 66:1007-1027.

LeVine, R. A. and LeVine (Lloyd), B.
   1966   Nyansongo: A Gusii community in Kenya. In *Six Cultures: Studies in Child Rearing,* Vol. 2, ed. B. Whiting. New York: John Wiley and Sons, Inc.

Longabaugh, R. H. W.
   1962   The Description of Mother-Child Interaction. Ed.D. dissertation, Harvard University.
   1973   Mother Behavior as a Variable Moderating the Effects of Father Absence. *Ethos* 1(4):456–65.

Miller, N. E. and Dollard, H.
   1941   *Social Learning and Imitation.* New Haven: Yale University Press.

Minturn, L. and Lambert, W. W.
  1964 *Mothers of Six Cultures: Antecedents of Child Rearing*. New York: John Wiley and Sons, Inc.

Munroe, R. L. and Munroe, R. H.
  1971 Male Pregnancy Symptoms and Cross-Sex Identity in Three Societies. *Journal of Social Psychology* 84:11–25.
  1973 Psychological Interpretation of Male Initiation Rites: The Case of Male Pregnancy Symptoms. *Ethos* 1(4):490–98.

Munroe, R. L., Munroe, R. H., and Whiting, J. W. M.
  1973 The Couvade: A Psychological Analysis. *Ethos* 1(1):30–74.

Murdock, G. P.
  1949 *Social Structure*. New York: MacMillan and Co.

Murdock, G. P. et al.
  1962- Ethnographic Atlas. *Ethnology* 1–5.
  1966

Murdock, G. P. and Whiting, J. W. M.
  1951 Cultural Determinants of Parental Attitudes: The Relationship Between the Social Structure, Particularly Family Structure and Parental Behavior. In *Problems of Infancy and Childhood*, ed. J. E. Senn. New York: Josiah Macy, Jr. Foundation.

Murray, H. A.
  1938 *Explorations in Personality*. New York: Oxford.

Sumner, W. G.
  1906 *Folkways*. Boston: Ginn and Co.

Tancock, B.
  1961 A Study of Household Structure and Child Training in a Lower-Class Barbadian Group. Ed.D. dissertation, Harvard University.

Weisner, T.
  1973 Studying Rural-Urban Ties: A Matched Network Sample from Kenya. In *Survey Research in Africa: It's Applications and Limits*, eds. W. M. O'Barr, D. H. Spain, M. Tissler. Evanston, Illinois: Northwestern University Press.

Whiting, B. B.
  1950 *Pauite Sorcery*. New York: Viking Fund.
  1965 Sex Identity Conflict and Physical Violence: A Comparative Study. *American Anthropologist* 67(6):123–40.
  1969 The Effect of Urbanization on the Behavior of Children. Graduate School of Education, Harvard University.
  1973 Folk Wisdom and Child Rearing. *Merrill-Palmer Quarterly of Behavior and Development* 20(1):1974.
  1973 The Problem of the Packaged Variable. In *Proceedings of the Biennial International Conference on Behavioral Development*, ed. K. Riegel. Ann Arbor, Michigan.
  1974 The Effect of Modernization on Socialization. Paper presented at Third Annual Meeting of the Society for Cross-Cultural Research, Boston.

Whiting, B. B., ed.
  1963 *Six Cultures: Studies in Child Rearing*. New York: John Wiley and Sons, Inc.

Whiting, B. B. and Edwards, C.
1973   A Cross-Cultural Analysis of Sex Differences in the Behavior of Children Aged Three through Eleven. *Journal of Social Psychology* 91.
Whiting, B. B. and Whiting, J. W. M.
1975   *Children of Six Cultures: A Psychocultural Analysis.* Cambridge, Mass.: Harvard University Press.
Whiting, J. W. M.
1954   The Cross-Cultural Method. In *Handbook of Social Psychology*, Vol. 2, ed. G. Lindsay, Cambridge, Mass.: Addison-Wesley.
1959   Sorcery, Sin and the Superego: A Cross-Cultural Study of Some Mechanisms of Social Control. In *Symposium on Motivation*, ed. M. R. Jones. Lincoln, Nebraska: University of Nebraska Press.
1964   Effects of Climate on Certain Cultural Practices. In *Explorations in Cultural Anthropology: Essays in Honor of George Peter Murdock*, ed. W. H. Goodenough. New York: McGraw-Hill.
1971   Causes and Consequences of the Amount of Body Contact Between Mother and Infant. Paper delivered at the 70th Annual Meeting of the American Anthropological Association in New York.
1973   A Model for Psychocultural Research. The 1973 Distinguished Lecture Address delivered at the Annual Meeting of the American Anthropological Association, in New Orleans, Annual Report 1974.
Whiting, J. W. M. and Ayres, B.
1968   Inferences from the Shape of Dwellings. In *Settlement Archaeology*, ed. K. C. Chang. Palo Alto: National Press Books.
Whiting, J. W. M. and Child, I. L.
1953   *Child Training and Personality.* New Haven: Yale University Press.
Whiting, J. W. M., Child, I. L., Lambert, W. W. et al.
1966   *Field Guide for a Study of Socialization. Six Cultures: Studies in Child Rearing*, Vol. 1. New York: John Wiley and Sons, Inc.
Whiting, J. W. M., Kluckhohn, R., and Anthony, A.
1958   The Function of Male Initiation Ceremonies at Puberty. In *Readings in Social Psychology*, eds. Maccoby, Newcomb, and Hartley. New York: Henry Holt and Co.
Whiting, J. W. M., Landauer, T. K., and Jones, T. M.
1968   Infantile Immunization and Adult Stature. *Child Development* 39(1):59–67.
Whiting, J. W. M. and Mowrer, O. H.
1943   Habit Progression and Regression: A Laboratory Study of Some Factors Relevant to Human Socialization. *Journal of Comparative Psychology* 36(3).
Whiting, J. W. M. and Whiting, B. B.
1971   Task Assignments and Personality: A Consideration of the Effect of Herding on Boys. In *Comparative Perspectives on Social Psychology*, eds. W. W. Lambert and R. Weisbrod, pp. 33–45. Boston: Little, Brown and Co.

The Author

VICTOR BARNOUW, Professor of Anthropology, University of Wisconsin, Milwaukee, was born in The Hague, Holland, in 1915. Soon after World War I his father was appointed Queen Wilhelmina Professor of Dutch Language and Literature at Columbia University. At that time the family moved to New York City and Victor Barnouw went to school at Horace Mann. He speaks for himself below:

For three summers in the 1930s I attended the Winold Reiss Art School in Glacier Park, Montana, where our models were Blackfoot Indians. It was a surprise to a city boy to find so much of the old Indian way of life in force. We went to Sun Dances at Fort Browning and also across the border in Canada, where tipis were ranged in a large camp circle, with Indians riding in on horseback from all directions in a scene that might have been painted by Catlin. To me this was astonishing and exciting. Between poses I wrote down lists of Blackfoot words elicited from our models—my first efforts in the direction of anthropology.

I left Princeton after my second year to attend the National Academy of Design for two years, and after that went to Mexico, where I lived for five months, painting and traveling. My experiences in Mexico strengthened my interest in anthropology. I went back to college—Columbia this time, and after graduation in 1940 I enrolled as a graduate student in the Columbia anthropology department. At about this time I attended a lecture symposium to commemorate the death of Freud, at which two of the speakers were Karen Horney and Abram Kardiner. I was much impressed by Kardiner's lecture; that helped to focus my interest in anthropology. My article in this book takes the story from there. In 1949–50 I wrote a novel about Chippewa Indians, *Dream of the Blue Heron,* which was not published until 1966.

I have taught anthropology for about twenty-five years: first at Brooklyn College Evening Session for three years, then for three years at the University of Buffalo, and one year at the University of Illinois. Since 1957 I have taught at the University of Wisconsin, Milwaukee. My three textbooks (1973, 1975*a*, 1975*b*) developed from the courses I've given. At present I am working on a book about Wisconsin Chippewa myths and tales.

Barnouw has published extensively on the Chippewa, and this work is

62

represented in his chapter for this volume. He is author of a major text in culture and personality, as well as in anthropology. He has also published on Nepalese marriage customs, the Sindhis, mercantile refugees in India, and with Oscar Lewis on caste and the Jajamani in a north Indian village and on village life in northern India. His work in India is nor represented in this chapter.

This Chapter

This chapter is particularly valuable in the context of this volume because it is the only one which pursues a research problem stimulated directly by the Kardner-Linton seminar at Columbia University that influences so many of the other workers whose contributions are represented in this book. It also develops in clear prose the concept of basic personality.

Victor Barnouw describes how he went to the Chippewa to pursue purposes essentially relevant to the Kardner-Linton seminar. He used the Rorschach and Thematic Apperceptoin Test (TAT) and collected authobiographies, which he regarded as particularly important. He illustrates the type of data coming out of the autobiography and shows how he used it interpretively and as related to the concepts of personality and culture current at the time he did the initial interpretations. He demonstrates also how myths and folktales can be used as a source of psychologically relevant themes and characterizations, given the psychocultural and analytic model he employed.

Of particular interest to many will be his discussion of the James and Hickerson criticisms of the "atomism" hypothesis and his rebuttal of them. This discussion, which was muted in the original draft of this chapter, was enlarged at the request of the editor who felt it was a significant issue that contemporary students of psychological anthropology should know about. It is not merely a methodological issue, though the credibility of data and methods does play a role. It is more a matter of basic differences in personal and intellectual orientation, virtually world view differences, and of political orientation. Barnouw discusses the issues with remarkable objectivity and fairness.

Another interesting problem discussed in this chapter, with its ethical overtones, is that of psychological characterizations ascribed to the Chippewa. When such characterizations are applied, characterizations that seem unflattering out of the total context in which they are believed to operate and particularly when they are believed to be persistent, the psycho-ethnographer is in a delicate position. Barnouw discusses this problem as well with his usual objectivity and candor.

G.D.S.

2 An Interpretation of Wisconsin Ojibwa Culture and Personality: A Review

VICTOR BARNOUW

When I was a graduate student in anthropology at Columbia University in the early 1940s, I was introduced to the field of culture and personality in the Linton-Kardiner seminars on Psychological Analysis of Primitive Cultures. While I was attending classes, there were larger events going on, continually brought to everyone's attention by staccato news broadcasts and large newspaper headlines. German armies were advancing over Europe. In those days the aggressive actions and speeches of the Nazi leaders, combined with the apparent support and involvement of the German people, gave new credence to the concept of national character. It seemed to me then that the actions of the Germans could not be explained in terms of economic and political pressures alone; perhaps one also needed to know something about the personalities of Adolf Hitler, his henchmen, and the German people in general.

In 1940, I was receptive to the notion of national character or "basic personality structure" as forming part of an explanation for human behavior in different historical circumstances. The purpose of the Linton-Kardiner seminars, led by Ralph Linton, an anthropologist, and Abram Kardiner, a psychoanalyst, was to test the applicability of Kardiner's concept of basic personality structure to some selected non-western cultures.

BASIC PERSONALITY STRUCTURE

The term "basic personality structure" was not meant to apply to human beings in general nor to a particular person. It had reference to a designated society such as that of the Zuni or Trobriand Islanders. It was hypothesized that members of such a society would tend to have certain personality characteristics in common which would differentiate them in some respects from members of other societies. The basis for this assumption lay in Kardiner's acceptance of the Freudian doctrine that an individual's personality is largely shaped by the time he is six or seven.

A definition of personality which I have used is as follows: "Personality is a more or less enduring organization of forces within the individual associated with a complex of fairly consistent attitudes, values, and modes of perception which account, in part, for the individual's consistency of behavior" (Barnouw 1973, p. 10).

From Kardiner's point of view personality is largely determined by the nature of parent-child relations mediated through such practices as suckling and weaning, toilet training, and sexual disciplines. These practices, like other aspects of culture, are apt to be relatively standardized within a society and may contrast with those of other societies. Although individual mothers may differ from one another in certain respects, they tend, within a particular society, to follow similar patterns in suckling, in the timing and manner of weaning, in the laxity or severity of toilet training, and in lenience or strictness about sexual matters. It was assumed that the children growing up in such a society generally respond in similar ways to the same gamut of childhood experiences and that they therefore come to share a common basic personality structure.

To demonstrate the applicability of Kardiner's theories it was necessary to gather ethnographic data, especially with regard to child training practices, from a range of different societies. As a psychoanalyst, accustomed to listening to the autobiographical outpourings of patients, Kardiner stressed the value of life history material. As an adjunct to this, Cora DuBois, an associate of Kardiner's, had demonstrated the usefulness of giving the Rorschach Test to subjects in the field.[1] DuBois had done this from 1938 to 1939 on the island of Alor in Indonesia, where she had also recorded eight autobiographies and collected children's drawings. These materials were subjected to "blind" analysis, with the Rorschach recordings being independently analyzed by Emil Oberholzer, the drawings interpreted by Trude Schmidl-Waehner, and the life histories by Kardiner. There turned out to be a good deal of agreement in the personality generalizations made about the Alorese in these separate analyses (DuBois 1944).

1. The Rorschach Test involves showing ten bilaterally symmetrical nonrepresentational ink blots to a subject, who is asked to tell what he sees in the blots. Among the advantages of this test for fieldworkers in non-Western societies is that it does not require literacy, it is not culture-bound as a series of representational pictures might be, and it can be given to people at different age levels.

There were high expectations in the field of culture and personality in those days. Strong negative criticisms of such research were yet to come (Orlansky 1949; Lindesmith and Strauss 1950; Hart 1954). Culture and personality was much discussed in the early 1940s. I attended lectures by Erich Fromm at the New School of Social Research, heard Karen Horney speak, and took courses given by Ruth Benedict on social organization and the religions of primitive peoples. Although there were differences in the views of these stimulating people, they all shared a strong interest in the relationship between culture and personality in different societies. Moreover, there seemed to be straightforward techniques to apply in field work: the observation of behavior, collection of life history material, and administration of projective tests. The use of blind analyses of data brought back from the field seemed to guard against undue subjectivity on the part of field workers. Hence, there seemed to be every reason for optimism in this unfolding field of research.

FIELD WORK IN NORTHERN WISCONSIN

I felt very fortunate, therefore, when I was given a summer research grant in 1944 to do field work among the Chippewa (Ojibwa) Indians of northern Wisconsin for the purposes of the Linton-Kardiner seminar. The Columbia Department of Anthropology and the Milwaukee Public Museum had sponsored a series of summer field trips at the Court Oreilles Reservation in which Robert Ritzenthaler of the Milwaukee Public Museum had worked first with Joseph Casagrande and later with Ernestine Friedl, who were then both graduate students in the Department of Anthropology. Ernestine Friedl had presented ethnographic data about the Wisconsin Chippewa at the Linton-Kardiner seminar. Before attempting to analyze the material, Kardiner felt it would be helpful to have more life history data from Chippewa subjects. My assignment, then, was to elicit some autobiographies and also to get Rorschach Test protocols. Before going to Wisconsin I studied Rorschach Test administration with Florence Miale. I also read up on works by A. Irving Hallowell, Ruth Landes, and others who had written about the Chippewa. While this would seem to be necessary preparation, it may also have given me a mental set about what to expect, a question to be discussed later.

Until relatively recent times the Chippewa Indians had a hunting-gathering base of subsistence, with small crops of corn and squash grown in summer, wild rice harvested in the fall, and maple sap tapped in the spring. Particularly in the more northern groups, the small summer villages tended to break up in the fall, with a dispersal during the winter months, in response to ecological pressures. A family unit of husband and wife could be mobile and relatively self-sufficient. The man did the hunting and trapping, while the woman did the cooking, made clothes, looked after the children, and so forth.

Northern Wisconsin was surprisingly isolated from the rest of the world until the 1870s, when the first railways crossed the state from the south and lumber companies began operations. Although acculturation did develop rapidly after that, much of the old culture, especially in the field of magico-religious beliefs, was still in evidence in the 1940s. I do not mean to imply there had been little acculturation before 1870, for there had been contact between Chippewa and Europeans since the seventeenth century, but I was surprised to learn that some of my older informants had lived in wigwams and traveled in birchbark canoes in their youth, had fasted for visions, and in general had lived an Indian way of life.

I spent one month at Court Oreilles, working mainly with a fifty-five-year-old man named Jim Mink; then I moved to the Lac du Flambeau reservation, where the population was more concentrated and where it was easier for me to get about from house to house. I was there for two months. I used no sampling techniques for either Rorschach or life history subjects. Time was short, and my problem was simply to find a few informants, preferably of different generations, who would be willing to talk about themselves. Presumably, if they were all Chippewa Indians, they should all manifest the same basic personality structure. I did succeed in finding three relatively talkative Indians at Flambeau with whom I spent most of my time: Tom Badger, a conservative Mide priest about seventy years of age, who had never been to school; his wife Julia Badger, half his age, who had had twelve years of schooling; and John Thunderbird, who was the same age as Jim Mink. (These are not their real names but pseudonyms.) I returned to Lac du Flambeau for a second summer's work in 1946, when I also collected drawings and gave the Thematic Apperception Test and Rorschach Test to a few more subjects.[2] In the summer of 1947 I again spent a few days at Flambeau. Some of my life history material was given a "blind" analysis at the

2. The Thematic Apperception Test (TAT) involves showing the subject a series of pictures for each of which he has to make up a story, explaining what led up to the scene depicted, the thoughts and feelings of the persons involved, and the probable outcome of the episode. In some non-Western societies modified TAT's have been used, drawn specially to accord with the local culture; but in this case I gave part of the standard TAT designed by C. D. Morgan and Henry A. Murray, using only some selected cards, as was done by William Caudill in his testing of Chippewa children at the Court Oreilles reservation, referred to later.

Linton-Kardiner seminar in the fall of 1944 by Dr. Milton Sapirstein, a psychiatrist, while Dr. Bruno Klopfer, a Rorschach specialist, presented an interpretation of the Chippewa Rorschach protocols.

Three of the biographies appear in the appendix of my *Acculturation and Personality among the Wisconsin Chippewa* (1950). Tom Badger's autobiography is in "Reminiscences of a Chippewa Mide Priest" (Barnouw 1954). Some of his wife's phantasy material appears in "The Phantasy World of a Chippewa Woman" (Barnouw 1949).

ACCULTURATION AND PERSONALITY AMONG THE WISCONSIN CHIPPEWA

The main data I brought back from the field were the four biographies. I had also secured a long origin myth told to me by Tom Badger, the Mide priest (priest of the Medicine Dance religion), and also his description of the Midewiwin or Medicine Dance (Barnouw 1955, 1960). I had various ethnographic notes and also had access to the abundant field notes kept by Ritzenthaler, Casagrande, and Friedl. These notes covered the whole range of ethnographic data from material culture to folklore. Ernestine Friedl's field notes had extensive information about child training practices.

The four life histories, admittedly, made up a very small sample, and they varied in quality. Tom Badger, my oldest informant, gave good information about early Indian life in northern Wisconsin, traveling by birchbark canoe, hunting, berry picking, and getting maple sap in the sugar bush. He talked about fasting for a vision, making a deer fence, and gave information about shamanistic curing practices, fears of sorcery, the Midewiwin, and other traditional topics. This material was not rich in psychological clues, however. From Tom's narrative one gets an impression of a rather dependent sort of person. Tom was the youngest of four children and was apparently his mother's favorite. Here is one of his early memories:

One time, when I was three or four years old, I wanted to nurse. My mother was cutting wood. It was in the winter time. So I went into the woods and told her there were some guests down at our log house. There really were no guests at all. But that's how I got her to nurse me. She left her work and came back to the house [Barnouw 1954, p. 85].

Tom blamed his mother for the fact that he never had a dream or vision of a guardian spirit. When he fasted, she took pity on him and fed him at noon. "I don't know nothing now. But it was my mother's fault'' (ibid., p. 88). ''Blind'' analyses of Tom Badger's drawings and Rorschach responses both made the point that he was a passive, dependent person (Barnouw 1973, pp. 358–59).

Jim Mink came from Court Oreilles, which was affected by acculturation earlier and more rapidly than was Lac du Flambeau; so his life history had a less ''aboriginal'' flavor than the other three. Jim went to school for nine years and then spent fourteen years away from the reservation ''trying to become like a white man,'' as he put it. Then he returned to the reservation, married a girl of conservative Indian family, and tried to become like an Indian. For the past eight years Jim had been understudy to the Mide priest at Court Oreilles. He was a nervous, restless person, quite different from the more stolid and even-tempered Tom Badger. Unlike the latter, he apparently had an unhappy childhood. Jim had been afraid of both his father's father and his own father. ''They were *mean*. If I was hungry, I'd reach over for some more bread; then they'd take it away from me'' (Barnouw 1950, p. 80). When Jim was sent out to fast, as a boy, he washed the charcoal off his face, and went elsewhere to get food.

Jim's life history was rambling and erratic, but toward the end of our sessions he told me five interesting long anecdotes, one after the other, which all dealt with the despotic power of an older male figure. In three of these stories this figure was a white man, an Indian agent or deputy agent. In the other two anecdotes the man was an uncle of Jim's father. These men, although somewhat distant, all acted in a very generous manner to Jim Mink. The Indian agent also made boastful statements: ''I'm a big man, that's what I am. I'm the Indian agent. I've got the whole United States government right back of me. I hold the Indians right in the palm of my hand'' (Barnouw 1950, p. 86). The agent allegedly offered to help Jim carry a minor legal issue straight to the Supreme Court. These powerful, benevolent father-figures seemed to be wished-for replacements for Jim's mean father and grandfather.

John Thunderbird was the same age as Jim Mink and in some respects had led a similar life. He spent several years in a government boarding school, then did some traveling away from home with a wild west show. John returned to the reservation, married a conservative woman, and then became involved with the traditional Chippewa religions. He was very proud of belonging to a Drum Dance group and of being a speaker. John did not simply tell me his life story; he orated it, as if addressing a large audience. His life history has material on fasting, dreams, and Drum Dance, school life, and John's feast for the first kill.

John Thunderbird's mother died soon after he was born, and he was brought up by grandparents. He seems to have been well treated by them, but nevertheless he spoke of being lonely and very quiet as a child. His father remarried, but John didn't like his step-mother and said she was mean and scolded him. Like Tom Badger, John complained about not having a fasting dream. "I didn't fast long enough. I don't know nothing now" (ibid., p. 95). In his TAT, John Thunderbird told stories which stressed themes of loneliness, bereavement, death of parents, anxiety, fear of spirits and sickness; but he also told stories about long family lines and themes of ambition. In a Rorschach analysis Maud Hallowell noted John Thunderbird had longings for warmth and affection but also felt suspicious and bitter about people. He was or had formerly been an ambitious person, but his ambitions had soured and he had become very depressed by life (ibid, p. 110).

Of the four life histories, by far the richest psychological document was that of Julia Badger, Tom Badger's wife. She was a fat, bulky woman of thirty-four, "wall-eyed," passive, and full of daydreams. She had always been sickly and had had periods of temporary blindness and paralysis in childhood. These ailments apparently encouraged her introversive, narcissistic tendencies. They also led to her exposure to most of the aboriginal curing practices: sucking cure, conjuring lodge, bleeding, Medicine Dance, and so on. This made Julia well informed about traditional Chippewa beliefs and practices, despite her eleven years of schooling. Commenting on her Rorschach record, Dr. Bruno Klopfer said, "In our culture she would be called schizoid." But Julia was regarded as rather queer in her own community too.

Much of Julia Badger's autobiography seemed to be improvisation and fantasy, partly designed to cover up and deny the unhappiness of her childhood years. Julia's father died when she was five, but before that she was transferred to the care of her father's parents, whom she thought were her real parents until she was fourteen years old. Benevolent father-substitutes figured prominently in her fantasies. Moreover, Julia's first husband was a sixty-year-old Winnebago peyote leader and Tom Badger, her third husband, was twice her age.

A common theme in the last three of these autobiographies was unsatisfied dependency needs, with restitutive fantasies of powerful and benevolent father figures. This pattern seems to have been a response to the emphasis on independence in Chippewa child training and a failure on the part of parents to satisfy their children's needs for security and affection. Chippewa children were often neglected and left alone. A kind of caution and fearfulness was evidenced in many interviews with

Chippewa informants. There seemed to be many sources for such attitudes. First there were the "scaring" techniques used in disciplining children, warnings of bogies, spirits of the dead, and the giant owls which were said to carry children away. On the part of older informants there was an avowed fear of medicine men and sorcery. Informants also mentioned the danger of being touched by a menstruating woman or a person in mourning, which could cause paralysis or death in a child.

Some clues to Chippewa personality patterns also came from the Rorschach protocols. A striking feature of Chippewa Rorschach records was an avoidance of color. I found that of 107 Rorschach records taken at Court Oreilles and Lac du Flambeau by Ernestine Friedl, Robert Ritzenthaler, and me, 53 records were without any color responses at all, and only nine individuals gave more than two color responses. Hallowell found the same pattern in three groups of Chippewa representing different levels of acculturation: two in the Berens River region in Canada and the third and most acculturated group at Lac du Flambeau (Hallowell 1955, pp. 350–51). In the Linton-Kardiner seminar Bruno Klopfer remarked that the rarity of color responses suggested the individual was under pressure to become as emotionally independent of his environment as possible and to expect very little from others. The fear of overt emotionality and its possible consequences led to a pattern of undemonstrativeness. While low in color, Chippewa Rorschach records tended to be relatively high in human movement and animal movement responses, suggesting a tendency to introversion and fantasy.

An individual's source of security lay in supernatural resources in the old days. Chippewa sent children out to fast for a guardian spirit soon after they were able to walk about and play by themselves. Until he received the right sort of dream or vision, the child was periodically sent off to fast. There was no pooling of supernatural power, as among some other Indian tribes. The only shared power was between a godparent and a newly born godchild. Among the people I worked with the traditional sources of security were going or gone. At the same time, when compared with Hallowell's less acculturated Canadian Chippewa, the Rorschachs of the Flambeau group showed "a great paucity of inner resources" (ibid., pp. 351–52).

I argued that the rather fearful and isolated personality was related to an atomistic social organization both in the past and in the present. "Atomistic" in this sense refers to a loose form of social organization in which corporate organization and political authority are weak. It is not difficult for the component units to break away from the larger society of which they are a part. "Atomistic" is not a personality characterization but refers to a type of social order. Rubel and Kupferer refer to an "atomistic-type society," a society in which the nuclear family is the major structural unit (Rubel and Kupferer 1968, pp. 189–90). The term "atomistic" was used for simple unstructured societies by Ruth Benedict in lectures given at Columbia University (Maslow and Honigmann 1970, p. 323). Ruth Landes characterized Ontario Ojibwa as atomistic in 1937 (1937, p. 102). Hallowell also used the term "atomistic" in reference to the Berens River Ojibwa of whom he wrote: "Prior to this time [1875] there were no chiefs in the modern sense, nor any formal band or tribal organization. Of institutionalized penal sanctions there were none, nor was there any juridical procedure provided in the aboriginal culture. No one, in short, was responsible for punishing crime or settling disputes" (Hallowell 1955, p. 120).

It seemed to me the situation had not changed very much under reservation conditions in Wisconsin and the increase in population density had not resulted in more cooperative activity. The main cooperative social unit was still that of husband and wife. I discussed the difficulties in organizing group projects, such as tourist pow-wows (Barnouw 1950, p. 17). Since contrasts with other groups help to highlight the distinctive features in a society, I made comparisons between the Chippewa and plains tribes such as the Cheyenne, not only to point out their differences in aboriginal social organization and personality development but also to show how these tribes had differed in responding to historical events, such as the coming of the whites.

The writings of Grinnell and Hoebel about the Cheyenne abundantly illustrate the strong sense of solidarity and *esprit de corps* which characterized that plains tribe, particularly during the summer months when the large camp circle sometimes consisted of as many as two or three thousand persons. There was a council of chiefs and soldier societies which policed camp and regulated the buffalo hunt. Communal hunting of the buffalo and institutionalized "sewing bees" and quilling societies among the women attest to the stress on cooperation. Where there was rivalry, such as the rivalry between warrior societies, it functioned to increase the efficiency of the group. Cheyenne children spent much more time in organized group play than did Chippewa children, who had access to fewer playmates. Very little has been written about the Chippewa.

I also made the point that, although they had reasons for anti-white hostility, on the whole the Chippewa readily accepted white domination, in contrast to the more cohesive and aggressive plains tribes. Nor did the Chippewa take to the Ghost Dance which swept through the tribes of the plains, although they had earlier taken over the Drum Dance or Dream Dance from the Dakota. The difference was that the Ghost Dance was strongly anti-white while the Drum Dance was not. The Chippewa early fell into a dependent relationship upon the trader and later the government agent, who were often addressed as "Father."

I contrasted Chippewa and Dakota acculturation as follows:

Although some friction and irritation were unavoidable during the contact period, the Chippewa adjusted without any real protest to the new state of affairs, because the white man brought many gratifications which they valued highly. The atomism of their society favored a gradual and piecemeal type of acculturation. The Chippewa did not have to undergo the traumatic disorganization experienced by the Plains tribes, for in their case there was no marked change in the social order attendant on the white man's assumption of power over them. Patterns of interpersonal relationships did not significantly alter, and consequently there seems to have been no change in the personality structure of the Chippewa.

Among the Dakota, on the other hand, where the aboriginal social structure was swiftly disrupted, there is evidence that there has been a change in personality structure since the beginning of the reservation period (Barnouw 1950, p. 76).

A more general conclusion was that personality variables need to be taken into account in understanding the responses of different social groups to historical events. I was opposed to economic determinist explanations of historical events such as George Hunt's *The Wars of the Iroquois,* which assumed any people placed in the situation faced by the Iroquois would have acted as they did.

In the foregoing analysis one can see the influence of the Linton-Kardiner seminars in my emphasis on childhood experiences, life history material, and use of the Rorschach Test. However, the influence of Ruth Benedict, chairman of my Ph.D. thesis committee at Columbia, is also apparent, first of all in my use of the concept of social atomism. It was Benedict's influence, too, which led to my comparison of the Chippewa with plains tribes such as the Cheyenne. Cheyenne culture and social organization made up a very different configuration from that of the Chippewa. Comparisons and contrasts between such groups highlight the characteristic features of each. When critics attack my application of the concept of social atomism to the Wisconsin Chippewa, they either ignore or discredit this crucial comparison with the much more organized, cohesive tribes in the plains. I owe the inspiration for this contrast to Ruth Benedict's comparative configurationist approach, exemplified in *Patterns of Culture* (1934) in her contrast between the Pueblo cultures of the southwest and other North American Indian cultures.

WISCONSIN CHIPPEWA MYTHS AND TALES

Before discussing the criticisms which have been made by my memoir, I want to say something about Wisconsin Chippewa myths and tales. Reference was made earlier to the lengthy origin myth told to me by Tom Badger in 1944. If one compares this narrative with other origin myths, two characteristics stand out. First is the lack of reference to women or family relations; second is an emphasis on anal motifs. The tale is about the erratic adventures of the trickster hero Wenebojo, whose mother is impregnated by the sun at the beginning of the tale, and who is given a set of "parents" by supernaturals at the end. There are two communal episodes in the course of the narrative, one when Wenebojo lives with some beavers and another when he travels with some wolves. Otherwise he is a loner. Early in the story Wenebojo causes the deaths of his two brothers. He creates the world we live on, but his other creations or discoveries are limited: some elm-tree food, tobacco, and a laxative. Wenebojo discovers a plant which makes him defecate so much he is engulfed in dung up to his lips. At one point in the story Wenebojo burns his rear end, leaving behind him a trail of blood and scabs, which becomes the origin of tobacco. In another episode Wenebojo's guts stretch out from his rectum. He hauls them in and throws them over a tree, thereby creating elm-tree food. Wenebojo's few creations are thus all related to the anal zone. They are also oral: Wenebojo chews the plant which makes him defecate; people eat elm-tree food and smoke tobacco. Feces come up to Wenebojo's mouth. In the absence of competing explanations, the best way of accounting for this oral-anal emphasis, it seems to me, is along Freudian lines. Hence my article, "A Psychological Interpretation of a Chippewa Origin Legend," stressed that approach.

In my book *Culture and Personality* I made a contrast between the Chippewa origin myth and a Navaho origin myth, or its first thirty-four pages to make the two narratives of comparable length (Barnouw 1973, pp. 379–92). A weakness of that comparison was that I chose only two myth sequences. Ideally, one should compare two or more complete bodies of folklore, which is what I have done more recently. Apart from the Chippewa origin myth I have a collection of 46 Chippewa myths and tales taken down at Court Oreilles and Lac du Flambeau between 1941 and 1944 by Robert Ritzenthaler, Joseph Casagrande, Ernestine Friedl, and myself; two stories collected later by Bernard J. James at Court Oreilles are included. This collection has been compared with 60 stories collected by Margaret Lantis among the Nunivak Eskimo, a hunting-gathering people (1946, pp. 153–323), and 104 stories in Ruth Benedict's collection from the Zuni, a sedentary agricultural and sheep-herding tribe in New Mexico (Benedict, 1935).

If we compare these three bodies of folklore, the relative absence of male-female stories turns out to be true of Chippewa folklore in general, not only of the origin myth. Perhaps because the Zuni have matrilineal descent and matrilocal residence, women play a much larger role in Zuni folklore. Seven of our Chippewa tales deal with courtship, while nineteen do in Nunivak; but Benedict gives thirty tales of courtship in volume one, which makes up nearly 180 pages. In addition, she summarizes about twenty more tales of courtship. Courtship themes occur in eleven more tales. In addition, twenty-four stories deal with husband-wife relations. Margaret Lantis rates husband-wife and other relations in Nunivak folklore as "good" or "bad," and I have done the same for the Chippewa and Zuni tales. This gives the following breakdowns for husband-wife relations in the stories: sixteen good and six bad in Nunivak; four good and four bad in Chippewa; ten good and fourteen bad in Zuni. Thus male-female relations are emphasized much more in both Nunivak and Zuni folklore than in Wisconsin Chippewa tales.

The social units in both Chippewa and Nunivak stories are small, but as might be expected they are often larger in Zuni tales. In Zuni origin myths mention is made of the Corn, Eagle, Bear, Crane, and Turkey clans. There is no reference to clans in any of the Wisconsin Chippewa myths or tales. As might be expected of a sedentary agricultural society, there are many references in Zuni tales to specific localities, lakes, springs, mountains, and villages. There are almost no such references in Chippewa tales. In these respects Chippewa folklore seems to reflect the former semi-nomadic way of life.

Oral themes, including cannibalism and fears of starvation, appear in all three bodies of folklore, but anal themes figure prominently only in Chippewa tales—not only in the origin myth but also in a number of other Chippewa stories. The fact that anal motifs also occur in the folklore of neighboring woodland and plains tribes does not reduce the significance of this pattern, it seems to me. I think there may be a relationship between the stress on anal themes and the de-emphasis of male-female relations in Chippewa folk tales. It suggests a tendency to sexual repression and a consequent attention to pregenital zones, as Freudian theory would assume. The tendency to sexual repression would be one manifestation of the general caution and uneasiness in interpersonal relations mentioned earlier.

CRITICISMS BY BERNARD J. JAMES

Since my *Acculturation and Personality among the Wisconsin Chippewa* covers a large canvas, it is vulnerable to criticism on various grounds. Since it deals with history, it is open to questions of detail, historical facts, and alternative interpretations of events. Since it makes generalizations about Chippewa personality, it is open to questions about personality theory. (Is there really such a thing as basic or modal personality? Are Chippewa actually introverted, and what is the evidence for it?) Since it makes use of Rorschach findings, it is open to questions about the validity of the Rorschach Test, and so on. However, the first printed response was a favorable one, an enthusiastic review by Weston La Barre in the *American Anthropologist* (1952).

But criticisms soon did appear, first from Bernard J. James and later from Harold Hickerson. These criticisms mainly concerned matters of history and the nature of early Chippewa social organization. James argued that findings by Hallowell and Landes for the northern Chippewa had been uncritically applied to the Indians south of Lake Superior. He cited some eighteenth-century references to communities in Wisconsin with populations well over two hundred. James admitted there were probably seasonal fluctuations but argued there must have been more opportunities for social contact than had been acknowledged. James also pointed to the fact that the southern Chippewa successfully engaged in fighting the Dakota and therefore cannot have been so atomistic and uncooperative. He argued further that much of the atomism of present-day Chippewa life could be attributed, not to the persistence of earlier patterns but rather to the consequences of a pauper economy and what James later called the "reservation situation." Hence Chippewa personality studies should be more *situational* (James 1954).

These were sensible criticisms. The question that remained was whether James had overstressed the differences between north and south, past and present. I commented in reply: "I am all in favor of 'situational' analyses, but are not the traditions, values, and attitudes of a people part of the total situation in which they find themselves?" (Barnouw 1961). I pointed out that the northern and southern Chippewa groups shared essentially the same culture, originating from a common base. While some Chippewa groups moved from Sault Ste. Marie into Wisconsin in the seventeenth and eighteenth centuries, others moved westward to the Berens River region where Hallowell later studied them. In both areas there was relative isolation from outside contacts until around 1870. I drew attention to the striking similarity in Rorschach profiles of the Chippewa at Lac du Flambeau with those in Canada tested by Hallowell, who argued that the Rorschach, TAT and other data pointed to "a persistent core of psychological characteristics sufficient to identify an Ojibwa personality constellation, aboriginal in origin, that is clearly discernible through all levels of acculturation thus far studied" (Hallowell 1955, p. 363; Caudill 1949).

In a previous section we reviewed some aspects of Chippewa myths and tales, which must be centuries old, judging from their wide distribution. There is an "atomistic" quality to these stories which must antedate the reservation period.

However, it is likely that modern conditions have often fostered a state of anomie at the same time that the traditional resources of the old culture have tended to disappear. Stephen T. Boggs lived in one of Hallowell's Saulteaux groups in Canada and also in a more acculturated community in Wisconsin, spending thirteen months in the field to observe parent-child interactions. He found there was less parent-child interaction in the more acculturated Wisconsin setting. Since a child is no longer put in a cradleboard (and taken off), there is less handling by the mother. Children are more often left at home untended by parents, and there is less instruction in passing on adult skills. "With older children, parents seem to be almost completely uncommunicative about any of life's problems" (Boggs 1958, p. 53). However, this very pattern of relative lack of communication may be traditional in nature, as Boggs suggested elsewhere: "There is no doubt in my mind that Ojibwa parents are verbally uncommunicative with children. In approximately 390 hours of observation of thirty-two children in two Ojibwa communities I categorized about two thousand instances of parent-child interaction, defining as interaction the occurrence of any behavior pattern by a child in the presence of an adult (or an older child acting in place of a parent). . . . In at least one-quarter of these instances the parent or older child provided no sign to the child and did not react to him, however slightly. . . . The general level of interaction was quite low. . . . In the less acculturated community children experience a drastic reduction in the amount of interaction with their mothers during the second year of life. Mothers simply become unresponsive to their attempts to continue any pattern of dependence" (Boggs, n.d.).

In two papers Bernard James has presented the kind of situational analysis of Chippewa personality that he called for in his first paper discussed above. James emphasizes the modern non-Indian aspects of the community of "Deerpoint" on the Court Oreilles reservation where he lived for a year from 1951 to 1952. From James' point of view the Indian culture is, for all practical purposes, dead, a thing of the past. The reservation is a rural slum, and its Indian inhabitants have more in common with other lower-class Americans than they do with their Chippewa ancestors. In his behavioral description and comments on personality James' account has much in common with those of previous writers. He discusses the prevalence of anxiety and drinking patterns but does not relate these manifestations to any persistence of early personality patterns. Rather, they represent responses to poverty, white racial prejudice and discrimination (James 1961, 1970).

In his greater stress on modernity and "de-culturation," James' picture of the Indian scene is different from mine, and I think the explanation for this lies in the different natures of our field experiences. I have talked with James about our respective field experiences, and he has let me read the field notes which he took at the time. James worked at Court Oreilles, while I did most of my work at Lac du Flambeau, which was somewhat less affected by acculturation. Moreover, my assignment on the reservation was to get life-history material; so I spent most of my time with three relatively conservative Indians: Tom Badger, a Mide priest, his wife Julia, and John Thunderbird. On the same evening that I arrived at Lac du Flambeau I attended a small War Dance, attended by a few conservative families, at which two elderly Chippewa told their fasting dreams to honor their godchild, a Wac corporal, for whom the War Dance was held. Tom Badger beat a drum and sang on this occasion, and everyone danced. During my stay on the reservation I was continually hearing about traditional Chippewa beliefs and customs. It is understandable, then, that I stressed links with the past and continuity in Chippewa beliefs and practices.

On the basis of James' field notes I got the impression he had not worked with the conservative old-timers like Tom Badger; I made this point in an early version of this paper, which I showed to him. In a note quoted below, James disagreed with this observation. He stated, however, that no one in "Deerpoint" was active in the Midewiwin at the time of his field work. James was there a little later than I—1951–52, as opposed to 1944 and 1946. He was engaged in studying community life in general, which involved a stress on the contemporary scene. Here is how he described his field work in a note to me: "I moved at all levels, with the kids (roller skating, hunting, games), bootleggers . . . priests, loggers, sugar makers, mothers, fathers, the cop, bartenders (whites), fishermen, guides, etc. It was this kind of day-to-day cross-sectional experience that made it a very 'situational' thing. I *did* work with 'old-timers' [three names mentioned], since I did take a lot of historical notes. . . . It's a matter of emphasis. I found the old folks pleasant . . . but not the main stream. In fact some of the older people were rather hermit-like, which may have helped make the present seem especially different from the past, from my vantage point.''

In 1941 Joseph Casagrande and Robert Ritzenthaler had as their informant an old shaman called John Mink, who was even older and more conservative than Tom Badger. He still performed the sucking cure in 1941, attended bear ceremonials, and was a ritual leader in the Midewiwin. Joseph Casagrande has written an account of him in *In the Company of Man* (Casagrande 1960). John Mink was not an isolated oddity. There were many other old-timers at Court Oreilles in the early 1940s, although none as old as he. There was a group of conservatives who tried to preserve the traditional ways as much as possible and who interacted with the more progressive and younger Indians. In other words, one cannot declare that at any particular point the Indian culture "died." There was an intergrading between generations, and I believe there was continuity in many respects.

James' situational approach does away with one problem, that of accounting for the persistence of Chippewa personality patterns from the early culture into the present. James' solution to this is simple: there has been no such continuity. As he has pointed out, the main evidence for such persistence has been projective test protocols. With the current decline of interest in projective tests that evidence may not carry much weight with some critics. My own view is that there has been persistence in Chippewa personality patterns largely because the general nature of the social order has not changed; it was atomistic before and remains so. Ernestine Friedl argued that the key to the persistence lay in the continual change which the Chippewa came to accept as a natural state of affairs. At the same time she pointed out that the general outlines of economic life have remained much the same—a variety of subsistence and economic activities supplemented by handouts. Formerly handouts were conceived to come from supernatural beings as well as from members of one's own society; now their main source is the government (Friedl 1956). As we have seen, the question of why Chippewa personality patterns have persisted is considered a false issue by Bernard James.

To summarize and conclude this section, it seems to me that Bernard James' criticisms of my memoir have been fair, well considered, and constructive. But while I may have placed too much emphasis on the past, I feel that James has erred in the other direction in denying the relevance of early Chippewa culture and social organization for the understanding of present-day conditions.

CRITICISMS BY HAROLD HICKERSON

Following James' lead, Hickerson attacked some aspects of my work in a series of papers. (He has also criticized some of the other writers on the Chippewa.) The background and motivation of his criticisms were different from James'. James was struck by discrepancies between published work on the Chippewa and his own field experiences, and he wanted to set the record straight. Hickerson had done no field work with the Chippewa or other Algonkian Indians but was drawn into ethnohistoric work on the Chippewa through Indian land claims investigations. As he made clear in his 1967 publication, Hickerson accepts the Marxist view of primitive communism, that hunting-gathering societies are cohesive and collective (Hickerson 1967). Accounts by Hallowell and Landes do not describe the Chippewa in this way but mention private family hunting grounds and an atomistic social order. Hickerson argues that this cannot have been an aboriginal state of affairs. What Hallowell and Landes described were latter-day remnants of displaced populations. The early Chippewa bands first encountered by Europeans at Sault Ste. Marie, however, did have the cohesive characteristics required by Marxist theory. This early communal way of life, following Hickerson's interpretation, was disrupted by the fur trade and the incursions of whites. Thus, if some groups of Chippewa became atomistic in the last few centuries, it was because of the impact of outside forces. In order to demonstrate the collective nature of aboriginal Chippewa culture Hickerson had to find evidence in the Jesuit Relations for communal hunting and clan organization, and he did manage to find such evidence, although it is often ambiguous (Hickerson 1960; Barnouw 1961). Hickerson has received support in this line of reasoning from Charles A. Bishop, who claims, on the basis of a study of journals of Hudson's Bay Company traders, that northern Ojibwa up to the late eighteenth century had "large and frequently aggressive clan-named groups, often numbering over thirty individuals in midwinter" (Bishop 1970). Over-hunting and decrease of game later led to atomistic conditions.

Hickerson has drawn up a reconstruction of stages of Chippewa history, based on traders' journals, missionary accounts, and other early sources (Hickerson 1962, 1970). In his account of the southwestern Chippewa, which includes the Chippewa of Wisconsin, Hickerson, like

James, draws attention to the role of warfare in strengthening social solidarity. Hickerson believes that, under the impact of sporadic warfare with the Dakota, the Chippewa imitated their enemies by forming military societies, for which they borrowed the Dakota word *akicita*. He argures that where the term *gigidag* or *ogičida* was used it must indicate the presence of a warrior society (Hickerson 1970, pp. 52–61). But here the evidence is very thin. *Ogičida* merely means "warrior." If the term was used, it does not mean that Chippewa warriors were organized as they were on the plains. We have no accounts for the Wisconsin Chippewa which compare with the detailed recollections about Cheyenne military societies which Hoebel recorded in the mid 1930s (Llewellyn and Hoebel, 1941), and there are no references to military societies in our collection of forty-six Wisconsin Chippewa tales.

Although I think he has sometimes gone too far in finding indications of cohesion and collective patterns where the evidence was slight, Hickerson has brought some historical perspective to the study of the Chippewa. To that extent his work has been constructive. He has also expressed scathing contempt for earlier workers on the Chippewa, especially those, like myself, who have worked in the field of culture and personality. He sees their findings as amounting to no more than stereotyped prejudices. Hickerson quotes the Soviet anthropologist Averkieva on this subject: "The psychological portrait of the Chippewa . . . the features attributed to Indians by supporters of the 'atomistic' theory such as sullenness, hostility, wariness, suspiciousness, etc. are quite clearly the fabrications of ethnologists who are racists" (Hickerson 1967, p. 321). Although Hickerson does not accuse his American colleagues of racism, he is similarly severe: "The notion of atomism becomes virulent . . . when negatively evaluated characteristics are ascribed to simple peoples as permanent (generic) traits. Such imputations, in emphasizing the moral defects and organizational deficiencies of these peoples, tend to justify their exploitation by Whites. We can ill afford to be identified with such a rationale" (Hickerson 1967, p. 327).

Because of criticisms such as this, I felt obliged in the revised edition of my *Culture and Personality* to justify the continuation of research in this field. I first presented the dilemma that now confronts a prospective field worker: "If the anthropologist wants to avoid such criticisms (and who would not?), he would have to write only favorable descriptions or else decide not to publish descriptions which have negative features. This dilemma could lead to the end of culture-and-personality research. The world is smaller now, literacy greater, and the writings of anthropologists are beginning to find their way back to the communities they have described. This dilemma is further compounded by the fact that culture and personality research has been largely an American enterprise. Hardly any work in this field has been done in Europe. It would thus be easy for critics to link culture and personality research with charges of American imperialism and prejudice. This poses a problem for anyone contemplating culture and personality as a field of research'' (Barnouw 1973, pp. 489–90).

I nevertheless suggested three reasons for continuing such research: (1) The anthropologist studies man in his natural sphere of action, neither as a patient, as a psychiatrist studies him, nor as the subject of a laboratory experiment. Culture and personality thus provides an alternative way of learning about human personality which can check and supplement the findings of psychiatry and psychology. (2) This kind of research contributes to an understanding of the relationship between culture and mental disorders, providing cross-cultural perspective on mental health not otherwise available. (3) Culture and personality research may contribute to an understanding of historical events, of why particular human groups responded as they did to particular challenges. This last consideration was the one that first drew me to the field of culture and personality and was emphasized in my memoir.

An author whose work has been attacked is likely to be defensive; so a concluding self-evaluation of my work may not carry much weight, but this is how I would assess it. When I wrote my thesis, I saw it as building on the work of others who had written about the Chippewa, particularly Landes and Hallowell, whose writings I greatly admired. Neither Landes nor Hallowell worked within the Linton-Kardiner framework of ideas; their emphasis was less on childhood experience and more on general cultural concepts affecting the Chippewa, such as belief in sorcery, and institutions such as the family hunting ground system.

The views of one's predecessors inevitably influence an investigator, who can either build upon them, as I tried to do, or else turn against them and offer a new way of looking at things, as Hickerson did. Scholarly research thus benefits from both followers of Vishnu the preserver and Shiva the destroyer. The influence of one's predecessors may become a source of bias in the investigator, leading to a "standardization of error," which some critics charge was the case in Chippewa culture and personality research. Since I had read the writings of Landes and Hallowell before going into the field, that may have led me to expect or look for certain patterns of behavior and may have influenced my perceptions. But I did hear stories about sorcery; they came from the Indians, not from my expectations. Moreover, Landes and Hallowell, who were doing fieldwork simultaneously in the 1930s, do not seem to have influenced one another, and their views, in many ways, have much in common, although Landes saw romanticism and a great deal of richness and drama in Chippewa individualism, a conception which does not seem to be echoed in Hallowell's writings. Both stressed a certain fearfulness and mistrust of others among the Chippewa, and they agreed on various other matters. One will also find much agreement in the writings of Jenness, Friedl, Boggs, Rogers, Watrous, Caudill, and others who have dealt with Chippewa culture and personality patterns, as well as in the writings of traders and early travelers in documents such as Peter Grant's *The Sauteux Indians: About 1804,* J. G. Kohl's *Kitchi-Gami: Wanderings Around Lake Superior* (1860), and *A Narrative of the Captivity and Adventures of John Tanner* (1830). Mutual influence and common orientation on the part of anthropologists may account for some of the consensus among those who have written about the Chippewa, but not all of it. Although some, like Bernard James, may reject it, there is also the evidence of projective techniques, Rorschach, Thematic Apperception Test, and drawing analysis (Lowenfels 1950). I don't think all this can be dismissed as "standardization of error." In addition, there have been studies along similar lines of other North American Indian tribes with similar cultures, such as those by the Spindlers of the Menomini and John J. Honigmann's of the Kaska. As part of this general mosaic, my own work tried to show that an understanding of historical events in a particular society requires knowledge of the prevalent culture and personality patterns which its members share.

Apart from its relationship to other studies of Algonkian Indians, I think my work may have some relevance to cross-cultural studies of societies designated as atomistic. I did not invent the concept of social atomism, but I seem to have made it better known. Although this term has often been misunderstood and sometimes ridiculed, the concept continues to be used. A collection of articles about social atomism by eight contributors appeared in *Human Organization* in 1968 (vol. 27, pp. 189–235). And I see some interesting parallels in Chippewa culture with the marginal Paliyans of India, who are described by Peter M. Gardner as avoiding both cooperatoin and competition. The Paliyans seem to have an atomistic social order in which nuclear families are the only units marked by cooperation. Village membership is fluctuating, and there are no corporate functions in village life. Reminiscent of Boggs' work among the Chippewa is Gardner's observation that there is little verbal communication among the Paliyans (Gardner 1966). I am hopeful, then, that my work may have some bearing on the research of others, both in relation to Algonkian studies and to the cross-cultural study of atomistic societies (Barnouw 1969, 1973 pp. 366–69).

REFERENCES CITED

Barnouw, V.
  1949 The Phantasy World of a Chippewa Woman, *Psychiatry* 12:167–76.
  1950 Acculturation and Personality Among the Wisconsin Chippewa. *Memoirs of the American Anthropological Association,* No. 72.
  1954 Reminiscences of a Chippewa Mide Priest. *The Wisconsin Archeologist* 25: 83–112.
  1955 A Psychological Interpretation of a Chippewa Origin Legend. *Journal of American Folklore* 68:73–86; 211–23; 341–55.
  1960 A Chippewa Mide Priest's Description of the Medicine Dance. *The Wisconsin Archeologist* 41:77–97.
  1961 Chippewa Social Atomism. *American Anthropologist* 63:1006–13.
  1969 Cross-Cultural Research with the House-Tree-Person Test. In *Advances in the House-Tree-Person Technique:* Variations and Applications, eds. J. N. Buck and E. P. Hammer, pp. 417–47. Los Angeles, Calif.: Western Psychological Services.
  1973 *Culture and Personality,* rev. ed. Homewood, Ill.: The Dorsey Press.
  1975a An Introduction to Anthropology. *Physical Anthropology and Archaeology,* vol. 1, rev. ed. Homewood, Ill.: The Dorsey Press.
  1975b An Introduction to Anthropology. *Ethnology,* vol. 2, rev. ed. Homewood, Ill.: The Dorsey Press.
Benedict, R.
  1935 Zuni Mythology. *Columbia University Contributions to Anthropology,* vol. 21. New York: Columbia University Press.
Bishop, C. A.
  1970 Comments on Bernard J. James, Continuity and Emergence in Indian Poverty Culture. *Current Anthropology* 11:444.
Boggs, S. T.
  1958 Culture Change and the Personality of Ojibwa Children. *American Anthropologist* 60:47–58.
          The Sources of Ojibwa Personality, unpublished paper.
Casagrande, J. B.
  1960 John Mink, Ojibwa Informant. In *The Company of Man. Twenty Portraits by Anthropologists,* ed. J. B. Casagrande, pp. 467–88. New York: Harper and Brothers.
Caudill, W.
  1949 Psychological Characteristics of Acculturated Wisconsin Ojibwa Children. *American Anthropologist* 51:409–27.

DuBois, C.
  1944   *The People of Alor. A Social-Psychological Study of an East Indian Island, with Analyses by Abram Kardiner and Emil Oberholzer.* Minneapolis: University of Minnesota Press.
Friedl, E.
  1956   Persistence in Chippewa Culture and Personality. *American Anthropolgist* 58:814–25.
Gardner, P. M.
  1966   Symmetric Respect and Memorate Knowledge: The Structure and Ecology of Individualistic Culture. *Southwestern Journal of Anthropology* 22:389–415.
Grant, P.
  1890   The Sauteux Indians: About 1804. In *Les Bourgeois de la Compagnie du Nord-Ouest,* ed. R. L. Masson. Quebec: Cote et Cie.
Hallowell, A. I.
  1955   *Culture and Experience.* Philadelphia: University of Pennsylvania Press.
Hart, C. W. M.
  1954   The Sons of Turimpi. *American Anthropologist* 56:242–61.
Hickerson, H.
  1960   The Feast of the Dead Among the Seventeenth Century Algonkians of the Upper Great Lakes. *American Anthropologist* 62:81–107.
  1962   The Southwestern Chippewa: An Ethnohistorical Study. *Memoirs of the American Anthropological Association,* No. 92.
  1967   Some Implications of the Theory of the Particularity, or "Atomism" of Northern Algonkians. *Current Anthropology* 8:313–43.
  1970   *The Chippewa and Their Neighbors: A Study in Ethnohistory.* New York: Holt, Rinehart, and Winston.
  1971   The Chippewa of the Upper Great Lakes: A Study in Sociopolitical Change. In *North American Indians in Historical Perspective,* eds. E. B. Leacock and N. O. Lurie, pp. 169–99. New York: Random House.
James, B. J.
  1954   Some Critical Observations Concerning Analyses of Chippewa "Atomism" and Chippewa Personality. *American Anthropologist* 56:282–86.
  1961   Sociopsychological Dimensions of Ojibwa Acculturation. *American Anthropologist* 63:721–46.
  1970   Continuity and Emergence in Indian Poverty Culture. *Current Anthropology* 11:435–52.
Kohl, J. G.
  1860   *Wanderings Around Lake Superior.* London: Champan and Hall.
La Barre, W.
  1952   Review of Victor Barnouw, Acculturation and Personality among the Wisconsin Chippewa. *American Anthropologist* 54:249–50.
Landes, R.
  1937   The Ojibwa of Canada. In *Cooperation and Competition Among Primitive Peoples,* ed. M. Mead, pp. 87–126. New York: McGraw-Hill.
Lantis, M.
  1946   The Social Culture of the Nunivak Eskimo. *Transactions of the American Philosophical Society* 35, part 3:153–323.

1953 Nunivak Eskimo Personality as Reflected in the Mythology. *Anthropological Papers of the University of Alaska* 2:109–74.

Lindesmith, A. R. and Strauss, A. A.
1950 A Critique of Culture and Personality Writings. *American Sociological Review* 15:587–600.

Llewellyn, K. N. and Hoebel, E. A.
1941 *The Cheyenne Way.* Norman, Oklahoma: University of Oklahoma Press.

Lowenfels, M. S.
1950 Free Drawings as a Projective Test in Cross-Cultural Investigations. Unpublished Master's thesis, University of Pennsylvania.

Maslow, A. H. and Honigmann, J. J.
1970 Synergy: Some Notes of Ruth Benedict. *American Anthropologist* 72:320–33.

Orlansky, H.
1949 Infant Care and Personality. *Psychological Bulletin* 46:1–48.

Rubel, A. J. and Kupferer, H. J.
1968 Perspectives on the Atomistic-Type Society: Introduction. *Human Organization* 27:189–90.

Tanner, J.
1830 *A Narrative of the Captivity and Adventures of John Tanner. Prepared for the Press by Edwin James.* New York: Carvill.

The Author

MARGARET MEAD is Curator Emeritus of Ethnology, the American Museum of Natural History, and Adjunct Professor of Anthropology, Columbia University. She took her B.A. from Barnard College in 1923 and her Ph.D. from Columbia University in 1929. These simple facts, or any number of them for that matter, cannot, however, convey the essence of this remarkable woman and her career. She has made thirteen significant trips to the field including, of course, Samoa, Manus, New Guinea, and Bali. She has written books that are for many Americans the epitome of anthropology, such as *Coming of Age in Samoa, Growing Up in New Guinea,* and *Sex and Temperament in Three Primitive Societies.* She is also interested in studying contemporary cultures in light of perspectives gained by the study of small, homogeneous, stable societies, and in the further development of cultural theories of human behavior. Her books *And Keep Your Powder Dry, Male and Female, The School in American Culture, Culture and Commitment: A Study of the Generation Gap,* and *The Twentieth Century Faith: Hope and Survival* are particularly diagnostic of this interest and her contribution to the understanding of our own culture. She has pioneered in the study of relationships between childhood experience and adult development, in adaptaitons to cultural and technological change, in studies of national character, and in the use of photography as a basic tool in ethnography and psychological anthropology. She is also a pioneer in contributing to the intellectual stream of development of the Western world beyond the relatively narrow reach of professional anthropology as such.

She says of herself:

Margaret Mead was born in Philadelphia, Pennsylvania, in 1901, the oldest child of parents who were both social scientists. She was educated by her grandmother who had been a teacher and who was deeply interested in modern methods of pedagogy. After early experimentation with painting, writing, public speaking, political organizing, and psychological research, she decided to become a scientist and chose anthropology because it offered work that had to be done at once or the opportunity would be lost forever. During her fifty years of sequential field work in Oceania, she tried to combine the insights gained from small homogeneous primitive societies and the needs of the emerging world community in accord with her acceptance of the task to cherish and protect the lives of all human kind and the life of the world itself.

This Chapter

In this chapter Margaret Mead engages with a wide variety of evocative materials ranging from the Stanford-Binet and Porteus Maze tests through the House-Tree-Person test and the Lowenfield Mosaics, to blank paper with crayons or paints available and glass chimes that tinkle in the breeze. Her extensive use of such evocative materials may seem surprising when one realizes she is one anthropologist who insists we must take the culture the way we find it—searches for adequate experimental settings are out of the question. They are too costly in time, when "time is running out." Although she contrived situations, as in her field work in Manus with children, she allowed the situations to become natural, reducing the threat of a formal test situation or structured interview. In this manner, for example, she collected 32,000 drawings from children who had never before used a pencil and paper. She showed enormous flexibility in her use of evocative materials. She made her own ink blots, she used Chinese glass chimes and Japanese paper flowers which unfold in water as forms of projective tests.

However, her paper is not only an exposé of her use of evocative materials in the field. It is also the story of the pursuit of certain interrelated problems centering on the ascription of animistic thinking to primitive peoples in general, and particularly to children, from primitive cultures or not. She has long been interested in how children think. Her work has had direct implications for the theories of Piaget and his followers.

She makes a strong argument for anthropologists to do substantial ethnographic background work. She makes a point that because of the dominance of research grant sections by psychologists "who treated field trips as if they were planned laboratory experiments and judged grant applications in the same terms" field workers over the past three decades have gone into the field with "narrowly defined problems and spent their energies collecting data without doing substantial ethnographic background work." Her own dependence on "instruments" declined when she could really define problems on her own terms, and not as defined by psychologically dominated research grant sections of major foundations. Many of us resonate to her point.

Her paper draws extensively from her previously published works and ties them together into a unified whole addressed to her central problem as well as to the use of evocative materials in the field. It is important to remember, however, that this problem of the study of animistic thinking is only one of the interests Margaret Mead has pursued vigorously in field research and in publications.

Her finding that Manus children show no evidence of tendencies toward spontaneous animistic thought, in fact are negative toward such explanations and are less animistic than Manus adults, was and still is a major challenge to Piaget, and to all findings based entirely on a Western sample.

G.D.S.

3 *The Evocation of Psychologically Relevant Responses in Ethnological Field Work*

MARGARET MEAD

Scientific anthropology differs from the experimental sciences in that it is almost never possible to set up a satisfactory experiment in the field. The enormous degree of effort involved in even a very small and limited piece of comparative experimental work, such as the study of recognition of illusions, was well documented in Segall, Campbell and Herskovits (1966). In general, with relatively isolated and well preserved primitive cultures becoming more and more rare, it is very doubtful whether the effort that is required to try to find adequate samples for experimental work is at all justified (Cole, Jay, Glick and Sharp 1971). Even Whiting and Whiting after setting out to do carefully prescribed comparative work in cultures which had been previously studied, in the end gave their field workers permission to follow their own impulses in pursuing the most valuable emphases in each culture (Whiting 1963).

The search for particular situations, with the right number of children of a given age, the perfect contrast among a set of villages and the specified differences in culture contact, all are likely to take up more time and money than is defensible. Time is running out; national states are closing their doors to anthropologists, the jungle is being bulldozed and roads are being built through the Kalahari Desert and the Ituri Forest. However much an anthropologist may be interested in exploring or demonstrating some point which has arisen in the course of conventional experimental work in psychology, he or she will in the end, I believe, do better to accept conditions as they come, learn to use every possibility within a given field context, make do and mend with givens, rather than spending months looking for perfect sites, different sized populations or predetermined contrasts.

One of the hardest things for anthropology students to learn is how to relate theory and available methodology to the field work situation in which he or she will eventually "find themselves." They must learn how to formulate a question so that directed field work will yield a useful hypothesis which—given the current state of theory—would have been impossible (or at least highly unlikely) to have been formulated otherwise. And, they must learn to phrase problems broadly enough so that their field work will always be productive (Mead 1942).

Ethnological field situations are not places to prove psychological theories; rather they are places where existing paradigms can be questioned, and where new hypotheses can be generated—hypotheses which can then be subjected to such tests as experimentalists can devise. So the first skill needed is the formulation of an existing theory, or a set of implicit assumptions, in such a way that field work can call them into question. Field work which is merely designated to confirm an existing assumption should, I think, be regarded as a waste of time. Any reasonably sound theory which has taken the culture of the formulator into account may well find support in many other cultures. It is the culture which does not support it that provides useful material for broadening or reshaping existing theory.

This point can be illustrated (at the *reductum ad absurdum* level) by considering a hypothesis advanced by a prominent child psychiatrist in the 1920s which stated that infants need to go through a period of wet diapers in their psychosexual development. No one had to do extensive field work to point out that the human race had survived for hundreds of thousands of years without diapers, and that this theory was culture-bound. However, as the use of diapers spread from civilizations which demanded cleanliness to those which did not do so in the same way, the experience of the culture-bound psychiatrist might be of use in answering questions about the way children, hitherto left to run naked, were subjected to new types of discipline. At a deeper level, the attention given to culture-bound clinical histories did direct the attention of anthropologists to the way children were cared for and disciplined (Mead 1954*b*). As details of child rearing practices accumulated, it was possible to formulate more culturally inclusive theories. This in turn formed the basis on which a group of us during World War II worked on hypotheses about national character (Mead and Metraux 1965).

However, our capacity to formulate questions for which the study of whole single cultures might be expected to provide useful answers has been rather heavily impaired by the kinds of controls on field funds which have operated during the last twenty-five years. The largest portion of anthropological field funds have been provided by the National Institute of Mental Health, where the research grant sections were dominated by psychologists, who treated field trips as if they were planned laboratory experiments and judged grant applications in the same terms. Increasingly during the last three decades, field workers, especially students looking for dissertation materials, have gone into the field with narrowly defined problems, and spent their energies collecting data without doing substantial ethnographic background work. As support for the psychologically dominated style of work dries up, and anthropologists depend on more broadly presented problems for funds, the older kind of hypothesis generation and theory questioning field work may again be of interest to students (Mead 1970*a*).

In this paper I propose to discuss the history of one piece of my own research which was directed towards the testing of psychological theories in the course of which a great many kinds of evocative materials were used. During the last fifty years, the development of a variety of cross-culturally usable tests has paralleled an increasing cooperation between psychologists, psychiatrists and anthropologists.

Under the blanket term, evocative materials, I classify the following kinds of instruments which have been developed by psychologists and psychiatrists and which have proven to be productive when used cross-culturally or in particular other cultures.[1]

Intelligence tests: Those which are culture-bound but contain elements which can be modified like the Stanford-Binet (Buros 1972); Raven matrices, both adult and children (Raven 1941); intelligence tests explicitly designed to be culture-free, such as the Porteus Maze Test (Porteus and James 1963); and the Stewart Ring Puzzle Test.

1. This list is not exhaustive. These are the tests which my collaborators and I have found useful.

Projective tests: Those which are ambiguous designs or situations into which the respondent is required to project his own experience (Frank 1948), like the Rorschach (Rorschach 1921; Mead 1974*b*), Thematic Apperception Test (TAT) (Murray 1943; Henry 1947), the Szondi Test (Deri 1949), the Horn Hellersberg Test (Hellersberg 1950), the Abel Limited Free Design Test (Abel 1938), the Anderson Story Completion Test (Anderson and Anderson 1954, 1961; Hanfmann and Getzels 1953), McClelland Achievement Tests (McClelland et al. 1953).

Objective tests: Those which produce a product that can be studied independently of the use of the language: the Goodenough Draw-A-Man Test (Goodenough 1926); The House-Tree-Person (HTP) Test (Buck 1949); Kohs Blocks (Anastasi 1958); the Lowenfeld Mosaic, Kaleidobloc and Poleidobloc Tests (Lowenfeld 1939, 1954; Anderson, Thornhill and Smith 1973); Witkin Cards (Witkin et al. 1954); and the Bender Gestalt Test (Benter 1938).

Arrays of materials: The Lowenfeld World Technique (Lowenfeld 1948), a large set of three dimensional representations in scale of the real world; complex or simple sets of home making toys (Erikson 1963*b*; Henry and Henry 1944), blank paper with crayons or paints, clay, and plasticine; and complex materials from another culture such as a magazine cover, a narrative, or a folk tale following Devereux's suggestion that any culture can be used as free association material for studying another culture (Devereux 1955).

Evocative materials shade the most carefully designed and rigid tests which have the least expectation of cross-cultural viability through projective, objective and evocative sets for the creation of drawings or sculpture, to the use of writing, tape recording and photography to create cultural products for subsequent analysis. The collection of materials which do not involve tests but may involve recording standard situations in standard ways includes Lomax's use of films and tapes in cantometric and choreometric analysis (Lomax 1968), Gregory Bateson's analyses of photographic stills and films (Bateson and Mead 1962, *1942;*[2] Mead and McGregor 1951; McQuown 1971), and analyses of kinesic behavior (Birdwhistell 1970; Byers 1972; Thompson 1969). In such collections the integrity of the original cultural behavior is retained and not broken up as it necessarily is in the use of evocative materials.

One of the best examples of the integration of test and technique designed in a Euro-American cultural and theoretical setting and applied simultaneously with the conventional methods of participatory

2. Dates in italics refer to the original date of publication.

and observational field work, is the work of Rhoda Metraux and T. M. Abel in Monserrat (Metraux 1957; Metraux and Abel 1957; Abel and Metraux 1959). Here, large batteries of tests (Rorschach, Szondi, Bender Gestalt, children's drawings, Mosaics) were used in combination with intensive field work by the anthropologist.

Another example is the extensive use of tests which has been made in cooperation with Theodore Schwartz and Lenora Foerstal on our successive cooperative ventures between The American Museum of Natural History Admiralty Island Expedition in 1953 (Mead 1955; T. Schwartz 1966; L. S. Schwartz 1959), and a series of follow-up expeditions in the 1960s and 1970s (L. R. Schwartz 1966; Heath 1973; Malcolm 1972) (see acknowledgements at the end of this chapter).

There are so many techniques and technical aids now available, including video tape, special Polaroid containers for regular cameras for the immediate assessment of records, and computer analysis of test results on transformed cultural products, that a tremendous amount of responsibility falls on the field worker alone in the field, faced by the complexity of a living culture and a specific historical situation.

I therefore propose in this chapter to give in considerable detail the ways in which my questions developed from the instruments and methods available and the literature and thinking of the period when I went to Manus in 1928, and how these were then used to evoke answers to the questions I asked.

PRE-MANUS EXPERIENCE (MEAD 1974c)

There was no formal field work training when I was a graduate student. Professor Boas gave a course which he called *Methods* in which he used known ethnographic materials to discuss and criticize the principal anthropological theories of the day.

Lévy-Bruhl (Lévy-Bruhl 1926), in assuming that "the primitive" thinks differently from the way in which civilized men think, was criticized by the presentation of evidence from ethnographic data which indicated that primitive man was as capable of thinking "rationally" as modern man, and that modern man was also capable of thinking in the ways which Lévy-Bruhl attributed to primitive man alone (Boas 1965). It was a sign of sophistication in anthropological thinking, when each of us, in turn "discovered" that Lévy-Bruhl was French, and thus considered the metric system to be a sign of civilized man's rationality, rather than the English measurements (hands, pecks, stones, etc.) which had all the concreteness of the allegedly characteristic thinking of primitive man.

Differences in the success of intelligence tests had been attributed to differences in cultural experience. Having studied the history of intelligence testing, I did my Masters degree in psychology on the subject of the effect of language spoken at home (Italian) on the test records of children (Mead 1926, 1927). In my study of Italian children I used the Otis Group Test and the individual Stanford Binet test, which contained much of the materials used in later group tests as well as the very early attempts at what were later named (by L. K. Frank 1948) projective tests. The Stanford Binet contained a projective picture interpretation section (the precursor of the Thematic Apperception Test [Murray 1943]), an objective test (Ball and Field Test) and a vocabulary test which provided for the intrusion of the kind of emotional factor which Jung had invented in his verbal association test (Fenichel 1945). The interpretation of proverbs also allowed for the evaluation of the development of moral understanding. Attention to the way in which the test had been developed, using different components (rote memory, reasoning, recognition) emphasized that intelligence was complicated and differed profoundly among individuals who might, however, attain the same IQ.

While I was in graduate school, I worked with Melville Herskovits in exploring the Downey Will-Temperament Test (Downey 1924; Herskovits 1972). Campbell describes this experiment in his introduction to Herskovits' posthumously published volume on *Cultural Relativism* (Campbell 1972; Herskovits 1972), but one important detail was omitted. Because Herskovits found no correlation between test results and intragroup ratings when the test was given to clusters of people who knew each other well, he discarded the results of the test. However, there was one interesting result which I noted: although the overall correlations were negative, the correlations between a high score on the Downey Will-Temperament and high ratings for the same trait, were high. Stated another way, the test did in some way measure the presence of a trait, but not its absence. This corresponds to what we know of IQ tests today; a high positive score is completely predictive of capacity to succeed in the American school system, but low scores have to be attributed to such a wide variety of factors that they do not have comparable significance.

When I went to Samoa in 1925, having some knowledge of the current state of testing, I wished to use some sort of measure to distinguish individuals in groups of adolescent and pre-adolescent girls I was studying. In an appendix to *Coming of Age in Samoa,* written in 1926 and published in 1928, I summarized the use I had made of tests, as follows:

Intelligence Tests Used

It was impossible to standardise any intelligence tests and consequently my results are quantitatively valueless. But as I had had some experience in the diagnostic use of tests, I found them useful in forming a preliminary estimate of the girls' intelligence. Also, the natives have long been accustomed to examinations which the missionary authorities conduct each year, and the knowledge that an examination is in progress makes them respect the privacy of investigator and subject. In this way it was possible for me to get the children alone, without antagonizing their parents. Furthermore, the novelty of the tests, especially the colour-naming and picture interpretation tests, served to divert their attention from other questions which I wished to ask them. The results of the tests showed a much narrower range than would be expected in a group varying in age from ten to twenty. Without any standardization it is impossible to draw any more detailed conclusions. I shall, however, include a few comments about the peculiar responses which the girls made to particular tests, as I believe such comment is useful in evaluating intelligence testing among primitive peoples and also in estimating the possibilities of such testing.

Tests Used:

Colour Naming. 100 half-inch squares, red, yellow, black and blue.

Rote Memory for Digits. Customary Stanford Binet directions were used.

Digit Symbol Substitution. Seventy-two one-inch figures, square, circle, cross, triangle and diamond.

Opposites. Twenty-three words. Stimulus words: fat, white, long, old, tall, wise, beautiful, late, night, near, hot, win, thick, sweet, tired, slow, rich, happy, darkness, up, inland, inside, sick.

Picture Interpretation. Three reproductions from the moving picture *Moana,* showing, (a) Two children who had caught a cocoanut crab by smoking it out of the rocks above them, (b) A canoe putting out to sea after bonito as evidenced by the shape of the canoe and the position of the crew, (c) A Samoan girl sitting on a log eating a small live fish which a boy, garlanded and stretched on the ground at her feet, had given her.

Ball and Field. Standard-sized circle.

Standard directions were given throughout in all cases entirely in Samoan. Many children, unused to such definitely set tasks, although all are accustomed to the use of slate and of pencil and paper, had to be encouraged to start. The ball and field test was the least satisfactory as in over fifty percent of the cases the children followed an accidental first line and simply completed an elaborate pattern within the circle. When this pattern happened by accident to be either the Inferior or Superior solution, the child's comment usually betrayed the guiding idea as aesthetic rather than as an attempt to solve the problem. The children whom I was led to believe to be most intelligent, subordinated the aesthetic consideration to the solution of the problem, but the less intelligent children were sidetracked by their interest in the design they could make much more easily than are children in our civilisation. In only two cases did I find a rote memory for digits which exceeded six digits; two girls completing seven successfully. The Samoan civilisation puts the slightest of premiums upon rote memory of any sort. On the digit-symbol test they were slow to understand the point of the test and very few learned the combinations before the last line of the test sheet. The picture interpretation test was the most subject to vitiation through a cultural factor; almost all of the children adopted some highly stylized form of comment and then pursued it through one balanced sentence after another: "Beautiful is the garland of the boy and beautiful is the wreath of the girl," etc. In the two pictures which emphasised human beings no discussion could be commenced until the question of the relationship of the characters had been ascertained. The opposites test was the one which they did most easily, a natural consequence of a vivid interest in words, an interest which leads them to spend most of their mythological speculation upon punning explanations of names. [Mead 1961*a*, *1928*, pp. 289–92]

The assumptions behind this discussion are fairly simple: intelligence tests were designed to get at elements of intelligence which were human, but were likely to be culture-specific in form; comparing the results from a very different culture to those from the culture in which the tests had been devised would be impossible without standardizing them anew. Bearing this in mind, various sorts of tests might be used exploratorially, both to discriminate among members of another culture, and to demonstrate, illuminate or communicate the characteristics of another culture to psychologically sophisticated members of our own culture.

INTERIM INTELLECTUAL CONTACTS

On the way home from Samoa in 1926 I met Reo Fortune, who had been doing experimental work on sleep, using his own dreams to criticize the theories of Freud and Rivers (Fortune 1926, 1927*b*). The following winter I read Freud's *Totem and Taboo* (Freud 1960, *1918*) and Piaget's first book, *The Language and Thought of the Child* (Piaget 1960, *1926*). Piaget, having been influenced by Lévy-Bruhl, equated the way in which French children think with the development of the high mental capacities required for science and philosophy. In Piaget I found the assumption that the "savage" and the "child" think alike;

in Freud that the "child," the "savage," and the "neurotic" think alike. To each a kind of animistic thinking (like Lévy-Bruhl's participation [Lévy-Bruhl 1926]) was attributed. In the light of the existing state of anthropological theory, and my own field experience, I raised three questions: If animism is a human trait, what had happened to it in Samoa where the type of thinking attributed to "primitive peoples" was very little in evidence? Was it possible that the kind of ambivalence of which Freud spoke in *Totem and Taboo* was simply a culturally patterned recognition of such matters as fear of the dead, which might be culturally reversed? And third, if "primitive" adults think like civilized children and neurotics, *how do primitive children think?*

I tried to answer the first question in a paper titled "A Lapse of Animism Among a Primitive People":

So all the contacts with the supernatural were accidental, trivial, uninstitutionalized. The individual whose religious interest and unstable temperament gave him a reputation for oracular powers was given no accepted place in a pattern where religion claimed so little attention.

And yet neither the examination of his institutionalized animistic attitude or of his everyday conduct convinces the observer of the essentially untrained nature of the Samoan's mind. When he pays any attention to the dead, when he can tear his attention from counting the number of mats presented at the death feast, he thinks of them as still potent for harm, insubstantial creatures who wander about at night, banded together in ghost boats, who may be scalded at noon day when they are at home in their graves, or caught in fish nets at night and beaten to final extinction. When he runs a nail into his foot he sticks it into a breadfruit tree to cure the foot; when a child is born cross-eyed a ghost is to blame.

And a flashlight which will not work he spontaneously pronounces dead. An alarm clock which rings undeterred by a command to stop is indignantly hushed. But so great is his absorption with the social ceremonial within which he lives and moves and has his being, that the other matters where his premises are wrong, seldom claim his attention. From morning to night, from one year to another year, he gives as little or less time to the pursuance of false clues, to the invocation of false animistic sequences, as does any uneducated man in western Europe. His culture has through some historical accident, some shift in emphasis, turned aside from speculating about those aspects of life upon which primitive man has poor data, and concentrated on that aspect which gave all the correct observation from which animistic false premises spring—human relationships. [Mead 1928, p. 77]

I considered the second question in "An Ethnologist's Footnote to Totem and Taboo" (Mead 1930), in which I discussed the ways primitive peoples treat the dead; the Chukchee (Bogoras 1907) and Koryak

(Jochelson 1908) of Siberia suppress expressions of grief, while the Bagobo (L. W. Benedict 1916) of the Philippines believed in two souls, one to be feared and the other to be sent to Paradise.

But granting that the existence of conflicting attitudes may result in serious conflicts, and even in real neuroses in particularly susceptible individuals, it is hardly in accord with the ethnographic evidence to assume that the same attitude will be uppermost and approved, and the same attitude be deprecated and outlawed, in all human societies. And as the conscious mind of the individual is molded and shaped by the traditions of his own society, so the attitudes which are permitted free uncensored play in any individual personality will vary from one civilization to another.

Attempts to clarify and explain the mourning behaviors of individuals in very different cultures in terms of the particular ambivalence of attitude which is institutionalized in our own culture, are likely to be misleading.

Among the Chukchee and Koryak of aboriginal Siberia the whole emphasis is laid upon the complete removal of the dead, the equipment of the spirit so that it will never return, the bewildering and baffling of the spirit so that it cannot find its way back to the abode of its relatives. In discussing the Siberian practices I shall reproduce Dr. Bogoras' and Dr. Jochelson's own words so as not to mar their accounts by the introduction of less vivid paraphrases. After death, among the Chukchee, "one man must stay all the time with the body, because should it be left alone it might revive and do harm. . . . Among other taboos connected with the funeral must be mentioned the interdictions against beating the drum for three nights during the time of the ceremony. The beating of the drum might call the deceased back to the house."

Bogoras quotes a farewell speech of a wife to the corpse of her dead husband. " 'Well, well, what can I do, we have lived together for so many years and now you are going away. Do not keep an evil mind against me. My head was never very strong. If I acted unfairly toward you, have no bad feeling toward me.' . . . At every hitch in this task (that of dressing the corpse in its burial clothes) the followers admonish the dead one, saying 'Leave off! Make haste! You have to go away, do not be so obstinate.' . . . In most cases the body is carried out of the tent not through the entrance, but through the roof . . . or under the folds of the tent cover, somewhere on the back side of the tent. Every trace of this improvised exit is immediately obliterated; and thus the deceased one, if he should come back, would not be able to recognize the way." After reaching the grave and going through a number of ceremonies "the fortifier" (officiant) "cuts the throat of the corpse and leaves the body. This last stroke is to prevent the spirit of the deceased from following the people of the cortege and is considered quite indispensable. On the way home, the order of march is reversed, and many ceremonies and incantations are performed—the fortifier throwing behind him several small stones which become a "mountain," a bunch of grass which becomes a "forest," and a cup which becomes a "sea;" magical defenses against the return of the dead. On the return home "all the members of the procession, holding one another by the hand, form a large ring, which is encircled by that part of the thong that was taken home from the funeral. Each of the members takes hold of it, and each one cuts off the part nearest to himself. This severs all connection between them; and the spirit of the deceased, if it should ever come back, would have to find them out one by one."

Summary

The concept of ambivalence which Dr. Freud (Freud 1960, *1918*) has used to illuminate the origins of funeral ceremonies and contradictory attitudes towards the dead might also include the possibilities:

I. That some cultures, rather than retaining a great number of contradictory elements, will tend to emphasize one aspect of the emotion, either grief and love as in our own culture, or fear, distrust, and hostility as in the Siberian cultures described; and that when one aspect is so heavily stressed, it is the other which, excessively developed, leads to conflict. Which aspect of the ambivalent attitude is culturally stressed will depend upon historical causes.

II. Other cultures, like that of the Bagobo, may develop an institutionalized attitude towards personality which, objectifying the conflict between contradictory emotions, presents a cultural solution of the conflict and necessitates no such suppression on the part of the individual. [Mead 1930, pp. 298–99, 304]

I submitted the paper to Ernest Jones, then editor of the *International Journal of Psychoanalysis,* who rejected it as more suitable for an anthropological journal but not "psychoanalytically interesting." However, White accepted it for the *Psychoanalytic Review.* It was not until twenty years later, after an extensive stay at the Menninger Clinic (the first psychoanalytic culture I had ever experienced in a whole community), that I realized what Ernest Jones had meant when he said, "The paper as it is written might mislead the reader into thinking that you had made a mistake in regarding the conscious attitude of the Chukchees to represent one of the two halves of the ambivalent attitude dealt with by Freud" (Mead 1963*b*). I will return to this later in this chapter.

The third question—what would primitive children's thinking be like—required field work with young children under six which I had not done in Samoa.

During the two year period between my field work in Samoa and the Manus field work, I continued to work with the broad assumption that while human potentialities were universal, which ones would be expressed and the form that they would take depended upon the culture.

In the summer of 1927, Reo Fortune and I met briefly in Germany. He had concluded and published his book on dreams (Fortune 1927*b*) and a thesis on imitative magic (Fortune 1927*a*) and was on his way to Australia to take up a research grant from the Australian National Research Council. We did not yet know that Manus would be the place we would work, but we were already discussing how my new interest in the relationship between the thought of primitive children and the imputed thought of primitive adults, could be carried out. He told me Spearman had said that ink blots are a good test of the imagination (Spearman 1927). Rorschach had developed his test by then (1921), but neither of us had yet seen it.

During the following winter (1927–28), while Reo Fortune was doing his basic field work for *Sorcerers of Dobu* (Fortune 1963, *1932*), I wrote *The Social Organization of Manu'a* (Mead 1969, *1930*). Meanwhile, Ruth Benedict was working on her first paper on culture as "personality writ large" (R. Benedict 1959, *1930*) which she planned to give at the Congress of Americanists in the summer of 1928. I had completed the manuscript of *Coming of Age in Samoa* (Mead 1961*a*, *1928*), (with the exception of the last two chapters on the implications for American culture) in the spring of 1927, which included an analysis of the deviant (chapter IX of *Coming of Age in Samoa,* "The Girl in Conflict"). This chapter was actually the first published application of the configurative theory of culture. That same winter I elaborated on this in *Social organization of Manu'a* (Mead 1969, *1930*). Here again I dealt with the question of animism as I then conceived it:

The formal relationship between the society and its deity, as between the household and its family god, might be characterized as one of dignified avoidance. Certain rules had been laid down, certain old tapus still held supernatural sanction; if man, careless of fitting behavior, transgressed these rules, he must make amends. Life in this world was glimpsed as only occasionally precarious; observance of the rules of the social life brought blessedness in its train. There was no concept of good or bad luck, impersonal, unearned beneficence or malevolence of providence, such as plays such a strong role with us. Rather there was deserved blessedness and deserved misfortune, neither one was arbitrary, both were functions of man's way of life. Walking gravely within his given paths, man no more hoped for special concessions from the gods than he feared special unmotivated onslaughts. On the edges of this dignified formal relationship with a fairly uninterested heaven, were the difficulties introduced by local spirits and ghosts. But these were never taken official notice of; the man who angered a spirit would suffer the spirit's malicious revenge. But this was guerilla warfare on the borders of good society; neither Tagaloa nor the fono deigned to take any notice of it.

Chiefly concerned then with their social pattern, the Samoans have time for little else. Pondering upon the exigencies of ordered society, they take small interest in the world of the supernatural, nor are they puzzled and perplexed by the world of natural phenomena. The wavering line which divides the animate from the inanimate, the personal from the impersonal, borders their field of attention instead of threading its way among their preoccupations. For an interest in the intractability of material, the unaccountable tendency of wood to split or gardens to languish, they have substituted an interest in the personnel of carpentering or gardening parties. It is not that they have a clearer knowledge of the properties of material things than the Maori, who must perform long rituals to remove the sacredness from a tree which they wish to cut down. Occasional particular tapus, explicit beliefs in some animate phenomenon, attest to their typical untrained confusion. But their all inclusive social formula gives them no acceptable basis of interest in the mysterious properties of material things or natural phenomena. As the development of a human personality may be expressed in terms of choices made between many interests in an effort to bring all parts of one's character within one coherent picture, so a culture like Samoa may be envisaged also. A diffuse cultural equipment which drew from attitudes widely distributed in the Pacific has been reshaped to an individual people's emphasis. White civilization, on coming in contact with a primitive people, may teach them that material things must not be regarded animistically or that their gods are false. So the adult's world takes the varied conceptions of the child, pooh-poohs its rituals, ridicules its tapus and insists upon an acceptance of the findings of science. But without definite pedagogic discipline, many children will make some of these selections for themselves in terms of their own temperaments; one child will spend all his strength striving to control the world by means of formulas; another will devote himself to a careful investigation of the properties of material things or the principles of mechanics; a third will throw all his energies in establishing social rapport with his fellows. So human societies, left to themselves, will select parts of their heritage for elaboration, and the original choice will gain in impetus from generation to generation until a coherent individual culture has been developed. A strong religious interest, a premium upon aberrant individual gifts, a permission to love without social sanction and give without stint to that which is loved; all these would disturb the nice balance of Samoan society and so are outlawed. Samoa may be said to have a formal social personality, to be a devotee of a careful observance of all the decreed amenities. [Mead 1969, *1930*, pp. 85–86]

THE MANUS EXPERIENCE

The choice of the Admiralty Islands as a field site was based on two considerations. Since one of my curatorial duties at The American Museum of Natural History was the responsibility for the entire Pacific collection, and as I had done both intensive library research and field work in Polynesia, I wanted to work in Melanesia next. I was then planning to marry Reo Fortune, who was working under Radcliff-Brown's direction for the Australian National Research Council. Radcliff-Brown selected the Admiralties for us as an area about which we had very poor ethnographic material (Parkinson 1907; Meier 1907–1909). Within the Admiralties we chose to study the lagoon-dwelling Manus people on the advice of a district officer doing a special course in Sydney, who said that working with the land people of the Admiralties would be very difficult. This choice was made early enough so that I could include the proposed locality in my application to the Social Science Research Council to study the thinking of the "pre-school child." The definition of these early years in terms of school age, is itself a vivid reminder of how very rudimentary were our conceptions of the developmental stages of childhood.

I then had to choose the materials with which to investigate the relationship of animism to the thought processes of primitive children. Since Goodenough had already started her work on *Draw-A-Man Test* (Goodenough 1926), drawing seemed to be the obvious point of departure. There was then no theory of what evocative materials might be, and as I had no idea at all of how many drawings I would need, I fortunately took a very large amount of rough brown drawing paper and boxes of colored crayons. I also planned to study the childrens' behavior, games and songs, and to evoke their explanations of events, as Piaget had done (Piaget 1960, *1926*). I wondered a little how it would be possible to collect small children in a village in which people went from house to house by canoe.

Just as the local group had been selected on the advice of a district officer, the village of Peri itself was selected because a school boy we were given as an interpreter came from Peri and we found a second adolescent boy from the same village in Lorengau, the district capitol. We had inadvertently chosen the village of highest prestige and one with the largest number of entreprenêural men and women.

On my return from Manus in 1929 I wrote an account of this research, "An Investigation of the Thought of Primitive Children, with Special Reference to Animism."

All the work was done in the village of Peri during the six months of December to June, 1928–29. I worked throughout this period in collaboration with my husband, Dr. R. F. Fortune, who was making an investigation of the general culture. This circumstance made it possible for me to shorten materially the time which must be consumed in getting an understanding of the general outlines of a primitive culture before any special problem can be isolated and studied. I learned the Manus language, and all work with the children was conducted in it. The Manus language is a simple Melanesian language; a month is sufficient to get a good working knowledge of it; it is strikingly lacking in idiomatic refinements or delicate nuances.

In the village of Peri there were 210 people, of whom 87 were young people under or just at puberty. Actual ages were unknown, and only approximations based upon the people's knowledge of relative age could be used. Division into small age-groups was, in any event, impracticable because of the small number of cases. Of the group specially studied, there were twenty-two children, eleven boys and eleven girls between the approximate ages of two and six, and nineteen children, ten boys and nine girls between the approximate ages of six and twelve.

These forty-one children were studied under the following conditions:—

(a) With their parents and their brothers and sisters in their own homes, in canoes, or in other houses during ceremonies.

(b) At play in groups in the shallow lagoons.

(c) At play in groups on the three small coral rubble inlets which constituted the only level ground in the village.

(d) At play on the wide verandahs of our house which had been built of native materials and with only slight modifications of the native style of architecture.

(e) Within the large living room of our house. Here play was sometimes random on rainy days, but more often devoted to drawing. I provided them with a large square table, 8 feet square and a foot and a half high, at which they could kneel and draw. The room also contained a number of low cedarwood boxes upon which the children could sit, or beside which they could kneel and draw. The floor was composed of narrow strips of split timber with wide cracks in between, corresponding exactly to the floor of a native house. The room also contained a high table, three chairs, shelves curtained with a native mat, a "children's shelf," which contained odd bits of coloured paper, string, crayons, pencils, etc. There were a few books on high shelves, a few small photographs on the walls, and a glass Chinese chimes hung from the central rafter. The children became perfectly familiar with the entire room, and entered and left it without permission from me. They were sent out by the older boys at meal times and during the siesta hour, and sometimes went to sleep on the floor or curled up on a box.

They learned to take me very much for granted, accepting the original situation which I laid down that I liked children, that I wanted as many children as possible to come to my house and stay as long as they liked. I never interfered in any way with their behaviour unless a situation seemed actually dangerous. Although I sometimes took part in their games, I more often claimed to be engaged in my own affairs, and they became accustomed to having me write or typewrite, or apparently read in their midst. Dr. Fortune worked in another house.

Environments b, c and e were all combined within easy access of our house, as the lagoon playground extended around it on three sides, and it abutted on one of the small islets on the fourth side. The children were in the water one minute, up on the island the next, sprawling on the veranda or romping through the house the minute after.

It should be remarked that Manus children are accustomed to going wherever they like about the village, and are in no fear of adults. The Manus men delight to humour and play with the children, so that my indulgence was in no sense out of character either to the children or to their parents. The children were originally attracted to the house by curiosity, in the wake of the adolescent boys and girls who did the house work, and by presents, balloons, balls, etc., which I dealt out day by day. Later they came to draw, and they came also from a quickly established habit of rendezvous.

Methods

As the existence of a primitive culture was in itself an experimental condition I utilized this fact as much as possible by observation of the children in normal social situations. In order to provide a more controlled situation and also in an attempt to elicit types of material which did not appear under ordinary observational methods, directly experimental methods were used. The methods employed fall under the following heads:

(a) Observation of a group of children, or of a child and an adult, or a group of children and adults, etc., in some ordinary social situation.

(b) Collection of spontaneous drawings.

(c) Interpretation of ink blots.

(d) Definite stimuli in the form of questions designed to provoke animistic responses.

(a) I handled this material in the form of running notes, with time records in two-minute intervals for certain types of play groups. It included questions from children to adults, children's responses to adult commands, explanations, etc., children's subterfuges, children's responses to situations of emotional stress, such as quarrels, severe illnesses, accident, fear displayed by adults, strangers in the village; birth and death; children's responses to storm, cyclone, animals, fish, birds, shadows, reflections, scenes between pairs of age-mates, between elder and younger children, between fathers and children, between mothers and children, between children and infants.

As these observations were all directed towards two particular ends, the definition of the type of child behaviour characteristic of children within the Manus culture, and the analysis of the thought of Manus children with a view to comparing it with the animistic thought said to be characteristic of children in western civilization, I proceeded as follows. Any particular type of situation, e.g. a child's behaviour when threatened by its parents with supernatural punishment, was observed each time it occurred until a type response was discerned; from that time on, each situation of the same type was observed, but not recorded in detail if it bore out the type findings based upon previous observations. All deviants or contradictions of the type-finding were recorded in detail. When a series was obtained the deviants were analysed and the deviating child investigated to determine whether special features of the child's family background, mentality, or temperament accounted for the deviation.

This method is possibly inferior to the laborious recording by a staff of stenographers of every response made by every child over many months. But one investigator attempting to cope with the difficulties of field-work in a primitive community in the few months allowed by climate and field funds, cannot hope to duplicate the voluminous methods of modern nursery school research. Such an investigator must confine himself to an attack upon the core of the problem and use methods like those outlined above to shorten field labour whenever possible. This method is open to less objection in a primitive culture than in a heterogeneous civilized society, because of the homogeneity of the subject's experience. The number of standardized type responses is far greater in a primitive society than in a civilized one.

(b) Drawings were collected to the number of 32,000 over a period of five months. No child had ever used a pencil and paper before. Any attempt at drawing had been confined to one game, outlining a shadow on soft soil with a sharpened stick used as a stylus. This game was only played by the older children and had never, so far as I could judge, been used to make original drawings instead of outlines. At least such use was not known to the group of children which I studied. As beginning drawing with the very young children would have involved actual instruction in the use of a pencil, I decided that a situation more closely analogous to the normal imitative educational situation could be produced if the older children were permitted to draw first and the younger ones led to imitate them. Five boys of about fourteen years of age were given pencil and paper and simply told to "draw," *taro we,* literally "to make a mark." They had seen us write and they had seen some half dozen Government officials write in record books. The brightest of the group, Kilipak, said, "Let's draw a human being." He and one other boy, Tamapwe, provided leads of this sort which the other three followed. The next day the next younger group, after having crowded about the older boys' elbows, were given pencils, until finally the youngest children were drawing without having received any instruction from me. I never passed any judgment upon the children's work, with the exception of a very generalized "That's splendid! That's fine!" type of encouragement to the younger children.

A definite regimen of behaviour was set up. When a child finished a sheet of paper, or tired of drawing with a half completed sheet, he must bring it to me. I wrote the name and date on the corner, and the interpretation of each picture on the paper. This procedure was standardized by the older children also; the older ones spontaneously explained their drawings; when the smaller ones failed to explain their unintelligible scrawls the older children insisted upon an explanation; this very simply became translated into a fixed rule. In this way the drawings bore most completely upon the problem under investigation.

For the drawing I used the large standard sheets of coarse-grained buff paper, and the children were given their choice between lead pencils and crayons. The crayons, although coloured, were never popular, and only selected when all the available pencils were in use; then most of the small children would select black crayons in preference to coloured ones. This seemed to be accounted for in terms of a preference for a sharp point and a lack of appreciation of colour. Only the fourteen- and fifteen-year-olds after four months of drawing hit on the idea of using the coloured crayons for realistic effects, and this was confined to drawing canoes and boats which they are accustomed to seeing painted.

(c) The interpretation of the ink blot test was used as a more controlled way of handling the children's responses. I made my own set of ink blots; they averaged about an inch and a half in greatest dimension, blue on a white surface. The child was shown one at a time and asked *"Tito ko no pwa tcha?"* "What is this like?"

The response was recorded without comment. If a child was slow or shy, I added an encouraging phrase or so: *"e ki la,"* "come on," or *"Oi tu pa sani, ne?"* "You understand, don't you?"

(d) I also presented the children with a series of problems, utilizing in several cases situations which originally occurred spontaneously. These problems were:

(1) The attribution of malicious intent to a canoe which had drifted from its moorings. *Ndrol tasitan muan, ne? i tu wek.* That canoe is bad, isn't it? It's drifting.

(2) The attribution of personality to Chinese glass chimes. This was of the type which can be purchased in Woolworths, rectangular pieces of glass suspended by clender cords from a supporting ring, and a piece of paper suspended from the whole so that the slightest wind will agitate the paper and cause the glass pieces to tinkle against each other. This was hung from a crossbeam of our house.

In this experiment I utilized an adult magical concept in an attempt to assimilate the chimes to native ideas of the supernatural. I said the chimes was a *ramus,* a property-getting charm. Manus adults have a variety of such charms, shells to be worn in the ear or hung on a betel bag, shell crescents with which food is magically crisscrossed, bird claws which are worn hanging down the back, elaborate constructions of grass and pig's tusks on the front house post, special drumsticks which, when used, make people bring the drummer the property for which he is asking—all these and others fall under the category of *ramus,* charms which cause other people to give you what you ask. It is a thoroughly magical concept, operating automatically without any intermediary. When I hung the chimes up I did so in the presence of adults, and remarked, "This is my *ramus.* It is crying out for Manus things which I want to take away with me to my own country." The adults accepted this explanation at once. One remarked, "What kind of property does it want?" Another said, "Is it asking for fish?" And a third said, "It is calling for beadwork."

In presenting it to the children I used this same conceptualization: "This is my *ramus*. It cries for native property. What do you think it is crying for now?"

I listened also for spontaneous comment upon the little chimes, which tinkled for the next three months whenever the wind blew.

(3) Presenting them with a dancing doll of the type which is constructed of paper so that arms, legs and the whole body have a tremendous extensibility like the paper chains made for Christmas trees. When these dolls are suspended they can be manipulated by very slight jerks of the string.

(4) The attribution of malicious intent to a pencil. When a child had made a drawing which he considered bad and had shown his displeasure by remarking on it: *"Tito muan,"* "this is bad"; or *"lo no tu taro we ka pwen,"* "I just drew, that's all," i.e. without definite intent to produce any result (this was a most frequent alibi). I would then seize the opportunity to say, *"Pensil muan, ne Pensil ne po mangas wiyan pwen,"* "The pencil is bad, isn't it? The pencil doesn't do good work."

(5) The problem of how the writing on the paper was made by my portable typewriter. This was a question in which the children took a tremendous spontaneous interest from the start. They would gather around the typewriter for an hour patiently trying to analyse the mechanism. I have listed this problem under posed problems, because the typewriter itself was an artificial situation which I had introduced into their environment.

(6) The problem of the Japanese paper flowers which open out when placed in water. An atmosphere of expectation was engendered; I remarked that something most important was about to take place; enjoined most careful attention and dropped one of the paper pellets into a bowl of water, and simply recorded the comments. This problem and No. 3 had to be posed to one child after another in immediate succession to prevent intercommunication. It was, therefore, a type which it was impracticable to use often, as I did not have the necessary assistance to segregate the children who had taken the test from those who had not. It meant persuading adults to act as warders in what seemed to them a meaningless piece of behaviour. Complicating the native social situation in this way is always of doubtful value, as it is impossible to estimate accurately the repercussions in other departments of native social life.

These six problems contained the following elements:—

(1) Personalization through ascription of motive to a moving inanimate object. This was a less extreme form of personalization than No. 4, for a canoe is less amenable to control than a pencil.

(2) The personalization of an instrument producing mechanical or rhythmical sounds.

(3) Presentation for explanation of an object in human form which made apparently voluntary dancing motions.

(4) Personalization through ascription of motive and separate will power to a pencil. This problem contained the additional element of offering an acceptable alibi for failure in execution.

(5) A mechanical device of such complexity that the connection between the visible movements of my fingers on the typewriter keys and the writing had to be deduced without any knowledge of the principles involved.

(6) An appearance of greatly accelerated but natural growth, or, alternatively, the presentation of an appearance of wonderful transformation from a pellet into a flower.

Results
(a) Observations of Spontaneous Behaviour

As the investigation was designed to discover and record spontaneous animistic thought as expressed in the conversation, games, etc., of children, I expected this aspect of the investigation to yield the most interesting results. The results, however, were virtually negative. I found no evidence for spontaneous animistic thought in the uncontrolled sayings or games of these Manus children during five months of continuous observations alone or in groups, when they were unconscious of being observed at all.

Before going further it is necessary to distinguish between what I am calling "spontaneous animism" and a child's acceptance of animistic categories which are explicit or implicit in the linguistic concepts of its elders. When an English-speaking child refers to a ship as "she," he is not being spontaneously animistic, he is merely conforming to a recognized category of gender. But when a child draws a picture of a steamboat, setting the steamboat on end, inserting a face on one end, and attributing human activities to the steamboat, (Fortune, 1927a) this is spontaneous animistic thought, although it may be, as I shall suggest later, rooted in a traditional linguistic usage. Similarly a child who talks to a dog, or a horse, or a cat, or a parrot, is not necessarily animistic, but is merely imitating traditional adult behaviour. On the other hand, an English-speaking child who has long conversations with a toy engine or with a tree has spontaneously attributed personality in a way which transcends the traditional pattern of its group. Similarly a child who says his prayers and asks God to make him a good boy and not let it rain to-morrow is showing no childish or spontaneous animism, while a child who invents an imaginary playmate, holds long conversations with the playmate and reports sayings and adventures of this imaginary playmate, is indulging in a type of thought which may, with due reservations upon how much stimulation the child has received from others, be called spontaneous, and nontraditional.

Therefore, I do not class it as spontaneous animism when a Manus child says, "The ghost of the wife of Pondramet married the ghost of Sori last night." In saying this the child is merely repeating a piece of gossip, as he would say, "A woman in the village of Rambutchon has had a baby." The Manus adults believe that the ghosts of the dead live all about them in the village; they are continually in communication with these ghosts through diviners and mediums, and marriages and quarrels on the ghostly plane are often reported by mediums. The children accept the alleged presence of the ghosts in general, and parrot their parents' comments. Only if a child spontaneously elaborated the idea of ghosts, talked with them, saw them, invoked them for his private ends, would I class remarks upon the ghosts as spontaneous.

So when a Manus child calls a pig by name and tells it to come and eat, which is exact reproduction of adult behaviour, I do not call this spontaneous. But had a Manus child ever been seen conversing with a dog or commenting upon a dog's feelings or even addressing a remark to a dog, this would indeed have been spontaneous, for Manus dogs are unnamed and never spoken to in words. The natives control them entirely by kicks, cuffs, and a low guttural call.

Also when a Manus child explained a woman's sickness by saying she had a snake in her belly, this was merely repeating a doctor's diagnosis, and from the child's point of view was a statement of fact, although the adults knew that the terrific distortion of the woman's abdomen was from no natural snake, but from a supernatural snake.

Similarly with the treatment of the concept of the *tchinal* or mischievous land devil, in the persons of whom the water-dwelling Manus people caricature and express their fear and distrust of their land neighbours. The adult describes the *tchinal* to the child in an attempt to intimidate him from wandering about at night and to explain to him why his presence is inconvenient when the parent goes to the market at the edge of the land. *Tchinals* have extraordinarily long arms, protruding teeth, hair which hangs matted over their eyes. Their fingernails are as long as their fingers, and they will pursue and eat men. If a child reported having seen a *tchinal*, or added more and personal detail to this traditional picture, or showed special fear of a special *tchinal* whom he declared to inhabit a special spot, only in such cases would these be declared to be evidences of spontaneous animistic thought.

To summarize, I considered strictly traditional behaviour, whether expressed in language or belief, as insufficient proof that a child spontaneously attributed personality to natural phenomena, animals or inanimate objects, or created imaginative non-existent personal beings.

I found no instance of a child's personalizing a dog or a fish or a bird, of his personalizing the sun, the moon, the wind or the stars. I found no evidence of a child's attributing chance events, such as the drifting away of a canoe, the loss of an object, an unexplained noise, a sudden gust of wind, a strange deep-sea turtle, a falling seed from a tree, etc., to supernaturalistic causes. This is the more remarkable when it is realized that if a stone falls suddenly in the bush near an adult, he will usually mutter, "a spirit," and the common explanation of the loss of any small object such as a knife, if the explanation of theft is rejected, is that a spirit took it. In adult theory spirits put ideas into people's minds, are responsible for any insane or unreliable behaviour—in the native idiom a spirit "twists the neck" of the unfortunate demented person. Also spirits send turtles to their mortal wards, or guide the feet of their wards to the turtles, and it is angry spirits which send cyclones to injure a sinning man's house. Furthermore, the adults believe that one spirit was recently turned into a crocodile, and that carved crocodiles can talk. So in this case the children not only did not construct new and spontaneous explanations to account for the behaviour of natural phenomena, animals or unexplained sounds or motions around them, but they actually largely neglected the stock explanations provided by the culture.

The evidence of observation was confirmed by the evidence from the drawings. There were no animals acting like human beings, no composite animal-human figures, no personified natural phenomena or humanized inanimate objects in the entire set of drawings. If a shark was drawn it was drawn either as a mere representation, as accurately as possible, or as part of a scene in which a man was spearing a shark. The sun and moon were not spontaneously selected as subject-matter for drawing; when I asked the children to draw them the sun was indicated by a circle, the moon variously as a crescent and a circle. There was no humanization.

The treatment of spirits was equally scant. I shall discuss this topic under two heads: (1) The treatment of the child's individual guardian ghost, and (2) the treatment of the subject of the general spirit population of the village.

(1) Little boys from the age of five or six, with a few exceptions in households where there are several children, have a guardian ghost assigned to them. This is usually either the spirit of a dead male child or a child born on the spirit plane. Occasionally a spirit of a grandfather who has been supplanted by some younger and more recently deceased ghost, will be given to the male child of the house. In theory this ghost goes everywhere with the child to protect him from all spiritual dangers, notably from the malicious attack of other ghosts. In order to appreciate the children's treatment of these guardian ghosts of theirs it is necessary to describe briefly the relationship between an adult male and his Sir Ghost (i.e. the special deceased male relative whose skull is hung in his house and upon whom he relies for protection).

A man communicates with his Sir Ghost through a medium, or a diviner. Through the medium he asks his Sir Ghost's opinions, and receives long and detailed replies. Through his divining bones, or those of another diviner, he asks his Sir Ghost questions which can be answered by signs meaning yes or no. If he is not a bone diviner, he may still consult his Sir Ghost by asking him a question, spitting on a betel leaf and watching which side of the leaf the juice runs down. Before this latter type of communication a man may chat aloud amiably with his Sir Ghost for several minutes. Similarly a man gives his Sir Ghost verbal orders to accompany other members of his household on danger-ous expeditions. If asked, a man can tell at once where his Sir Ghost is.

All this the children have seen and heard. But to their own guardian ghosts they pay no such attention. Most of them can tell the name of their ghosts, but not always the relationship. No child claimed to have seen his ghost, nor knew of any other child who had ever seen his ghost. Only one child had ever talked with his ghost, and he, Bopau, was regarded as aberrant by his companions. No child was ever heard to ask his ghost to do anything for him, such as help him win a race, etc. When I questioned the older children, aged twelve to fourteen, in more detail on the subject of the helpfulness of their ghosts, they all expressed great scepticism. "Probably he wouldn't be there." "There is no use talking to him. I think he isn't there." "No, don't ask him. Do it yourself."

Also the boys never boast of having spirits when the girls do not, although the men make just this point against the women.

Against this background of general sceptical lack of interest, little Bopau stood out strongly. He was the case which deviated from type; if my observations and conclusions were correct the reasons why Bopau took a creative interest in his ghost where the others did not, should complement my findings in the other cases. This they did. Bopau was an orphan. His father had been dead only two years, and although Bopau lived in the house of his father's younger brother, he was not beloved there. His dead father, Sori, was the Sir Ghost of this younger brother, Pokenau. Pokenau had assigned to Bopau a spirit-child of no importance named Malean. But Bopau claimed that Sori, his father, was his ghost, and that Sori talked with him and he with Sori. He rejected the ghost assigned to him. He was a lonely, shy, unloved child, compensating for his loneliness by imaginary intercourse with his ghostly father.

(2) In the treatment of spirits in general the children show very little interest. There are only half a dozen drawings which are said to be ghosts rather than human. These had no distinguishing ghostly attributes. The children hear a good many reports of ghostly activity, some of which they remember. When a child is ill a séance is held over it. Often the child himself, even a child of thirteen or fourteen, does not know the spiritual diagnosis of the sin which has caused his illness. (It is never his sin, but always a transgression of some older relative.) They go to sleep during séances, imitate ghostly whistles to frighten their elders, and use the argument which their parents use to them, *"Kor e palit,"* "the village is ghost-ridden," i.e. dangerous, to keep unwanted younger children from accompanying them on some expedition, and the younger children soon learn to answer, *"Kip e aua,"* "You are lying." The children play no games involving the ghosts.

The question of the children's treatment of the *tchinals,* land devils, differs somewhat in accordance with adult habit. The ghosts are an important constituent of the adult world; adults obviously act most of the time with reference to ghostly wishes; the names of ghosts are always on adult lips. With the *tchinals,* however, it is different. The parents threaten the children with them if they go to a slightly distant islet to play, yet the parents go carelessly to that islet. The parents speak of the wishes of ghosts, but never discuss *tchinals* among themselves. The children accept the concept of the *tchinal* with good humour, but slight real belief. Once I saw them playing a game of seizing each other and shouting, "I am a Sir *Tchinal*. I eat men." This only happened once, however. In their drawings they adopted the habit of branding any drawing of a human being which was a failure as a *tchinal*. Analysis of the drawings of the group and of individuals revealed that there was no style of depicting a *tchinal;* it was simply a faulty or accidentally grotesque attempt at drawing a human being. Even the traditional aspects of the *tchinal,* the long matted hair and the long fingernails, did not appear in the drawings. The children not only failed to elaborate imaginatively upon the traditional concept, but they even neglected to utilize some of the salient traditional features.

One other point deserves special mention here, the question of reflections in water. The adults believe that if the image of a Manus falls in fresh water, part of his soul stuff will remain there, in the power of a fresh-water demon, and magical rites are necessary to recover the soul. The elders avoid taking children to the mainland because the children will not take this belief seriously, but instead enjoy peering over the edge of the canoe at their shifting images in the water. This is a case where the children actually reject the concept that the image is an inextricable part of the personality, a prelogical concept which should have been, on the old hypothesis, particularly congenial to the immature mind.

(b) The Evidence of the Drawings

This has already been touched upon in the discussion, and can be merely summarized here. The drawings showed no personalization of inanimate objects or animals or natural phenomena. They showed only a few drawings which were said to be ghosts, although the ghosts occupy fully a third of adult thought and conversation; the drawings of ghosts contained no special features; many faulty attempts at depicting the human form were classed as *tchinals*. There were no scenes of *tchinals* eating men or *tchinals* turning into other things, such as occur in the tales. There were no scenes in which ghosts killed men or stole their soul stuff, or any other scenes depicting the traditional intercourse between ghosts and men. There were no drawings of skulls, although a skull, the bodily abode of the ghost, hung from the rafters of almost every house in Peri. The only scenes which were drawn were strictly realistic—fights, games of ball, boat races, scenes of fishing for turtle or shark.

(c) The Ink Blot Test

The ink blot test also provided no results which indicated a tendency to spontaneous animistic thought on the part of the children. The children's responses could be divided into three groups which have no correlation with either age or sex.

(1) Children who genuinely tried to discover what the ink blot was meant to be, and having hit upon an answer gave it with conviction and sometimes with an explanatory detail showing which part of the blot convinced them that their interpretation was correct. Most numerous group.

(2) Children who began an attempt to discover the proper interpretation, but whose interest soon wavered, and who then offered the same explanations in more or less regular alternation throughout the series. So the replies would be god, pig, man, pig, dog, man, etc.

(3) Children to whom the ink blots suggested so little that they had to look about them for suggestions, and then named the ink blot after a pot, or an article of furniture. Least numerous group.

A few children followed the pattern already established in their drawings; when the ink blot showed too little resemblance to the object named they would add "of a *tchinal.*" So Popoli said "a house . . . hym . . . I think it is the house of a *tchinal.*" All the children gave only one answer; they did not permit their imaginations to play with the material. Once a child had said, "That is a crocodile," he accepted the ink blot as a depiction of a crocodile, and turned away from it without further interest. The most intelligent children scrutinized the drawings most carefully, and in a few cases failed to find any close counterpart within their own experience. They then suggested things of which they had heard but never seen, "a cassowary," "a telephone" (of which a work boy had brought home the tale), "part of a foreign canoe," "a horse." The replied did not show a high standard of community response. For example, No. 8 was interpreted as head of a man, island, bird, bird, stone, rat, ball, tattoo mark, pig, mirror, cloud, pepper leaf, tree trunk, a whirlwind, I don't know, human being, a snake, head of a man, human being, mirror, head of a man, pig, pig, pig, verandah, pig, tree, etc.

(d) Definite Stimuli

Space does not permit my reporting here in full the answers to the six experimental situations. In this preliminary report I shall merely quote one set of answers for twenty children, and give the type answer for the other five tests.

(1) The attribution of malicious intent to a canoe which had drifted away. The stimulus question, "That canoe is bad, isn't it? It has drifted away."

Answers

Girls between three and six years of age:
    Masa: No; Popoli[3] didn't fasten it.
    Kawa: No; the punt (used to fasten canoes with) slipped.
    Maria: No; it wasn't fastened.
    Pwailep: No punt.
    Ngalowen: Popoli is stupid; he didn't fasten it right.
    Sapa: No; no punt to fasten it.
    Itong: No; it wasn't fastened right.
    Molung: Not fastened.
    Saliko: I can fasten a canoe; Popoli can't.
    Alupwa: No; no fastening; no punt.

3. The name Popoli is used throughout for the child who did not fasten the canoe properly. Actually different names occurred as the experiment was repeated under different circumstances.

Boys between three and six years of age:

Bopau: No punt through the outrigger.

Mee: No punt; bad Popoli.

Ponkob: The canoe floats. No punt, no punt, no punt.

Pokus: No; where's the punt?

Pope: No; no punt; it floats away.

Topal II: Popoli didn't fasten it; Popoli will lose his canoe.

Salemon: It will float away; there is no punt in it to fasten it.

Tchokopal: No; I fasten my canoe, my canoe, my canoe. Then it does not drift.

Pomitchon (aged six): Popoli is a stupid boy; he doesn't know how to fasten a canoe; when I fasten a canoe, it doesn't drift; I understand.

The Glass Chimes

(2) The children know very little of the *ramus* concept beyond applying the name to the wrappings and pigs' tusks on house posts, which are stationary *ramus*. Their interest was not caught by the word. They turned instead immediately to studying what made the sound. The type answer for the children of five or six was: "The wind winds the paper. It shakes the strings. Then the glasses hit and it sounds." The type answer for the younger children was of this order: "The paper moves. It pushes. It sounds," or "The wind winds. The glass hits. It sounds."

(3) The dancing doll.—The responses here were of two types. Some of the youngest children responded first by imitating the loose-jointed movement of the doll. Only afterwards did they speculate on the source of movement. The older children wanted to manipulate the doll at once. Younger child's type response, after imitative dance for a minute: "She pulls the string. It's dancing." Older child's type response: "Let me pull the string and shake it. Let me make it dance."

(4) The attribution of malicious intent to the pencil.—Younger child's response: "I drew it." "I made it." "I made it badly." Older child's type response: "No, I didn't make it right," this of one's own work. Bystander comment: "No, she did it wrong." "No, she is stupid. She doesn't know how to draw right."

(5) The typewriter.—This was a more complicated problem and mainly interesting for method of attack. The children's first question was: "How does it work?" Then followed a series: "She hits those white things, there." "When she hits them those things jump." "There's a string under there." "No, a stick which moves when she hits the white things, and then the stick moves and pushed the other thing (type) up." "Then it hits the black cloth and that makes the mark." "Why?" "There's a mark there," points to type. This was typical for the age of five-six. The younger children watched without comment.

(6) The Japanese paper flowers. Younger child's typical response: "The water gets inside and makes it bigger, like a hibiscus" (the Manus have no

general word for flower). Older child's typical response: "It's rolled up. The water loosens it. It's like a hibiscus, isn't it?''

In evaluating the accuracy of this response it should be borne in mind that these children have spent their lives in the water, and understand the action of water far better than civilized children.

Discussion of Results

The results of these various lines of investigation show that Manus children not only show no tendency towards spontaneous animistic thought, but that they also show what may perhaps legitimately be termed a negativism towards explanations couched in animistic rather than practical cause and effect terms. The Manus child is less spontaneously animistic and less traditionally animistic than is the Manus adult. This result is a direct contradiction of findings in our own society, in which the child has been found to be more animistic, in both traditional and spontaneous fashions, than are his elders. When such a reversal is found in two contrasting societies, the explanation must obviously be sought in terms of the culture; a purely psychological explanation is inadequate.

There are two alternative explanations, both of which involve a cultural determinant, which may be offered in the light of the Manus evidence. The contention that a tendency to spontaneous animistic thought is a function of immature mental development must, of course, be dismissed. It may, however, be argued that the human mind possesses a tendency toward animistic thought, and also a tendency towards non-animistic practical observations of cause and effect relationships. Proceeding upon this premise, the argument would be that in modern society the methods of education now in vogue tend to discourage the animistic tendencies of the human mind, until such tendencies are almost entirely suppressed, while in Manus the system of education tends to discourage the practical non-animistic thought processes so that the growing individual becomes progressively more animistic and less matter-of-fact in his thinking. This theory recognizes a psychological substratum tending towards animistic thought, and allows culture only a suppressive, non-creative role.

An alternative explanation would disallow the contention that the human mind had a universal tendency towards animistic thought, and limit this tendency as an idiosyncrasy of some human minds only. It would further propose that animistic tendencies of individual adult minds had left their impress upon the human language and human institutions in such a way that an individual born within a human society had a set of animistic conceptions and premises ready-made for his acceptance. Upon this theory children born into our society would first be made animistic by their culture, and then, through later processes of education this animistic tendency would be criticized and in large measure eliminated.

Before considering these alternative possibilities further it is necessary to enquire what evidence can be derived from Manus culture. Here again it will be necessary to summarize briefly and leave fuller statement for more extended publication. Analysis of the Manus culture, including the language, religious beliefs, mythology, folk beliefs and methods of education, leads me to the following conclusions.

The matter-of-fact nature of Manus child-thought is dependent upon the following conditions:—

(1) The fact that the Manus language is a bare simple language, without figures of speech, sex gender or rich imagery.

(2) The fact that the Manus child is forced at a very early age to make correct physical adjustments to his environment so that his entire attention is focussed upon cause and effect relationships, the neglect of which would result in immediate disaster in terms of severe punishment.

(3) The fact that the adults do not share the traditional material of their culture with their children.

These three factors in the situation deserve some further explanation. The Manus language belongs to the Austronesian stock, but it is conspicuously bare, and lacking in metaphor. In the course of hundreds of texts recorded by Dr. Fortune only three similes were found. The use of verbs which apply to the specifically human action of persons to describe the action of inanimate objects is also absent. The wind winds. The sun does not smile or waken. There is only one third person pronoun for all genders. The language provides the child with no stimulating leads to spontaneous animistic thought.

Compare this condition with the wealth of metaphor and animistic suggestion in English. Children are taught the distinctions between he, she and it, and then find the moon personalized as "she," and ships described in animistic terms which would bewilder a Manus adult. Children are taught poetry in which natural phenomena and animals are continually personalized in language and ascribed behaviour. This is, where the Manus language provides no linguistic base for spontaneous animism, the English language does.

The second reason, the enforced physical adjustment of the child, is also very important. As I have described the physical education of Manus children at some length elsewhere (Mead 1962), I shall not go into detail here. Suffice it to say that Manus children are taught the properties of fire and water, taught to estimate distance, to allow for illusion when objects are seen under water, to allow for obstacles and judge possible clearage in canoes, etc., at the age of two or three. Matter-of-fact adjustment which permits of no alibis, for a child is punished for awkwardness or physical failure, forces the children's thought along practical lines. Furthermore, the material environment offers no mechanical complexities such as elaborate machines, beyond the comprehension of the child, and so conducive to animistic speculation. The simple mechanical principles upon which a Manus native builds and navigates his canoes, or builds his house, present no mysteries. The child is not discouraged from an attempt at matter-of-fact understanding by explanations which he cannot follow, nor does the adult find the attempt at explanation too difficult and fall back upon fanciful explanations like the example in which a mother told a child who had already spent hours exploring the internal structure of a piano that the sounds were made by little fairies who stood on the wires and sang. Also the Manus adult is careful not to discourage children in their efforts towards a physical control of their environment. Children are never told they are "too little," "too weak," "not old enough" to do anything. Each child is encouraged to put forth its maximum effort, in terms of its individual capacity always, and not in terms of invidious comparison with other children (Mead 1931). It is never intimidated. If a child attempts something beyond its capacity it will be diverted, but not openly discouraged. The child is therefore not constrained to manufacture alibis in terms of seven league boots or imaginary playmates who possess the skill and adult licence denied to him. A child's attention is always concentrated upon what he can do now, not upon what he is unable to do. It is unnecessary to labour comparisons with the educational methods of our own society, methods in some measure imperative because of the dangerous mechanical complexity of modern life, in some part merely the result of traditional attitudes towards precocity.

The third reason suggested to explain the Manus child's lack of animistic thought is the peculiar educational attitudes of the Manus in respect to their non-material culture. Children are taught early and painstakingly how to walk, swim, climb, handle a canoe, shoot a bow and arrow, and throw a spear accurately. They are taught to talk. But they are not given any instruction in the social and religious aspects of adult life, beyond occasional threatenings with ghosts or *tchinals,* which, occurring only in this particular context, the children soon learn to recognize as bogies only. Children are told no stories of any kind, nor are they expected to be interested in stories, which are for "men and women, not for children." As myths play a very slight part in Manus life, and are seldom told—the average adult cannot tell more than four or five complete tales—the children do not overhear them. They are not required to conform to the will of the ghosts; when they are ill it is for an adult sin, and they are neither told nor expected to understand the intricacies of the religious life. They are permitted at ceremonies, but take no part in them, regarding all social, economic and religious ceremonial as tiresome things which adults do, but from which children are exempt. If they were actively shut out from adult life their curiosity might be stimulated; as it is they are prevailingly indifferent. Thus it is that they learn very late, near puberty for girls, often past puberty for boys, the religious concepts of the Manus, concepts which would be a rich background for spontaneous animism if taught them as children, as our children are taught traditional theology, myths and fairy tales.

Within the Manus culture itself it is, therefore, possible to find explanations of the differences between Manus child-thought and Manus adult-thought. The language offers no stimuli, the method of education fixes the children's attention along antithetical lines; the adult culture, which provides each generation grown to maturity with a set of traditional animistic concepts, provides the children with no background for animistic constructs. Contrasting conditions occur in our own society, the language is richly animistic, children are given no such stern schooling in physical adjustment to a comprehensible and easily manipulated physical environment, and the traditional animistic material which is decried by modern scientific thinking is still regarded as appropriate material for child training.

Upon the strength of one experiment, in one native culture, it is possible to draw only negative conclusions. Animistic thought cannot be explained in terms of intellectual immaturity. Further research will be necessary to determine whether animism must be regarded as a tendency of all human minds which may be stimulated or suppressed by educational factors or merely as an idiosyncrasy of some human minds, which has become crystallized in the language and institutions of the human race. [Mead 1932, pp. 173–89]

In *Growing Up in New Guinea* (1930), I discussed not only the lack of animism among Manus children but the whole process of character formation—the phrase itself had not yet been introduced into my vocabulary. Here Reo Fortune contributed by insisting my major finding was that regardless of the detailed sequence or style of learning, children in an isolated homogeneous culture develop into reasonable replicas of their parents. So, although Manus children were extraordinarily free, cooperative, and pleasant, as they grew older, both sexes became absorbed into an exploitive, competitive system.

They are as like their forebears as peas to peas. The jolly comradeship, the co-operation, the cheerful following a leader, the delight in group games, the easy interchange between the sexes—all the traits which make the children's group stand out so vividly from the adults'—are gone. If that childhood had never been, if every father had set about making his newborn son into a sober, anxious, calculating, bad tempered little businessman, he could hardly have succeeded more perfectly.

The society has won. It may have reared its children in a world of happy freedom, but it has stripped its young men even of self-respect. Had it begun earlier, its methods need have been less abrupt. The girl's subjection is more gradual, less painful. She is earlier mistress of her cultural tradition. But as young people, both she and her husband must lead submerged lives, galling to their pride. When men and women emerge from this cultural obscurity of early married life, they have lost all trace of their happy childhood attitudes, except a certain scepticism which makes them mildly pragmatic in their religious lives. This one good trait remains, the others have vanished because the society has no use for them, no institutionalized paths for their expression. [Mead 1960, *1930*, p. 210]

1929–1953 RETURN TO MANUS

During the years following my Manus field work, after having completed *Growing Up in New Guinea, Kinship in the Admiralties* (Mead 1934) and "An Investigation of the Thought of Primitive Children" (Mead 1932) and after Reo Fortune's completion of *Sorcerers of Dobu* (Fortune 1963, *1932*) and *Manus Religion* (Fortune 1965, *1935*) my interest turned to new problems. This was undoubtedly partly due to the total lack of response on the part of Piaget and his associates to my findings. (Wayne Dennis [1943] had launched an attack on my work in which he completely failed to understand my point.)

Unlike my first two field trips to Samoa and Manus which had focused on the assumptions of psychology and psychiatry, the third focused on the way culture molds the expected personalities of men and women. Having already explored the significance of cultural stylization in adolescence, personality, and child thought, the next step was to study the extent to which cultural determination influences the personality of the sexes.

As I did not have to ask for funds from grant-giving organizations which insisted on a narrow definition of a problem, I could simply phrase as my goal a very open ended approach. My dependence upon "instruments," tests, and evocative objects declined significantly.

On reviewing this history, I conclude that I have used instruments to examine or challenge the approach formulated by a psychologist or psychiatrist, but that when a problem was phrased in cultural terms, I tended to use traditional field work methods of close participation, event analysis (Fortune 1965, *1935*; Mead 1947b, 1954d), child and adult drawings, verbatim tests, film, and photographic sequences of behavior. I have actually reserved the use of evocative objects for cross referencing to previous work, or for communication with psychologists and members of other disciplines on return from the field (AAA1954; Mead 1974b). Our brief field work among the Omaha in 1930, which was not long enough to justify work on the language, involved no tests or evocative situations of any kind (Fortune 1932; Mead 1966a).

For *Sex and Temperament in Three Primitive Societies* (Mead 1963a), I used children's drawings, a doll and snake as part of my repertoire of simulating objects, and I had been asked by child psychiatrist David Levy to try out the Rorschach. I did ten Rorschachs; there were no localization charts then (I later made my own in the field.) Two protocols without localization charts were translated and shown to Bruno Klopfer on my return in 1933. He could make nothing of them, and expressed contempt for the results. As I knew I could not get better results in the field, I neither wrote up the other eight, nor used the Rorschach again in ensuing field work in Bali and Iatmul. Later, in 1946, when I was writing the last section on Unabelin in *The Mountain Arapesh* (Mead 1949), I looked at Unabelin's Rorschach and realized that it was in fact a perfectly good protocol. Having phrased it in the formal terms that Klopfer had developed, Jane Belo, who had worked with me in Bali (Belo 1970), presented it to Klopfer who, after many years of dealing with cross-cultural materials, now found it worthy of interpretation.

These two episodes, in which I had tried to work responsively in formulating my problem in the direction of psychological work, and then met with disapproval or blank indifference, should contain some lessons for interdisciplinary workers. The cultural anthropologist goes into the field with a tremendous load of queries, possibilities, theories, and methods; choice among them is difficult enough. The knowledge that there will be an intelligent consumer (as Gardner Murphy was, for example, when, at his request I wrote him observations about Manus séances, or Muzafer Sherif was about color categories), will encourage fieldworkers to continue along the same lines. Indifference is likely to have the opposite effect.

My original interest in the relationship between culture and temperament was reinforced in the course of my investigation of the determinative effects of cultural expectations on sex typed behavior. *Sex and Temperament in Three Primitive Societies* (Mead 1963a, *1925*), therefore, became primarily a statement on the way one of several human temperaments could be standardized for one or both sexes. However, the cultural climate in 1933 made the investigation of invariant characteristics of human beings unwise (Mead 1972; Sheldon 1970a, 1970b; Tanner 1953).

Stimulated by my interest in Erik Erikson's formulations of the Freudian position (1963a, *1950*) and an earlier interest, while I was among the Arapesh, in Roheim's psychoanalytic studies of different cultural types (1932), the work of Abraham (1925), and John Dollard's *Criteria for the Life History* (1949), I turned instead in Bali and Iatmul to an investigation of the ways in which psychocultural development and basic sex differences could be expressed in culture (Bateson 1958, *1936*; Bateson and Mead 1962, *1942*).

When I met Margaret Lowenfeld in 1948, I became acquainted with the tests she called objective, that is, evocative materials which were arranged by the subject and did not depend on deriving mediating and inaccessible mental images. Mosaics, Kaleidoblocs and Poleidoblocs (Lowenfeld 1939, 1954) all have the advantage over Rorschachs, TATs, Szondis, or even Horn Hellersberg tests in that they can be displayed together in such a way that cultural or individual differences over time can be made simultaneously visible.

Science has advanced in proportion to the ability of the scientist to present sequential material in a simultaneous visual form, using tables and charts. This became clear when I examined Margaret Lowenfeld's exhibits for the World Conference on Mental Health in 1948, and for subsequent congresses, and in the exhibits Rhoda Metraux, T. M. Abel and I prepared for the American Psychological Association in 1960 (APA 1960) and the American Anthropological Association in 1954 (AAA 1954). Objective tests which can be drawn or photographed and juxtaposed have great advantages. Discussion of test results—objective or projective—and of Rorschach results—as in the use of Rorschach in the interdisciplinary project of Research in Contemporary Cultures (Mead 1974*b*; Mead and Metraux 1953; Mead and Wolfenstein 1963) clarifies the relationship between thought process and culture. Stated most simply, communication depends on the existence of shared materials within interdisciplinary research groups, whether these be artistic products, films of behavior, or recorded interviews, the visible product of objective tests, or the verbal response of projective tests.

Through the 1930s a greater understanding developed of the relationship between child rearing, available forms of cultural expression and character structure (Bateson 1958, *1936*; Dollard 1949; Mead 1961*b*, *1937*). I could thus add to my original inquiries into Manus thought and development a discussion of Manus personality and the application of theoretical positions which saw each culture as a kind of neurosis, with a specific plot or central trauma (Mead 1935, 1939). I gave a talk to the Psychiatric Institute in 1934, discussing the way Manus material fitted in with theories of anality and compulsion neurosis, a theme Spitz developed independently while he was still in Europe (Spitz 1935). In 1949 I re-examined my material on all seven South Sea cultures, and I characterized the Manus in the following way:

They present the curious anomaly of a small group of people at Stone Age level without monotheism, without any political forms more complex than kin grouping held together by the affinal ties and exchanges, who have developed a form of character structure that in its puritanism, its capacity to postpone pleasure for economic gain, its industriousness, its capacity to exploit other individuals for profit, and its high free level of intelligence—including great ease with machinery—is curiously like the character structure associated with the rise of Protestantism and modern capitalism in western Europe. [Mead 1967, *1949*, p. 414]

In a chapter on the relationship between social anthropology and psychiatry prepared for the first volume of Alexander and Ross's *Dynamic Psychiatry* (Mead 1952), I discussed viewing all cultures as instances of the institutional development of a nuclear trauma in which we could take account of various ways in which specific types of character formation could be seen as rewarding instead of deforming.

An even greater complication is introduced when we consider the Manus who show such close resemblances to many emphases in our own culture. They do not, like the Samoans, emphasize a balance between need and fulfilment, between body and outer world, so perfect that almost all aberrant behavior— whether of initial receptivity to trauma or to blessing—is barred out, but, instead, live in a one-sided world in which intelligence, competence, a high standard of living, and an alert, inquiring, interested attitude toward the outer world are maintained by a method of child rearing in which competing tendencies, any desire to listen to one's own heart, to see visions, to find beauty, remain well below the surface. Rorschachs of the Manus would show, undoubtedly, great impoverishment in the fantasy life. Observation of their way of life and study of their institutionalized kinship arrangements show that there are many human potentialities of which they make little. They work with an intensity and drive which accord but ill with life on the Equator. They die young. Yet in a society which offers no competing vision of another way of life from which the Manus, with his pattern of repression, is barred out, attention only to the degree ot traumatization would not be a full answer. Rather, Manus may be seen as a culture which has a set of institutions and a method of learning that provide one of the possible fits between human impulses and social forms, when the relationships between all human beings, including mother and child, are construed in terms of intervening material objects, when the attention is directed outward to the observable relations between objects, and human intelligence is given free play to probe into and manipulate such relationships. [Mead 1952, p. 437]

By this time, I was explicitly including primary process thinking, seen as composed of affectively linked sequences, body based thinking and elements that are repressed in the course of individual experience— three aspects which also seem to characterize the language of poetry, dreams, myths and rituals. The idea that preverbal thinking develops in early childhood introduced, in a new form, some of the original assumptions of Freud and Piaget, which implicitly assigned nonrational thought, within which spontaneous animism could be placed, to an earlier period in the development of the child. So I wrote:

. . . dream thought need not become a disturbing rival form, opposed to "rational thought." It is possible to see that the only alternatives are not either high adjustment to the external world, paid for by a break with this early preverbal way of thought, which is completely relegated to an unconscious, kept precariously out of ordinary waking functioning, or a break-through of a kind of thinking so culturally unpatterned that it obscures adjustment to the external world, such as is found in schizophrenia. In those societies in which there is articulate social use of these primary processes of thought, it is not only the extraordinarily gifted individuals who are able to preserve their creativity—as in our society—but each member of the society is provided with a medium through which the inarticulate ways of thought of the infant and the culturally disciplined mature observation of internal and external world can be articulated into a pattern which provides meaning to both. We know too little of the cultural conditions for creativity, but there are suggestions that types of reliving of very early experience which are permitted by cultural forms may be significant, as when children pass through not only a stage of dispossession by the next younger sibling but stay within the family circle long enough to watch the dispossessor dispossessed (Mead 1940, 1947*a*) or, contrastingly, when very little counterpointed patterning is imposed upon the primary learnings of the first year of life (Gorer and Rickman 1962, *1949*). [Mead 1952, pp. 431–32]

and,

A culture may be seen as the historically developed way in which the human potentialities for internally oriented, medially oriented, and externally oriented feeling-thought are regulated, canalized (Murphy 1966*a*, *1947*) and patterned so that they may be learned, shared, and perpetuated, and individuals who share them may live together in societies. [Mead 1952, p. 440]

and,

Social change takes place today on a world stage, and in each country the insights and practices of physician and social scientist are only a part of the whole changing climate of opinion within which men are seeking to come to firmer grips with the forms of their culture. But these insights and practices are nevertheless significant and may, perceptively and responsibly exercised, sometimes be crucial. [Mead 1952, pp. 443–44]

My original interest in animistic thinking had become submerged by the greater consideration given to the potential capacities for different kinds of feeling-thought displayed by individuals and manifested in the institutional forms of different cultures. A whole series of dimensions, some of them incomparable, had been introduced. This included preverbal thought in the first year of life, which might be either inner- or outer-oriented; types of thought which are congenial to different modal zonal emphases, which in turn are fitted with stages of psycho-sexual development; types of thought which are more characteristic of some constitutional types than others, with cultural consequences if a given constitutional type be taken as a model for the ideal type in the culture; and possibilities of either inner-oriented or outer-oriented thought styles becoming dominant in a culture. The Manus, for example, demonstrated an outer, "reality" orientation as their conscious form. In Trobriand culture on the other hand, as analyzed by Dorothy Lee (1940), there was verbal negation of "rational sequences" such as the relationship between semen and a foetus, food and growth, seed and mature plant, the beginning of a road and its destination, while at the same time in everyday life the Trobrianders related efficiently to the world around them.

RETURN TO MANUS—1953 (MEAD 1954c)

My return to Manus was primarily influenced by my desire to use my previous knowledge of the culture and of individual members of the society, in order to understand the process of rapid cultural change within one generation (Mead 1954c). As the design of the project was also based on methods I had used before, I sought a graduate student associate who, in addition to having a good basic knowledge of cultural anthropology and culture and personality studies, would also have training in psychological approaches to culture and personality, in photography, and in practical and theoretical electronics. In Theodore Schwartz I found such an associate who was prepared to use a great variety of tests and instruments on the expedition. We took with us Rorschachs, a modified form of the TAT, the Bender Gestalt Test, the Stewart Ring Puzzle Test and Lowenfeld mosaics. The three of us, including Theodore Schwartz, Lenora Shargo Schwartz, and myself gave tests, collected drawings and modelings in clay, and reproduced earlier test situations.

During the twenty-five year interval, the Manus had undergone a complete cultural transformation (Mead 1966b, 1966c; T. Schwartz 1962). There had been a political movement with a cargo cult base, and schooling had been introduced on a very rudimentary level. In general, the test results confirmed previous testing. In response to TAT cards, one typical response by an adult whom I had known as a child was, "I see a half a man and a half a woman. I can see both hands of the man and only one hand of the woman. This drawing is very indistinct. I do not know any more about it. If I knew something about the man who made it, I might be able to tell you more" (Mead 1966b, 1956, p. 367).

They wrestled with the Rorschach for long periods, silently attempting to fit some actuality to the image on the card. When I asked a group of the men who had drawn for me as little boys to draw again, they repeated the exact style of their drawings as they had made them twenty-five years before. The changes we found in their test results were congruent with the changes that had gone on in the society. We found a slightly lessened sense that they could discern cause and effect relationships; while they had understood the unfolding Japanese flowers perfectly twenty-five years before, when these were presented again, the children asked if some chemical had been put in the water. Where children had drawn with a happy disregard for the shape and area of a piece of drawing paper (which I had tested by giving them drawing paper cut into semi-circles), they now fitted their drawings to the contours of the paper, reflecting the fact that they had developed a closed political system, where once it had been open (Mead 1953, 1954a, 1955).

Perhaps the most significant finding was an explanation for the way in which the children had rejected adult ceremonial and religious behavior in the past. I found that as the adults embraced their new social forms with enthusiasm, the children embraced them also. I had been puzzled by the way in which children imitated all adult physical activities but none of the social. I now realized that indeed they had imitated the adults there also, but what they had imitated was the hostility of the adults toward their subjection to a driving economic system which had been grafted onto their experience of cooperation in childhood (Mead 1954a, 1955). As a result, I tempered my original pessimism regarding educational innovation as a source of change (Mead 1974a); I found that when external circumstances provided the proper setting, the cooperative childhood experiences of the Manus could again be invoked to underwrite a new social order.

Working with the test materials of 1953, Theodore Schwartz has done further comparative explorations of Admiralty Island thought patterns and of Manus capacities for learning, which have not yet been published. Both of us made return trips to Manus in the 1960s (Mead 1970b).

CONFRONTATION WITH PIAGET: THE ORIGINAL EVOKER

In 1953, I became a member of the World Health Organization Working Group on Child Development, of which Jean Piaget and Bärbel Inhelder were members (Tanner and Inhelder 1957–1960).

Toward the late 1950s, Lévy-Bruhl, on whose work Piaget had based his views on the primitive mind, had virtually retracted his earlier insistence that difference in kind existed between the thought of primitive and modern man (Lévy-Bruhl 1949). I had by then gained a far deeper appreciation for what Freud had found when he acquainted himself with excerpted accounts of the rituals of primitive men, and thinking they represented earlier forms of humanity, had equated them with archaic thought patterns in his patients (Mead 1952; Knapp 1963).

At the end of the fourth year, Professor Piaget was asked to summarize the proceedings of the three preceding conferences. He addressed a series of questions to each of the participants, and we all took pains to have the replies from English speakers translated into French in the hope that they might receive more serious attention. The questions he addressed to me were:

1. Everything varies from one society to another, in particular the systems of numeration and the circumstances under which one learns to count. But why is it generally accepted that $1 + 1 = 2$ or $2 + 2 = 4$? This is not innate. It is not learned from experience, since two objects are not equivalent to ''two'' unless they are counted (= activity of the subject). Is it ''social'' as thought by Durkheim? But he was then obliged to suggest that ''under all civilizations lies *the* civilization'' and consequently to postulate a certain common functioning which seems to me characteristic of the laws of equilibrium (which apply equally well to operations between individuals and to the operations of the individual himself). Does Margaret Mead accept the possibility of arriving, thanks to the mechanisms of equilibration, at such common elements despite the diversity of the cultural points of departure?
2. When an individual is transplanted from one civilization to another or subjected to a new *training,* can any similarity be perceived between the order of things learned during this kind of ''Aktualgenese'' and the developmental order observed in the growth of the child as studied among us? Example: the acquisition of the operations of measurement? [Tanner and Inhelder 1957–1960, p. 25]

My response:

In replying to Professor Piaget's challenging paper, I find that I must first distinguish between two approaches which appear in his statement. On the one hand he appears to say that in order to have a unified theory of development, itself dependent upon a common language, which will make it possible to bring our various materials together, we must recognize the three traditional divisions of (a) hereditary factors, (b) the action of the physical environment, and (c) the action of the social environment, brought together in terms of a fourth factor, that of development, for which he proposes a formulation in terms of contemporary equilibrium theory. With this general position I am in full accord; I believe the development of such a theory is practicable and that its expression by the use of contemporary mathematical models may be fruitful, although I reserve judgment as to whether the adoption of economic emphasis —calculations of strategy based on gains and losses—is the most rewarding model from amongst the available ones. This aspect of the problem is, however, the domain of General System Theory represented in our Group by Dr. Von Bertalanffy, and I shall not address myself to it further.

However, throughout Professor Piaget's paper there appears from time to time a second and quite contrasting approach, in which the recognition of the importance of individual differences—as opposed to "average" performance of individuals at a given "stage"—the recognition of the role of the culture in advancing or retarding any of these assumed sequences, and the recognition of continuity rather than "stages" in physical growth (p. 11)—are all treated, not as providing additional and needed material for a general theory of the development of the child, but rather as opposing theories of disproportionate emphases upon one of these three traditional factors. If this approach were followed it would be tantamount to saying that it is possible to establish stages if one confines oneself to the study of the cognitive and affective behavior of children in twentieth century Euro-American culture, and leaves out of account material on their physical development, and material on children in other cultures. As such an expectation contradicts the whole intention of Professor Piaget's integrating formulation, I merely mention it here, at the beginning, to stress that I am addressing myself to my alternative understanding of his paper, and not to the assumption that study of the factors of physical growth and culture automatically results in disagreement.

In regard to the question of "general stages," our present cross-cultural evidence, admittedly very fragmentary, suggests that it becomes decreasingly possible to relate different aspects of the child's behaviour to its age or other measure of development, as age increases. The duration of development may nevertheless be of some significance in explaining different configurations of learning. I say "duration" to allow for periods of illness or regression, or for extreme differences in the amount of interpersonal interaction in the life of a given child, who may, for example, be said to be equivalent—in this widest developmental sense—to a much younger or older child, because of the intervention of factors of acceleration or arrest in interpersonal contacts. For infants and very young children, the gross developmental conditions of learning to walk and talk also seem to introduce, in all known cross-cultural contexts, a certain degree of generalization into all other types of learning occurring at the same time. It must also be recognized that in regard to such things as walking and talking, different individual constitutions and different arrangements for learning in different cultures—as for example when children are kept swaddled or cradled beyond the period when they could walk, or hear phrases stated in their name long before they could formulate them themselves—may both vary to such an extent as again to make any idea of general stages appear useless.

If a theory of stages is conceived as a progressive series of equilibria, disequilibria and re-equilibria levels, in which successive equilibrium levels, even of momentary duration, may be distinguished, but in which in any given process certain fixed sequences may occur, this formulation can be applied, with our present knowledge, to the investigation of human development within different cultures. As Professor Piaget now formulates the problem, such exploration would have to be done in very great detail, using tests which were formally identical and culturally comparable on a series of identified children, whose physical development had also been studied, over a sufficient period of time so that *transitions* might be examined and analysed in the case of these identified children. The question of the average age for the appearance of a stage while useful as a corrective for ethnocentric overgeneralization from studies on children of a particular culture, seems to me to be of only very limited significance. Only when the actual *succession* of stages in the development of any process can be followed in identified individuals, in an identified culture, within an identified social unit (that is a group in which each individual's place in relation to each other individual is known) can we begin to relate together the three factors affecting development. I would maintain this as necessary because if, as Professor Piaget suggests, there are no general stages, then retardation or acceleration—(in terms of chronological age or developmental duration)—in any one process, attributable either to culture or to constitution, may have the most profound effects on the configuration of learning, and thus on the development of the personality. It may be that our must acute understanding of the constant sequences in any process may come in those processes where averaging is possible—a position which has not, I believe, yet been demonstrated fully—but that for the understanding of total development, it will still be necessary to take account of the effects of different combinations among these constant or fixed sequences, which are themselves systematically associated with genetic or with cultural patterns.

The specific study of identified individuals makes the distinction which Professor Piaget (p. 20) draws between *molar* phenomena and *molecular* phenomena less significant, for it makes it possible to address research immediately to the molecular level. When the general system of culture is examined as manifested in the behaviour of identified individuals in their interaction with a new member of the society—a formulation which permits more exact study than a formulation in terms of "generations"—it is then possible to relate this behaviour not only to the whole system of culture (which may be expected to be sufficiently redundant to allow for the total genetic range of contemporary survival possibilities of *Homo sapiens*), but also to the peculiarities of certain stocks within the society which have become isolated by various breeding barriers—such as class, cult, sect, occupational lines, etc. In this way it will be possible to investigate the degree of facilitation or inhibition existent, for example, in cultural systems which make a very slight use of mathematics, or in which the perception of time-space relations are very differently organized.

To address myself to the specific questions of Professor Piaget (p. 25, III):

I would not say (with Durkheim) that "under all civilizations lies *the* civilization," but that all civilizations express the conditions of being human (la condition humaine), in that *Homo sapiens* is dependent for his humanity— his survival as a species in the form we call human—on a system of socially transmitted learned behaviour. This learned behaviour shows certain regularities which can be related to the requirements of man's biological characteristics —long infancy, properties of the central nervous system, etc.—in combination with the rest of the environment on this planet. Without such an assumption of regularities all comparative work between different cultures would obviously take a very different form, and such an assumption does underlie all contemporary work in cultural anthropology.

The way in which children learn natural languages may be regarded as a case in point. As far as is known children learn languages which on other grounds may be classified as easy or difficult, and of many different types of complexity, at the same age in all cultures. This can be attributed to two factors—the redundancy of natural languages and the fact that all first languages are learned in interaction between speakers and those who have not learned to speak at all, in the same way. The nature of speech, and the particular language spoken are communicated together. With the rationalization of the cultural understanding of languages, the development of such ideas as "a language," "grammar," "word," "alphabet," "verb," "predicate," "utterance," "phoneme," "morpheme," the process of linguistic learning is becoming progressively transformed. So, in response to Professor Piaget's second question, if an adult had to learn a language as a child learns it, without the intervention of any categories of linguistic analysis, there would undoubtedly be found many similarities in the order of acquisition. However, in all known societies, a difference occurs because the idea of the existence of different languages has already been formalized, and while the child learns to speak, the adult, having learned to speak, learns to speak a second language. It is quite conceivable that the systematic and very early teaching of the alphabet and of reading and writing might introduce into the first learning of the child a new factor which would make learning language in complex, fully literate societies no longer comparable with learning languages in non-literate or slightly literate societies, and that some effects of this sort may be making themselves felt in the present difficulties which are being encountered in efforts to give a type of early education designed for children of the literate to children of the non-literate.

However—still in response to Professor Piaget's second question—it would appear that every cultural system contains within it the provision for the way in which it must be learned by children during their normal development, including sufficient leeway for a range in this normal development—in such respects as type of imagery, capacity to organize, type of memory, etc. One route to a comprehension of another culture, or some complex part of a culture, such as the language, the legal system, the ritual idiom, etc., is to repeat the steps taken by children learning this system. This contrasts with the way in which a linguistically sophisticated adult masters the "grammar" of another language in a matter of hours, or a mathematically sophisticated adult masters a new type of mathematics. It would seem that once having traversed the steps necessary to become human, in any culture, one may transfer that learning, at an adult level, to any other culture, but that cultures differ in the developmental levels which they call into play in certain areas of experience. So western culture has now developed to a high degree the type of thinking necessary for scientific endeavour, but leaves in a quite uncultivated state various capacities for introspective experience developed in Indian culture. For members of cultures which have not elaborated our type of scientific thinking, immediate transference of previous learning into understanding of our culture may be possible only for the exceptionally gifted as it may mean an imaginative act of transference covering a whole series of missing stages, in the form in which they have been culturally elaborated in our own society. For the less gifted, it may be necessary to include in any education in another culture a re-experience of earlier stages of learning, in the different cultural form. As I have understood Professor Piaget's discussions in our meetings this formulation is one which he feels is compatible with his material. [Tanner and Inhelder 1957–1960, pp. 48–52]

THE PRESENT STATE OF THEORY

A result of the four Child Development Conferences was the first integration of cultural anthropology, general systems theory, ethology, psychoanalysis, child psychology and work on the brain. These were followed by five Josiah Macy Jr. conferences on group processes (Schaffner 1955–1960), and it became clear that after a preliminary inclusion of work on creatures as diverse as geese, penguins, and sheep, the next major step in the development of a theory of human behavior would have to come from work on the brain. There had been hints for several decades of important lines between different kinds of thought, variously called primary and secondary processes, rational and non-rational, linear and circular, in the scattered work on eidetic imagery (Klüver 1933) and problems of left handedness (Wile 1934). Both of these problems, however, became unfashionable in the 1940s and very little work was done on them until the 1960s. Today however, we have an impressive amount of relevant work on the differences between the right and left hemispheres of the brain (Pribram 1970; Sperry 1971) and new work on the triune brain is emerging (MacLean 1973).

In conclusion, the problem I tackled initially in Manus dealt with the relationship between certain kinds of thinking and stages in child development, differences in culture, possible systematic difference among types of individuals and problems associated with culture change, the second question which Jean Piaget addressed to me in 1956. This last problem is the one which Theodore Schwartz is working on with new Manus materials collected in 1973 and 1975. It is possible that the next few years will see all of these efforts brought together and give us new clues about which forms of education will permit a more rapid transformation in learning style for individuals reared in one type of culture who wish to enter another.

ACKNOWLEDGEMENTS

The work described in this chapter has been done: as a Fellow of the National Research Council, 1925–1926; as a Fellow of the Social Science Research Council, 1928–1929; during expeditions financed by the Voss Fund of the American Museum of Natural History; during the New Guinea Admiralty Island Expedition, 1953–1954, under a Rockefeller Foundation Grant; during projects under National Institute for Mental Health Grant (NIMH-07675-06), 1963–1968, National Science Foundation Grant (NSF GS-642), 1965–1969, and grants from the Institute for Intercultural Studies and The Jane Belo Tannenbaum Fund of the American Museum of Natural History, 1971–1975.

The following permissions have been granted:
M. Mead. "An Investigation of the Thought of Primitive Children with Special Reference to Animism." *Journal of the Royal Anthropological Institute* 62(1932), pp. 173–189.
M. Mead. "Some Relationships between Social Anthropology and Psychiatry." In *Dynamic Psychiatry*, F. Alexander and H. Ross, eds. Chicago: University of Chicago Press, 1952, pp. 437, 431–432, 440, 4443–444.
M. Mead. *Growing Up in New Guinea.* New York: Morrow, 1962 (first published in 1930), p. 210.
M. Mead. *Coming of Age in Samoa.* New York: Morrow, 1961 (first published in 1928), pp. 289–292.
M. Mead. *social Organization in Manu'a.* Honolulu: Bishop Museum Press, 1969 (first published in 1930), pp. 85–85.
J. M. Tanner and B. Inhelder, eds. *Discussions in Child Development,* 4 vols., (195701960); vol. IV (1960), pp. 25, 48–52.

132 MARGARET MEAD

REFERENCES CITED

Abel, T.
  1938 Free Designs of Limited Scope as a Personality Index. *Character and Personality* 7:50-62.
Abel, T. M., and Metraux, R.
  1959 Sex Differences in a Negro Peasant Community: Montserrat. *Journal of Projective Techniques* 23:127-133.
Abraham, K.
  1925 The Influence of Oral Eroticism on Character Formation. *The International Journal of Psycho-Analysis* 6:247-58.
American Anthropological Association (AAA)
  1954 Projective Techniques Exhibit, Meeting. September, New York City.
American Psychological Association (APA)
  1960 Projective Techniques Exhibit, Meeting. November, Minneapolis, Minnesota.
Anastasi, A.
  1958 *Psychological Testing,* 3rd ed., pp. 238-39. London: Collier-Macmillan.
Anderson, H. and Anderson, G. L.
  1954 Children's Perceptions of Social Conflict Situations: A Study of Adolescent Children in Germany. *American Journal of Orthopsychiatry* 24:245-47.
  1961 Culture Components as a Factor in Child Development. 1. Image of the Teacher by Adolescent Children in Seven Countries. *American Journal of Orthopsychiatry* 31:481-92.
Anderson, V., Thornhill, R. G., and Smith, M.
  1973 *Lowenfeld Poleidoblocs.* With Introduction by M. Lowenfeld. Harlow and Essex: Educational Supply.
Bateson, G.
  1958 *Naven,* 2nd ed. Stanford: Stanford University Press. (First published in 1936.)
Bateson, G. and Mead, M.
  1962 *Balinese Character: A Photographic Analysis.* New York: New York Academy of Sciences. (First published in 1942.)
Belo, J.
  1970 A Study of Customs Pertaining to Twins in Bali. In *Traditional Balinese Culture,* pp. 3-56. New York: Columbia University Press.
Bender, L.
  1938 *A Visual Motor Gestalt Test and Its Clinical Use.* New York: American Orthopsychiatric Association.
Benedict, R.
  1959 Psychological Types in the Cultures of the Southwest. In *An Anthropologist at Work,* ed. M. Mead, pp. 248-61. Boston: Houghton Mifflin. (First published in 1930.)
Birdwhistell, R. L.
  1970 *Kinesics and Context.* Philadelphia: University of Pennsylvania Press.
Boas, F.
  1965 *The Mind of Primitive Man.* New York: Free Press. (First published in 1911)

Bogoras, W.
   1907   The Chukchee, Part II: Religion. *Memoirs of the American Museum of Natural History,* vol. 6, part 1. New York.

Buck, J. N.
   1949   The H-T-P Technique. *Journal of Clinical Psychology* 5:37–74.

Buros, O. K.
   1972   *The 7th Mental Measurements Yearbook,* vol. 1, pp. 767–73. Highland Park: Gryphon Press.

Byers, P. E.
   1972   From Biological Rhythm to Cultural Pattern: A Study of Minimal Units. Ph.D. dissertation, Columbia University.

Campbell, D. T.
   1972   Introduction. In *Cultural Relativism,* ed. F. Herskovits, pp. v–xxvi. New York: Random House.

Cole, M., Gay, J., Glick, J. A., and Sharp, D. W.
   1971   *The Cultural Contexts of Learning and Thinking: An Exploration of Experimental Anthropology.* New York: Basic Books.

Dennis, W.
   1943   Animism and Related Tendencies in Hopi Children. *The Journal of Abnormal and Social Psychology* 38:21–37.

Deri, S.
   1949   *Introduction to the Szondi Test.* New York: Grune and Stratton.

Devereux, G.
   1955   *A Study of Abortion in Primitive Societies.* New York: Julian Press.

Dollard, J.
   1949   *Criteria for the Life History.* New York: Smith. (First published in 1935.)

Downey, J. E.
   1924   *The Will-Temperament and its Testing.* Yonkers: World.

Erikson, E. H.
   1963a Childhood and Society, rev. ed. New York: Norton. (First published in 1950.)
   1963b Sex Differences in the Play Configurations of American Pre-Adolescents. In *Childhood in Contemporary Cultures,* eds. M. Mead and M. Wolfenstein, pp. 32–41. Chicago: University of Chicago Press. (First published in 1955.)

Fenichel, O.
   1945   *The Psychoanalytic Theory of Neurosis,* p. 23. New York: Norton.

Fortune, R. F.
   1926   The Psychology of Dreams. *Australian Journal of Psychology and Philosophy* 4:119–40.
   1927a On Imitative Magic. Diploma thesis, University of Cambridge, unpublished.
   1927b *The Mind in Sleep.* London: Kegan Paul.
   1932   Omaha Secret Societies. *Columbia University Contributions to Anthropology,* vol. 14. New York: Columbia University Press.
   1963   *Sorcerers of Dobu.* New York: Dutton. (First published in 1932.)
   1965   *Manus Religion.* Lincoln: University of Nebraska Press. (First published in 1935.)

Frank, L. K.
   1948   Projective Methods. Springfield: Thomas.
Freud, S.
   1960   *Totem and Taboo.* New York: Random House. (First published in 1918.)
Goodenough, F.
   1926   *Measurement of Intelligence by Drawings.* Yonkers: World Book.
Gorer, G. and Rickman, J.
   1962   *The People of Great Russia.* New York: Norton. (First published in 1949.)
Hanfmann, E. and Getzels, J. W.
   1953   Studies of the Sentence Completion Test. *Journal of Projective Techniques* 17:280–94.
Heath, B. H.
   1973   *Somatotype Patterns and Variation Within a Melanesian Population.* Ninth International Congress of Anthropological and Ethnological Sciences. Chicago.
Hellersberg, E. F.
   1950   *The Individual's Relation to Reality in Our Culture; an Experimental Approach by Means of the Horn-Hellersberg Test.* Springfield: Thomas.
Henry, J. and Henry, Z.
   1944   *Doll Play of Pilaga Indian Children.* Research Monograph no. 4. New York: American Orthopsychiatric Association.
Henry, W. E.
   1947   *The Thematic Apperception Technique in the Study of Culture-Personality Relations.* Provincetown: The Journal Press.
Herskovits, M.
   .1972   *Cultural Relativism,* ed. F. Herskovits. New York: Random House.
Jochelson, W.
   1908   Material Culture and Social Organization of the Koryak. *Memoirs of the American Museum of Natural History,* 10, part 2. Leiden: Brill.
Kluver, H.
   1933   Eidetic Imagery. In *A Handbook of Child Psychology.* 2nd rev. ed., ed. C. Murchison, pp. 699–722. Worcester: Clark University Press.
Knapp, P. H.
   1963   *Expression of the Emotions in Man.* New York: International Universities Press.
Lee, D.
   1940   A Primitive System of Values. *Philosophy of Science* 7:355–78.
Lévy-Bruhl, L.
   1926   *How Natives Think,* translated by L. A. Clare, p. 16. New York: Knopf.
   1949   Les Carnets, pp. 49–50, 61–62, 70, 129, 157. Paris: Presses Universitaires de France.
Lomax, A.
   1968   *Folksong Style and Culture.* Symposium Volume No. 88. Washington: American Association for the Advancement of Science.
Lowenfeld, M.
   1939   The World Pictures of Children: A Method of Recording and Studying Them. *British Journal of Medical Psychology* 18:65–101.

1948   The World Test. In *Projective Techniques,* ed. J. E. Bell, pp. 468–73. New York: Langmans, Green.

1954   The Lowenfeld Mosaic Test. London: Newman Neame.

MacLean, P. D.

1973   The Brain's Generation Gap: Some Human Implications. *Zygon* 18:113–27.

Malcolm, L. A., et al.

1972   The Distribution of Blood, Serum Protein and Enzyme Groups on Manus Island. *Human Heredity* 22:305–32.

McClelland, D. C., et al.

1953   *The Achievement Motive.* New York: Appleton-Century-Crofts.

McQuown, N. A., et al., eds.

1971   *A Natural History of an Interview.* MS. 95, 96, 97 and 98 (series 15) of the Microfilm Collection of Manuscripts in Cultural Anthropology. Chicago: University of Chicago Library.

Mead, M.

1926   The Methodology of Racial Testing: Its Significance for Sociology. *American Journal of Sociology* 31:657–67.

1927   Group Intelligence Tests and Linguistic Disability Among Italian Children. *School and Society* 25:465–68.

1928   A Lapse of Animism Among a Primitive People. *Psyche* 9:72–77.

1930   An Ethnologist's Footnote to Totem and Taboo. *Psychoanalytic Review* 17: 297–304.

1931   Two South Sea Educational Experiments and Their American Implications. *University of Pennsylvania School of Education Bulletin* 31:493–97.

1932   An Investigation of the Thought of Primitive Children, with Special Reference to Animism. *Journal of the Royal Anthropological Institute* 62:173–90.

1934   Kinship in the Admiralty Islands. *Anthropological Papers of the American Museum of Natural History* 34:183–358.

1935   Review of the Riddle of the Sphinx by Geza Roheim. *Character and Personality* 4:85–90.

1939   Researches in Bali, 1936–1939. *Transactions of the New York Academy of Sciences,* ser. 2, vol. 2, no. 1, pp. 24–31.

1940   The Arts in Bali. *Yale Review* 30:334–47.

1942   Anthropological Data on the Problem of Instinct. *Psychosomatic Medicine* 4:396–97.

1947a Age Patterning in Personality Development. *American Journal of Orthopsychiatry* 17:231–40.

1947b The Mountain Arapesh III, Socio-Economic Life, and IV, Diary of Events in Alitoa. *Anthropological Papers of the American Museum of Natural History,* vol. 40, part 3, pp. 163–419. New York.

1949   Character Formation and Diachronic Theory. In *Social Structure: Studies Presented to A. R. Radcliffe-Brown,* ed. M. Fortes, pp. 18–34. Oxford: Clarendon Press.

1952   Some Relationships Between Social Anthropology and Psychiatry. In *Dynamic Psychiatry,* eds. F. Alexander and H. Ross, pp. 401–48. Chicago: University of Chicago Press.

1953 *Manus Revisited,* pp. 15–18. Annual Report and Proceedings, Papua Scientific Society, Port Moresby.

1954*a* Cultural Discontinuities and Personality Transformation. *Journal of Social Issues, Suppl. Ser.* 8:3–16.

1954*b* The Swaddling Hypothesis: Its Reception. *American Anthropologist* 56:395–409.

1954*c* Manus Restudied: An Interim Report. *Transactions of the New York Academy of Sciences, Ser. II* 16:426–32.

1954*d* Research on Primitive Children. In *Manual of Child Psychology,* ed. L. Carmichael, pp. 667–706. New York: Wiley. (First published in 1946.)

1955 Energy Changes under Conditions of Cultural Change. *Sociometry and the Science of Man* 18:201–11.

1960 *Growing Up in New Guinea.* Apollo Editions. New York: Morrow. (First published in 1930.)

1961*a* *Coming of Age in Samoa.* Apollo Editions. New York: Morrow. (First published in 1928.)

1961*b* *Cooperation and Competition Among Primitive Peoples.* Boston: Beacon Press. (First published in 1937.)

1962 Retrospect and Prospect. In *Anthropology and Human Behavior,* eds. T. Gladwin and W. C. Sturtevant, pp. 115–49. Washington, D.C.: Anthropological Society of Washington.

1963*a* *Sex and Temperament.* Apollo Editions. New York: Morrow. (First published in 1935.)

1963*b* Totem and Taboo Reconsidered With Respect. *Bulletin* of the Menninger Clinic 27:185–99.

1966*a* *The Changing Culture of an Indian Tribe. Cap Giant.* New York: Capricorn Books. (First published in 1932.)

1966*b* *New Lives for Old: Cultural Transformation—Manus, 1928–1933.* Apollo Editions. New York: Morrow. (First published in 1956.)

1966*c* *Continuities in Cultural Evolution.* New Haven and London: Yale University Press. (First published in 1964.)

1967 *Male and Female.* Apollo Editions. New York: Morrow. (First published in 1949.)

1969 *Social Organization of Manu's.* Honolulu: Bishop Museum Press. (First published in 1930.)

1970*a* The Art and Technology of Field Work. In *A Handbook of Method in Cultural Anthropology,* eds. R. Naroll and R. Cohen, pp. 246–65. Garden City: Natural History Press.

1970*b* Field Work in the Pacific Islands, 1925–1967. In *Women in the Field,* ed. P. Golde, pp. 293–331. Chicago: Aldine.

1972 *Blackberry Winter: My Earlier Years.* New York: Morrow.

1974*a* What I Think I have Learned About Education 1923–1973; Epilogue. *Education* 94:388–97.

1974*b* A Note on the Evocative Character of the Rorschach Test. In *Toward a Discovery of the Person: The First Bruno Klopfer Memorial Symposium, and*

Carl G. Jung Centennial Symposium, ed. R. W. Davis, pp. 62–67. Monograph of the Society for Personality Assessment, Burbank, California.

1974c Margaret Mead. In *History of Psychology in Autobiography,* vol. 6, ed. G. Lindzey. New York: Appleton-Century-Croft.

Mead, M. and Macgregor, F. C.

1951 *Growth and Culture: A Photographic Study of Balinese Childhood.* New York: Putnam.

Mead, M. and Metraux, R., eds.

1953 *The Study of Culture at a Distance.* Chicago: University of Chicago Press.

Mead, M., and Metraux, R.

1965 The Anthropology of Human Conflict. In *The Nature of Human Conflict,* ed. E. B. McNeil, pp. 116–38. Englewood Cliffs: Prentice Hall.

Mead, M. and Schwartz, T.

1960 The Cult as a Condensed Social Process. In *Group Processes, Transactions of the Fifth Conference, October 1958, Princeton, New Jersey,* ed. B. Schaffner, p. 87–187. New York: Josiah Macy, Jr. Foundation.

Mead, M. and Wolfenstein, M., eds.

1963 *Childhood in Contemporary Cultures.* Chicago: University of Chicago Press. (First published in 1955.)

Meier, J. P.

1907- Mythen und Sagen der Admiralitasinsulaner. *Anthropos* 2:646–67, 933–41;
1909 3:193–206, 251–57; 4:354–74.

Metraux, R.

1957 Montserrat, B. W. I.: Some Implications of Suspended Culture Change. *Transactions of the New York Academy of Sciences,* ser. 2, vol. 20, no. 2, pp. 205–11.

Metraux, R. and Abel, T. M.

1957 Normal and Deviant Behavior in a Peasant Community: Montserrat, B. W. I. *American Journal of Orthopsychiatry* 27:167–84.

Murphy, G.

1966 *Personality.* New York: Basic Books. (First published in 1947.)

Murray, H. A.

1943 *Thematic Apperception Test.* Cambridge, Mass.: Harvard University Press.

Parkinson, R.

1907 *Dreissig Jahre in der Sudsee.* Stuttgart: Strecker and Schroeder.

Piaget, J.

1960 *Language and Thought of the Child.* Cleveland: World Publishing. (First published in 1926.)

Porteus, S. D. and James, G. A.

1963 Studies in Intercultural Testing. *Perception and Motor Skills* 16:705–24.

Pribram, K. H.

1970 *Languages of the Brain.* New York: Academy Press.

Raven, J. C.

1941 Standardization of Progressive Matrices, 1938. *British Journal of Medical Psychology* 19:137–50.

Roheim, G.
    1932   Psycho-Analysis of Primitive Cultural Types. *International Journal of Psycho-Analysis* 13:1–222.

Rorschach, H.
    1921   Psychodiagnostik, Methodik und Ergebnisse eines wahrnehmungsdiagnosti-schen Experiments (Deutenlassen von Zufallsformen). In *Arbeiten zur ange-wandten Psychiatrie,* vol. 2, ed. W. Morgenthaler. Bern: Bircher.

Schaffner, B.
    1955-   *Group Processes,* 5 vols. New York: Josiah Macy, Jr. Foundation.
    1960

Schwartz, L. R.
    1966   Conflicts Fonciers a Mokerang, Village Matankor des Iles de L'Amiraute. *L'Homme; Revue Francaise d'Anthropologie* 6:32–35.

Schwartz, L. S.
    1959   Cultural Influence in Perception. Master's essay, Stella Elkins Tylor School of Fine Arts of Temple University, unpublished.

Schwartz, T.
    1962   The Paliau Movement in the Admiralty Islands, 1946–1954. *Anthropological Papers of The American Museum of Natural History,* vol. 49, part 2.

    1973   Cult and Context: The Paranoid Ethos in Melanesia. *Ethos* 1:153–74.

Schwartz, T. and Mead, M.
    1961   Micro- and Macro-cultural Models for Cultural Evolution. *Anthropological Linguistics* 3:1–7.

Segall, N. H., Campbell, D. T. and Herskovits, M. J.
    1966   *The Influence of Culture on Visual Perception.* Indianapolis and New York: Bobbs-Merrill.

Sheldon, W. H.
    1970a   *The Varieties of Human Physique; An Introduction to Constitutional Psy-chology.* New York: Hafner. (First published in 1940.)

    1970b   *The Varieties of Temperament: A Psychology of Constitutional Differences.* New York: Hafner. (First published in 1942.)

Spearman, C. E.
    1927   *The Nature of "Intelligence" and the Principles of Cognition.* London: Macmillan. (First published in 1923.)

Sperry, R. W.
    1971   How a Developing Brain Gets Itself Properly Wired for Adaptive Functioning. In *The Biopsychology of Development,* eds. E. Tobarth, L. R. Aronson and E. Shaw, pp. 27–44. New York and London: Academic Press.

Spitz, R. A.
    1935   Fruhkindliches Erleben und Erwachsenenkultur bei den Primitiven, Bemer-kungen zu Margaret Mead Growing Up In New Guinea. *Imago:* 21:367–87.

Tanner, J. M.
    1953   Growth and Constitution. In *Anthropology Today,* ed. A. L. Kroeber, pp. 750–70. Chicago: University of Chicago Press.

Tanner, J. M. and Inhelder, B., eds.
  1957- *Discussions on Child Development*, 4 vols. New York: International Univer-
  1960 sities Press.

Thompson, B. L.
  1969 A Psychological Interpretation of a Recurrent Pattern in Early Parent-Child
        Relationships in Bali, D.Ed. Thesis, Teachers College.

Whiting, B. B., ed.
  1963 *Six Cultures: Studies of Child Rearing.* New York and London: Wiley.

Wile, I. S.
  1934 *Handedness, Right and Left.* Boston: Lothrop, Lee and Shepard.

Witkin, H. A. et al.
  1954 *Personality Through Perception.* New York: Harper.

The Author

FRANCIS L. K. HSU is Professor of Anthropology and Chairman of the department at Northwestern University, Evanston, Illinois. He was born in a village in Manchuria. After grade and high schools in Manchuria he attended the University of Shanghai, where he received his B.A. in Sociology (1933). In 1937 he won a four-year fellowship to study anthropology in the London School of Economics (London University) and received his Ph.D. in 1940. Returning to then Free China in 1941, he met his wife Vera Yi-Nin Tung, whom he married in 1943. A year later, they came to the United States at the invitation of Columbia University, travelling in a U.S. troop ship with 3000 GI's and officers, quite a few becoming lasting friends. That was their first introduction to America. He joined Northwestern University in 1947 after two years at Cornell University. He specializes in psychological anthropology and comparative studies of large civilizations, with special reference to China, Japan, India, and the United States.

He has done field work in North Central China, 1935–36; Southwestern China, 1941–42 and 1942–43; Hawaii, 1949–50 and 1970–71; India, 1955–57; and Japan, 1964–65. His main research emphasis is not on areas as such, but on the unifying psychological factors (testable or inferable) underlying the behavior patterns in each culture which make them predictable and which distinguish one culture from another. He characterizes his work as a "Grammar of Culture."

At various times he was a visiting professor of Psychological Anthropology (Kyoto University); of American Studies (Hawaii); Senior Specialist, East-West Center and fellow, Anthropological Survey of India. Besides consultantships in the United States Labor Department and psychiatric hospitals, he has lectured widely in different parts of the United States and abroad to both academic audiences and the general public.

In 1972 he made a nine-week tour of the People's Republic of China with Mrs. Hsu, their two American-born daughters, Eileen and Penny, and their son-in-law, Richard Balzer. The trip took Dr. Hsu and his family to cities and rural areas in South, Central and North China as well as Manchuria. They spent days with their relatives and interviewed various individuals—from tri-ricksha operators and barbers to university professors and former industrial tycoons. Part of the results of this visit is published as *China Day by Day* (1974), a pictorial book Dr. Hsu co-authored with his older daughter and her husband.

Dr. Hsu is the author of some one hundred articles in learned journals and some nine books, which include: *Under the Ancestors' Shadow; Americans and Chinese; Clan, Caste and Club; Psychological Anthropology; Kinship and Culture; Iemoto: The Heart of Japan.*

This Chapter

In contrast to many of the contributors to this volume, Francis Hsu is searching for unifying forces that make some characterization of large, national wholes possible, and in identifying continuity in these large scale factors. He is not working with a modal personality concept but has developed his own model of psychological homeostasis. The meaning of this concept in the context of Professor Hsu's work will be left for the reader to discover.

Hsu is acutely aware of the extent to which the culture and world view of anthropologists affect their perceptions and interpretations. He points out that the significance of kinship, magic, science, etc. in other cultures may easily be perceived by Western anthropologists but not so easily understood in their own culture. He feels strongly that anthropologists should know their own culture and stresses the ethnocentrism of western scholars.

He emphasizes the constants of human affect in contrast to economic, scientific, or technological change. He derides the notion, for instance, that the American family has really changed. And he traces certain persistencies back through the biblical flood myth as central features of Western culture.

Professor Hsu interweaves his personal and professional experience into an impressive unity. Every step of his life, from his early experience in China, to his trip from Bombay to the United States with American troops, his encounters with English ladies, his experience on a Mediterranean cruise, as well as his field work as such, is a contribution to the development of ideas and the progressive evolution of his thinking.

His chapter does not deal with "national character," as such, but it demonstrates how one may ask pertinent questions and make useful observations about culturally patterned behavior and culturally influenced personality characteristics in the context of large and complex national wholes.

G.D.S.

4 *Passage to Understanding*

FRANCIS L. K. HSU*

The germ of my interest in the importance of the psychological factors in human behavior across national lines began when I studied two novels, *Silas Marner* and *Les Miserables,* as a sophomore at the University of Shanghai.

Through *Silas Marner* I came to appreciate, for the first time in my life, how a lonely man's money could substitute for his need for human company. Yet how easily Silas Marner changed the object of his attachment when his money was stolen and the little girl Eppie walked in. I had heard of *shou ts'ai noo* (''wealth-guarding slaves'') in Chinese communities before this time. These were rich but overly stingy old men who were disliked, but never had I heard or read about a Chinese *shou ts'ai noo* who lived in such loneliness or who made a Marner type of switch.

Victor Hugo's novel filled me with more amazement. Why would Javert, a mere police officer, take it upon himself to pursue Jean Valjean all over the map to a bitter and mutually destructive end? Jean Valjean's only real crime was to get some bread for his hungry widowed sister and her seven children, for whom he was practically the sole support. Was Javert not also a father, son, husband, brother, who would understand Jean Valjean's desperation? Furthermore, Javert never consulted his wife or parents, or even his superiors at work before embarking on his relentless mission. Was he insane?

I had then only a peephole view of Western literature. I had not read other Western classics such as Homer's *Iliad* or Melville's *Moby Dick.* Hemingway's *Old Man and The Sea* was yet to be written. I did read a few other Western novels such as *David Copperfield* and *Return of the Native,* but none of them impressed me the way *Silas Marner* and *Les Miserables* did. In another English class we even studied Emerson's essay on ''Self Reliance,'' but while its beautiful rhetoric sounded good, its psychological significance eluded me. Our teachers were native white Americans. They had been in China for several years, but they could not speak or read Chinese and they knew little and cared less about the Chinese way of doing things. They taught Western books in terms of the

*I am greatly indebted to my wife, Vera Y. N. Hsu, who helped me much in writing this paper.

universal truths they conveyed. Our salvation lay in the extent to which we succeeded in absorbing them.

This was in the 1930s when China was suffering from foreign intrusion. Western powers such as Britain, France, the United States and even Belgium each had their well-protected territorial, political and economic interests, and Japan was coming in fast. First she took Manchuria. Then she invaded Shanghai. North China was becoming a haven for Japanese criminals and drug pushers and a military training ground for the conquest of China and Asia. Dr. Sun Yat-sen, who had led the 1911 Revolution that toppled the Manchus but who could not stop the warlords and the foreign aggressors, told the Chinese that Japan could conquer all China in twenty-four hours.

There was a rush of ideas on how to save China. Only three of them caught more than my passing attention. One was the notion of "Save the Country through Religion (Christianity)" *(chung chiao chiu kuo)*. A second was "Village Development to Save the Nation." The third notion, promoted by some professors, was "Total Westernization" *(ch'uan p'an hsi hwa)*, from government to family, from education to technology, and from ethics to literature.

One thing could not but puzzle most thinking Chinese. Few societies have consciously borrowed from another as much as Japan has from China: clothing, housing style, city planning, writing, even flower arrangement—the list is long. Before the Meiji Restoration the phrase *t'ung wen t'ung chung* ("common language and same race") was often used by Japanese writers to express their feelings about China, and the Chinese continued to repeat it even after Japan embarked on a course of total aggression. Yet Japan was able to deal effectively with Western efforts at domination, and to rise rapidly among the powers, while China lagged far behind.

That was a riddle I did not have the opportunity to work on until years later (Hsu 1975). It persisted as part of my life-long interest in the differences between peoples.

INTRA-SOCIETAL AND INTER-SOCIETAL DIFFERENCES

This interest stayed with me even when I was doing practical work. From 1934 to 1937 I was a social worker in the Rockefeller Foundation-sponsored Peking Union Medical College Hospital. The role of a social worker at that hospital was twofold. The primary role was to assist the doctors in administering and completing medical treatment. Some patients claimed they could not afford the cost of the treatment. The social workers were to find help after determining that the claim was justified. Some patients would fail to return, or returned only after they had tried traditional Chinese medicine, including acupuncture. Our duty was to get these patients to return and to complete treatment at the hospital.

The other duty of the hospital social worker was to augment the medical diagnoses and remedies by ascertaining the relevance of social factors, and then mobilizing them.

Our basic technique of investigation was case work through interviews and home visits. In this way I came into close contact with Chinese of diverse walks of life, mostly the urban poor and the peasants, from many parts of China. Through these interviews and home visits I came to appreciate two things. One, Chinese people of modest means from different provinces were quite similar in many basic ways. To be sure they spoke dissimilar dialects, some of which were unintelligible to me. But their approaches to religion and to medical treatment were the same. For example, my Christian patients did not accord their churches any more importance than my non-Christian patients gave to their temples. In both cases religion did not make any difference as to whom they would hire, work for or associate with. Temple-visiting Chinese never confined themselves to one temple, for no one was a member of any one temple.

Chinese from different regions shared a common approach to medical treatment. They tended not to stay with one kind of treatment. Those who appeared in the hospital for treatment of, for example, some liver ailment, thought nothing of getting serious advice and drugs from herbal doctors, especially if the Western treatment did not give the desired results in a hurry. And some who were in the care of herbal doctors or Western-style physicians also made use of the services of diviners or acupuncturists or shamans or elderly men of their home towns known for wisdom and experience.

The phenomenon which astonished me most was the violent conflicts between my patients and the Peking Union Medical College-trained Chinese doctors. The major conflict was over the patients' custom of seeking other traditional help while in the doctors' care. Instead of educating their patients the doctors looked down upon them. They would revile them or refuse to see them when they returned. Explosions bordering on temper tantrums were not rare.[1] What should

1. Until recently practitioners of Chinese herbal medicine and acupuncture were hardly distinguished from diviners and shamans in the eyes of Western physicians. Times have changed. Today quite a few doctors in the West have begun to take many traditional Chinese cures seriously, especially acupuncture.

have been a minor aspect of the social worker's work often consumed most of our time and energy. We became peacemakers between doctors and patients, explaining to the former the traditional Chinese psychology in medicine and to the latter the mores of "Western" doctors. These doctors, though Chinese by birth and ancestry, seemed totally ignorant of Chinese ways and seemed to be more Western in their professionalism than even their Western counterparts. In three years I found no exceptions to this.

I became convinced of the power of social and cultural factors in human psychology.

MALINOWSKI AND HIS BASIC NEEDS

Having thus been sensitized to intergroup differences I went to the London School of Economics to study under Bronislaw Malinowski in 1937. There I learned much about the Trobriand Islands, but his views on what he designated as the basic needs of man caught most of my attention.

According to Malinowski all cultures are anchored on "basic needs." These basic needs then lead to cultural "imperatives" or derived needs which are then translated into cultural "responses." For example, man's basic need for food is met in specific cultures by certain technical skills and tools and patterns of human cooperation for hunting, planting, raids or whatever. Once these tools and measures are adopted by a society they become the cultural imperative or derived needs of its members. The sum of such derived needs in a given society is its cultural response in the form of economy.

Malinowski never went beyond food, sex and bodily safety in his discussion of basic needs in the late thirties. A longer and more precise formulation of them and their cultural derivations was to appear much later, posthumously (Malinowski 1944, pp. 91-131). I was not satisfied with Malinowski's theory of needs because it only accounted for some of the common denominators of dissimilar cultures, but not the elements and trends which made them different both at the societal level and, on a probability basis, at the individual level. For example, why were most of the world's missionaries Westerners rather than Chinese or Japanese?

Even at the level of common denominators, the basic needs cannot account for some cultural phenomena. For example, what basic need or needs account for the universality of art? On the other hand, why do animals and humans differ so much in their behavior even though they share the same basic needs?

However, Malinowski's theory of basic and derived needs led me to think in a new direction, namely the psychic factors underlying human behavior. During the first spring recess I visited Paris and noted an English-French difference. Before arriving in London I had been prepared for social formality among the English and for greater social freedom among the French. Yet English girls went out with boys without chaperones, but French girls on dates were invariably accompanied by mothers or aunts. This was the first intercultural contrast which enabled me to appreciate the difference between inner control and external control.[2]

These experiences strengthened my interest in inter-societal comparison and contrast, which in turn laid the foundation of my work on the U.S.A. (Hsu 1953, 1970), on India (Hsu 1963) and on Japan (Hsu 1975). But in those days Western anthropologists were not interested in studying their own cultures, much less in substantive comparison of "primitive" peoples with themselves. Where they did a sort of comparison, the results were a mixture of facts and fantasy, as in the area of incentives to work.

According to scholars dealing with the subject at the time, modern Western incentives to work are mercenary and calculable, betraying self-interest pure and simple, while in the "primitive" societies the economic incentives are invariably interwoven with rituals, the desire for public approval, community requirements and other noneconomic considerations which often negate or obliterate self-interest. (Firth 1929, pp. 156–59, 162; Miller 1937, pp. 423–44; Thurnwald 1932, pp. 280–81).

I saw this contrast as invalid. Self-interest is evident in every society, but self-interest rooted in the individual's feelings and aspirations is everywhere subject to social and cultural conditioning and limitations. Consequently even in the industrialized West incentives to work are, to the extent that the individualist must be a member of his society and a product of his culture, also not free from noneconomic factors. However, the boundary of self-interest may be confined to one individual, as zealous Calvinists would have it, or it may encompass a nuclear family, a giant household, or a whole tribe. (Hsu 1943, pp. 638–42). Differences in the boundaries of self-interest were germane to my later formulation of situation-centered Chinese versus individual-centered Americans (Hsu 1953, 1954a, pp. 318–64). It also contributed to my model of Psychosocial Homeostasis (PSH) (Hsu 1971a, pp. 23–44).

2. Later I was to develop the difference in my paper on suppression versus repression (See Hsu 1949, pp. 223–42).

WITCHCRAFT AND SORCERY

Two other relevant ideas occurred to me at that time. One concerned witchcraft and sorcery, and the other the problem of the unity of Chinese social organization.

Quite a few of Malinowski's students and visitors to his seminar were presenting papers on witchcraft and sorcery. In due course I read Evans-Pritchard's *Witchcraft, Oracles and Magic Among the Azande* (1937), the issue of *Africa* on witchcraft and sorcery put together by S. F. Nadel (1935), and other reports of comparable phenomena in the South Seas and India.

The results of our discussions proceeded along the following lines: that witchcraft and witch hunting are related to law and order; that witchcraft can have serious effects among people who believe in it; and that witch hunting is an outlet for psychic tensions. But as I listened to descriptive details of how witches or sorcerers worked and their punishment I became greatly interested in two things.

First, the rarity of the phenomenon in China. During a rash of theft in my grade school in eastern Manchuria I heard some talk about how to catch a thief. Put a dead cat or doll in a boiler, stick a number of needles into it, and boil. The thief will at once develop pains all over his (or her) body and confess. Some forms of sorcery found their way into a few traditional Chinese novels, such as when a wife tries to increase her attraction to win her husband back from his concubine.

But I never saw a Chinese sorcerer in action, nor met a Chinese who did. Furthermore, while Chinese historical records contain a few instances of the use of sorcery in intrigues among the inmates of some emperor's harem, they say nothing about witch hunts. In fact, I do not remember any serious discussion at all about witchcraft or sorcery among my Chinese fellow students. Why did Western scholars devote so much of their research time and energy to it?

This led me to read more on witchcraft and sorcery in the West, and it was an eye opener. G. L. Kittredge's *Witchraft in Old and New England* (1929) and Montague Summers' *The History of Witchcraft and Demonology* (1926) led me to a second point. Witch hunting, as it was found in Europe, had one outcome. Rarely were the lives of "convicted" witches spared; usually they were burned, hanged, drowned or otherwise executed. There was no way they could redeem themselves by compensating their victims for their alleged crimes. There could be no counter-witchcraft to which their alleged victims could safely and openly resort, for to possess counter-witchcraft was tantamount to having truck with the Devil. The estimates of scholars on the number of witches put to death in Europe vary greatly, from 30,000 to several million (Summers 1926, p. viii). A noted American historian told me of travelers in southern Europe during the Middle Ages reportedly using the witch burning pyres to illuminate their way.

On the other hand, witch hunting as it occurs in the non-Western world usually showed the following relativistic characteristics unknown in the West:

1. The lives of condemned witches or sorcerers can be spared if they or their kinsmen make compensation to the victims. Sometimes public confession of guilt is enough. In other instances the victims take action for the sole purpose of getting retribution payments. After confession and/or damage payment the guilty one returns to society without further difficulty.

2. Counter-witchcraft measures or white magic, which are the same sort of acts as those of witches or sorcerers, are highly valued by the people. Their possession even leads in some instances to positions of power and influence (Browne 1929; Hogbin 1934, p. 216).[3]

3. Where witches or sorcerers are reportedly "executed," they are more commonly put to death by angry avengers related to the "victim," or by mob action. Where a chief exists with trial-conviction-punishment procedures, the penalty usually befalls only those sorcerers who have resorted to plain poison to assure results (Hsu 1960, pp. 35–38).

I then understood why my fellow Western anthropologists were so concerned with the witchcraft and sorcery phenomenon while my fellow Chinese were not. We came from different historical backgrounds, one absolutist, all-or-none, the other relativist, more or less. Those who believe in only one true and all-prevailing God must fear the existence machinations of only one Devil whose sole purpose is to overthrow or undo the good work of their only God. How then can they leave the Devil and his followers alone?

KIN TERMS AND UNITY OF CHINESE CULTURE

Before anthropology came to China, Chinese and Western scholars used to speak of China as one social and cultural entity. One of the areas frequently written about was the Chinese family and kinship system. Wilkinson (1926), Chen and Shryock (1932), and Feng (1937) are some examples.

H. T. Fei (1936), on the other hand, pointed out that the spoken kin terms used in different parts of China are often entirely different

3. Raymond Firth confirmed this point much later (1954, pp. 103, 113–115.)

from each other and from the literary terms. He concluded there was not one Chinese system of kinship but many. However, noting the presence of the same literary terms in all of China, I raised the question with Malinowski as to which should be considered closer to reality, the variable spoken systems or the literary system. Malinowski opined that, of course, the spoken system should.

Sometime later I did an experiment. I substituted a set of alphabetical letters for all the actual terms used in each spoken system. The results showed great unity in the underlying principles: generation, sex, lineage and age (Hsu 1947, pp. 618–24).[4] These results strengthened my conviction that Chinese society and culture are marked by unitary features more than by diversity, and gave me additional assurance later when I worked on the national character of China in contrast to that of America.

THE ENGLISH WIFE

In the meantime, one day during the third year of my English sojourn, after my thesis was completed and passed by the examiners, I suddenly realized I might have something to say about the English family. This was followed by some ten months of reading and research before I returned to then Free China via Africa, India and the Burma Road.

In writing the manuscript on *The English Wife* I had an early opportunity to see how biased some quantitative research could be. At that time *The Material Culture and Social Institutions of the Simpler Peoples* (Hobhouse et al. 1915) was still very much the talk of the academic community. Using roughly the Hobhouse et al. rating scale, Hornell Hart wrote a book entitled *The Technique of Social Progress* (1931). According to Hart modern Britain and the U.S.A. represented the two highest points of development in the human marital relationship. Britain had maximum scores or high positive scores on such items as "consent of bride," "equal divorce right," "equality in court," "liberal education" and "wide social contacts," etc. In "leisure" the modern British women were supposed to have the maximum enjoyed by any other group of women in the Euro-American world.

I found his tabular representation extremely misleading. It failed completely to account for the discrepancy between actual conditions and the formally emphasized patterns, not due to class differences alone. For

---

4. In that article I added two more spoken systems, one from South Manchuria and the other from Yunnan.

one thing, up to World War II, while English women enjoyed universal education and suffrage, and women could enter some previously all-male professions, they were far from having achieved equality with men in general. Furthermore, whatever progress toward equality occurred was confined to the non-marital scene.[5] Even among the middle and higher strata of society the inequality between men and their wives was very evident. It was worse among the lower middle-classes and glaring among the lower-classes. (Rice 1939, pp. 94, 96–102, 121, 131–32; Eyles 1922).

How could a respected British scholar be so oblivious to reality and give British marital life such high marks in his tabulation? Throughout my years in England I often felt the need for the English scholars to know themselves better as a counterweight to their views of others. Had they taken steps in that direction, the English scholars might have had a sounder understanding of the English marital relationship. The English wife suffered from the contradiction between a highly egalitarian ideal and a very unequal reality. In this regard her condition contrasted sharply with that of her Chinese sister in old China. The Chinese wife was subordinate to her husband. That pattern was glorified in the ethics and philosophy governing traditional Chinese family and society, which was also the pattern of marital conduct in reality. I concluded the English wife probably experienced less contentment, because her expectations were far above reality as she found it, than her Chinese sister, whose expectations and reality nearly matched each other.

Through my inquiry into the English marital bond I came to the idea of what I described as an inverse Oedipus complex. I was well aware of Malinowski's notion of the replacement of the father by the mother's brother in the Oedipal situation among the Trobriand Islanders. I also read Freud's *New Introductory Lectures*. What I noted in the English family was a strong tendency by mothers to favor their sons and often to be the cause of the sons' marital difficulties with their wives because of their interference. On the other hand I found no evidence of comparable interest by adolescent and adult sons in their mothers.[6]

5. A wartime booklet issued by the British Council intending to show people abroad the life of the British women listed the following items of legislation as due to their influences: "The raising of the age at which marriage is permitted to the young; the raising of the age of consent to sexual intercourse in girls; the granting of money allowances to widows and orphans; laws regulating the employment of children and dealing with the youthful lawbreaker. . . ." The writer added, "These and other measures *of the same kind* (italics mine) are distinctly traceable to the new influence in British political life" (Hamilton 1940).

6. I had not looked into the British psychoanalytic literature at the time, so had no knowledge of the psychic tendencies of boys of younger ages and their mothers.

I asked myself why this great attachment by English mothers to their sons. My answer was that it was attributable to their psychic needs arising from the incongruity between their heightened expectations and their inferiority in reality vis-à-vis their mates. I even met one English woman who said to me, "Which mother does not think of sleeping with her son at one time or another!"[7] I never had a comparable encounter with a Chinese mother, nor could I imagine any Chinese mother saying such a thing.[8]

KINSHIP, PERSONALITY AND DYNASTIC CYCLE

Returning to wartime China from England I soon embarked on field work in "West Town" (pseudo-name for Hsichow, Western Yunnan) which led eventually to *Under the Ancestors' Shadow* (Hsu 1948, 1971*b*), and *Religion, Science and Human Crises* (Hsu 1952*a*, 1973*d*). I had not yet heard of Culture and Personality as a subdiscipline, although I already read Ruth Benedict's *Patterns of Culture* (1934), and three books by Margaret Mead: *Coming of Age in Samoa* (1928), *Growing Up in New Guinea* (1931), and *Sex and Temperament in Three Primitive Societies* (1935). I even read Linton's *The Study of Man* (1936), but the significance of its chapter on culture and personality eluded me. I dreamed of doing a functionalist community study in China and that was what I did, first in 1941–1942 and then during part of 1943.

While working on my materials at the local level my mind kept running to wider issues. I had never been convinced that local variation was more important than overall pattern, especially for any society which had functioned as one political entity for so long. I added the kin terms of "West Town" to Fei's eight systems, subjected them to the same test, and found that the "West Town" system did not deviate significantly from the overall Chinese pattern.

At about this time I noted the cyclical nature of Chinese history and became interested in finding a link between local facts and larger historical trends. Specifically, each imperial dynasty continued itself along family lines, mostly by primogeniture. Beginning with the First Emperor of Ch'in in 221 B.C. the founder of a dynasty was intent upon maintaining this imperial succession in perpetuity. But all dynasties fell

7. By that remark she thought that she was substantiating Freud's theory of Oedipus complex. But she was not, because she was speaking about the mother's desire and not that of the son.

8. Although I finished the manuscript on *The English Wife* in 1941, I never published it.

and were replaced by new dynasties. The founder of a dynasty was usually an energetic and able man while his descendants suffered from progressive degeneration in personal quality.

As I listened, looked, and probed around in "West Town," I became more than ever convinced of the social importance of the father-son tie and its influence on the psychic characteristics of the sons. I concluded the concatenation of kinship forces favored reduction in ability and achievement motivation on the part of the sons of the rich and highly placed. Consequently they or their sons would fail to live up to their ancestors' shadows, thus unavoidably making room at the top for the sons of the poor and not-so-well placed. A family and kinship system which seemed to protect the continuation of the social status of its male descendants had built into its very system forces which led to the opposite trend, thereby giving traditional Chinese society a remarkable degree of social mobility in the long run.

My next step was to seek a measure to test this hypothesis. I used two indices to identify kinship links among Chinese who achieved prominence through the ages. My first concerned those Chinese who reached national prominence and my second, those who became celebrities at the district level. The results confirmed my hypothesis that the prominence of any given family did not last for more than two or three generations either at the national level or the local level. They also indirectly supported my conclusion from my "West Town" study as to the deleterious effects of the father-son identification in Chinese kinship. The details were given in Appendix IV, "A Study of Family Prominence" in *Under the Ancestors' Shadow* (Hsu 1948, pp. 301–10). Twenty-two years after its publication I had the opportunity to examine later works by other scholars on social mobility in China and found nothing to contradict my earlier conclusion (Hsu 1971*b*, pp. 297–315).

The parallel between the pattern of rise and fall of dynasties and that of kinship groups led me to think that the same social forces had generated the same personality characteristics in both situations. I realized then (and do now) that the rise and fall of a ruling dynasty was a much more complex affair than that of a single prominent family. No simple equivalence between the two is scientifically defensible. However, we are not precluded from seeing the smaller situation as in some ways providing a clue, or being related, to the psychosocial forces operating in the larger arena. In my view the principle justification for village studies in a large society is how the local facts will illuminate the national picture (Hsu 1973*a*, pp. 527–36).

Before coming to the United States my knowledge of American national character came from reading. In Bombay, India, where my wife and I boarded a troopship for America, one of the three books I bought was Margaret Mead's *And Keep Your Powder Dry* (1942). As we began the thirty-six day voyage with some 3000 home bound GI's and officers, I read the book with increasing fascination. Mead's analysis gave me my first look into the American mind and the GI's and officers were the first Americans we had met who were not out to sell Christianity, gadgetry or democracy. Instead, they were mostly concerned with ending the war and getting on with their own private lives. We became friends with a few of them and our friendships have continued in some cases up to today.

There was a small-boned GI, a second generation Italian-American, who had won $3000 shooting craps before he came aboard. He cut out all gambling during this voyage because he was keeping the money for a down payment on a little house in Flushing, N.Y. where he would live with his widowed mother. There was a lieutenant, an attorney in civilian life, who constantly complained about how the beastly war had disrupted his career.

A sergeant from California could not understand why the government in wartime China severely punished hoarders and price manipulators. "We in America," he would say, "were taught that the more money you make the better it is for the country, for then you give jobs to more people." My best advice about how to get on in the United States came from an officer who was also a Lincoln-Mercury dealer in upstate New York. "Just get up a bank account of $20,000 and you will have all the respect you need." We were introduced for the first time to the American way in sex while on the officers deck one day. Some Australian wives were necking with their American husbands in public. "Are they not embarrassed being seen like that?" we thought in passing.

ANTHROPOLOGY AND PSYCHOANALYSIS

My formal introduction to culture and personality occurred when I gave a series of presentations on my "West Town" findings in the Linton-Kardiner seminar at Columbia University. There I received a massive dose of psychoanalysis. I read Freud's works more systematically than before, and those of his followers and his opponents including Joseph Jastrow (1940).

I soon became dissatisfied with Kardiner's interpretation of culture and personality, in particular his preoccupation with the maternal care of infants, especially patterns of breast feeding and diaper control, and how these would determine the personality and culture of the adult world. Kardiner was not unaware of the importance of later social and cultural influences, but when I looked into his actual interpretation of the field data at his disposal I found he down played it.

The case of the Alorese illustrates this point well. Kardiner concluded the Alorese hated their mothers and had no effective personality structure for constructive action. The reason? Extremely poor maternal care.

Besides the failure of much of his evidence to support his major thesis,[9] Kardiner even misread some items of the original data, and unintentionally omitted others contrary to his thesis. For example, he held the fact that Alorese youngsters use epithets to revile their elders as evidence for the lack of idealization of the mother as well as the "preponderance of hatred and aggression toward her."[10] But the actual data on which this conclusion was based reads as follows: "The children imitate their elders by using obscene words in anger. Words for genitalia are common epithets of derogation. Violent cuss words are: 'Sleep with your mother; your father can't'."[11] What the Alorese do is revile their enemies' mothers and not their own mothers. One reviles the mother of one's enemy because it hurts him. The more he cares for his mother the more the epithet is going to hurt. This phenomenon is common among Chinese, Russians, and Italians.[12]

Through the experience of the Linton-Kardiner seminar, consultantships in several psychiatric hospitals,[13] and reading and in my role as organizer of a culture and personality symposium,[14] I found much inconsistency and confusion. Some scholars did an elaborate study of the infantile and childhood experiences of a people, then pointed out, in a general fashion, that these experiences did not really mean as much as had been supposed, and left the subject just where it became interesting. Some insisted on the importance of later experiences as reinforcing or altering forces, but gave little indication in their actual interpretation of the field material that this insistence was more than lip service.

9. For example, Kardiner used the fact that some Alorese women ran away from their husbands and refused to return or yield to their sexual advances until the men had paid up as evidence that love is mixed with hatred. (See Kardiner 1945 for this and other similar "evidences": pp. 147, 150, 132, 150–51 and 133–34.) My question is, are there no American women who will leave their husbands because their men show public signs of inattention or because they value their money more than their wives? How many words are there in the American vocabulary indicating deception?

10. See A. Kardiner, *The Psychological Frontiers of Society* (New York: Columbia University Press, 1945), pp. 150–51.

11. Ibid. p. 138.

12. For other Kardinerian fallacies see Hsu 1952, pp. 227–50.

13. At various times I served as consultant at Rockland State Hospital, Orangeburg, New York; Fort Meade VA Hospital, Md.; Chicago VA State Hospital; and Downey Hospital, Downey, Ill.

14. Its results were later published as *Aspects of Culture and Personality* (Hsu 1954*b*).

Others emphasized the present situation to the virtual exclusion of the early phases of life. Still others pointed out the importance of everything, from birth to death, from the biological peculiarities of each individual to the entire cultural history of the society. I came to the conclusion that, for a more balanced view of the relationship between culture and personality, we had to distinguish firmly between the insights from anthropology and from psychiatry (Hsu 1952*b*, pp. 227–50).

NORMAL VERSUS ABNORMAL

It became clear to me that a balanced view of the relationship between culture and personality must begin with the recognition of the differences in objectives between anthropology and psychiatry. Social sciences such as anthropology and sociology are concerned with whole groups of individuals who are normal functioning members of their society, but clinical disciplines such as psychiatry and psychoanalysis are essentially concerned with single individuals who are ill and are having difficulty with their environment.[15]

Of course the demarcation line between the normal and the abnormal is not so clear. Who has not experienced headaches, backaches, running noses, or a general malaise that kept him from work or play? What we live by, instead, is a common sense definition that separates those who are disabled by physical ailments from performing their usual roles and those who are not. Can we not use the same basis for the distinction between the mentally ill and the mentally well?

The core difference between the two groups is tremendous.[16] The pathological person is one who clings consciously or unconsciously to the past much more than he does to the present. Frustrations turned into traumas, the psychic scars of the past in the form of unconscious fears

15. It is true there are a few clinicians whose aim goes beyond the therapy of single individuals. But it is also true there are some physicists or ornithologists who have schemes for saving mankind. However, if the work of the vast majority of anthropologists is compared with that of the vast majority of psychiatrists, there will be little doubt about the validity of the statements made here.

16. In this discussion I was excluding organically-based illnesses. Studies on glandular imbalance in connection with cases of schizophrenia and such a well-known phenomenon as paresis show that, in the long run, it may become possible to cure such individuals by ordinary medical means. Oneirophrenics studied by Meduna of the Illinois Medical School show all the symptoms of true schizophrenics but will recover quickly by medical reduction of their blood sugar level. At the time I was also not aware of what Hervey Cleckley (1964) calls "psychopaths," individuals who are accepted members of society, but who exhibit gravely bizarre behavior now and then.

and obsessions continue to carry significant influence in his present behavior. In short, to such a person past experiences, especially frustrations, are much more important than present ones, even satisfactions.[17]

On the other hand, the normal, functioning member of any society tends to focus his or her attention on the present much more than on the past. All human beings have all kinds of internal tensions and stresses. The normal, functioning member of a society tends to learn from past experiences, but will be too busy solving present problems to be psychically immobilized by the past (Hsu 1952b, pp. 227-50).

However, although I was against obsession with early childhood experiences in formulating our culture and personality theories, I never was interested in shifting to the opposite position, namely that culture is superorganic, and originates and changes according to laws of its own, with little or no reference to the individual.[18]

What we needed, I concluded then, was a formulation which would link the individual (including his childhood experiences and personality characteristics) with his society and culture. This need gave further impetus to my thinking about Psychosocial Homeostasis (PSH).

At this point, although I saw the tug-of-war between early and later experiences as scientifically unproductive polarization (Hsu 1952b, pp. 248-49), I was much more in favor of later experiences. I was to change this opinion several years later.

ROLE VERSUS AFFECT

What led me to the change was my realization of the much greater importance of affect in human behavior, both individually and nationally, than role.

In spite of the fashion among social scientists to regard economics or natural resources as the primary determinant of patterns of society and culture (poverty, ecology, the impact of industrialization or modernization), I have always held the view that man's most important

17. The mentally ill person may, of course, create a past to which to cling (e.g., the hysterical women observed by Freud who all confessed to having been seduced by their fathers) instead of the actual past. However, all memories of, or unconscious reactions to, the past usually involve addition to or subtraction from it so that created past and the true past in the minds of the individuals concerned are not qualitatively different. Another thing is that some mentally ill persons are said to be going through a process of regression so that, instead of clinging to the past they may have fallen back on the past when present going becomes difficult. This again is not qualitatively different from the views expressed.

18. For an exposition of this theory see Leslie White (1950). White seems, however, to carry the theory to an extreme that was probably not intended by Kroeber (1948, pp. 253-54).

environment is the social environment. In all societies human beings relate to each other through role (usefulness) and through affect (feeling). We know role in terms of skilled and unskilled labor, white collar or blue collar, dentist or diamond cutter, housekeeper or politician. In role relationships we tend to be rational and calculating. As society has grown in complexity, the number and variety of roles have grown with it. In fact, role differentiation is the major concomitant of the growth in societal complexity. For example, in today's American society, each candidate for national office is supported by an army of experts including speech writers, public relations men, technicians, and foot soldiers beyond the imagination of the small town politicians of yesteryear. Giant corporations often have more diversified personnel and more workers and specialists on their payrolls than many small member states of the United Nations.

This development is inevitable as a large society becomes more industrialized. The number and variety of laws have increased, as have bureaucratic departments, crimes, problems of production, and of course the size and complexity of machines.

On the other hand, while roles have proliferated in number and quality, affect has not. Americans still have the same kinds of feelings as their ancestors who lived two or three thousand (probably more) years ago: love, hate, rage, despair, hope, anxiety, forbearance, loyalty, betrayal, and so forth. The list is not long, and many of the terms can be partially or wholly subsumed under each other. That is why great literature (fiction, poetry), great art (painting, sculpture) and even great philosophy and ethics survive the ages, for we moderns feel the same agony and joy and the same loyalty and duplicity as the ancients. We can relive their lives through what they have written; and they too, were they alive today, would understand our problems with our children, parents, friends and enemies, employers and employees, sweethearts and spouses. By contrast, old books of science and technology are useless to us except as curiosities or material for histories of science and technology. Not only the ancients, but our fathers and even our older brothers have found it hard to catch up with our present developments in science and technology.

CULTURE AND AFFECT

However, the patterns of affect which operate among some peoples are different from those which motivate others. My first awareness of some Western-Chinese contrasts came when, as I indicated at the beginning of this essay, I read *Les Miserables* and *Silas Marner*. These contrasts became sharper. Westerners may experience love, hate and despair as do the Chinese and the Japanese, but the ways in which they express love, hate and despair, and the factors which make them love, hate or despair are not universal.

I performed a systematic scrutiny of Western novels, drama and art in comparison with their Chinese counterparts. Since the details were given in the first and second editions of *Americans and Chinese* (Hsu 1953, pp. 19–35; 1970, pp. 35–41), I will only briefly state here the two outstanding psychological contrasts, using novels only. First, Chinese novels usually concentrate on what the characters do in their social roles as generals or common men, while their Western counterparts focus on what the characters do, *think* and *feel* as individuals. There are no pre-modern first person Chinese novels. Second, in contrast to their Chinese counterparts, Western novels are mostly preoccupied with sex. Sex is not absent in Chinese novels but even when sex forms the central theme the novel usually deals with how it is later channeled into socially acceptable contexts, not simply with how the separated lovers conquer the difficulties and eventually possess each other, as more typically happens in Western stories.

In the 1970 edition of *Americans and Chinese* I showed that the post-1949 new novels have not departed from their traditional Chinese characteristics (Hsu 1970, pp. 35–51). They combine new objectives with old patterns of affect, stressing the overwhelming importance of the interpersonal nexus over individual aspirations. In the same way the Chinese have now combined Chinese and Western techniques in art, Chinese and Western forms of music and musical instruments, and Chinese and Western medicines. Western-trained Chinese doctors in the old Peking Union Medical College Hospital (now Capital Hospital) and elsewhere not only work side by side with traditional herbal doctors, acupuncturists, and finger pressurists, but actively learn from them and vice versa.

The basic patterns of affect of each society tend to persist over time, in spite of changes in role structures through economic development, acculturation or revolution. A single member of one society transplanted into another at birth or at a few years of age can easily acquire the patterns of affect of his adopted society, but there is no evidence that a whole society changes that way.

DOMINANT KINSHIP DYAD HYPOTHESIS

Given my assumption that man's most important environment is his fellow men, I came to the conclusion that the kinship constellation, the first human network of the individual, is of overwhelming importance. The reasons are twofold. First, in human affairs patterns of affect determine the maintenance, change and escalation of roles. The latter are rational while the former are not. Among most social scientists today the fashion is to speak of the impact of the auto, TV, industrialization or whatever on the family or personality. That is putting the cart before the horse. For example, autos and factories will separate people from their families only if they have the desire to leave first, in the name of identity seeking, or simply the need for new experiences or self-fulfillment. As the process gets under way, of course, more autos and more factories will have some feedback effect. But there is no question that the desire to separate comes first.

The other reason is that patterns of affect are acquired early in life. In our schools we learn the three R's, but it is from our parents and siblings that we learn how we feel about ourselves, about our fellow humans and about the rest of the world. The reader will recall my previous criticisms against an obsession with early experiences. Now I realize the overwhelming importance of the first human network, kinship. But the importance that I attribute to it is very different from that based on Freudian or individualist assumptions.

Instead of concentrating on infant care practices and psychosexual development during the earliest months or years, I looked into the total network of family relations of the child and how he or she is socialized throughout the growing up years. Seeing the pitfalls of arguing from the individual, especially the pathological individual, I looked into the differing kinship systems for factors which would link individual behavior tendencies with the larger social and cultural patterns in which they are found. In this endeavor I tried to ignore the typical anthropological ways of looking at kinship, such as the link between forms of marriage and residence rules, or the componential analysis of kin terms, and ask myself the question: What messages does each kinship system transmit to its members which are also evident in the larger society and culture that encompass it? My task was not unlike that of the student of nutrition. Granted food is necessary for the maintenance and growth of the human organism, what food elements are necessary for what parts of the human organism and how? For that purpose the nutritionists use terms such as carbohydrates or vitamins instead of green peppers and rice. For my task, I discarded most traditional concepts such as matrilineality or cross-cousin marriage, and looked for elements centrally relevant to interpersonal behavior in general, such as continuity and exclusiveness.

My Dominant Kinship Dyad hypothesis[19] is designed to do the following things: first, going beyond Radcliffe-Brown and others, I hope to show not only that one kinship relationship can influence another, but that these influences can originate from one relationship and extend to all other relationships so as to shape the entire kinship system.

Second, when these influences exert themselves in this way, the effector relationships do not simply change into secondary versions of the affector relationship, as Radcliffe-Brown and others have argued— and the kinship systems in question may make no assumption of such formal change either. Instead, what occurs much more generally is that the qualities and patterns of interaction in the effector relationships assume characteristics similar to those of the affector relationship, so that the husband-wife relationship or the father-son relationship in one kinship system, for example, appears drastically different from that in another.

Third, those influences within the kinship system become visible in the qualities and patterns of behavior among those other members of the same society not related through kinship. In other words, there is a definite link between interaction patterns in a kinship system and characteristic modes of behavior in the wider society of which that kinship system forms a part.

The hypothesis is designed to reveal the crucial importance not merely of certain limited child rearing practices, but of the broader aspects of interpersonal interaction in the nuclear family to personality orientation. The particular personality orientations fostered by particular kinship systems in turn provide the affective forces (or motivation) for the maintenance, change or escalation of particular social organizations and culture patterns.

With the aid of this hypothesis and of Adamson Hoebel's idea of cultural postulates, I re-examined the Chinese and American ways of life. The results are given in *The Study of Literate Civilizations* (Hsu 1969, pp. 61–83). I developed a number of subsidiary hypotheses, relating specific kinship attributes to a variety of patterns of interpersonal behavior, of cultural tendencies and of deviation (Hsu 1969, pp. 84–96).

The Dominant Kinship Dyad hypothesis has been used to understand several other peoples (Hsu 1963, 1975; Tatje 1974). It has also been subjected to certain ethnographic tests in other societies and cultures (Kopytoff 1971, pp. 69–86; Barth 1971, pp. 87–95; Howard

19. For fuller details concerning this hypothesis see Hsu 1965, pp. 638–61; 1966, pp. 999–1004; and 1971c, pp. 3–29.

1971, pp. 96–105; Hunt 1971, pp. 106–43; Rohlen 1971, pp. 144–57; Berndt 1971, pp. 158–245; Newell 1971, pp. 271–83; Strodtbeck 1971, pp. 291–317; Edgerton 1971, pp. 318–36; Fernandez 1971, pp. 339–66; and Wallace 1971, pp. 367–70).

One of the major findings of Tatje's work among Blacks in Chicago is that "mother-daughter kinship content is not limited to poor ghetto dwellers with unstable economic, social and marital situations. There are important continuities . . . that obtain across income and class lines, and differ significantly from the dominant white middle class American kinship system in which the focal relationship is that of husband and wife" (Tatje 1974, p. 408). Some other efforts to test parts of the Dominant Kinship Dyad hypothesis which have seen print are found in Moodey (1971) and Strodtbeck, Moodey and Yu (1974, pp. 90–98).

PSYCHOSOCIAL HOMEOSTASIS (PSH) AND *JEN*

My formulation of Psychosocial Homeostasis (PSH) followed field work in India from 1955 to 1957 (Hsu 1963) and in Japan from 1964 to 1965 (Hsu 1975), but especially a Mediterranean cruise in 1969.

We toured a number of Greek islands including Rodos (Rhodes), Paros, Ios and Naxos. In the evenings when we were in port and had time off from sightseeing, our host and hostess arranged epic reading sessions among the assembled party of about fourteen. We began with *Agamemnon* and took turns reading the parts aloud. After one session I became bored because I prefer card playing to epic reading.

Nevertheless, the Greek epics, of which my wife and I were ignorant up to that point, caught our fancy. During the cruise and shortly afterward we read the *Iliad, Agamemnon,* the *Odyssey* and many other books and articles. We scrutinized them with special reference to motives, objectives and means. We had read about the Trojan Horse before, but were now astonished to find that all that human suffering and expenditure of materials and lives were for the purpose of getting a mere Helen back. And our greatest astonishment was that the leader of the war was not even the husband of the seduced woman, but her husband's brother, who saw Achaian honor at stake. I then perceived the link between *Les Miserables* and later Western classics such as *Moby Dick* and *The Old Man and The Sea* with the Greek epic. That is, Western man extols the virtue of fighting to the finish, regardless of consequences, because he is obsessed with the fulfillment of individualist ambitions. The Chinese would have asked Agamemnon and Captain Ahab and the "Old Man," "Is this trip necessary?"

This study of the Greek epics only confirmed and intensified the conclusions I had derived twenty years before from studying other Western and Chinese literature (Hsu 1953). The absence of significant roles for parents and other relatives in these epics and novels led my wife and me to reflect on kinship in the West and China. The usual view is that the Western family has undergone great changes in history, as a result of the Industrial Revolution. I had my doubts about this; now we made a systematic comparison of the Biblical flood story with its Chinese counterpart.

The results of this comparison were given in the 1970 edition of *Americans and Chinese* (Hsu 1970, pp. 442–44). Briefly, in the Western myth not only did Noah leave his parents to perish (and his wife, her parents), but even afterwards when the chosen man Noah, his wife, his three sons and daughters-in-law were the only survivors in the entire world, they did not stay together. The family was pulled asunder by quarrels with sexual overtones and by curses. In contrast, in the Chinese myth not only did the gods play no part, but the people as a whole did not choose moving away in a boat as a solution. Instead, a minister appointed by the king eradicated the flood and saved the people in their original habitats, and what the minister failed to accomplish his son continued to a successful conclusion.

This contrast is not merely academic. The Biblical version of the myth seems to have a genuine hold on the Western mind. In 1968, 1969 and 1971 I performed the following little experiment in three separate classes at Northwestern University and at the University of Hawaii. I asked my students to exercise their imaginations and rewrite the flood myth with an entirely different plot. None of the stories deviated from the Old Testament themes, or even remotely approached the Chinese model (Hsu 1974, pp. 163–68). The Biblical myth was a psychocultural germ which Western man was to develop and escalate into his present institutions and cultures.[20]

The contrasts between the flood myths are commensurate with those between Western and Chinese art and literature, and those between their respective historical trends in social and cultural development. They led me finally to make my formulation of Psychosocial Homeostasis (PSH) (Hsu 1971a, pp. 23–44).

This formulation is founded on two assumptions. First, all human beings need to receive and give affect which, in interpersonal terms, is intimacy. Second, their most preferred universal source and object of affect is fellow human beings. For this reason I propose the substitution

20. I never concern myself with original origin.

of the Chinese interpersonal *Jen* to replace the individualist term "personality." But when and if human beings are not available, the human tendency is to seek substitutive sources, such as things (animals, machines, money, etc.) or gods (religions, political creeds, Transcendental Meditation, Thoreau's Solitude, etc.). These non-human substitutes are one-sided: the lovers of things and gods lavish affect on them, but except for dogs, there is no reliable evidence that the latter reciprocate in kind. This one-sided intimacy also characterizes the relationship of a patient with his psychotherapist. The patient exposes himself and may develop affect for the therapist, but the therapist only listens and explains for payment.

In the PSH formulation I first assume the cultural heritage of each society to be an independent variable as follows:

Cultural heritage
↓
Social organization
(kinship system)
↓
Individual behavior

The individual is born with potential but no predetermined patterns of role or affect. He acquires particular patterns of affect through his kinship system which is in turn guided by the larger social organization and cultural heritage of his society. The latter reaches the individual as messages from parents and siblings, through the schools and churches he goes to, and through the literature and movies he enjoys. Throughout this process, affective or PSH needs determine role learning and performance.

As the individual grows from infancy through adolescence to adulthood a parallel but reverse process also takes place as follows:

Cultural heritage
↓ ↑
Social organization
(kinship system)
↓ ↑
Individual behavior

In this reverse process the individual will act out the messages he has received through the kinship system, thus maintaining, changing and escalating the inherent tendencies of his social organization and cultural heritage. Throughout this reverse process the affective or PSH needs of the individual also dictate role choice and performance.

Thus, for a majority of Chinese their father-son dominated kinship system inculcated in them, among other things, the attributes of continuity and inclusiveness. These attributes led them to retain their kinship ties, to add to them through birth and marriage, to be unconcerned and uninvolved with the outside world, and to seek solutions to their new problems through traditional human resources found within kinship, local and pseudo-kinship spheres.

Their social organization and cultural heritage provided them with ready-made and automatic sources of affect. They did not have to form or enter into secondary groups to work hard for their PSH. Consequently most of them failed historically to follow their ambitious rulers and colonize distant territories or missionize alien peoples. Internally, they had rebellions to replace tyrannous rulers, but not revolutions aimed at changing the system of government, business and industry or education. Instead, the Chinese tended to escalate their cultural heritage by adding new acts of filial piety or increasing the rules for accentuating already elaborate status differences between the emperor and his subjects. Their centripetal outlook did not propel them to be more spiritual than others, or to be interested in exploration of the inner recesses of the mind. Consequently their literature suffered from what one modern student describes as "psychological poverty." Absolutist and expansionist Christianity never took hold among the Chinese.

Among a majority of Americans, their husband-wife dominated kinship system has inculcated in them, among other things, the attributes of discontinuity and exclusiveness. These attributes led them to discard or wish to discard their kinship ties, to replace them with peers in cause-oriented clubs, to be adventurous, to seek expansion of all boundaries in order to achieve new experiences, to form new ties and to gain new worlds.

Their social organization and cultural heritage make it impossible for them to enjoy the ready-made and automatic sources of affect in kinship, their first human grouping, so their PSH is always uncertain and precarious. Everything is subject to change without notice among peers. This uncertain PSH leads Americans to seek the certainty of objects, of gods, or of self through inner exploration, to compensate for the uncertainty of human relations. Consequently pet foods have become a better business than baby foods. Furthermore where they have to deal with human beings Americans seek to escalate the role element at the expense of affect, so that human relations become externalized into what money can buy, machines can manipulate, or power can control (Hsu 1974*b*).

The result is that Americans have given themselves a most dynamic society in which progress, improvements, creativity and change are constants. But theirs is also a society where T groups, Esalin, Maharishi and Maharaj Ji, drugs to expand inner consciousness, psychoanalysis, horoscopes, divorce and violence will become increasingly popular as affect among humans becomes increasingly scarce or useless. They will need to move inward to explore their own inner selves or outward to conquer new worlds to control scarce sources for PSH. Thus the American individual, in his inevitable search for PSH, cannot but escalate over the generations the mobile, dynamic and expansionist tendencies already extant in his social organization and cultural heritage, unless some dramatic and fundamental changes occur in the process.

With the PSH formulation I was able to identify *iemoto* as the most basic Japanese secondary grouping, and develop it as a new key to understanding Japanese characteristics in the arts, education and government as well as in religion, militarism and industry (Hsu 1975). A comparative study of the PSH patterns among the Jews of North Metropolitan Chicago and of Istanbul, Turkey, was done by Mark Glazer from 1971 to 1972 (Glazer 1973). His findings provide limited support to the thesis that the pattern of PSH is positively correlated with behavior (Glazer 1973, pp. 169–74).

In my PSH formulation the existence of the Freudian unconscious and preconscious is not denied; they are acknowledged (as layers seven and six in my psychosociogram or PSG) but I think it is unnecessary to take them into account for us to understand the behavior patterns of a majority of normally functioning members of any society. Gravitation also exists in our universe, but have social scientists found it necessary to build their theories around it?

LOOKING AHEAD

Understanding one's culture. It seems to me that the most important need in our profession is for the conscientious and systematic understanding of the anthropologist's own culture as a prerequisite to ethnographic work, especially work in psychological anthropology. Students in elementary psychology are taught various errors in perception due to illusion. A good deal of evidence besides that revealed by the old Muller-Lyer test leaves no doubt as to the distortion effect of optical illusion, the McCulloch effect, simultaneous contrast and afterimages. The Edgar Rubin devices for distinguishing between figures and the spaces between figures are classic and well known to all students in introductory psychology.

This elementary lesson in psychology has yet to be driven home to anthropologists, especially psychological anthropologists. We never see the tribe or village we study with a truly open mind. The mind of the ethnographer is invariably cluttered with assumptions about his own society and culture which are bound to distort his observation. For example, coming from a culture where the kinship web is small and temporary, American students cannot but be overly impressed by the strength of kinship in Hindu India. Having been raised in a society where the kinship web is very extensive, I naturally saw kinship in India as of far less importance (Hsu 1963). Starting from Europe where science and rationality were held to be the accepted and only true standard of "civilized" behavior, Malinowski could not but see magic as an outside element filling the gap of science. Having come from another cultural background in which magic, religion, custom and empirical knowledge are a traditional mixture, I was able to see that the Malinowskian distinction between magic and science is nowhere a clear-cut reality in the minds of the majority (even in the West) and that modern Western science and scientific practices, if they are to become part of a majority of human societies, must compete with traditional customs (Hsu 1952a, pp. 4–8, 97–118). Furthermore, while making no claim to judge the subjects of their study by the standards of their own cultures, many anthropologists cannot but reveal that is precisely what they do, as I have demonstrated after a cursory examination of books by Beals and Hoijer, Herskovits, Murdock, Forde, Hoebel, Levi-Strauss and Keesing (Hsu 1969, pp. 53–54).

Offhand or implicit comparisons are scientifically useless, and possibly even dangerous. They may be full of unintended ethnocentrism. What we need is to make explicit and systematic comparison between the subject of our study and the society and culture of which the ethnographer is a part. In this way the student puts himself on record and can rationally scrutinize the results of his comparison. He will also enable others better to judge the factual or logical bases of his comparison and its merits or demerits.

Of course not every present anthropologist has studied his or her own society and culture. That simply is one of our professional defects that needs remedying. All psychoanalysts have to undergo analysis. Why should not the students of anthropology, especially psychological anthropology, analyze their own cultures which necessarily influence their perceptions of the world around them?

The need for comparative approach. When *Americans and Chinese* first appeared (1953) it was not even reviewed in the *American Anthropologist,* which was not so much the fault of any one editor as of the *conscience collective* of American anthropology as a whole. The decision of an individual editor at the time must be seen as reflecting the *feeling* of most anthropologists that *Americans and Chinese* was not anthropology. The same thing happened with *Clan, Caste and Club* (1963). I am glad to see lately a more active interest among my colleagues in studying America, but find some of them still treat it in the same way they did "primitive" societies before, without intersocietal comparison (Hsu-Balzer and Hsu 1975, pp. 20–23).[21]

Beyond gaining explicit knowledge of their own cultures, psychological anthropologists must insist on the comparative approach. Here we should distinguish comparative studies from cross-cultural studies. Cross-cultural studies, which deal with a few variables in a large number of societies, are only one kind of comparative study. They use statistical techniques and computers and are usually done in the privacy of offices and laboratories. By comparative studies I refer to those involving in-depth field work among two or more societies and cultures, and the results of which may form the basis for cross-cultural exercises later.

All anthropological field work involves perception on the part of the fieldworker. He or she can employ tests and take head counts, but unless we can reduce all statements about human behavior to quantitative terms (so that we can speak of thirty-two degrees of oppression according to the Secrest Scale or Strodtbeck Meter, and so on), our qualitative statements about human affairs must be comparative to have any meaning at all. There are no exact measurements to enable us to see more life in absolute terms. How do we measure despotism? How do we measure sibling rivalry? How many fights or quarrels or lawsuits must we see for a relationship to be termed rivalrous? We must realize that despotism and rivalry are relatively easier entities to gauge than others such as religiosity or prejudice.

Furthermore, even after we have obtained quantitative figures, their interpretation is often a matter of opinion based on feelings or beliefs rather than of rationality and reality. For example, do we know the optimum or acceptable unemployment rate in the U.S. since it has

21. Some publishers seemed to reflect a reluctance toward the comparative approach similar to that among some anthropologists. When I first offered half of *Americans and Chinese* in 1951 in manuscript form to a publisher its managing editor asked if I would eliminate the Chinese material in it and confine myself to the United States. In fact he offered to publish both if I would separate it into two books, one on China and the other on the United States. Just about that time I sold a piece to *Parents' Magazine* comparing Chinese and American ways in adolescence. While the article was in press, the Korean war broke out. Thereupon the magazine's editor informed me that my article was "killed." The magazine could not afford any cultural comparison in which the American way did not come out all superior.

been raised from three percent in the fifties to five percent in the sixties? Can we definitely measure the goodness of a particular government by the number of inmates in its jails? In these and other matters we must depend on comparison of ethnographic data from different societies to make our conclusions about any one of them scientifically useful. Those anthropologists who feel the pressure from the physical sciences for quantification and computerization should remind themselves that, in spite of their use of dazzling formulae and sophisticated hardware, our celebrated economists give us contradictory answers when our national and individual needs for sound remedies are most urgent. Sophisticated methodology and manipulative techniques will lead us nowhere unless we first understand the significance of the variables we are dealing with.

What we most need in comparative studies is more cooperation among anthropologists in investigating those psychosocial attributes most relevant to our understanding of behavioral characteristics and social and cultural development. The investigation should be carried out on different levels. For example, how long do different kinds of affective relationships last in American society as compared with Japanese or Alorese society? Are the comparative lengths of such relationships correlated with the rates of continuity in their role relationships? What is the effect of parent-child exclusiveness or inclusiveness on the performance of pupils in schools?

The problem of intellectual prejudice. Ethnocentrism is not confined to any human society and culture. However, Western ethnocentrism (of which American ethnocentrism is a part) has a peculiarity not shared by others. Universally, ethnocentrism means a firm belief that one's own culture is superior. The ethnocentrism of Westerners in general and Americans in particular means also that whatever makes their ways superior should be the standard for all mankind. That is why all the world's missionaries are Westerners. From that kind of ethnocentrism it becomes easy for Western scholars to assume the universal validity of their findings. In the physical sciences this approach may be admissible, but in the social and psychological sciences it can lead only to blind alleys and absurdities. I have explained the latter in some detail, including the obsession with economic determinism, the mistaken belief in the changing American character and the absurd notion that instincts propel men to violence, war and self-destruction (Hsu 1973*b*, pp. 1–19; 1973*c*, pp. 4–14). Being products of a culture where affect among humans is scarce, even the anthropologists from it tend to give undue importance to substitutes for human relations such as gods and objects and mobility or the idea of change. They fail to see that many of their working hypotheses are expressions of people in search of more certain sources of Psychosocial Homeostasis.

Pointing out some mistakes by a science or by some of its practitioners is far from having found the means for correcting either. For example, in spite of public outcry and government efforts against racism and prejudice, my fellow social scientists have yet seriously to consider my propositon that extreme individualism is at the root of both (Hsu 1961, pp. 220–25).

One of my colleagues and a good friend often tells me that I am a man who has found his culture. I do not entirely agree with him. I am a man born and raised in one society who has operated reasonably well role-wise in another society where roles have escalated at the expense of affect. But beyond my family and my small circle of friends, I am very much in search of continuous affective relationships among my fellow scholars, and especially in need of cooperation with those who care, in the hope of turning my adopted society and culture around, even by a minor degree.

REFERENCES CITED

Barth, F.
  1971   Role Dilemmas and Father-Son Dominance in Middle Eastern Kinship Systems. In *Kinship and Culture*, ed. F. L. K. Hsu, pp. 87–95. Chicago, Ill.: Aldine Publishing Co.

Benedict, R.
  1934   *Patterns of Culture*. Boston, Mass.: Houghton, Mifflin & Co.

Berndt, R. M.
  1971   Social Relationships in Two Australian Aboriginal Societies of Arnheim Land: Gunwinggu and Murngin. In *Kinship and Culture*, ed. F. L. K. Hsu, pp. 158–245. Chicago, Ill.: Aldine Publishing Co.

Browne, C. R.
  1929   *Maori Witchery: Native Life in New Zealand*. London, England: J. M. Dent & Sons, Ltd.

Chen, T. S. and Shryock, J. K.
  1932   The Chinese Family: Organization, Names, and Kinship Terms. *American Anthropologist* 29(3): 623–69.

Cleckley, H.
  1964   *The Maks of Sanity*, 4th ed. St. Louis, Mo.: C. V. Mosby Co.

Edgerton, R. B.
  1971   An Examination of Hsu's "Brother-Brother" postulate in Four East African

Societies. In *Kinship and Culture,* ed. F. L. K. Hsu, pp. 318–36. Chicago, Ill.: Aldine Publishing Co.

Evans-Pritchard, E. E.
1937 *Witchcraft, Oracles and Magic Among the Azande.* London, England: Oxford University Press.

Eyles, Margaret L.
1922 *The Woman in the Little House.* London, England: Grant Richards.

Fei, H. T.
1936 The Problems of Chinese Relationship Systems. *Monumenta Serica* (Peking) 2(1):125–48.

Feng, H. Y.
1937 Chinese Kinship System. *Harvard Journal of Asiatic Studies* 2(2).

Fernandez, J. W.
1971 Bantu Brotherhood: Symmetry, Socialization and Ultimate Choice in Two Bantu Cultures. In *Kinship and Culture,* ed. F. L. K. Hsu. Chicago, Ill.: Aldine Publishing Co.

Firth, R.
1929 *Primitive Economics of the New Zealand Maori.* London, England: Routledge and Kegan Paul.

1954 The Sociology of "Magic" in Tikopia. *Sociologus* 14:113–15.

Glazer, M.
1973 Psychological Intimacy Among the Jews of North Metropolitan Chicago and the Sephardic Jews of Istanbul, Turkey. Ph.D. dissertation, Northwestern University, Evanston, Ill.

Hamilton, C.
1940 *The English Woman.* London, England: Longmans, Green & Co.

Hart, H.
1931 *The Technique of Social Progress.* New York: H. Holt & Co.

Hobhouse, L. T., Wheeler, G. C., and Ginsberg, M.
1915 *The Material Culture and Social Institutions of the Simpler Peoples.* London, England: Chapman & Hall, Ltd.

Hogbin, I. H.
1934 Law and Order in Polynesia. New York: Harcourt, Brace & Co.

Howard, A.
1971 Some Implications of Dominant Kinship Relationships in Fiji and Rotuma. In *Kinship and Culture,* ed. F. L. K. Hsu, pp. 96–105. Chicago, Ill.: Aldine Publishing Co.

Hsu, F. L. K.
1942 *The English Wife,* unpublished.

1943 Incentives to Work in Primitive Communities. *American Sociological Review,* December:638–42.

1947 On a Technique for Studying Relationship Terms. *American Anthropologist* 49:618–24.

1948 *Under the Ancestors' Shadow: Chinese Culture and Personality.* New York: Columbia University Press.

1949 Suppression versus Repression. *Psychiatry* 12(3).

1952a *Religion, Science, and Human Crises: A Study on China in Transition and Its Implication for the West.* London: Routledge and Kegan Paul.

1952b Anthropology or Psychiatry. *Southwestern Journal of Anthropology* 8:227–50.

1953 *Americans and Chinese: Two Ways of Life.* New York: Abelard-Schuman, Inc.

1954a Cultural Factors. In *Economic Development: Principles and Patterns,* ed. H. F. Williamson and J. A. Buttrick, pp. 318–64. New York: Prentice-Hall, Inc.

1954b *Aspects of Culture and Personality* (ed.). New York: Abelard-Schuman, Inc.

1960 A Neglected Aspect of Witchcraft Studies. *Journal of American Folklore* 73, 287:35–38.

1961 *Psychological Anthropology: Approaches to Culture and Personality.* Homewood, Ill.: Dorsey Press.

1963 *Clan, Caste and Club: A Comparative Study of Chinese, Hindu and American Ways of Life.* Princeton, N.J.: Van Nostrand & Co.

1965 The Effect of Dominant Kinship Relationships on Kin and Nonkin Behavior: A Hypothesis. *American Anthropologist* 67:638–61.

1966 Dominant Kin Relationships and Dominant Ideas. *American Anthropologist* 68:997–1004.

1969 *The Study of Literate Civilizations.* New York: Holt, Rinehart and Winston.

1970 *Americans and Chinese: Purpose and Fulfillment in Great Civilizations.* Revised and enlarged edition of *Americans and Chinese: Two Ways of Life,* 1953. New York: Natural History Press.

1971a Psychosocial Homeostasis and *Jen:* Conceptual Tools for Advancing Psychological Anthropology. *American Anthropologist* 73(1):23–44.

1971b *Under the Ancestors' Shadow.* Stanford, Calif.: Stanford University Press.

1971c *Kinship and Culture* (ed. and contributor).

1973a Methodology of Studying Literate Civilizations. In *A Handbook of Method in Cultural Anthropology,* ed. Naroll and Cohen, pp. 527–36. New York: Columbia University Press.

1973b Prejudice and Its Intellectual Effect on American Anthropology: An Ethnographic Report. *American Anthropologist* 75:1–19.

1973c Kinship is the Key. *The Center Magazine* 6:4–41.

1973d *Religion, Science and Human Crises: A Study of China's Transition and its Implications for the West.* Westport, Conn.: Greenwood Press, Publishers.

1974a Kinship, Psychosocial Homeostasis (PSH) and Learning. In *Cultural Factors in Learning and Education,* pp. 163–76. Fifth Symposium on Learning, Western Washington State College, Bellingham, Washington.

1974b Individual Fulfillment, Social Stability and Cultural Progress. A paper presented at a Multi-Disciplinary Symposium on Social Change and Social Character, Oct. 23–24, University of Delaware, Newark, Delaware.

1975 *Iemoto: The Heart of Japan.* Cambridge, Mass.: Schenkman Publishing Co.

Hsu-Balzer, E. and Hsu, F. L. K.

1975 The Anthropology of American Life Is in Need of the Cross-Cultural Perspective. *Reviews in Anthropology* 2(1):13–24.

Hsu-Balzer, E., Balzer, R. and Hsu, F. L. K.
   1974   *China Day By Day*. New Haven, Conn.: Yale University Press.
Hunt, R. C.
   1971   Components of Relationships in the Family: A Mexican Village. In *Kinship and Culture*, ed. F. L. K. Hsu, pp. 106–43. Chicago, Ill.: Aldine Publishing Co.
Jastrow, J.
   1940   *Freud: His Dream and Sex Theories* (first published under the title, *The House That Freud Built*). New York: Tower Books.
Kardiner, A.
   1939   *The Individual and His Society*. New York: Columbia University Press.
   1945   *The Psychological Frontiers of Society*. New York: Columbia University Press.
Kittredge, G. L.
   1929   *Witchcraft in Old and New England*. Cambridge, Mass.: Harvard University Press.
Kopytoff, I.
   1971   The Suku of the Congo: An Ethnographic Test of Hsu's Hypotheses. In *Kinship and Culture*, ed. F. L. K. Hsu, pp. 69–86. Chicago, Ill.: Aldine Publishing Co.
Kroeber, A. L.
   1948   *Anthropology*. New York: Harcourt, Brace and World.
Linton, R.
   1936   *The Study of Man*. New York: Appleton-Century-Crofts.
Malinowski, B.
   1944   *A Scientific Theory of Cultures and Other Essays*, ed. H. Cairns. Chapel Hill, N.C.: The University of North Carolina Press.
Mead, M.
   1928   *Coming of Age in Samoa*. New York: William Morrow & Co.
   1931   *Growing Up in New Guinea*. London, England: G. Routledge & Sons.
   1935   *Sex and Temperament in Three Primitive Societies*. New York: William Morrow & Co.
   1942   *And Keep Your Powder Dry*. New York: William Morrow & Co.
Miller, N.
   1937   *Primitive Economics in the Light of Consistency in the Mores, in Studies in the Science of Society*, ed. G. P. Murdock, pp. 423–44. New Haven, Conn.: Yale University Press.
Moodey, R. W.
   1971   Masculinity and Femininity Among Students in Delhi and Jaipur. Ph.D. thesis, University of Chicago, Chicago, Ill.
Nadel, S. F.
   1935   Witchcraft and Sorcery. In *Africa* 8(4).
Newell, W. H.
   1971   Hsu and the External System. In *Kinship and Culture*, ed. F. L. K. Hsu, pp. 271–83. Chicago, Ill.: Aldine Publishing Co.
Rice, M. S.
   1939   *Working-Class Wives*. Harmondsworth, England: Penguin Books.

Rohlen, T. P.

1971 Father-Son Dominance: Tikopia and China. In *Kinship and Culture*, ed. F. L. K. Hsu, pp. 144–57. Chicago, Ill.: Aldine Publishing Co.

Strodtbeck, F.

1971 Sex Role Identity and Dominant Kinship Relationships. In *Kinship and Culture*, ed. F. L. K. Hsu, pp. 291–317. Chicago, Ill.: Aldine Publishing Co.

Strodtbeck, F., Moodey, R. W., and Yu, E. S. H.

1974 Dominant Dyads in Hindu and Confucian Families: The Uneasy Case Relating Unconscious Masculinity and Pragmatism. In *Comparative Family and Fertility Research*, ed. H. Y. Tien and F. D. Bean, pp. 90–98. Leiden: E. J. Brill.

Summers, M.

1926 *The History of Witchcraft and Demonology*. London, England: K. Paul, Trench, Trubner & Co., Ltd.

Tatje, T. A.

1974 Mother-Daughter Dyadic Dominance in Black American Kinship. Ph.D. dissertation, Northwestern University, Evanston, Ill.

Thurnwald, R.

1932 *Economics in Primitive Communities* (published for International Institute of African Languages and Cultures by H. Milford). London, England: Oxford University Press.

Wallace, A. F. G.

1971 Handsome Lake and the Decline of the Iroquois Matriarchate. In *Kinship and Culture*, ed. F. L. K. Hsu, pp. 367–76. Chicago, Ill.: Aldine Publishing Co.

White, L.

1969 *The Science of Culture*, rev. ed. New York: Farrar, Straus and Giroux, Inc.

Wilkinson, H. P.

1926 *The Family in Classical China*. London, England: Kelly and Walsh, Ltd.

Woodside, M.

1946 Courtship and Mating in an Urban Community. *Eugenics Review* 38(157): 29–39.

The Author

LOUISE SCHAUBEL SPINDLER was born in Chicago, Illinois where her father had been born in 1854. His German father and French mother were descendants of immigrants to America seeking religious freedom. They had come to Illinois from Pennsylvania and established a farm that included the area that later became Oakpark, near Chicago. When she was three years old the family went West to southern California—open, beautiful country in the 1920s and 1930s. She spent summers near played-out gold mines in the Sierras in which her father was interested. In this special milieu she came to know and understand highly individualistic and diverse personalities. And nature, at its best in the Sierras, then and later became a source of inspiration and solace for her.

She moved to the middle West before her college years and attended Carroll College in Wisconsin, majored in romantic literature and drama, and experienced the special attention one is likely to receive only in a small school. After graduating from college she taught high school English and literature in northern Wisconsin where she met and married George Spindler who was teaching biology and general science. After World War II she came into contact with anthropology through Scudder Mckeel at the University of Wisconsin which she attended only part time in order to be with their young daughter, Sue, during her formative years. She continued her part time graduate career at U.C.L.A. and at Stanford, obtaining her Ph.D. in 1956—the first granted by the department. She owes a great deal to her unusual mother, Cora Field, who supported her in every way in her attempt to combine a scholarly career and family life.

She has always been interested in the personal autobiographic aspects of actors and persons in literature and drama. This interest was transferred to anthropology and bore fruit in her development of an expressive autobiographic interview technique applied to a sample of Menomini women in various states of acculturative adaptation, and in her development of the concept, latescence. She also brought concepts of role and self, stemming from G. H. Mead, into the analysis of field data.

In collaborative field work with George Spindler, besides the innovations mentioned above, she has been particularly influential in calling for equal samples of males and females, thus exhibiting her conviction that the two sexes do adapt differently and that the world view of women in different cultural contexts is poorly understood. She has been mainly responsible for the elicitation of data from women informants on matters such as witchcraft and the personal aspects of sex roles. These were data that would be difficult or impossible for a male in the field to attempt to elicit from women.

She is at present Research Associate and Lecturer in the Department of Anthropology at Stanford University, and series editor with George Spindler for Holt, Rinehart and Winston.

She has published collaboratively with George Spindler on male and female adaptations in culture change, modal personality techniques and the study of acculturation, psychology in anthropology, the Instrumental Activities Inventory, a joint book on the Menomini, *Dreamers without Power,* and a text in cultural anthropology with Alan Beals and George Spindler. She has published independently on the changing roles and perceptions of Menomini women, witchcraft in Menomini acculturation, on culture change and modernization, and a recent chapter on the Menomini in the new handbook of North America, Smithsonian Institution.

This Chapter

In this chapter Louise Spindler provides a case study of methodological and theoretical development in the work of George and Louise Spindler on psychocultural change and urbanization from 1948 to 1974. Many of the problems grappled with by other workers are represented in their work and the case study is placed in this context.

She deals briefly with early attempts by others to deal with this problem area then moves to the beginning of the Spindlers' field work in 1948 with the Menomini Indians of Wisconsin. She discusses various research strategies including the use of the Rorschach, the expressive autobiographic interview, the sociocultural index schedule, and ethnographic observation. She describes an attempt to produce an analytic model for Rorschach data that avoids some interpretive problems and then moves to her own attempt to interrelate goals, roles, values and perceptual structure in the study of Menomini women adapting to cultural change.

The last part of the chapter is concerned with the development of a new theoretical model, and a related technique, the Instrumental Activities Inventory, its use among the Blood Indians of Alberta, Canada, the Mistassini Cree and in urbanizing German villages, and with the movement in the Spindlers' work toward a cognitive, social action model.

This chapter provides an example of how anthropologists beginning in the 1940s and 1950s with the "somewhat inchoate model" referred to by Mel Spiro in his chapter have applied it to their research problems and have adjusted to new discoveries and interests and to the changing socio-intellectual milieu of our times. Both of the Spindlers have a strong sociological as well as anthropological and psychological orientation and this is evident at a number of points, such as in the attention to role and social interaction, especially in Louise Spindler's work, and the development of the IAI model and eliciting technique, which focuses on the nexus of social action and cognitive organization.

G.D.S.

5   *Researching the Psychology of Culture Change and Urbanization*

LOUISE SPINDLER

Worldwide urbanization and industrialization are bringing hundreds of small, technologically and politically emergent societies under the pressures of heretofore unfelt new and upsetting problems of adaptation.[1] The era of urbanization and industrialization was preceded by and still intermingles with the era of culture change and acculturation brought about by the dramatic expansion of western culture during the nineteenth century. Anthropologists have become more and more interested in these processes. The conditions leading to demoralization and disintegration, versus those associated with successful adaptation, are underlying foci of attention, though not always explicitly stated. At some undefined point the study of acculturation and culture change

1. This chapter has been substantially revised from a paper published in *Psychological Anthropology*, ed. Thomas R. Williams (The Hague: Mouton, 1975).

grades off into the study of modernization and urbanization. Psychological processes have always been included, but with varying degrees of emphasis and adequacy of formulation.

The earlier attempts to deal with these kinds of processes focused on the specific cultural traits that were selected or excluded during the cultural contact situation, rather than on the psychological mechanisms involved. The major part of the "Memorandum for the Study of Acculturation," sponsored by the Social Science Research Council in 1936, was devoted to a scheme for the analysis of cultural traits (Redfield et al. 1936). Under the section on "psychological mechanisms," the individual is the unit of analysis, with emphasis on his personality and social status. The equation of the individual with psychological process leaves the problem at an idiosyncratic level. This equation was one reason for the rejection of psychologizing by some anthropologists; they saw such a focus as a form of reductionism from the cultural level that was likely to lead nowhere (G. and L. Spindler 1963, p. 521). The 1936 memo does, however, include a form of psychology as a major dimension and indicates that anthropologists interested in cultural change felt the need to move toward a more adequate formulation of the psychological process even at that early date.

Anthropologists tried again in 1954, under the auspices of the Social Science Research Council to devise an orderly approach to the study of acculturation (SSRC 1954). In the 1954 memorandum, individuals, as such, were not included, but "intercultural roles" were. This memorandum seems more advanced in its use of psychological concepts, as it includes ideological, motivational, and perceptual sets as factors in role-playing. The frame of reference is, however, still cultural. As the process of acculturation is conceived, a coherent, organized system (culture) responds, through people, to the impact of another system.

This orientation has contemporary overtones. A major criticism to be leveled against it, however, is that when the cultural system begins to disintegrate and individuation takes place, the formulation is no longer adequate. This frame of reference cannot explain why or how the system disintegrates unless neopsychological formulations, such as "anxiety about the efficacy of traditional solutions," or "striving for prestige in emergent status systems" are utilized. Both the 1936 and 1954 memos explicitly acknowledge the existence of a psychological dimension, but both appear to place a heavy burden upon the culture concept, often requiring reification (G. and L. Spindler 1963, pp. 520-24).

A. Irving Hallowell was one of the first anthropologists to design his research on acculturative processes with the focus on psychological adaptation. In his well-known research with the Ojibwa (1952) he utilized psychological tools and concepts to relate psychological processes to changes in culture as people adapted to changes wrought in the conditions of their existence by the impact of Euro-American culture, economics, and political power.

The problems George Spindler and I have encountered over the past twenty-five years in our research are shared by many workers interested in the psychology of culture change. A variety of strategies used in combination with a variety of data will be covered. Each model and strategy we employed was built with knowledge acquired about the shortcomings of earlier models and strategies. We feel after building models and devising new techniques the anthropologist should return to the field to retest and revise his creations. The publications referred to begin with "An Experimental Design in the Study of the Psychology of Culture Change" (G. Spindler and W. Goldschmidt 1952) and end with *Dreamers Without Power: The Menomini Indians* (G. and L. Spindler 1971), and *Burgbach: Urbanization and Identity in a German Village* (G. Spindler 1973).

AN EXPERIMENTAL DESIGN

The specific aim during the first periods of research, starting in 1948 with out first study of the Menomini Indians of Wisconsin, has been to find a way to relate the manifest aspects of socioeconomic and cultural life to the manner in which people in change perceive and respond to the world about them. Our interest, however, was never in the individual as such, but rather in the shared processes of psychocultural adaptation. The Rorschach projective technique was used in the first phases of the Menomini study as an expression of perceptual structure.[2] A sociocultural schedule with 23 indexes and 180 coded items ranging from the mode of living—house type, income—to items on the belief system (G. Spindler 1955) represented the manifest sociocultural dimension. In a sense, both the Rorschach responses and sociocultural indices could be considered products of an individual's perceptual organization. It was necessary, however, to keep them rigorously separated for analytic purposes. With our aims in mind and with these

2. The term "perceptual structure" is used to mean the way in which an individual organizes his perceptions of the world about him. We are, of course, hedging a bit here, for we go beyond this meaning when we infer emotional states. However, even here, we are concerned with the way these states appear to influence perception. Also, since perception in the sense used here requires cognition, or is the first step in cognition, we might claim the Rorschach reveals cognitive structure and process, and sometimes we verge in this direction.

particular techniques decided upon, George Spindler and Walter Goldschmidt devised a model that was an approximation of an experimental design (Spindler and Goldschmidt 1952). The focus was on the covariance between processes. The four statistically validated (G. Spindler 1955) levels of acculturation constituted what may be regarded as the independent variable and the patterns of perceptual structure derived from statistical treatment of Rorschach indices the dependent variable.

We now regard the concept of "levels" of acculturation as too passive. In *Dreamers without Power* (1971) we analyze the acculturative "levels" as forms of coping, as adaptive strategies that deal actively with the situation created by the confrontation between two highly divergent, in fact incongruent, psychocultural systems—the Menomini and the North American-European. "Acculturative levels" infers a kind of passive assimilation into the latter by the former. While assimilation did occur, and will continue to occur, it is not all that did or will happen. Each of our "levels" of acculturation were represented by groups that we termed sociocultural categories. Each of these resisted or adopted, or adopted only partially, the dominant culture, or created new combinations from old and new. The shift in interpretation can be seen clearly in the difference between any of our publications in the fifties and this most recent one (1971) on the Menomini. It is interesting that the change in stance is not solely a result of new scientific knowledge or accumulated theory. It is in part an adaptation of the anthropologist to a change in the tenor of the times. The terminology in this chapter must fall short of a full expression of these trends, for if it were reformulated, it would not be an accurate representation of what we actually did. This is a part of the case study we are presenting of our work.

In the initial stages of designing our research, we were heavily influenced by Hallowell's study of the Ojibwa (1952). In this pioneer study, Hallowell isolated three Ojibwa groups representing different levels of acculturation (terms as used then). Through analyses of Rorschach protocols utilizing composite group profiles comprised of averages of special Rorschach determinants he found continuity of the same basic psychological pattern through three stages of acculturation—with a persistent core of generic traits which could be identified as Ojibwa (1951, p. 38).

In our research with the Menomini we were able to isolate four sociocultural groups on the basis of religious identification (G. Spindler 1955). Statistical tests were applied to socioeconomic and cultural indices, such as house type, education, use of medical facilities, etc., to validate a posited continuum of acculturative adaptation running from a native-oriented through transitional to two acculturated groups. The

Rorschach technique was then applied to a sample of sixty-eight adult males drawn from the four sociocultural categories in the continuum and to twelve white males living on the reservation. The females were dealt with later (L. Spindler 1962) and compared to the males (L. and G. Spindler 1958). The differences between the sociocultural categories, on the basis of Rorschach as well as sociocultural indices, proved to be statistically significant, numerous, and consistent. The two ends of the adaptive continuum, most unlike in the sociocultural dimension, were most unlike in the psychological dimension. The sociocultural continuum and the distribution of Rorschach responses were not, however, isomorphic. There was evidence, for example, of considerable persistence in certain native-oriented perceptual patterns through the transitional categories. The highly socioculturally deviant Peyote group was also differentiated more frequently in Rorschach scores from every other Menomini group than any other acculturative category was. An intensive study was therefore made of the Peyotists, with collections of visions, autobiographic interviews, conversion experiences and extensive observations of both ritual and everyday behavior (G. Spindler 1952; G. and L. Spindler 1971, pp. 94–140). It was clear that the cult represented a systematic deviation, a term developed by E. M. Lemert (1951). The psychological deviation, as revealed by Rorschach responses, is expressed in ways that are strikingly parallel to the unique directives and behaviors that distinguish the Peyote Cult as a special group within the sociocultural continuum. It is the only Menomini category in which human movement responses (and they express a ruminative quality) exceed the animal movement responses, where introspective responses are numerous, and where overt, relatively uncontrolled emotions are displayed in Rorschach responses. The Rorschach responses, the peyote ritual, and peyote belief system are highly integrated—virtually expressions of each other. The fantasy expressed in their responses revolves about the relation of the individual to the supernatural. These fantasies also express deep anxiety and self-doubt—attitudes revealed in the autobiographical interviews and in behaviors and beliefs in the ritual content. (This analysis is given complete expression in *Dreamers Without Power* [1971].) These kinds of relationships between perceptual organization and behavior patterns, we felt, were interesting and offered important clues for further research.

Methodologically speaking, even without interpretation of the presumed psychological meaning of Rorschach scores, this pattern of deviation and differentiation among all the categories appears to tell us something about the covariance of psychological and sociocultural process in acculturative adaptation. We could posit that changes in external behaviors and symbols representing behavior during the acculturative process are paralleled by changes in the perceptual structure representative of each group, but there were significant deviations from this paralleling.

Perhaps we should have stopped here. However, after making the questionable validity of many standard interpretive hypotheses applied to Rorschach scores explicit, we proceeded to apply them consistently to the already demonstrated differences between sociocultural groups as these seemed to at least offer clues to the meaning of these complex relationships (G. and L. Spindler 1963, pp. 527–28). In general, the application of these interpretive hypotheses produced results highly congruent with ethnographic observations, and also led us to new hypotheses that we could, and did, investigate in the field. Whether we would have been wiser to forego the Rorschach, given its problematic character, is a moot question. Given the assumption current when we began using it—that the whole personality was the object of study—it was a reasonable, perhaps inevitable, choice.

COMMENTS ON THE RORSCHACH

Anthropologists using concepts such as world view, basic premises, or personality must adduce these from what informants do and say in cultural context. Unless the researcher has data derived by techniques external to the particular cultural system, his approach is culture bound, almost wholly idiographic, and emic if he has used native views as direct data in his approach.[3] He has no way of generalizing. Using the approach of the ethnoscientist, the fieldworker can only collect emic responses to culturally phrased questions. The ethnoscientist's aim is to get to the point where he can predict what the informant's response will be in reference to a specific domain being investigated within a cultural system. In all of these kinds of strategies, the old circularity trap becomes a problem, insofar as cognitive structure and process is of interest, as it was in a different way for the early workers in the field of culture and personality. All of these approaches are teleological in that the

3. We make a distinction, often overlooked, between an "emic" approach, referring to ethnography based on native views and classifications of reality, and an idiographic approach, referring to the analysis of interrelationships within a cultural system. Both are concerned with the unique qualities of a given culture or personalities-in-culture and are not direct contributions to generalizing, or nomothetic science (until they are so exploited), but they are not the same thing.

researcher derives cognitive or perceptual products from cultural products. Culture, cognitive and perceptual structures become expressions of each other.

We decided in the early phases of our research that in order to elicit relevant forms of psychological response we must use an instrument external to the culture being studied; one that would allow the respondent to make a novel response not anticipated by a cultural pattern. This is essentially the problem of the cross-cultural cognitive psychologist. Our approach at that point began to become etic and nomothetic. The Rorschach furnishes stimuli from outside the culture. We may not know exactly what the responses to these stimuli mean. But when consistent changes in Rorschach patterning occur in different sociocultural categories, we surmise differential psychological adaptations are being expressed by different perceptual patterns. We can then try to figure out what these differential adaptations are, using categories meaningful across cultural domains. At the same time, the Rorschach approach is emic (Lindzey 1961) to the extent that it elicits the subjective reality of the informants in a specific cultural milieu in a way impossible with objective-type schedules and questionnaires.

Our use of the Rorschach was quite tangential to the conventional applications of the Rorschach as an instrument for personality assessment of individuals in our own society. We used standardized but culturally ambiguous stimuli to elicit culturally variant responses. The results are cryptic and often difficult to assess, but seem to furnish data sufficiently abstracted from the highly unique, emic, cultural-relevant responses (as those in life histories) to permit controlled comparisons of culture cases.

The Rorschach activates a set of complex processes which are little understood. Responses to the Rorschach are products of a person's cognitive-perceptual process, weighted by bioemotional factors, influenced by situational definitions, and formed within a cultural milieu. Our position has been that they can be used to detect whether the psychological (perceptual) organization of persons, and groups of persons, is changing in correspondence with change in the sociocultural conditions of existence, even though their specific meaning can be only partially or ambiguously inferred, and requires extensive contextualization for an extension of meaning.

Since the Rorschach interpretations were formulated with implicit assumptions held in Western culture, one must be extremely cautious about using standard qualitative interpretations. There are, however, many levels of interpretation possible. It is possible, for example, to examine the parts of the inkblots used by the informant in percept formation. Some, for example, create integrated wholes. Others dwell on minute, isolated details, white space, or projections from the body of the inkblot, rather than the inner details. It is also possible to use the content of responses to adduce areas of preoccupation or special concern. Or one can do symbolic analyses. The most problematic level is one requiring the inference of emotional states. But this level is most problematic regardless of the technique used. We felt it was better to regularize our observations and interpretive procedures than to use the insight method that seemed to characterize much personality and culture work at the time. And as stated, for certain analytic purposes we attempted to eliminate or reduce this level of interpretation to the absolute minimum.

Both justified and unjustified criticisms have been leveled at studies using Rorschach results. In some cases the criticisms stem from misuse of the tool and the data produced by it. Statistical problems have dogged the use of Rorschach data from the start. We pride ourselves on being among the first to use a rigorous statistical design employing probability tests of differences in distributions, thus avoiding the problems inherent in the use of measures of central tendency as criteria of difference. Our research design also involved the use of a control group of whites, as stated, and rigorous separation of quantifiable sociocultural and psychological indices. Many Rorschach studies have been done without sufficient attention to these matters. But no test or instrument can produce results that should be regarded as *the* basic data of an anthropological study. Our work made use of the Rorschach data in conjunction with sociocultural indices, interview materials, data from participant observation, and the expressive autobiographic interview technique and above all, basic ethnography. We take pride in our ethnography, in its totality. *Dreamers without Power* expresses our ethnographic orientation perhaps better than any other single publication.

Because the expressive autobiographic interview technique afforded substantial materials on the life adjustments of a reasonably large, selected sample of informants, representing both typical and deviant adaptations within each acculturative category, it needs a few words of explanation. The expressive autobiographic interview (EAI) is a cross between a structured interview and a chronological autobiography. The respondent is asked to tell the story of his or her life, but intervention by the anthropologist at critical points relevant to special foci (i.e., value conflicts, experiences in Whiteman society, witchcraft, sex), turns the autobiography to relevant considerations and permits an economy of time not possible with the full autobiography. This technique furnishes a useful complement to Rorschach data. In cases where an individual's Rorschach pattern is radically deviant, the fieldworker can elicit data on the special kinds of environmental stimuli to which the individual has had to adapt. The technique is most successful after the anthropologist knows enough about his people and their culture to be able to identify the key points around which to center inquiries. We selected our EAI sample on the basis of Rorschach as well as sociocultural indices, thus identifying socially and psychologically deviant as well as modal individuals. (For more complete detail see L. Spindler 1952, and G. and L. Spindler 1970.)

Both the Spindlers and Hallowell, in their use of the Rorschach, committed two fallacies. One is the global fallacy and the other the jumping fallacy. They are both typical anthropological fallacies insofar as studies of the psychology of acculturation are concerned and so merit some discussion. The global fallacy may be defined as the attempt to deal with a complex holistic construct like "personality" or "perceptual structure" as a variable. This is apparent in nearly everything that has been said about the Menomini and Ojibwa. It raises rich, complex issues with respect to the covariance of psychological and sociocultural process. It also raises serious methodological problems which cannot be lightly dismissed.

The jumping fallacy may be defined, following Leonard Doob (1960), as the application of unvalidated interpretive hypotheses concerning the meaning of Rorschach scores and profiles. At times the jumping strategy had value for us. We asked: "What will happen if we set up the most parsimonious standard interpretations available in the literature on projective techniques and apply them to a sample of persons whose characteristic overt behaviors are intimately known to us?" The results seemed to us to justify the decision. The interpretations based on Rorschach scores, even at the third level—inferring emotional states—seem too congruent with our other observations to be discarded.

It is apparent we were applying a clinical, phenomenological, interpretive approach, as well as a more controlled statistical method. We were aware of the dangers of *ad hoc* reasoning and the closure tendencies we all exhibit in the search for plausibility. We attempted to control these tendencies with a rigorous research design and systematic quantitative as well as qualitative analyses. The consistent relationships between Rorschach data and sociocultural observations led us to the conviction that the Rorschach was tapping significant psychological process in depth, and with sufficient reliability to allow us to use it as a complex index of psychological process. The Rorschach seemed to work for us but we assume, in today's context, that others will remain unconvinced.

AN ATTEMPT TO PRODUCE A NEW ANALYTIC MODEL
FOR RORSCHACH DATA

In 1958, acutely aware of the disrepute into which the Rorschach had fallen, we attempted a new strategy in our efforts to reduce distortion of data. We used it in an attempt to describe differences between adult Menomini men and women in psychological adaptations to the exigencies of sociocultural change (L. and G. Spindler 1958, pp. 217–33). At that time these differences were a little studied area.

In the first phases of this analysis we discarded all conventional interpretations of the meaning of scores in analyzing the covariance of psychological process with manifest sociocultural adaptation and dealt exclusively with the concentration and dispersion of Rorschach scores in the various acculturative categories and in comparisons of males and females. By means of this approach we felt we were able to say at what point in the acculturative continuum significant changes in psychological structure occurred, whether sociocultural deviation is accompanied by psychological deviation, what differences there were between the sexes, and how relatively homogeneous various of our groups were psychologically.

The strategy may be described as follows: the four acculturative categories for males and females had been validated statistically on the basis of sociocultural indices. Statistically significant differences were found in the distribution of Rorschach indices between those categories for the men, but *not* for the women. However, significant differences were found between males and females as two whole groups without respect to acculturative categories (L. and G. Spindler 1958, p. 220). With the knowledge that psychological differences as indicated by Rorschach responses did exist between males and females in the sample, the problem became one of finding a technique that would make it possible to refine and exploit the meaning of these differences.

A modal technique applied to Tuscarora Indian Rorschachs by Anthony Wallace (1952) seemed a useful first step, despite our reservations concerning the use of any measure of central tendency. In contrast to the application of the technique by Wallace, we used a modal Rorschach profile for each sex as a measuring stick against which the Rorschach responses of males and females for each sociocultural category could be compared. We were trying to explain a phenomenon we had observed using other data manipulation techniques. We were able to identify, at a certain level of plausibility, the contribution of each sociocultural category to the modal profile for each sex and compare modal profiles for all groups.

All of the differences uncovered by the statistical tests of male-female differences were represented by the differences between the Rorschach profiles of the modal groups of males and females, and these differences were now a part of what appeared to be a meaningful gestalt. They did not appear to be the result of a fortuitous convergence of fractionated indices drawn from diverse psychological types. We were also able to say that the modal male profile was most like the modal profile of the transitional acculturative category, and that the one for the females was most like that of the native-oriented group. In a spasm of terminological proliferation we called these "psychocultural centers of gravity."

We were never satisfied with the statistical methods we employed then, and we know now that we were right. There is no way of getting around the fact that any expression of central tendency and inclusion of Rorschach profiles within a modal group rests upon assumptions about the independence of scores that are not justified. Nevertheless, the convergence of the results gained by this method with those gained by other methods remains impressive to us nearly two decades later.

For example, the modal Rorschach profile for the women is correspondent with that of the native-oriented group. It exhibits continuity throughout the acculturative continuum until the elite acculturated position is reached. At this point there is a sudden shift in modal pattern. This correlates nicely with our observations of social interaction and our interview and biographic data on how women viewed themselves. For the males the situation appeared to be the reverse, that is, the modal male profile was correspondent with an acculturated level, and exhibited sharp divergence with the native-oriented profile. Both relationships received substantial support from an examination of social and cultural materials for each person in the modal groups, contextualized within the continuum as a whole. (L. and G. Spindler 1958, pp. 226–31; L. Spindler 1956, 1962).

The danger with this kind of manipulation is that one begins to create a very complex interlocking, and potentially self-supporting analytic and inferential system. It is fun to play with the materials this way but the results should not be taken too seriously. What faith we have in them is because we maintained our anthropological values, and kept relating other observations to our statistical processing. The style of thinking, however, we still support: the integration of quantitative and qualitative data and the styles of inference related to them, the detection of interesting avenues for exploration, and the complex model of psychocultural and sociocultural adaptation itself.

ROLES, VALUES, AND PERCEPTUAL STRUCTURE INTERRELATED

Two new variables were introduced in "The Study of Menomini Women and Culture Change" (L. Spindler 1962); they were role playing behaviors and values. The previous studies had utilized relationships between sociocultural and psychological variables, but social interaction, in contrast to cultural patterning, had been de-emphasized. Symbols representing value orientations (i.e., house type, use of native medicines, etc.) had been included in the sociocultural index schedule. It seemed important now to include social interaction, in terms of role playing, as an important variable with a high potential for tying together social, cultural and psychological data. The main focus of this study was to find the relationships existing between the social (represented in interaction patterns via role playing), the cultural (represented by values), and the psychological (represented by Rorschach materials) variables during the process of culture change.

After the basic changes in these variables were determined for the representative women in each category on the acculturative continuum, the problem involved the tracing of interrelationships between the three dimensions in each of the sociocultural categories (established by means of the same statistical procedures as those used for the males) and between categories, describing *how* the shared values and value orientations of a group were implemented in role-taking and social interaction and how the perceptual structuring was or was not related to the other two dimensions. Although these dimensions in any individual are all related aspects of social behavior and perceptual-cognitive process, by treating them as separate entities it is possible to define with greater rigor which kinds of values and value orientations and what manner of role-taking is associated most directly with changes in the patterning of perceptual structuring.

The materials for value orientations and specific values were derived from expressive autobiographic interview materials (described earlier), observations of overt behaviors, and specific value preferences expressed in the sociocultural indices collected. It was found, for example, that a continuum of values (i.e. display of native objects, use of Indian medicines) was concomitant with the continuum of acculturative categories, and that a sharp break occurred between groups whose members have been identified with Menomini religious groups and those that have not (L. Spindler 1962, p. 92). Data for role-taking as mother, wife and social participant in reference groups were drawn from autobiographical materials supplemented by direct observation. The range was from the model for the conservative Menomini woman, who was a recipient of social action, interacting in a "latescent" manner (L. Spindler 1962), to the model of the elite acculturated woman who was an originator of social action.

With the data in the social, cultural, and psychological dimensions, it was possible to draw conclusions and formulate hypotheses about their interrelationships. Some correlations were statistically demonstrable. For example, "the modal perceptual structure (Rorschach) is associated with the expression of specific Menomini values," and "the two extremes of the posited acculturative continuum are distinguished by a distinct set of interrelated social, cultural and psychological attributes" (L. Spindler 1962, pp. 94–95). Other relationships were drawn mainly from autobiographical materials and were more inferential. For example, "basic attitudes towards the supernatural are crucial factors in effecting changes in the perceptual structure" (L. Spindler 1962, p. 96). And, on the basis of the results from our attempts to this point, we remained convinced that, as Fred Voget once wrote:

> The extent to which the different variables [in a socio-cultural system]; continue to form (or may need to form) an interrelated system through change phases is crucial to the understanding of structuring processes. [Voget 1971]

CONTROLLED COMPARISONS AND THE INSTRUMENTAL ACTIVITIES INVENTORY

In 1954 Fred Eggan wrote on the method of controlled comparison, which offered good leads for introducing further checks and controls for fieldworkers (Eggan 1954). The studies done by Hallowell with the Ojibwa and ourselves with the Menomini used a type of research design that might be called "comparative," in that the several sociocultural categories are compared with each other. However, neither study attempted to compare beyond the boundary of a single culture.

After completing the first phases of the Menomini study, we hypothesized the same reformulation of perceptual structure found among the most acculturated Menomini would occur in other situations where the conditions were approximately the same and Western culture was dominant. After a reconnaissance of North American Indian communities, we chose the Blood Indian Reservation in Alberta, Canada. Here we could attempt to control some of the major variables in the psychocultural adaptations of the two groups. In both cases there were the relatively isolated reservation community, the prejudicial attitudes of surrounding whites, and the unique feature of a highly productive industry using rich natural resources within the boundaries of the reservation; in the Menomini case, the lumber industry; in the Blood Indian case, cattle ranching and wheat growing. It was hypothesized that the elite Menomini represented a psychological as well as socioeconomic transformation because success, recognizable in the terms of the dominant culture, was available to them, with the possibility of identifying with the goals of this culture. Thus, we expected a similar type of adjustment process.

We knew many aspects of the old Blood Indian culture were still alive, so we posited a sizeable native-oriented or traditional group, comparable to that of the Menomini. The fact that the Blood were also Algonkian speakers was of some relevance in searching for controls and independent variables.

We used the same techniques in studying these two communities, including the Rorschach, autobiographies, interviews, a sociocultural index schedule, extensive participant observation, relevant ethnohistorical data and a new kind of eliciting technique which we devised for use in the Blood Indian research called the Instrumental Activities Inventory (IAI) to be discussed later (G. and L. Spindler 1965). Again, our aim was to compare the relationship between manifest cultural change, including changes in material culture, group membership, religious practice, subsistence, etc., and psychological adaptation, in both its perceptual-cognitive and affective dimensions. Through the use of this controlled comparative approach, some important and unanticipated kinds of data were made available.

The Blood Indian sample could, it appeared, like the Menomini be divided into categories on the basis of overt sociocultural indices. We were able to distinguish two extremes in overt acculturation—"old timers" (including some middle aged and even younger people) who spoke little English and identified with the traditional culture, and the young Blood who had attended school, spoke English more comfortably than their own language, and knew little of the old culture. The bulk of the population was, however, culturally between these two extremes at the time of our study (1958–1964).[4] Most of the Blood still speak their own language and many belong to traditional organizations, evidencing considerable cultural homogeneity. The research revealed that acculturative adaptation and socioeconomic status were not necessarily concomitant among the Blood Indians. Some men and women who were highly successful ranchers, for example, spoke their native language well and belonged to traditional societies. Rorschach data clearly indicated less difference between posited sociocultural categories than among the Menomini. Even the apparently most acculturated persons were rarely differentiated Rorschach-wise as a group from others, though there is a Blood Rorschach pattern. Unlike the Menomini, we surmised, the Blood were able to cope with the demands of the surrounding "Whiteman" cultural system without a corresponding psychological reformulation.[5] And the socioeconomic elite and culturally conservative alike were able to keep a strong cultural identity. To present the hypothesized reasons for this type of adaptation would go beyond the focus of this paper (see G. Spindler 1968; L. Spindler 1973).

The initial causes must lie in the differences in sociological, economic, and ecological conditions to which the two groups had to adapt. That radical psychological reformulation appears to have been unnecessary for the Blood to cope successfully with the dominant white culture must be considered a potentially significant variable. The Blood appear to have many of the required psychological features, such as social aggressiveness, practicality, and open display of emotions that were lacking in the native-oriented Menomini adjustment. It might seem that researchers using a method of controlled comparison as just described could be taking a first step in resolving the conflict in orientation existing today between those using an idiographic and partially "emic" approach and those using an etic and nomothetic approach, since the approaches are combined here. For example, the two cultures were first thoroughly studied separately, with emphases on the inter-relationships within the community between social and psychological processes and upon what informants said about their own circumstances. The Blood and the Menomini were then compared in an attempt to generalize

---

4. We have done field work with the Blood intermittently since 1964, but with somewhat different objectives that are tangential to the focus of this paper.

5. We use the term "Whiteman" because the Blood do. It is not a racial designation. The more traditional Blood regard Blacks as "Whitemen."

about relationships between sociocultural and psychological variables at a more universal, cross-cultural level. This analysis is still in process at the time of this writing and there may be other surprises in store for us.

THE INSTRUMENTAL ACTIVITIES INVENTORY AS A TECHNIQUE

Notwithstanding the collection of comparable data for the Menomini and the Blood, we did not feel we really understood how the Blood perceived themselves or the Whiteman and his culture. In an effort to remedy this, we developed the IAI. It consists of twenty-four line drawings, drawn by a professional Blood Indian artist, representing Indians engaged in activities—activities instrumental to achievement and maintenance of life styles and socioeconomic statuses recognizable and valued in the Blood community. There are three major classes of instrumental activities within the Blood community representing the range of adaptations to the outside world. These include activities instrumental within the framework of the most traditional aspects of the culture, such as being a medicine man; those instrumental in the community in its more contemporary and less traditional aspects, such as participating in rodeos; and those instrumental within the terms imposed by the western economy and social system, such as being a store keeper or accountant (G. and L. Spindler 1965).

PROJECTIVE TECHNIQUES ANTECEDENT TO THE IAI

Like most tools, the IAI is a lineal descendant of others. It is in part a projective technique in the tradition of Henry Murray's Thematic Apperception Test (TAT), though we prefer the term "eliciting technique." The IAI is broadly related to all projective techniques in that the user must make the assumption that what people say in response to visual stimuli bears some significant relationship to their psychic organization as well as to their behavior, though this relationship need not be linear. We designed the technique to elicit responses more directly related to actual behavior on the one hand, and to the cognitive organization of those behaviors on the other, than those generated by the Rorschach or TAT. It is not intended as a rigorous psychological "test" but as a semi-controlled eliciting device.

Starting with William E. Henry's development of a TAT for use with Hopi and Navajo Indians (Henry 1947) modifications of the TAT have been made for particular cultures. The assumptions and purposes of the researchers using these modifications are basically the same as those using the original TAT. These modifications approach the IAI in that they are attempts to make the stimuli operationally meaningful in the context of the respondent. They suffer methodologically, however, in that it is difficult to analog the original Murray TAT interpersonal situations in variable cultural contexts. Thus, the value that might be claimed for standardization of stimuli is destroyed. The Rorschach technique has a better claim for standardized stimuli, since the inkblots themselves contain no specific cultural content.

Of the various inventions of picture techniques by anthropologists, we owe the most to the experiment developed by Walter Goldschmidt and Robert Edgerton for the study of values applied to the Spindler sample of Menomini sociocultural categories (Goldschmidt and Edgerton 1961). The authors claim the most important difference between their technique and the TAT is that they are attempting to measure culturally established patterns of behavior rather than individual personality dynamics. Edgerton administered a set of eleven cards, each presenting two alternatives in value choices on a single card. Significant variations in responses of Menomini individuals for the various acculturative categories were obtained, thus, incidentally, providing additional confirmation of their meaningfulness as categories. While the IAI and this picture technique exhibit certain features in common, the rationale for each differs in certain important respects. We believe that the focus in the IAI upon instrumental activities leads to a more total conception of the individual's relationship to his social environment. Also, in the IAI each picture represents only one instrumental activity. In this manner we felt we could avoid imposing dichotomous choices upon the respondent in the stimulus frame of a single picture. It is possible that dichotomies that are real in western culture are false within the framework of the conservative groups in other cultures. We wanted to elicit the *native* perception of instrumental relationships. The Blood IAI presents twenty-four specific alternatives from which the respondent can choose in any order and with any emphasis he wishes. Only after the respondent has made free choices do we "force" some choices between pairs and trios of drawings and on the basis of the respondent's first choice. Respondents are also asked to explain why they made the choices they did.

Sets of instrumental activities drawings were later designed and used by us for a study of Mistassini Cree teenagers and for a study of German schoolchildren, their schools, their teachers, and their parents (G. Spindler 1973, 1974). Other adaptations have been made by other researchers for various projects that are now in progress, including a study of social class differences in instrumental preferences in elementary school teacher behavior (Slobodin 1977).

We found the IAI extremely useful in eliciting data relevant to our several objectives. One objective was to discover how evaluative choices of instrumental alternatives are related to antecedent experience as indicated by sex, schooling, socioeconomic status, religious affiliation, etc. Another objective in using the IAI was to be able to describe the specific values projected into the rationales given for choices by our respondents. (We came later to call these "supporting values" [G. Spindler 1974].) Data relevant to this area is in accord with the general hypothesis that the Blood community is relatively homogeneous in its basic cultural substrata but also provided us with highly specific information about Blood values and their dynamic interrelationships. Another important objective in using the IAI was to isolate persistent cognitive orientations that pervade the specific perceptions and evaluations of instrumental activities. We were able to isolate integrating principles and types of thinking operative in the Blood Indian management of perceived social reality and the manner in which they were able to maintain cognitive control of potentially conflicting instrumental alternatives (see G. and L. Spindler 1965; and G. Spindler 1968, 1974). The data showed, for example, that the Blood exhibited a low tendency towards stereotypic thinking, that they rarely thought conditionally (in retrospect or into the future). Things are as they are or were as they were and one cannot make them different in fantasy. A number of other cognitive orientations were drawn from the IAI data.

A THEORETICAL MODEL FOR USE WITH THE IAI

The instrumental model first developed in the Blood Indian study was further refined in a study of urbanization processes occurring in two villages in southern Germany. The IAI was, of course, redrawn with a series of pictures specially designed for the area. The sample was drawn from several classrooms of children at educational levels ranging from the third to the ninth grade and from their parents and teachers. We emphasize here the theoretical model rather than the results of the research (see G. Spindler 1973, 1974, for the complete analysis).

The broad premises and concepts included in the theoretical model can be stated as follows: The behaviors we term instrumental are means to goals, such as states of being or possessions, associated with desired life styles. The relationship between activities and goals can be termed an *instrumental linkage*. Instrumental linkages are systematized, interrelated, and constitute the core of any cultural system (as rationalized within this model). Cultural belief systems are a statement of key instrumental relationships in idealized form and help maintain the credibility of these linkages. Children are taught what they are, how they work, and why some are better than others, in homes, schools, churches, and initiation ceremonies. The result of this teaching in the individual is a perceptual-cognitive structure that is a kind of working model of the cultural system but that varies somewhat with each individual. This working model permits the individual to maintain control of his life space in a cultural system, as long as the established instrumental relationships continue to function. Cognitive control as socially relevant is therefore the ability of the individual to maintain a working model, in his mind, of potentially productive instrumental linkages and their organization, so that he or she can make appropriate choices from the total range of instrumental possibilities. This model, as we have said, is formed in the mind by cultural transmission and the total experience of the individual. During rapid culture change established instrumental linkages are challenged by new information, new behavior models, and new instrumental possibilities. Alternative linkages are recognized, acquire credibility and become operable. This process may be studied and constitutes, for us, a key focus in the study of the psychology of cultural change and urbanization. In using this model one may be concerned with either the culture system processes (such as technological or economic) that result in new instrumental linkages, or with the perception, selection, and cognitive ordering of alternative linkages by individuals (G. Spindler 1973, p. 118).

The purpose of administering the IAI with this theoretical model in mind was to discover how the children cognitively managed instrumental choices and ranking when the cultural system was transforming during rapid urbanization. Line drawings were modified to include activities instrumental to the attainment of goals considered appropriate in the Remstal Valley of southern Germany, in the traditional as well as urbanizing sectors.

With the data from the IAI analyzed in terms of the relevant theoretical assumptions, we were able to isolate and identify the cognitive organizations of the children as well as of parents and teachers in the sample. The cognitive organizations pivoted around three potentially conflicting dimensions. The analysis permitted us to see how the children managed to maintain cognitive control in a changing milieu, and what role the school played as a culture transmitting agency (G. Spindler 1973, p. 131; 1974).

RORSCHACH-IAI COMPARISONS

We find that the data produced by the IAI and the Rorschach techniques intergrade. The Blood, for example, perceive real objects, people or animals in the Rorschach inkblots, usually in an action context; they usually encompass relatively small, sharp details in the ink-blots; and the meaning ascribed to them is concrete and specific. These features of Blood Rorschach responses are congruent with what the IAI revealed about the thinking processes of the Blood Indians, particularly with respect to cognitive orientations concerning activity, stereotypic thinking, immediacy and practicality, and literality.

The Rorschach moves the fieldworker further into an ill-defined area we can call the personality structure than does the IAI—into the psychic control areas, the management of anxiety and of emotions as well as the perceptual structuring, and into the respondent's fantasy life. These are admittedly problematic areas. We tried to avoid the worst problems by the strategies described. The IAI is not concerned with "personality" in this sense, and is more concerned with what people do or think they can do in the real world. The respondent selects from a number of different instrumental relationships and supports his decision by explaining why he or she made those choices. The IAI moves us directly into the area of the respondent's cognitive management of perceived social realities. It is, however, essentially an emic approach. However, we feel that given a theoretical model of instrumental linkages in cultural systems, we are in a position to utilize our elicited data etically, regarding instrumental relationships in given cultural domains as conceptually equivalent across cultures. The road to this development is not entirely clear and much work remains to be done.

If we had to choose between one or the other of the two techniques, we would be reluctant to forego the depth and understandings the Rorschach data provide, despite their problematic character. However, we would choose the IAI because it moved us into an area of perception and coding of alternative cognitive modes which are more directly relevant to the study of culture change.

THE PAST AND THE FUTURE: CONCLUDING REMARKS

In reviewing the attempts of researchers, including ourselves, in the field of psychological anthropology in general and psychocultural change in particular, we are convinced of the importance of using eclectic, experimental approaches in a context of solid background ethnography (see L. Spindler 1977). Models and techniques must be flexible and adaptable to new knowledge gained from many fields (i.e., physiology, psychology, anthropology, psychoanalysis, ethnology, and ecology). And it is incumbent upon anthropologists, with a large number of testing grounds, to test their models, return to the field, collect data, and change their techniques again. We have attempted to do this. Though there is continuity in our work, especially in its orientation towards a perceptual-cognitive approach, we are at a very different place now than we were when we began by using the Rorschach. Our purposes have remained essentially the same, but our theoretical models and instrumentation have changed. We have moved toward a different conception of culture and personality and of psychocultural process, toward a conception that places the continuously adapting, changing choosing individual in a network of social interrelationships and shifting instrumental possibilities. We must now find ways of making our emic and idiographic results more generalizable. We must make our instrumentation, or more properly, the data produced by the instrumentation, more codable and more quantitatively manageable.

Whatever techniques are utilized, most psychologically oriented anthropological research is dependent upon data from language. The ethnoscientist assumes that the events and things in a people's conceptual world are mirrored in the semantic categories of their language (Tyler 1969). Yet the psychological validity of a componential analysis inferring a covert taxonomy is not high. Further, the structures used, which may not be as free of western cultural bias as they seem, are static and do not refer to process—to changes in time. The anthropologist using instrumentation such as the projective techniques, autobiographies or eliciting devices such as the IAI is subject to other constraints.

Gregory Bateson suggests we seek means other than language for delineating deep, underlying cognitive patterns. He contends the human mind is a deep structure, with its conscious aspect dealing only with bits and pieces. On the other hand, the deep values of unconscious thought deal with relationships and patterns, rather than with things. And these kinds of relationships defy coding and linguistic description. He argues that man projects these whole patterns in art, which should offer many clues to the psychocultural anthropologist. At present we are observing and coding only a distorted picture of how the mind codes knowledge, Bateson writes. This situation may continue until we have new breakthroughs in the field of neurophysiology, which could allow mapping more directly the cognitive processes involved in ingesting the desiderata of a culture (Bateson 1972).

These concerns are beyond our ability to cope with now or in the foreseeable future, though they must be acknowledged. We must continue to do the best we can with verbal elicitations, controlled but not forced, and contextualized with good background ethnography.

COMMENT BY GEORGE D. SPINDLER

Louise Spindler has mentioned only indirectly our pervasive feeling of not being quite respectable because of our interest in projective techniques—particularly the Rorschach. When we were at the Center for Advanced Study in the Behavioral Sciences in the mid-fifties we were called aside by a senior social scientist and told everyone thought we were intelligent and competent but couldn't understand why we were "hooked on the Rorschach." This was simply one in a series of instances stretching back to graduate training and extending into the present. As a compensation for this pervasive feeling we made strenuous attempts at respectability through the use of control groups, careful statistics, operational definition of variables and sound background ethnography. It is probable that our work was generally accepted as being among the more rigorous of its kind.

Whatever we may say about the pros or cons concerning the use of the Rorschach as a means of eliciting personality-relevant responses, it is true that we cannot imagine how we could have done without it in much of our work. We found the Rorschach stirred the imaginative processes in such a way that ordinarily laconic people became talkative and expressive. We also found it gave us something to do that was both specific and non-threatening. And once an individual had talked to us about what he or she saw in the Rorschach it was possible to go on to almost any question. It also gave us entrée into homes and long hours of sitting patiently listening or waiting to listen as we observed social interaction, use of material artifacts and space, voice levels, etc. Therefore when we say we have a sample of sixty-one Rorschachs of Menomini women or a sample of sixty-eight males it is also correct to say we have a *case* sample in some depth. These are case studies of individuals and the context in which they function most relevantly.

We have always tried to combine qualitative and quantitative approaches. Our training in statistics at the University of Wisconsin with Professor Tom McCormick, extending over three long semesters, has stuck with us. We believe as we were taught: if it happens you can count it. That is you can if it is an event, but sometimes things happen that one can't count because one doesn't know when the event begins or ends. Judgments must be made in the act of counting and of placing instances in given classes. We have, therefore, come to regard statistical applications as entirely expedient to a given purpose in a given locus. And we feel statistics of any sort are as easily manipulated both consciously and more often unconsciously as any other type of data refinement procedure. We have come to feel that it is the total transaction in the field, with all the senses unstopped and the unconscious working full time, that makes it possible for us to produce anything useful to our discipline and to a better understanding of human behavior.

It is also true, however, that we are interested in new forms of instrumentation, as long as we don't forget what we have learned about instrumentation or what it is we are after. Our movement to the Instrumental Model and the Activities Inventory is symptomatic of a broader interest in individual adaptation, decision making, cognitive processing and control—but always in a social context. We are trying to move closer to where we think the action is, to the nexus of social forces, cognitive patterning and affective loading. To make our instrumental model complete we must go much further than we have. We need new ways of conceiving of life space and life style, of networks of relationship that make operative the instrumental choices made by individuals, and of the ways these social phenomena connect to perceptual and cognitive organization. And we need to understand much better than we do at present what we mean by "cognitive control." Of course these problems are not ours alone. We have, however, phrased them in our own way.

REFERENCES CITED

Bateson, G.
    1972 Grace and Information in Primitive Art. In *The Study of Primitive Art,* ed. R. Firth. New York: Oxford University Press.
Doob, L. W.
    1960 *Becoming More Civilized, a Psychological Exploration.* New Haven, Conn.: Yale University Press.
Eggan, F.
    1954 Social Anthropology and the Method of Controlled Comparison. *American Anthropologist* 56:743–63.
Goldschmidt, W., and Edgerton, R.
    1961 A Picture Technique for the Study of Values. *American Anthropologist* 63:26–45.

Hallowell, A. I.
  1951 The Use of Projective Techniques in the Study of Sociopsychological Aspects of Acculturation. *Journal of Projective Techniques* 15(1):27–44.
  1952 Ojibwa Personality and Acculturation. In *Acculturation in the Americas, Proceedings and Selected Papers on the XXIXth International Congress of Americanists,* ed. S. Tax. Chicago: University of Chicago Press.
Henry, W.
  1947 The Thematic Apperception Technique in the Study of Culture-Personality Relations. *Genetic Psychology Monographs* 35:3–135.
Lemert, E. M.
  1951 *Social Pathology.* New York: McGraw-Hill Co.
Lindzey, G.
  1961 *Projective Techniques and Cross-Cultural Research.* New York: Appleton-Century-Crofts.
Redfield, R. et al.
  1936 Memorandum for the Study of Acculturation. *American Anthropologist* 38:149–52.
Rubinfine, D. L.
  1961 Perception, Reality Testing and Symbolism. In *The Psychoanalytic Study of the Child,* vol. 16, eds. H. Hartmann, M. Kris, A. Freud, R. Eissler. pp 73–89. New York: International University Press.
Slobodin, C.
  1977 Relationships Between Parents and Teachers of Preschool Children: A Study of Values. Unpublished doctoral dissertation, Stanford University.
Social Science Research Council
  1954 Acculturation: An Exploratory Formulation. *American Anthropologist* 56:973–1002.
Spindler, G. D.
  1952 Personality and Peyotism in Menomini Indian Acculturation. *Psychiatry* 15:151–59.
  1955 *Sociocultural and Psychological Processes in Menomini Acculturation,* vol. 5. Berkeley: University of California Press.
  1968 Psychocultural Adaptation. In *The Study of Personality: An Interdisciplinary Appraisal,* ed. E. Norbeck. New York: Holt, Rinehart and Winston, Inc.
  1973 *Burgbach: Urbanization and Identity in a German Village.* New York: Holt, Rinehart and Winston, Inc.
  1974 Schooling in Schönhausen: A Study of Cultural Transmission and Instrumental Adaptation in an Urbanizing German Village. In *Education and Cultural Process: Toward an Anthropology of Education,* ed. G. Spindler. New York: Holt, Rinehart and Winston.
Spindler, G., and Goldschmidt, W.
  1952 Experimental Design in the Study of Culture Change. *Southwestern Journal of Anthropology* 8:68–83.
Spindler, G., and Spindler, L.
  1963 Psychology in Anthropology: Applications to Culture Change. In *Psychology: A Study of a Science,* ed. S. Koch. New York: McGraw-Hill Book Co., Inc.

1965   Instrumental Activities Inventory: A Technique for the Study of the Psychology of Acculturation. *Southwestern Journal of Anthropology* 21:1–23.

1970   Field Work Among the Menomini. In *Being an Anthropologist,* ed. G. D. Spindler. New York: Holt, Rinehart and Winston, Inc.

1971   *Dreamers Without Power: The Menomini Indians.* New York: Holt, Rinehart and Winston, Inc.

Spindler, L.
1956   Women and Culture Change: A Case Study of the Menomini Indians. Unpublished doctoral dissertation, Stanford University.

1962   Menomini Women and Culture Change. *American Anthropological Association,* vol. 64, no. 1, memoir 91.

1973   Culture Change. In *Culture in Process,* 2nd ed. A. Beals, G. and L. Spindler, eds. New York: Holt, Rinehart and Winston, Inc.

1977   *Culture Change and Modernization: Case Studies and Mini-Models.* New York: Holt, Rinehart and Winston.

Spindler, L., and Spindler, G.
1958   Male and Female Adaptations in Culture Change. *American Anthropologist* 60:217–33.

Voget, F.
1971   Cultural Change. In *Biennial Review of Anthropology,* ed. B. J. Siegel. Stanford: Stanford University Press.

Wallace, A. F. C.
1952   The Modal Personality Structure of the Tuscarora Indians as Revealed by the Rorschach Test. *Bureau of American Ethnology Bulletin 150.* Washington: U. S. Government Printing Office.

The Author

ANTHONY F. C. WAL-
LACE was born in Toronto,
Canada. He subsequently
became a naturalized U.S.
citizen and served in the
A.U.S. from 1942 to 1945.
He took his B.A. in history
from the University of Pennsylvania in 1947, his M.A.
from the University of Penn-
sylvania in 1949 and his Ph.D. in anthropology from the same institution in
1950. His major ethnographic field work was done with the Tuscarora Seneca
Indians. He is at present Professor of Anthropology, Department of Anthropology, and Medical Research Scientist III, Eastern Pennsylvania Psychiatric
Institute. He served as president of the American Anthropological Association
(from 1971 to 1972).

His publications range well beyond the particular interest developed in his
chapter in this volume. Particularly notable in this respect are his ethnohistoric
writings on psychological aspects of the Delaware, the Tuscaroras, and the
Seneca. He has applied psychoanalytic theory to the interpretation of some of
his materials but has focused more on a psychiatric-anthropological approach
represented in this chapter. He says of himself:

I was born in Toronto in 1923 and came to the United States with my
parents when I was two years old. My father and his family were all college-
affiliated people, my mother's family were connected with a cotton manufac-
turing firm in Manchester in England. In a genealogical mood, I might
attribute to this conjunction of career lines, my interest in combining the
humanistic with scientific and technological approaches to the study of man.
Be that as it may, this dual line of interest continued from high school, when I
reveled in science fiction and wrote lots of unpublished poetry and short stories,
through college when I majored in history with a minor in physics, to the time
when I discovered in Frazer's *Golden Bough* that anthropology was the one
field that seemed to accept this sort of intellectual combination. To be sure, I
have discovered since that there are other kinds of anthropology than Frazer's;
but nonetheless, I still recall the pleasure I felt in realizing, as I read him, that
here was an intellectual community which believed that to the trained eye the
richly textured tapestry of history might reveal general laws.

Although the researches described in the accompanying paper can hardly be called historical, they do in fact derive from an initially historical approach to the subject of revitalization movements. The "general laws" in question here have to do with the conditions under which prophets achieve their revelations, and there appears to me to be no virtue in insisting that such historical laws must eschew psychological or physiological processes and remain purely social. The reductionism involved is legitimate because it has to do with the timing not the subject matter of the vision.

This Chapter

Wallace's research on the Handsome Lake religion, "mazeway resynthesis," revitalization movements, and stress is well known. He early formulated the hypothesis that "endocrine mechanisms involved in stress probably set up a physiological milieu in the brain which facilitated the kind of resynthesis which can be observed in religious prophets, in Indian youths during the vision quest, and in paranoid schizophrenia." A series of papers emerged from this basic hypothesis. He found a suitable milieu for his interest in the Eastern Pennsylvania Psychiatric Institute.

He became concerned with measuring semantic capacity as an approach to better understanding and diagnosis of critical phases of schizophrenia. This led to yet further inquiry upon the nature of semantic and cognitive processes. In this context he developed a concern for Arctic hysteria in its various forms. He explored the possible role of dietary deficiencies in the etiology of the syndrome. This work was taken up by psychiatric anthropology students, who found clear evidence of abnormally low serum calcium in cases of Arctic hysteria. This in turn has led to further work on physiological factors, including dietary deficiencies, as conditions related to schizophrenia. This chapter describes the chain of circumstances and concepts tying this part of Anthony Wallace's career together. It is unique in the context of this volume because of its attention to a physiological dimension and because it is concerned with applied projects, and with the developing organization of one long-term research interest.

G.D.S.

6 Basic Studies, Applied Projects, and Eventual Implementation: A Case History of Biological and Cultural Research in Mental Health

ANTHONY F. C. WALLACE

My aim in this brief paper is to write a case history: to put down, as well as I can remember without consulting old files, a record of my own and some of my students' work on the interplay of biology and culture in mental illness. It begins with a description of basic research some twenty years ago and follows an irregular line of investigation through increasingly applied projects to the eventual production of useful tools. The paper does not in any sense pretend to be a survey or history of ideas and findings in the general field of biological and cultural interrelationships. Indeed, its purpose is to show how various ideas and sources of support interweave as a research program moves toward the possibility of useful implementation in the "real" world.

I apologize to my colleagues for the autobiographical mode of presentation; although the proper mode in academic writing is austere and impersonal, I believe personal history is the only immediate way of coming to grips with this kind of material. The program described has not produced any great scientific breakthrough and it has not revolutionized any part of American life. But it does pose the hard question: is our research ever really put to use? This case history does, I would suggest, represent reasonably well a typical, if not necessarily the most desirable, situation, where practical application is accomplished only after a long time, a decade or more of increasingly focused study, and when multiple lines of interest and support converge with and continuously redirect the research line, so that its course resembles the confluence of streams in a watershed rather than a straight road (or even a winding lane) connecting two points labeled "theory" and "application."

INITIAL ORIENTATIONS TO THE PROBLEM

During my years in the service in World War II, I read Sir James Frazer's *Golden Bough* and was inspired to go into anthropology by its grand evolutionary perspective on human culture and history. Anthropology seemed to offer an opportunity to blend scientific and humanistic ways of thought, which I had earlier somewhat awkwardly tried to accomplish by majoring as an undergraduate in history with a minor in physics. After the war, at first as a veteran supported by the G.I. Bill and later by a couple of university fellowships, I completed my degree in history and went on to anthropology as a graduate student at the University of Pennsylvania. There I was tutored first by Frank Speck, an American Indianist who took me on in spite of my admiration for Frazer. Speck had been trained by Franz Boas and believed in meticulous ethnographic field work, not in literary syntheses of cultural evolution. About 1948, A. I. Hallowell, one of Speck's earlier students and colleagues, came back to Penn from Northwestern, bringing with him, in addition to interests in American Indian ethnography and ethnohistory, his own special interest in the small but growing field of "culture and personality."

I turned enthusiastically to culture and personality. As Hallowell's student, I studied the Rorschach test and other projective techniques at Bruno Klopfer's summer institute. I took courses in psychological statistics and clinical psychology with the psychology department, studying with persons who were interested in such things as the evaluation of psychosurgery, particularly frontal lobotomy, and the problems of test and measurement. And I underwent a two-year program in educative analysis with the Philadelphia Psychoanalytic Institute. My dissertation concentrated on the collection and analysis of a set of Rorschach records from an American Indian reservation.

After receiving the Ph.D. in 1950, I stayed on at Penn as an instructor in sociology and as the administrator of a Ford Foundation grant for promoting interdisciplinary research in the behavioral sciences. I also applied at once to the Social Science Research Council for, and received, a Faculty Research Fellowship for a biographical study of a Seneca Indian religious prophet named Handsome Lake (*c.* 1749–1815). (I had published an Indian biography earlier, in 1948, and enjoyed working with historical materials, which while scanty and inflexible, are also more intimate in some respects than interview data, because original documents are the communications themselves, frozen in time, rather than cautious responses of informants *about* their communications.) It was during the work of Handsome Lake that my first real awakening to the problem of relating biological to social and cultural events in an individual life occurred.

The Seneca Indians were one of the Five Nations of Iroquois (or Six, after the arrival of the refugee Tuscarora from North Carolina) who occupied New York State west of the Hudson River. These people had a Neolithic culture that combined sedentary agriculture, conducted by the women and centered around their villages, with extensive and far-ranging hunting, war, and diplomatic expeditions by the menfolk. Their system of marriage was adapted to these circumstances, which required continuous residence by the female lineages in their villages while the men foraged abroad, by encouraging easy separation and remarriage. To European eyes, indeed, the reckoning of matrilineal descent for lineage and clan membership, the important role of women in influencing decisions with respect to war and peace by their privilege of urging warriors to take vengeance for killings, and the women's political role in nominating members of the chief's council, added up to a true "matriarchy." In their medical beliefs, the Iroquois depended heavily on a theory of dreams which, in a way, was remarkably similar to that of psychoanalysis later, emphasizing the need to diagnose unconscious wishes and gratify them. An apparatus of ritual and of "secret" medicine societies was available to carry out this diagnosis and to find means for satisfying the wishes of the soul.

The presence of the two great contending colonial powers, France and England, placed great strains on this way of life. During the seventeenth and eighteenth centuries, the Iroquois were hard put to preserve their lands, their economy, and their independence. At last, with the end of the American Revolution (during which most of the Iroquois fought with the British), the system came to an end and by 1797 all of the Iroquois in New York State and Pennsylvania were confined to a number of scattered reservations.

Handsome Lake, a resident of a small tract of land called the Cornplanter Reserve along the Allegheny River near the New York-Pennsylvania line, was an ex-warrior and a chief of the great Iroquois confederacy. He experienced a religious vision in June 1799, and the event was recorded in detail by Quaker missionaries from Philadelphia who were living with the Indians at the time. The prophet, a chronic drunkard, collapsed one morning, lay motionless for hours with cold extremities and imperceptible breathing and heart beat, and was laid out as a corpse. When he awoke, he described a remarkable vision, the first of several, in which messengers of God revealed a new gospel to him that eventually became the bible of a new religion that still survives among the Iroquois. These visions in effect revealed the blueprint of a new way of life, better suited to accommodation with whites and to circumstances of reservation life. It emphasized the need for men to take over agriculture from the women, using the new techniques of plowing and fenced fields; it asserted the priority of the nuclear family household over the matrilineal lineage; it attempted to blame the ills of the Indians on alcohol and witchcraft; and provided ritual means to ensure a termination of these evils. I did a little comparative reading in sources like James Mooney's old classic, *The Ghost Dance Religion,* and found that a great many new religions seemed to have originated similarly in a vision by a prophet who achieved the formulation of his ideas for the improvement of society while in an altered state of consciousness.

Here was the problem! Although the feelings, values, ideas, and memories embodied in these visionary revelations obviously were the product of the prophet's earlier experience, the actual work of reassembling them into a new Gestalt was done while the prophet was oblivious to his surroundings. The similarity of the accounts of prophetic visions from widely different parts of the world suggested that the process was common to humanity and occurred under predictable conditions. But precisely what sort of conditions? It seemed worth considering that the event had something to do with psychological stress—at least, that is what most of the prophets and their observers said. But psychological stress does not occur without a concomitant pattern of physiological stress. Could it be the altered physiological milieu was responsible not only for the loss of consciousness but also for the fact that a radical resynthesis of cognition and values (or what I called a "mazeway resynthesis") was typically made suddenly, and permanently, during a trance rather than gradually in the course of meditation? In other words, could a biological upset be necessary to this kind of psychological resynthesis and therefore to the cultural changes which followed?

A byproduct of these considerations was the elaboration of the concept of "mazeway" as a system of cognitive maps and meanings which the individual constructs from his experiences and which he uses to plan his behavior. Similar to Boulding's concept of the Image, mazeway appeared to me to be a construct necessary for two functions: to link individual behavior with those generalized patterns or regularities which are connoted by the term culture; and to identify the field upon which neuro-physiological variables could act.

STRESS AND REVITALIZATION

I was so entranced by the perspective opening up before me of studies delineating the processes of individually and culturally adaptive change in response to stress, that I postponed the completion of the work on Handsome Lake in order to take up the cross-cultural study of revitalization movements and the associated psychological processes. (The Handsome Lake study was finally published in 1970.) About 1954 I applied successfully to the National Institute of Mental Health for a three-year research grant to study revitalization movements and about 1956 for a supplementary grant to study the hallucinatory experiences of shamans as reported in the anthropological literature (Grants M–883 and M–1106). In the midst of all this it became apparent to the sociology department that my interests did not coincide with theirs and that I could not expect advancement there, so in 1955 I took advantage of an offer from the director of the newly opening Eastern Pennsylvania Psychiatric Institute to join their staff as a medical research scientist. About the same time I was invited to affiliate with the Anthropology Department at the University of Pennsylvania as a Visiting Associate Professor.

The situation at Eastern Pennsylvania Psychiatric Institute was stimulating because of the presence of laboratory scientists who, in contrast to most anthropologists and sociologists, were interested in biological and chemical determinants of human experience. There were people from the Massachusetts Institute of Technology and the Army Chemical Center who had been working on nerve gas and sought to explain the physical chemistry of nerve impulse transmission; some of them had just invented a glass electrode which measured sodium ion activity in biological fluids. Some people were experimenting with and testing the then newly introduced tranquilizers and others were playing with lysergic acid diethylamide and other hallucinogens which seemed to offer the prospect of turning model psychoses on and off for clinical study. Still others were studying stress hormones. Biological theories of the etiology of schizophrenia were very much in the air and there were hot debates between the hard scientists in Basic Research and the socially and clinically oriented people devoted to psychoanalysis, learning theory, or milieu therapy. And at this time, inspired by the work of Cannon on homeostasis and Selye on physiological stress, equilibrium theories of biological, social, and psychological varieties were very much in the air. The early formulations of General System's Theory, and other sources, all pointed toward the need for a general theory of behavior which would unite all approaches to the study of man. As yet, however, the conceptual, let alone methodological, problems of bringing together articulated processes from biological, social, and psychological systems had not fully revealed themselves. It was not, for instance, clear that the concept of stress would be a troublesome one to work with. Developed first to denote the application of distorting forces to a mechanical system, in which it produced a resultant *strain,* the term stress was applied to the analogous situation in disease in man and animal by Hans Selye and his collaborators. They demonstrated that a fairly regular *general adaptation syndrome* (the analogue of structural strain) was produced by a number of different stressors (e.g., infection, cold, heat, surgery). It was tempting to me, and to others in anthropology like Caudill, to view the condition of whole societies in a comparable way, identifying such impacts as over-population, environmental change, or political and economic difficulties as stressors and various "pathological" responses as the resultant structural strains. The hope that a unified science of human behavior would soon be emerging was implicit in such formulations.

In all of this I felt my studies of the revitalization processes were conceptually central because they linked the biological and the psychological, social, and cultural via the concept of *stress.* I was not trained in the chemical and medical sciences, however. For a time I toyed with the idea of going on to medical school, or of taking a Ph.D. in biochemistry, but it seemed to me there were plenty of well-trained people in this area, and it would be unwise to postpone the development of my own work for half a decade or more for the sake of being able to spread myself even more thinly over a still wider range of interests. In some ways, I regret not going into the laboratory, for not doing so has meant that my suggestions for desirable research have not all been acted on as promptly as I might wish (or, indeed, not at all). But having observed the agonies of delay in laboratory programs that result from difficulties with purchasing, with calibrating instruments and debugging procedures, and with pursuit of methodological red herrings, I am also sometimes glad I did not put on a lab coat.

I therefore left the pursuit of the actual physiological mechanisms involved in the process of mazeway resynthesis with the suggestion, expressed in several papers, that the endocrine mechanisms involved in

stress probably set up a physiological milieu in the brain which facilitated the kind of resynthesis which can be observed in religious prophets, in Indian youths during the vision quest, and in paranoid schizophrenics. A series of papers on these and related subjects, and a trail of
subsequent publications, were the personal outcome of this line of
thought.

THE PROBLEM OF SCHIZOPHRENIA

I began now (in the late 1950s) to feel it would be more productive
to work collaboratively with physiologists, psychologists, and psychiatrists directly on the problem of schizophrenia. The revitalization research had raised questions about the cultural importance of, as well as
the biological conditions preparatory to, paranoid processes. ("Paranoid
processes" may be defined as those kinds of thinking in which the
individual constructs for himself a set of new, idiosyncratic assumptions
about the nature of the real world in order to reduce his own anxiety by
changing his own cognitive framework. In general these assumptions
violate the conventional common-sense wisdom of the community.
Often these assumptions are "not true" from the standpoint of a
supposedly unbiased observer but a paranoid assumption can be "true"
and still be paranoid because of its function in the individual's psychic
economy.) I now began to ask myself questions about other kinds of
symptoms which were common complaints of persons labeled schizophrenic. I was particularly interested in the sense of alienation described
by many schizophrenics in such metaphors as, "It's like being enclosed
in glass." I collected a series of patient autobiographies which revealed
very clearly that some schizophrenics were acutely aware, in the early
phases of their illness, of episodes of detachment when meanings of
familiar objects and experiences became lost. I was also impressed by the
anxiety such patients experienced when they realized that familiar
objects, people, and culturally standardized learned procedures—such
as ironing a shirt, or getting through a revolving door—became impossible. From this emerged a generalized model of schizophrenic types of
psychosis as an episodic, recurring condition of desemantication, whose
varying levels of symptomatology could be tracked through the period of
onset and hope fully associated with such events as medications, illnesses, life crises, and so on. The problem of the chronic, backward
schizophrenic then could be seen as that of a partially, or occasionally,
desemanticated person who had given up trying, who had set his

identity values lower, and had devised a suitable theory of his illness, in order to avoid anxiety.

I now began to cast about for a research design to tie all this together into a testable set of hypotheses (and I suppose I can say I am still involved in the effort to design valid and reliable operations). There were three requisites, I argued: one, a measure of the currently effective level of semantic capacity; second, a procedure for recording in day by day detail the course of the patient's illness before hospitalization; and third, a procedure for repeated and concurrent measurement of relevant fractions of blood and spinal fluids deemed suspect by biologically oriented colleagues.

The search for a procedure for measuring semantic capacity led me at once (this would be about 1957 or 1958), with the aid of John Atkins, to the recently published work of Ward Goodenough and Floyd Lounsbury on the componential analysis of meaning. The aspect of meaning which was immediately relevant to psychiatric concerns, of course, was its cognitive structure. What does a symbol (such as a word) denote for a particular person when he hears or uses it? Some procedures in semantic analysis did not pretend to do more than simulate human behavior— that is to say, they provided a calculus by which culturally correct behavior could be predicted but did not necessarily employ a calculus actually used by the native. Our purpose demanded we be able not merely to predict what word the native would use but also the exact criteria he used in reckoning. To achieve this sort of ''psychological'' validity in semantic analysis turned out to be no simple task. As a result, I have been working at the subject of cognition and semantics now on and off for years, and a number of papers have emerged, of more interest I suspect to anthropologists than to psychiatrists (and certainly not even very interesting to many anthropologists). The efforts I made to test the operating semantic levels of individual patients' use of kinship terms were interesting but I felt more needed to be done to understand basic semantic structures before anything like a test was devised. A by-product of this also was a study of the semantic structure of the terminology of emotions in use by a group of patients and therapists at Eastern Pennsylvania Psychiatric Institute.

A procedure for reconstructing the patient's immediate past (up to six months before the hospital) was worked out by Ray Fogelson and others of my assistants. It proved to be possible, by careful and detailed interviewing, to recapture a great deal of minute information about the patient which was, we felt, relevant to his own theory of illness and also to possibly pathogenic events, such as the number of patient's close kin who had been hospitalized for psychiatric illness, the patient's untoward responses to anesthesias during and sedatives after surgery, and the administration of various psychotropic drugs.

The third requisite—mobilizing the laboratory sciences to do broad blood studies, and then zeroing-in on suspected parameters which appeared to be associated with lowered semantic level on testing and/or with episodes of desemantication reported during the history-of-illness interviews—proved to be administratively impossible. At the Institute —for good reason, I hasten to say—there had from the first been a tradition of academic freedom, and as Director of Clinical Research at the time I was zealous in defending it from encroachments from out-side. This policy left everyone free to do his own thing, and thus made any sort of programmed research of the kind I was talking about almost impossible. One would have, in effect, to set up his own research center, control budget, personnel, and space, and carry through a prolonged program of studies with ruthless consistency, in order to accomplish what I was trying to do.

THE ARCTIC HYSTERIA PROJECT

Along with the development of the schizophrenia program, I undertook to try to develop a more general procedure for relating the incidence and prevalence of psychiatric illness to the culture of the community. Many such efforts were unsatisfying because questions of etiology were begged; I felt the understanding of cultural influence had to go hand in hand with an understanding of individual etiology. I looked about for an "ethnic psychosis"—that is to say, a psychosis whose symptom pattern appeared to be confined to a unique milieu— and settled on two possibilities.

One useful case was Geoffrey Tooth's report on *trypanosomiasis* in West Africa. This form of sleeping sickness, communicated to man by the bite of an infected tsetse fly, produces at a certain stage of illness a panoply of symptoms allegedly indistinguishable, on clinical grounds, from schizophrenia: delusions, hallucinations, flat affect, and catatonic posturing, among others. But while this case had some heuristic value, it was less intriguing than arctic hysteria. This latter term has been tradi-tionally used by anthropologists to denote two kinds of symptoms: episodes of uncontrollable mimicry in persons who have been startled (this syndrome being most commonly described among Siberian peo-ples); and fits of grand hysteria with nudity, flight, and convulsive seizure the conspicuous symptoms among the Polar Eskimo visited by the explorer Robert Peary and others in northwest Greenland. My assistants and I at the Eastern Pennsylvania Psychiatric Institute launched an initial library study of *piblokto,* as the Polar Eskimo called this hysteria, and also a companion study of the so-called *windigo* psychosis among the northeastern Algonkian hunters. The latter study was carried to completion and was published by Raymond Fogelson, who was working for me at the time. In it he suggested the possibility of nutritional deprivation as a determinant of this cannibalistic sort of paranoia.

The first problem to be solved in the *piblokto* study was to develop procedures for differential diagnosis. A. A. Brill, a psychoanalyst, had on the basis of overt similarities in symptomatology concluded that *piblokto* was a true functional hysteria caused by a "lack of love." Two anthropologists who had worked on the problem, Gussow (1960) and Parker (1962), had proposed somewhat more general but related hypotheses, both based on the assumption the syndrome was functional in nature. Gussow suggested *piblokto* was a characteristic response of the Eskimo personality type in the presence of psychological insecurity, a seductive "invitation to be pursued." Parker similarly interpreted the Eskimo personality type as essentially extroversive and it was therefore in line with Eskimo character when in trouble to express dependency needs and "call attention to his plight." We questioned these diagnoses on *a priori* grounds and sought to develop the record more fully in order to prepare a research design by which a differential diagnosis could be accomplished, allowing the possibility of various combinations of functional and organic etiologies. Robert Ackerman and I published this programmatic research design. As we explored the matter, we became intrigued by the possibility that dietary insufficiency of calcium, aggravated by lack of sunlight, might be producing symptoms of tetany rather than hysteria; somewhat later, we realized that the attacks were probably being precipitated by hyperventilation. Tetany—a neurological syndrome marked in mild cases by characteristic muscular contractions of the extremities, and in more severe cases by a melange of symptoms, including in some cases flight, depression, delusions, and major convulsions—is most often seen in Western societies today as a consequence of surgical removal of the parathyroid glands which are located behind the thyroid in the neck. But various other processes can contribute to tetany, including digestive disorders and diets extremely deficient in calcium and vitamin D. As we followed this up, we discovered that at the time Freud was doing his fundamental studies in hysteria in Europe in the latter part of the nineteenth century, the differential diagnosis between tetany and hysteria was regarded by neurologists and psychiatrists as being indeed a difficult problem, and that there were actual epidemics of tetany among the working classes in European cities!

Having developed a general method, we now set about to use in the field at Thule the epidemiological model we had been working on, and to test in particular our calcium hypothesis. We mobilized a team consisting of a Danish psychiatrist then working at Eastern Pennsylvania Psychiatric Institute, the basic research labs of Gilbert Ling, also there at the time, Ackerman, and myself. I applied to the National Institute of Mental Health and was asked to withdraw the application! The Arctic Institute offered funds if the National Institute of Mental Health would make a grant. Finally, despite the efforts of Froelich Rainey and other Arctic anthropologists, and the promise of cooperation from the resident Danish physician at Thule, the Danish government failed to come through with a visa. The reason for their reluctance stemmed, I am told, from an unwillingness of the hunter's council at Thule to be studied by anthropologists. The proximity of the study to Thule Air Base, a highly restricted Strategic Air Command installation, may also have been a factor.

So the initial field study was not made. Indeed, not long after this I resigned as Director of Clinical Research at Eastern Pennsylvania Psychiatric Institute and in 1961 moved to the University of Pennsylvania, where duties as chairman of the department, and other interests, made further pursuit of the *piblokto* problem impractical. I retained a part-time affiliation with Eastern Pennsylvania Psychiatric Institute, however, which I still hold. Raymond Fogelson went on to Seattle to the University of Washington and then to the University of Chicago. Robert J. Smith, another research assistant, went to Ossawatomie, Kansas, where he worked in a psychiatric setting, and then moved on to one of the Michigan State campuses. Robert Ackerman went to the University of Oregon and to his continuing career in archaeology.

A SECOND GENERATION TAKES UP THE *PIBLOKTO* PROBLEM

In my administrative work in anthropology at Penn, I was determined to establish a section in physical anthropology which was strong in what might be called human biology and physiology in addition to the traditional paleontology and growth studies. I also was encouraging to young resident psychiatrists who wished to obtain Ph.D.'s in anthropology. And I continued to teach the potential virtues of a view of culture and personality which included biological as well as cultural or psychological dimensions.

These efforts eventually bore some fruit. The department is now occupying a new wing in the University Museum which has laboratories for research in physical anthropology, including (if necessary) blood chemistry. And I was able to interest one of the graduate students in physical anthropology, Solomon Katz, in the calcium hypothesis and the *piblokto* problem, suggesting we needed an electrode similar in principle to the one that had been in design in the basic research labs at Eastern Pennsylvania Psychiatric Institute. As it turned out, Orion Instrument Company in Cambridge was just then putting a calcium ion electrode into experimental production. I was able to secure an appointment for Katz at Penn and also at Eastern Pennsylvania Psychiatric Institute, and so we began to develop a calcium (and other electrolyte) research program at Eastern Pennsylvania Psychiatric Institute again, beginning about 1967. There we gained as colleagues and Ph.D. candidates in anthropology two psychiatric residents, Edward Foulks and Robert Kraus. Foulks did his field work in Alaska studying arctic hysteria, among other things, and Kraus has just returned from a year in Alaska investigating Eskimo suicide. Both men paid their way by doing medical service for the Public Health Service in Alaska and Kraus in addition has received substantial National Institute of Mental Health grants.

Foulks' dissertation received the John Gillin award of the American Anthropological Association in 1972 and was published under the title *The Arctic Hysterias*. Foulks found that in some of his ten cases of *piblokto*-like "hysteria" in Alaska, there was clear laboratory evidence of abnormally low serum calcium. In addition, he reported on the unpublished work of Bohlen, which showed that the absence of regular night and day alternations during much of the Arctic year is selectively disturbing to the circadian rhythm of calcium in the human body. Furthermore, as we had found for northwest Greenland, the calcium poor diet and the limited exposure to sunlight were predisposing factors. In effect, Foulks' study showed that problems of calcium metabolism did indeed contribute significantly to the etiology of *piblokto*-like syndromes among the Alaskan Eskimo.

Katz's work has now moved on to a different level. For a while we worked at the National Institutes of Health Clinical Center on the floor devoted to patients suffering from electrolyte imbalance, particularly calcium problems. He more recently completed analyzing blood samples from eight state hospitals (where all patients were studied, some 20,000 in all) looking for electrolyte abnormalities. A large number of undiagnosed cases of hyper- and hypocalcemia were found (of whom a number have since been under treatment). State agencies are actively interested in the proposal that these blood chemistry surveys be performed routinely for all state hospital patients in Pennsylvania. Katz and I have collaborated in all this in a loose and general way, discussing research results, problems, and strategies, and combining to advise research people in the field. And Katz has my support in his current enterprise: to set up a large ecological/medical research center at Point Barrow, where, among other things, the *piblokto* problem may eventually be solved.

RETROSPECT

This has been a brief case history, describing the main lines of my own training and research experience in the borderland of anthropology and psychiatry. I am by no means satisfied with the results. But at this point, I do think I can make some evaluation. First, I feel some sense of discomfort, a feeling of not having reached closure on most of the problems I undertook to solve. This is not surprising, for the problems are not really likely to be solved by one person; but it is precisely the sense of not having reached closure that keeps me interested. Two administrative observations also are in order. First, although I was, as I have noted, tempted to add technical skills in biochemistry in order to be able to work both sides of the street, I am really doubtful whether I would have been any more effective in problem solving than I have been without these skills. There simply is not enough time for one person to manage all of these operations personally. Hence, the only recourse is to work with a team. And here a second observation, which I have made many times over the past fifteen years, must be voiced. The tradition of academic freedom and individualized research—which is essential in most universities and research centers—does not, I believe, yield maximum efficiency in solving a particular problem (like the *piblokto* problem or the problem of the schizophrenias). Here what one would need to have is control, real authority, to hire, promote, and transfer professional personnel, to manage an installation, to purchase equipment and supplies, to carry out a coherent and step by step research program over a period of decades. Without some one master plan, research efforts are diffuse and unrelated and much effort is frittered away in academic competition. There are obvious risks in this authoritarian model too, not only its lack of freedom, but also in the possibility of grimly running down a blind alley long after the error of the choice has been shown. But it should be tried more often.

REFERENCES CITED

Foulks, E. F.
  1973 The Arctic Hysterias. *Anthropological Studies, American Anthropological Association*, no. 10.
Gussow, Z.
  1960 Pibloktoq (Hysteria) Among the Polar Eskimo: An Ethnopsychiatric Study. In *Psychoanalysis and the Social Sciences*, ed. W. Muensterberger. New York: International Universities Press.
Parker, S.
  1962 Eskimo Psychopathology in the Context of Eskimo Personality and Culture. *American Anthropologist* 4:76–96.
Tooth, G.
  1950 *Studies in Mental Illness in the Gold Coast*. London: H. M. Stationery Office.
Wallace, A. F. C.
  1956a Mazeway Resynthesis: A Biocultural Theory of Religious Inspiration. *Transations of the New York Academy of Sciences, series II*, 18:626–38.
  1956b Revitalization Movements. *American Anthropologist* 58:204–81.
  1956c Stress and Rapid Personality Changes. *International Record of Medicine and General Practice Clinics* 169:761–74.
  1959 Cultural Determinants of Response to Hallucinatory Experience. *A.M.A. Archives of General Psychiatry* 1:58–59.
  1960 The Biocultural Theory of Schizophrenia. *International Record of Medicine* 173:700–714.
  1961 *Culture and Personality*. New York: Random House.
  1969 The Trip. In *Psychedelic Drugs*, ed. R. E. Hicks and P. J. Fink. New York: Grune and Stratton, Inc.
  1970 *The Death and Rebirth of the Seneca*. New York: Knopf.
  1972 Mental Illness, Biology, and Culture. In *Psychological Anthropology*, ed. F. L. K. Hsu. Cambridge, Mass.: Schenkman Publishing Company, Inc.
Wallace, A. F. C. and Ackerman, R.
  1960 An Interdisciplinary Approach to Mental Disorders among the Polar Eskimos of Northwest Greenland. *Anthropologica* 11:1–12.
Wallace, A. F. C. and Atkins, J.
  1960 The Meaning of Kinship Terms. *American Anthropologist* 62:58–80.

The Author

GEORGE A. DEVOS, Pro-
fessor of Anthropology at the
University of California at
Berkeley, is the product of an
interdisciplinary education at
the University of Chicago,
with a B.A. in sociology in
1946, an M.A. in anthro-
pology in 1948, and a Ph.D.
in psychology in 1951. With
considerable experience as a clinical psychologist, and extensive research
activities in Japan, he has dedicated himself to the comparative approach of
anthropology with a focus on psychological motivation in social contexts. His
intellectual mentors led him to an eclectic orientation that continues to find
fruitful stimuli in the works of social structuralists Max Weber, Emile Durkheim, and to a lesser degree Karl Marx. Pioneers such as Freud, Mead,
Malinowski, Kardiner, Erikson, and Piaget have greatly influenced his work in
what has become known as psychological anthropology.

DeVos's sustained field work has centered on Japan. He has shown a
special interest in collaborating with researchers in other cultures. He is both an
advocate and a critic of psychological testing as a means of measuring the effects
of culture on individual development and personality disorders. He remains
optimistic about the further development of psychological methods as part of
disciplined field work. His theoretical interests have been nurtured by problems of human belonging and social constraint. His research has been specifically directed toward such problems in modern cultures as mental illness,
crime, delinquency, suicide, and the effects of minority status. Among his
present research activities he is carrying out a psychocultural study of the
Korean minority in Japan.

His major books include: *Japan's Invisible Race: Caste in Culture and
Personality*, University of California Press, Berkeley (1972), with Hiroshi
Wagatsuma; *Socialization for Achievement: Essays on the Cultural Psychology
of the Japanese*, University of California Press, Berkeley (1973), a collection of
his principal papers on Japanese culture and personality over the past twenty-
five years, much of this done in collaboration with Japanese colleagues;
*American Japanese Intercultural Marriages: Personality Patterns and Problems
of Adjustment*, The Chinese Association for Folklore (Taipei) 1973; *Migration,*

Ethnic Minority Status and Social Adaptation, United Nations Social Defence Research Institute (Rome) 1973, with Otto Klineberg; and *Ethnic Identity: Cultural Continuities and Change*, Mayfield Publishing Company (Palo Alto) 1975, with Lola Romanucci-Ross. Forthcoming is a trilogy with Hiroshi Wagatsuma, Professor of Anthropology at the University of California at Los Angeles, reporting the results of ten years of joint research in an urban lower-class district in Tokyo, beginning with *Heritage of Endurance: Psychocultural Continuities and Delinquency in Japanese Urban Lower-Class Families*, ready for publication with companion volumes in preparation.

This Chapter

In this chapter George DeVos focuses, as does Francis Hsu in his, on the results of observation and field work in complex literate cultures. Professor DeVos started with studies of the adaptation and acculturation of Japanese-Americans in Chicago. The question of adjustment had particular meaning as a result of the incarceration of Japanese-Americans in concentration camps in the United States during World War II. From this and related work came an article that became a classic in personality and culture circles, ''Achievement, Culture, and Personality: the Case of the Japanese-Americans'' (with William Caudill). This article emphasized the convergence of values in Japanese society and American middle-class culture.

Later DeVos worked in Japan, in a fishing and in an agricultural village, as part of a massive team project. He discusses in this context various research techniques, problems of scale conversion, the use of depth interviews, adjustment tests, and the projective techniques—the Rorschach and modified TAT.

In his most recent collaborative research in Japan he has focused on three problem areas: juvenile delinquency and youth problems in a period of rapid social change; minority status for the Ainu, Korean, and Baraku, and its consequences; and experiences of personal alienation. These are very central problems, with both practical and theoretical implications in any complex modern society. He has also recently researched suicide in Japan, utilizing a variety of approaches.

His research and the interpretation of data are characterized by attention to complex interrelationships discerned through various forms of observation of natural phenomenon ranging from newspaper articles and other mass media to statistics on suicide rates in relationship to age, sex and periods of time, and also to elicited data such as individual biographies and projective test data. He applies theories and concepts from a broad interdisciplinary spectrum.

G.D.S.

7 The Japanese Adapt to Change

GEORGE DE VOS

For over twenty-five years I have been exploring how Japanese culture influences the adaptation of its members to rapid social change. As an anthropologist as well as a clinical psychologist, I have been concerned with patterns of positive adaptation as well as with symptoms of maladaptation and maladjustment.

In this chapter I will illustrate how I pursued my general interests, using specific methods ranging from the quantitative use of psychological tests to the analysis of literature and biography. In my Japanese research I have been able to do collaborative field work with Japanese colleagues. Secondary data are provided by the numerous publications of other Japanese social scientists. There is also statistical material available gathered by the government bureaucracies that function as an integral part of a highly literate culture. Working in an urban-industrial society is different from working in situations where intense field work by single individuals in the form of direct personal contact is the only means available for gathering data.

In addition to my academic background in sociology and anthropology and my training and experience as a professional psychologist employing diagnostic and therapeutic methods with individuals suffering from psychoses and psychoneuroses, I have made use of the insights gained from personal psychoanalysis. My training as a psychologist dealing directly with individual maladjustments has resulted in making me forever critical of any formal social science generalization that leaves out concern with the intense reality of subjective personal experience. I have found that I can best reconcile my psychological orientation and the structural study of society within the multidisciplinary approach of "culture and personality" as it was developed in the late forties as an integral part of anthropology. I was most impressed at that time by the works of Kardiner, Mead, Bateson, Hallowell, and Cora Du Bois. W. Lloyd Warner, my principal mentor in anthropology at the University of Chicago, was in the intellectual lineage of Durkheim and Radcliffe-Brown. He made no distinction between the social theory developed in sociology and anthropology. Therefore, I have continued to respond to the intellectual stimulation of work derivative from the orientation of Emile Durkheim and Max Weber, reconciling these approaches to social dynamics as best possible with the clinical literature of psychoanalysis.

Late in my graduate studies at the University of Chicago I began to feel a lack of specific training in controlled research methods. I had become increasingly intrigued by the possibilities of the intensive testing devises known as "projective techniques." A variety of techniques were being developed to elicit spontaneous expressions of personality either in the form of perceptual patterns, or in the form of attitudes about interpersonal relationships. At the time of my graduate work at the University of Chicago, there were a number of specialists working both with Rorschach inkblots and the Thematic Apperception Test. A variety of courses on projective tests were being given at the university and at a number of clinics and hospitals in the Chicago area. I spoke with Dr. David Shakow who was then serving as chief psychologist at the Illinois Neuropsychiatric Institute. Although I was a graduate in anthropology, he allocated to me one of the psychological internships funded at the institute. He had been sufficiently impressed by the enthusiasm of a young graduate and had himself the breadth of interest to encourage the cross-cultural application of psychological methods. I soon found that psychological testing was not something one could take on casually as a side interest. Therefore, I committed myself thoroughly for several years to the field of psychodiagnosis.

In the Army I had two and one-half years of special training in Japanese language and culture. Ruth Benedict's "The Chrysanthemum and the Sword" was published in 1946. I found it a stimulating, provocative attempt to integrate some of the major themes manifest in Japanese psychocultural behavior. Just subsequent to this publication, in early 1947, I heard that William Caudill and Setsuko Nishi were planning a study of Japanese-Americans who were relocating in large numbers in Chicago after leaving the internment camps where they had been confined during the war. Encouraged by Irving Hallowell and by William Henry, Caudill had determined to do his doctoral research in anthropology using the Thematic Apperception Test as his principal investigative device. Setsuko Nishi, a graduate student in sociology, was to study the voluntary organizations formed by the Japanese resettling in Chicago. Charlotte Babcock, a psychoanalyst with the Chicago Institute of Psychoanalysis, quickly joined us and began intensive psychoanalytic studies with a number of Japanese-American patients. I determined to use the Rorschach test on the same sample of subjects interviewed by Caudill and Nishi, having, for my part, received intensive instruction in this test from psychologists Al Hunsicker and Hedda Bolgar. Subsequently Estelle Gabriele, a psychiatric social worker, and sociologists Lee Rainwater, Alan Jacobson, and Adrian Corcoran joined our project.

The orienting concern for our joint research was the nature of Japanese-American social adaptation. We presumed we would be able to document the ill effects of the collective social trauma resulting from the wartime hysteria which caused Japanese-Americans to be forcefully removed from their homes in California. We were prepared to find evidence of a great deal of social and personal malaise. We were quite surprised by what we actually found. The Japanese community as a whole had been able to surmount the difficulties encountered without manifesting much evidence of either social disorganization or personal maladjustment. A number of community groups had quickly organized among the Japanese themselves. They sought little in the way of outside help. The existing social agencies in Chicago were seldom called upon to provide assistance. In our own direct contacts we did not find a group of disorganized or distraught individuals. Rather, the Japanese-Americans were quickly adapting to life in Chicago. They found housing for themselves and they re-established a very effective community network. Work opportunities opened up. Our survey of employers found that a favorable stereotype was formed after an initial reluctance to hire. Both Issei, i.e., the immigrant Japanese, and their American-born Nisei children quickly established a reputation for themselves as effective workers, and were soon sought out as employees. Our preliminary contacts, therefore, raised an intriguing question. Why were the Japanese-Americans able to adapt so well in spite of a history in America of racial and social discrimination?

ACHIEVEMENT, CULTURE AND PERSONALITY, THE CASE OF THE JAPANESE-AMERICANS

My direct contribution to the cooperative research on the Japanese-Americans in Chicago was to gather samples of Rorschach Test protocols as a means of systematically comparing a normative non-Japanese-American sample with the personality patterns of the Japanese-American-born generation as well as those of their immigrant parents. I gathered samples of fifty immigrant Issei and sixty American-born Nisei, men and women, and a smaller sample of thirty Kibei. These were Nisei who had been sent to Japan for several years of schooling during childhood. In effect, they were brought up, for some years at least, in a

Japanese peer group rather than an American one. I compared my 140
Japanese-American records with Rorschach samples of normal, neurotic,
and schizophrenic American subjects that were being collected as part of
a clinical research project. This project was conducted at the same time
at Michael Reese Hospital under the direction of Samuel Beck, a renowned specialist in psychodiagnosis. From those materials I selected my
American control sample of 160 normal and 50 neurotic and 50 schizophrenic records.

Although I initiated my Rorschach research with considerable skepticism, by 1949 I had become deeply impressed with the results. Differences in the perceptual patterns contrasting the generations were
clearly apparent. In contrast with those of the Issei, the Nisei norms
approximated in many respects the statistical norms of the American
groups. Our Kibei sample varied widely, but when averaged the norms
were generally found to fall between those obtained for the Issei and the
Nisei. In subsequent interdisciplinary work at Nagoya University between 1953 and 1955 the Rorschach results of a sample of eight hundred
Japanese in Japan were very similar to the norms I had obtained from
the much smaller sample of Issei immigrants in Chicago.

The Rorschach results on the Chicago samples are published in
detail in my doctoral dissertation and subsequent publications (DeVos
1952, 1954, 1955). I cannot present a brief summary table as it is
characteristically done statistically for Rorschach findings because I do
not agree with the validity of such use of the Rorschach. Lee Cronbach
(1949) among others has offered some trenchant criticism of the statistical techniques generally used in the Rorschach research presented by
anthropologists. For example, simple statement of means and standard
deviations are inappropriate forms of analysis for many of the variables.
Certain statistics cannot be used in Rorschach research because summary
scores do not meet certain basic assumptions, such as a normal distribution or equal distance between categories. In my work, therefore, I made
a serious attempt to overcome these limitations. The detailed statistics I
have presented in my work generally take the form of numerous chi-
square comparisons. Chi-square can reveal the level of confidence with
which one can assume that differences in distribution are not due to
chance factors. To illustrate: some reports are content to state the
means and standard deviations of color responses. I found such reporting a poor way to compare groups. While mean number of color
responses tells us something, it does not tell us enough about how one
group is actually handling color in comparison to another group. Therefore, I prepared a series of Chi-square tables in which the color was

compared with other research variables in a number of "show/don't show" 2 x 2 comparisons (DeVos 1952, 1954).

The most striking feature of the Issei Rorschach records was the emphasis on total configurations, uniting individual elements in complex comprehensive percepts. The Issei would indicate a sense of failure when they were unable to give such a total response to each of the blots. This pattern was modified in Nisei records toward an American readiness to attend to details as well as to whole configurations. There were also striking differences between Issei and Nisei in patterns of rigidity and maladjustment which seem to shift greatly with acculturation (DeVos 1955). The Nisei manifested an overall flexibility not very different from that found in the normative American group. In such differences one can immediately see some possible generalization about the greater psychological flexibility operative in American culture in contrast to the social rigidity demanded by the traditional culture of Japan. Simpler patterns of relatively higher rigidity were demonstrated later in the 1954 research in Japan. The Nisei in the American schools could be assumed to have come in contact with modifying influences that oriented them toward adopting types of personality controls prevalent in the American middle-class. Differences between Nisei and the Japanese-trained but American-born Kibei in terms of rigidity and maladjustment seem to indicate that the peer group influences to which the Nisei had been exposed in American education in contrast to those experienced by the Kibei in Japan tended to produce lower levels of rigidity.

The Nisei showed a higher mean maladjustment score than did the American normal group; however, they did not score nearly as high in this regard as the Issei and Kibei. I found, in brief, individual characteristics comprising the total maladjustment score shifted with acculturation. The Nisei women as a whole showed the most extreme shift away from the norms of the Issei. The shift between Nisei and Issei men was less radical. This greater difference in women was due in part to the fact that the Issei women showed far higher levels of rigidity and maladjustment in general than did the Issei men.

Later in Japan, however, we found no similar significant differences in the structural components of personality between the sexes as measured in the Rorschach Test. We must presume there was selectivity of those men and women who immigrated. The picture brides in some instances may have been individuals showing personal maladjustments which would have interfered with marriage in Japan, therefore they came to the United States.

As far as general measurements of psychopathology are concerned, I could not characterize the group as a whole as showing any strong propensity for any particular kind of psychoneurosis or psychosis. The records were highly varied. There was evidence in some records of obsessive-compulsive personality defenses, others could be characterized as hysteroid or paranoid. But it must be noted that such tendencies were found within the American normal control sample in equally varied proportions.

The Nisei were most like the Issei in the intellectual sphere. The Rorschach evidence from both generations strongly supported the concept of a group dedicated to accomplishment. The American control sample in contrast to the Nisei showed more sluggishness in intellectual approach. However, when broken down into socioeconomic levels, the Nisei records resembled those Americans in the control group who were classified in an executive occupational category in contrast to skilled, semi-skilled, or unskilled occupations. The similarities were in organizational drive and in the active orientation symbolized in movement responses. Some Nisei showed tendencies to strain beyond their available capacity. As a group however, they were able to demonstrate a high potential for bringing off this ambition-striving in a satisfactory fashion as far as their capacity to achieve was concerned.

The Rorschach evidence fits in with what we found from our interviews within the Japanese community and from the background statistics of education about the relatively high levels of attainment and other forms of manifest occupational success within the community. William Caudill (1952) found strikingly corroborative material on achievement drive in his TAT findings.

Caudill and I combined our findings in an article, "Achievement, Culture and Personality: The Case of the Japanese-Americans" (Caudill and DeVos 1956). This publication stressed the finding that acculturation as far as Japanese-Americans at least, did not necessarily mean total congruence of personality variables with Americans. In the case of Japanese-Americans, Japanese values find expression in modes of behavior which oriented the Japanese toward middle-class educational, occupational, social behavior. We emphasized the role of culture as creating a persistence which causes each immigrant group to the United States to respond in a characteristic way to patterns of relative acceptance or rejection or discrimination. Simply examining this process in a psychological framework on the one hand or a sociological framework on the other is not sufficient. Cultural continuity is found in modalities of socialization experienced within the primary family. Indeed, when looking at some of the emotional variables on the Rorschach, we found characteristic patterns of affective symbolism continuing through the two generations. I developed, therefore, a scoring system which permitted statistical comparisons of affective symbolism. Subsequently this scoring system has found use in clinical psychology in a number of different studies. Unfortunately, in cross-cultural studies there has been little attempt to do any systematic comparative analysis of symbolic material with the Rorschach (DeVos, Chapter 23 in Kaplan 1961). In the Japanese-American sample we found, for example, content responses indicating passivity. However, when these responses are seen in the total context of the record and measured against the relative number of active and passive movement responses and other indications, they assume somewhat less significance. These responses are evidence of a submerged current of passive dependency running through the Nisei male population. It is interesting that there is a slightly different tone to the dependency symbolism in the records of Nisei women. Their responses are of a childish nature which may have a happy and active quality rather than suggesting the kind of passivity found in the male responses. The movement responses of many of the Nisei women also indicate a submerged active aggressiveness. In the Nisei at least one sees in the Rorschach symbolism some contrasting patterns in symbolic content. Aware of this difference in the symbolic content I sought to develop some methods of quantification which could systematically test differences.

The tendency for both Issei and Nisei Japanese-Americans to give anatomical responses with sado-masochistic overtones was not replicated in the Rorschach material later obtained from Japan. I now consider such material related specifically to the peculiarities of minority status and the attendant pressures of discrimination inherent in American race relations. The content symbolism of the Rorschach seems to be more susceptible to situational pressures than other features considered in standard scoring. The patterns of approach indicated by the relative use of whole responses compared with large / smaller / rare details, the proneness to use color, movement, texture, etc., seems to remain more stable than does the symbolic content of the responses themselves.

I compared the prevalence of sado-masochistic anatomical responses in the Japanese-American sample with responses Horace Miner obtained from Algerian Arabs living in the Casbah of Algiers. These city Arabs differed from others tested by Miner living apart from direct French social domination in the outlying oasis. The city Arabs gave numerous responses depicting mutilation of flesh. Similarly, Goldfarb reported a prevalence of sado-masochistically toned anatomical material in the Rorschachs of an American Negro sample studied clinically by

Kardiner and Ovesey (1951). Theodora Abel and F. L. K. Hsu (1949) also reported the presence of anatomical material in the Chinese-American records they examined.

Finding this similarity in various minority group samples, I considered it possible to offer the hypothesis that sado-masochistic anatomical material can reflect in some way social constraints faced by individuals living in minority status. Such individuals develop characteristic defense mechanisms governing the expression of emotions. These responses specifically seem to reflect a sense of vulnerability to violence, that is to say a sense of susceptibility to aggressive penetration from the outside. A society that contains a threat of violence toward given minorities deepens the sense of vulnerability in those so threatened. They respond by characteristic unconscious as well as conscious controls exercised over the external expression of their responding aggressive feelings. These feelings are too dangerous to admit to full consciousness.

Another recurring theme that was very much in evidence in our Rorschach material as well as in the TAT material on American Japanese gathered by Caudill were feelings of personal inadequacy and concern over potential failure. The Issei records particularly gave considerable evidence of hostility turned inward on the self rather than toward the source of frustration.

The general conclusions from my studies in collaboration with Caudill and others were twofold. First, on the social-psychological level the facility of acculturation exhibited by Japanese-Americans was due principally to the peculiarities of superego formation within Japanese culture which allowed for optimal adaptive advantage in meeting social requirements of achievement in the context of American occupational requirements. Second, this successful adaptation was due to the fact that the system of values inculcated in Japanese culture converged with that operative within middle-class American society. This correspondence, however, did not imply total congruence. In fact, there was much to indicate, as both Caudill and I found in our later studies, that patterns of socialization in Japan exhibited characteristic differences from those pertaining in the United States.

SOCIAL VALUES AND PERSONAL ATTITUDES IN RURAL JAPAN

After an intensive period of professional activity in research and training acquired through working in a mental hospital as a chief psychologist, circumstances permitted me to turn again to a study of Japanese personality and culture. Dr. Tsuneo Muramatsu visited the United States and heard about our study of Japanese acculturation in

Chicago. He immediately turned to the possibility of conducting such research in Japan itself, using similar techniques. He sought to combine the talents of Japanese sociologists and psychiatrists as well as psychologists in a concerted effort on a larger scale to study the effects of change so visible to the Japanese themselves. From 1953 to 1955 I joined this collaborative project, applying for financial assistance from the Rockefeller Foundation and the Foundation Fund for Research in Psychiatry. We set up a research design which involved large-scale interviewing with social attitude scales and the use of smaller samples of projective tests in both urban and rural settings. We selected three representative villages, one a farming village, another a fishing village, and the third a mountain village involved both in forestry and marginal agriculture. We sampled a good proportion of the members of these villages. In the city samples we used block sampling methods using National Census tracts, selecting ahead of time a particular member of a family to be interviewed. We employed students majoring in sociology and psychology, specially trained by our staff in general interview and test administration. Depth interviews were conducted by senior staff members who were either social workers or psychiatrists. Opinion Schedules were used selectively together with a basic questionnaire given to a sample of twenty-four hundred individuals. Included were all the items of the F-scale of the "Authoritarian Personality" study (Adorno et al. 1950); excerpts from the tough-tender, liberal-conservative scale developed by Eysenck (1953); a direct opinion scale on the Japanese family system (the J-scale) measuring various attitudes about lineage, family obligation, forms of deference, family roles; and finally an indirect liberal-conservative scale of Japanese psychological attitudes (measurements of Japanese-type superstitions, forms of obligation, attitudes toward child rearing, etc.). This larger sample of opinion scales was then in selective instances coupled with samples of eight hundred Rorschach tests, eight hundred Thematic Apperception Tests (modified from the original Murray set, as to features of face, dress, and background detail), items adapted from the Insight Test of Sargent which we termed a "Problem-Situation Test" and some spontaneous figure drawings. Lastly, we did intensive interviews with selective family units.

Our staff consisted of more than thirty individuals. It was a unique opportunity to gather a considerable body of psychological data on the same subjects. Unfortunately, the overall potential of this study was not realized in what was ultimately published in Japan by Professor Muramatsu and his associates in 1962. This summary volume is more descriptive than analytical and lacks interpretation. The lack of published conclusions and inferences from this large-scale study has been a disappointment to me, knowing the potential richness of the material. Unfortunately it is a characteristic of Japanese group research generally, to subordinate individual interpretations to a bland consensus offensive to none.

In my own work, I have attended most to intensive materials gathered from Niiike and Sakushima, the agricultural and fishing villages. I based many of my generalizations about the use of projective methods in Japan on the materials from these two sites (DeVos 1973).

The work of translating opinion scales from one culture to another turned out to be difficult but not impossible. Cultural attitudes were revealed in an attempt to understand, together with colleagues from another culture, the psychological implications of particular items. In translating items from the F-scale, for example, it became apparent that some implicit cultural assumptions can be so radically different that some of the items of the F-scale seemed to be nonsensical to the Japanese. I remember in particular, as we worked on translation, that there was serious talk about dropping some items, since they were considered so absurd. One item in the scale, for example, relates to the idea of punishing homosexuals. An affirmative answer to this item weighs toward a high authoritarian score. My Japanese colleagues thought this particular item made no sense. Homosexuality in Japan is seen as an immaturity or an aberration, but does not evoke any idea of possible punitive social sanctions. As one of my colleagues confided, such an item deepened his suspicion that Westerners were indeed cruel and aggressive compared with Japanese.

A major problem in translation is not simply the question of different ideas but a problem of creating a natural way of expressing ideas, so that we could create psychologically equivalent items going from one language to another.

One subgroup took on the development of items stimulated by Helen Sargent's so-called Insight Test. This test (which we retermed a "Problem Situation Test") was used to supplement TAT pictures by creating a series of dilemmas that would lead to answers directed either toward individual behavior, lineage behavior, or to some expression of obligation to family or to individual goals. For purposes of analysis we grouped our items into six general categories: (1) child-parent relations; (2) marriage and parental obligations; (3) possible marriage choice and attitudes toward arranged marriage; (4) marital discord and family tensions; (5) problems of reputation and personal sensitivity; and (6) problems of duty obligations and responsibility.

We constructed such items as following: (Item 21) A young man gets into trouble. If he tells his parents they can help him, they will be very disappointed and will strongly disapprove of what he has done. (Japanese values stress the role of the child as a representative of his family. His disgrace brings disgrace on his parents. Such an item sought to elicit the degree to which such considerations are of spontaneous concern.) Another, (Item 12) for example, measured marriage and parental obligations: "A man's parents were habitually indebted to an individual for help. One day this individual asks the parents to accept his daughter as a bride for his son. The man's parents are very happy about the request." (A marriage as a fulfillment of obligation—*giri*—demands a child sacrifice his future as a repayment for obligation.) See Table 1.

The distribution of responses to Problem Situation Test Item 12 shows the difference between men and women in the village suggesting, as the other items, that older women are the most conservative in their attitudes concerning village life. In this item, three of the fourteen men queried, including one adolescent, directly accepted marriage on such terms, but five men definitely rejected the idea of marriage for obligation and there was a great deal of hedging in the replies gathered from the other men. Among the women, however, we see eleven of the sixteen queried on this item, including all nine women over thirty-five, accepted the idea of a marriage of obligation. Most of their replies explained directly that if one's family owed much to another family, one must pay in returning the favor because one owed so much to one's parents and because it would "set the parents at ease." In women under thirty-five more conflict appeared. One woman refused to answer, one hoped for future "investigation" since one cannot be married more than once, and two girls under eighteen directly refused to get married because of the "shame" or "dislike" for the person selected as a potential mate.

These responses represent rather clearly an interesting value differential operating in the village tested. All but the youngest women showed little conflict between filial piety and obligation, on one hand, and individual choice on the other. They clearly accepted the older collective virtues. Adolescent girls were troubled but they had little tendency to phrase their concern in terms of principles. They probably had no experience in defending their feelings by an appeal to such ideals as "woman's rights." Men of all ages, however, generally showed a hesitancy and a qualification in their answers and were more visibly caught in a dilemma between a sense of obligation and gratitude toward the parents and respect for individualism. As a group they appreciated the value of self-will as opposed to passive submission to obligation. In

TABLE 1
DISTRIBUTION OF RESPONSES TO PROBLEM SITUATION TEST ITEM 12

A man's parents are indebted to an individual for help.

(Men) One day he asks the parents to accept his daughter as a bride for their son. The man's parents are very happy about the request.

(Women) One day he asks for their daughter as a wife for his son. The woman's parents are very happy about the request. What would he (or she) do?

Age codes:	18+(a)	25+(y)	35+(m)	50+(o)	65+(s)	Men (total)	Women (total)
Men	3	3	4	3	1	14	
Women	5	2	5	2	2		16

I—Not marry

						Men (total)	Women (total)
						5	2
1. because he dislikes the other person							1(a)
2. because he already has a lover and dislikes the other person						1(a)	
3. because one should get married by one's own choice						3(a-y-s)	
4. because it is better to give things as thanks for receiving help						1(o)	
5. because he is ashamed							1(a)

II—Marry if the other person is suitable

	Men (total)
	3
1. because people should get married for themselves, not for parent and family or obligation	3(y-m-o)

III—Investigate

	Women (total)
	1
1. because one can't get married more than once in a whole lifetime	1(y)

IV—Marry

	Men (total)	Women (total)
	6	12
1. for obligation	3(a-m-o)	5(m-m-m-o-s)
2. for setting the parents at ease		6(a-y-m-m-o-s)
3. because he has had the will to be married	1(m)	
4. because he finds the other a suitable person	2(y-m)	1(a)

the hedging that appeared, however, it is evident there was only a veneer of active masculine self-will acquired over deeper attitudes signifying submission to possible family pressure.

In general, we found the problem situation test an extremely helpful technique, especially when used with other opinion scales and the TAT to assess the various levels of consciousness on which values exist in a changing situation. We found, for example, that TAT stories, less directly conscious, spontaneously reflected more conservative attitudes than did answers to the Problem Situation test. On the other hand, we could elicit by direct yes-no questions rather liberal statements which, in a sense, did not conform to underlying emotional attitudes.

This type of difference was found on different levels of consciousness and was so blatant I have written about an obvious "psychological lag" in Japanese culture. This psychological lag is behaviorally most apparent today in the fact that one can elicit by a standard attitude schedule anywhere in Japan much more liberal attitudes toward free marriage than one sees manifest in rates of free marriage. In effect, the overall rate of arranged to free marriages has not changed radically in the last twenty-five years, although the willingness to espouse—theoretically at least—a free marriage as an ideal example of autonomy is very prevalent wherever one asks for direct opinions concerning the subject.

In the modification of the TAT for use in Japan we had considerable discussion over what cards to use and whether or not to change the Western settings so that the decor and features of people would seem more natural to Japanese. We called on an excellent artist to try to alter the original cards used by Murray and change them into Japanese settings. In some instances we had alternate cards drawn and did extensive pre-testing on college students in Nagoya to see which cards would produce results similar to the original Murray set. Our results were somewhat surprising because, with minor exceptions, we found almost no difference between responses to the Japanese set we developed and to the American set when the cards were kept deliberately equivalent. My present conclusion is that we would have obtained almost identical results in Japan whether we had bothered to alter the set into a Japanese version or not.

In addition to the original set of cards used by Murray, we developed some cards of our own taken from various sources—from magazine illustrations as well as some deliberately commissioned, drawn to our specifications.

We ran alternative cards for card 1 which is a picture, in the American set, of a boy looking at a violin. Alternatively, in Japan we also used in half our sample the boy looking at a book. We had some initial doubt a violin would be seen with equivalent meaning as a symbol of achievement in Japan. Those who were skeptical, however, were proven wrong. The boy with the violin and the boy with the book served equally well to draw forth achievement themes and, in effect, these themes are more apparent in Japanese stories than those reported in samples of Americans in the United States. This emphasis on achievement themes on this card held true for rural villages as well as city samples.

Retrospectively, the one legitimate argument for using a separate Japanese set, therefore, was that although the Murray cards could be directly used in Japan to elicit stories, there would have been a sense of strangeness if on some of our cards we used Caucasian faces and then interspersed these with original Japanese scenes. Selected to test out some interpersonal topics not covered by the Murray cards, this switching of background perhaps would have aroused some undue attention to the fact that we were using Caucasians in some and not in others. The major reason for developing a "Japanese" set therefore was to use only cards with Japanese faces.

Our in depth interviews were a real challenge. It was the first time this sort of inquiry had been conducted by members of the psychiatric and psychological professions in villages. The period of preparation and organization was indeed exhilarating for me as a participant. The Japanese capacity to work together toward common objectives and to organize people efficiently into cooperative groups was very evident. Everyone worked hard and diligently and our preparations were concluded in an amazingly short time considering the difficulties involved. Most of our field work was conducted in the spring and summer of 1954. I learned the simple social pleasures of doing everything together—eating together, sleeping together under mosquito nets in one large tatami-room, and having our recreational time together. What is often seen as a status-conscious society does not feel separated by status when individuals are actually performing a common task. Those of high status and low status worked equally well together with a minimum of distraction by such concerns. There is a readiness to give and take between subordinates and superiors. Japanese seek out consensus and unanimity by being sensitive to possible disagreements and avoiding them. They accomplish this not by pulling rank but by patient persuasion wherever possible.

These social virtues facilitate organization and performance. They become a source of considerable frustration, however, to an American at a point where analysis and interpretation of data becomes necessary. At this point I found that Japanese are unnecessarily cautious and self-limiting, hesitating to make any interpretations which are not the common consensus of the entire group.

THEMATIC CONCERNS IN HUMAN RELATIONS

My work with projective tests in Japan, principally the TAT, led me to develop a system for analysing manifest content in story materials. The method I developed (see Table 2) is derived from a number of studies of social attitudes. Most obviously embedded in it are the type of analysis done initially by Henry A. Murray with the Thematic Apperception Test. But also visible are such influences as that of Parsons and Bales (1955) who attempted to analyze primary family role behavior in terms of "instrumental" and "expressive" categories.[1] Table 2 contains the essential categories I found to be important for the consideration of interpersonal role concerns. Among the five instrumental concerns are: achievement, competence, responsibility, power, and what I termed mutuality (cooperative-competitive concerns). I find these to be basic elements observable in instrumental concerns—whatever the cultural material I have attempted to categorize. (See Table 2.)

These concerns are interwoven with five expressive concerns: harmony, affiliation, nurturance, appreciation and pleasure (or their opposites). It is in the molecular pattern, in the interweaving of these elemental themes, that I find culturally based attitudes. When one goes beneath the surface appearance, for example, of family attitudes in Japan to understand motivations, one finds a very complex network of attitudes and expectations in which various instrumental and expressive motives are inextricably interwoven. One also finds expressions of cultural modalities in role interaction characteristic of various possible role positions in the society. These consistencies can be defined in formulating an ideal normative picture of Japanese life within the primary family, which I have attempted to do in several publications which have been summarized in my recent volume, *Socialization for Achievement* (1973). It is impossible to briefly recapitulate the major arguments of this book. I will simply attempt to illustrate here how I have come to the conclusion, out of thematic materials, that Japan is not, as many would

1. Instrumental behavior is *goal oriented* behavior—behavior that is a means toward actualizing some end either for oneself or in response to role expectations. "Expressive" behavior is emotional behavior which is its own end. It is not performed as a means but in order to experience what occurs when one acts.

TABLE 2
BASIC THEMATIC CONCERNS IN HUMAN RELATIONS

Thematic Concerns	Positive (Socially Sanctioned)		Negative (Socially Unsanctioned)	
	Active, initiated and/or resolved	Passive or Indeterminate — Passive or unresolved	Active, initiated and/or resolved	Passive, withdrawal and/or resolution
INSTRUMENTAL BEHAVIOR				
Achievement (will do) internalized goals (S)	Goal-oriented activity	Internal conflict, over-commitment, role diffusion, day-dreaming	Goal-oriented criminal activity	Anomic withdrawal, alienation from social goals
Competence (can do) internalized standards of excellence (S)	Avowel of capacity	Doubt about capacity, worry, diffuse anxiety, chagrin	Failure due to personal inadequacy	Sense of incapacity and inadequacy
Responsibility (ought to do) internalized moral standards and controls (S)	Sense of duty, assumption of obligation *Some forms of "altruistic" suicide* *	Remorse, guilt, regrets over acts of commission or omission	Profligacy, irresponsibility	Avoidance, escape *Some forms of 'anomic" suicide* *
Control-Power (must do) external power *superordinate:* (V)	Legitimate authority, power— mastery, persuasion	Defensive insecurity	Authoritarian dominance, security, control through destruction of feared object	Failure to assert proper authority (spineless, gutless)
subordinate: (V)	Liberation, autonomy or compliance	Ambivalence about authority or power	Rebellion, trickery	Submission

Thematic Concerns	Positive (Socially Sanctioned)	Passive or Indeterminate	Negative (Socially Unsanctioned)	
	Active, initiated and/or resolved	*Passive or unresolved*	*Active, initiated and/or resolved*	*Passive withdrawal and/or resolution*
Mutuality (with or against) interpersonal ethics				
competitive: (H)	Regulated competition, games, contests	Envy	Unethical competitive behavior	Capitulation withdrawal from competitive situation
cooperative: (H)	Concerted behavior (mutual trust)	Distrust, disagreement	Plotting, deception of a cohort	Sense of betrayal
EXPRESSIVE BEHAVIOR				
Harmony (with, emotionally) (H-V)	Harmony, peaceful relationships	Jealousy, fear of threat, emotional discord	Violence, injury, revenge *Some "egocentric" suicides**	Withdrawal into hostility and resentment
Affiliation (toward someone) (H)	Affiliation, intimacy, union, responsiveness, contact	Isolation, loneliness, alienation	Rejection of another	Sense of loss due to rejection or separation *Some "egoistic" suicides**
Nurturance (for someone) (V)	Nurturance, care, help, comfort, succor	Dependency	Withholding	Sense of personal, social, or economic deprivation *Some "egocentric" suicides**

Table 2 continued

Thematic Concerns	Positive (Socially Sanctioned)		Passive or Indeterminate (Socially Unsanctioned)	
	Active, initiated and/or resolved	Passive or unresolved	Active, initiated and/or resolved	Passive, withdrawal and/or resolution
Appreciation (from someone) *others:* (H-V)	Recognition of achieved or ascribed status	Feeling ignored, neglected, unappreciated	Disdain, disparagement	Sense of degradation *Some "anomic" suicides**
self: (S)	Self-respect	Doubt about worth, sense of shame	Self-abasement, self-depreciation	Sense of worthlessness *Some "egoistic" suicides**
Pleasure (within oneself) self-expression (S)	Satisfaction, sense of curiosity or creativity, enjoyment	Indifference, boredom	Masochistic behavior, asceticism	Suffering
		FATE		
Fortune Health, social, economic conditions	Good luck, fortunate circumstances	Anxiety over environmental or health conditions	Bad fortune, accident, injury, bad economic circumstances	Handicap, illness, death

Note: In each category the relationship between actor and others changes relative to the observer's perspective in the thematic concerns. Some categories are actor initiated and some are actor responsive. There are internalized concerns (self-oriented) coded (S) and other-oriented themes concerned either with horizontal interactions coded (H) or vertical interactions coded (V).

have it, a "shame" culture. Rather, Japanese are motivated by internalized guilt.

For example, I found in the TAT materials numerous expressions of a sense of guilt related to possible parental suffering. Stories will often have a sequence as follows: A daughter marries against her father's opposition but her husband dies and she becomes unhappy. Another story sees a mother strangling to death a woman who tempted her innocent son. Subsequently, the mother becomes insane and dies. The son begs forgiveness.

Very often stories in the TAT show the death of the parent followed by reform and hard work leading to success. There are stories such as that of a son scolded by his father. The son walks out of the house. The father dies. Subsequently the son reforms, works hard and becomes successful. Or, a son becomes more thoughtful of his mother after his father's death, leading to his ultimate success in life.

Some stories show how the blame for the socially intolerable action of a child is put on the mother whether she deserves it or not. The son, knowing this would happen to her, becomes sensitive about bringing suffering on his mother by having her blamed for his improper behavior.

One story sees a child dropping his father's precious vase. The father gets angry and scolds the mother for having allowed the child to hold it. The child grows up to become a fine man—a most startling type of sequence to be found in a TAT story plot. What is implicit in this story is the mother is "responsible." The son feels guilty because the mother is blamed. He expiates by hard work.

We also find failure leading to suicide. To Murray card "3," a slumped figure, I have received some stories of failed examinations leading to suicide. Such stories demonstrate the pressure felt about having to succeed and an inability to face failure, a tension felt by many Japanese. There are other examples found not only in projective tests but also in interviews, suggesting how strong guilt is aroused when there is failure in the performance of expected role behavior.

Among Japanese, there is little verbalizing of guilt or otherwise negatively toned attitudes expressed toward the direct physical expression of sexuality per se. Rather, one finds that guilt, whether the word is used or not, is easily evoked when there is possible loss of self-control, or the individual strays from his prescribed social role and becomes involved in a love relationship that interferes with his future-oriented life goals. For many Japanese it is the loss of occupational or family purpose more than sexual expression itself that is a source of guilt in heterosexual relationships. I have come to regard this emphasis on internalized guilt related to parental expectations and potential parental injury as a major dynamic that explains the Japanese concern with achievement. There is a Calvinistic-like need in many Japanese to validate oneself through performance. This tendency plays a significant part in the collective efforts of Japanese society and has shaped its pattern of adaptation to modernization and industrialization (cf. *Socialization for Achievement,* 1973).

SOCIAL PROBLEMS IN JAPAN: DEVIANCY AND ALIENATION

The cultural definitions of achievement and normative role expectations in any society have their negative as well as their positive sides. Economic and social conditions have negative as well as positive influences. In any complex society one finds various forms of deviant behavior including crime and delinquency and relative rates of suicide and mental illness, the dark side of desired ideals and values. There are statistical indices available to suggest at least the relative incidence of such systems of personal and social malaise. However, to simply analyze the maladaptive features of society in such strictly sociological terms is insufficient. Only by combining some knowledge of psychodynamic principles with investigation of social determinants can one gain a true integrative perspective on both the subjective and objective conditions —the positive and negative possibilities faced by individuals in culture.

Starting from a sociological perspective Durkheim's basic theory of anomie is a valid and useful one. Anomie is a condition found in societies that have lost social cohesion. A-nomia (absence of regulation) results in individual malaise—alienation. The individual without social constraint becomes disorganized—his behavior becomes deviant or he suffers internal conflicts. This concept helps us examine how social determinants influence the meaning of deviant social behavior. However, as used by sociologists it does not refer directly to psychological states or personal experience. As actually experienced, however, personal difficulties are only in the most indirect way related to the overall conditions of social cohesion existing in a society. Knowledge of social conditions does not preclude studies on a psychological level.

In my collaborative research with Japanese I have concentrated on three social problem areas: juvenile delinquency and youth problems in a period of social change, minority status, and experience of personal alienation. From 1960 to 1970 I worked with various Japanese collaborators doing research on the general issue of delinquency in Japan, analyzed from a cross-cultural, comparative perspective. During this period of time I worked with Hiroshi Wagatsuma on questions of the present fate of the Japanese outcastes the Burakumin or former ''Eta''—a residual pattern of social discrimination continuing from feudal times. We sought to draw conclusions concerning the psychocultural determinants of a general theory of caste behavior (cf. DeVos and Wagatsuma,

Japan's Invisible Race, 1966). The methods used in these latter studies were less specifically oriented around psychological testing. We conducted intensive interviewing, obtaining life history material as well as test material from selected families. We paid a great deal of attention to secondary sources, obtaining statistical compilations from government records. We also turned to individual biographies and literary productions.

It is my contention that social science demands flexibility in the use of methods and that, indeed, some problem areas can only be approached with multi-disciplinary efforts. The role of the anthropologist in such endeavors is to keep a focus on the cultural variables involved in the various forms of social behavior examined. With Keiichi Mizushima I made a historical examination of attitudes toward what is deviant or criminal. We went into considerable detail exploring the nature of the Japanese underworld and its organization, using mostly secondary sources but also taking advantage of some opportunities to interview individuals who are part of underworld organizations in Japan. One can, in certain instances, take advantage of the neutral position as a foreigner in Japanese culture to gain candid interview material that is not always possible for social scientists working directly within their own culture. In assessing how the underworld is organized in Japan, it quickly became apparent there are some cross-cultural parallels between Japanese Yakuza organizations and the Sicilian Mafia. One apparent similarity between the Japanese and the American criminal social scene is the conservative political ideology of the underworld which tends to support rightist political causes and conservative social ideas. In Japan there is periodic covert or even overt conflict with leftist elements of the present social structure.

The social attitudes found in the underworld are directly opposite to those dominant among Japanese students alienated from, and critical of, their modernizing society. The postwar social scene in Japan has been characterized by noticeable trends towards some forms of more assaultive crimes and political confrontation among youth. I try to distinguish in my writings between characteristics of politically motivated deviant behavior such as in confrontation of student groups and behavior more characteristically lower-class which takes less political-ideological forms in the expressions of deviant attitudes.

The present-day student movements in Japan must be seen in their total historical and cultural context. They are the results of processes of modernization, and the peculiarly marginal status of the uncommitted student is a feature not only of modern Japanese society but of industrial societies throughout the world. There are certain alienating features of what has been termed "adolescence" which characterize different class levels of modern societies differentially. Increase or decrease in lower-class alienation is most often neatly represented by statistics on delinquent behavior. But in middle-class youth it is represented by eloquent and disturbing vocal, political as well as social criticism.

In relating student malaise to the general pressure toward accomplishment discussed above, I find it is not that middle-class youth have lost their need for achievement, it is more that they raise questions concerning the total context on the direction being taken by their society —achievement for what? for what ultimate social ends? Evidence of the presence of social anomie in Japan as elsewhere is found represented in the severe questioning of implicit goals in a society which has come to be structured in terms of economic objectives with loss of regard for other social values.

MINORITY STATUS AND DEVIANCY IN JAPAN:
THE CASE OF THE BURAKUMIN

In the United States, many of the negative aspects of failure are related to problems of ethnic pluralism. Japan, strictly speaking, is not a pluralistic society. Nevertheless one finds that in Japan four percent of the population can be classified in one way or another as part of some recognizable minority (Weatherall and DeVos 1974). Some of these groups are indeed small in number. The Ainu population in Japan in no way proportionately approximates the relative number of American Indians, our aboriginal population. Nevertheless, many of the problems of the Ainu are similar to those found by American Indians. There are, numerically at least, more besetting problems related to the minority Koreans and Burakumin, who together comprise about two and one-half to three percent of the Japanese population. The Korean minority approximates six hundred thousand, the outcaste minority of former untouchables is estimated to be more than two million.

Modern Japan and the present-day United States share the sustaining ideology that all social strata and ethnic subdivisions, whatever their number, are imbued with sufficient goal-directed achievement motivation to undergo the sustained periods of vocational training after puberty required to equip the oncoming generation with all the specialized skills necessary to maintain a very complex technological society in efficient operation. At the same time, it has long been evident to American social scientists that such an ideal of training everyone to technical competence is not being realized. From the vantage point of the psychological anthropologist, one can contend there are very manifest, limiting psychological, as well as sociological forces operating to prevent optimal educational-vocational advancement among the members of specific minority subgroups. Japan, as the United States, reveals similar evidence of social dislocation and deviancy in specific minority groups that seem to indicate that some form of social inhibition is operative which prevents optimal exploitation of "human resources."

It is apparent to Americans that particular ethnic minorities in the United States respond to being barred from full participation in society by behavior that is very often disruptive both to themselves and to the majority. There is no doubt that discriminatory practices have had adverse effects that can be well documented. Discrimination has long-term generational effects on the members of disparaged groups. Concepts of self are negatively influenced by social discrimination. Socialization experiences within disparaged minorities become different through time if they are not already so. Patterns leading to self-debilitating forms of social response become inevitable. To illustrate our research approach in this area, I will concentrate on some of our findings related to attitudes toward authority which we found to be present among the Japanese former outcastes.

In doing our overall delinquency study in Japan, we had no initial intention of concentrating very specifically on minority problems. However, through fortuitous circumstances we gained the trust of members of the outcaste minority and were able to do a great deal of individual interviewing as well as gathering available statistical materials. This opening into the outcaste community developed while we were working in the city of Kobe going through the records of delinquents having contact with the family court system. In my work as a consultant with research projects on American delinquents in the United States, I had previously made a survey of various statistics on arrest rates and other forms of police contact recorded for the various minority groups in the state of California. There is no doubt there is differential attention paid by police toward minority group members. Nevertheless, this social factor is insufficient to explain the very high rates of arrest of youths from the black and Mexican-American communities in California. There is some representation in these statistics of actual behavior differences found in these groups, especially when one examines the type and nature of offence for which the individuals are institutionalized. We knew that in official legal practice there is no overt discrimination toward the outcastes in Japan. They are not recognized in any way in official documents. Nevertheless, in such cities as Kobe there are maps available that very carefully delineate the boundaries of the various ghettos in which the outcastes live. We made use of such a map to spot on it the residency of those youths arrested by the police over a period of several months. We also looked at names and were able to draw out a list of individuals with Korean backgrounds. By this means we established there was an arrest rate among Koreans seven times, and among the Burakumin four times, that of the majority population.

In the process of this research on differential delinquency patterns, we were able to gain contact with members of the outcaste community and do intensive interviewing with them. We found the expression of social attitudes toward social authority differed radically with what we had found among majority Japanese. These differences related to what I term "differential socialization experiences," "differential role expectancies," "different types of social self-identity," "different forms of reference groups" and "selective permeability to experiences"—all of which characterize outcaste youth in comparison with those of the majority culture. Let me illustrate briefly.

Differential Socialization within the Buraku Community

Our informants confirmed that within the outcaste ghettos one is more apt to find open expressions of impulsive and volatile behavior. While hostility within the community is muted, expressions of hostile aggressive behavior toward outsiders are somewhat implicitly encouraged. According to our observations and interviews, fathers of outcaste children are prone to use physical punishment more than fathers in the lower-class majority community. At the same time outcaste children are told to control themselves so they will not be a disruptive factor within the community. But hostility, hate and aggression developed within the family or peer group are less negatively sanctioned when they are displayed toward members of the majority community who are judged to merit such hostility because they are prejudiced and practice discrimination toward outcastes. Lacking sexual inhibitions, children from the outcaste community are more likely to be aware of the sexual practices of adults than the children living in a majority community. Buraku adults are more apt to talk openly about sex. Children, therefore, have more opportunity to learn about sexual behavior verbally as well as visually in the very tight living conditions found in many of the outcaste urban ghettos.

Differential Role Expectancy

Although the vast majority of the dwellers in the ghetto are on the lowest economic level, the urban Buraku community shows certain types of socioeconomic stratification. Generally there is considerable casualness about marriage ties and sexual fidelity and temporary liaisons are reported to be fairly common. Whereas traditionally a husband's infidelity is expected in every stratum of Japanese society, women in the outcaste community are also prone to take up temporary liaisons without experiencing heavy negative community sanctions. Physical aggression from husband to wife and from parent to child is frequent. In the Buraku, however, the upper-class outcaste families are more muted in their expression of aggression and practice patterns closer to those of the majority middle-class society. However, identification as a member of the Buraku makes members of middle-class families feel a sense of vulnerability about their inability to control their passions. The self-identity of the Burakumin carries with it, even among higher-status individuals, the likelihood of a pejorative self-image.

Self-Identity as a Burakumin

The most poignant material gathered in our study was that related to the social self-identity of Burakumin. In this respect our material resembles some of that described in Kardiner and Ovesey in their 1950 studies conducted on the New York black community. One must state that this prevailing pattern of social self-disparagement among American blacks seems to have been radically altered by the social and political events occurring subsequent to 1950. It is also apparent that recent political movements in the outcaste community had a similar salutary effect on many of the outcastes as they attempted to assert for themselves a more affirmative, positive self-image. Nevertheless, a great deal of our material demonstrated that an internalized negative attitude toward the self reflects many of the majority attitudes, even among those who are consciously making strong efforts and diligently work to overcome the effects of a disparaged social position.

With one story reported in our volume I will illustrate how difficulties of self-acceptance operate. Sometimes a child living in a family attempting to "pass" only becomes aware of his disparaged social self after reaching adolescence.

The journal *Buraku* reported a tragic case of self-discovery and its aftermath: Etsuko took her life at eighteen years of age using an agricultural chemical obtained at school. A local newspaper reported that her suicide was due to a nervous breakdown resulting from excessive adolescent sentimentality, and the national newspapers, the *Mainichi* and the *Asahi,* each reported a different cause. The *Mainichi* reported that the girl killed herself because she had been suspected of theft, and the *Asahi* attributed her suicide to discrimination at her school. The complete story was complex. One of Etsuko's friends at school, also a Buraku girl, was quoted as saying, "Etsuko is the only Buraku girl in her class; therefore, it was she who was suspected when there were a number of thefts in her classroom. I am certain she did not do it but she became very upset when she was suspected. Shortly before, a thoughtless inquiry had been made at the school to identify the Buraku students in every class. I am not saying that this inquiry made Etsuko kill herself but it certainly was one of the causes. It was thoughtless of her school to make such an inquiry; instead of giving warmth or help to Etsuko who needed it, the school actually increased discrimination by carrying out such a strange inquiry." [DeVos 1973, pp. 405ff.]

Etsuko's father was of the Buraku but in attempting to pass he had moved out of the Buraku community a long time before, and had very little subsequent contact with his former community. The family was relatively well off, and the parents did not want to inform their children about their Buraku status. Etsuko and her three sisters grew up without any knowledge of their outcaste background. Further, according to Etsuko's friend, Etsuko had even exhibited some prejudice against Buraku people. However, in some manner or other, shortly before her death she learned about her own identity. At school there were some students who became suspicious about her hidden background. Then came the inquiry by the school held supposedly for the purpose of finding "Buraku" problems in the school. Etsuko must have developed a complicated ambivalent feeling toward her own identity as a Buraku person. The inquiry at the school which made all the students aware of Etsuko's origins must have been a severe shock. This was followed by the suspicion of being a thief which is sufficient explanation for the tragic suicide that followed.

We have found expressed in our interviews considerable unconscious and suppressed negative self-images. When we asked one informant whether he thought that Buraku people are visibly discernible, his answer was affirmative. He said, "Yes, the Buraku persons are usually identifiable," and hastened to add, "at least for other Buraku members they are identifiable." He mentioned too that when he sees or meets somebody with a Buraku background who is successfully passing, he can rather easily tell that person's hidden nature. We asked him specifically how, but he could not give us any precise explanation. After thinking for a while, he finally made this statement: "Living conditions within the outcaste community are terrible—torn-down houses, unsanitary conditions, distasteful occupations, dirty food, bad language, violence, fighting, laziness—everything that is bad and ugly is found in outcaste districts.'' He believes that these conditions produce what he has termed ''something vicious, something dirty, something unnamable, as something that can be felt like a strong odor. This something horrible permeates the people who are born and reared and live in this area, something like a bad body odor. Even when an individual leaves the community, wherever he may go there is something horrible, which is discernible and always accompanies him.'' This something can be found in speech, or mannerisms, or facial expressions. He said he believes that a Buraku person gives an impression that differs from what one receives from a non-Buraku. Here we see an example of a man from such a community inadvertently expressing that he himself has a terrible image of his own people as somehow unclean. We cannot assess how much of this negative feeling he directs consciously toward himself (DeVos and Wagatsuma 1966, pp. 405ff.).

In addition to such statements we obtained a great deal of anecdotal material about attitudes directed against outside authorities whether in the form of welfare cheating or in the form of deceit. The evidence was clear that when one is part of a discriminated group there can occur a certain assuagement of one's disparaged self-image by being deviously clever against the hated majority.

Educational Problems Among the Burakumin

Another striking parallel between disparaged minorities in the United States and that of the Burakumin in Japan is the evidence of difficulty in obtaining jobs. Statistics showed that the Burakumin are systematically kept out of the large-scale industries by some method of informal screening. This type of screening is most directed toward those with lower scholastic attainment, that is to say, ordinary Japanese with poor school background are much more apt to obtain jobs than Burakumin with poor school background. The higher the Burakumin manages to achieve educationally the less likely he is to face easily recognizable social discrimination. It is our conviction that discrimination occurs even in the higher occupational levels; although it may be harder to document it is still very evident.

As far as school attainment itself is concerned, it is clearly evident that the Burakumin do poorly. They also do poorly on the various forms of IQ tests administered within the Japanese educational system. According to Tojo (1968), the results of the Tanaka-Binet group I.Q. test administered to 351 fifth and sixth grade children included 77

TABLE 3

COMPARISON OF THE TANAKA-BINET I.Q.
TEST SCORE PERCENTAGES OF BURAKU
CHILDREN WITH THOSE OF MAJORITY
GROUP CHILDREN IN A CITY NEAR OSAKA

I.Q.	Non-Buraku children (274)	Buraku children (77)
Above 125	23.3	2.6
124–109	31.8	19.5
108–93	23.3	22.1
92–77	11.7	18.2
Below 76	9.9	37.6

TABLE 4

COMPARISON OF TANAKA-BINET TEST
SCORES OF PRIMARY SCHOOL CHILDREN
IN FUKUCHIYAMA CITY

	I.Q. average
Buraku boys (10)	89
Buraku girls (9)	87
Non-Buraku boys (10)	105
Non-Buraku girls (12)	103

TABLE 5

COMPARISON OF GRADE-POINT AVERAGES
IN PRIMARY AND JUNIOR HIGH SCHOOL
IN FUKUCHIYAMA CITY

Primary School	
Buraku boys (12)	2.29
Buraku girls (10)	2.59
Non-Buraku boys (10)	3.29
Non-Buraku girls (15)	3.16
Junior High School	
Buraku students (8)	2.2
Non-Buraku students (11)	3.3

Buraku children. This test was done at a school in Takatsuki City near Osaka. As in other reported illustrations, the I.Q. scores of Buraku children are markedly lower than those of the non-Buraku children.

The implications of such results and the others illustrated in the accompanying table are obvious. Living in a disparaged minority status position in society does something to the self-concept which becomes reflected in their performance scores. This is not to say that whatever happens does not become part of the functioning ego of the child. In effect, in such sad circumstances children are in some ways severely debilitated. At an early age they are prevented from reaching anywhere near their biological potential.

In the instance of the Japanese Burakumin, difference in "racial" origin does not serve as a possible explanation. Social discrimination itself has a deleterious effect on the development of a type of intellectual functioning that serves well in school performance.

Another study in Japan done by Nomura (1956) illustrates graphically how pejorative social attitudes can affect performance. In Izumo in Shimane prefecture on the seacoast of southwestern Japan, there are still found the remnants of a long tradition of fox possession. Japanese folk beliefs in this area have it that a fox can possess individuals against their will. There is also the belief that given families have a relationship with a "fox" who helps them just as the devil in New England was thought to help certain families to prosper. Families who are suspected of having a fox are called "black" in this area in contrast with "white" families who are "pure" and have had no such evil contact. In many communities in this area people are either classified as "black" or "white" and these classifications continue through several generations. In effect, marriage across the "black" or "white" line has been tabooed because it is believed that if a member of a "white" family marries a member of a "black" family, all the other members of the "white" family become "black." In this area one finds Burakumin who are treated even more stringently as outcastes than elsewhere. They are ranked socially below the "black" families, of course. Nomura compared the "intelligence" of students in three junior high schools where children of "white" families, "black" families, and Burakumin matriculated together. Using two different kinds of intelligence tests, he found that the results were uniform. "White" children average significantly higher on these tests than the children either from "black" families or from the Buraku ghettos in the vicinity.

Again one notes it is social disparagement here that must be considered a significant variable, rather than possible considerations of genetic differences.

SUICIDE IN JAPAN: A PSYCHOCULTURAL APPROACH

To illustrate another possible psychocultural explanation of social phenomena, I would like to cite briefly findings of my work and that of Wagatsuma related to the appearance of extreme forms of alienation in Japanese that can lead to suicide. For the past ten years I have been gathering examples, from the press and other sources, of suicidal behavior in Japan, seeking to find patterning which can be related in some form to a psychocultural explanation. During this period Wagatsuma and I have examined the writings of well-known Japanese authors who have written about suicide. We have done intensive analysis of biographical materials on these authors and related their life history to their writings about self and society. I find that neither the usual Durkheimian sociological explanations of suicide on the one hand, or those forwarded by psychoanalytical writers on the other are sufficient to explain my data. I have attempted, therefore, to combine what is satisfactory in these two disparate approaches in developing categories of suicide which I have set up in classifying the materials gathered. I find that one can, in effect, separate six themes in Japanese suicidal tradition that have fair reoccurrence and that suggest a Japanese cultural flavor to self destruction.

Overall, I feel that foreign attention to Japanese suicide has been drawn by the spectacular nature of some forms of traditional suicide. It is not true that Japan has more suicides than elsewhere. Although, shortly postwar, the Japanese rate indeed was very high and close to the top of countries reporting, the present rate of suicide in Japan has fallen to approximately sixteenth position among the countries represented in the documents of the World Health Organization. The statistics available on suicide do, however, reveal certain overall Japanese characteristics.

First, more than in most countries, suicide is committed most frequently by individuals under thirty. There is a U-shaped curve in suicide graphs with a dip in the middle years, then a rise to a high level in old age. Second, proportionate to European and American statistics, women in Japan commit suicide with greater frequency.

The social phenomena of suicide in Japan raises certain questions in terms of psychodynamic and sociological factors that, I contend, are operative cross-culturally. In Japan as elsewhere there are observable social, cultural, economic, and political pressures that have characteristic effects through the generations in producing a fairly constant number of individuals who resolve both external pressures and inner dilemmas

TABLE 6
DEVIANCY AND ALIENATION

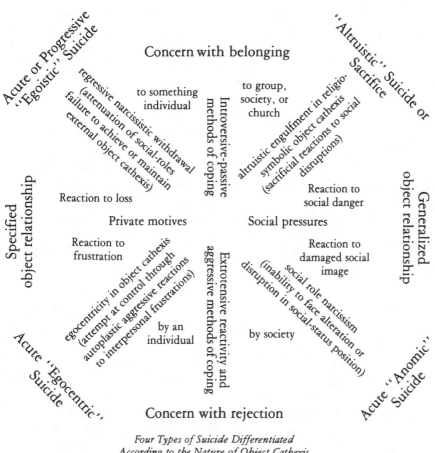

Four Types of Suicide Differentiated
According to the Nature of Object Cathexis
and Personal-Social Polarities of Suicidal Motivation

through suicide. There are also acute social, economic, and political convulsions occurring periodically that cause overall fluctuations in the rate. The question then arises: what makes Japanese at a particular age or social segment particularly vulnerable to the logic of suicide?

Patterns in Japanese Suicide

Self-sacrifice and dedication. There are special culturally stressed themes of sacrificial suicide in Japan related to Durkheim's concept of altruistic suicide. From the suicidal courage of the Japanese warrior

Samurai to the deaths of Kamikaze pilots in World War II, there are numerous instances citing the use of suicide as some form of instrumental behavior related to the protection of the collectivity. Suicide, indeed, is related to the concept of dedication to role. It is a form of sacrifice. It can be seen as an act of responsible dedication or an assumption of responsibility for the failure of one's subordinates. Taking responsibility can also require suicide as a form of reproach to underlings who are not functioning properly.

The traditional cultural logic of Seppuku or Harakiri contains a central belief that suicide is an honorable act preserving the status of the house of the offender and relieving other members of the family of any responsibility and punishment for the unsanctioned behavior of one of its members. By submitting positively to a demand for ritual suicide, the offender affirms his own responsibility and cleanses himself and his subordinates of past deviation.

I have also had reported to me numerous examples of mothers who threaten suicide as a way of bringing wayward children to proper behavior. The children respond to such a threat because they know that it has considerable weight and may indeed be carried out by a mother who feels "responsible" for the bad behavior of her child.

Responsibility and a rupture of social role. Durkheim's conception of anomic suicide appears in many dramatic forms in Japan. According to Durkheim's concept, a rupture of social cohesion—for example an acute economic slump—disrupts the social roles of individuals. In this normless state, they may find adapting to a different lifestyle intolerable; hence, they resort to suicide.

There are numerous social situations in Japan in which harmonious adjustment to a given social role is by circumstances irrevocably disrupted. To the Westerner these situations do not seem as severe as to a Japanese. To us, therefore, there seems in Japanese suicide an undue involvement of sensitivity to the potential of irrevocable damage to one's self-esteem. I termed my explanation of this "role-narcissism." I have discussed at length how the Japanese sense of dedication involves a sense of vulnerability to a disruption of status (Chapter 18, DeVos 1973). Role narcissism is an intense identification of one's total self with one's professional or social role, leading to the exclusion of other social meaning. Therefore, should there be a rupture in status, the individual has no other alternative means for adjusting himself to a different role in his society. On the surface, at least, some Japanese suicides related to a rupture of status seem to be acts resulting from over-rigid interpretation of responsibility. Sometimes, examined more closely however, what one finds is an apparent unwillingness to face circumstances that would force one to live with the consequences of irresponsibility. Whatever the case, such suicidal acts are characterized by the inability to live with the permanent alteration of one's image as seen by others. This is the chief ingredient of anomic suicide as defined by Durkheim.

Suicides of social attenuation. Examples of Durkheim's "egoistic" suicide are also found in Japan. In some suicides one finds a profound expression of a sense of loss of meaning, and an incapacity to overcome a chronic inner state of alienation. Intensely introspective individuals do not accept the same levels of belief or social belonging that satisfy the uncritical. Those who seek an idiosyncratic meaning for life may suffer the consequences of a profound alienation and an inability to sustain themselves by adherence to some form of collective belief. In Japan, for traditional cultural reasons, some forms of religious conversion available to Westerners do not work well. One cannot assuage one's sense of aloneness and helplessness by an overwhelming commitment to a transcendent god as is possible in many Western religious conversion experiences. The ultimate loyalty of a Christian was belief in such a god. For a Japanese it was to his given role of service to family and social authority. Religious transcendence is not as quickly available to the distressed, alienated Japanese intellectual. Suicide may be his only alternative.

Loss and suicide. One finds that many Japanese have developed a type of narcissistic capacity to find in one's physical and mental prowess a substitute for a meaningful interpersonal relationship. In such individuals the processes of aging and a diminution of vigor are severe challenges to the maintenance of meaning. For others, the loss of a loved one in old age results in either a devitalization that withdraws the individual from proper attention to body needs, or it can result in such a sense of total loss that suicide results. Statistically Japan reports one of the highest rates for suicide among those above sixty years of age.

Suicide as an attack on a vulnerability to guilt. A type of suicide not discussed in sociological analysis is one that is very common in Japan. A suicidal act can be some form of expressive retribution or an ultimate attempt to compel action. These suicides which I have termed "egocentric" suicides in Japan at least presume an implicit knowledge that others are potentially guilty for inflicted suffering—as I described in reference to the inculcation of guilt in Japan. One's own suffering can be manipulated as a means of compelling action on the part of others. This mode of suicide is particularly open to individuals who are in some dependent status either emotionally or socially. According to Takeo Doi, the noted Japanese psychiatrist, the dependent person in Japan practices *amae* ("a form of emotional manipulation practiced by the subordinate toward a superior to induce nurturant behavior toward a dependent").

Suicide as a collaborative act. Finally, in Japan one finds numerous instances in which suicide is done with another person. Some of these suicides are in effect collective family expressions of bankruptcy in which severe economic distress cannot be faced. In effect, family suicide which occurs with some frequency is a form of anomic suicide in which the status of the family as a collectivity is so hopelessly impossible that the husband in agreement with the wife kills her, the children, and then himself.

Another frequent form of suicide is the dual suicide of a heterosexual pair. Contrary to the supposition that these are always lovers who had an intense involvement, sometimes we find that such supposed "love suicides" amount to a coming together of two individuals who share a like-minded sense of despair about life. They support one another to the extent that their suicidal resolve is maintained. Each individual feels it is impossible to carry out the act alone; but in collaboration with one another, they manage to bring it to conclusion.

Vulnerability to Suicide and Japanese Socialization

Having found some means of categorizing patterns in Japanese suicide, the challenge was then to relate these to socialization experiences that would lead to the suicidal act. What causes vulnerability to suicide in Japanese culture? In attempting to answer this question I had to return to the same themes that helped me explain the intense sense of dedication to achievement found in Japanese.

The first prevailing culture theme is that of intensity of care given to children resulting from the mother's sense of strong dedication to nurturance. There is no doubt Japanese mothers express a degree of selflessness and absorption in a child's life that can scarcely be matched in other societies. The pattern does not stop with the intensity of dedication to the maternal role during early childhood. The mother, in this sense, continues until her children, in turn, internalize a necessary dedication to role. The modes of socialization practiced not only teach the patterns of self-sacrifice but those of suffering as a means of producing guilt in others. That is to say, traditional Japanese parents, especially the mother, suffered when they witnessed the bad behavior of their children. A child becomes increasingly aware that his or her bad behavior causes suffering in parents, therefore the child begins to sense a terrible capacity to hurt loved ones. This induction of guilt results in a more severe internalization than that which results from threat of punishment, retribution, or abandonment. In addition, Japanese socialization also depends upon the use of the outside community as a sanctioning agent. A child's behavior can result in the family suffering through negative community attitudes directed toward the family as a whole. Japanese are made acutely sensitive to a need to maintain social belonging and to develop a strong sense of interdependency with others.

In Japan, therefore, one finds a continuous cultural reinforcement of the type of maternal dedication to the child through which the male child especially seems in some sense to become an extension of the mother's masculine principle, to be indulged and directed by subtle controls toward future male social role realization. The social role becomes "libidinalized" for many children. Japanese mothers continually reinforce the male child's growing concern with a future need to accomplish and to justify (to himself and to others) his social worth in what is covertly if not overtly a competitively organized outer world. The female child conversely learns to assume her future role, that of a whole-hearted dedication to assisting a husband and afterwards her male children toward the adequate assumption of male occupational roles. An intense, lifelong bond to the mother is the heart of the continuing closeness of the family unit.

In Japan as elsewhere, an early problem over maternal attachment may produce a later inability to transfer a sense of intimacy to others. It may give rise to a strong regressive tendency that prevents any transfer of libidinal intensity to later "objects." In Japan the body remains a source of pleasure. The individual may remain intensely aware of both positive and negative body experiences leading in some instances to forms of body narcissism. He or she may develop the body as an object of hate as well as love. This psychodynamic involvement with the body may only appear as a suicidal propensity late in life. The effects of early socialization may take their toll even in old age. In other individuals where there is a somewhat higher level of psychosexual maturation, a narcissistic preoccupation may be transmuted directly to the social role. The occupational and social expectancies placed on the individual become excessively cathected. His investment in his role substitutes for satisfaction that cannot be attained in interpersonal intimacy. Within such individuals in Japan there is a continuous sensitivity to the judgment of others about success or failure. It is not surprising therefore that adult Japanese who conform well to expectations can make their social occupational role the ultimate moral meaning of life, be it that of the male in the external world or the mother within the primary family.

There is, according to Doi and others, a difficulty for Japanese to realize *jibun*—an individual sense of self. One finds, for example, that, despite cultural readiness for introspective probings and preoccupations, Japanese are characteristically resistive to psychoanalytically oriented forms of psychotherapy. To the more individualistically oriented Westerner the immediate explanation occurs that Japanese cannot, for some reason, face underlying ambivalent feelings toward parents that go counter to a deeply inculcated sense of filial piety. While this is descriptively accurate, if we leave the explanation at this point, we still do not achieve a fully dynamic explanation of why Japanese cannot readily criticize parents or face the fact that a mother or father may not be ideal in realizing parental role expectations. The fact is that the Japanese have no alternative direction to go in order to seek deep psychological security. They do not have a transcendent religion providing an imagined god or goddess which satisfies deep needs for nurturance as in the Christian illusions of intimacy with Jesus or the Judeo-Christian concern of a loving God. The Japanese must maintain their illusion of an all-nurturant mother in real life rather than find it in a transcendent supernatural relationship.

Internalization of Aggression

The explanation why Japanese develop such a strong sense of social role and in some instances carry this to the point of a suicidal response to social disruptions is incomplete without some examination of how the aggressive component that goes into suicide is turned in on the self. In Thematic Apperception Test material I have noted in various contexts elsewhere the proneness to masochistic propensities in the internalization of aggression in Japanese culture. This is especially apparent in the women's role but is found also in men located in subordinate status. A continual emphasis on assuring future success as a result of enduring present privation predisposes individuals to what is termed "moral masochism," as Reik discusses it in *Masochism and Modern Man* (1941). The equation has it that present suffering will be repaid by future triumph. He who endures triumphs in the end. The supreme virtue of endurance in Japanese culture is exemplified by the strong sense of accomplishment in the direction of long-range goals. The Japanese mother's most powerful disciplinary weapon is the very self-sacrifice with which she dedicates herself. The child learns the vulnerability of the loved one and is frightened by its own capacity to injure. The mother who exhausts herself on behalf of her child, produces a sense of guilt that a Japanese cannot escape and which he can, in times of crisis, turn back into acts of aggression on himself. A man in the traditional culture could bend aggression into more acceptable channels, but a man was never free to direct his aggression toward a constituted authority. He learned from his mother to turn potentially aggressive feelings toward or for authority back on the self. All authority represents for him an idealized distant father whom the mother has taught him to respect at all costs.

The intensive affective relationship of a mother and son in traditional Japanese culture influenced the way in which the infantile sexuality could be transmuted into adult relationships. Emphasis on lineage tended to de-emphasize the conjugal relationship in favor of a mother-child oriented concern with succession and continuity. For the male child the mother becomes the symbol of lifelong dedication and sacrifice, the father an image of unapproachable authority. At the same time sacrifice and masochism are taught to be unconscious forms of control so that there too, the Japanese learn that injuring the self is the ultimate means of inducing others to the behavior expected of them.

Lastly, the type of attenuation found in Japanese egoistic suicides can be explained in terms of a maternal deprivation which in given instances results in a continued primary narcissism and an incapacity to develop relationships. Individuals in countries other than Japan suffer such early deprivation but in the peculiar context of the expected pattern of Japanese socialization, the Japanese individual responds to difficulty with affective bonds in a characteristic Japanese way. He can only seek out culturally available forms. In the West a sense of deep personal isolation can be assuaged by religious conversion and the solace of an imagined personal relation with god. This outlet is not as readily available in Japan as is a suicidal gesture that symbolizes a loss of self in a spasmodic act of group dedication, even to death. Thus, in a curious way, Japanese religious conversion, if it may be termed that, can often lead to a suicidal "patriotic" or familial act rather than a new dedication to life.

Crisis and social cohesion within Japanese society. As a coda, one can turn from the psychological back to the social and see that the U-shaped curve of suicide in Japan has to be seen in terms of life-stage crises characteristic for Japanese culture. It is at the point of adulthood that many Japanese find their most stringent crisis over individuation. It is at that time that many young women feel most strongly the conflict between their own personal inclinations and the social directives of submissiveness to the family and to an imposed marital choice. Young men and women both feel pressured to subordinate individual considerations to family decisions. Men especially must commit wholeheartedly to prescribed goals through active accomplishment whether or not they find the deep willingness to do so within themselves. In their need for commitment, young men must perhaps compress the expansive view of society to which they have been stimulated in adolescence and adjust themselves to the narrower confines of a minor bureaucratic position or an insignificant role in a large company.

Once this crisis is passed and resignation to role has occurred, the suicide rate in Japan goes down. The culture meets commitment with security and it is only in old age that the enveloping protection of a secure position within a group is challenged once again by the dissolving effects of retirement and the loss of the enveloping sense of belonging that has marked the middle years.

Compared cross-culturally the Japanese seem unduly preoccupied with standards of excellence. The Japanese internalize such standards. They worry about how they appear to others and sometimes less obviously, they worry about how they appear to themselves. This preoccupation with standards makes the Japanese particularly vulnerable to social vicissitudes. Many Japanese so internalize standards of social expectations with respect to their roles that they become highly vulnerable to any rupture. Thus the Japanese show a unique subtlety or degree of sensitivity to what others may consider a minor assault on social presence. Status concerns are much more pronounced in middle-class than lower-class individuals. In considering suicide we have turned full circle, returning to a consideration of the Japanese pressure to achieve. A culture pattern as a totality is not without cost for the individuals who maintain its continuity.

REFERENCES CITED

Abel, T. M. and Hsu, F. L. K.
  1949 Some Aspects of Chinese Personality as Revealed by the Rorschach Test. *Rorschach Research Exchange and Journal of Projective Techniques* 13:285–301.
Adorno, T. W. et al.
  1950 *The Authoritarian Personality*. New York: Harper.

Caudill, W. and DeVos, G.
  1956   Achievement, Culture and Personality: The Case of the Japanese Americans. *American Anthropologist* 58(6):1102–1126.
Cronbach, L. J.
  1949   Statistical Methods Applied to Rorschach Scores: A Review. *Psychological Bulletin* 46(5):393–429.
DeVos, G.
  1973   *Socialization for Achievement.* Berkeley, Calif.: University of California Press.
  1955   A Quantitative Rorschach Assessment of Maladjustment and Rigidity in Acculturating Japanese Americans. *Genetic Psychology Monographs* 52:51–87.
  1954   A Comparison of the Personality Differences in Two Generations of Japanese Americans by Means of the Rorschach Test. *Negoya Journal of Medical Science* 17:3.
  1952   A Quantitative Approach to Affective Symbolism in Rorschach Responses. *Journal of Projective Techniques* 16:133–50.
DeVos, G. and Miner, H.
  1958   Oasis and Casbah—A Study in Acculturative Stress. In *Culture and Mental Health,* ed. M. Opler, pp. 333–50. New York: Macmillan Co.
DeVos, G., and Wagatsuma, H.
  1966   *Japan's Invisible Race: Caste in Culture and Personality.* Berkeley, Calif.: University of California Press.
Eysenck, H. J.
  1953   Primary Social Attitudes: A Comparison of Attitudinal Patterns in England, Germany, and Sweden. *Journal of Abnormal and Social Psychology* 48(4).
Kaplan, Bert
  1961   *Studying Personality Cross-Culturally,* ed. B. Kaplan. New York: Harper & Row.
Kardiner, A. and Ovesey, L.
  1951   *The Mark of Oppression.* Cleveland and New York: The World Publishing Co.
Reik, T.
  1941   *Masochism in Modern Man,* translation by M. H. Beigel and G. M. Kurth. New York: Grove Press.
Wetherall, W. O. and DeVos, G.
  1975   Ethnic Minorities in Japan. In *Discrimination Across the World* (provisional title). De Hague, Netherlands: Foundation for the Study of Plural Societies.

The Author

WESTON LA BARRE, James Duke Professor of Anthropology at Duke University, was born in Pennsylvania and "counts among his forebears two Pennsylvania Dutch grantees of William Penn, the Quaker minister John Woolman, and a Governer-General of New France." He graduated from Princeton *summa cum laude,* and from Yale with honors. His thesis was the *Peyote Cult.* As Sterling Fellow of Yale his third field trip was to Desaguadero, after which he was SSRC research intern at the Menninger Clinic. Trained as a parachuter for naval intelligence in Asia, after the war he was a Guggenheim Fellow and received the Róheim Award. He has taught at six universities other than Duke, and has visiting-lectured at dozens more. He has spent two years in China, India, Ceylon, and Southeast Asia, has studied a dozen North American Indian tribes, lived twice in South America, crossed Africa twice, lived twice in the Caribbean, and has lived in twenty-five countries of Europe. He has been twice Fellow of the National Science Foundation. His major books are *The Human Animal* and *The Ghost Dance: Origins of Religion.* Editor of over 150 volumes of *Landmarks in Anthropology,* La Barre has published over 100 books and articles of his own in six languages. Married to Maurine Boie, author of the *New York City Baby Book* and now a psychiatric social worker, the couple have "one beautiful and two handsome children" and live by a woodland stream in the "climax formation forest" near Chapel Hill, North Carolina.

This Chapter

Like George Devereux, Weston La Barre is committed to a strong psychoanalytic position. He seeks a kind of anthropological holism and this search is apparent throughout his works. He regards the comparative approach as the "glory of anthropology." This theme, too, is apparent in his published studies and in this paper.

In the first two-thirds of this paper he develops his position first by dissecting sociology and psychology, and particularly experimental psychology, in its academic context. Readers will find his dissection decisive, scathing, and telling. He is no less critical of anthropological foibles and failings, however, and many anthropological readers will read his frank commentary with delight if not total agreement. With the ground clear he says quite correctly, "The reader, having inevitably put together the opinions and evidence in this paper, should now have some idea of where I stand as an anthropologist." He provides an all too brief but clear and concise statement of his intellectual and personal antecedents and discusses the salient features of his major works in the following pages.

Like George Devereux, Weston La Barre also sees much of scientific methodology as a vigorous defense against threatening self-involvement. In this context he gives us a penetrating analysis of the role of statistics and the nature of counting. It is apparent that he is not against quantitative methodology as such, but wants it to be used in a sophisticated manner.

He uses a double-acrostic puzzle to illustrate the nature of field work on cultural wholes.

G.D.S.

8   The Clinic and the Field

WESTON LA BARRE

The kind of anthropologist one becomes depends greatly, beyond motivation and need, on his view of the nature of his data. There is long and basic disagreement among anthropologists as to whether their discipline is potentially a science or, more properly and essentially, one of the humanities—whether human data are quantifiable and able to yield durable "hard" scientific generalization, or whether by their nature these data are overly malleable to the motivations of the researcher, set in his own ethnographic time and psychological life-space.

Among methods anthropology might borrow from other sciences, the *experimental method* would seem to be wholly repugnant, out of a decent humanistic concern for the data, other human beings. Besides, since the experimenter is himself a human being and motivated to find his own psychic homeostasis, the controlled experiment tends to control out of his data his own anxieties and prevents the very edifications an unmanipulated naturalism might give him. A further difficulty with the experimental method, and I think an insurmountable one, is that anthropologists enculturated to one culture could hardly frame objective and culture-free hypotheses concerning another culture or cultures.

Consider the sociologist. At one time, notably at the early University of Chicago, sociologists were actually field workers, entranced and open-ended observers of subcultures in their own society, and they produced such fine naturalistic studies as *Gold Coast and Slum, The Saleslady, The Jack-Roller*[1] and others, which the anthropologist can still admire. The tradition is not yet extinct (in a sense, in the phenomenological approach of Goffman, Luckman and others), and yet most contemporary sociologists would prefer to think of themselves more prestigiously as quantifying scientists, with "testable" hypotheses. Now, any such hypothesis derives from common sense, a basic "insight" (unwitting awareness of his own culture). That is, one wants a *plausible* hypothesis that, it is to be hoped, will find verification. But to the plausible the hypothesis must derive from that covert consensus, unexamined contemporary local ethnography. Lest the sociologist be detected in obviousness, the hypothesis is lost in an arcane and fatuous pomposity of vocabulary, and any obviousness of his conclusions merely testifies to the soundness of the method. Thereupon the sociologist sets out to "collect his data"—commonly a noun entity to be measured against a predicated adjectival quality—to be calibrated against the opinions of his selected "subjects." Next he brings heaps of protocols, puts them on punch-cards, and lays them at the feet of the Truth Machine untouched by human mind. Finally he pushes the button, and Science emerges. The more elaborated the programming "model" (his equations), the more "sophisticated" his results. But he does not seem to realize that his results have already been programmed by a far more sophisticated (or sophistic) computer, his mind—the unexamined, motivated, enculturated, time-serving human mind.

If the sociologist is lucky, his results will indicate an overlap of two intersecting circles—never concentric, unless he has produced an authentic tautology, though the more tautological the more impressive—the common area of which can be expressed statistically (if the circles are not even tangent he has flubbed it). That is, his new scholasticism has discovered and measured a semantic overlap, a pooled consensus of the connotations and denotations of a noun and an adjective in selected tribesmen's minds. It is an obscure recognition of this circularity and ethnocentricity in what the sociologist has been doing, chasing his tail in his own back yard, that is at the heart of the anthropologist's charac-teristic and chronic vexation with the sociologist. The man and his ma-chine have labored mightily and brought forth: contemporary folklore. He has not only discovered, but what is more *proven,* a fragment of ethnography much more expeditiously produced by simple old Chi-cagoan ethnography. He has discovered the obvious, however preten-tiously, to which all can agree. Can the sociologist ever be even the folklorist of his own society, unless he discovers and acknowledges that this is what he is really doing? The anthropologist can congratulate himself that at least he has flung a much wider net upon the human than has the sociologist. But ignoring for the moment the enormous crosscultural differences in doing even this, is it possible that the anthro-pologist can ever do more than simple ethnographic description?

In a spirit of fun, but also with a modicum of ironic seriousness, I once wrote an account of Professor Widjojo,[2] a fictive native ethnog-rapher visiting the "Usans" (pronounced either "Us-ans" or "U.S.A.-ans" as one chooses, since no phonemic table was provided by Widjojo), who attended an occidental *futbol* game and systematically misinter-preted all he saw in terms of what he thought were Usan categories. The battle over the sacred pigskin produced fallen warriors, but these were miraculously resurrected (evidently in accordance with Christian myths) under the aegis of an Alma Mater and her animal totem, the animal mascot of the men's society, aided by the magical chants of the moiety-communicants. The totem was not, however, of an exogamous group, for careful diachronic kinship studies showed that communicants as often married within as outside of the totemic Alma Mater moieties, etc., etc. The *koktel parti* after the ceremony was even more gro-tesquely misunderstood, though, in all fairness, by that time as a participant observer Professor Widjojo may have become tiddly.

The spectacle of the sociologist should chasten the anthropologist. Is he, too, imprisoned in the nature of the cultural situation when he attempts to play the scientist? Is he, too, not to be trusted to frame objective scientific hypotheses, even after the most earnest and compendious bird watching? Early anthropology is replete with ex-amples in which, having an ax to grind, the anthropologist sets up an hypothesis, subtly or flagrantly ethnocentric, and then sets out on a world tour for confirmation. Sir James George Frazer, no fieldworker to be sure, is usually cited as a notorious example of this tendency since he assumes, *a priori* and unexamined, a "psychological unity of mankind" which is precisely what should be established first, empirically and inductively, before using an Australian myth, say, to explain folklore in the Old Testament,[3] as though it had any ethnographic relevance whatever.

This "daisy-picking" method tears the datum brutally from its tribal context, and (without our espousing Malinowski's anti-historical and anti-areal tunnel-vision that would treat each single culture as explainable sufficiently and only in terms of itself) surely we have learned from functionalism the critical significance of *context*. Indeed, surprisingly, Frazer sometimes succeeds in illuminating an apocopated or overly terse Old Testament myth, such as "The Origin of Death," when citing a nearby African Semitism, relevant precisely because it is related in ethnographic space and historic time. Otherwise, depending as it does on unproven psychological unity—which Malinowski's insistence on the *sui generis* nature of each tribe does much to destroy—Frazerian comparativism is quite useless as distribution studies. My point is not a now uselessly didactic beating of a dead horse, but a necessary polemic one. For Freudian psychology, which I employ, also depends on unities—but here rooted in demonstrably pan-human biology, a psychology founded presumably too much in biology, for which Freud has been so roundly criticized. As for Malinowski's "synchronic" shibboleth, often the only meaning of a dysfunctional element is to be found in the history of a culture. The understanding of a society's culture depends as much on ethnographic history as does the Freudian understanding of personality through individual history. Lack of method is no excuse to erect Trobriand lack of literacy into a rigidly anti-historical principle. Indeed, in a similarly "historyless" hemisphere, Sapir[4] brilliantly summarized many sound and useful techniques for discovering *Time Perspective in Aboriginal American Culture*.

It is usually assumed that Frazerism is defunct. But what are we to think of the implied unity-of-mankind psychologism of the French Jungian who, after a few weeks of rapid travel through Bororo country, sits in Paris and spins out volume after volume of myths from his own mind? And what are we to think of Chomskian universalism, even when at last jounced from its Indoeuropean back yard into Finnish and Samoan studies? All languages, we are told, show a mystic sameness—which shows that Chomsky as little understands the unique quiddities of languages as Lévi-Strauss does those of cultures, for neither language nor culture is quasi-neurological. But when Chomskians are pressed to elucidate this mystical sameness, it turns out that all languages have sound, sense, and structure—which means that language is by definition oral (and not, as has been wickedly suggested, modulated flatus, which is within the realm of biological possibility though not of the tautological definition of language) and has a finite number of discriminable gamuts of sound or phonemes, varied as these are, instead of white noise; that sense is necessary for any communication, human or animal, since language is a form of communication, and that is what communication is, transduction of meaning; and that, finally, languages are structured, alarmingly incommensurate as these structures are. If the generalized Chomskian "similarities" are not these tautological banalities, we get at best such universals as something functionally resembling pronouns—as if man were a social primate, though divided up into discrete metazoan bodies, and some men talk to and about others! What hath God wrought? The human mind grinds everywhere with the same cogs!

As to other scientists whose methods the anthropologist is invited to emulate, consider the experimental psychologist. But when Wundt went into his laboratory to contrive the "controlled experiment" did not his hypotheses subtly control out of the data everything anxiety-laden that would teach the psychologist anything properly *psychological* about *people?* Instead of the bread of psychological understanding of human beings, we get from them the stone of a disguised neuroanatomy and neurophysiology of birds and animals, with human analogies at best on this crude biological level of perception, sensation, and learning. But rats and pigeons lack infantile dependency of any significant amount, they lack the nuclear family, the incest taboo, symbolism, language, and culture—in fact all the species-specific traits that make human beings human. Or when social psychologists actually do use people in their "experiments," say, in measuring attitudes through (culture-bound, deductive) questionnaires, are these "attitudes" true statistical comparables, and are they not still buzzing with unexamined quiddities and semantic incommensurabilities? Questionnaires are no more than Gallup polls that pool and mask the many remaning dynamically significant differences in individuals, and are at best unwitting ethnography—or psychiatry. For example, some die-hard opinions about Mr. Nixon seem to reveal only irrational Oedipal dispositions toward authority figures or the degree of personal psychopathy of the pollee.

Only the clinical psychologist, far less prestigiously "scientific" than the experimental psychologist, continues to observe the unmutilated naturalistic phenomenon, the individual person with his idiosyncracies, and allows him through a structurally *meaningless* Rorschach card to speak projectively of himself and his own meanings, or through the diagnostically useful MMPI to display a sizeable number of the varying psychiatric components of his unique personality configuration, in similarly open-ended fashion. Experimental psychologists, one observes, are self-recruited from among individuals who have appreciable psychological problems that evidently motivate them to psychological research. Honest compulsives, they obscurely suspect the truth is not in them, so they armor themselves more and more with protective method. However, since self-therapy is largely impossible, academic psychology becomes a kind of institutionalized compulsive neurosis: a new method-obsessed scholasticism that to obtain the reliable has given up the threateningly significant. (Of course a different character diagnosis can similarly be given for most anthropologists.) For good reasons clinically blind, the experimentalist can be elaborately scornful of the "hunch artist" clinician who states naturalistically precisely the psychological dynamics that arouse the experimentalist's anxieties, which his "method" successfully avoided.

Here one is reminded of the scorn often meted out to the clinically oriented culture and personality anthropologist, whose statements about group-ethos are said to mask constantly remaining differences among finer categories of individuals; indeed, Sapir himself, the founder of culture and personality studies, noted that as we refine these social categories more and more, the closer we get to the psychological individual. Oddly enough, anthropologists are happily content to make large *ethnographic* generalizations about generic group behavior, but are curiously alarmed at *psychological* statements about generic ethos. However, "culture" and "personality" are both abstractions, on different levels,[5] *from the same data,* reverberant interindividually influenced behavior in a social animal. Culture is the abstraction of the regularities of behavior among members of a group —resulting from the influence of individuals upon individuals.[6] Personality is an abstraction of the regularities of behavior in an individual—resulting from the influence of individuals upon an individual. Those who denigrate culture as an abstraction should remember that Society and Structure are equally abstractions from the same socially reverberant behaviors of the same animal. It is simply a matter of the abstraction one feels comfortable with and allows no invidious name-calling with respect to "abstraction."

Because of the semi-tautologous relationship of culture and personality, society and structure, it early occurred to me that a concept of the "social cynosure" would be dynamically more significant than the "modal personality" and similar concepts. The cynosure is not the modal person, not the "successful" or otherwise desirable to become, not even the most to be emulated person in the society, but simply the one who receives the most massive and continuous *attention* in any society. Cynosures in American, Chinese, central Australian, British, Indonesian, Japanese, African, Aztec, Indian, German, American Indian, French, classic Greek, Balinese, and Northwest Coast cultures were examined, with indications of how the study of these cynosures afforded insights into the dynamics and structure of their respective societies. Contemporary "women's libbers" might relish my sympathy with women in our society as clotheshorses, male consumer-appanages, and mere sex objects in male games of invidious prestige, in this my first paper written at Duke University, with notes hastily sketched on the back of an envelope from the Dean, when I was suddenly asked to address one of Gillin's anthropology classes as part of the slave-market scrutiny of a potential new academic property. But I also brought into evidence both businessmen and consumers as unwitting victims of our system. Although the article has been anthologized and also published in French, the concept of cynosure has been used, to my knowledge, only by Warren Morrill in Bucknell. The concept had not been a mere renaming of the familiar concept of ethos, and both the English and French versions appeared in obscure publications.[7]

The glory of anthropology is its comparative perspective. Perhaps one could take the position that the "experiments" in being human have already been made for us in the naturalistic ethnographic world, and with more extravagant differences than any culture-bound experimenter could imagine. Onerous as cultural difference is intellectually, the historically looming disappearance of ethnographic difference is in a sense frightening. Cultural imperialism in a world village may produce the monolithic which still remains, in fact, merely a culture—which is the reason why any utopian who becomes omnipotent had better be one hundred percent omniscient and omnibenevolent as well! For only the spectacle of cultural difference has enabled us to discover the fact of culture itself.

We have ventured to dissect the sociologist and the psychologist. What are the anthropologist's motivations and behaviors, beyond the obvious wish to escape his own stultifying and punitive culture, in the discontent with his own civilisation? Edmonson[8] has shrewdly observed that "in its nativistic aspect anthropology is nascent internationalism."

If so, is the anthropologist actually bent on the destruction of his data? Anthropology is basically a reaction to the intellectual crisis posed by the Renaissance, the massive encounter—first the classic past, and later world horizons opened by trade—with the fact of other cultures, alarmingly varied in space and time, and consequent attempts to attain some nomothetic rock of ages amidst the sea of idiographic relativism. Like every other voyager, the anthropologist passes between Scylla and Charybdis, between the rock of dogma and the whirlpool of mysticism in Joyce's metaphor, the institutionalized and the subjective "truth" respectively. The metaphor is even more painful than it first appears: the monster consumes whatever human passes by, the whirlpool engulfs it. The relativist flounders, but every would-be nomothete distorts and transforms. In a sense, consumed by dogma, the anthropologist *becomes* the man-eating monster on the rock and turns ethnography into its own substance, which surely constitutes no scientific superiority over swirling in a sea of relativism.

Perhaps the only intellectual escape is honestly to recognize the predicament: the nomothetic aspect of any culture as a postulational system is a psychic defense mechanism—which is why we detest this defeatist insight. But cultural truth is no more apodictic than a Riemannian, Bolyaian, Lobachevskian or Euclidean Fifth Postulate—including the private culture of the anthropologist and his need for intellectual homeostasis. He is inescapably a symbol-manipulator. "Man depends on symbols because he cannot endure a threat to his powers of comprehension."[9]

Anthropologizing thus resembles the behavior of participants in a crisis cult, the intellectual crisis inherited from the Renaissance. A fifty-year perspective on the history of anthropology shows it to be, ironically, quite like the history of any other science. Kuhn[10] has shown us that science "progresses" not in a steady, cumulative, linear fashion but by a series of disjunctive leaps, when, after a crisis of reigning "normal" science, men suddenly begin to look at the world with new hypothetic myths. In our urge to be scientific we should not ignore the predicament of the other sciences! Nor are we entitled to be epistemologically condescending to Tillich[11] when, after a masterly and courageous survey of existentialism, he obdurately leaps to the postulate of a "God beyond God." The human wish is only more nakedly exposed in religion than in science, the defense against nescience.

However repugnant to our intellectual pretenses, the dour recognition that anthropologizing is crisis behavior, as in any other science, is intended with deadly seriousness. Consider only how, phenomenologically, we *behave*. The last fifty years of anthropology is not so much an unbroken cumulative endeavor as it is disconcertingly like a straggling parade of charismatic characters and their entourage. When viewed in context, the statement of each messianic *guru* makes each anthropology into a species of autobiography, or lyric poetry. The personal motive is even embarrassingly exposed, as in eminent anthropologists anyone could name. And from Malinowski to Lévi-Strauss there is an unmistakable aura of the messianic, certainly in the reflex behavior of journeyman communicants who during a period of "normal" science dutifully repeat and prove the master's dicta. This is not meant with contumely. It is only that the more eminent the leader, the more his clientele expose the fact in their behavior, and both Malinowski and Lévi-Strauss were in their day inarguably very eminent anthropologists.

Consider the case of Malinowski. Staunch Boasians like Lowie[12] responded to the meteoric rise of Malinowski with a truly vituperative tone, all the more remarkable in this ordinarily judicial-minded, good gray historian of ethnological theory. Malinowski makes "apocalyptic utterances" in "messianic mood," his "favorite pastimes" consisting in "battering down wide open doors . . . or petulantly deriding work that does not attract him." Malinowski "thumbs his nose at technology, flouts distribution studies, sneers at recognition of the past" —and all his acolytes piously respond. Disdaining any larger human context, areal or distributional, that might help make sense of his chosen people, Malinowski "treats each culture as a closed system except insofar as its elements correspond to vital biological urges." For Malinowski, however, unlike Durkheim, this windowless-monad society was not the unit, and "Malinowski came to regard the family as the fundamental unit in all human society." But Malinowski never attempted an adequate human biology beyond this vague postulate. As to any psychoanalytic ground for this postulate (another anathema to Lowie), although Lowie mistakenly thought Malinowski a representative of this school, Malinowski was quite inadequately informed in this area and plainly anti-psychoanalytic, which makes it grossly unfair to use Malinowski as a whipping-boy for it.[13]

Like Radcliffe-Brown, Malinowski "avowed a disdain, largely but by no means uniformly indulged in practice, for history"—and acolytes learn to chant the cant word "diachronic" pejoratively. For a presumably biology- and psychology-based theorist, Malinowski also curiously disdained the individual, though Radcliffe-Brown, remarkably considering his derivation from Durkheim, later included the individual as a legitimate object of anthropological inquiry. Like Radcliffe-Brown, Malinowski considered that any particular culture "is normally a systematic or integrated unit in which every element has a distinct function"—ignoring the fact that many elements are plainly dysfunctional, or even functionally irrelevant as inherited from past culture-history. Worse yet in the view of contemporary anthropologists, like the notorious Bastian Malinowski would apply anthropology to colonial government. For Lowie, when "functionalism is reduced to what it is—a worthy program for ascertaining what intracultural bonds may exist," Malinowski remains "an ethnographic provincial" with an "adolescent eagerness to shock the ethnological bourgeois."

Thus from an eminent contemporary of Malinowski. Regard, again, his fate at the hands of his students. Considering that, for whatever reasons, their distinguished mentor had fallen into neglect, a group of Malinowski's students[14] joined in writing an intended rehabilitation of his reputation. But each specialist, in turn, concluded that Malinowski did not really understand kinship, or handled economics inadequately, or linguistics or whatever, though all could at last enthusiastically agree that, after all, as even Lowie conceded, Malinowski was a superb field worker. But then even this laudatory consensus evaporated on the lamentable publication, posthumously in 1967, of A Diary in the Strict Sense of the Term[15] in which it transpired that Malinowski really "hated his niggers" and preferred to cling to companionship with European colonials, to waste his time reading cheap romantic novels, or to suffer Portnoy's complaint. It looks very much as though, diachronically, Malinowski had become the Scyllan monster.

The extremeness of the range between messiah and monster may lead one to wonder whether it pays to become an eminent anthropologist, even if one could. Better to remain the hierodule of the reigning cognitive king! Stay "normal" scientist and be counted "sound"! The unreasonable and unrealistic range of attitudes toward another prominent colleague, Margaret Mead, is another case in point. The phenomenon is also current in the career of Lévi-Strauss, who, although incompletely translated at this writing, by some younger American anthropologists has already been solemnly pronounced "dead." In none of the social sciences, I suggest, is there such a swift passage between hyperdulia and contumely as in anthropology. Field work at the next yearly convention of the American Anthropological Association should confirm or disconfirm this hypothesis.

If eminence is a function of other anthropologists' opinions, then this should be a proper arena of inquiry. Perhaps anthropologists could learn some anthropology through scrutiny of themselves. This is a growing concern, most ably exemplified in Devereux's sophisticated study of countertransference to one's data,[16] but also evidenced in recent writings of other sensitive anthropologists.[17] Is it that, by definition self-alienated from his own culture, the maverick anthropologist has a consequently inordinate thirst for conformity to the current culture of fellow-anthropologists?[18] There is certainly a marked professional camaraderie among these social exiles. But such an explanation for a perhaps peculiarly American need to belong does not accord with the savage one-upmanship hierarchy of British social anthropologists, who in their fun and games often appear more tiresomely eager to advance the anthropologist than anthropology as a discipline. Or is this latter merely a matter of the notorious rudeness in British establishment circles, employed to keep others in their proper place? Or is it a question of the paucity of Oxbridge university jobs? Again, why is it that the French can tolerate only one ranking official intellectual at a time, now Sartre, now Lévi-Strauss? But prestigious academic jobs are not plentiful in classical studies either, and I seem to discern far more decorous an urbanity and even polemic grace among Hellenists, who appear resigned to being ethnologists who are merely humanists. Or do all anthropologists suffer a fanatically religious *odium theologicum* because anthropologizing is everywhere truly crisis cult behavior, still attempting to surmount the Renaissance trauma? Laymen constantly and eagerly interrogate us for the truth, and in the public eye it all makes anthropology seem an excitingly fast-moving game, and the anthropologist a waggish fellow. Certain it is that anthropology obeys Kuhn's rules, often with unseemly alacrity.

Thus far, this phenomenological ethnology of ethnologists would appear only to expose motives. But every scientist has motives, and we do not darkly question physicists and chemists about theirs. The reason is that these scientists are not people studying people, and it remains true that the motives of "social scientists" should always be carefully scrutinized, lest they discover only what they *need to,* autobiographically. By analogy, but far more exquisitely, the psychiatrist must know himself, through a rigorous and often painful didactic analysis, *for he will not be able to see in his patients what he cannot afford to see in terms of his own defenses.* He must constantly ask "What am I doing in saying this or asking that?"—that is, he must carefully watch his own countertransference to the patient. ("Am I seeking power over my patient? Am I showing what I know, indulging in one-upmanship? Am I being impermissively aggressive, in terms of my own needs and not my patient's? Why am I vexed with him at this moment? What anxieties does he arouse in me, and why? Am I projecting my own meaning, or patiently seeking his? And however firmly clear I finally am about the pattern, have we shared enough examples of it from his behavior now for the patient to be able to see his present anxiety level, or should we wait?''—etc., etc.) As a psychiatrically oriented anthropologist, I find the imperative of self-awareness inexorably imposed also on all anthropologies.

What are the altnernative *methods* anthropologists use, and hence what are the subtypes of anthropologists? Largely, I think, the difference between the anthropological scientist (nomothete) and the anthropological humanist (idiographic naturalist) ultimately resolves into whether he chooses to use numbers or words as his model. What are the differences between numbers and words?

In the hands of physical scientists, number can undeniably accomplish spectacular results. In 1950, H. C. Urey examined a Jurassic belemnite roughly 150 million years old. From the isotopes of oxygen present, and their amounts, he was able to show that the animal was hatched in the spring, lived almost four years, and died in the spring; and that, during its lifetime, the temperature of the water in which it lived ranged from 68 to 70 degrees Fahrenheit in summer, and from 59 to 64 degrees in the winter. What an elegant scientific demonstration this is! How devoutly we would wish to be able to do this in the social sciences!

Now, the reason Dr. Urey was able to sustain these astonishing insights with confidence was that the *last significant difference* between the comparables consists in the differences between the isotopes of oxygen. Having no other differences, the isotopes were then fit to be counted and compared: number itself is only one step further denuded of all qualities. Knowing the biochemistry of organisms, Urey could make these statements because an atom of isotope X of oxygen is observed *always* to behave exactly like another atom of this isotope under the same circumstances of temperature. Indeed, the laws of chemistry are based on quite daring extrapolations: all isotope X atoms of an element behave exactly alike whenever they occur in time. So too in physics: if we observe anything with respect to magnetism-gravity in our portion of the universe, and are sure we are dealing with comparables, in this case energy-mass, then we can extrapolate the same principles to the farthest galactic system.

The elegance and precision of the physical sciences has led to quite premature attempts to take over the statistical methods of the physical sciences into the social sciences—premature largely because we sorcerer's apprentices have nowhere in our analyses reached anything like the *last significant difference* among "comparables" in the human data we observe. This statement is not to be taken as an indiscriminate attack on the use of quantitative techniques as such, but only to maintain a proper respect for them. All we insist upon (and numerologists think they have) are authentic comparables. It also helps to know qualitatively what we are measuring. The famous example from physical anthropology is Dixon's measurement and correlation of three indices of the head and nose, surely an "objective" and exact enough procedure. Thereupon Dixon[19] found "Melanesians" among the Pueblo Indians and "Australoids" in South America. What a superb method to trace racial, and hence cultural diffusions! The quietus on this scholasticism was rendered by Boas,[20] in his study of the children of immigrants in New York: children of dolichocephalic Italians became successively more brachycephalic the younger they were in the family, whereas children of brachycephalic Ashkenazim Jews became successively more dolichocephalic. And now long shelves of patient craniometric studies became waste paper for they had been measuring what was not genetically there. (Had they had illegitimate racist motives that anthropological reality failed to sustain?) One German scientist perfected over two hundred such indices! If only he had had the computer then, we would doubtlessly have had the triumph of computeroscopy for all time.

Social scientists often believe they are dealing with admissable comparables in their data because they have *defined* them as such. But there's the rub: words have now entered the picture. I firmly believe that, just as one is seemingly born a Platonist or an Aristotelian, a Parmenidean or a Heraclitean,[21] so apparently one is born a quantifier or a qualifier, possibly even through comparative brain-hemisphere dominance. Quantifiers say qualifiers do not understand numbers. But qualifiers say that quantifiers do not understand words *or* numbers. In any case, numbers-minded and word-minded persons do differ widely in their judgment of what constitutes authentic comparables in the social sciences. Numbers, say the rigorously verbal-minded, can be manipulated only if the comparables are denuded *in nature* of every other single quality but one and have qualitatively reached the level of "last significant difference." Words cannot be made to jump through numerical hoops. They unfortunately cannot be made comparables "by definition" because words are slippery in their Protean connotations and denotations, and a Procrustean lopping off of heads and feet does a certain damage to the human data.

Eagerly quantitative individuals shirk all the remaining *and perhaps functionally significant* differences in their still-global data in order to reach their putatively number-stark "comparables"—but qualifiers believe they have thus mutilated and impoverished their data. The problem is peculiarly insuperable with respect to ethnological data: perhaps one must be born into a culture in order to handle its categories with any astuteness connotatively and denotatively. Besides, emic *pattern* and *context* are what we should really attend to (data orientation), not fragmental etic numerical manipulation (method orientation). But may we not legitimately compare apples with oranges if we have rigorously *defined* both as "fruits" and not "vegetables"?

No, says the verbal-minded person, acutely sensitive to the semantic arbitrariness and cultural subjectivity of such labels in any verbally-defined category. Any etic mode is one possible butchering of the world, admits the emic-conscious person, and perhaps the Boston mode is as good as the differing butchering method of Omaha meatpackers when it comes to the eating, depending only on one's preferences for cuts of meat. But any etic mode is ethnographically *irrelevant* when it ignores native context and pattern in the living culture. And it mixes up the desired scientific truth with the observed ethnographic fact. Further, can we be sure we have categorized as economic what is more importantly religious in native eyes? Again, is not every etic enterprise an attempt (wished) to translate (transmogrify) sometimes irrational(?)—(!)—human behavior into what is cognitively comfortable (rational) to the researcher (the old Renaissance trauma again)? For all our yearning loyalty to science, is not social science always subtly ethnocentric? Given our motives, cognitive homeostasis, is it really possible to be scientific about ourselves and others? Perhaps it is. But it means becoming clinical, and perhaps only humanist in the process.

Now, by no means are all nomothetic endeavors necessarily quantifying, any more than the designation "empirical" belongs exclusively to the quantifiers, as many of them seem easily to assume. There are many non-quantifying ways of being empirical. Consider the superb work of non-quantifying psychological experimentalists such as McClean on functional brain areas, or the productive naturalism of Dement on REM states. The clinical is a case in point. Ordinarily we would readily agree, a valid generalization necessitates $N + 1$ instances for it to be minimally established—and yet Freud's case of "Little

Hans" did not really need Ferenczi's case of "Little Arpad" to prove what can easily stand on its own as a complex and self-consistent organic whole. To my mind, also, the Indoeuropeanist Bender sufficiently established that "-ock" is an archaic dualizing suffix in the single word "buttock" and does not really need the reduplicated pluralizing of "ballocks" to prive it, for this repluralizing merely confirms again that the suffix is archaic and now nonfunctional. Similarly, Malinowski's contrast of lagoon versus deepsea fishing in the Trobriands alone is sufficient to establish a useful heuristic principle, widely applicable to secular versus magico-religious behaviors elsewhere. It is not really necessary to make an exhaustive statistical study of all inhabited Pacific atolls in order to use this insight, though it might be good for a grant.

There is also something to be said for expertise, and for being massively "soaked in the data." Many good ethnographers can confidently reply to the query, "How would the Bobobobo you studied react in this situation?," even though they might need to correct some implicit and irrelevant assumption of the questioner. Shall long experience count for nothing in making sound judgments? The "intuition" —nothing mystical but literally "imbedded learning"—of medical diagnosticians is sometimes of so high an order that the doctor can merely walk through his waiting room and know with assurance that "this is a gall-bladder case." His well-programmed mind has worked almost instantaneously to sort into a meaningful whole a complex of observations that he might even have difficulty in verbally articulating bit by bit without long explanation.

I once witnessed a brilliant Rorschacher, on the basis of a scant handful of responses, state flatly, "This man has a tumor in his right frontal lobe"—and upon operation a right-frontal tumor was found and removed. The procedure seems almost magical to those ignorant of Rorschach technique. But it produced verifiable results. The Rorschacher may later, somewhat painfully, point out consistent "organic signs" in the protocol—and did you notice the lack of speech slurring there would have been if it were on the left?—etc., etc. The Rorschach test may sometimes seem to be only window-dressing for sheer clinical insight. But the Rorschacher meanwhile is surely demonstrating the ability to operate with "large W's" that is a sign of intelligence itself. Some individuals have this reticulated mode of clinical insight. Many linear thinkers do not. Nor may they have the experience and the open Gestalt preparedness to see the data that are waiting there.

Counting does have its uses in the social sciences. But in anthropology cultures are molar complexes, with reticulated meanings—that informants can tell us about best. Numbers here can only operate with etically-fragmented shards assembled from maimed wholes. The less trivial and the more complex the data, the less legitimately available is the quantitative method. Besides, relevant quantifying can only operate on the basis of prior insight. Statistical voyagers from atoll to atoll would be mere camp followers of a masterly Malinowskian insight. The cultural statistican, curiously, cares little for insights into functioning wholes but seems principally enamored of his method. "Have method, will travel"—and from guru to guru as these kaleidoscopically change. "Empirical sociology" is already a mere branch of statistics, which is the main subject. However, we repeat, social science statistics are often useful in proving what we already know. Or think we know.

It may be impossible to show the numbers-minded why their manipulations are so unsatisfactory in the social sciences. Their statistical operations may be mathematically impeccable, the equations marvelously "sophisticated" (read, complex), but they have missed the boat. I have in mind here Whiting's[22] elegant Rube Goldberg contraption for explaining circumcision—in such rainy *kwashiorkor*-afflicted regions as, say, the *locus classicus* deserts of the pastoral-Semitic Near East, with polygyny thrown in free. In my view, the Semites have already explained the real motive for circumcision in their abundant documents, though it depends on only a single constantly reiterated and deeply imbricated symbol, the immortal snake.[23] If etically-defined research later discovers that the wives of circumcised men have a lower incidence of cervical cancer, that is very interesting, and a triumph of etic science for us. But it is not the late-Old Stone Age motive for circumcision.

What is wrong with the quantifier is not only his locus of meaning but also his unexamined semantic predicament. Who cares about seventy percent truths anyway? This simply means that the numerical baskets are thirty percent full of irrelevant noncomparables. Some qualitatively undiscerned cobblestones have somehow gotten in with the apples and the oranges. The supposed entities turn out to have been only slippery words after all. They have evidently been dealing with something else, perhaps only round things. In the early days of anthropology, assuming that a field worker is manufactured through mere attendance at classes, Boas used to ask a single question of students returning from the field: "Did you find your Indians?" The question to be asked of the social scientist quantifier is, "Have you found your entities?" Are verbally-defined data enough? Are words entities?

By no means. Let us push words to their limits. Take the quanti-fiably testable question, "How many seats are chairs?" Quantifiers too easily believe that *definition* safely confines discrete number-like en-tities that can then be manipulated numerically. But how do words behave semantically? Is a "seat" a chair, bench, bar stool, or some-thing in a car, ski lift, train or plane? Is it an elective office in the legislature, a country place, a capital? Is a seat the rear of one's pants, or a privilege one buys at a ball game or concert for various prices depending on its location, has free on the floor in front of the TV, struggles to keep on a horse or tractor, but (depending on sexist training) should not keep when a lady is present? For that matter, is a "chair" a kind of formal public leadership, usually exercised standing up—no, it is a "bench" on the judiciary, *other* people stand up and the process begins when the man sits down, or when several judges sit, not on one bench but in separate swivel chairs—or is the chair what a judge gives murderers to their dismay, or a university professorship one avidly seeks and exercises mostly standing up, leaning on a podi-um or sitting affably on the corner of a table? As for "table," that favorite object of philosophers, well, that is a protean word we should probably table here.

In vain the quantifier insists, "This is ridiculous; we all know what I mean!" But do we? As very speakers of the same complexly connotative and denotative language, we amiably consent, perhaps unwittingly, that a seat is a chair is a bench is a table, and much else besides. At best, quantifying here is merely the impressive manipula-tion of already covertly accepted comparables, a *fait accompli,* so why bother?—but here we are back again at the sociologists' overlapping circles. Consequently, for me, the main interest in a quantifying article lies in the proposition the author intends to prove. And of course he will, since negative results do not display his astuteness in framing hypotheses, and scholastic exercises in not-even-tangent circles are unpublishable. Meanwhile the only plausible "models" rest on prior consensus, which is unexamined ethnography.

For this, and other reasons, "problem-oriented" field work, even when unquantified, is so often dubious, especially if the results are "positive." How do we know which island to select for such research? Are Arapesh and Mundugumor and Tchambuli all waiting there on one island to illustrate one's problem? Or would our crudely statistical probability sense feel more comfortable if Redd adventitiously found Tribe A in Ulan Bator, White found Tribe B in Kuala Lumpur, and Blu Tribe C in Uttar Pradesh—and no one was even looking for them? How did one fieldworker, setting up a theoretical paradigm while in New Guinea, presciently know the missing link would be found in Bali? Mead has borne much of the onus for her presumably psychoanalytic field work—but how accurately and justly, since much of it has been devoted to systematically "disproving" Freud's chief propositions: that passage from childhood to adulthood is for Oedipal reasons inevitably marked by the turmoil of adolescence, that psychic ontogenesis universally follows biological paradigms, and that masculinity and femininity are psychologically shaped by the vicissitudes of the kind of body one has?

Authentic field work, I submit, is far more open-ended, discursive, and multi-dimensional. In not going to the field armed with prefigured questionnaires (which find only what they are shaped to find), culture-bound hypotheses (one is motivated to verify), models (based on what verbal analogies), and problems (whose?), anthropological field work is more like the naturalism of the clinical method. Beyond the hypothesis that human beings can communicate about themselves if only one listens and watches, how much does one really know beforehand when he goes to a new tribe, beyond a vague perception of his own somehow universal humanity? But from this he must constantly delete his own cultural presuppositions, as the clinician must constantly subtract his personal countertransference distortions. The associations are the patient's, the meanings the informant's. Learning a culture is much like learning an unknown language, with all kinds of unguessed symbols, structures, semantics. We guess that the language communicates. But we have to learn it.

The process of learning a new language is almost identical with that followed by the psychiatrist Sechehaye when she arduously learned the bizarre symbolisms of her patient and gradually traced out semantic associations in a unique schizophrenic system; the only difference is that they shared much the same syntactic structures, as in a cognate Indoeuropean language, their common humanity. The intuition of such psychiatrists as Grete Bibring and Lucie Jessner is almost uncanny. But they had only more deeply experienced their own humanity than have most of us.

Field work on cultural wholes is much like a double-acrostic puzzle—and if anthropology is so much like a game, ignoring for the moment why we play it, what are the rules of the game we are playing? In a double-acrostic puzzle we are given a number of blanks, prefigured by the culture so to speak, the meanings of which we laboriously piece together with what we find out from our informants. Their meanings and their contexts make up the answers. In a double-acrostic puzzle, each fragmentary meaning is part of a larger consistent whole: each word that satisfies the meaning occupies an exact number of spaces, and the puzzle maker, the society studied, directs us to place each meaningless phoneme into a statement; each letter-space is keyed to a larger pattern of meaning. Each definition-word is rigorously governed by the sense of the final statement and, as so often in field work, it may be that one is not sure of the right meaning until very late in the game. But as meaning gradually begins to emerge, one can read back and forth from diagram to definition, as well as the other way. Further, in a classic double-acrostic, the initial acronyms of the definitions, read vertically, give the name of an author and his book title. All these consistencies control the final solution; in anthropology, whatever consistencies are involved in biology, economics, religion, and a kinship system—all the functional relationships that knit a culture into a consistent whole—control and criticize the answer.

Now, the person who is busy with double-acrostic ethnographizing is scarcely concerned with scrutinizing his single steps (any more than the diagnostician is), or in making explicit why he assumes what he does. He easily discards a minor false inference, for he has no large ego-involvement in a fragmentary part-hypothesis. He knows, for example, that in an English sentence – – – – – is likely to be o-f t-h-e, but he could be mistaken. It could be "to, at, by, on, in, if, as, or" etc., plus "the"—or it could be something else again. He can only establish this by minute and implicit computer-fast *ad hoc* hypotheses (constantly checking with his informant), and then testing back and forth constantly for consistency, meaning, and relevance. The inferences that crowd upon him are so low-level as hardly to deserve the name of hypotheses!

Part of his sense of procedure is contributed to by his awareness of the characteristic way single letters combine in the language (English words do not end in q, nor begin with ng). Let us say it is his morphophonemic sense, here close to a "clinical sense" (the clinician does not expect manic warmth in a schizophrenic, an hysteric denies the obvious and a compulsive is only pretending to seek it, a paranoiac does not load himself with depressive guilt, etc.). Perhaps the double-acrostic puzzle solver is indeed a "hunch artist"—but is not the physical scientist allowed even more grandiose hypotheses? He is not so much interested in procedures in his own mind as in relevance in his subject's. He knows that false solutions will be thrown out by their internal inconsistency with the whole (no one can "fake" a Rorschach). Thus, if the t-h-e he inferred turns out to be a-r-e, he has to erase part of it and try again. It is the multi-dimensional controlling consistencies that force a meaningful answer upon him. It is not irresponsible hunch artistry because the rules of the game (his clinical "methodology") will trip up all false hasty inferences. The pattern that emerges may still have minute errors left, but the chance of two completed solutions to a double-acrostic being both correct is astronomically remote. The clinician and the Rorschacher, the ethnographer and the analyst are all alike here: they soak themselves in the unreconstructed data, in naturalism as uncontaminated by the examiner as is humanly possible, in minute synthetic working on the richly reticulated qualitative details of holistic pictures. As hungry as the next man for nomothetic heurisms, I trust them all only with a benevolent skepticism and feel my feet more on the ground with sustaining idiographic detail. My model is Antaeus, not Pythagoras.

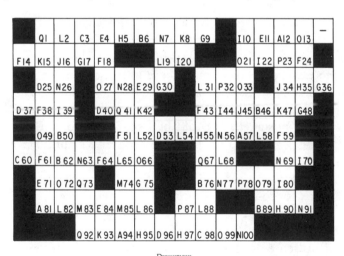

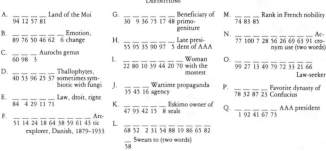

DEFINITIONS

A. _ _ _ _ Land of the Moi
94 12 57 81

B. _ _ _ _ _ _ Emotion,
89 76 50 46 62   6 change

C. _ _ _ _ Aurochs genus
60 98 3

D. _ _ _ _ _ _ Thallophytes,
40 53 96 25 37 sometimes symbiotic with fungi

E. _ _ _ _ _ _ Law, droit, right
84 4 29 11 71

F. _ _ _ _ _ _ _ _ _ _ _ Arctic
51 14 24 18 64 38 59 61 43 explorer, Danish, 1879-1933

G. _ _ _ _ _ _ _ Beneficiary of
30 9 36 75 17 48 primogeniture

H. _ _ _ _ _ _ _ Late president of AAA
55 95 35 90 97 5

I. _ _ _ _ _ _ _ _ Woman
22 80 10 39 44 20 70 with the mostest

J. _ _ _ _ Wartime propaganda
35 45 16 agency

K. _ _ _ _ _ _ Eskimo owner of
47 93 42 15 8 seals

L. _ _ _ _ _ _ _ _ _ _ _
68 52 2 31 54 88 19 86 65 82
_ Swears to (two words)
58

M. _ _ _ Rank in French nobility
74 83 85

N. _ _ _ _ _ _ _ _ _ _ _ _ _ Acronym use (two words)
77 100 7 28 56 26 69 63 91

O. _ _ _ _ _ _ _ _ _ _ _
99 27 13 49 79 72 33 21 66
Law-seeker

P. _ _ _ _ _ Favorite dynasty of
78 32 87 23 Confucius

Q. _ _ _ _ _ AAA president
1 92 41 67 73

Instructions

When a Definition is guessed, pencil it in the spaces given. Then write in the letters again in the puzzle Diagram, distributed as directed (A94, A12, A57, A81). In "O" for example, the word for "law-seeker" might be "plaintiff" since the number of letters fits—but it must obey other consistencies. For, when completed, the Diagram will read across horizontally (1, 2, 3, 4, etc.) as a complete sentence quotation from a book; further, the first letters of the Definitions (A, B, C, D, etc.) read vertically will give both the author and the title of the book from which the quotation is taken (there is no other "vertical" rationale, as in a crossword puzzle, but because of complex internal consistencies one *knows* he has the right answer and does not need to wait until next week's filled-in Diagram). One may make low-level hypothecations back and forth between Diagram and Definitions: for example, M74 and G75 in the Diagram/G might be "of"—or "it" or "is" or "he"—but it must fit the Definitions. So, too, E71, O72, Q73 might be "who"—or "for" or "she" or "the" or "but"—but always depending on fit both with the sentence-meaning and the Definitions. Correct meanings will be constantly rewarded with new insights, as in field work, until, gradually, an irrefutable meaning will emerge, for any incorrect inference will be brought up short by inconsistency with the multiple logic of the method.

Definitions

A. **L A O S** Land of the Moi
94 12 57 81

B. **A F F E C T** Emotion,
89 76 50 46 62 6 change

C. **B O S** Aurochs genus
60 98 3

D. **A L G A E** Thallophytes,
40 53 96 25 37 sometimes symbiotic with fungi

E. **R E C H T** Law, droit, right
84 4 29 11 71

F. **R A S M U S S E N** Arctic explorer, Danish, 1879–1933
51 14 24 18 64 38 59 61 43 tic

G. **E L D E S T** Beneficiary of
30 9 36 75 17 48 primogeniture

H. **G I L L I N** Late president of AAA
55 95 35 90 97 5

I. **H O S T E S S** Woman
22 80 10 39 44 20 70 with the mostest

J. **O W I** Wartime propaganda
35 45 16 agency

K. **S E D N A** Eskimo owner of
47 93 42 15 8 seals

L. **T E S T I F I E S O**
68 52 2 31 54 88 19 86 65 82
N Swears to (two words)
58

M. **D U C** Rank in French nobility
74 83 85

N. **A S I N I T I A L** Acronym use (two words)
77 100 7 28 56 26 69 63 91 cronym use (two words)

O. **N O M O T H E T E**
99 27 13 49 79 72 33 21 66
Law-seeker

P. **C H O U** Favorite dynasty of
78 32 87 23 Confucius

Q. **E R N I E** AAA president
1 92 41 67 73

The reader, having inevitably put together the opinions evidenced in this paper, should now have some idea of where I stand as an anthropologist: not a scientist if, as usually in the social sciences, "scientist" means only the quantifier, for these quantifiers seem to me monumentally naive semantically, and quite hopeless in understanding what numbers are and can be made to do. Not an experimentalist, since social science hypotheses tend so painfully to display autobiographical origins and motivations, and are, I think, inescapably ethnocentric. Instead, the anthropological holism I seek requires biology, primatology, human biology, folklore, anatomy, archaeology, linguistics, clinical psychology, *belles lettres,* history, psychiatry, art, and any other discipline that promises perspective on our complex human data; one is not impressed by what any of the "social sciences" have given us to date, and I think I know why they have not. For me, the books of Job and Genesis, *Moby Dick* and *Ulysses,* the Parthenon and Senlis, Mozart and Bloch are all equally texts in anthropology, and I would as soon learn about the human from *Lophophora williamsii* as from a schizophrenic girl or a half-mad Siberian shaman. If anthropological holism means *Nil humanum alienum a me puto,* I would aspire to be called a humanist, if one ever knew enough about the human animal to deserve the appellation.

By training primarily an Americanist taught by Sapir, Spier, Wissler, Murdock and Osgood, I have also benefited from the cultural anthropology of the Indonesianist Kennedy, the Africanist Herzog, and the Polynesian Te Rangi Hiroa (Sir Peter Buck), but could never get enough of Asia, though I lived for some years in China, India and Ceylon, and have visited Japan, Taiwan, Hong Kong (all three twice), Thailand, Singapore and central Malaysia. An insatiable traveler, I have lived and traveled for six months in Bolivia, Chile, British Guiana, Peru and Brazil, as well as visiting the Caribbean four times in Cuba, Puerto Rico, Bermuda (twice, for a total of two months) and have traveled across Africa twice, from the Gold Coast to Khartoum and from Cairo to Casablanca. I know most of the large cities and many of the college towns of the United States from many speaking tours and scientific congresses, as well as Canada (including Nova Scotia) and twice Mexico. Whatever linguistics I know came from Sapir and Bender, a Princeton professor who wrote all the etymologies of the second unabridged Webster, and the Anglo-Saxonist Elsasser, as well as the language teachers of the five languages I can speak adequately. Bender thought I should be a linguist when he sent me to Sapir, but at Yale slightly older graduate students already there were Voegelin, Whorf, Swadesh, Newman, Haas and others, and after the culture shock of a course in Navaho with Sapir, I never aspired to compete with these formidable older colleagues in linguistics, though I remained an avid Indoeuropeanist as far as my abilities permitted and have lived and traveled over the years in twenty-five countries of Europe. My favorite tribes are the classic Greeks and the Jews, partly for technical reasons but also because they are my intellectual ancestors.

But the major influence on my anthropological thinking has been analytic psychiatry. Sapir considered that no one was prepared for certain kinds of field work, such as religion and culture and personality studies, unless he knew analysis thoroughly. Hence it was the fashion in the thirties at Yale to undergo a didactic analysis, and reading the classic works of Abraham, Jones and Ferenczi was taken seriously. A post-doctoral fellowship year as research intern at the Menninger Clinic confirmed this interest, and I later had two more analyses, including a violently negative transference to a celebrated New York analyst, from whom I finally learned only decades afterward on my own. My third therapist made me his colleague in teaching at the Medical School of the University of North Carolina at Chapel Hill, and my wife and I have long been colleagues in psychiatry there and at Duke University and have published together.[24] Trained as a parachuter for the Office of Naval Intelligence, I was kidnapped from duty with them in Calcutta, Kunming and Chungking by the Office of Strategic Services, successively in the China-Burma-India unit in Delhi and the South East Asia Command in Kandy where I spent a much-remembered seven months (every anthropologist has a Goona-Goona land, and mine was Ceylon), and ended up attached to the Staffs of the Commander Destroyers Atlantic Fleet in Casco Bay and the Commander-in-Chief Atlantic Fleet in Bermuda; no warrior, I hasten to add, even parachuting was for me primarily a profoundly psychological experience, and my jobs were invariably in intelligence. I have taught anthropology at Rutgers, in summer sessions at Washington Square College, Wisconsin, Northwestern, Minnesota, North Carolina (also for some years in the UNC Medical School), and am now the James B. Duke Professor of Anthropology at Duke University. I have been a Sterling Fellow of Yale and a Guggenheim Fellow (also fellow of the Santa Fe Laboratory of Anthropology, American Museum of Natural History and Yale Institute of Human Relations, SSRC, Viking Fund, and twice NSF), and the initial recipient of the Róheim Award. As editor-in-chief of the *Landmarks in Anthropology* series, I have edited some 129 books in approximately 178 volumes. One of the professional honors I count highest has been my being invited some twenty times as consultant in the three-day biannual conferences of the Group for the Advancement of Psychiatry, founded by William Menninger after the war, working with the Committee on Adolescence with whom I have also published.[25] In consequence of being an anthropologist with psychiatric training, I am pleased to be called on for such rewarding chores as speaker on a panel with Robert Stoller and the Johnson-Masters team at the American College of Psychiatrists in New Orleans, with Linus Pauling and Stanley Szurek on the President's Panel of the American Orthopsychiatric Association in San Francisco, and more recently as incumbent of the Simmel-Fenichel Lectures in Los Angeles. In descent, I am of so-called Old American pre-Revolutionary stock, including the Quaker divine John Woolman and Pennsylvania Dutch grantees of William Penn in Lancaster County. But the bar sinister in my French patronymic family was burned at the stake in 1766 at the age of eighteen in Abbeville, from which strain I may have inherited a certain maverick streak; his grandfather was Governor of New France just after Frontenac and lost a disastrous war with the Iroquois, which swung this powerful tribe to the side of the infant American colonies. Perhaps like him I am a spectacularly poor administrator, and (as was darkly alleged of my spiritual father, Edward Sapir) much prefer to "waste my time on students"—being delighted to help choose as departmental chairman a lady who promptly became president-elect of the American Anthropological Association. I like to think these mongrel origins make a case for "hybrid vigor," improved again in three stunning children by my marriage to a descendant of Danish sod house pioneers in frontier Minnesota, herself then the editor of a professional journal in New York and lately a winner of the Isabel Carter Award. *Haec sunt mea gaudia,* to which must be added extreme good fortune in my friends.

The *apologia pro opera sua* can best be done by simply exposing the methods used. *Native American Beers,*[26] my first professional article, was a distribution study, made from leftover data on psychotropic substances zealously compiled in one of twenty-two appendices to my doctoral dissertation; my thesis advisor, Leslie Spier, suggested I publish it in the *American Anthropologist* (he edited it at that time). This earliest effort achieved the distinction of a brief news article in *The New York Times,* affording the kind of feedback and appreciation

so encouraging to a young writer. Although the article, like the dissertation itself, was thoroughly an example of then "normal" science, in
my more innerdirected later efforts I have come to value the famous
but little regarded words of Henry David Thoreau: "Why should we
be in such desperate haste to succeed, and in such desperate enterprises? If a man does not keep pace with his companions, perhaps it is
because he hears a different drummer. Let him step to the music
which he hears, however measured or far away."

The Peyote Cult[27] was modeled after Spier's admirable study of
the Sun Dance, though the study of peyotism afforded abundant oral
history, collected by myself and generous colleagues, with no need to
rely on statistical study of trait-distributions as Spier had. The publication of this dissertation by three publishers in some dozen imprints
and new editions, though gratifying, is the result merely of a later
unanticipated interest of the counterculture in its subject matter, for
the book has no merit of innovation in method and is largely a
meticulously compiled ethnography only. In this connection it is
amusing that, when setting up a new tribal peyote cult, Indians have
repeatedly consulted the rather jejune descriptive core of the monograph for details, with the result that scarcely any culture change
in ritual has occurred in the past fifty years. This is further discomfit-
ing, since one hardly expected to be the prophet in a religion of the
book—for what if the young graduate student had made some error,
thus to mislead later generations! Fortunately the conjectural elements, notably those on the Red Bean Cult, have been amply supported by archaeologists from Campbell and Troike to Adovasio and
Fry.[28] In some cases, fieldworkers on specific tribes have tended to
push back the date of acquisition to earlier cult-bringers; but peyotism
has often been introduced several times into a tribe, and such field
work is a useful refinement of my own. I have myself had second
thoughts on the provenience of peyotism, and wish we had more
information from the little-known tribes of Texas and northeastern
Mexico for another look at the matter. Spier was rigidly anti-psychological and allowed no such material in the published version, edited
while I was in South America, though some surreptitious psychological
glints did get by in a few footnotes. And I learned, as does every
graduate student, that no one should count himself a free agent
intellectually in his doctoral dissertation. Indeed, both Róheim[29] and
Hultkrantz[30] criticized the book—and quite rightly—for its dearth of
individual psychological materials, though in the end I can scarcely
be justly accused of being anti-psychological. For myself, I prefer to

the original text the again mounting appendices to the book, for these five- and ten-year supplements allow more perspective and reassessment.

Once interested, perhaps one is always interested in a subject, and out of this grew the concept of a New World "narcotic complex" (I would now prefer the term "psychotropic" as being more accurate),[31] and an ethnological understanding of the Old World/New World problem of botanical statistics on psychotropic plants; when a botanist noted the New World natives knew some eighty psychotropic plants, whereas the Old knew only a half-dozen, though the Old World was longer inhabited by men, had a larger land area, and certainly as varied plants and climates as the New, I suggested that perhaps the reason was that, ethnographically, American Indians in their concepts of "medicine power" were in a sense culturally programmed to discover psychotropic plant sources of such power.[32] Another study gives a larger perspective on American psychotropics.[33] It is a matter of some pride that on my second field trip, his first, I took along a Harvard graduate student named Richard Evans Schultes, who after more than a dozen years of field work in Amazonia has become the ranking authority[34] on the ethnobotany of New World psychotropic plants, as I may be of the ethnology.

My first properly psychological, indeed psychiatric, paper was *The Psychopathology of Drinking Songs*,[35] a rather light-hearted scrutiny of limericks collected at Princeton beer parties and at Morey's at Yale, showing the content of the "normal unconscious" when the superego is liquidated in alcohol. It seemed that limerick singers were preoccupied with, of all things, Oedipal revolt, lampooning of authority figures, youthful atheism, male and female sexuality (including perversions and fixations), autoerotism, anality, coitus and its variants, and (often unintended) pregnancy and other anxieties. The study was first presented as a paper at an evening meeting of the senior staff at the Menninger Clinic, none of whom appeared startled at its disclosures, though it achieved attention in an article with the clever title "Beneath Genteel Externals" in a weekly news magazine.

Some Observations on Character Structure in the Orient: I. The Japanese[36] was a psychoanalytically oriented culture and personality study, based on War Relocation Authority internees at Topaz, Utah, and on wartime interrogation of Japanese prisoners in the Red Fort at Old Delhi during the war. Anthropologists and sociologists, plainly upset by its analytic clinical approach, have long found it a convenient target as a presumably "early impressionist" culture and personality study, without any method beyond hunch-ethnography. It was not. Roiled by the method, critics quite failed to discern the method. The method was deductive. Observing that the Japanese encountered were markedly compulsive, I carefully listed all the traits which clinical work indicates are characteristic of the compulsive personality, together with the life history vicissitudes that ontogenetically and regularly produce the compulsive. Thereupon, voluminous ethnographic data were cited in order to ascertain whether there was a deductive matching between the clinical and the ethnographic. There was. QED, I thought. But I did not know then the degree of anxiety and anger aroused in people by a method that unpleasantly informs them of what they do not want to know about themselves. However, a baker's dozen of later studies of the Japanese ethos, using the Rorschach and other more acceptable methods, have uniformly demonstrated that the Japanese are, surprisingly, compulsive. Since that time, of course, there are many younger[37] psychological anthropologists quite adequately qualified to use analytic theory; and Margaret Mead,[38] at the outset of her masterly summary of the work of a large psychological congress at Houston in 1968, stated that in four decades of culture and personality studies the basic stratum of theory has been the psychoanalytic. Twenty years was a long time to wait.

Curiously, a second and longer such study, on the Chinese, much more discursively ethnographic despite its implicitly analytic method, aroused no such indignation and it has been placidly anthologized and excerpted ever since. The experience taught me that method is what alerts colleagues, not the subject matter delineated: the method is the message. But it takes stamina for the young anthropologist to stand in a rain of contemporary disfavor. *The Aymara of the Lake Titicaca Plateau, Bolivia*[39] would be, if nothing else, a thoroughly standard ethnography. The fate of this monograph is curious. John Gillin, a superbly qualified reviewer, was assigned the book. But shortly afterward he was to undergo a potentially grave major operation, and my reaction to my old friend and admired predecessor at Duke University was, "John, please don't bother about it now!" Gillin sturdily survived the operation for some decades, and the book was never reassigned from so obviously appropriate a reviewer. Although it was a Memoir of the American Anthropological Association, the monograph was never reviewed and is almost entirely unknown. To me this was a minor and perhaps undeserved professional disaster, since long argument with the Memoir editor, John Alden Mason, had finally succeeded in including a long section on the uncustomary subject of

"Native Knowledge, or Folk Sciences." These included ethnometeor-
ology, ethnohistory (read, folk history), ethnobotany, ethnoanatomy
and ethnophysiology, ethnoanthropology, ethnopsychology, ethnoeth-
nology, and ethnogeography. Since the Aymara are specialists in it,
ethnomedicine required additional, separate treatment and further
articles, while the data on ethnobotany were so voluminous as to
require a separate monograph, published in my favorite Italian city,
Firenze. As a result, I have long privately thought that "the new
ethnography" was not so new after all, being already present in this
monograph of 1948, indeed in still earlier articles of 1942 and 1947.[40]

Publication of my Aymara field work has taught me, if nothing
else has, the sometimes wide discrepancies between one's own and
others' judgments of his work. As a last scraping of the bottom of the
barrel, there were left some field notes on the potato taxonomy of the
Aymara which, not valuing them much, I published in an obscure and
now extinct journal.[41] But the fantastically omnivorous Lévi-Strauss
found it! It is the only work of mine he has ever cited (though I did
send him *The Human Animal* in thanks for his serving as my NSF
sponsor in Paris), but I nevertheless remain puzzled to find it in the
canon of the younger social anthropologists. The Aymara have an
interesting binomial system of plant nomenclature, but I had never
done anything in writing this article, I had only carefully reported
voluminous categories of the Aymara, and to them belonged any
credit! Perhaps sheer information is still the more to be valued than
the fanciest "method" in ethnography, of which this paper had quite
none at all. Consequently, any kudos with respect to the Aymara field
work has come from a simple reportorial minor article, not from
innovations in an unknown book.

Other Aymara work concerned their ethos.[42] I found them "tru-
culent, hostile, silent, and unsmiling in all their dealings with
whites." Now, field work in the barren and cold windswept Titicaca
plateau, as in many other places, is admittedly not pleasant physically.
After several experiences of attempted kindness met with treachery, I
began to blame myself and to be concerned with "countertransference." What, possibly, was I myself contributing to this untoward
judgment? I had always liked the straightforward temperament of the
Plains Indians among whom I had worked on two earlier field trips.
Post-field library work, however, quickly revealed that earlier students
had expressed still harsher judgments. A Frenchman found them
"cruel, awkward, and repulsively ugly" (Grandidier, in 1861); a Scot,
"silent, and uncommunicative, intensely suspicious and distrustful"

and filled with "deep-rooted and inveterate hatred" (Forbes, 1870); an American, "more sullen, and more cruel" than the Quechua, and "a people notoriously morose, jealous, and vindictive" (Squier, 1877); and another Frenchman, "hard, vindictive, bellicose, rebellious, egotistical, cruel, and jealous . . . lacking in will, except the will to hate" (Walle, 1914). Indeed, shortly before my stay, another American had considered them "the most difficult of all Andean peoples to cultivate . . . disagreeable . . . dishonest and generally unreliable. . . . Here is a rare opportunity for the ethnologist who is looking for a tough job" (Hewlett, 1938). Better to have gone to Wetar in Indonesia, as I had at first planned, until it was learned that Du Bois was going to Alor! One writer even invoked for the Aymara a degenerative "racial or ethnic disease" (Adams, 1915). Indeed, the Aymara themselves had a word, *qaiya,* for their sullen melancholy. I returned several times to the problem, to measure these multinational "subjective" assessments of ethos against "projective" data in the form of the Aymaras' own folktales. A 100% sample of tales, collected earlier for linguistic studies, was examined and finally a psychological-historical explanation was offered for the findings: "If the Aymara, as evidenced in their folk tales (and indeed throughout the rest of their culture), are apprehensive, crafty, suspicious, violent, treacherous, and hostile, one important reason for this may be that such a character structure is an understandable response to their having lived for perhaps as long as a millenium under rigidly hierarchic and absolutist economic, military, and religious controls"—successively of the ancient Colla empire (when chiefs were carried in litters), the conquering Inca, the Conquistadores, the colonial Spanish, and the post-colonial Bolivians. Curiously, in the last two decades, younger Aymarists (Heath, Plummer, Carter, Cole, Hickman) have taxed me with giving a wholly inaccurate picture of the Aymara, whom they found friendly, cheerful and cooperative during the post-Revolution field work of these students. Moreover, the new fieldworkers are mutually consistent in the matter. Was a whole generation of earlier workers mistaken, despite the range of time and variety of nationalities represented? Perhaps this only demonstrates that ethos, a learned complex, is not necessarily stable dischronically and that non-genetic ethos can be as changeable as culture. The ethnographic "experiment" here prepared for us by history, I would observe, has given results not inconsistent with the findings of clinical psychologists when describing the contrastive effects on children's groups of authoritarian versus permissive treatment by adults. Historically, the Bolivian peasant rebellion seems in fact to have been one of the few authentic revolutions in Latin America, with real changes between the thirties and the sixties in basic politico-economic structure beyond the usual mere circulation in personnel. If this is true, the answer may remain culture-historical: with drastic change in social conditions, the Aymara ethos has apparently veered 180°. Since the new Aymarists are manifestly competent and mutually consistent, any humanist will be thoroughly gratified with their findings.

The Human Animal[43] was a first venture into anthropological holism, into what I did not then but might now call the "ethology of culture." The experience of all my major book manuscripts, save for *The Aymara*, has uniformly been rejection by a dozen publishers each. The first version, of article length, was rejected by Benedict, as advisory editor of *Psychiatry*, for being "too Spencerian." However, like most students of the Boasian tradition, I had been restive with ethnography as mere piles of ethnographic information, and was in search of some unifying principle. Could this not be done by putting together physical anthropology, ethnology and linguistics, and trying to make sense of the whole? But my generation of graduate students had been rigorously drilled to accept that biology (race) and culture have two entirely distinct modes of filiation, biological and sociological, and never the twain could meet. Perhaps, also, an honorable field-oriented anthropology had totally failed to sustain racist superstitions. Nevertheless, could not an adequately species-specific *human biology* encompass all these aspects of man? This biology I found in analytic psychology—which was doubly to damn it. Melville and Frances Herskovits, citing their own successful encounter with the formidable Boas over Africanisms in the Americas, encouraged my heresy, without necessarily agreeing with it. One celebrated physical anthropologist jeered at this heretical holism and strongly urged rejection by the ultimate publisher. But a stubborn editor, since established as one of the foremost publishers of anthropological materials in the United States, Alexander Morin, with whom it is only fair to say I rewrote the book, persisted. A comforting irony is that several physical anthropologists, including my irate reader, have since compiled symposia on man's biological adaptations to culture and the species-specific grounds in human biology for culture-bearing. Of later physical anthropologists, Frederick Hulse, James Spuhler, and Alice Brues have most elegantly handled these ideas. As Heller[44] has noted, the history of an idea is to begin as heresy, and to end a commonplace banality. But again the irony of the Japanese study: the conclusions were readily adopted, but the method of reaching them contemned.

They Shall Take Up Serpents: Psychology of the Southern Snake-Handling Cult[45] was forced on me as ethnography lying virtually at my front door, since an interstate conference of snake-handling churches was held in 1948 in Durham, North Carolina. My relationship with the organizer of the conference, the snake-handling minister "Beauregard Barefoot," was long and clinically edifying, though I ended up with a certain humanistic sympathy for him and his poor-white clientele, and the snake-handling cult itself was reassurance to me that anthropologists would not necessarily be technologically unemployed with the final acculturation of the last "untouched" tribe in highland New Guinea or central Amazonia. The method of the book was quite simple and clear from its divisions: first, the ethnography and history of the cult movement, then its Old World origins and symbolisms in the Old Testament, and finally the autobiography of the snake-handling preacher, which was of necessity treated as a clinical document. The study furthered my understanding of the relationship between personality and culture, and the data dynamically illustrated Freud's observation that hysteria and psychopathy are two sides of the same coin, for the acting-out leader and his repressed clientele were symbiotically made for each other. Cultist snake-handling has largely died out, as I predicted, in the urbanizing and industrializing Piedmont, but a number of workers are studying the continued persistence of snake-handling in Appalachia, among whom I consider the present authority on the snake-handling cult to be Steven Kane, now a graduate student at Princeton.

Another interest has been kinesics and non-verbal communication. *The Cultural Basis of Emotions and Gestures*[46] has been considerably anthologized, but I regard *Paralinguistics, Kinesics and Cultural Anthropology*[47] and *Ethology and Ethnology*[48] as more developed studies. An international conference at Royaumont on dreams—and especially association there with the psychologist William Dement and the Hellenist E. R. Dodds—further stimulated my interest in the relationship of REM state dreams to the charisma and visionary innovations of the culture-hero founders of crisis cults.[49] As a prolific reviewer, I consider the book review an art form, demanding much of the discipline of a short story or *haiku*. Of mine, the favorite half-dozen that best succeed in saying what I wanted to, may be still worth reading.[50]

The culmination of a holistic interest in human biology and culture is my major work, *The Ghost Dance: The Origins of Religion*.[51] It is a complex book, with several main themes. Anthropologists

have long puzzled over the definitions, taxonomy, and institutionalization of magic and religion, but it seems to me that the difference lies
not so much in differing real objectivities in the outside world as in
their being basically different subjective ways of apperceiving the
unknown. That unknown is here less outside than inside man. Since
religion appears to be inclusively and exclusively human, its roots must
lie in human biology, and these sources can be studied ontogenetically
through dynamic psychiatry, as well as "phylogenetically" though
archaeology, explicit history, comparative ethnography, and species-
specific human biology. Further, no earlier anthropologist had ever
concerned himself with the question *why magic and religion have such
emotional plausibility,* since both are so often in manifest conflict with
explicit rational experience. These origins lie emotionally in the onto-
genetic development of each individual personality, and as universally
as the developmental stages in neotenous *Homo sapiens.* Indeed, the
universally present *types* of magic, I believe, must ultimately rest on
the universal human experiences of learning to walk and to talk. To
walk is to learn an impressive new voluntary control of one's body and
much of the material environment, a potency that includes "alloplastic" evolution as a peculiarly human evolution culturally. But,
regressively in crises of ego-technique controls, this valid and experienced control of one's organism is illegitimately extrapolated if it is
supposed that control of part of an enemy's substance, his exuviae,
means affecting his now-discrete organism. Exuvial or contagious
magic thus misconstrues the nature of organism. Similarly, to talk is to
discover the almost magical power of symbols in adapting to and even
managing other human beings. But this valid and experienced power
does not operate, as homeopathic magic assumes, through mere verbal
means, on the puppet that merely *symbolizes* the enemy, for this is
falsely to extrapolate the nature of symbols. Thus, exuvial magic mis-
apprehends the nature of organic things, effigy magic the nature of
symbols. Again, since in sober fact all our information about the
"supernatural" comes exclusively from charismatic personalities, our
relation to which can be examined psychiatrically, why not then examine cultural crisis situations, in which dependency on personal authority is substituted for our experience of reality. Since the *de facto* source
is always clear, why not give up *de jure* wranglings over *truth* arrived
at by unexaminable "supernatural" means, and instead study naturalistically these charismatic utterances as clinical and ethnographic *fact,*
together with a study of these vatic culture heroes and the sociocultural conditions under which they operate. An earnest cultivation of

the scientist's careful discrimination between what is inside (hypothesis) versus what is outside (phenomena) could only end in perceiving that the secular is adaptive to "outside" but the sacred only to "inside" realities. The contrast of sacred and secular, religious and rational, is further the contrast of two experienced epistemological modes, REM state and waking state.

This rigorously secular approach to religion implies ultimately a benevolently skeptical attitude even toward culture itself, and as such is perhaps shocking. A medical student taking a reading course with me in psychoanalytic psychiatry, after he had read *The Ghost Dance* remarked amazedly, "Sir, you would say *anything* if you thought it was true!" When I survey the customary reaction to my often ungenteel and group-unchastened statements, perhaps his amazement is justified with respect to religion, the understanding of which has been traditionally so hampered by our emotional vested interests, and hence by the privileged position we give religion as presumably unexaminable subjective human experience. But the subjective *is* examinable clinically. The procedure is likely to infuriate all true believers, and many other people besides, but I had long since decided in lone battle that I knew what I knew about secular psychiatry. The locus of the "*super*natural" world is the "*sub*conscious" mind, as projected in the crisis-cult revelation-vision of the leader while in a dissociated state; but REM dreams and all other dissociated states are equally open to secular scrutiny.[52] The Ghost Dance is one type of the seemingly endless and ubiquitous crisis cults in societies suffering cultural trauma (the discovery of the fallible defensive nature and limitations of one's own culture). But the social context of these traumata also can be examined, both historically and ethnographically as well. With insights derived from psychiatrically sophisticated human biology into the nature and purpose of culture, and the abundant comparative ethnography of crisis cults in their social context, insights gained into culture heroes and their charisma can then be applied to our own Graeco-Hebraic tradition. Charisma, which seems to be a "supernatural" *rightness* streaming from the charismatic individual, is merely the emotional welcomeness of his message, *déjà vu* in the prepotent unconscious wishes of each communicant. A somewhat startling discovery on examination of occidental culture-history was that Platonism and the whole Great Tradition in Western philosophy and religion can be traced and unmistakably demonstrated continuously clear back to Old Stone Age origins. In another book I intend to pursue study of this tenacious *continuity* of culture, in the context of an amazingly

292   WESTON LA BARRE

widespread superstition about ourselves, before embarking on the third work of a proposed trilogy, begun by *The Human Animal* and continued in *The Ghost Dance,* to be titled *The Singing Head.*

REFERENCE NOTES

1. H. W. Zorbaugh, *Gold Coast and Slum* (Chicago: University of Chicago Press, 1929); Frances R. Donovan, *The Saleslady* (Chicago: University of Chicago Press, 1929); and Clifford R. Shaw, *The Jack-Roller* (Chicago: University of Chicago Press, 1930).

2. "Professor Widjojo Goes to the Koktel Parti," *New York Times* Magazine, 9 December 1956, 17ff.; republished, "Totemistic Celebrations," *The College Years,* ed. A. C. Spectorsky (New York: Hawthorne Books, 1958), pp. 396–98; R. W. Hoffmann and R. Plutchik, eds., *Controversy* (New York: G. P. Putnam Sons, 1959), pp. 129–32; "The Koktel Parti," *Background and Foreground,* ed. Lester Markel (Great Neck, N.Y.: Channel Press, 1960), pp. 256–61; "Professor Widjojo's Field Trip to the Us-ans," *Duke Alumni Register* 50 (January 1954) 4–7.

3. Sir James G. Frazer, *Folklore in the Old Testament* (London: Macmillan, 1919), 3 vols.

4. E. Sapir, *Time Perspective in Aboriginal American Culture, A Study in Method* (Ottawa: Canada Department of Mines, Geological Survey Memoir 90 [#13 Anthropological Series], 1916); reprinted, New York: Johnson Reprint Corp., 1968.

5. M. E. Spiro, "Culture and Personality, The Natural History of a False Dichotomy," *Psychiatry* 14 (1951) 19–46.

6. W. La Barre, *The Ghost Dance: Origins of Religion* (New York: Doubleday, 1970; London, Allen & Unwin, 1972); revised paperback edition (New York: Delta Books, 1972), pp. 46–48.

7. W. La Barre, "Social Cynosure and Social Structure," *Journal of Personality* 14 (1946) 169–83; reprinted in *Personal Character and Cultural Milieu,* ed. D. G. Haring (Syracuse: Syracuse University Press, 1956), pp. 535–45; "Cynosures (points de mire) et structures sociales," *Revue de Psychologie des Peuples* 8 (1953) 362–77; Warren Morrill, "Social Cynosure and Cultural Adaptation," *Anthropology Tomorrow* 6 (April 1960), 8–12.

8. M. S. Edmonson, "Nativism, Syncretism and Anthropological Science," *Nativism and Syncretism* (New Orleans: Middle American Research Institute, Tulane University, Publication 19, 1960, 183–203), pp. 186–88.

9. Barbara G. Myerhoff, *Peyote Hunt: The Sacred Journey of the Huichol Indians* (Ithaca: Cornell University Press, 1974), p. 230.

10. T. S. Kuhn, *The Structure of Scientific Revolutions* (Chicago: University of Chicago Press, Phoenix Books, 1962).

11. Paul Tillich, *The Courage To Be* (New Haven: Yale University. Press, 1952).

12. Robert H. Lowie, *The History of Ethnological Theory* (New York: Farrar & Rinehart, 1937), pp. 230–42.

13. W. La Barre, "The Influence of Freud on Anthropology," *American Imago* 15 (1958) 275–328, pp. 281, 292–294. See also S. Axelrod, review of Hendrick, *American Anthropologist* 61 (1959) 548–49; and a letter of R. Benedict to M. Mead, *An Anthropologist at Work* (Boston: Houghton Mifflin, 1959), p. 305.

14. R. W. Firth, ed., *Man and Culture: An Evaluation of the Work of Bronislaw Malinowski* (London: Routledge & Kegan Paul, New York: Humanities Press, 1957). Ronald Cohen (review of M. Gluckman, *American Anthropologist* 67 [1965] 954) wonders "why a man who in the passage of time had been so wrong on so many counts, had during his lifetime been hailed as such an all-encompassing leader not only of his discipline, but of western intellectual life as a whole."

15. B. Malinowski, *A Diary in the Strict Sense of the Term* (New York: Harcourt Brace and World, 1967).

16. G. Devereux, *From Anxiety to Method in the Behavioral Sciences*, with a preface by W. La Barre (The Hague: Mouton, 1967); *Angst und Methode in den Verhaltenswissenschaften*, Verwort von W. La Barre (Munchen: Hanser Verlag, 1973).

17. R. M. Wintrob, "An Inward Focus: A Consideration of Psychological Stress in Field Work," *Stress and Response in Field Work*, eds. F. Henry and S. Saberwal (New York: Holt, Rinehart & Winston, 1969), pp. 63–76; A. N. J. den Hollander, "Social Description: The Problems of Reliability and Validity," *Anthropologists in the Field*, eds. D. G. Jongmans and P. C. W. Gutkind (Assen: Van Gorcum, 1967; New York: Humanities Press, 1970); Eleanor Bowen (Laura Bohannan), *Return to Laughter* (New York: Harper & Sons, 1954); Fred Gearing, *Face of the Fox* (Chicago: Aldine Press, 1970); Kenneth Read, *High Valley* (New York: Scribners, 1965); G. W. Berreman, *Behind Many Masks* (Ithaca: Society for Applied Anthropology Monographs, 4, 1962); Hortense Powdermaker, *Stranger and Friend* (New York: Norton, 1966); W. La Barre, *The Ghost Dance*, pp. 52–53; Barbara Gallatin Anderson, "Adaptive Aspects of Culture Shock," *Abstracts*, 67th Annual Meeting of the American Anthropological Association, 1968, p. 4; G. D. Spindler, ed., *Being an Anthropologist: Field Work in Eleven Cultures* (New York: Holt, Rinehart & Winston, 1970); M. Freilich, ed., *Marginal Natives: Anthropologists at Work* (New York: Harper and Row, 1970).

18. La Barre, *Ghost Dance*, pp. 4, 52–53, 289–290.

19. R. B. Dixon, *The Racial History of Man* (New York: Scribners, 1923).

20. F. Boas, "Changes in Bodily Form of Descendants of Immigrants," *Race, Language and Culture* (New York: Macmillan, 1940), pp. 60–75.

21. La Barre, *Ghost Dance*, pp. 507–8, fn. 23.

22. J. W. M. Whiting, "Effects of Climate on Certain Cultural Practices," *Explorations in Cultural Anthropology: Essays in Honor of George Peter Murdock*, ed. W. Goodenough (New York: McGraw-Hill, 1964) pp. 511–44.

23. W. La Barre, *They Shall Take Up Serpents: Psychology of the Southern Snake-Handling Cult* (Minneapolis: University of Minnesota Press, 1962; New York: Schocken Books, 1969), pp. 78–84, 107. See also, W. La Barre, "The Snake-Handling Cult of the American Southeast," Goodenough, *op. cit.*, pp. 309–33; reprinted, *Bobbs-Merrill Reprint Series in Anthropology*, 1971.

24. Maurine and Weston La Barre, "The Worm in the Honeysuckle; A Case Study of a Child's Hysterical Blindness," *Social Casework* 47 (July 1965) 399–413; "The Triple Crisis: Adolescence, Early Marriage, and Parenthood," *The Double Jeopardy, The Triple Crisis* (New York: National Council on Illegitimacy, 1969).

25. *Normal Adolescence: Its Dynamics and Impact* (New York: Scribners, 1948, GAP Report No. 68); *Come Costrire l'Adolescente Normale, La curiosita l'esigenza di liberta la maturazione sessuale* (Milano: Ferro Edizione, 1969); *Ungdommen og Samfunnet, En bok om vanlig ungdom for foreldre, oppdragene, ungdomsledere og de unge selv* (Oslo: H. Aschenhoug & Co., 1969); *Dinamica da Adolescencia, Aspetos biologicos, culturais e psicologicos* Sao Paolo: Editora Culturix, 1970). Other articles on childhood and adolescence: W. La Barre, "Toward World Citizenship," *Survey Graphic* 85 (March 1949) 153–56, 187–89, reprinted as a training document (Washington: State Department Foreign Service Institute, 1949); "Child Care and World Peace," *The Child* 13 (1949), 157–57, also reprinted as an FSI training document; "Wanted: A Pattern for Modern Man" (New York: National Committee for Mental Health pamphlets, 1949), reprinted in *Child-Family Digest*, 1 no. 3 (August 1949) 17–31, and in *Sociology: A Book of Readings*, eds. S. Koenig, R. D. Hopper, and F. Gross (New York: Prentice-Hall, 1953); "The Age Period of Cultural Fixation," *Mental Hygiene* 33 (1949) 209–21; "The Family, Its Functions and Future," *Child-Family Digest* 2 (June 1950) 3–16; "The Family: Fundamentals versus Filigree," *Child-Family Digest* 5 (July 1951) 3–13; "Family and Symbol," *Psychoanalysis and Culture: Essays in Honor of Geza Roheim*, eds. G. W. Wilbur and W. Muensterberger (New York: International Universities Press, 1951), pp. 156–67; "Appraising Today's Pressures on Family Living," *Journal of Social Casework* 32 (1951) 51–57; "Self Respect and Mental Maturity," *Child-Family Digest*, 13 (September 1955) 3–16, reprinted in Michigan Society for Mental Health *Mental Health Bulletin*, 12 no. 2 (1955) 1–6; "The Social Worker in Cultural Change," *Social Welfare Forum*, 1957, pp. 179–93; "The Social Cell," *Saturday Review*, 38 no. 17 (23 April 1955) 17, reprinted *Child-Family Digest*, 12 (June 1955) 74–76; "The Patient and His Families," *Casework Papers* (New York: National Conference on Social Welfare, Family Service Association of America, 1958), pp. 61–71, reprinted, *Child-Family Digest* 18 (January-February 1959), 9–18; "Adolescence: Lesson in History," *Child Study* 36 (1959) 10–15; "How Adolescent Are Parents?"

National Parent-Teacher, The PTA Magazine 54 (December 1959) 4–6; "Relations Between Parents and Children," *Understanding Family Dynamics* (Pittsburgh: Family Living Institute, 1960), reprinted *Child-Family Digest,* 19 (July-August 1960), 15–16, and "Les relations entre les parents et les enfants," *Medicine et Hygiene* (Geneva, Switzerland), 20 no. 559 (30 July 1962) 604–606; "The Well-Disciplined Parent," *Christian Home,* 20 no. 2 (February 1961) 12-14, reprinted in *Adult Teacher,* 14 no. 5 (May 1961) 4–6; "The Trouble with Young People Nowadays is . . . ," *Carnegie Review* 10 (January 1967) 3–12; "Adolescence, the Crucible of Change," *Social Casework* 50 (January 1969) 22–26; "Authority, Culture Change and the Courts," *Loyola Law Review* 18 no. 3 (1971–1972) 481–92.

26. W. La Barre, "Native American Beers," *American Anthropologist* 40 (1938) 224–234; "Aboriginal Americans Liked Their Liquor," *New York Times,* 6 March 1938.

27. W. La Barre, *The Peyote Cult* (New Haven: Yale University Publications in Anthropology, 19, 1938); reprinted (Hamden, Conn.: Shoe String Press, 1959, 1964, 1968, 1970, 1975; New York: Schocken Books, 1969, 1970, 1975). For defenses of peyotists see Franz Boas, A. L. Kroeber, A. Hrdlicka, J. P. Harrington, M. R. Harrington, W. La Barre, V. Petrullo, R. E. Schultes, Elna Smith, and Chief Lookout, "Statement against the Chavez Senate Bill 1349," *Congressional Record,* 8 February 1937; and W. La Barre, D. P. McAllester, J. S. Slotkin, O. C. Stewart, and S. Tax, "Statement on Peyote," *Science* 114 no. 2970 (30 March 1951) 582–83. For reviews see W. La Barre on J. S. Slotkin, The Peyote Religion, in *American Anthropologist* 59 (1957) 350–60; on D. F. Aberle and O. C. Stewart, Navaho and Ute Peyotism, *American Anthropologist* 60 (1958) 171; on C. B. Dustin, "Peyotism and New Mexico," *Western Folklore* 21 (1962) 211; and the film review of Peter Furst, "To Find Our Life: The Peyote Hunt of the Huichols of Mexico," *American Anthropologist* 72 (1970) 1201.

28. W. La Barre, "Mescalism and Peyotism," *American Anthropologist* 59 (1957) 708–11; T. N. Campbell, "Origin of the Mescal Bean Cult," *American Anthropologist* 60 (1958) 156–60; R. C. Troike, "The Origin of Plains Mescalism," *American Anthropologist* 64 (1962) 946–63; J. M. Adovasio and G. F. Fry, "Prehistoric Psychotropic Drug Use in Northeastern Mexico and Trans-Pecos Texas," Paper, *Seventy-First Annual Meeting, American Anthropological Association,* Toronto, 1972, mimeographed.

29. G. Róheim, Review, *Psychoanalytic Quarterly* 8 (1939) 248–49.

30. Ake Hultkrantz, in "Twenty Years of Peyote Studies," *Current Anthropology* 1 (1960) 45–60, p. 57.

31. W. La Barre, "The Narcotic Complex of the New World," *Diogenes* 48 (1964) 125–28, reprinted in *Bobbs-Merrill Reprint Series in the Social Sciences,* 1969, *Bobbs-Merrill Reprint Series in Anthropology,* 1971; "Le complexe narcotique de L'Amerique autochtone," *Diogene* 48 (1964) 120–134; "El complejo narcotico de la America Autoctona," *Diogenes* 11 (1964) 102–112. The term "psychotropic" is suggested in *Twenty Years,* p. 54 (p. 204, in 1964 and later editions of *The Peyote Cult).* See also Carol C. Barber,

"Peyote and the Definition of Narcotic," *American Anthropologist* 61 (1959) 641–46.

32. W. La Barre, "Old and New World Narcotics: A Statistical Question and an Ethnological Reply," *Economic Botany* 24 no. 1 (1970) 73–80.

33. W. La Barre, "Hallucinogens and the Shamanic Origins of Religion," *Flesh of the Gods: The Ritual Use of Hallucinogens*, ed. P. T. Furst (New York: Praeger, 1972), pp. 261–78; "Anthropological Perspectives on Hallucination and Hallucinogens," *Hallucinations: Behavior, Experience, Theory*, ed. R. K. Siegel and L. J. West (New York: John Wiley and Sons, in press 1975).

34. Richard Evans Schultes and Albert Hofmann, *The Botany and Chemistry of Hallucinogens* (Springfield, Illinois: Charles C. Thomas, 1973).

35. W. La Barre, "The Psychopathology of Drinking Songs," *Psychiatry* 2 (1939) 203–12; "Beneath Genteel Externals," Time, 10 July 1939. In "the largest collection of limericks ever published," G. Legman *(The Limerick, 1700 Examples, with Notes, Variants, and Index*, Paris: Hautes Etudes, 1953) incorporated my long manuscript collection, but gave credit for those in the *Psychiatry* article. Other psychiatric articles: W. La Barre, "Primitive Psychotherapy in Native American Cultures: Peyotism and Confession," *Journal of Abnormal and Social Psychology* 24 (1947) 294–309, reprinted in *Bobbs-Merrill Reprints in the Social Sciences*, 1965; "The Apperception of Attitudes," *American Imago* 6 (1949) 3–43; "Obscenity: An Anthropological Appraisal," *Law and Contemporary Problems* 20 (1955) 533–43; "Psychoanalysis in Anthropology," *Science and Psychoanalysis*, ed. J. J. Masserman (New York: Grune & Stratton, 1961), vol. 4, pp. 10–20; "Trandference Cures in Religious Cults and Social Groups," *Journal of Psychoanalysis in Groups* 1 (1962) 66–76; "Confession as Cathartic Therapy in American Indian Tribes," *Magic, Faith, and Healing*, ed. Ari Kiev (New York: Free Press, 1964), pp. 36–49; "Geza Roheim," *Psychoanalytic Pioneers*, ed. F. Alexander, S. Eisenstein and Martin Grotjahn (New York: Basic Books, 1966) pp. 272–81; "Clinical Approach to Culture," *Contemporary Psychology* 11 (1966) 397–98; "Personality from a Psychoanalytic Viewpoint," *The Study of Personality, An Inter-Disciplinary Approach*, eds. E. Norbeck, D. Price-Williams, and W. M. McCord (New York: Holt, Rinehart and Winston, 1968), pp. 65–87; "Anthropological Perspectives on Sexuality," *Sexuality: A Search for Perspective*, eds. D. L. Grummon and A. M. Barclay (New York: Van Nostrand, Reinhold Co., 1971), pp. 38–53; "Culture and Personality: An Overview," *Psychotherapy and Social Science Review* 5 no. 11 (1971) 17–19.

36. W. La Barre, "Some Observations on Character Structure in the Orient: I. The Japanese," *Psychiatry* 8 (1945) 319–42, reprinted in *Japanese Character and Culture*, ed. B. S. Silberman (Tucson: University of Arizona Press, 1962), pp. 325–59; "Some Observations on Character Structure in the Orient: II. The Chinese," *Psychiatry* 9 (1946) 215–37 and 375–95; a portion of this has been reprinted as "Chinese Food and Drink," *Alcohol Intoxication: Social Attitudes and Controls*, ed. R. G. McCarthy (New Haven: Yale University Center of Alcohol Studies, 1954). A third in the series, on India, lies on my five-foot shelf of unpublished manuscripts.

37. "The Influence of Freud on Anthropology," *American Imago* 15 (1958) 275–328, was intended to continue the survey by Clyde Kluckhohn, "The Influence of Psychiatry on Anthropology in America during the Past One Hundred Years," in *One Hundred Years of American Psychiatry*, eds. J. K. Hall, G. Zilboorg, and H. A. Bunker (New York: Columbia University Press, for the American Psychiatric Association, 1944). The survey should be continued from 1958 to the present by some qualified young anthropologist.

38. M. Mead, "Problems and Progress in the Study of Personality," in eds. Norbeck, Price-Williams, and McCord, *op.cit.*, pp. 373–81. P. 373.

39. W. La Barre, *The Aymara Indians of the Lake Titicaca Plateau, Bolivia* (Menasha, Wisconsin: Memoirs of the American Anthropological Association, 68, 1948). "The Uru of the Rio Desaguadero," *American Anthropologist* 43 (1941) 493–522, and "The Uru-Chipaya," *Handbook of South American Indians*, ed. J. H. Steward (Washington: Bureau of American Ethnology, Bulletin 143), II:575–83, 1946—were also products of this field trip.

40. W. La Barre, "Aymara Biologicals and Other Medicines," *Journal of American Folklore* 64 no. 252 (1951) 171–78; *Materia Medica of the Aymara, Lake Titicaca Plateau, Bolivia* (Firenze: Istituto Botanico dell'Università, 1960; *Webbia*, XV no. 1 [1959] 47–94). But my interest lay still earlier in "Folk Medicine and Folk Sciences," *Journal of American Folklore* 55 no. 218 (1942) 197–203, and "Kiowa Folk Sciences," *Journal of American Folklore* 60 (1947) 105–14.

41. W. La Barre, "Potato Taxonomy among the Aymara Indians of Bolivia," *Acta Americana* 5 (1947) 83–103.

42. *Aymara Indians*, pp. 39–40; "Aymara Folktales," *International Journal of American Linguistics* 16 (1950) 40–45; "Aymara Folklore and Folk Temperament," *Journal of the Folklore Institute* 2 (1965) 25–30; "The Aymara: History and Worldview," *Journal of American Folklore* 79 no. 311 (1966) 130–44, and in *The Anthropologist Looks at Myth*, ed. John Greenway (Austin: University of Texas Press, 1966), pp. 130–44.

43. W. La Barre, *The Human Animal* (Chicago: University of Chicago Press, 1954; Phoenix Books, 8th impression, 1968); *L'Animal humain* (Paris: Payot, 1956); an Italian edition is in press (Milano: Bompiani, 1975). Portions of the English edition have been reprinted as: "Strange Patterns of Marriage," *Science Digest* 36 no. 5 (November 1954) 23–26; "Universal Biological Features in the Family," *Marriage and Family in the Modern World*, ed. Ruth S. Cavan (New York: Crowell, 1960), pp. 16–19; "People Are Different," *Midway* 7 (1961) 62–83; "Human Abilities," *Perspectives on the Social Order*, ed. H. L. Ross (New York: McGraw-Hill, 1963), pp. 48–51; "Superstition and the Soul," *Prose as Experience*, eds. T. C. Altschuler, M. M. McDonough, and A. J. Roth (Boston: Houghton-Mifflin, 1965), pp. 180–92; "The Human Animal in Biological Perspective," *Culture Shock*, ed. P. K. Bock (New York: Knopf, 1970), pp. 5–15. Further articles developed from viewpoints in *The Human Animal:* "The Biosocial Unity of the Family," *Exploring the Base for Family Therapy*, eds. N. W. Ackerman, F. L. Beatman, and S. L. Sherman (New York: Family Service

Association of America, 1961), pp. 5–13; "Introduction to the Science of Man," *Anthropology Today* (Del Mar: CRM Books, 1971), pp. 5–21; "The Development of Mind in Man in Primitive Cultures and Society," *Brain and Intelligence: The Ecology of Child Development,* ed. F. Richardson (Hyattsville, Md.: National Educational Press, 1973), pp. 21–38.

44. Erich Heller, *The Disinherited Mind* (Baltimore: Penguin Books, 1961), p. 232.

45. See reference note 23; also W. La Barre, "Snake-Handling: The Present and Recent Past," *Readings in Anthropology: The Evolution of Human Adaptations,* eds. P. J. and G. H. Pelto, and J. J. Poggie, Jr. (in press, 1975).

46. W. La Barre, "The Cultural Basis of Emotions and Gestures," *Journal of Personality* 16 (1947) 49–68; reprinted in *Selected Readings in Social Psychology,* ed. S. H. Britt (New York: Rinehart, 1949), pp. 49–56; *Personal Character and Social Milieu,* ed. D. G. Harding (Syracuse: Syracuse University Press, 1949: 489–506; 1956: 547–63); *Bobbs-Merrill Reprint Series in the Social Sciences,* 157, 1961; *Modern Sociology: An Introduction to the Study of Human Interaction,* eds. A. W. and H. P. Gouldner, J. R. Gusfield, and K. Archibald (New York: Harcourt, Brace and World, 1964), pp. 26–32; *Workbook in Group Dynamics,* ed. Jeanne Noble (New York: New York University Bookstore, 1968), pp. 49–68; *Interpersonal Dynamics, Essays and Readings in Human Interaction,* eds. W. G. Bennis, E. H. Schein, F. I. Steele, and D. E. Berlin (Homewood, Illinois: Dorsey Press, 1968), pp. 197–205; *Selected Readings,* ed. Phillip L. Stern (New York: Associated Educational Services Corp., 1969); *Make Men of Them,* ed. Charles G. Hughes (Chicago: Rand McNally, 1972), pp. 94–104; *Communicating Interpersonally: A Reader,* eds. R. W. Pace, B. E. Peterson, and T. R. Radcliffe (Columbus, Ohio: Charles E. Merrill Publishing Co., 1973); *Man and Culture,* ed. James M. Henlin (Boston: Holbrook Press, 1974); *The Social Aspects of the Body,* ed. T. Polhemus (New York: Random House, 1974); D. P. Gilfillan, *Nonverbal Behavior* (Evanston, Illinois: Northwestern University, 1974); *Anthropological Aspects of Movement,* ed. Martha Davis (New York: Arno Press, 1975); and "Die kulturelle Grundlage von Emotionen und Gesten," *Kulturanthropologie,* eds. W. E. Muhlmann and Ernst W. Muller (Koln-Marienburg: Kiepenheuer & Witsch, 1966), pp. 264–81.

47. W. La Barre, "Paralinguistics, Kinesics, and Cultural Anthropology," *Approaches to Semiotics,* eds. T. A. Sebeok, A. S. Hayes, and M. C. Bateson (The Hague: Mouton, 1964), pp. 191–220; *The Human Dialogue, Perspectives on Communication,* eds. F. W. Matson and Ashley Montagu (New York: Free Press, 1967), pp. 456–90; *Intercultural Communication: A Reader,* eds. L. A. Samovar and R. E. Porter (Belmont, California: Wadsworth Publishing Co., 1972), pp. 172–80; and "Paralinguistica e Cinesica e Antropologia culturale," *Parlinguistica e Cinesica,* eds. T. A. Sebeok, A. S. Hayes, and M. C. Bateson (Milano: Bompiani, 1970), pp. 279–321. 279–321.

48. W. La Barre, "Ethology and Ethnology," Semiotica 6 (1972) 83–96. Related publications: "Comments on the Human Revolution," *Current Anthropology* 5 (1964) 147–50, reprinted *Bobbs-Merrill Reprints in the Social Sciences,*

1965; "Some Comments Concerning Hockett's and Ascher's Contribution on the Human Revolution," *Current Anthropology* 7 (1966) 201–203; "Comments on Proxemics," *Current Anthropology* 9 (1968) 101–102, reprinted in *Culture: Man's Adaptive Dimension,* ed. Ashley Montagu (New York: Oxford University Press, 1968), pp. 50–55.

49. W. La Barre, "El sueño, el carismo y el héroe cultural," *Los Suenos y las Sociedades humanas,* ed. L. Echávarri (Buenos Aires: Editorial Sudamericana, 1964), pp. 453–61; "The Dream, Charisma, and the Culture Hero," *The Dream and Human Societies,* eds. G. E. von Grunebaum and Roger Caillois (Berkeley: University of California Press, 1966), pp. 229–35; "Le rêve, le charisme, et le héros culturel," *Le Rêve et les Sociétés humains,* eds. R. Caillois et G. E. von Grunebaum (Paris: Gallimard, 1967), pp. 205–21.

50. W. La Barre, reviews of D. G. Mandelbaum (ed.), "Selected Writings of Edward Sapir," *Survey Graphic* 86 no. 263 (May 1950); Rattray Taylor, "Sex in History," *Book Find News,* November 1955; Charles Winick, "Dictionary of Anthropology," *Southern Folklore Quarterly* 21 (1957) 322–23; Ashley Montagu (ed.), "Man and Aggression," *American Anthropologist* 71 (1969) 912–15; R. Gordon Wasson, "Soma, Divine Mushroom of Immortality," *American Anthropologist* 72 (1970) 368–73; R. L. Birdwhistell, "Kinesics and Context: Essays on Body Motion Communication," *American Journal of Sociology* 77 (1972) 999–1000; E. F. Torrey, "The Mind Game: Witchdoctors and Psychiatrists," *Social Casework* 55 (1974) 57–58; and W. McKee Evans, "To Die Game: The Story of the Lowry Band, Indian Guerrillas of the Reconstruction," *American Anthropologist* 76 (1974) 409–10.

51. *The Ghost Dance* (see reference note 6); W. La Barre, "Materials for a History of Studies of Crisis Cults," *Current Anthropology* 12 (1971) 3–44. See also "Les mouvements réligieux nés de l'acculturation en Amérique du Nord," Histoire des Religions, tome 2, *Encyclopédie de la Pléiade* (Paris: Gallimard, 1969) 29:1–40.

52. W. La Barre, "Anthropological Perspectives on Hallucination and Hallucinogens," in R. K. Siegel and L. J. West, (eds.), *op. cit.*

The Author*

JOHN J. HONIGMANN was born in the Bronx, New York, took his Ph.D. from Yale University in 1947 and is now Professor, recently Chairman, of the Department of Anthropology, University of North Carolina. He has done extensive field work with the Fort Nelson Indians, the Sarsi, the Kaska of British Columbia, the Attawapiskat of James Bay, on the Great Whale River, in West Pakistan, in rural Austria, with the Eskimo of Probisher Bay, and the Inuvik. He describes his intellectual development:

I cannot claim to have been drawn to anthropology as a result of some youthful proclivity or by familial example, for my parents and other mature kin came from poor European backgrounds and had very little formal education. I did not even know the discipline existed, nor did I ever dream of college, until far along in evening high school, when I was twenty-two years old and working full time during the day, I decided to follow the example of my future wife and attend evening college classes (free in New York City in those days). At Brooklyn College, around 1940, I met Abraham H. Maslow, whose enthusiasm for culture and personality and the work of Ruth Benedict infected me. From him I heard about field work, for he had spent a season observing the Northern Blackfoot Indians whom he described as a psychologically secure people with high self-esteem. A course with May Mandelbaum Edel using Margaret Mead's *Cooperation and Competition* helped set my mind on graduate training. In 1941 I was not quite bold enough to quit my job in the classified department of the *New York Times* but with my wife's encouragement applied and got a year's leave of absence to try graduate study at Yale, with financial assistance of course. I took the necessary ethnography, ethnology, and archeology courses and, with much more relish, absorbed as much culture and personality as I could from John Dollard, Leo Simmons, John Whiting, Eugen Khan's presentations in the psychiatry department, and books for which I combed the tiers of Sterling Library. Field work among the Kaska allowed me, with my mentor Cornelius Osgood's interest and support, to apply the concepts, theories, and methods I had absorbed. The next big influence in my intellectual development I trace to membership in the Department of Soci-

*Editor's Note: Professor Honigmann died as this volume was going to press. We are grateful for this chapter, one of his last contributions to our field, and lament his loss.

ology and Anthropology and Institute for Research in Social Science at the University of North Carolina. Although I remained largely unsympathetic to quantitative research and theory testing such as the sociologists favored, some of their epistemological appreciation for the method rubbed off and added a considerably different dimension to the research approach I had learned before and vigorously defended in discussions. How, at the age of sixty-one, I am trying to bring those two traditions of scholarship together is told in the chapter I have written for this volume.

This Chapter

In this chapter John Honigmann contrasts the personal approach, which regards the personal element of the individual researcher as a key feature in the way knowledge is produced, to the objective approach which suppresses the personal element as far as possible. As he says, the two approaches are not merely contrastive but in competition with each other. This is a basic division among social scientists in general and can be readily detected in the chapters of this volume. Most of the workers represented here have attempted to combine the two approaches, despite their competition. This appears to be one of the distinguishing criteria of an emerging psychological anthropology, and it was true of some of the earlier culture and personality work as well.

The objective approach is associated with replicability, validity, reliability, agreement between observers and data control. The personal approach is associated with opportunistic sampling, postulation of covert factors, insight, and understanding of whole, complex, processes. It appears on the surface that scientists would choose the first and artists would choose the second.

Honigmann goes on to show how his generalized neo-Freudian framework, which most of us shared or share, derived from Kardiner, Horney, Fromm, Maslow, and David Levy, guided his selection of data, their interpretation, and the development of explanatory models in his work. He was concerned more with demonstration than with testing hypotheses. And he was very much concerned with inferring underlying, covert, postulated factors from observed facts such as an artifact, an action, or a statement. In this context the perceived act becomes an expression of something not immediately apparent. Honigmann discusses the pros and the cons and the difficulties of such an approach in the light of hindsight. Though appropriately reserved about the personal approach Honigmann comes essentially to the conclusion that it is the one he would even now elect though he would add attention to causal sequences including those involved with social structure, ecology, or historical events.

He discusses how an assertion or interpretation can be regarded as true. What is the nature of truth value? And how does one attain it? In this context he uses essentially a coherency, rather than a correspondence test of validity.

G.D.S.

9   *The Personal Approach in Culture and Personality Research*

JOHN J. HONIGMANN

The loss of confidence in culture and personality resulting from the critical barrage directed against it after its heyday came almost simultaneously with the beginning of my professional career. It disturbed me, but I did not attempt much explicit rebuttal of the attacks. Still the problem was always with me. Recently I began to see a possible basis for justifying not only the traditional approach in descriptive culture and personality but in ethnography generally. I tried to clear my mind of as many stereotypical ideas about science, scientific method, validation, and "good" anthropology as possible. What were we doing in the forties, I asked, and why did it then seem commendable? In identifying our method then, I was helped by knowing something about the method endorsed by the critics and by the temper of positivism which has tended to prevail, at least in what anthropologists claim they do. My paper makes clear how strongly I have myself been affected by this temper and the considerable value I see in empiricism. My delineation and justification of what I call the personal approach is my answer to this methodological re-examination. In defining it, I think I identify the traditional method of ethnography and offer a philosophical justification of it, brought out in biographical fashion as I re-examine my early research among the Kaska Indians.

AN INTRODUCTORY EXAMPLE

Among a North American subarctic group of Indians who normally display considerable reticence, suppressed emotion, stoical self-containment in interpersonal relations, and inhibitory attitudes toward sex, adolescence brings a flurry of heterosexual activity. Young people's sexual behavior, taking place in the late evening, begins with teasing initiated by either sex or roughhousing in which the boy takes the lead. At some point the teen-age girl runs away, the boy in pursuit. Then once distance has guaranteed privacy, the girl may be caught and sexual relations follow. The seemingly earnest desire of the girl to avoid capture may easily fool someone unfamiliar with the people's norms into thinking that the boy is attempting rape.

As an anthropologist analyzing this culture pattern, I regarded it as a symbolic acting out of ambivalence. More or less unconsciously, I wrote, the Indians simultaneously conceive of sexual relations as both pleasurable and threatening. With a passing nod recognizing newly awakened glandular processes involved, I explained the young people's premarital sexual behavior as motivated by a desire to break through a culturally derived barrier of reticence and suppressed emotionality, the goal being to secure affection without entering into a too-intense relationship with anyone.

This brief example of psychological anthropological thinking in the 1940s, when psychoanalytic theory dominated culture and personality research, illustrates a traditional style of ethnographic work that I call the personal approach. Contrasting with it is another method that I name objective. The tension of choosing between the two approaches, which has been with me for a number of years, affects the whole of cultural anthropology and also troubles other disciplines studying human behavior and other cultural phenomena. With the prospect of writing this chapter before me, I saw an opportunity to deal with the tension existing between the personal and objective approaches and to consider the extent to which the former may retain a place in cultural anthropology. That, as the title indicates, is the major theme of the chapter.

TWO APPROACHES COMPARED

With few exceptions (Mead and Métraux 1953; Mead and Wolfenstein 1955; Berreman 1966; Honigmann 1963, pp. 306–07; 1971), you will find little in print to guide you in applying the personal approach followed in traditional culture and personality research by myself and others. On the other hand volumes have been published about the contrasting method based on objectification of knowledge through which, Pelto (1970, pp. 39ff.) and others argue, one can obtain more credible results.

Both methods have a place for imagination and intuition, two modes of thinking without which scholarship in any discipline would stagnate. Both apply empiricism, the philosophical theory that knowledge of external events depends in the first place on sensory experience. Each in the manner of all science and art simplifies the portion of the world it studies. Each hopes to reach conclusions that are true, though inevitably investigators using both sometimes realize they have erred. And both acknowledge that the personal element associated with human investigators affects how empirical knowledge is produced. The outstanding difference between the two styles of research lies in the variant attitudes with which each regards the personal element in the production of knowledge and the manner in which they deal with that element.

The personal approach in traditional culture and personality and other branches of cultural anthropology assumes that a qualified investigator possessing a unique combination of interests, values, aptitudes, and sensibilities will in a largely unrepeatable manner reach significant conclusions about a culture that others can accept as credible. The value of what he discovers and communicates depends not only on what is phenomenally given but to a substantial degree on his unique personal characteristics and the vantage point he employs. Reading his personal conception of a culture or personality, the reader appreciates the part played by his idiosyncratic makeup in what he presents (Sullivan 1949, p. 167). At its most extreme the personal approach states that what is prizeworthy in research is not correspondence between the researcher's observations and external events but the richness, insight, originality, or some other quality in his experience of those events. We all momentarily adopt such an attitude when moved by a powerful new theory. Then, quickly caught up in the tradition of objective verification, we demand that its proponents either corroborate the view or disprove it. One part of me admires the extreme personal approach applied to culture and personality, but simultaneously I recognize it to be more appropriate for poetry and fiction than for scholarship. I also know novels like *Christ Stopped at Eboli* and *Call the Next Witness* and works like *Patterns of Culture* fruitfully employ a fairly extreme personal approach in dealing with matters of interest to cultural anthropologists;

but the conventions of anthropology do not permit a professional anthropologist to present data in the form of a novel or even in the vivid manner of *Sketches by Boz*.

Whereas the personal approach regards the personal element of the individual researcher as a key feature in the way knowledge is produced, the objective approach suppresses the element as far as possible. The objective method aims at agreement between observers, not personal knowledge. It assumes a degree of independence exists between knowledge and the particular individual who produces it. Knowledge is objective to the degree that it can be replicated by independent investigators. Hence, even though only a single investigator is at work, the goal of objectivity requires him to employ techniques of observation and of analysis that are as public as possible, meaning they allow others to follow the steps taken and allow for future agreement between him and others who apply the same steps. Counting, rating scales, questionnaires, tests, ethnoscience methodology, and experimentation exemplify objective research (W. Wallace 1971, ch. 1). The personal element has a valid place in objective research only in the originality with which an investigator formulates a problem, method, or theory that he then carries out with due regard for objective criteria. At a minimum the criteria demand unambiguous definitions of what one is observing and explicit rules of procedure.

The two approaches do not merely contrast with one another; they are also in competition. Proponents of more objective methods for anthropology claim that only by adopting them will we be in a position to produce credible knowledge, meaning that the knowledge is produced in a form allowing future investigators to discover essentially the same results by replicating the research (Pelto 1970, chapter 1 and pp. 38–44). With the favorable regard that many anthropologists bestow on the possibility of replication, the personal approach has come to be widely regarded as deficient. Perhaps it suited an earlier day, but now it must be refurbished and more standardized ways of collecting and analyzing data adopted.

The traditional method of research in cultural anthropology has even been accused of departing from empiricism when in fact a responsible scholar following the personal method respects empirical facts as much as an objective researcher. Both confine conclusions to what the senses reveal. The impression of a lack of empiricism arises because the personal approach allows one to exploit more potentialities in empirical data. The investigator need not restrict his reasoning and conclusions only to what others can readily replicate. The objective method, on the other hand, sacrifices some insight for the sake of public knowledge for that is the value it gives highest priority.

For many years anthropologists have sought to combine the two approaches in their research, the proportions varying in particular instances. Using the personal approach part of the time—as I did in the work described in this chapter—investigators carefully define their more important concepts, describe their techniques, and manifest other evidence of respect for objectivity. The competition between the approaches has not yet driven anthropologists generally to abandon the personal approach. For one reason, no adequate substitute for reliance on the personal investigator's many tacit procedures exists when it comes to studying a culture comprehensively over many months.

ASSUMPTIONS AND THEORY

I now return to the research alluded to in the introductory example that I carried out using mainly the personal approach. The research took place between 1944 and 1946 when, as a Yale University graduate student working on a Ph.D. dissertation, I collected and analyzed data about personality in culture among the Kaska Indians in northern British Columbia (Honigmann 1949; for field role and other technical matters, Honigmann 1970a, pp. 40–54). I had three objects: first, to write an account of the personality characteristic of the Kaska Indians; second, to write a comprehensive account of a modern Indian culture, something for which few precedents existed as ethnographic reconstruction still dominated Amerindian research; and, third, to relate the personality characteristics to the culture. My interest in culture and personality had begun while I was an undergraduate student studying psychology with Abraham Maslow. His interest in cultural influences on personality and his use of the culture based psychoanalytic theories of Karen Horney and other new theories in psychoanalysis aroused my interest. Maslow's references to personality research he had conducted among the Northern Blackfoot Indians further stimulated me. Clinical psychiatric reports read in those years showing how psychoanalysts interpret patients' dreams, other statements, and behavior, exerted a potent influence on techniques I subsequently used in Kaska research. During a semester of graduate study at Columbia I attended a tremendously exciting class in culture and personality taught by Ruth Benedict who, however, neither emphasized a psychiatric approach nor applied psychoanalytic theory. Seminars at Yale with John Dollard and Leo Simmons dealing with life-history analysis provided further training in psycho-dynamic analysis.

To set down the guiding concepts, assumptions, and theory which thirty years ago guided my work amounts more to retrospection than to history. Today I think about those ideas against a background of reading and other experience totally lacking in 1944. Controversies have surfaced over some of those matters. Above all, using them taught me a great deal about their limitations. My most important conceptual tool in the Kaska research, the concept of socialization, I have since found to be theoretically problematic.

With those remarks let me begin by saying I used an inclusive concept of personality, one that includes overt behavior as well as covert dispositions and other hidden states. I still prefer such an inclusive notion to the more common one which restricts the meaning of person-ality to nonobservable behavior. But I perceive problems with the inclusive concept that I did not fully realize thirty years ago. If person-ality includes both nonobservable and observable behavior then it commits one to the view that personality and culture (meaning behav-ior, not artifacts) are two aspects of a single system, not two separate interacting systems. I proposed to study the interaction of personality and culture, as if the two were conceptually independent, when in fact what I did was look at the same events from two sides.

I used the term culture then, as I still do, for the system of artifacts, activities, ideas, feelings, and motives conceived of as belonging to a society. Personality encompasses most of the same elements (excluding artifacts) but conceives of them as distributed among individuals or as inherent in a generic individual, *the* Kaska Indians.

One of my assumptions in 1944 held that cultures differ qualita-tively from one another in pervasive qualities perceivable in the system as a whole. A culture has a holistic ethos. The assumption has been severely criticized as overly subjective and conjectural, the criticism then being directed at the personal approach wherein the idea originated (among humanists before anthropologists adopted it). I recognize the personal element in holistic cultural characterizations, yet I continue to accept them as credible, somewhat heartened by the fact that statistics have been able to objectively demonstrate cultural syntalities (Cattell 1950). Ruth Benedict's configurationalism provided a model of holistic thinking that never left my mind in those years. However, unlike her *Patterns of Culture,* I favored studying cultural qualities psychologically, as emanating from personality. I recognized more explicitly than she did that cultures might be disharmonious and inconsistent in their overall ethos because of inconsistency in underlying personality traits.

Holistic descriptions of culture imply a high level of uniformity in the behavior of a social system; they imply that, despite individual differences and deviance, similar behavior recurs from person to person. People are assumed to share similar psychological characteristics, though these are always modified by age, sex, and other factors influencing experience. The assumption of uniformity has perplexed me considerably during the past three decades as I confronted the ably presented, and apparently contrary, position maintaining that social life consists of organized diversity. Reflection leads me to accept both positions as working assumptions for different purposes. One can study a social system to demonstrate uniformities and regularities or to bring out differences between categories of individuals. Among the Kaska Indians I mostly did the former; many years later studying the far northern Canadian town of Inuvik with Irma Honigmann I did primarily the latter (Honigmann and Honigmann 1970).

In 1944 I gave considerably less thought than today to the epistemological foundations of knowledge, although in my graduate training Cornelius Osgood stressed the importance of knowing one's philosophical presuppositions. At present I consider myself an antirationalist who assumes the insufficiency of reason and imagination by themselves to produce satisfactory knowledge. Scholarly activity requires facts, evidence of what is said or done; on that the mind goes to work. A combination of facts and cogitation produces knowledge. During recent years I have found myself increasingly demanding facts to support analytical conclusions, certainly evidence of a growing appreciation for objectivity in research. In my Kaska study, guided by psychoanalytic theory, I rationalistically allowed mental activity to outrun facts more than I tolerate now in myself or others. Yet my fieldwork collected abundant facts. During some ten months among the Kaska Indians I accumulated many richly detailed field notes and other records. In my monograph I occasionally provide pertinent facts—statements by informants and examples of overt activities extracted from field notes—to let the reader see the relationship between psychological interpretations and the independent evidence from which they derive. Of course facts stored in field notes or even audiotapes already bear the personal stamp of the investigator. They are much less independent of him than, say, the documents consulted by a historian as a basis for his conclusions.

A version of psychoanalytic theory deriving from Kardiner, Horney, Maslow, Fromm, and David Levy played an essential role in specifying what to look for in studying Kaska Indian personality and its relationship to culture. According to that theory, which stresses conscious and unconscious motivation, the key dispositions in personality are culturally engendered, not biologically given. Even when the theory posits certain innate tendencies, such as the Oedipus complex or the biological drive of sex, it postulates that they assume a cultural guise through social patterning and therefore differ between societies. From time to time I admit current reservations about the usefulness of such theory. Three decades ago, in the years when Abram Kardiner's work was fresh and exciting, I had few doubts about it.

In studying the Kaska I paid attention to how people felt, consciously and unconsciously, and considered feeling states to be closely related to motivation. Feelings of anxiety, curiosity, anger, and others become aroused when a motive instigates behavior. The feelings stimulate further behavior, or in cases where they conflict, may arrest action. Feelings register whether the motivated behavior is succeeding in reaching its goal, and hence provide subjective evidence of adaptation. Apart from using the Rorschach test, I made no attempt to enhance reliability in identifying feelings, for example, by using objective devices analogous to the sentence-completion test or the Semantic Differential technique.

As I have said, the inclusive conception of personality I held, which views cultural acts as part of personality, fits rather clumsily with the theory that culture and personality interact with one another. According to this very basic notion in culture and personality research, which guided my work, culture first shapes the biological drives and inculcates other motives in members of a society and defines the feeling tones which motives register when activated, frustrated, or gratified. Child rearing plays a very large part in such patterning of personality. Then, once the emotionally tinged motives have been culturally implanted, they influence the culture through the way the individual in society projects them in behavior. Hence the same culture traits in different societies acquire a distinctive character by virtue of being based on different personality systems. "Projection" is Kardiner's term; it means that individuals express personality features in their interpersonal relations, in relationships with supernatural figures, and in myths or folk tales. I used dreams and folk tales as well as attitudes expressed toward supernaturals to infer people's motives, feelings, and conflicts between motives or feelings. Naturally, considering the sources of my theory, I regarded dreams as the king's highway to knowledge of motives and feelings. Concerning folk tales, I regarded the circumstances in which someone narrated them as a vital key to understanding the dispositions and feelings they revealed.

Taking those ideas, I constructed a moderately original theory of my own, maintaining that the major emotionally toned, culturally patterned motivations acquired by a population become expressed in behavior and material artifacts. In the "dominant motivations" resides the way people apprehend the world as well as their values and their generalized life goals. In Kluckhohn's (1943) words the dominant motivations represent a "master configuration . . . the integrating principle of the culture." Whereas nowadays I would use the term "ethos" as a label only for the qualitative features perceived in behavior and artifacts resulting from the dominant motivations, then I used the word to designate both the motives and their expression in behavior and artifacts.

What I have written shows the centrality of socialization theory in my research. I attached great importance to early socialization, especially to indirect learning or nonverbal communication in the form, for example, of early frustrations and gratifications through which the infant and two- or three-year old comes to acquire certain early and lasting dispositions. Socialization, I believed, enables children to acquire basic motivations attended by specific feelings that remain active throughout life. To some extent my views regarding early indirect learning have remained constant since those years. I find objective confirmation for some of them in the work of John W. M. Whiting and his associates using cross-cultural methodology; their work supports psychoanalytic theory bearing on the crucial importance of early experience in setting lifelong personality orientations. Occasionally I have continued to use early socialization theory but with the awareness that despite early learning people remain capable of adapting to new social conditions. Early socialization can explain the persistence of certain broad, personality traits such as I concentrated on in the 1940s; but it fails to take into account situational adaptation, and that constitutes a serious limitation.

My method of using these theories remained one of demonstration rather than testing; that is, I marshalled evidence that supported the relationships postulated by the theory but made no attempt to find data that might contradict the theory. Subsequent experience has made me better able to appreciate the difference between demonstration, favored in traditional anthropological research and congenial to the personal approach, and testing theories through deducing hypotheses susceptible of being proven or disproven. Demonstration, I am now convinced, is never satisfactory for a theory explaining causal relationships; under such circumstances research accomplishes much more when it shifts to an objective approach and tests the relationships empirically. I will return to this matter.

THE ASSUMPTIONS AND THEORY APPLIED

Illustrating from my Kaska Indian field work, I will cover the steps by which an anthropologist working in the traditional manner obtained a collection of facts to analyze and incorporate into an ethnography of culture and personality. The critical comments, being the products of thirty years of reading, thought, and experience continue, of course, to be retrospective.

Sampling

All fieldworkers sample because of the impossibility of observing everyone and everything at every time. Traditional ethnography relies on opportunistic sampling to select people and situations for observation and questioning, the fieldworker collecting information from people willing to cooperate with him and whom he finds congenial (for details see Honigmann 1970*b*, pp. 267–74). He joins their activities and receives them as visitors to his household. Even the topics they talk about are frequently those they choose. At the time I carried out such opportunistic sampling among the Kaska, I lacked any logical justification for the procedure. Only many years later did I read Margaret Mead's (1953*a*, pp. 645–55; 1953*b*, pp. 41–47) explanation of the method and her defense of its use. The object of such sampling is not to learn how many informants said something or how often a behavioral feature occurred but to specify as precisely as possible the source or context of a given bit of information. The ethnographer regards every sampled individual and event as in some way representing the culture. What is represented varies from one person or event to another, but it must be systematically understood, for example, in terms of the informant's age, sex, type and length of experience with the culture and other cultures. Each bit of information—even if it is only a posture or a tone of voice— is considered in relation to the person who revealed it and the situation where it took place. Such sampling contrasts with representative sampling used when the goal of research is not to formulate descriptive patterns but to show how often or how strongly certain features of behavior occur in a community. Opportunistic sampling fits the personal approach very well: the individual investigator personally and in a comprehensive way synthesizes what he discovers. Representative sampling on the other hand suits the standards of the objective, for it lends itself better to replication.

I am sure I fell short of Mead's advice while doing field work among the Kaska Indians and failed to consider all the characteristics of informants and situations relevant to the information they provided. On the other hand, I know that I recognized the importance of such factors as an individual's mixed tribal background, age, or widowhood or an event's abrupt termination due to an unwelcome interruption.

Observation and Interviewing

In culture and personality research one observes people in order to secure intimate knowledge about their life style, feelings, motives, defenses, and inner conflicts. Such observation, continuing over many months, requires repeated contacts with the individuals in a variety of circumstances and a warm, confident relationship between them and the ethnographer. The anthropologist maintains a receptive interest in what people say and do and a noncensorious attitude so that fear or shame will not block information. No doubt complete openness is an unachievable ideal, but ideals help to set high standards.

Interviewing among the Kaska often consisted of assiduously cultivating undirected conversation, the informant's contribution to which I recorded verbatim in handwriting as often as possible. I also arranged a few formal interviews during which I solicited life-history material, and dreams with free association.

In addition to observation and interviewing I administered the Rorschach Inkblot Test to gain information about personality but utilized the instrument far less systematically than other anthropologists (e.g., A. F. C. Wallace 1952). Today even more than in 1944 I much prefer to collect what people do and say in natural situations rather than to give tests.

If as yet I have said no word about the ethical aspects of the highly personal observation and interviewing I conducted, it is because in the 1940s anthropologists did not cultivate today's heightened consciousness of ethical matters. In retrospect I perceive ethical problems in my work that did not occur to me then. Of course I recognized the highly intimate character of the information I received and sought to protect subjects' privacy by disguising names but, except in one article, I did not conceal the name of the group. I see no point in doing so now, but I have regretted not having consistently suppressed it.

Here is an excerpt from information obtained through a formal interview. The subject is a young woman whom I call Dorothy and whom I got to know well. The events she narrates occurred in Tahltan Indian country, many miles downriver from Kaska territory, where as an illegitimate child Dorothy was raised by her maternal grandmother, a Kaska woman.

Another time we was small, and daddy tell us to trap, and wolverine got caught. We scared [of] him, and we caught big stick, and throw at him. We throw that last ax at him. He got our ax. I get one stick. I reach to him. Pretty soon he catch me. My brother take the ax before he turn around. He kill him. We go further up. My brother got stick and put it on martin's back, and I stand on it. That martin lift me up. Pretty soon my brother find stick and kill that martin.

Like any facts unillumined by theoretical concepts this incident reveals little of cultural or personality significance. At an appropriate time (I will show how) once her account is interpreted with the aid of theory and put together with other information Dorothy provided, it reveals a major motivational component in her personality. Actually theory intruded even before interpretation began, for the theoretical ideas I had learned before going to the field led me to solicit biographical material from Dorothy and other informants. Many incidents, however, I recorded without initially asking how I could use them in analyzing the relationship to culture or personality. I am sure I also failed to record things people said and did because I did not recognize their psychological or cultural significance, especially if they occurred early in field work before I began to formulate the main themes of Kaska personality. Highly standardized observation and interviewing would have utilized a strict frame of reference from the outset specifying the type of behavior to look for or inquire about. Such checklists, however, can never anticipate everything likely to be observed in an unfamiliar culture, and probably don't improve on the "observation guide" a psychological anthropologist has in his head as a result of the theory and ethnographies he previously read and assimilated.

Four Types of Propositions

Following the collection of factual data by observation and interviewing, ethnography enters an analytical stage in which the anthropologist uses his facts to construct four major types of propositions. The illustrative example opening this chapter contains examples of each. The first sentence represents a pattern or factual generalization describing certain features of Kaska Indian personality. Factual generalizations constitute the bulk of statements found in ethnographic reports. Each such statement, although founded on a number of discrete observations, is expressed in general terms. Some ethnographers rely primarily on ready-made patterns offered by informants (in that manner Spradley

[1972] obtained his knowledge about the adaptive strategies of urban nomads) but others, including myself, prefer also to construct patterns from unstructured incidents.

The second paragraph of the opening example opens with an interpretation, a statement inferring meaning (plus feeling) from behavior. The same sentence could also be read as illustrating a third type of proposition, a noncausal relationship, or an equivalence, between sexual activity and an internal, psychological state of affairs. Then we have a causal explanation in the statement linking the young people's sexual activity to a motivational component of personality.

In the next four sections I propose to show how, in following the personal approach, these types of propositions, starting with interpretations, are derived from factual data obtained through observation and interviewing.

Interpretation

Often an ethnographer obtaining information through observation or interviewing simultaneously interprets the meaning, feelings, or motives lying behind what the actors do or say. Ethnography, you see, is not the neat, sequential process represented by my conceptual model in which analysis comes after data collection. Interpretation occurs

Interpretation in psychological anthropology, as in psychoanalysis, means that from observed facts—an artifact, action, or statement—the ethnographer infers underlying, covert, postulated factors—motives, conflicts, defenses, feelings, or identifications—which, theory says, the observed facts mean. Thus, applying psychoanalytic theory with reference to the Kaska Indians, an adult's denial of illness reveals anxiety against which the person is defending himself; and sexual teasing in adolescence represents an ambivalent way of seeking affection. The meaning found in observable phenomena may have use solely for the ethnographer; the person being studied not sharing it. But an anthropologist following psychoanalytical principles more likely assumes that whatever he infers is also understood, perhaps only unconsciously, by the subject. Psychoanalytical interpretation such as I adopted in the Kaska research, is highly deductive, but interpretation may also proceed largely inductively, as it does when meanings are formulated that apply specifically to a particular community or individual.

Taking the incident Dorothy narrated in her life-history, I proceeded from the events (her brother took a stick and killed the wolverine) to what they meant to her. I perceived Dorothy to be identifying with her brother and thereby to be expressing self-assertion. Her references to conquered fears, killing, standing on the martin, and to her brother mean she is vesting herself in those forceful, masculine (from the standpoint of the Kaska) qualities. Standing on the martin symbolizes successful accomplishment.

Looking back, I have no doubt that I should have been less deductive or probed harder for evidential support of those meanings, which now strike me as too rationalistic and probably unconvincing to anyone uncommitted to psychoanalytic theory. During the ensuing years I have become much more reluctant to interpret what people say or do in terms of unconscious meanings. Who can objectively prove them true or false? Deductive interpretations guided by psychoanalytic principles or any other *a priori* key in which one has unquestioning faith stunts critical thinking and invites shoddy workmanship. I much more favor an inductive approach to personality analysis in which interpretation is constrained by facts in hand and one asks what does this mean for the actors in their particular context. I have become sufficiently impressed by criteria of objectivity to maintain that interpretations not directly based on what informants say should be supported by as much contributory evidence as possible. And the reasoning by which the meaning is inferred should be presented. For someone who has the necessary data, the financial means, and the time, objective tests of interpretations could be designed. Such tests would employ the hypothetico-deductive method of experimental research in somewhat the following manner (the illustrative examples again pertain to Kaska Indian data): If a man's worrying about illness is interpreted as signifying dependence, then one could predict that appropriate scoring procedures (which must be devised and given preliminary trials) will reveal the most hypochondriacal complaints to come from men who give evidence of being most involved in conflicts over dependence and independence. If a folk tale of homosexual women is interpreted as based on tension over relationships between men and women in the society where the story is told, then logically such tales should more often be found in cultures where such tension is strongly developed than where it is weak. Later I will describe how somewhat in this manner, but without sufficiently rigorous controls against contaminating the results with prior expectations, I used Rorschach test responses to check an interpretation of Kaska motivation. Such tests, which represent the ideal of objectivity in research, are impossible to carry out properly for the hundreds of items an individual researcher interprets in the course of traditional anthropological field work. At best they can only be employed for the most strategic interpretations. Although I admire the use of such methods, I would be satisfied

with a more modest approximation of the objective approach in interpretation, namely, as I have said, a full statement of the evidence on
which the interpretation is based and an account of the personal manner
in which one reached it.

Patterns

An interpretation provides a consciously built cognitive scheme for
knowing cultural and individual facts. Patterns, or factual generalizations, represent another kind of model of behavior. During the last
decade or so I have thought much about how ethnographers construct
patterns; hence, what I am about to say far exceeds anything I understood in 1944 about this essential feature of anthropological reporting.

In making patterns from data the ethnographer scans specific acts,
items communicated to him verbally, as well as his interpretations for
significant attributes they share. The pattern thus derived may also
include the circumstances under which the attributes occurred. The
circumstances may simply specify the sex or age category of the persons
manifesting the pattern or they may name the place, the social makeup
of the group involved, and the purpose for which the group assembled.
When patterns reach a great point of specificity they become nearly
invariant generalizations, akin in some respects to causal relationships,
although the ethnographer does not intend them to explain anything in
theoretical terms. In constructing patterns an ethnographer bears in
mind, more or less explicitly, only attributes relevant for his interests. A
psychological anthropologist interested in cognition will scan data for
indications of how people apprehend their world, whereas another
investigator especially interested in emotion will be attuned to indications of how people feel. Although the relevant attributes may not be
listed in a systematic observation guide, they are often definite enough
to enable a researcher to note the absence of certain expected features
and report them in the form of negative ("zero") patterns (e.g., "the
Kaska avoid idealizing sexual relationships").[1]

Since quite diverse patterns could be constructed by different

1. The reader may feel impelled to go to ethnography to see what patterns he can
discern. The task will be frustrating. Patterns form the backbone of ethnographies, but
being styled by language, they often run together and are accompanied by illustrative
case material and the author's comments about the pattern which make specific patterns
difficult to find. Better look at a culture element list; the one on the North American
Plateau culture area (Ray 1942) contains seventy-six hundred elements, almost any one
of which could be converted into a pattern by regarding it as a generalization of a feature
found in a Plateau culture.

investigators guided by different criteria of relevance looking at the same events, pattern construction ideally illustrates the personal approach as it operates at a fundamental level of ethnography. Conceivably, objective rules could be adopted to operationalize pattern finding by specifying relevant attributes to be heeded. Machines recognize patterns in that discrete fashion (Watanabe 1971), but human beings, as Gestalt psychologists have pointed out, do not apprehend the form of events by adding together constituent, atomic features; neither do ethnographers.

Going back to the introductory example, the first four sentences report the circumstances under which adolescent Kaska Indian boys and girls initiate premarital sexual relations. I constructed the pattern after having observed several instances of the behavior it generalizes. I also brought an early version of my pattern forward in conversation with informants to learn their reaction to my discovery, and one man spontaneously referred to the hectic nocturnal activity of adolescents. In effect the informants affirmed the factual generalization I had reached. In the manner of other traditional ethnographers, I expressed this and most other patterns without stating the frequency with which they occurred and also without recognizing that some adolescents may not have behaved according to the generalization. In other words, the pattern does what traditional ethnographies often do: it ignores situational and individual variability and gives an impression of timeless homogeneity of behavior. Recent criticism of traditional ethnography has attacked precisely that feature and I realize now that I should have made some effort to discover when or for whom the pattern does not occur; had I done so my pattern would have been strengthened.

Returning to the incident from Dorothy's life-history, one of the personality patterns I constructed from that and information revealing similar attributes (for example, a young woman having killed a porcupine with her ax exclaimed, "I'm as good as a man!") states that women seek to emulate male roles. Their behavior in a variety of contexts reveals attributes of self-assertion and independence, traits they ideally associate with men. Using a psychoanalytic concept, I named the personality pattern masculine striving. But here my report does contain the warning that some feminine behaviors run contrary to the generalization.

In the course of analysis, ethnographers combine patterns thereby constructing more embracive factual generalizations. Female masculine striving, men's identification of successful hunting with sexual potency (something I learned from dreams), and similar patterns including the predominance of good form (F +) in Kaska Rorschach test protocols constituted evidence for a pattern that I called a dominant motivational trend characteristic of Kaska personality, and named "egocentricity." The Kaska evaluate personal independence highly, possess a strong sense of personal responsibility, and a keen sense of achievement (features resembling Horney's (1945, pp. 75–81) detached personality type). Through further combinations, far less systematically and critically executed than I would now encourage, I synthesized half-a-dozen such motivational trends to obtain a couple of highly general personality patterns labeled the world- and self-views. The Kaska Indian's view of the world wavers between an idea that experience is manageable and an awareness that life is threatening and difficult. In his self-view he normally regards himself as self-reliant but in time of crises lapses into a feeling of relative helplessness.

Causal Relationships

In discussing interpretation I described how an investigator endows observed events with certain meaning through inferring underlying motives, purposes, or feelings. The perceived act or statement thereby becomes an expression of something not immediately apparent. In psychological anthropology, relating an observed event to the hidden condition that motivates it also often serves as a causal explanation. Bear in mind, however, that even in psychological anthropology covert psychological conditions represent only one kind of cause. Other causal relationships include environmental conditions and childrearing techniques as the explanatory antecedents.

Causal relationships on the basis of a theory connect two or more concepts, one of which, the antecedent or independent variable, constitutes the agency producing the other, the consequent or dependent variable. My account of Kaska culture and personality, guided by psychoanalytical and other theories of motivation, frequently employs motivation as the antecedent that accounts for people's actions or something they said. Referring once more to the introductory example, note how I explain young people's premarital sexual behavior as motivated by a desire to break through the barrier of reticence and suppressed emotionality, patterns characteristic of Kaska Indian personality. And in analyzing Dorothy's story about her brother killing the martin, I suggested that in telling the story she was motivated by self-assertion and masculine striving.

Such purely psychological explanations seemed useful to me and other anthropologists in the mid-1940s when psychological anthropology and other synchronic approaches had only recently replaced the historical perspective formerly dominant in cultural anthropology. Nowadays I regard explanations cast in solely motivational terms as less useful than propositions in which a causal sequence also includes social structure, ecology, or historical events among the antecedents of the thing to be accounted for (cf. Pelto and Pelto n.d., p. 22). Take Dorothy's narrative. We gain comparatively minor knowledge about human behavior by deriving it solely from a motive (self-assertion) compared to what would be gained if those tendencies could be related to, say, ecological conditions. What I endorse has, of course, been the trend in culture and personality research since Whiting and Child (1953, p. 310) listed "maintenance systems" as the antecedent at the head of a causal chain linking child training practices with personality variables and the latter with projective systems (see also Harrington and Whiting 1972, pp. 491–92).

Almost as frequently as motivation, I utilized early child rearing to account for people's acts, dreams, and fantasies and also to explain the origin of the dominant motivations governing Indian behavior. My ethnography especially emphasizes the importance of a discontinuity in early Kaska child care that occurs once the mother begins to withhold a good deal of her earlier emotional warmth and generous attention and becomes more aloof (Honigmann 1949, pp. 307–10). As I interpreted what happens, the child is traumatically disappointed in the self-confident, optimistic expectations which it had learned earlier when the mother behaved more indulgently. Such disappointment, I maintained, explains affect hunger, emotional suppression, and various projective systems unconsciously created to deal with the persisting traumatic effects of the discontinuity. I now question having put so much emphasis on early experience as a source of personality formation and seriously doubt I had sufficient evidence for the elaborate interpretation I made of the young child's perception of the discontinuity or the feelings it experienced. There could have been little realistic basis for rationalistically emphathizing so deeply into Kaska children. The consequences I drew from the discontinuity derived from psychoanalytic theory, in which, as I have said, I had greater confidence then than I do now. I have also become aware of the danger lurking in the cross sectional method when it is substituted for longitudinal study of individuals. I did not observe emotional withdrawal practiced by mothers of the adolescent children and adults whose emotional restraint I observed. How could I know those individuals had experienced that childhood "trauma"? The cross sectional method assumes homogeneity, but in this case I lack any information about how widespread the pattern of maternal emotional withdrawal was among the mothers of Kaska society. After all, only a few mothers had children two or three years of age, the age when emotional withdrawal is instituted.

Noncausal Relationships

In addition to constructing causal relationships during analysis, ethnographers also relate independent sectors of culture in noncausal fashion. Patterns of personality may, for example, be compared with patterns of culture to show how both reveal similar values. Such relationships are not designed to explain why anything happens, but they nevertheless contribute to understanding.

In my Kaska report I point to congruence between the atomistic social structure and the strong inclination for independence characteristic of the personality. A common emphasis on individualism runs through both sets of patterns and connects them one to the other. A different type of noncausal relationship, on the level of personality, points out conflicting personality patterns between tendencies to independence and dependence. The gap between what the Kaska Indians say they would like and what their culture brings them illustrates another kind of noncultural relationship. Adults rationalize a desire for children by speaking of the economic contribution a child will make to the family. Yet old and infirm people can actually count very little on the support of grown children. The link between ideal and real amounts to a discrepancy which adds information about Kaska life but in itself explains nothing. Noncausal relationships sometimes link geographical characteristics with culture or personality. Arthur Hippler (1973, p. 1539) conceives of the subarctic environment as nonnurturant and also identifies nonnurturance as an attribute in Indians' maternal behavior. He then relates one to the other: "Athabascans faced with a harsh nonnurturant environment developed non-nurturance as a defensive tactic to cope with it. . . ." Almost imperceptibly he slips across the boundary between noncausal and causal relationships as he implies that the environment exerted an influence in the trial and error process that led to child rearing processes.

Some noncausal relationships, instead of linking patterns through common elements or because of congruity or its lack, assert quantitative covariation. For an example I leave the Kaska Indians and proceed to a study of native people in the Mackenzie River town of Inuvik (Honigmann and Honigmann 1970, p. 145). Here we find two styles of child rearing. Families little committed to the norms of mainline Canadian culture but strongly espousing the frontier culture of the western subarctic practice one style which is permissive and flexible. Those strongly committed to mainline norms tend to follow a stricter pattern. But again it would not take much to read this statement of covariation between child rearing and cultural values as a causal explanation in which different values become the antecedent factors governing different styles of child rearing. The process of shifting from a noncausal to a causal relationshp is so easy, and for us so natural, that it often happens unbeknown to the writer.

ASSESSING TRUTH

I have given four main types of propositions that ethnographers commonly construct in culture and personality as well as other research and illustrated them with examples mostly taken from my Kaska work. Another step remains for the ethnographer, namely judging whether ethnographic propositions are true. Here the divergence between the personal and objective approaches to knowledge shows up most strikingly. Again I point out that compared to my knowledge of epistemological questions and the importance I attach to them today, they interested me very little in 1944. Hence this section will be heavily retrospective.

All persons engaged in scholarly activity feel some concern about the truth value of the knowledge they produce, but scholars in all fields do not exert the same effort to discover whether their propositions are true. The fact that some disciplines don't regularly make strong efforts to assess truth value is important because there is a tendency for a proposition one constructs to automatically acquire the appearance of validity. The longer we work at it, the more plausible it appears and the greater the deliberate effort that must be made in subjecting it to questioning.

In both the personal and objective approaches truth arises, existentially speaking, when a person or a category of persons, say a profession, comes to believe something. The difference between the two approaches lies in operations performed by followers of each to ascertain believability.

Believability, the truth value of a proposition, can arise by several means, each means itself the subject of credibility. In school, believability may derive from a teacher or other authority who presents a proposition or an operation for ascertaining believability in a persuasive manner. Credibility may also stem from the fact that a proposition is printed rather than spoken. If a sophisticated person does not endow an authority or print with inherent power to make things believable, then those means will not affect the truth value of propositions they transmit. In regard to some means, say a psychological test, considerable effort may be made to assess the credibility (called validity) of the means. Historians make credibility assessments of documents and anthropologists of informants before they are prepared to trust them.

In scholarly work the credibility of propositions frequently results, first, from having used means and sources in collecting and analyzing the data which the investigator deems believable and second, more strongly, from operations deliberately performed to critically test the propositions after they have been formulated. Experimentation is one of the most powerful means civilization has devised for this purpose, but it cannot always be applied. Credibility testing forms an intrinsic part of personal and objective research, but it is less rigorously carried out in the personal approach for reasons I have mentioned. No matter how rigorous or objective a technique of verification may be, ultimately it rests on a personal conviction that the operation is itself believable. Exclusively objective knowledge is chimerical, a contradiction in fact, for only a person knows anything, including knowing when a proposition he knows is true. As Kepler said when he assessed the worth of the evidence in favor of the Copernican system, "I have attested it as true in my deepest soul."

Western thought in the humanities as well as the sciences during the past five centuries has given increasing credence to propositions that could be shown to correspond closely to the phenomena to which they refer. A variety of procedures allow an investigator to make a correspondence test, but basically the method consists in ascertaining that a proposition agrees with new facts pertaining to the same object, facts which are different from the facts on which the proposition was originally based. The supposition is that the new facts independently confirm the existence of the phenomenon to which the proposition refers. To illustrate: the mock-rape pattern of Kaska adolescent sexuality became more believable as additional instances of the activity and confirming informant testimony became available. The inference that certain Kaska behaviors indicate an underlying motive of self-assertion gained credence as additional behaviors strengthened the inference and especially as signs in Rorschach test protocols confirmed it. Causal relationships are more difficult to confirm. A correspondence test (really an experiment) confirming a causal relationship which connects a particular motive as cause to a certain act, its effect, requires that additional people who possess the motive perform the act significantly more often than those lacking the motive. Obviously, the first task is to establish the motive in one group and its absence in another. A noncausal relationship asserting a common feature to link two or more patterns of behavior can be more simply tested by asking if independent researchers agree with the assertion. If the noncausal statement specifies quantitative covariation between two groups, then measurement is required to prove that the quantity or degree of the trait in question varies between the two groups.

Correspondence tests may be highly objective—and that is the ideal in following the objective approach—or they may be largely personal, as in most of my work among the Kaska Indians. Thus, questioning my pattern, I established the truth of the pattern that Kaska mothers use low emotional intensity in interacting with their children by relying on further observations, and—here a slight degree of objectivity appears—relying on the corroborative testimony of my wife. We did not, however, attempt to objectify degrees of emotional intensity and train ourselves or others to use such a scale. For interpretations and highly embracive patterns of personality, I used additional data selectively or illustratively, rather than marshalling it experimentally to see if the proposition stands up. Having discovered emotional self-restraint to be an aspect of Kaska personality, I looked for further evidence corresponding to the proposition and described it to document my conclusion.

Even today many anthropologists (some of whom would deny any affiliation with the personal approach) make no effort to collect a number of subjects or situations to see if the concurrence they perceive between antecedent and consequent factors occurs dependably, that is more often than by chance. Ethnographers assert causality; they rarely test for it. When I employed objective tests, it was in a highly personal manner. To mention one occasion: I compared responses given by twenty-eight Indian subjects to two kinds of Rorschach inkblots in order to give evidence for a certain kind of anxiety. This anxiety, according to theory, is experienced by individuals who shy away from emotional contact and has its roots far back in early life experience. Rorschach theory maintains that in response to certain inkblots, individuals possessing such anxiety will manifest signs of unease by inhibiting their productivity and manifest other signs. I assumed the Kaska Indians, with their emotional restraint and with their early traumatic encounter with the mother's emotional withdrawal, would possess such anxiety and would therefore show the expected signs. Elementary statistics revealed that the sample of twenty-eight respondents responded to the cards as expected. In effect I had conducted an experiment, seeking independent evidence which would objectively confirm a pattern of Kaska personality. I had crossed the boundary between the personal approach and the approach that seeks knowledge in objective indicators such as a test. But I am aware of several methodological weaknesses in this test. I had no control group of subjects lacking the traumatic early experience and, let us assume, the anxiety supposed to come from it. Had I used such a control group and had they given fewer signs than the Kaska, my confidence in the test would have been more advisable. Also, I have only my hunch that the anxiety which the Rorschach test measures is similar to the meaning I attached to emotional restraint. Nevertheless, I was aware of the importance of obtaining independent confirmatory evidence, and I have shown how I went about obtaining it.

I assume everyone outgrows methods and theories, and it is not surprising I should be critical of those I used thirty years ago to assess truth value of propositions. I realize my critical remarks may obscure the fact that I still believe many features of my ethnography and my characterization of Kaska Indian personality to be true. I still trust my perceptions then and believe that my length of stay and relationship with the people enabled me to make sound judgments of their psychological makeup. Participant observation provides the personal approach with a sense of cultural indwelling that leads to confidence in factual generalizations and other propositions.[2] Sometimes, however, the confidence can be misplaced, and I think that happened in the way I dealt with causal relationships in my report on Kaska culture and personality. I think I erred methodologically (regardless of whether my propositions were right or wrong) in simply asserting causal connections between certain features of early child rearing and later life personality patterns. Assertions of that sort are but the first step in causal research. They constitute theory which must be verified, either by comparative study of individuals within a single social system or, in the manner of hologeistic research exemplified by John W. M. Whiting and his coworkers, by comparing social systems.

Participant observation isn't the only basis of believability in ethnography following the personal approach. In my Kaska work, I realize now, I frequently employed another well-known basis of assessing truth value: coherency testing. Where correspondence tests seek empirical agreement between propositions and nonpropositional facts, coherency testing, which is primarily rationalistic not empirical, never

2. For the use of indwelling in personal knowledge see Polyani 1966, pp. 16ff.; also De Laguna 1960.

steps beyond the propositions to look at empirical facts. In coherency testing one looks to see if a pattern, interpretation, or relationship is consistent with other propositions he has constructed, or he assigns causes solely by logically following a theory (such as psychoanalysis) without testing to see if facts support the conclusion. I did this when I believed Kaska child rearing to be the cause of personality patterns because what I posited agreed with psychoanalytic theory. Similarly when I appraised the truth value of the meanings and purposes lying behind what people did, I asked myself whether I had remained faithful to psychoanalytic theory. I inspected interpretations to detect contradictions between them, sometimes explaining away contradictions in rationalistic fashion. In the end, the truth value I attached to my ethnography depended heavily on the consistency I discovered in my interlocking patterns, interpretations, and causal as well as noncausal relationships and on the confidence I had in the assumptions, theories, and method I followed. As befits anyone following the personal approach, I also had confidence in myself as capable of presenting a true version of Kaska culture and personality and offered such a picture for others to accept as true.

The history of science clearly reveals that any truth, and proposition to which someone at sometime attaches truth value, is notably unstable. In the long run it makes no difference for the stability of a proposition whether it is based on correspondence or on coherency testing. Hence we can predict the conditions under which credibility in a proposition will disappear. It will waver whenever new facts come to light which contradict the proposition; or when new testing procedures give different results; or when new theoretical perspectives are accepted which lead to a different perception of the old facts. Knowledge need not be contradicted to lose a substantial degree of truth value; only the organizing concepts of a discipline need shift for doubt to arise. Thus as psychoanalysis gave way to other ways of conceptualizing data, the ethnographic interpretations that I had cast in psychoanalytic concepts became increasingly less convincing.

CONCLUSIONS

Berreman (1966, pp. 349–50) believes that anthropology's distinctive method with its inexplicitly defined intuitive element (his term for what I call the personal approach) can be made more subject to verification, more objective, without itself being destroyed. But in taking steps to make traditional ethnographic data collection and analysis more explicit, as Berreman urges, would not fundamental changes have to be made in the personal approach, thereby destroying it? The personal approach in scholarship is never wholly subjective or intuitive, but its objectivity cannot increase indefinitely without eradicating the distinctiveness that Berreman and I value.

Berreman by-passes an important question: is the personal approach at all defensible? Should it be encouraged as an approach to cultural knowledge?

Before tackling those questions, I remind you that in evaluating my Kaska ethnography I offer the objective approach as a point of comparison, but the fact that the personal approach I followed fell short of objective criteria is not the main ground on which I unfavorably criticize certain aspects of my work. I continue to believe in certain information I obtained with the personal approach among the Kaska; for example, in the patterns of reticence and emotional restraint which I discovered forming part of the Indians' personality. Since 1945 there have even been indications that my conclusions with respect to that pattern as well as other patterns of personality were reliable; the evidence comes from investigators who have worked in cognate subarctic communities.

But I have admitted a decline in truth value concerning some things in my report on the Kaska Indians. My loss of believability stems partly from loss of confidence in theories of unconscious motivation and other features in psychoanalytic theory, especially the determinative effects which the theory ascribes to early socialization. I am also dissatisfied with the cross sectional method I employed to establish connections between childhood and adulthood and with the extent of rationalism in my work, especially when it came to inferring motivational states and making other interpretations from overt behavior. Such dissatisfaction has made me much more positivistic, reluctant to make inferences, in my recent ethnography. My chief objection to the personal approach, whether used by myself or others, relates to its total inadequacy for establishing causal relationships. Something serious is wrong with relying on coherency testing alone in constructing causal explanations. Recent work I have done, where I use objective means to test causal hypotheses (Honigmann and Honigmann 1970) convinced me of the superiority of objective methods when it comes to claiming causal relationships to be true.

I see no reason to extend the same criticism to patterns, interpretations, and noncausal relationships unconcerned with quantitative co-variation. For those one can employ coherency testing to the personal approach, remembering that in scholarship this method is never completely subjective. Neither the investigator nor the reader should confuse the validity of personal judgments with validity obtained by objective methods, such as rating scales, multiple observers whose reliability is measured, etc. Propositions based on the personal approach, the truth value of which is assessed largely through coherency testing, should be judged by their logic and consistency. Appraise them for the perceptiveness and sensitivity they reveal or fail to reveal, and for the comprehensiveness with which they deal with relevant data. Judged on that basis I accept as true Ruth Benedict's conception of Plains and Pueblo cultural orientations; Lloyd Warner's interpretation of American Christianity and other symbols in our national culture; Lévi-Strauss's structural insights into myths, totemism, and other symbolic products of culture; and Francis L. K. Hsu's comparisons of Chinese, Americans, and other nationals, although I know that their theories have not been tested to the satisfaction of those who only espouse highly objective scholarship.

One must bear in mind that information collected through the personal approach with its unstandardized methods can be used to only a limited extent for comparative purposes. No problem exists when the same investigator using the same perspective, so to speak, compares personality traits, folk tales, or other cultural features in different societies or entire cultures. But using material collected by different investigators for comparison requires knowing the theoretical interests and other aspects of the personal element governing each researcher in order to account for distinctive emphases and biases in the data. Thereby their accounts are standardized after a fashion. One criticism of hologeistic research has been that it treats all ethnographers as equally unbiased and attentive to the objective facts. "Data quality control," a recent innovation in cross-cultural surveys (Naroll 1970), attends to a few influential factors (such easily recognized ones as length of time in the field, use of the native language, etc.) but ignores many others that it is hard to obtain information about.

A major difficulty connected with following the personal approach stems from some anthropologists' unwillingness to tolerate patterns, interpretations, and relationships reached by that method. Our standards have changed and we rationalize our newly acquired appetite for objective procedures as intellectually healthier, more rigorous, etc. With respect to causal relationships and, to a lesser extent, interpretations drawn from overt behavior, my standards have changed too, but on practical and logical grounds I retain confidence in the capacity of the personal approach. From what I said near the beginning of this chapter, the personal approach provides a kind of knowledge that cannot as yet be furnished by objective methods alone. If it is desirable to have such knowledge, then the personal approach belongs in anthropology.

REFERENCES CITED

Berreman, G.
    1966   Anemic and Emetic Analysis in Social Anthropology. *American Anthropologist* 68:346–58.
Cattell, R. B.
    1950   The Principal Culture Patterns Discoverable in the Syntal Dimensions of Existing Nations. *Journal of Social Psychology* 32:215–53.
De Laguna, G.
    1960   The *Lebenswelt* and the Culture World. *Journal of Philosophy* 57:777–91.
Harrington, C. and Whiting, J. W. M.
    1972   Socialization Process and Personality. In *Psychological Anthropology*, ed. F. L. K. Hsu. Cambridge, Mass.: Schenkman.
Hippler, A.
    1973   The Athabascans of Interior Alaska: A Culture and Personality Perspective. *American Anthropologist* 75:1529–41.
Honigmann, J. J.
    1949   Culture and Ethos of Kaska Society. *Yale University Publications in Anthropology*, no. 40.
    1963   *Understanding Culture.* New York: Harper and Row.
    1970a   Field Work in Two Northern Canadian Communities. In *Marginal Natives*, ed. M. Freilich. New York: Harper and Row.
    1970b   Sampling in Anthropological Field Work. In *A Handbook of Method in Cultural Anthropology*, eds. R. Naroll and R. S. Cohen. Garden City, New Jersey: Natural History Press.
Honigmann, J. J. and Honigmann, I.
    1970   Arctic Townsmen. Ottawa: Canadian Research Centre for Anthropology, Saint Paul University.
Horney, K.
    1945   *Our Inner Conflicts.* New York: Norton.
Kluckhohn, C.
    1943   Covert Culture and Administrative Problems. *American Anthropologist* 45:213–29.
Mead, M.
    1953a   National Character. In *Anthropology Today*, ed. A. L. Kroeber. Chicago: University of Chicago Press.

1953*b* The Study of Culture at a Distance. In *The Study of Culture at a Distance,* eds. M. Mead and R. Metraux. Chicago: The University of Chicago Press.

Mead, M. and Metraux, R., eds.
1953 *The Study of Culture at a Distance.* Chicago: University of Chicago Press.

Naroll, R.
1970 Data Quality Control in Cross-Cultural Surveys. In *A Handbook of Method in Cultural Anthropology,* eds. R. Naroll and R. Cohen. Garden City, New Jersey: Natural History Press.

Pelto, P. J.
1970 *Anthropological Research.* New York: Harper and Row.

Pelto, P. J. and Pelto, G. H.
n.d. Intra-Cultural Diversity: Some Theoretical Issues, unpublished paper.

Polyani, M.
1966 *The Tacit Dimension.* Garden City, New Jersey: Doubleday.

Ray, V. F.
1942 Culture Element Distributions: Xii, Plateau. *Anthropological Records,* vol. 8, no. 2. Berkeley.

Spradley, J. P.
1972 Adaptive Strategies of Urban Natives. In *Culture and Cognition,* ed. J. P. Spradley. San Francisco: Chandler.

Sullivan, J. W. N.
1949 *The Limitations of Science,* Mentor Books. New York: New American Library.

Wallace, A. F. C.
1952 The Modal Personality Structure of the Tuscarora Indians. *Smithsonian Institution, Bureau of American Ethnology Bulletin* 150.

Wallace, W.
1971 *The Logic of Science in Sociology.* Chicago: Aldine Atherton.

Watanabe, S., ed.
1971 *Frontiers of Pattern Recognition.* New York: Academic Press.

Whiting, J. W. M. and Child, I. L.
1953 *Child Training and Personality.* New Haven: Yale University Press.

The Author

MELFORD E. SPIRO was born in 1920, in Cleveland, Ohio. He received his B.A. from the University of Minnesota in 1941, and his Ph.D. from Northwestern University in 1950. He has taught at Washington University (St. Louis), and at the Universities of Connecticut, Washington (Seattle), and Chicago, before moving in 1968 to the University of California, San Diego, to found the Anthropology Department on that campus. His interest in culture and personality, which was stimulated while a graduate student of A. I. Hallowell, has informed almost all of his work. As he views it, culture and personality is not a specialty within anthropology, but a distinctive theoretical approach to the various problems posed by the investigation of cultural and social systems. With respect to these latter systems, he has been primarily interested in the family and in religion, one or both of which he has studied in Micronesia, Israel, and Burma.

This Chapter

In this chapter Melford Spiro demonstrates how what he has come to regard as his early, over-deterministic, cultural model was modified by continuing field experience beginning with the Ifaluk, continuing through his study of the Kibbutz to the present in his work in Thailand and Burma. He began in the early 1950s with an "inchoate model" of determinism and a personality theory composed of about equal parts of neo-Freudianism and social learning. In this he was like the rest of us who began our work in the early 1950s. Though still operating with a basically culturally deterministic and relativistic model his Ifaluk field work resulted in significant modifications, which he discusses. His Kibbutz field study caused him to take the matter further and forced him to conclude that many of man's basic motives are universal, and that his previous model was misguided. His work on Buddhism in Thailand and Burma inspired originally by Max Weber's views on religion and world view—an essentially culturally relativistic model—resulted in his concluding that cultural differences in certain basic cognitive orientations are more apparent than real. He came to see certain invariant dispositions and orientations as stemming from pan-human biological and cultural constants. His present position is a clear challenge to the "new ethnography," ethnosemantics, and ethnoscience, since they stress the noncompatability of cultures.

Professor Spiro's chapter is notable both as an analysis of the evolution of certain central ideas in the thinking of a significant contributor to the field and as a perspective on major theoretical-philosophical shifts that have taken place in the discipline as a whole and not only in the more restricted domain of psychological anthropology.

G.D.S.

10 Culture and Human Nature

MELFORD E. SPIRO

Although the editors have asked the contributors to describe the development of their research findings and ideas, I cannot describe *what* I have done, or how I did it, without explaining *why* I did it.[1] Much of this paper, therefore, will be concerned with intellectual motivations and research strategies rather than with research operations or detailed research findings. Moreover, since I believe that any valid explanation is ultimately historical (genetic, evolutionary, developmental, etc.), a reliable account of *why* I did what I did cannot begin with my anthropological research, but must rather be rooted in my intellectual history. Hence, I shall first describe the intellectual (and other) interests that brought me to the study of culture and personality, and I shall then discuss one of the themes that, until relatively recently, has run through

1. I am grateful to Theodore Schwartz for his extremely helpful criticisms of an earlier draft of this paper.

331

a great deal of my research. Since I am concerned with explaining the over-determined motivational structures that lie behind research choices, and the complex decision structures on which research strategies are based, I do not have space to discuss other themes, or to describe my more recent interests.

BEGINNINGS

In an important sense, my intellectual interests have always been more philosophical than scientific, and just as in the Middle Ages philosophy was the handmaiden of theology, so for me anthropology has been the handmaiden of philosophy, a tool for the empirical investigation of some central issues concerning the nature of man. Although I have worked in four different societies—the Ojibwa, Ifaluk, an Israeli kibbutz, and Burma—I have never been interested in ethnographic description, *per se*; and although I have published on a variety of institutions—family, kinship, politics, socialization, and religion—I have had little interest in institutional analysis, as such. Ultimately—so, at least, I have believed—these enterprises are useful to the degree that they can illuminate some aspect of the nature of man. Since, however, anthropology is primarily interested in society and culture, and since until recently it has been much more concerned with social and cultural differences than with universals, my choice of anthropology—rather than, for example, psychology—might seem rather strange. In the light, however, of the intellectual and political *zeitgeist* of the intellectually formative years of my life, this choice was not so strange after all.

For liberal intellectuals, like myself, coming to maturity in the late thirties and early forties, politics was an overriding concern. Existentialists without knowing it, we had to come to grips with the twin traumata of our time—the great depression at home, and the rise of the Fascism abroad. Having escaped the seductions of Soviet Communism, while yet deploring the "poverty amidst plenty" which seemed to be characteristic of capitalism, we perceived in democratic socialism the only viable alternative to the horrors of both Fascist and Communist totalitarianism. As Marxists—and, in some sense, we were all Marxists in those days—we believed that men were the creatures of their social systems. If American society was characterized (as we thought) by competitiveness, exploitation, and injustice, these characteristics were not expressions of human nature, but of a particular social system. Hence, to abolish these evils it was only necessary to change the social system that produced them. In a social system, such as democratic socialism, whose institutions were based on equality and justice, they would disappear.

If Marxism was the ideological inspiration for these convictions, their intellectual underpinnings, at least for me, were derived from my philosophical studies. As a philosophy major, I had been persuaded— to be sure, I was prepared to be persuaded—by Locke, Hume, Rousseau, and the philosophers of the Enlightenment that man comes into the world as a *tabula rasa;* that anything that is eventually inscribed on the blank slate is put there by experience; and (though this was not shared by all these thinkers) that the most important types of experience are those derived from encounters with social institutions. Hence, the notion of a society in which men are motivated by cooperation, altruism, and mutual aid was not viewed as a utopian quest—nor was it viewed as a secular derivative of the religious visions of Amos or Isaiah, those Hebrew prophets who had earlier influenced me—but as a logical de- duction from the social theories of the eighteenth century philosophers of Reason. For if, indeed, man has no "nature," then his characteristics must be a product of history, as the latter is distilled by and concretized in the social institutions of his society.

But the capstone—and "proof"!—of the thesis of the malleability of man, and the omnipotence of social institutions, came from the writings of Durkheim, for Durkheim (as I viewed him) was not just another speculative philosopher; he was, rather, an empirical scientist. And if, as he had shown in *The Elementary Forms of the Religious Life,* the very forms of thought (space, time, causality, etc.) are ultimately derived from the structure of society, what else could be said on the subject? Durkheim, though a sociologist, had used anthropological data to sustain his arguments. This convinced me that it was from anthro- pology that I could best derive future intellectual nourishment, and when some years later I decided to pursue graduate studies in the social sciences, I turned to anthropology.

Although I earlier discovered Durkheim was not in good favor in anthropology—mostly because of Goldenweiser's critique of his theory of totemism—the regnant anthropological notions of that time were entirely consistent with (indeed, they might just as well have been derived from) Durkheim's view of society and culture. Still, these no- tions—cultural determinism and cultural relativism—provided a dif- ferent conceptual, as well as rhetorical, basis for my views concerning the relationship between man and society. Since cultures vary across space and time, and since behavior is culturally variable, the inference that

334 MELFORD E. SPIRO

man's nature is similarly culturally variable seemed irrefutable. The concept of culture not only seemed to provide the definitive refutation of the notion of a universal human nature, but it appeared to be a refined tool for understanding group differences in behavior. Unlike the vague and rather metaphysical concept of social or historical "forces," the concept of culture could not only be broken down into observable units of empirical investigation, but it generated theories which seemed to account for group differences. (The culture theories of the time were inadequate to account for cultural invention, change, or deviance, but I did not perceive this as impugning their validity.)

Having discovered anthropology, I lost whatever interest I might otherwise have had in sociology or psychology. Focused on only one cultural variant—that of Western man—the findings of sociology, so it seemed to me, could shed little light on Man. Similarly, psychology, with its concern with subcultural psychological processes (learning, perception, cognition, and the like) as they could be studied in the laboratory, also seemed unlikely to shed important light on Man. Its findings were based either on the study of lower animals who, since they had no culture, seemed inappropriate models for the study of humans; or, they were based on the study of Western subjects, and since, as I believed, psychological processes are culturally shaped, these findings seemed culture-bound. Anthropology, on the other hand, seemed admirably suited to my interests. If man is the creature of culture, then the proper study of man, so I believed, is the study of culture; and since culture is variable, then the proper study of Man is the study of culture in all of its variability. If, moreover, each culture (as Ruth Benedict had argued in her seductive metaphor) has carved out a different arc from the total circle of cultural variability, and if (as she also contended) each primitive culture constitutes a natural experiment in cultural variability, then it further followed that the proper study of cultural variability entailed the study of primitive cultures. For me, then, anthropology was clearly the science of choice. This being so, it is important to sketch in greater detail the dominant anthropological notions concerning culture and human nature of that time, notions to which I (and most of my contemporaries) became, if we not already were, committed.

Since human behavior is culturally determined, and since cultures vary enormously, the only valid generalization that can be made about human nature is that it is enormously malleable ("plastic"). The existence of cultural universals does not require any qualification of this conclusion since culture, being "superorganic," does not reflect (and, hence, cannot be "reduced" to) noncultural, pan-human, biological or psychological attributes. Although, so far as biology is concerned, such anatomical attributes as hair form, eye color, and so on, are biologically determined (subject of course to cultural selection), biology has little, if any, determination on social behavior. Since the latter can be explained, without residue, by cultural determinants, the organism, like the psyche, is conceived as either an "empty" or a "black box." Since, according to one "empty box" model, culture affects behavior by a kind of Newtonian action-at-a-distance, the box remains perpetually empty. According to a second model, however, the empty box does not long remain empty for, as a consequence of "enculturation," the external culture is somehow incorporated by the social actors. Nevertheless, since the resultant "inside" (psychological) determinants of behavior are merely the "outside" (cultural) determinants that have become "internalized," and since, therefore, they vary as culture varies, these psychological determinants can hardly constitute the basis for a species-specific human nature. The "black box" differs from these two "empty box" models in that it does not deny the existence of "inside" variables; it merely denies their influence on social behavior. Since the latter, so the argument goes, is culturally variable, how can it be explained by biological or psychological determinants which are constant? Hence, even if these "inside" variables may be said to constitute or to determine a species-specific human nature, the latter is irrelevant to the understanding of man's social behavior.

Whatever the differences among these three models, it will be noted that all agree (if only by implication) there can be no conflict between the individual and culture. If there is nothing inside the individual (the first model), or if what is inside is either orthogonal to, or represents the internalization of, culture (the third and second models respectively), then the individual and culture are in a state of harmony. That is, what the individual wants to do is identical with what his culture requires him to do.

It should also be noted that although all three models explain behavior by reference to culture, culture itself is left unexplained. To explain culture by reference to some set of biological and psychological determinants (construed as the core, or nucleus, of human nature) is not only inconsistent with the empty and black box models, but it illustrates the fallacy of "reductionism." (For unexplained reasons, reductionism was taken to be a self-evident fallacy.) Hence, like Aristotle's First Cause, culture remains an Unmoved Mover. To be sure, since culture is in large part a symbolic system, man must everywhere have the capacity to invent, transmit, and acquire cultural symbols, and to that extent symbolization is to be included with plasticity as a second attribute of human nature. (Indeed, functionally, or adaptively viewed, symbolization is to human plasticity what instinct is to animal specificity.) But since symbolization is culturally variable, the universality of symbolic processes does not imply the universality of symbolic meanings. Hence, so far as content is concerned, there is no universal human nature; there are only culturally specific—and therefore culturally variable—character structures.

Lest the above conceptions be used as a handle for racist arguments, the concept of cultural relativism—according to which all cultures, and therefore all culturally variable character structures, are equally valuable —was enlisted to do battle against racist notions in general, and the notion of primitive mentality, in particular. It should be noted, however, that cultural relativism was also used, at least by some anthropologists, to perpetuate a kind of inverted racism. That is, it was used as a powerful tool of cultural criticism, with the consequent derogation of Western culture and of the mentality which it produced. Espousing the philosophy of primitivism—akin to, but not identical with, Rousseau's notion of the Noble Savage—the image of primitive man was used by some few anthropologists as a vehicle for the pursuit of personal utopian quests, and/or as a fulcrum to express personal discontent with Western man and Western society. The strategies adopted took various forms, of which the following are fairly representative. (1) Attempts to abolish private property, or inequality, or aggression in Western societies have a reasonably realistic chance of success since such states of affairs may be found in many primitive societies. (2) Compared to at least some primitives, Western man is uniquely competitive, warlike, intolerant of deviance, sexist, and so on. (3) Paranoia is not necessarily an illness, because paranoid thinking is institutionalized in certain primitive societies; homosexuality is not deviant because homosexuals are the cultural cynosures of some primitive societies; monogamy is not viable because polygamy is the most frequent form of marriage in primitive societies. Needless to say, the anthropologists of that period were neither the first, nor—as recent politically motivated resolutions advocated at meetings of the American Anthropological Association indicate—the last to use anthropological ''findings'' as ''scientific'' support for personal and political *Weltanschaungen*.

QUALIFICATIONS

Although many years were to pass before I finally discarded as untenable many of the ideas described in the previous section, the corrosive process began when I encountered the theories of A. I. Hallowell, my mentor at Northwestern University, and (through him) psychoanalytic and learning theory. From Hallowell's writings and teachings I came to realize that culture does not impinge directly on behavior, but is mediated through personality processes relating to individuals. The contours of these processes, I came to believe, were best delineated by Freud. It was the work of Kardiner, however, that persuaded me of the importance of the family and of socialization in the formation of these processes. From Kardiner, too, I became convinced of the importance of "projective systems" for the understanding of those aspects of culture that are not "reality" based. There remained, however, a missing ingredient. If social actors monitor their own behavior in accordance with cultural norms and rules, it was necessary to explain the acquisition of culture in each generation of social actors. Here, the social learning theorists—and especially Miller and Dollard—provided the key.

Hence, when I completed graduate work, my theoretical framework comprised an inchoate synthesis of cultural determinism, and cultural relativism, neo-Freudian personality theory, and social learning theory. In this loosely integrated synthesis, culture was viewed as a kind of master plan for group adaptation; it was transmitted primarily in the family, and in the early years of life, by traditional methods of socialization and enculturation, it was acquired as part of the personality by techniques of social reinforcement; its acquisition ("internalization"), however, often conflicted with and frustrated other personality "needs"; the conflict was resolved by the disguised satisfaction of these needs through culturally mediated symbolic systems ("projective systems").

It will be noticed that this synthesis, by including explicit attention to "personality," represented an important qualification of my earlier thinking. But this shift from a cultural to a culture-personality framework did not alter my earlier notions concerning human nature; on the contrary, it strengthened them. For, although influenced by psychoanalytic thought, the main thrust of the culture-personality school was precisely the reverse of psychoanalysis. While the latter postulated invariant stages and processes (and even invariant symbol formations and symbolic meanings) in the formation, structure, and functioning of personality, culture-personality (with some important exceptions) was primarily concerned to demonstrate their cultural variability. Since, according to this school, personality was determined by, and constituted the internalization of, culture, the range of personality variability across groups could hardly be smaller than the range of cultural variability. Indeed, since personality characteristics and personality configurations, respectively, were viewed as isomorphic with cultural characteristics and cultural patterns, the notion of a pan-cultural human nature was viewed as highly unlikely. On the contrary, it was assumed as almost self-evident that Zunis, Germans, Hawaiians, and Thais are much more different, not only in culture but also in personality, than they are similar.

These, then, were the views which I took with me on my first field trip—to the atoll of Ifaluk in the Central Carolines.

FIRST FIELD TRIP—IFALUK

In those far off days—it was 1947-48—very few anthropologists thought of going into the field with a "problem," let alone with a hypothesis for "testing." Rather, the typical fieldworker immersed himself in the local society and culture and, with luck, he then came up with a problem that might provide the basis for a doctoral dissertation. This, too, was my approach, and the problem I came up with was aggression. The choice of this problem was hardly accidental. In the first place, after some few months on the atoll, I was struck by the fact that I had not observed a single act of overt aggression. Reflecting on this remarkable fact, and reflecting on my own adjustments to atoll living, it was hard to escape the conclusion that the control of aggression was *the* central—or at least *a* central—problem confronting any group of 250 people attempting to live together on a land mass six-tenths of a mile square.

But, of course, the decision to study aggression was not that simple. What about the kinship system? The Ifaluk had a matrilineal descent system, based on matrilineages—a subject we knew very little at that time. What about the political structure? Ifaluk, though a small face to face society, had a complex system of hereditary chieftanship—a combination which would have evoked the attention of scores of anthropologists with backgrounds different from mine. What about the complicated redistribution system? The products of the fields and the oceans were periodically redistributed in Ifaluk by a mechanism which any Oceanist worth his salt would have investigated in minute detail. Although these, and other equally fascinating aspects of Ifaluk social structure commanded and deserved as much attention as aggression, there must have been other reasons for choosing the latter for study.

First, given my interest in human nature, it is understandable I would have been much more interested in social processes than in social structure. Second, among these processes, aggression had been a salient concern even prior to my trip to Micronesia, beginning with my political interest in the viability of socialism. This interest was supported by the culture-personality literature of that period, which had persistently held up the Pueblos as examples of nonaggressive, noncompetitive peoples, who constituted refutations of the Western notion that aggression and competition were universal social characteristics. Indeed, in this literature, the Hopi and Zuni were constantly contrasted with the Kwakiutl and Dobuans in support of the cultural relativist thesis concerning aggression and cooperation, and the Ifaluk seemed to offer yet additional support for this thesis. More immediately, as a student of Hallowell, my interest in aggression had been stimulated by three brilliant papers he had published on the psychocultural determinants of, and solutions to, the problem of aggression among the Berens River Saulteaux. These had left a deep impression on me. Finally, under Hallowell's guidance, and together with a group of graduate students, I had conducted field work on the Lac Du Flambeau (Wisconsin) Ojibwa reservation the summer prior to leaving for Ifaluk, and I had been struck with (what I thought to be) a high incidence of aggression on that reservation. It was found at the social level (in interpersonal and intergroup behavior), at the cultural level (spontaneously told jokes and folk tales almost invariably displayed an aggressive theme) and at the personality level (as revealed in the Rorschach test). Since the Ojibwa and Saulteaux are the same people, and since, though separated in space and living under different ecological and economic conditions, they yet exhibited similar aggressive tendencies—which, in turn, were similar (as Hallowell had shown in an ethnohistorical analysis) to those of their historical forbears—was an exciting finding, which reinforced my interest in aggression.

It is little wonder, then, that when observations in Ifaluk revealed almost no manifest aggression, I was struck by the contrast with what I had observed among the Ojibwa only six months earlier. The near absence of aggression in Ifaluk seemed clearly to support my views concerning cultural relativism of human nature, and the cultural determinism of personality. Since the Ifaluk had a cooperative social system, since their ethos stressed the value of nonaggression, since there were few cultural pressures for competition for scarce resources, and since in this sociocultural context there was no observable aggression, it seemed to follow—as the Pueblo data had already suggested—that aggression is a function of historically specific cultural determinants, rather than an attribute of "human nature." This conclusion was also consistent with, and lent support to, the leading psychological theory of aggression—the frustration-aggression theory. For, when formulated in psychological terms, the Ifaluk observations seemed to indicate that in the absence of sociocultural frustration, there is no aggression.

After some additional work in Ifaluk, other observations however, not only began to intrude on my attention, but they eventually compelled a change in my views about Ifaluk aggression. First, I had begun collecting personality data—Rorschach and TAT protocols and dreams —which clearly revealed the existence of hostile impulses at the personality level. In short, from the absence of aggression—a behavioral variable—in Ifaluk, I had wrongly inferred the absence of hostility—a psychological variable. (Here, and in what follows, "hostility" refers to such motivational and affective variables as anger, rage, hatred, and so on, while "aggression" refers to observable social action—verbal and behavioral—whose intent is harm, injury, damage, and so on.) Second, I had begun collecting data on cultural systems—folk tales, myths, and religious beliefs—which revealed important aggressive themes; and on the assumption that these systems constituted projective expressions of personality dispositions, these cultural data, too, revealed the existence of hostility in Ifaluk.

These findings not only challenged my conception of Ifaluk personality, but they posed two immediate problems. First, in the absence of a competitive culture, what explanation, other than recourse to the outmoded notion of "instinct," could be offered for Ifaluk hostility? Second, given the existence of hostility, why was it not expressed in aggressive social behavior?

Actually, I had been aware of what later appeared to be a partial solution to the first problem even prior to the empirical challenges to my original observations. Shortly after arriving in Ifaluk I was (rather annoyingly) awakened every morning by the cries of babies who, at dawn, are brought by their mothers to be bathed in the chilly waters of the lagoon. Invariably, the infants would react to this experience with cries of rage, and although I could not say the experience was traumatic, there was no doubt that it was painful for the infants. When queried, mothers said they knew that it was a painful experience, but custom nevertheless required that infants be bathed in that way and at that time. When, some months later, I was perplexed by the presence of hostility in people living in a cooperative and nonfrustrating culture, it occurred to me that it might be related, at least in part, to this bathing experience. Since Ifaluk *adults* did not suffer important frustrations, perhaps, so I reasoned, their hostility was not situational, but characterological, their hostile impulses representing motivational dispositions

produced by those conditions that are formative of personality dispositions in general, *viz.,* infant and childhood experiences. Although it
seemed to me doubtful that one type of frustrating and painful experience—even one that was repeated daily for a long period—could produce a permanent character trait, it seemed reasonable that perhaps
other types of early frustrating experiences might also be discovered.
Hence, changing the focus of my study from adults to children, I began
a three-pronged program of investigation, including observations of
parent-child interaction, interviews of parents and of children concerning processes of socialization, and interviews of children concerning their
reactions to these socialization processes and their consequent feelings
toward parents and siblings.

From these investigations it was discovered that in addition to their
early bathing experience, Ifaluk children do indeed have other frustrating (perhaps traumatic) experiences, and I became increasingly convinced that adult hostility in Ifaluk was traceable to this configuration of
early childhood frustrations. Although, as is the case with all naturalistic
studies, the absence of controls did not permit this conviction to be
converted into a conclusion, its status as a highly likely hypothesis
seemed warranted on theoretical-deductive grounds. That is, on the
assumption that hostility is not "instinctive," and on the further assumption that it is produced by frustration, then, since there appeared
to be few situational determinants of hostility in Ifaluk adulthood, it
seemed to follow that it was produced by the frustrations of childhood.

Having discovered a tentatively satisfactory answer to the first question raised by Ifaluk hostility, I still had to find an answer to the second:
given that the Ifaluk do indeed have hostile impulses, what accounts for
their nonaggressive behavior? Why isn't hostility expressed in observable social aggression? Two answers suggested themselves—one based
on the Freud-Kardiner theory of religion, the other on my observations
of chieftainship. Since Ifaluk religion postulates the existence of a class
of spirits who are purely evil—their sole aim is to cause human suffering
—I reasoned that much of the hostility of the Ifaluk is expressed (both
displaced and projected) in their hostile feelings to the *alus,* as these
spirits are called. Moreover, since rituals are periodically performed to
drive away these evil spirits, I inferred that much of their hostility is
discharged in the performance of these "aggressive" rituals. Since the
characteristics of these spirits are, on a number of dimensions, isomorphic with those of the parents of their childhood, the expression of
hostility in this form could be seen as a symbolic expression of the

hostility which, though repressed, was originally aroused by the frustrating parents. In short, viewed as a projective system, Ifaluk religion seemed to afford one avenue for the expression of hostility.[2]

Although, *ex hypothesi,* religious beliefs and rituals channeled the expression of hostility, permitting the discharge of hostile impulses through projection and displacement, this hypothesis did not explain why the Ifaluk complied with this culturally approved form of aggression, rather than expressing their hostility in aggression against their fellows. Why, in short, did they follow their cultural ethos, which prohibits any social aggression? The ethos itself, so I assumed, is a highly adaptive cultural trait for a group living in a tiny land mass (in which physical avoidance of others is impossible), but, like any other functional explanation of culture derived from biological evolutionary model, it does not explain the conditions for the persistence of the ethos, or for compliance with its dictates. The latter condition must be explained not by some functional requirement—a "final" cause—but by some condition in the immediate social field of the actors—an "efficient" cause. This condition, it seemed to me, consisted in the institution of hereditary chieftanship, especially the prescribed behavior and *persona* of the chiefs, *qua* chiefs.

In Ifaluk, the chiefs are moral mentors. At periodic assemblies they exhort the people to do "good," and much of this exhortation is concerned with admonitions to behave in accordance with the ethos of nonaggression. In addition, they periodically monitor the behavior of their subjects by regular inspections of their districts—there is one chief for each district—to assure that this ethos is complied with. The chiefs, to use their own expression, are the "fathers" of their people. Moreover, from observations of the Ifaluk in interaction with the chiefs, and from interview and test protocols, it seemed as if, reciprocally, the chiefs were, in the people's eyes, benevolent parental figures, whose approval was of vital importance for their self-esteem and positive self-image. Desire for the approval of chiefs, and fear of their disapproval, seemed to be the most important social determinant of the Ifaluk adherence to the ethos of nonaggression.

With this, I felt that I had tentatively, and in large part, solved the problem of aggression in Ifaluk, and in a manner entirely consistent with my views of culture and human nature. However disappointing,

2. Since that time, I have become convinced that there are sources of frustration—especially related to esteem—in the adult social system, and that there are other expressions of hostility in addition to projective expressions. Moreover, Theodore Schwartz (personal communication) has called my attention to the aggression in the Ifaluk treatment of infants and children.

especially after my original impressions, to discover hostility in the Ifaluk, this discovery neither supported the notion of a pan-cultural human nature, nor did it challenge my own notion of historically specific cultural determinism. Although the social system did not engender hostility, the socialization system did, and this clearly supported my view that hostility is culturally relative. For, if the Ifaluk socialization system engenders hostility, then, so it seemed to me, other socialization systems could surely be found which do not. Moreover, despite the presence of hostility at the personality level, the Ifaluk case demonstrated that its expression, like its instigation, is culturally relative. Instead of permitting hostility to be expressed in social relations, Ifaluk culture directed its expression into other, less disruptive, channels.

Although for me, at least, the foregoing interpretation of the instigations to, and vicissitudes of, aggression in Ifaluk seemed convincing, it was obvious, as I have already indicated, that its various hypotheses remained unproven. Without controls there can be no proof, and in naturalistic studies of society and culture, there are really only two types of controls. One can study different groups under the same conditions (this, in effect, characterizes the comparative method in all of its variants), or the same group under different conditions. The latter method (which, for reasons I cannot develop here, is the much more satisfactory) exploits historical change to test interpretations previously offered for the *status quo ante*. Thus, if my interpretations of Ifaluk aggression are valid, it follows that were its religious beliefs and rituals to change, and were chieftanship to be abolished (or otherwise lose its meaning), then—if there were no functionally equivalent structural alternatives for these institutions—hostility should be expressed in overt social aggression, or (if it is inhibited by external sanctions) in predictable clinical symptoms. This prediction not only provides a clear empirical test of the hypotheses discussed above, but it is now possible to perform this test. In the quarter century that has elapsed since my study of Ifaluk, there have been important changes both in its religious and its political system. Christianity, introduced by the missionaries, has replaced the traditional religion, and elective government, introduced by the United States, has replaced traditional chieftanship. I hope to return to Ifaluk to assess the psychological consequences of these changes and, thereby, to test the hypothesis described here.

SECOND FIELD TRIP—ISRAEL

Although the Ifaluk findings were consistent with traditional culture-personality views, they nevertheless left unanswered the basic question with which I had been concerned—can culture (in the holistic sense) form the psychological structure of human beings into any mold it chooses? Still, I was sufficiently wedded to the traditional anthropological paradigm to remain committed to the conventional culturalist answer to this question. In 1950, having recently completed my Ph.D. thesis on Ifaluk aggression, I decided to explore this question in an Israeli kibbutz.

Although I still believed, on the grounds adduced by Benedict, that anthropology ought to be concerned with primitive societies, the rationale for studying this, a modern group, was precisely that which Benedict had offered for the study of primitives—it represented yet another, and an unexplored, arc of the total circle of cultural variation. Within this particular arc, I was concerned with two problems especially. First, since children are reared outside of the domestic family, to what extent do they exhibit the same stages of psychosexual development which psychoanalysis had postulated as universal, and more especially, to what extent do they develop an Oedipus complex? Second, adverting back to the Ifaluk study, to what extent had the kibbutz succeeded in producing children without hostility? It seemed particularly desirable to explore the second question in a kibbutz since the latter is not only one of the few *modern* examples of a cooperative group, but it is one that practiced a form of democratic socialism which had been of such great interest to me in my early life. Here, I shall treat the latter question only.

On the basis of the meager available literature, it was evident that the kibbutz movement had ushered in a new type of human society. Rejecting the traditional social structures of the West, this movement had initiated a radical experiment in voluntary, comprehensive, cooperative living. Not only were the means of production collectively owned, and not only was the system of distribution based on the socialist principle of, "from each according to his abilities, to each according to his needs," but even the children were raised by (and for) the community, rather than in individual families. Living in communal children's houses, rather than with their parents, they were reared by professional nurses and teachers, whose primary goal was the transmission of the cooperative values of kibbutz culture. If, then, there is no universal human nature, if the psychological characteristics of social actors represent the internalization of the historically specific cultural values of their group—if, in a word, personality is the culture writ small—then, if the kibbutz values of sharing and cooperation were in fact internalized by the children, it would be expected that they would exhibit little if any competitive or hostile characteristics. This at least was the premise which guided my kibbutz field work.

The findings of the kibbutz study had a strong—and thus far a lasting—impact on my image of man and on my conception of anthropology. Although the kibbutz children were raised in a totally communal and cooperative system; although their socialization had as its primary aim the inculcation of a cooperative, noncompetitive ethic; although the techniques of socialization were mild, loving, and permissive; although the target responses were properly reinforced; although, in a word, almost all of the culture conditions were designed to exclusively promote cooperation and sharing, the data clearly indicated that kibbutz children, like other children, do not wish to share scarce and valued goods—they want them for themselves and they resist the attempts of adults to get them to share them. They view as rivals those with whom they are obliged to share, and they aggress against those who frustrate their desires to monopolize (or at least to maximize) these scarce goods. Although they learn to cooperate, their cooperative motives do not lead to the extinction of their learned competitive and rivalrous motives. In short, although they learn to view aggression as wrong, when they are frustrated they become angry, and their anger—when not controlled—leads to overt aggressive behavior.

This does not mean, I hasten to point out, that the kibbutz has been unsuccessful in transmitting its ethic of sharing, equality, mutual aid, and cooperation to its children. It has, on the contrary, been surprisingly successful, if "success" is defined as the perpetuation, by successive generations of adults, of the social and cultural systems for which they were socialized. But if "success" means not only the internalization of the above values, but the absence of any competing and conflicting tendencies—i.e., if "success" means the development of a "new man," (as the kibbutz puts it)—one without competitive, hostile, or acquisitive motives—then, of course, the kibbutz has not been successful. But only a utopian or—what is the same thing—a radical cultural relativist would have ever thought that the creation of such a "new man" was possible. Indeed, from a nonutopian point of view the real mark of the kibbutz success is that although its children have developed competitive and acquisitive, as well as cooperative and sharing dispositions, when, as adults, they experience conflict between them, they usually resolve the conflict in favor of the latter dispositions. In short, the kibbutz values have penetrated to that part of the personality which is the true measure of the internalization of cultural values—the superego.

On the basis of the kibbutz study (and on the basis of everything I have studied, read, and reflected upon since) I slowly and painfully came to the conclusion that the belief that competition, rivalry, hostility, and so on, are culturally relative rather than generically human is a misguided and false notion which, invented by Rousseau, continues to be perpetrated by the latter day believers—true believers—in the noble savage. This is so, I came to believe, because although the intensity of competitive and hostile motives is culturally (and individually) variable, and although culture can tame and domesticate these motives, it is culture itself (interacting with characteristics of man's mammalian biology) which also, and universally, creates them. This conclusion is based on a number of assumptions that will be examined in the last section of the paper.

THIRD FIELD TRIP—BURMA

From my earlier exposure to Durkheim, I had acquired a persistent interest in the study of religion, but it was the influence of Max Weber, whose religious sociology I became acquainted with only after returning from Israel, that led me to turn my research attention to religion. *The Protestant Ethic* opened my mind to a point of view and method of analysis which were revolutionary and enormously exciting. Moreover, Weber's essays on the sociology of religion, and especially his work on the religions of India, stimulated an interest in Asia and Asian religions which has not yet run its course. Again, however, this interest was very much related to my concern with human nature. Although man's basic motives, I had already decided, are culturally universal, Weber's work strongly suggested that world views are culturally relative, and the religions of India, Hinduism and Buddhism—but especially the latter—seemed to constitute convincing proof for this thesis. If the adherents of one of the world's great religions believe that the self is an illusion, that there are no gods, that life is suffering, that suffering can only be avoided by rejecting the world and all worldly desires, that (therefore) the quest for immortality is a quest for eternal suffering, that salvation consists in the cessation of life (i.e., of rebirth)—if, that is, Buddhists believe in these, and in many other, principles that are directly opposed to accepted Western principles, it seemed to follow that world views—those fundamental cognitive orientations by which men order their lives—are historically conditioned and therefore culturally relative.

In order to study both the determinants and the consequences of the Buddhist world view "on the ground," I determined that my next field trip would take place in Asia, and from 1961 to 1962 I was fortunate to have the opportunity to conduct such a study in Upper Burma. Subsequently, in the summers of 1969 to 1972 I continued these studies among the Burmese expatriates in Thailand. As an anthropologist, especially one committed to functionalism, I did not, of course, restrict my studies to Buddhism. But I shall avoid any discussion here of the findings concerning kinship and politics, of folk religion and folk medicine, not to mention aggression, though the latter is directly related to the previous sections of this paper. Instead, this discussion will be confined to elements of the Burmese Buddhist world view in their relationship to human nature.

As was the case in the earlier field trips, the expectations I took to Burma proved to be chimerical, for I discovered that the religious beliefs of Burmese Buddhists—and subsequent studies of other scholars revealed this was also the case in Ceylon and Thailand—were in many respects rather discrepant from those described in Western works on Buddhism, not excluding that of Weber. The discrepancies were based on two errors. One error was mine, in expecting congruence between canonical texts and beliefs held by religious actors, for, of course, it is never the case that the belief systems of religious actors accurately mirror their canonical texts. The other error was that of Western interpreters of Buddhism, who, by their often inaccurate renditions of canonical beliefs, had presented a distorted conception of Buddhism. One example of such a distortion is the alleged atheism of this religion. Although in the metaphysical or theological sense of denying the existence of a Creator or Redeemer, canonical Buddhism is indeed atheistic, it is nevertheless far from being the kind of Ethical Culture movement that it is often portrayed to be. On the contrary, Buddhism explicitly affirms the existence of a host of superhuman beings—gods, godlings, and spirits—and it prescribes various types of ritual for enlisting the help of the benevolent, and appeasing the wrath of the malevolent, ones. It is metaphysically important that these superhuman beings are not eternal, that they, like humans, are subject to the law of karma and, hence, to the wheel of rebirth, but it is irrelevant to the religious concerns of the Buddhist actor who, like religious actors everywhere, turns to these beings for help in time of need, and invokes their activity to explain his suffering. For him, life is inconceivable without the help of the benevolent superhuman beings, and most of life's vicissitudes are inexplicable without his belief in the malevolent.

To be sure, the superhuman helpers of Buddhism are of no assistance—as they are in some other religions—in the Buddhist's quest for salvation, for their help is confined to this world. Even the Buddha, Himself, though He has shown the Path to salvation, is not—as is Christ, for example—a Savior. To be saved every man must walk alone on that Path, without external guidance or intercession. Man, as it were, must save himself. To this extent, Western interpretations of Buddhism are correct. What they usually fail to observe, however, is that this Path is not one on which many Buddhists desire to walk because its soteriological goal, nirvana, is not one which they usually aspire to attain. The reason is simple. Nirvana, a knotty concept at best, is not a state of being—not, at least, in the ordinary sense of "being." Indeed, in the latter sense, nirvana is best characterized as a state of nonbeing, signalling the end of the wheel of rebirth in all of the planes of existence postulated by Buddhist cosmology. But Buddhists, for the most part, are no more interested in the extinction of their future rebirths than are Westerners in the extinction of their *present* birth. Although paying lip service to the notion of nirvana, most Buddhists, in fact, conceive of salvation in highly concrete and material terms, much as it is conceived in most other religious systems. That is, salvation for them is a state of being in which wants and desires are fulfilled, and in which suffering is extinguished. Such a state of affairs they project into future rebirths, in which they are reborn either as wealthy human beings, or—if they dare to aspire to it—as gods in one of the Buddhist material heavens. (They explain that they do not aspire to the normative goal of nirvana by the fact that their present spiritual attainments are still underdeveloped. They hope, however, that after many future rebirths they will eventually develop higher spiritual qualities by means of which they will be able to aspire to this superior vision of salvation. In this regard they are like the young St. Augustine, who prayed he might achieve celibacy, "but not yet.")

But in addition to these findings, there were still others that also disabused me of my earlier view that basic human cognitive orientations are entirely culturally relative and wholly historically conditioned. Thus, for example, the all too human hope which the Burmese evince for a continuous existence is expressed not only in their desire for continuous rebirths, but also in the prevalence of alchemic beliefs and practices whose aim—like the alchemic aims of China—is not the transmutation of base into precious metals, but the attainment of "immortality." To be sure, this goal is not defined as immortality because, as Buddhists, the Burmese profess belief in the normative doctrine of the impermanence of sentient existence. Hence, this goal is defined as—and the alchemic beliefs hold up the possibility of—a continuous existence of only sixty thousand years duration. One could, of course, debate the issue (though probably without much profit) of whether, for the average human mind, sixty thousand years is or is not tantamount to immortality.

Now in pointing, by implication, to the similarities between certain dimensions of the Burmese world view and those of traditional Western culture, I am not suggesting the two are similar on all dimensions. Since, even within the same social group, there are individual differences in cognitive orientations, it is *a fortiori* the case that there are group differences in cognitive orientations, as well, and the latter are obviously a function of cultural differences. I am suggesting, however, there are some basic cognitive orientations that are not culturally variable (though they may be culturally determined), and among these must be counted those mentioned here in this brief description of some of the cognitive orientations found in Buddhist societies, *viz.:* the desirability of life, and hence the desire for its prolonged duration; the desirability of material and physical pleasures, and hence the desire to maximize these pleasures; belief in superhuman beings, both of good and evil, and the corollary belief that human action (religious ritual, etc.) can influence their activity by invoking the assistance of the former and repelling the harm of the latter. It is especially instructive that Buddhist actors share these pan-human orientations because in their case these orientations (except for the third) are in direct opposition to the normative teachings of the religion which they genuinely—indeed passionately—revere.

In sum, although the differences in the normative values and official codes of different cultures may, in some instances, lead to the conclusion that culturally constituted cognitions are so different as to constitute (as many contemporary ethnoscientists believe) incommensurable world views, on the basis of the Burmese study I have come to believe this conclusion is entirely unwarranted. I now believe, on the contrary, that when the values and codes of social actors are studied directly, rather than inferred from normative cultural concepts, many cultural differences in basic cognitive orientations are seen to be more apparent than real; to a large extent these differences are merely the manifest expressions of the same underlying cognitive orientations which, being historically conditioned, take different cultural forms.

In short, just as the kibbutz and Ifaluk studies convinced me that many motivational dispositions are culturally invariant, the Burmese study convinced me that many cognitive orientations are also invariant. These invariant dispositions and orientations stem, I believe, from pan-human biological and cultural constants, and they comprise that universal human nature which, together with received anthropological opinion, I had formerly rejected as yet another ethnocentric bias.

CONCLUSIONS

Having described how I gradually and painfully came to discard much of the received anthropological wisdom, I now wish to explore (what I consider to have been) the fallacies in traditional anthropological thinking that led to the adoption of cultural determinism and, hence, to the cultural relativistic view of human nature.

I have already noted that in the traditional conception, "culture" referred to all aspects of a group's environment, except the physical, and to all aspects of man, except the biological. Given, then, that man constitutes a single biological species and that, nevertheless, social behavior reveals a wide range of cross-cultural variability, it seemed to follow that the organism is an empty or a black box, and that social behavior, therefore, is determined by culture. Given, too, that personality characteristics were believed to exist in a one to one relationship with behavioral characteristics, the former being thought to be *directly* deducible from the latter, it seemed to follow that personality is also culturally determined. This meant that no psychological characteristic—no affect, no need, no wish, no belief—could be part of human personality unless culture put it there. Given, moreover, that culture is variable, personality (it was further argued) must similarly be variable; historically specific cultures produce culturally variable personality characteristics. Given, finally, that depending on their culture, human beings may acquire *any* empirical subset of the total conceivable set of human psychological characteristics, any member of the latter set (it was concluded) is culturally relative; none is an invariant characteristic of a universal human nature. Any psychological characteristic—the feeling of love or hate, the wish for mortality or immortality, the belief in the talion principle or its reverse—might or might not be found in any social group as a function of its cultural program.

Skipping over some logical and empirical problems in its global[3]

3. The logical problem raised by the global conception of culture is easily stated. If culture includes (among other things) behavioral patterns and personality traits, to say that culture determines behavior and personality is obviously circular. Although this difficulty is easily resolved—by excluding behavior and personality from the definition

and holistic[4] conception of culture, this conceptual structure falters, I believe, on two related, but separable, theses, both of which are (I believe) untenable. These are (1) culture is the exclusive determinant of personality, and (2) personality consists exclusively of the internalization of culture. Let us begin with the first.

Culture is the exclusive determinant of personality. Culture determinist theories of behavior and of personality were developed in the first instance as alternatives to and refutations of biological determinism. Given the demonstrable cross-cultural variability in behavior and personality, anthropology (validly) argued that social behavior cannot represent an expression of instincts, and personality formation cannot represent an unfolding of genetically programmed psychological traits. Rather, both must be (in a large part, at least) a result of learning, which is to say (since anthropology is concerned with group, rather than individual, variability) that they are the products (in large part, at least) of social and cultural determinants. So far, so good. To have concluded, however, that cultural determinism implies the absence of any invariant (pan-cultural psychological characteristics—in short, that all such characteristics are culturally relative—is an invalid conclusion which is based, I believe, on three interrelated fallacies.

The fallacy of assuming that the cross-cultural variability in social

---

of "culture" and thereby rendering the culture concept less global—yet another problem with respect to personality remains. For if personality is not part of culture, and, moreover, if personality (as we shall see below) is not isomorphic with behavior— if, on the contrary, personality is viewed as a system of cognitive, perceptual, motivational, and affective dispositions "underlying" behavior—it cannot be so blithely assumed that cultural (and, therefore, behavioral) variability is associated with personality variability. This latter thesis now becomes an empirical hypothesis, to be tested by direct examination of personality, rather than an *a priori* assumption whose proof consists in pointing to the cross-cultural variability in behavior. In short, if personality is not, merely by definition, a part of culture, and if the isomorphism of personality and behavior is not accepted as an unchallenged assumption, then the question of pan-cultural psychological characteristics remains open.

4. The empirical problem raised by the holistic conception of culture is also easily stated for, given this conception, it is difficult to know which of the various elements comprising a culture are the determinants of personality: Art styles? Religious beliefs? Descent systems? Modes of production? Child rearing? Some of these? All of these? In short, so long as culture is taken as an undifferentiated whole, a seamless web, the thesis of cultural determination of personality is not very illuminating, since (even in the now restricted conception of culture) the only things that are excluded as possible determinants are characteristics of the organism and of the physical environment. Even Margaret Mead, much of whose work has concentrated on (and has illuminated so much of) the relationship between child training and personality, has disclaimed any notion that the former is an especially important cultural determinant; rather, she claims, it is merely a convenient way of entering into the total configuration of cultural determinants.

behavior and personality implies that the organism is an empty or black box. Despite the variability in culture, it does not follow that man has no invariant psychological characteristics, because some, at least, are biologically determined. Far from being an empty or black box, some of the properties of the organism are important determinants of social behavior as well as personality. Although space does not permit a detailed, let alone an exhaustive catalogue of these properties, I might mention a small subset, *viz.*, those relevant to the problem of hostility and aggression discussed in earlier sections of this paper.

Because of prolonged helplessness, requiring dependency on others for the satisfaction of their survival needs, children are everywhere raised in family or family-like groups, whose members, to a greater or lesser extent, provide them with nurturance, gratification, and protection. As a result, children everywhere have the following characteristics: the need to receive love from, and the motivation to express love for, the loving and loved objects; feelings of rivalry toward those who seek love from the same (scarce) love objects; hostility toward those who would deprive them of these objects; and so on. In short, everywhere (due to Oedipal struggles and conflicts with siblings) children's need for love is necessarily thwarted, as well as gratified, to some extent. Moreover, because everywhere man lives in social groups—yet another biological requirement of the human organism—and since the requirements of a human social order demand that children learn to behave in compliance with cultural norms, everywhere their needs, desires, and wishes are necessarily frustrated, as well as gratified, to some extent. Everywhere, therefore, if for only these reasons, hostile, rivalrous, and competitive feelings, as well as those of love and mutual aid, will be found to some extent.

The expression, "to some extent," underscores the fact that the intensity of these various types of frustrations, and hence the intensity of these feelings, are highly culturally variable. Similarly, and for the same reason, the targets of these feelings, the degree to which they are permitted expression in aggressive behavior, the social domains in which they are permitted expression (whether in kinship, religion, politics, and so on), the manner in which they are expressed (whether directly, through displacement, projection, and so on)—all these are culturally determined and culturally variable. Nevertheless, although different cultures channel these feelings in a bewildering variety of social and cultural forms—some more, some less, adaptive—all cultures produce them to some extent. They are, in short, among man's invariant psychological characteristics.

The fallacy of confusing "a culture" with "culture" in the expres-

sion "cultural determinism." The theory of cultural determinism was based on the following (valid) argument. Given that human beings are born without instincts, the gratification of human "needs" depends on learning. Given, moreover, that they are born entirely helpless, they are wholly dependent on adults for the acquisition of the means for their gratification. Given, finally, that they live in social groups, these means must be shared, and, therefore, prescribed, *i.e.,* they must be cultural. Thus, the properties of the organism, interacting with those of the social environment, *require* that a human existence be a culturally constituted existence. In short, if other animals adapt by means of species-specific biological specializations, human adaptation is achieved by means of a species-specific nonbiological specialization, *viz.,* culture. If this is the case, then, for a human primate to be classified as man—i.e., to be characterized as more than a bipedal, big-brained, primate—it is not enough that he have those biological characteristics a zoologist would designate as the distinguishing features of Homo sapiens. It is also necessary that he have those characteristics—socially shared and transmitted symbols, values, rules, and so on—that an anthropologist would designate as the distinguishing features of a cultural mode of adaptation. But if culture is as important an adaptive human requirement as food or water, then culture and the psychological products of culture—the drives, needs, cognitions, and the like, that are produced by culture—are as much a part of man's nature as his biological characteristics and *their* psychological products. Indeed, since many of man's biological, and biologically derived psychological characteristics are found in the entire class of mammals, it may be said that since his cultural and culturally derived psychological characteristics are man's species-specific characteristics, they are the uniquely *human* part of his nature.

These, then, were the insights that were originally captured by the notion of cultural determinism. They were valid then and, in my opinion, they are valid now. When, however, anthropology became increasingly impressed with cultural differences, this original notion of cultural determinism underwent (as we have seen) two changes. First, instead of being taken as *a* determinant, culture was taken as *the* determinant, of human nature, for when anthropologists began to view culture as internalized by social actors, they also began to argue that culture was the exclusive (or the exclusively relevant) content of the black or empty organism. Second, since culture is found in a bewildering variety of local manifestations, anthropologists came to view each culture as a more or less historically unique creation, each producing a culturally unique human nature. Consequently, it came to be believed that there is little basis for postulating any set of invariant psychological characteristics that might comprise a universal human nature.

Almost without recognition, therefore, the meaning of "cultural determinism" has undergone a gradual shift. Beginning as a statement about man's nature, it has come to be a statement about his history. From a theory of the generic cultural determination of single pan-cultural human nature, it has become a theory of the historically specific cultural determination of many culturally relative human natures.[5] The fallacy in this shift is obvious. Since cultural variability does not mean that culture is distributed across space and over time in a series of discrete configurations, each incommensurable with every other; since, on the contrary, culture is known to be distributed in a series of over-lapping configurations; since, in short, despite the variability of culture, there is clearly discernible (what Wissler termed long ago) a "universal culture pattern," then, if personality is determined by culture, there must also be a universal personality pattern—a set of invariant psycho-logical characteristics produced by all cultures. In sum, even an exclu-sively cultural determinist theory of personality does not entail a cultural relativistic theory of human nature. For if certain cultural characteristics are pan-cultural, then, *ex hypothesi,* certain personality characteristics are also pan-cultural, and they, at least, comprise man's pan-cultural human nature.

The fallacy of not distinguishing the phenotypic from the geotypic, or (using a more fashionable metaphor) surface structure from deep structure, in culture. Culture, as man's most important adaptive special-ization, mediates the interaction between the properties of his psycho-biological organism and those of his social and physical environments. But in its role as mediator, culture is necessarily variable across space and over time because, as a product of man's symbolic capacities, culture can (and must) vary with a host of variable historical conditions—ecological settings, diffusionary opportunities, politically powerful or charismatic leadership, unpredictable physical and social events (war, drought, invasions), and so on. If, then, culture is the means by which men and groups adapt to the functional requirements of individual and group existence, it is not surprising to find a wide range of differences in the

5. Certain trends in current anthropology are even more relativistic. Thus, for example, the movement alternatively referred to as the "new ethnography," ethno-semantics, or ethnoscience, rejects the very notion of objective categories of ethno-graphic description. Arguing that cultures are incommensurable, the members of this movement insist that "etic" (i.e., cross-cultural) categories distort, when they do not falsify, the meanings of intracultural concepts, and that "emic" categories alone can convey their meanings. In my view this is not only the *reductio ad absurdum* of cultural relativism, but it leads to the demise of anthropology as a science.

form and content of culture as a function of an equally wide range of differences in man's historical experience.

Variability in the form and content of culture does not, however, imply variability in the substance of culture, nor, *a fortiori,* does it entail variability in personality. Indeed, identical psychological structures can be associated with (and eventuate in) manifestly dissimilar cultural structures, for though phenotypically different, the latter may be genotypically identical, *i.e.,* they may be functionally equivalent structural alternatives for coping with the identical functional requirements of individual and group existence. Different religions, for example, exhibit wide variability in their belief and ritual systems, and yet these different systems may all satisfy (among other things) a common human wish for dependency on powers greater than man. Thus, the gods of different cultures may differ in form and content (cultural phenotype), but, as powers greater than man (cultural genotype), they all reflect a pancultural human psychological characteristic (dependency need).

If, then, differences in cultural phenotypes do not imply differences in genotype, culture is less variable than it seems. Hence, phenotypic cultural differences do not in themselves justify the inference of personality differences, and phenotypic cultural variability does not in itself imply the cultural relativity of human nature. Unless these phenotypic differences can be assumed to be more than historically conditioned variable expressions of the same cultural genotype, such differences are entirely compatible with a pan-cultural human nature.

The foregoing critique of cultural determinism, and its corollary, cultural relativism, may be summarized as follows: the nature/history dichotomy is a false dichotomy; although personality, to some extent, is culturally relative, man has a nature as well as a history; this is so because even a radical cultural determinism does not imply a radical cultural relativism; however much societies may differ, they all must cope with man's common biological features, especially his prolonged infantile dependency; the adaptively viable means for coping with the latter condition exhibit common social and cultural features across a narrow range of social and cultural variability; these common biological, social, and cultural features are a set of constants which, in their interaction, produce a universal human nature.

Personality consists exclusively of the internalization of culture. Although the thesis that culture is the exclusive determinant of personality accounts, in part, for the traditional denial of a pan-cultural human nature, the thesis that personality is the internalization of culture has been even more decisive in this regard. For since culture is variable, and since, *ex hypothesi,* personality is merely culture as it is internalized in social actors, it follows necessarily that there can be no pan-cultural human nature; there can only be culturally relative human nature. But this undifferentiated model of personality (personality as constituted exclusively of culture) is even less tenable than the global model of culture held by its champions. If, instead, we were to adopt a more sophisticated model of personality—one in which personality, conceived as a system, consists of differentiated structures, each with distinctive functions—cultural variability need not imply personality variability (and, for that matter, cultural similarities need not imply similarities in personality).

Consider, for example, the Freudian model according to which personality, as a system, consists of three differentiated, but interrelated structures. Over-simply put, these structures consist of an impulse system, or id; a cognitive-perceptual system, or ego; and a normative-prescriptive system, or superego. This model is not only much more complex than the internalization-of-culture model, but one of its postulated structures—the id—comprises wishes and desires, many of which are in frequent, if not persistent, conflict with culture. Moreover, since the id is only one structure of the personality, and since another of its structures—the superego—comprises (among other things) inter-nalized cultural values, many wishes of social actors are not only in conflict with the cultural requirements of their group (external conflict), but one part of their personality is frequently in conflict with another (internal conflict). In the latter case, the ego experiences conflict between impulses which seek gratification and internalized cultural values which proscribe their gratification. To complicate the picture even more, this conflict may be unconscious, as well as conscious.

According to this model of personality, social behavior is often neither a direct expression of an undifferentiated personality, nor a simple result of the influence of external cultural norms. It is more likely to be the end product of a chain of interacting psychological events, including impulse (id), cultural and personal values (superego), conflict between them, and defense against conflict (ego), which only then eventuates in behavior. In most cases, to be sure, behavior—the end product of this chain—conforms to cultural norms, for the actor usually complies with his superego, and resolves the conflict by controlling the forbidden impulses—either by the conscious mechanism of suppression, or by a variety of unconscious mechanisms of defense (including the defense of repression). In short, according to this model of personality, social actors are not merely the creatures of their culture, formed in its mold, and reflecting its values. Although typically conforming with them, a comprehensive description of their values is only a partial description of their personality. Indeed, their values, which comprise one part of their motivational system, are often in conflict with equally strong motives which oppose them. The latter may be kept under control, but since control does not mean extinction, culture, as Freud argued, necessarily produces "discontents"—a condition in which the social actor is frequently at odds with himself and with his culture.

Since both models of personality, the Freudian structural model and the internalization-of-culture model, make the same behavioral predictions—both predict behavior will conform with cultural norms—what difference does it make regarding which of the two one chooses? (Indeed, the principle of parsimony would suggest the adoption of the latter, or cultural determinist model.) Although this choice makes little difference for the prediction of social behavior, it makes a great difference for the understanding of personality (not to mention the understanding of the psychic costs of culture, mental illness, social deviance, and so on). According to the internalization-of-culture model, behavior is the direct (unconflicted) expression of cultural norms as they are internalized in the personality. Hence, for example, if one observes little aggressive behavior in some social group, it could be inferred that, having internalized a set of cultural values opposing aggression, the social actors are nonhostile—for hostility, according to this model, is determined by cultural values which favor aggression. According to the Freudian model, however, this inference may be entirely unwarranted, for these nonaggressive actors may (as a result of any number of punitive and frustrating conditions) have strong hostile impulses which, however, because of strong superego disapproval of aggression are kept under rigid control.

Just as the internalization-of-culture model may invalidly deduce personality from behavior, it may similarly invalidly deduce culture from behavior. Thus, if one were to observe a great deal of aggression in a social group, then, in accordance with this model, it could be inferred that the actors have internalized a set of cultural values which favor aggression. According to the Freudian model, however, this may not be the case at all. Rather than expressing cultural values, aggressive behavior may in fact be in direct violation of them. The aggression (stemming from socially induced hostility) may instead be the result of an immature ego (with little impulse control), or a weak superego (which has insufficiently internalized the cultural values opposing aggression), or of a powerful id (with strong hostile impulses).

In sum, when personality is viewed as a system with differentiated structures and functions, the simple isomorphism between culture, behavior, and personality postulated by the internalization-of-culture model is frequently found wanting. As we have seen, a group which exhibits very little aggressive behavior may, nevertheless, be characterized by strong (probably unconscious) hostility; and a group which exhibits a great deal of aggressive behavior may nevertheless be characterized by cultural values which oppose aggression. (In the latter case, of course, the aggression will probably be expressed—displaced, projected, and the like—in socially acceptable forms). To take a classic case, the Hopi may be no less hostile than the Sioux, despite the fact that the latter exhibit much more social aggression, and that their cultural values concerning aggression are much different. Rather than reflecting differences in hostility, resulting from differences in culture, the differences in their aggressive behavior may instead reflect differences either in the social canalization of aggression, or in the relationships among the id, ego, and superego components of their respective personalities. Indeed, their strict avoidance of interpersonal aggression might suggest the hypothesis that Hopi hostility may be even stronger than that of the Sioux, but that, because of a stricter superego, they inhibit their dangerous hostile impulses.

This example suggests that although group differences in behavior say a great deal about differences in culture, in themselves they may say little about differences in personality, and even less about the cultural relativity of human nature. It also suggests that different models of personality do indeed make a difference for our understanding of human nature. The internalization-of-culture model, which assumes that personality differences are isomorphic with behavioral and cultural differences, leads to the cultural relativistic view of human nature. The model of a structurally and functionally differentiated personality, which makes no assumptions about social-culture-personality isomorphisms—and which therefore requires that personality be investigated independently of both behavior and culture—supports the view of a pan-cultural human nature.

REFERENCES CITED

The following entries pertain exclusively to the author's three research projects discussed in this chapter.

Ifaluk
    1953   *An Atoll Culture* (with E. G. Burrows). New Haven: Human Relations Area Files.

1950 A Psychotic Personality in the South Seas. *Psychiatry* 13:189–204.

1951 Some Ifaluk Myths and Folk Tales. *Journal of American Folklore* 64:280–303.

1952 Ghosts, Ifaluk and Teleological Functionalism. *American Anthropologist* 54: 497–503.

1953 Ghosts: An Anthropological Inquiry into Learning and Perception. *Journal of Abnormal and Social Psychology* 48:376–82.

1959 Cultural Heritage, Personal Tensions, and Mental Illness in a South Sea Culture. *Culture and Mental Health*, ed. M. K. Opler. New York: Macmillan.

1961 Sorcery, Evil Spirits, and Functional Analysis. *American Anthropologist* 63: 820–24.

Kibbutz

1956 *Kibbutz: Venture in Utopia.* Cambridge, Mass.: Harvard University Press. (New augmented edition, 1971, with a new chapter.)

1958 *Children of the Kibbutz.* Cambridge, Mass.: Harvard University Press. (New augmented edition, 1975, with a new chapter.)

1954 Is the Family Universal? *American Anthropologist* 56:839–46.

1955 Education in a Communal Village in Israel. *American Journal of Orthopsychiatry* 25:283–92.

1957 The Sabras and Zionism: A Study in Personality and Ideology. *Social Problems* 5:100–110.

Burma

1967 *Burmese Supernaturalism: A Study in the Explanation and Resolution of Suffering.* Englewood Cliffs, N.J.: Prentice-Hall.

1971 *Buddhism and Society: A Great Tradition and its Burmese Vicissitudes.* New York: Harper and Row.

1965 Religious Systems as Culturally Constituted Defense Mechanisms. *Context and Meaning in Cultural Anthropology,* ed. Melford Spiro. Glencoe: Free Press.

1966 Buddhism and Economic Saving in Burma. *American Anthropologist* 68: 1163–73.

1968 Religion, Personality, and Behavior in Burma. *American Anthropologist* 70:359–63.

1968 Politics and Factionalism in Upper Burma. *Local Level Politics,* ed. Marc Swartz. Chicago: Aldine.

1969 Religious Symbols and Social Behavior. *Proceedings of the American Philosophical Society* 113:341–50.

1969 The Psychological Functions of Witchcraft: The Burmese Case. *Mental Health in Asia and the Pacific,* ed. Caudill and Lin. Honolulu: East-West Center Press.

1972 Violence in Burmese History: A Psychocultural Interpretation. *Collective Violence,* ed. Short and Wolfgang. Chicago: Aldine.

1973 Social Change and Functional Analysis: A Study in Burmese Psychocultural History. *Ethos* 1:263–97.

1974 The Oedipus Complex in Burma. *Jr. Nerv. and Mental Disease* 157:389–95.

n.d.   Psychodynamic Explanations of Cultural Belief Systems: A Burmese Example. *Memorial Volume for Fritz Schmidl,* in press.

n.d.   Symbolism and Functionalism in the Anthropological Study of Religion. *Proceedings of the International Association for the History of Religion,* in press.

n.d.   The Psychodynamic Dimensions of Household Composition in Upper Burma, *International Jr. of Comp. Sociology,* in press.

n.d.   *Kinship and Marriage in Burma,* forthcoming.

The Author

PROFESSOR GEORGE DEVEREUX is Directeur d'Etudes (ethnopsychiatry), Ecole des Hautes Etudes en Sciences Sociales, Paris. He was born in 1908 in Lugos, Hungary. He studied mathematical physics at the Sorbonne from 1926 to 1927 with Mme. Curie and Jean

Cliche: Editions Flammarion, Paris

Perrin. He has diplomas from the Institut d'Ethnologie, University of Paris, 1931; the Ecole Nationale des Langues Orientales, Paris, 1931; a Licence es Lettres from the Sorbonne, 1932; and a Ph.D. in anthropology from the University of California, Berkeley, 1935. He is also a graduate psychoanalyst (Topeka Institute for Psychoanalysis, 1952) and a licensed psychologist (University of the State of New York, 1959). He is Docteur es Lettres et Sciences Humaines (University of Paris V:Rene Descartes) 1971. He has done some field work with the Hopi, has worked extensively with the Mohave Indians, very briefly with the Roro (Melanesians), and the Karuama of Papua very extensively and among the Sedang Moi of South Vietnam. He has done many years of clinical work and research at several psychiatric hospitals and was in private psychoanalytic practice in New York City during 1959–63. Before his present appointment at the Ecole des Hautes Etudes in Sciences Sociales, Paris, he had taught at the University of Wyoming, and Menninger School of Psychiatry at Topeka, Kansas, at Columbia University (chiefly in the School of General Studies) and at Temple University School of Medicine, Philadelphia. He has published eleven books and some 230 articles. His areas of special interest include the epistemology of the sciences of man; ethnopsychiatry, ethnopsychoanalysis, psychological anthropology, ethnology, and clinical psychoanalysis. In addition to the nonliterate communities in which he has worked, he also has devoted a number of books and studies to ancient Greek literature, mythology and history. He says of himself:

For reasons stated in the introductory section of the paper, I have been absorbed all my life in the problem of truth in human affairs . . . including its deliberate or unwitting (countertransference) distortion. Viewing culture and society as inductively reached constructs, I have rejected culturalism. This approach requires one to start from sense data, derived from individuals. I have, however, avoided both psychological and cultural (social) reductionism, by postulating that each human phenomenon calls for a psychological *and* a sociocultural explanation and that these two explanatory discourses stand in a complementarity relationship to each other; the two discourses can neither be mingled nor held simultaneously. This, I believe, is the real charter which guarantees the autonomy of both anthropology and psychology; it certainly guarantees it better than does culturalism or a purely biologically oriented "psychology." Apart from fundamental theoretical and methodological problems, I have been interested mainly in concrete facts and in their scientific exploitation. My general orientation was, for decades, outside the mainstream of anthropological thinking. The tide has turned only recently: several of my formerly remaindered books have been reprinted, volumes of my collected papers are appearing in rapid succession and my work is being translated into various languages. This suggests that though I have labored alone, I did not labor in vain.

This Chapter

Readers who are not acquainted with basic psychoanalytic concepts, or with the differences between classical psychoanalysis and neo-Freudian psychoanalysis may find certain particulars of Professor Devereux's summary and commentary on his own writing elusive. It is hoped that some of these unsolved puzzles will move the more curious of these readers to explore at least a part of Professor Devereux's writings directly and to go back to some of the relevant writings of Freud. Devereux is one of the very few who know the craft and content of anthropology as a professional, who have applied classical psychoanalytic concepts to the analysis of ethnically embedded phenomena (though he goes far beyond the initial formulations by Freud in this direction). His emphasis for instance, in *Reality and Dream* on the formation of ethnic personality during the Oedipal stage rather than in early training, and not by child rearing techniques as such but by "the mood of the parents while mediating such techniques" is a potent challenge to the emphasis on early childhood training and related environmental variables that characterizes much culture and personality work. The relational context is what teaches. It is constituted of the total environment of spatial, structural, and symbolic elements, as well as by the mediation of parents and surrogates.

For psychological anthropologists interested in educational anthropology his *Therapeutic Education* is essential reading. His concepts of ethnicization and re-ethnicization would be useful in the modern context of misalignments between ethnic groups and customary schools.

362

In *Mohave Ethnopsychiatry* Devereux pursues an emic, ethnoscientific approach to Mohave knowledge of psychological and psychosomatic disorders. But he applies etic categories of mental illness to interviews with Mohave informants in an attempt to relate these conceptions to modern psychiatric usage. His abiding interest in Mohave culture and psychology is carried further in his as yet uncollected essays on Mohave sexuality and childrearing.

Devereux's *From Anxiety to Method in the Behavioral Sciences* takes up the problem of the objective-subjective or humanistic-scientific interaction of the anthropologist with informants and the data produced by this interaction. It seems his approach has the potential of transforming a major handicap in field studies to a major source of data and insight. Readers will find this publication of direct relevance to a numberof chapters in this volume but particularly to John Honigmann's in his contrast between personalistic and objective research approaches, and to Weston La Barre's.

Professor Devereux's essays in general ethnopsychiatry are worthy of serious readings. They constitute the core of his theoretical position. This collection of essays is not yet available in English (it is in French, German, Spanish, and Italian). Nor is his *Ethnopsychoanalyse Complementariste* (1972), also containing his principle substantive theoretical essays separately published in English.

Ethnopsychoanalytic Studies of Greek Tragedy and Poetry and *Dreams in Greek Tragedy* represent some of Professor Devereux's recent work on ancient Greece, for which he acquired competence "from scratch" as he puts it, in the absence of opportunity to do more of the usual kind of anthropological field work. Though at first glance this material may seem less directly related to redefining psychological anthropology than much of his other work, this is not the case. Ultimately all ethnography becomes ancient history or historical-literary epic. Devereux has demonstrated that this material is accessible to ethnopsychiatric scrutiny, thus broadening the scope of psychologized anthropology.

The points made in "Perspectives for the Future" ending the Devereux chapter are of great significance for psychological anthropology. The problem of living with what appears to be sure knowledge (that may turn out to be false) and of tolerating what seems dubious (but that may turn out to be truth) is particularly difficult in the sciences of man, and particularly in that subdiscipline devoted to the interrelationships between person and milieux, where perceptions are important facts and often determine "reality." Devereux makes the point that distortion of fact is maximal in our work, but that the analysis of the process of distortion and the need to distort can produce very important data. The sciences of man will have to face up to the inside/outside, object/observer problem. Some readers will want to solve the problem by what Devereux calls "asceptic packaging." Others will accept the tactic Devereux advocates of stepping directly into the conflict as a participant-observer-analyst, at several levels of simultaneous discourse. Whatever the inclination, the thoughtful reader will acquire a new level of awareness of the problem and its consequences.

Professor Devereux's chapter is different from the others in this volume in that he summarizes and comments on a number of his major writings, one by one, rather than writing an integrated overview essay. It is apparent from the scope and character of his work that such an essay would be extremely difficult for anyone to write, and, besieged by graduate students, demands by publishers for translations and new writings, and faced by the necessity of continuing a full teaching and administrative schedule, he is hardly in a position to attempt it. Since many of Professor Devereux's most important publications are unknown to American students and professionals alike, this summary and commentary on major works is of great utility.

G.D.S.

11   *The Works of George Devereux*

GEORGE DEVEREUX

Nothing I have ever written confronted me with as many difficulties as the present account of my contribution to psychological anthropology.

In the first place, writing survey articles, especially in the field of the history of ideas, requires a kind of gift which I lack: even writing book reviews is difficult for me. Also, writing accounts of work already done is psychologically very different from doing concrete new work. My natural inclination is to write either meticulous analyses of concrete facts or else papers or books dealing with high level theoretical and methodological problems.

My difficulties are further increased by a kind of reluctance (which the French call "pudeur" and the Greeks called "sophrosyne") to speak of my own work, especially at the present time, for in the course of the last five years the appraisal of my work has changed radically. This requires me to revise my self-image and to view my work as being *now* within the mainstream of scientific endeavor.

A more concrete difficulty is created by the quantity of my publications: eleven books and some 230 papers. Some of them are clearly not relevant in the present context. However, a number of primarily clinical papers, or papers in the field of psychiatric-psychoanalytic theory, are likely to be eventually used in research on psychological anthropological problems. It is hard to decide which of them should *not* be mentioned here.

In order not to make this paper unduly long I have limited myself almost entirely to discussions of my books (three consist of collected articles) and have mentioned many other papers not included in these volumes only in passing. Almost the only exception to this rule is my series of papers on the Mohave—papers which are actually chapters of a book on Mohave sexuality and child rearing, for which I still hope to find a publisher some day.

A few words may be said of how I came to anthropology. I was born in a trilingual, tricultural small Hungarian town, which was given to Rumania after World War I when I was a little over ten years old. I therefore learned to cope with a multicultural situation, especially because I discovered very soon that even seemingly factual statements were unreliable. At age ten, I learned in the Hungarian high school that, in a certain battle, the Hungarians had defeated the Rumanians. Next year, in the Rumanian high school, I was taught the opposite.

I also encountered emotional hypocrisy quite early. In the first year of the Hungarian high school my Rumanian classmates had to write essays inspired by Hungarian patriotism; next year, in the Rumanian high school I had to write patriotic Rumanian essays. Things were not much better in other sectors of my childhood and adolescent experience. I therefore looked for affective sincerity in great music—and found it there.

As to objective truth, I hoped to find it in the study of mathematical physics at the Sorbonne. Unfortunately, in 1926–27, parts of the theory of radiation were still based on Newton's particles theory; others presupposed Fresnel's wave theory. As a result, I abandoned physics— prematurely, as it turned out, for the very next year the works of Heisenberg and de Broglie resolved these contradictions. It is therefore not fortuitous that Heisenberg's indeterminacy relationship (and Bohr's complementarism), as well as Bertrand Russell's theory of the Epimenides-type paradoxes, should, to this day, play so great a role in theoretical thinking.

Subsequently I learned anthropology, primarily from Marcel Mauss but also from Paul Rivet and L. Lévy-Bruhl (whose work seems to me to merit infinitely more attention than it receives today). The *craft* of anthropology I learned from Kroeber and Lowie.

When, in 1935, I returned to Berkeley from field work with the Hopi and Mohave, the Roro and Karuama of Papua and the Sedang of South Vietnam, I realized that the interpretation of much of my material required a psychological competence which I did not possess. Having (to my misfortune) read in Indochina one of Róheim's books which my ignorance of psychoanalysis did not enable me to understand, I remained an anti-Freudian until, in 1938, my Mohave informant taught me psychoanalysis, as Freud's patients had taught it to him (see the section on the Mohave). This explains why, until 1938, I read practically only non-Freudian psychological and psychiatric works. I completed my training as an analyst in 1952.

From 1939 to 1940 I studied sociology with Sorokin at Harvard and, simultaneously, did research at Worcester State Hospital, thus also acquiring basic clinical experience.

Between 1939 and 1963 I earned a living chiefly because I knew psychiatry and/or sociology; only occasionally was I given a chance to give a course on "real" anthropology. Before the war I held minor teaching jobs in sociology; after the war I held research and teaching jobs in psychiatry and ethnopsychiatry. Between 1959 and 1963 I was also engaged in the private practice of psychoanalysis.

In 1963 I decided I had no future in anthropology in the United States and therefore accepted a professorship in ethnopsychiatry in France, where I have been living. In the same year I also took another drastic step: having received no grants for field work during the preceding twenty-five years and having not even had a chance, since 1953, of doing clinical work with an American Indian patient (as a substitute for field work), I acquired (from scratch) a competence in Greek philology: the study of ancient Greece served as a stimulating substitute for field work with a new ethnic group.

Fortunately for me, the hellenists—and especially the British hellenists—gave a favorable reception to my studies on Greece, to which I have devoted much of my time ever since. Of course, as Margaret Mead pointed out in summing up the panel on "Psychoanalysis and Anthropology" (American Anthropological Association Meeting, 1974), I continued doing with Greek material exactly what I had been doing all along with traditionally anthropological material.

I prefer—understandably—not to speak further of my nearly forty years in outer limbo, now that the tide has turned and my work is receiving the attention which, as many now concede, it should have received long ago. Others than I (Besancon 1971; Weidman and Witt-kower 1973; Wulff 1974) have recently pointed out I anticipated by decades certain basic interpretations and theories which others formulated only much later. I am able to account neither for the long indifference to my work, nor for its sudden recognition since 1970. But this is something that matters only to myself; it seems unnecessary to discuss it further at this time.

This brief introduction indicates how difficult it is to summarize my contributions to psychological anthropology, especially as many of my relevant contributions are to be found in primarily sociological, psychiatric, psychoanalytical, and philological publications.

REALITY AND DREAM

Reality and Dream: The Psychotherapy of a Plains Indian (1951a, 2nd augmented edition; 1969a, French edition in press) is probably still the only published verbatim account of any psychotherapy; it also lays the theoretical foundations of the technique of cross-cultural (intercultural) psychotherapy, and instances it.

Four preliminary chapters discuss the problem of disguising the patient's identity, environment, life history, and hospitalization. Part I is devoted to theory and technique. Chapter 1 evolves the concepts of areal culture pattern and areal ethnic personality. Briefly stated, in times of sociocultural decay, Crow Indian culture, like Crow ethnic personality, reflects the generic Plains ethos and personality more than specifically Crow ethos and personality. Hence, the patient identity could be disguised by calling him a member of the imaginary Wolf Plains tribe. Throughout this chapter culture is treated as a construct. The formation of the ethnic personality is determined not by child rearing techniques but by the mood of the parents while mediating to him, through such techniques, the culture of his tribe. The role of adult experiences in the formation of the areal ethos is strongly emphasized, since ethnic personality manifests itself mainly in interpersonal relationships; it is shaped *not* during the pregenital stages (the age of partial object) but during the Oedipal stage, which (though still "pregenital") is the age of tridimensional complete objects. This highly condensed account of ethnic personality formation is compatible with the classical psychoanalytic outlook and, therefore, incompatible with Kardinerian and other neo-Freudian theories of ethnic personality formation. This chapter also confirms Kroeber's view that the culture area concept is primarily a means of cultural synthesis and not of cultural analysis.

Chapter 2 discusses the values of the Plains Indians life style and its role in the present day self-image of the Plains Indian.

Chapter 3: Working Hypotheses:

  I. Psychic instances:
    1. The Wolf superego is patchy and nonpervasive.
    2. The Wolf ego cathects the body ego; this determines a tendency toward somatization and toward a strong libidinization of the musculo-skeletal system. The relative ranking of defense mechanisms is determined by cultural factors.
  II. Psychosexual development:
    1. The oral stage, being gratifying, accounts for dependency cravings and improvidence.
    2. Anal expulsiveness is not much inhibited; social pressure encourages generosity and inhibits anal retentiveness.
    3. The phallic-urethral stage underlies traditional competitiveness and boasting.
    4. The Oedipal stage is characterized by an early dispersion of positive and negative cathexes.
    5. The latency period is absent.
    6. At the genital stage excessive object cathexes are lacking; jealousy is motivated primarily by social prestige requirements.
  III. Dependency and aggression:
    1. Dependency cravings, expected to be conspicuous, justified the use of expressive-supportive therapy.
    2. Aggression was expected to be hard to manage. Self-destructive aggressions had to be controlled, legitimate aggression encouraged.

Chapter 4: symptoms were numerous and included many categories, from organic symptoms to management problems.

Chapter 5: transference and kinship behavior. The therapy confirmed the expectation that types of transference would be patterned on the model of kinship relations obtained in Wolf society. Professor Erich Wulff, M.D. (1974), recently wrote that my relevant findings were confirmed independently, though much later, both by Parin and Morgenthaler and by himself.

Chapter 6 repudiates the pseudo-Freudian "atom bomb" conception of the unconscious and revives Freud's original view that only repression makes the instincts monstrous.

Chapter 7 concerns dreams and their managements. Since Wolf society greatly values dreaming and since the patient dreamed a great deal, the "interpretation" of the *manifest* content of dreams was used as an ultimately self-abolishing cultural-therapeutic lever. The patient's dream behavior was discussed with him as though it were *real* behavior. This made many characterological interpretations possible and high-lighted transference problems. The reality testing and conflict solving— i.e., autodidactic—functions of the dream could also be exploited.

Chapter 8: since more than twenty-five years ago, when this therapy was carried out, a Plains Indian with little education had no chance to function as a middle-class white. Even if the therapy could have turned him into one, the objective of the therapy was the successful and gratifying reintegration of the patient into the Wolf community.

Part II contains the verbatim account of thirty therapeutic sessions and summarizes some post-treatment conversations. An additional chapter contains a minute survey of developments in the course of the treatment which was successful and produced lasting results.

Part III, written by Professor R. R. Holt, reproduces in full the batteries of tests given to the patient both at the beginning of therapy and at its end.

Part IV, written by the author, contains accounts of the modified body image projection test and finger painting tests, which the author administered to the patient in the course of the therapy.

The late William Caudill, in his review (Caudill 1951) correctly pointed out that my countertransference was not discussed in this work. This remark induced me to put the finishing touches to my work on countertransference (1967*a*).

ABORTION

A Study of Abortion in Primitive Societies (1955*a*, 2nd augmented edition 1976) contains a theoretical-methodological chapter which was reprinted in a volume of my theoretical essays (1972*a*) and will be discussed in connection with that book.

Data on abortions—many of them exceedingly brief and sketchy— from some four hundred tribes are reproduced in the terminal ("source book") section of this work. Some sixty traits related to the abortion complex as a whole are tabulated tribe by tribe.

The methodological problem this book seeks to clarify is whether *sketchy* data on a given topic from a *large number* of tribes can enable one to analyze the abortion problem as a whole *in depth*. My point of departure was the mathematician's ergodic hypothesis: the same results can be obtained by simultaneously tossing a very large number of identical coins and by successively tossing the same coin a very large number of times. Thus, methodologically, this book provides a model for the in depth exploitation of sketchy data concerning a given item derived from a large number of groups—or persons.

The focus of my concrete inquiry was the range—the variety—of items (motives, attitudes, techniques, etc.) related to abortion in a large number of tribes. In this connection I showed that even sketchy data on abortion from a great variety of groups permit one to understand the "abortion complex" *in depth* and that psychologically inferred meanings and predictions that a certain practice must exist somewhere can be substantiated by further research. One inferred meaning and one predicted practice could be confirmed only after the book had already gone to press; the relevant confirmatory data were inserted into the galleys. The inference was that the illegitimate child is often fantasied as the result of incest. The predicted practice was that a taboo, whose violation causes *miscarriage,* may be *deliberately* violated to procure an *abortion,* in at least one ethnic group.

The second edition (1975*a*) contains a new chapter in which three insights (which I already had in 1955 but could not substantiate at that time for lack of data) are presented with supporting material. One finding is that some women do not abort because they are pregnant, but become pregnant so as to be able to abort. This appears to represent a denial of the fantasy that women are "born castrated." Another idea was inspired by the fact that infanticide usually occurs before the onset of nursing, i.e., at a time when the infant *ceases* to be invested with narcissistic libido but is not yet invested with object libido. At *that* moment the child is not the object of any kind of libidinal investment; this makes infanticide tolerable. The critical transition from narcissistic to object libidinal investment appears to occur at times already during pregnancy; this makes abortion psychologically tolerable at that time. The third finding is that the interruption of *any* ongoing natural process is traumatic. Persons who had to obey orders at once in their childhood, thus interrupting not yet completed action-sequences, tend to have few *authentic* childhood memories. The latter findings are incompatible with the Kinsey group's (Gebhard 1958) subsequent assertion that abortion does not traumatize the woman.

The only ethical aspect of abortion is the obligation to create the kind of world in which the abortion of a presumably normal and viable baby cannot, in any humane frame of reference, be viewed even as the lesser of two evils.

THERAPEUTIC EDUCATION

Therapeutic Education 1956*a*) is not primarily a contribution to psychological anthropology. Rather it tends to apply psychoanthropological insights to the problem of the efficient therapeutic education of defective or disturbed children and adolescents; it discusses reciprocal education in the peer group.

Relevant for psychological anthropology are attempts to differentiate between therapy and education, discussions of wrong methods of ethnicization and re-ethnicization (or of enculturation and re-enculturation), an analysis of the differences between discipline and punishment.

Of special importance is a new theory of the formation of the superego. I define it as the residue of all experiences which the child was unable to master *through its own resources* (means) at the time these experiences occurred.

A chapter entitled "The Wrong Patient" formulates the concept of the "deputy lunatic": quite often the child expresses the illness of its symptom-free milieu. This view anticipates the little that makes sense in so-called anti-psychiatry, which achieved great notoriety by wrapping one sound insight into pretentious rhetoric.

Therapeutic Education is the only one of my first five books not to have been reprinted as yet. I am confident this book, too, will eventually obtain recognition, for there is much in it that I believe to be new even twenty years after its original publication.

MOHAVE ETHNOPSYCHIATRY

Mohave Ethnopsychiatry (1961, 2nd augmented edition 1969) differs radically from all other studies of psychological illness in tribal societies known to me in that it is primarily a study of the Mohave's *knowledge* of psychological and psychosomatic disorders. It could actually serve as a textbook from which budding Mohave shamans, preparing to specialize in psychiatry, could learn their craft.

An introductory section provides a brief sketch of Mohave culture. Part I discusses the fundamentals of Mohave psychiatry and the status of the psychologically disturbed. Part VIII analyzes the genesis and validity of Mohave psychiatry. An appendix is devoted to the problem of alcoholism.

Parts II–IV and VI–VII describe and discuss, one by one, various named Mohave psychiatric psychosomatic disease entities. Each section presents first the data and case histories provided by the informants and ends with an ethnological and psychoanalytic scrutiny of the data. The reader is never in doubt as to whether a given passage contains Mohave data or the author's interpretations.

Part V differs from the others in that it contains information provided in response to queries formulated by the investigator in terms of modern psychiatric knowledge. The absence of schizophrenia is noted, as is the incapacity of even the best Mohave informants to recognize descriptions of obsessive-compulsive neurosis, which is almost unknown in tribal cultures.

It is to be observed that the Mohave do not group various named categories of disorders. This grouping, which was indispensable for the proper organization of the book, was therefore effected by the author in terms of broad modern nosological categories, such as: disorders of the instincts, mood disturbances, etc.

The 140 cases cited range from a few lines (concerning, as a rule, dead and only dimly remembered persons) to detailed case histories, some of which include long interviews reproduced verbatim.

A book containing nearly half a million words cannot be summarized in a few lines. I can highlight here only three points. (1) A variety of disorders and even one ritual are held by the Mohave to constitute forms of suicide. This is striking, for Mohave culture is not a tough or morose one. The tendency of suicides to occur in clusters is of special interest. (2) Mohave psychiatric ideas often have striking affinities with the psychoanalytic outlook. (3) These affinities are so obvious that during my 1938–39 field trip, in the course of which many of the data used in this book were collected, I ceased to be anti-Freudian (see the introduction to this paper).

I stress in particular that the nature and the organization of my data are basically ethnological. The real subject matter of this book is ethnoscience, which my psychiatric psychoanalytic competence simply helped me to reproduce and to interpret meaningfully, exactly the way a knowledge of botany helps an anthropologist write a competent account of the ethnobotany of a given tribe.

I note, as an afterthought, that I have collected similar data amongst the Sedang Moi, but have not published them because no one expressed interest in publishing it. Yet such a book would be a valuable pendant to my *Mohave Ethnopsychiatry*, because Sedang Moi ethnopsychiatry (viewed as an ethnoscience) differs radically from Mohave ethnopsychiatry. The Mohave are psychologically perceptive; the Sedang are not. Sedang informants show no interest even in the psychological motivation of suicides: psychological disorder and / or psychosomatic distress are, in Sedang culture, linked with economics, law and super-naturalism, rather than with psychology, human motivation and suffer-ing. Their ethnopsychiatric "science" is therefore very rudimentary. Thus, the Mohave have some two dozen named psychiatric disease entities whereas the Sedang have only two: *kok* ("neurotic, queer") and *rajok* ("insane"). The Mohave therapy of psychological distress is psy-chologically oriented; Sedang "psycho"-therapy is purely ritual and legalistic. Also, were the Mohave seek to clarify, e.g., the suicide's motivation, the Sedang seek to determine chiefly who could be *fined* for having caused it.

Whether support for the writing and publication of Sedang ethno-psychiatry will ever materialize remains to be seen, though the value of such a book would, I feel, be considerable.

ANXIETY TO METHOD IN THE BEHAVIORAL SCIENCES

From Anxiety to Method in the Behavioral Sciences (1967) is, in a very real sense, my first book. Some of the questions it asks go back to my adolescence; at least one of its key theories (chapter 22) was formu-lated in 1931. Most of the book was drafted in Indochina (1933–35). These facts disprove a remark in Price-Williams' review (1968), that some views expressed in it are not exactly new. I note he gives *no* example of such allegedly "no longer new" views. I hold that this book is radically innovative even today, though it had to wait about forty years for a publisher to take a chance on it.

The account I give of this book consists entirely of excerpts from its "Argument," to which I have nothing to add.

Countertransference is the most crucial datum of all behavioral science, because the information derived from transference can usually also be obtained by other means, whereas that provided by the analysis of countertransference cannot.

The scientific study of man is: (1) impeded by the anxiety arousing overlap between subject and observer, (2) which requires an analysis of the nature and locus of the partition between the two; (3) must compen-sate for the *partialness* of communication between subject and observer on the *conscious* level, but (4) must avoid the temptation to compensate for the *completeness* of communication between subject and observer on the *unconscious* level, (5) which arouses anxiety and therefore also coun-tertransference reactions, (6) distorting the perception and interpreta-tion of the data, and (7) producing countertransference resistances mas-querading as methodology, which cause further *sui generis* distortions.

(8) Since the existence of the observer, his observational activities and his anxieties (even in self-observation) produce distortions which it is not only technically but also logically impossible to eliminate, (9) any effective behavioral science methodology must treat these disturbances as the most significant and characteristic data of behavioral science research, and (10) must use the subjectivity inherent in all observation as the royal road to an authentic, rather than fictitious, objectivity, (11) which must be defined in terms of what is really possible rather than in terms of what "should be." (12) When ignored, or warded off by means of countertransference resistances masquerading as methodology, these "disturbances" become sources of uncontrolled and uncontrollable error, although (13) when treated as basic and characteristic data of behavioral science they are more valid and more productive of insight than any other type of datum.

In short, behavioral science data arouse anxieties which are warded off by a countertransference inspired pseudo-methodology; this maneuver is responsible for nearly all the defects of behavioral science.

The best—and perhaps the only—way of attaining a simplicity congruent with the facts is to frontally attack the greatest complexities by means of the extremely practical device of treating the difficulty *per se* as a fundamental datum, not to be evaded, but to be exploited to the utmost—not to be explained, but to be used as an explanation of *seemingly* simpler data.

Each of these filters, while "correcting" some distortions due to subjectivity, produces specific—and usually unrecognized—distortions of its own. Even the invisible observer must ultimately say: "And this I perceive." He must, moreover, at some point say also: "This means that. . . ." This is technically a "decision" and it is a fundamental fact that the "theory of games" cannot yield decisions; it can only define consequences and appraise their probability. The decision—which in science consists in saying: "This means that . . ."—is still made by the behavioral scientist in terms of the same subjectivity and in response to the same anxieties which confront him when he uses no filters of any kind. I therefore do not advocate the elimination of filters; I urge only the elimination of the illusion that they abolish all subjectivity and entirely neutralize anxiety. They do neither; they only slightly *displace* the locus of the partition between subject and observer and *postpone* the exact moment at which the subjective element (decision) intervenes. The scientist should cease to exclusively emphasize his manipulation of the subject and should seek to understand concurrently—and sometimes primarily—himself *qua* observer. The subject most capable of manifesting scientifically exploitable behavior is the observer himself.

Not the study of the subject, but that of the observer gives us access to the *essense* of the observational *situation*.

The data of behavioral science are, thus, threefold: (1) the behavior of the subject; (2) the "disturbances" produced by the existence and observational activities of the observer; (3) the behavior of the observer: his anxieties, his defensive maneuvers, his research strategies, his "decisions" (all equaling his attribution of a meaning to his observations).

The last chapters of this book show how to use as bridges precisely those situations which are usually treated as barriers. Behavioral science will become simple when it begins to treat the behavioral scientist's own reactions to his material and to his work as the most basic of all behavioral science data. Until then, we will only have the illusion of simplicity.

I note, in conclusion, that had this book been understood—and published—in the 1930s, my career may have been very different. The fact that it was *not* published *then* attests its originally pioneering character. The fact that it is *still* innovating is proven by La Barre's *Preface,* by Spiro's review (1969) and also by the interest it has elicited, particularly in Germany: it was a German Scientific Book Club selection and is now in its second edition in Germany as an Ullstein Pocketbook. (French, German, Spanish and Italian translations are about to go to press.)

ESSAYS IN ETHNOPSYCHIATRY

Essais d'Ethnopsychiatrie Générale (1970*a*), presents my basic theory of ethnopsychiatry in a volume containing sixteen papers sublished between 1939 and 1966. In a sense, this volume contains the theoretical part of a treatise of ethnopsychiatry in several volumes, planned since 1935, which I could never write because of lack of adequate grants. German and Spanish editions are available; English and Italian editions are in press and the third French edition (1977) has been published.

Chapter 1, "Normal and Abnormal," sharply distinguishes between normality or sanity which are psychiatric concepts and adjustment or adaptation which are sociological concepts. In a pathological society the normal can be badly maladjusted and the abnormal well adjusted. The concept of normality used is that of Freud, completed by the criterion of adequate sublimations and the capacity for continuous creative readjustment without losing the sense of continuity of self (non-opportunism).

The unconscious segment of the ethnic personality contains what each culture forces its members to repress; the idiosyncratic unconscious contains that which nonroutine subjective experiences force a person to repress. A trauma occurs when an individual is not provided with resources enabling him to cope with the situation or is denied access to culturally provided defenses. As elsewhere (1951a), I hold that the ethnic character is a product of parental psychological attitudes and not of child rearing techniques. Four types of ethnopsychiatric personality disorders are enumerated: (1) type disorders related to social structure (see chapter 10); (2) ethnic disorders related to the group's culture pattern; (3) sacred disorders of the shamanistic type; and (4) idiosyncratic disorders.

The view that the adjustment of the shaman proves his sanity is refuted in detail; this unacceptable theory is due to a failure to distinguish between mere (erroneous) beliefs and pathological experiences (e.g., trances, visions) instancing such beliefs.

Ethnic disorders tend to be highly patterned culturally and possess considerable cultural mass, but are none the less Lintonian "patterns of misconduct." This Lintonian model also underlines simulation. It is important to note that ethnic disorders always impair the ethnic personality. There often exist highly specific procedures for triggering at will seizures of ethnic disorders.

Type disorders are, as noted, products of flaws inherent to the social structure; more will be said of this in chapter 10.

In idiosyncratic disorders the underlying conflict is culturally atypical and culture provides no defenses against it, nor patterns of misconduct for socializing it.

Chapter 2: all behavior results from a structured selection of certain patterns for implementation, and a structured rejection of patterns *not* to be implemented. All behavior can be analyzed in terms of four frames of reference: biological, experiential, cultural and neurotic.

My approach also permits a fivefold classification of disorders in terms of the way in which one handles cultural materials.

1. Normality: cultural materials known to be exogenous are used and experienced in an up-to-date manner; they are internalized though their external origin is recognized.

2. Immaturity: the external origin of culture is recognized but the material constituting it is appraised and handled in a historically and/or chronologically obsolete manner (king = boss = father).

3. Neurosis: cultural material is recognized as exogenous but its meaning is transposed from the level of psychosexual maturation to which it belongs to an inappropriate stage of maturation (e.g., a neurotic woman apprehended coitus as a nursing situation, see chapter 15).

4. Psychosis: cultural material is no longer recognized as being of external origin and the meanings assigned to it are subjective and psychotic (e.g., toilet = throne).

5. Psychopathy: the psychopath is aware of the external nature of culture. He has no loyalties to it, though he specializes in the exploitation of the cultural loyalties *of others* for personal ends.

Chapter 3 concerns "social negativism." In order to be able to alleviate tensions, a symptom must be at variance with cultural requirements. All symptoms are pseudo-individual solutions of meta-individual problems. Social negativism is a key concept of my theoretical outlook. (Written in 1940, before counter-cultures came into being, this chapter seems almost prophetic.)

Chapter 4: "The Voices of Children" takes things up at the point where Ferenczi left off in his "Confusion of Tongues" between adults and children, which the ultra-orthodox consider controversial. On the one hand it deals with meta-language and, on the other hand, with divergences between what the child means and what the adult thinks the child means. Special attention is paid to conscious and unconscious refusals to understand. A crucial distinction is made between: (1) the *childlike* child—a complete specimen of a young organism within the framework of psychobiological norms, but an incomplete specimen of the adult in terms of sociocultural norms, and (2) the *puerile* child—an incomplete and distorted young organism within the framework of psychobiological norms, but a complete specimen of the child in sociocultural terms. This distinction was already made in (1956*a*). Much so-called child psychology is a vicious circle: society trains the *puerile* child and then considers it a specimen of the "natural" childlike child.

I add as an afterthought that authentic psychoanalysis must reject equally paleopsychology and Eibl-Eibesfeld's notion of the "preprogrammed man," on the one hand, and the excessive psychologism of the advocates of man's infinite conditionability.

Chapter 5 shows that Kleinian (spurious) cannibalistic wishes imputed to the infant are actually projections, upon the child, of *genuine* adult teknophagic impulses.

Chapter 6 provides a clinical basis for the view enunciated elsewhere (1953*b*), that the Oedipus complex is not innate but is a reaction to the parent's Laïus and Jocasta complexes. It also clinically substantiates the views expressed in the same study that the outgrowing of the Oedipus complex implies an at least fantasied retaliatory homosexual triumph over the father, since both the myth and the complex of Laïus have aggressive homosexual components.

Chapter 7 distinguishes between neurotic crime and criminal behavior. It postulates the psychopathic criminal is not "instinct ridden" but "superego ridden." This paper reinforces Freud's conceptions that neurosis, perversion and criminality are inherently different phenomena.

Chapter 8 shows the sexual delinquency of young girls in a puritanical society is wrongly conceived. The behavior of such girls is not sexual but anti-sexual (masochistic-regressive). They are feminine neither sociologically nor psychologically. These girls are not even juvenile but puerile (see chapter 4). The adults' obsessive rejection of adolescent sexuality literally teaches these girls the most efficient way of aggravating adults. In short, the young female sexual delinquent is a caricature of the puritan; she can be cured not by reinforcing her hatred of sexuality (masochism), but by teaching her to love; only this is conducive to self-respect.

Chapter 9 proposes *one possible* sociological theory of schizophrenia. One cause of schizophrenia is disorientation in a type of society which (1) contains far too many traits to permit an over-all view of it, and (2) is structured on many different layers of abstraction, making orientation by extrapolation (which is the schizophrenic's preferred method of reasoning) otiose. I have shown elsewhere (1959) that the bizarreness of schizophrenic thinking is logically rooted in paradoxical shifts from one level of abstraction to the other.

Chapter 10 views schizophrenia as the ethnic psychosis of occidental cultures and shows that such cultures systematically inculcate the schizoid model. They encourage aloofness and hyporeactivity, lack of affect in sexual life, partial or fractional involvements, dereism, the obliteration of the frontier between the real and the imaginery, infantilism, fixation and regression (including "momism"), and depersonalization.

Hence, it is difficult to cure a schizophrenic living in a schizoid society. I also criticize the *logic* underlying current attempts to find an organic basis for schizophrenia. If such research is done at all it should seek to determine what proportion of persons with an organic defect are (in addition) *also* schizophrenic. It is noted that, owing to acculturation, schizophrenia is rapidly spreading to so-called under-developed countries where it previously did not exist.

Chapter 11 is a study of neurotic fatigue. Wild animals cannot stand the hard and sustained work which domestic animals can furnish as a result of selection. Ancient mine slaves were almost the first men who had to work hard and continuously. Excessive fatigue (e.g., frantic ritual dancing) produces a kind of drunkenness owing, perhaps, to biochemical self-intoxication. Also, for some neurotics orgasm is chiefly a hypnotic—the coital pleasure simply a secondary gain. By analogy, dreaming may well be a means of obtaining a restful sleep. I therefore divide hypnotics in two classes: those which help to dream so that one can sleep, and those which make one sleep so that one can dream.

In some cases seemingly neurotic fatigue has an anticipatory character. It anticipates the fatigue one would experience had one actually performed the work one is expected to do. I explicitly recognize that this theory of neurotic fatigue accounts only for a few aspects of the phenomenon in question.

Chapter 12 discusses masochistic blackmail on the cultural level. Some groups destroy their property, so as to "force" the arrival of "Cargos." Some neurotic adults remain helplessly dependent on their parents so as to force them to be immortal, never withdrawing their supports.

Chapter 13 is a general theory of the diagnostic process. The key notion is that diagnosis implies not a *negative* finding (X is not normal) but a *positive* one (X is yes-ill or yes-crazy). The diagnostic process includes several steps: (1) a singularity is present in me (in you); (2) this something concerns the healer; (3) this something concerns the psychological healer. This last admission is very threatening to the self because it recognizes that the very core of one's self is flawed.

Psychological disorder is often believed to be contagious: his didactic psychoanalysis is supposed to enable the analyst not only to plunge into the depths of the unconscious, but also to re-emerge from it intact. A common defense against the thought that one is psychologically disturbed consists of an attempt to represent the disturbance as peripheral to the self ("I was bewitched" or "It is something I ate"). Some psychological symptoms have as their real purpose the signaling that one is "crazy" rather than, e.g., "criminal." In short, any diagnosis is formulated in terms of the conformity between a "singularity of behavior" and a marginal model, never in terms of a deviation from the norm. Hence, neither statistical methods nor the point of view of cultural relativism can solve the problem of normality and abnormality.

Chapter 14: belief in pathogenic dreams is common in many societies. The ethnopsychiatrist may call a dream "pathogenic" only if the dreamer's culture specifies the *nature* of the bond between dream and illness and considers this bond to be a *causal* one. When this is not so, one may speak only of prophetic, symptomatic, pathognomonic, autoscopic, etc. dreams. A clarification of this important specification is made very difficult by the lack of systematic accounts of primitive dream theories.

Chapter 15: cultural factors play a role even in psychoanalytic therapy. Culture and the human psyche are coemergents. Both are species-characteristics of man. Most personality disorders involve some de-differentiation and de-individualization, i.e., an impoverishment of the personality. Abnormal behavior, which is hard to understand in sociocultural terms, is easy to comprehend in psychiatric terms.

One must differentiate between three types of psychotherapy: (1) intracultural psychotherapy (patient and therapist share the same culture; (2) cross-cultural or intercultural psychotherapy (patient and therapist belong to different cultures but the therapist is familiar with his patient's culture); and (3) metacultural or extranscultural psychotherapy (patient and therapist belong to different cultures; the therapist is unfamiliar with his patient's culture but understands the nature of culture per se.[1]

The therapist must be both affectively and culturally neutral; he must not allow his interest in his patient's culture to make him lose sight of his therapeutic objectives. Otherwise the patient will "feed him" anthropological "tidbits" which play the role of "red herring resistances" (cf. Freud's Egyptologist patient). The rule that one must first interpret that which is closest to consciousness may not be violated, but one must bear in mind that the patient's culture may determine which of the several meanings of his conduct is actually nearest consciousness in *his* case.

A special difficulty arises in metacultural psychotherapy. Exploiting the therapist's ignorance of his culture, the patient may distort the real meaning of those cultural traits he mentions in his treatment. With acculturated patients it is sometimes difficult to determine whether a given item should be interpreted in aboriginal or in modern cultural terms. Valid clues are sometimes furnished by the manner in which cultural material is handled in psychiatric illness (chapter 2).

Chapter 16 investigates psychoanalysis as an anthropological field technique. It is particularly suitable for determining the variety of matrices to which a cultural item belongs and also which of these matrices is the primary or secondary one. Of special interest are over-emphasized items, elaborated out of all proportion with their real importance: the Mohave homosexuality complex is as highly elaborated as the warfare complex. Many items not really belonging to a given trait-complex are often brought into a relationship of forced compendence with it. Cases where a given item belongs to mutually contradictory matrices are also interesting (see section on the Mohave papers). Every

---

1. Originally I called this therapy "transcultural psychiatry" (1951a), taking psychi-*atry* to mean psycho*therapy*. Those who did not grasp this point illegitimately applied this term to the field of ethnopsychiatry as a whole. I therefore no longer use it.

highly cathected pattern or belief has (in the *same* culture) also a less elaborated (and/or latent) contrary manifestation ("man's best friend" —"dirty dog"). Some of these negatively appreciated items can give rise to important sublimation (1976*b*, chapter 1). At other times one of two divergent accounts of a given trait may reflect its conscious meaning and the other its unconscious meaning. Newly acquired cultural items may be inserted into traditional matrices (1972, chapter 8). Conversely, Mead notes that some traditional Manus items were detached from their original matrix and integrated with some matrix of their post-war culture.

Culture can be defined both as an internal experience and as a manner of experiencing. Culture is a manner of apprehending both the individual components and the general configuration of man's world and of his vital space (contrast "this girl has sex appeal" with "this girl is my daughter"). Culture also determines whether man is viewed as inherently good or bad. The intrusion of cultural biases can even stultify science, impeding its development (1972, chapter 10).

In short, the total comprehension of a cultural item implies not only an awareness of the variety of matrices to which it can belong but also the interplay between these matrices. One must also take into account that the selfsame item can belong to a variety of matrices in different cultures. Even the systematic affirmation of a belief necessarily implies the negation of the opposite belief and this negation is as much a part of a culture as is the affirmation. As Hadas remarked, in a monotheistic society the atheist *does not* believe in *one* god.

Psychoanalysis is the only psychology which claims to be exclusively a human psychology. Ethnology, too, studies a uniquely human phenomenon. A collaboration between the two is the last bastion of the notion that man is an end in himself.

ETHNOPSYCHANALYSE COMPLÉMENTARISTE

Ethnopsychanalyse Complémentariste (1972) contains my principal substantive theoretical essays written between 1940 and 1972. The introductory *Argument* is almost impossible to summarize. It rejects interdisciplinarity and advocates pluridisciplinarity, postulating the total interdependence of the sociological and the psychological *datum* and the total independence and inherent completeness of both psychological and sociological *explanations*. This principle is the real charter of the autonomy of the social sciences and makes all sociological or psychological reductionism impossible.

The observed is always the individual; the observed group is a construct of the mind. The separation between psychological and sociological discourse can be effected in two ways. (1) The criterion of yield: when the law of diminishing returns begins to operate in the sociological explanation one must switch to a psychological explanation—and vice versa. (2) The observer as a source of constraint. In sociology the observer is, by definition, "outside;" in psychology he is, by definition, "inside."

In each case the awareness of being observed constrains behavior. A distinction is made, in passing, between society and small groups. In society the influence anyone can exert needs the support of a social status; in a small group it does not. Crucially important is Bohr's *Abtötungsprinzip:* an overly precise study or even explanation of the subject destroys that which is observed (Bohr 1937). This, too, reflects the principle of complementarity. Generally speaking, any phenomenon requires a complete explanation both psychologically and sociologically, but the two discourses may neither be mingled nor held simultaneously.

On a practical level, what in psychological explanation is an operant motive is an instrumental motive in sociological explanation, and vice versa.

There also exists a complementary relationship between Lévy-Strauss' technique of discovering structural invariants and the psychoanalytic explanation which discovers the invariants of affective content in various myths (1955*a*, 2nd edition; 1975*a*, chapter 8).

What has been called the "excessive power" of Chomsky's transformational grammar can be avoided by realizing that any human activity implies, on the one hand, a *structured* preselection of the number of structures to be submitted to transformations and a structured prerejection of structures characteristic only of the species as a whole. The structures governing selection and those governing rejection may well stand in a complementarity relationship to each other. Returning to the *Abtötungsprinzip,* the excessive sociological explanation of a phenomenon causes the disappearance of the very object of sociological discourse, leaving in place only what is most psychological about man. The reverse is also true, of course. Such overdone explanatory discourses within *one* frame of reference also become automatically tautological. Of course were it possible to enunciate simultaneously two complementary discourses (which is impossible), the result would be a vicious circle. Hence, complementarism is not a "theory" but a methodological generalization only.

Chapter 1 must also be greatly condensed, for its argumentation relies heavily on the logic of modern physics. Broadly speaking, it shows it is possible to elaborate a conceptual scheme of society which presupposes nothing about the individual *qua* object of psychological contemplation. Hence, several of my theorems and corollaries are inspired by the laws of statistical mechanics. This scheme also assumes that society is a chronoholistic system: a complete knowledge of its state at time t_0 does not suffice for the prediction of its behavior at time t_0 + Δt; all its antecedent history must be known.

After a discussion of the possibility of conceiving both social time and social space in a manner compatible with certain sophisticated concepts of modern physics, several methods involving no psychological conception whatsoever of individual behavior are proposed.

The method of the least path: the structure of society determines which of the several paths leading from a to b demands the least expenditure of energy. The method of transformation studies the characteristics which remain invariant when a set is subjected to a series of transformations. (It is important here to note the date of publication of this article as 1940.) The method of quantum mechanics involves the concept of complementarity or indeterminacy. One cannot speak of the burglar's superego when a policeman is present, nor of social constraint when the policeman is absent.

I next turn to the structure of social space, viewed as a gravitational field in which the concept of the "social mass" of the individual plays a crucial role as a nucleus of attraction. The "social mass" of an individual contributes to the structuring of the social space surrounding him. The ongoing relationship between two individuals can be analyzed via the transformation of systems of coordinates. This permits one to view society as a space so curved that for Y the least path will be that which passes near X. The "curvature" of the social space can also be called customs or morals.

I next consider stability and change in terms of the third law of thermodynamics and recall once more that all living systems, society included, are chronoholistic systems which must be described in integro-differential equations *not* reducible by any amount of differentiation to differential equations involving a "one point memory;" these equations must involve statistical macro-parameters. I conclude with the observation that sociological theory resembles an investigation of the "metrical" properties of "social space." The scheme presented here is compatible with any logically coherent sociological theory.

Chapter 2, though published only in 1966, is based on an insight reached in 1931 and, in a way, provides the point of departure for all my theoretical and methodological thinkings. Only its formulation was facilitated by Bohr's subsequent work on the partition between object and observer (i.e., between inside and outside). The paper formulates this problem in terms of the problem of stress. A stress is endogenous when a minute external change produces considerable internal changes; it is exogenous when a minute change in the organism produces major changes in the environment. As discussed elsewhere (1967a, chapters 20 to 24) the partition between inside and outside can be conceived in a manner inspired by the Dedekind cut, with one difference: instead of the point of interest being situated where one increasing and one decreasing series *meet,* it is located where two such initially overlapping series *separate.* After briefly stressing that the central nervous system (which centralizes and structures our behavior) was originally *not* in the service of unification but in that of segmental autonomies and noting also that the specialization of tissues can be *maintained* only within a complex system forming an organism, I urge that the real locus of phenomena of interest in human sciences is precisely the Jordan's curve which in theory, "separates" but in practice, "unifies" man and his environment. The "externalist" says that interactions occur on this curve; the "internalist" says that the perceived phenomena of interaction actually *create* and *are* this curve. In practice, this conception is of crucial interest to the psychosomatician.

Originally, chapter 3 was chapter 4 of *Therapeutic Education.* It advances two fundamental propositions.

1. The methodological proposition: the intensive analysis in depth of a single practice in a single tribe—or of the proverbial Viennese patients—leads to universally valid propositions. Conversely, the selfsame propositions can be reached by a cross sectional "surface" study of a particular trait in many societies or of a problem in many subjects. This thesis is based upon the ergodic hypothesis of mathematicians (see my discussion 1976b).

2. The substantive thesis: a full catalogue of all cultural data (practices, beliefs, etc.) compiled by anthropologists would fully overlap with an equally complete catalogue of intra-psychic material obtained by psychoanalytic clinicians. This implies each man is a complete specimen of Man and each culture is a complete specimen of Culture. As to the substantive thesis, it does not exclude diffusion in ethnology nor learning in psychology. The role of both is simply to bring out into the open and to implement possibilities already present in a germinal form. Such outlandish items as coprophagous monsters, the reversible penis and beings without anuses are found on the individual level in the form of fantasies, and as beliefs in many cultures between whom diffusion was impossible. The inverted penis idea, in particular, can belong in

various cultures to different cultural matrices, as matrices are defined (1970*a*, chapter 16). As already noted (1955*a*), these theories permitted me to predict the existence of certain customs "somewhere" or to infer their meaning long before I could find actual data substantiating my predictions or interpretations.

Chapter 4 provides suitable logical foundations for culture and personality theories. Both *personality* and *culture* are treated as constructs—a view incompatible both with culturalism and neo-Freudianism. As in all my work, psychological and sociological discourses are rigorously separated. This extremely intricate article cannot be summarized, particularly since it makes extensive use of Russell's theory of mathematical types, his interpretation of "Epimenides type" paradoxes and his conception of *what* is and *who* is "typical."

Chapter 5 argues for the use of two types of modal personality models. It shows that all behavior can be completely explained either sociologically or psychologically and, as noted in my summary of the *Argument,* indicates that what, in sociology, is operant motivation is, in psychology, instrumental motivation and vice versa. This theory explains why both spontaneous and organized social movements and processes are possible. Even though *psychologically* the persons participating in such a process are differently motivated, *sociologically* they must be held to be identically motivated.

A few words must be said of the history of this paper. It dates from a 1956–57 team study of Hungarian refugees. Its writing was triggered by a discussion meeting of the team: the sociologists and political scientists of the group proposed uniform sociological motivations; the psychologists, psychiatrists and psychoanalyst (myself) stressed the variability of individual motivations. This article first appeared in Bert Kaplan's volume *Studying Personality Cross-Culturally* (1961). Though the review of that book in the *American Anthropologist* did not even mention it, the article was reprinted only two years later, as the lead-off article of the anthology *Personality and Social Systems* (1963) edited by N. J. Smelser and W. T. Smelser.

Chapter 6 discusses ethnic identity. Identity has two meanings. (1) The absolute uniqueness of individual *A* is determined by at least one operation *so precise* as to make *A* the sole member of a class. For example, only John Smith has a certain weight. If that weight is determined to the tenth decimal he is the sole person of the class of "things" having exactly that weight. (2) Uniqueness can also be defined by means of a *nonreproducible accumulation* of *imprecise* determinations. The degree of imprecision must be specifiable. There is, presumably, only one person American, male, age over eighty, over six feet tall, gynecologist, named Smith—though there are countless other Americans, old people, tall people, etc. I distinguish between ethnic personality and ethnic identity as such: ethnic personality is a conceptual scheme derived, inductively, from concrete data, consisting of the statements of observers and of the subject's own statement concerning his behavior in terms of his ethnic membership (Epimenides the Cretan says: "All Cretans are liars"). Ethnic identity is difficult to define because it is, in practice, abusively contaminated by ethnic personality. The moment anything is predicated about ethnic identity other than *"A* is, while *B* is not, a Mohave," ethnic identity begins to function as an ideal all or nothing model (contrast spy with traitor).

Any activity which can be predicted or explained through a knowledge of the subject's ethnic personality must be viewed as a manifestation thereof. By contrast, since ethnic identity is not an inductive generalization, it cannot be expected to describe any basic aspect of the personality of e.g., a Mohave. Ethnic identity *models* are dissociative; many new culture traits are the results of antagonistic acculturation (cf. chapter 8).

There also exists a complementarity relationship between the explanation which considers Brasidas' courage as an inevitable manifestation of his Spartan personality and the explanation which views his courage as an intentional display of his Spartan ethnic identity.

Ethnic identity can be underlined by autoplastic means (e.g., a Mohave teaching himself to be brave) or by alloplastic means (the Nazis making the Jews wear the yellow star of David).

Ethnic identity ritualism may become exaggerated in times of decline (the Roman-dominated Spartans exaggerated their ancient Spartan customs). Some ethnic identities involve the claim of incarnating an areal climax; Athens called itself the Hellas of Hellas. A group may also have a *double* ethnic identity self-mystique. In pursuit of expansionistic goals, Sparta claimed now a Dorian and now an Achaean ethnic identity. Some ethnic identity models are constraining: Spartans could only be soldiers. By contrast, Athenian ethnic identity permitted the individual to be Athenian in many ways.

A hypercathected ethnic identity, which overrides all other identities, ceases to be a tool and becomes a strait-jacket and, therefore, proves to be dysfunctional: the person becomes one-dimensional. Ethnic identity is truly functional only if it involves the uninvidious appreciation that *"B* is a *Y* by being a non-*X."* "Black is beautiful" can be true and functional only if it subsumes that "White is also beautiful" (in a different way) and vice versa, of course. Any ethnos incapable of recognizing this elementary fact condemns itself dissociatively to a slow drift, as a closed system, toward utter meaninglessness. The obsessive stressing of one's ethnic (or any other "class") identity reveals a flaw in one's self-conception as a unique multidimensional entity. It represents a first step toward a "protective" renunciation of true identity: if one is nothing but a Spartan, a capitalist, a proletarian or a Buddhist, one is next door to being nothing and therefore even to not being at all.

Chapter 7 proposes an explanation of the notion of kinship rather than simply of kinship. It gives a special interpretation of the exchange of women, whose importance I stressed long ago (1939), a point Lévi-Strauss cited. After some preparatory material which indicates that there is a special pleasure and even a social distinction derived from having sexual relations with two women closely related to each other (mother and daughter, two sisters), I analyze in detail a clinical example which indicates that the latent meaning of a patient's dream was that having seduced his friend's sister, his friend now had the right to have anal intercourse with him. In dream, the patient's anus was symbolized by the "farting vagina"—first that of his wife and then that of his sister. It is then indicated that the sexual "soiling" of a woman is held to soil even more her male kin—father, brothers, husband. Everything indicates that having to give a kinswoman in exchange for a wife is a bitterly resented compromise. In fantasy the strong take and give nothing in return; he who must yield his female kin (be it in an exchange) is weak, castrated, feminized. Marriage ritual puts a pleasant mask on the bitterly resented renunciation of the bride's kin and disguises the groom's triumph by the pretence of submissive greatfulness.

The exchange of women is governed not by equity but by the rule of talion. In the above mentioned patient's dream, he must appease his friend whose sister he seduced by offering him a feminine substitute for his own anus as the lesser of two evils. Primitive exchanges of women, like modern swinging, serve to ward off anxiety over homosexual retaliation for heterosexual seduction. What matters in the circulation of women is, thus, not heterosexual reciprocity but the warding off of homosexual counteraggression.

Chapter 8 (in collaboration with E. M. Loeb) discusses negative reactions to diffusion. Some resistances concern the borrowing of an item, others the lending or revealing of an item. Only a few of the many varieties of antagonistic acculturation can be cited. Defensive isolationism can concern places (Lhasa), social contact (silent barter) suppression of cultural items (embargo, boycott), or the adoption of a new or borrowed means, the better to defeat the (sometimes unwilling) lender. Thus, the Hebrews asked the prophet Samuel to give them a king to improve their military chances when facing foes led by kings. However, since means and ends often form a unit, borrowing the one without the other is sometimes destructive. Most important is dissociative/negative acculturation: many Jewish customs were developed in opposition to the cultural practices of their neighbours. The flight of Jewish scientists contributed to Nazi Germany's defeat. Regression in times of social stress, deliberate differentiation (upper-class accent), the evolving of practices in deliberate opposition to those of another group (Coran, Sourat 109) all instance antagonistic acculturation. Published during the War (1943), this paper did not receive much attention. Had its findings been taken into account in planning the post-war world, many costly errors could have been avoided.

Chapter 9: among the Mohave the power to perform any feat is supposedly obtained in dream. By listening, anyone can learn a shaman-istic curing song. But singing them has a curative value only if it is validated by a proper power-giving dream. Each shaman and singer professes to have had the proper dream and to sing the proper text. Divergences from his ideal model in the accounts and practices of other shamans will anger him and incite him to bewitch the deviant. Yet individual differences are unavoidable because of personal elements determining the shaman's vocation and (alleged) dream experiences. The problem of the subjective element in shamanistic accounts, claims, and practices is greatly illuminated by the clinical study of modern "borderline cases" who claim to possess supernormal powers.

Chapter 10 discusses the influence of cultural thought models upon primitive and modern psychiatric theories. The problem under con-sideration is made more difficult to analyze by the fact that an "in-correct" thought model can be formally scientific (phlogistic theory of heat), while another which happens to be "correct" may not be formally scientific (Mohave theories of hystero-epileptic convulsions). A primitive drug may actually have the effect claimed, though the ration-ale given in explanation may be radically supernaturalistic. I cite primi-tive neuropsychiatric theories rooted solely in cultural thought models: in the Sedang theory of nerve conducivity and their awareness of the seductiveness of the psychotic; and the Mohave theory of convulsions.

Adaptation. Modern psychiatric theories have similar models. The illegitimate prestige that the notion of adaptation (a sociological con-cept) had in American psychiatry had at its root America's problems with the enculturation of immigrants. Behavioral conformity was ex-pected to play the role of a still lacking national ethos.

Organicism. Organicism is rooted in the physician's need to be accepted as a bona fide scientist, and scientism, motivated by the need of the practitioners of certain sciences to ape the exact sciences, though the "real" sciences are exact only because they deal with phenomena much simpler than are those the student of man has to study.

The (primary) death instinct. The (primary) death instinct, which is clinically useless and logically untenable, is rooted in six different cultural thought models. (1) The physicalistic model is a misinterpretation of the second law of thermodynamics. (2) The biologistic model is a concession to organistic psychiatry. Instead of *slightly* revising his theory of the wish in the light of the repetition compulsion, Freud chose to invent a second instinct. (3) The theological model is the struggle between God and Devil, or Ormuzd and Ahriman; in short, between Good and Evil. (4) The ethical model is provided by three concepts: original sin, predestination, man's inherently evil nature. (5) The historico-cultural model is a kind of megalomaniac individualism which holds that man can die only of his own will. This recalls the belief of some primitives that every death is due to sorcery. (6) The clinical model: since we have the patient on the couch while his cruel parents, unfair boss, unfaithful wife, are not within reach, it is easy *and wrong*— as Loewenstein has pointed out—to blame everything on the patient's moral masochism.

Real science is culturally neutral. The Ionians borrowed Near Eastern temple science and, by lifting it out of its cultural matrix, caused it to progress. When Greek science became hellenized it became fairly static. The same process was repeated when the Arabs borrowed Greek science and the Renaissance Graeco-Arab science. The Age of Reason once more made science culturally neutral but at the cost of making it an idol of the market place. The same process of de-culturation and re-culturation is also found in the history of psychoanalysis. At present it is being re-enculturated, partly for support of Western ideology but partly also (in a typically Western manner) for use *against* occidental culture (Fromm, Marcuse). Whether headed for Greenwich Village or for Park Avenue, psychoanalysis is now also becoming an idol of the market place and, in so doing, it risks ceasing to be a culturally neutral objective science.

The English and the German translations of this book (1972) contain one extra chapter, "Time: History versus Chronicle," that is not included in the French, Spanish and Italian. It discusses socialization as culture pre-experience, differentiates history from chronicle and highlights that no society can exist if behavior is based wholly on here-and-now, trial-and-error learning. This complex paper cannot be summarized adequately.

ETHNOPSYCHOANALYTIC STUDIES OF
GREEK TRAGEDY AND POETRY

Tragédie et Poésie Grecques—Etudes Ethnopsychanalytiques
(1975) is my first collection of essays on Greek subjects. Two of the
papers it contains have not been published before. (Two further volumes of Greek essays, one on history and one on mythology, are
contracted for.)

Part I (two chapters) deals with general problems of esthetics in
relation to creativity. Chapter 1 disagrees with Freud in considering
creative genius explicable. The work of art results from a tension between tabooed material and culturally imposed rules of arts. Beauty
serves to bribe the superego, the way, according to Freud, humor can
bribe it. But the coin of beauty so used must be "legal tender" in the
culture to which both the creator and the consumer of art belong—
hence the difficulty of appreciating exotic or innovating art.

Chapter 2 shows that Aristotle *(Poetics)* grasped the similarities
between the structure of the psyche and that of the tragedy. Only one
example can be cited here. The irrational (that which precedes or follows
the tragedy or else occurs off-stage) is contrasted by Aristotle with the
"rational," which is shown on-stage. This relationship resembles that
between the beautiful public statue of the deity in the public part of the
Greek temple and the hidden and archaic statue, which *is* the deity and
was located in some secret chamber of the temple.

Part II deals with psychological problems. Chapter 3 shows the
psychological realism of Aeschylus' accounts of dreams. This poet observed, *inter alia,* the occurrence of eye movements while dreaming and
the fact that long dreams can be dreamed in a few minutes. He was also
aware of the conflict between wish and censor in dreams.

Chapter 4 shows that an ambiguous word in Sophokles' *Antigone*
(v. 414) must not be emended: its ambiguity well reflects the ambivalence of the speaker.

Chapter 5 (in collaboration with Jane W. Devereux) shows Sophokles' unconscious at work in *The Women of Trachis* (vv. 293 ff.).
Disregarding the mythical model of a virile Deianeira, he made his
heroine a proper Athenian lady. But—in a way recalling "the return of
the repressed"—he also introduced a *non*-system-adequate innovation.
His hyper-feminine Deianeira kills herself with a sword, like a man, and
not by hanging as did Greek women, including even the Amazon-like
Deianeira of the myth. The myth plays with respect to the tragedy the
role the day residue plays in dreams.

Chapter 6: Pace Verrall, Euripides described in the *Heracleidae* not the rejuvenation of an aged Iolaos, but the temporary remission of a rheumatoid arthritis—as did André Gide in *Les Caves du Vatican.*

In chapter 7 I cite two overlooked (Christian) testimonia, indicating that Stesichorus wrote more than one Palinode in order to recover his sight, which Helen of Troy, angered by his earlier condemnation of her, had caused him to lose. (Hypothesis: the poet had two attacks of hysterical blindness.) A Himera coin (reproducing a statue of the aged Stesichorus), shows him blind. This suggests that in old age he suffered from an *irreversible* (senile) blindness.

Chapter 8: in describing the encounter between Heracles and Leto's children (Apollo and Artemis), whose hind he had captured, Pindar used an ambiguous word meaning either a friendly reception or a hostile ambush. He did so because he was notoriously reluctant to describe unseemly clashes between Gods and mortals. I also prove Brommer's analysis of a statue showing Heracles with the hind is wrong. Brommer thinks Heracles is *not* harming the hind, but a scrutiny of the play of his arm muscles shows that he is breaking off her horn.

Part III (Chapter 9) discusses quadrupedal locomotion in tragedy and the unreliability of the interpretations of this performance of scholiasts and philologists alike. The scholiast says that at the beginning of Aeschylus' *Eumenides* the old prophetess is running on all fours. This she *cannot do* wearing a long skirt. Actually, she is running with the help of a cane. In Euripides' *Hecuba* the blinded Polymestor says that he is running on all fours, "my hands following my feet." H. Weil tried to emend this text with "My feet follow my hands." This is impossible for a crawling man wearing long royal robes. Actually, Polymestor is *backing out* of the tent on all fours, his hands following his feet. In Euripides' *Rhesus,* Dolon describes how, clad in a wolfskin, he plans to spy on the Greeks. Though the scholiasts criticized this plan, a careful reading of the text shows the plan to be feasible. I conclude that the transmitted text of poets must take precedence over its interpretation by scholiasts and philologists.

DREAMS IN GREEK TRAGEDY

Dreams in Greek Tragedy (1976a) is, I believe, the first attempt to scrutinize major literary masterpieces in the light of psychological anthropology. Anthropologists have of course, occasionally studied modern society in an anthropological perspective but they do not seem to feel that the methods of their science could also be profitably applied to the study of some of the greatest artistic masterpieces of mankind.

This book is an ethnopsychoanalytic study of dreams contained in *completely* transmitted Greek tragedies; dreams found in the surviving fragments of the Greek tragic poets were not studied because they were transmitted out of context. This immediately indicates that, in the analysis of a dream found in a surviving tragedy, the rest of the tragedy was used as "free associations" to the dream. Parallel passages in other Greek texts, in Greek culture as a whole, relevant clinical material, and comparable ethnological data were also used in the attempt to analyze dreams in tragedy.

General Introduction. Most Homeric dreams are mere allegories; dreams in tragedy are authentically dreamlike—more so than many dreams found in Artemidoros' *Dream Book.* But the psychological *plausibility* of tragic dreams becomes evident only in light of psycho-analytic scrutiny; an *ad hoc* pseudo-psychological "common sense" psychology is of no use in their study. The Greek tragic poets were great psychological realists; this explains their capacity to move us, even after almost 2500 years. In devising dreams, the Greek tragic poets did not begin by studying Freud. I had to study Freud in order to demonstrate the psychological plausibility of their dreams. It is noted in passing that Aristotle had a remarkable insight into what dream interpretation really involves.

Chapter 1—Atossa's dream in Aeschylus' Persae. The excellent preservation of the text—which contrasts with the corrupt transmission of more obviously dreamlike (i.e., anxiety arousing) texts—together with the transparent images first led me to believe this is a quasi-Homeric allegory rather than a dream. However, once the members of my seminar brought out the latent counter-Oedipal content of the dream narrative, its oneiric nature became evident. Better still, as soon as this was seen as a counter-Oedipal dream, it was completely congruent with *authentic* biographical facts concerning the historical Atossa. The poet apparently used historical data as the equivalent of a day residue.

Chapter 2—Io's dream (Aeschylus' Prometheus Bound*).* Briefly stated, this highly dreamlike dream almost certainly has cultural impli-cations: the coupling of Io (transformed as a heifer) with Zeus (her father Inachos) indicates the existence of a (copulatory) pastoral fertility right, discernible behind the dream's Oedipal façade.

Chapter 3—Menelaos: reactive depression and dream (Aeschylus' Agamemnon*).* This chapter contains probably the first attempt to re-store and emend a corrupted text on the basis of psychoanalytic con-siderations. In one instance even the psychodynamics of the copyist's *lapsus calami* could be reconstructed. The description of the deserted Menelaos' depression is practically an epitome of Freud's "Mourning and Melancholia."

Chapter 4—The dream of the Erinyes (Aeschylus' Eumenides*).* This chapter exemplifies the kind of dreams in which an action which should be performed in reality is simply dreamed, thus making awakening unnecessary. The alleged transformation of the fierce Erinyes into well-disposed Eumenides is shown to be very limited in scope; this sheds light on the ethically neutral character of archaic divinities.

Chapters 5, 6 and 7 form a whole; they examine the dreams which three different poets devised for Clytaemestra (Clytaemnestra).

Chapter 5—Stesichorus' Oresteia. The dream survived in the form of a two line fragment: the King (Orestes) is born from the split skull of the snake (Agamemnon). The dream's content can be correlated with miraculous cures recorded on votive inscriptions at Epidaurus, with Zeus's cephalic birth and with Greek beliefs concerning the reproduction of the viper.

Chapter 6—Aeschylus' Choephoroi. This chapter sheds light on many clinically attested fantasies and also on some primitive beliefs. Clytaemestra gives birth to a baby serpent who bites her breast and whom she then swaddles. Subsequently, when Orestes is about to kill her, she bares her breast (in a traditional way) and beseeches her son to spare her. The analysis discusses Greek breast-feeding "on demand," the biting of the nipple, the masochistic and ultra-feminine dream behavior of the virile Clytaemestra, the fantasy of poisonous milk, and the social function of the tyranny of the maternal breast.

Chapter 7—Sophokles' Electra. The latent content of this dream is buried under layers of cultural material. The dream itself has affinities with Near Eastern (Biblical, Mesopotamian) "culture pattern dreams." It represents a symbolic coitus between the murdered Agamemnon and his murderous wife. Extremely rich in cultural symbols, the latent content of this dream is poorer than the dreams Stesichorus and Aeschylus devised for Agamemnon's murderous Queen. This may explain why Euripides invented no dream for her in his *Electra:* the dream motif used by three great poets had become stale.

Chapter 8. The three Euripidean dreams *(Rhesus'* Charioteer, *Hecabe, Iphigenia)* are all variations on the "primal scene" theme, especially in the form in which the child spectator is, in fantasy, caught between his parents' cohabiting bodies as between millstones. There are also marked (not strictly psychoanalytic) affinities between the three dreams: the structuring of space, the circularity of time, the arrangement of colours in space, the symbols and the processes of symbolization. Also, if one breaks down the primal scene into some twenty traits, it can be shown that all twenty are present in the three dreams taken *together,* with more than fifteen present in *each* of the three. This has a direct bearing upon the (still controversial) authorship of the drama *Rhesus.* Since the *Hecabe* and the *Iphigeneia among the Taurians* are genuine works of Euripides, the possibility that the dream in the *Rhesus*, which has countless inner affinities with the two genuine Euripidean dreams, was not written by Euripides himself is negligible. The *Rhesus* we have was, thus, written by Euripides.

Chapter 9. Aeschylus' *The Suppliant Women* contains a dream metaphor whose text is extremely corrupt. The only thing that is clear is that the Danaides (about to be kidnapped and forced into marriage with their cousins by the Herald) compare their experience to a nightmare—and the Herald, himself, to a spider and to a snake. Exploiting only the intelligible parts of this corrupt text, clinical data and Greek beliefs about snakes and spiders, typical snake and spider dreams are discussed and correlated with the image of the phallic mother in suffocating, immobilizing nightmares. In short, what is being analyzed is not the dream metaphor—*qua* dream—but two types of typically Greek (and human) anxiety dreams.

This brief summary of a long and complex book cannot fully reflect its substantive context. It does show, however, that even literary master-pieces of the highest order are accessible to ethnopsychoanalytic scrutiny. This is an innovation and considerably broadens the scope of psychoanthropological research.

MISCELLANEA

Mohave Sexuality and Child Rearing

As noted in the beginning, almost the only exception to the rule that I deal here only with my books is my series of papers on the Mohave. They were written from the start to constitute chapters of a book for which I have not found a publisher. It should be borne in mind that they were written in the 1930s and 1940s. Many of them consider a variety of problems from the viewpoint of culture and personality; nearly all of them use the psychoanalytic approach. Both these types of approach were innovating in those decades and I am convinced that a revival of these approaches is urgently needed in the overly intellec-tualistic climate of current anthropology.

I cannot begin to summarize so long a series of papers. For this reason I list those I do cite in a chronological order. My paper on

Mohave homosexuality (1937), rejected by Ernest Jones for the *International Journal of Psychoanalysis*, remains the most complete account of homosexuality in tribal society; it has been repeatedly reprinted, excerpted and translated. A basic insight of my paper on incest (1939), that incest resembles avarice and excludes the incestuous from tribal interaction, was quoted in Lévi-Strauss's book on kinship. A study of twins (1941) revealed that side by side with repeatedly recorded beliefs exalting twins there existed a second set of condemnatory attitudes regarding twins. Together the two beliefs reflect the inevitable ambivalence that occurs when some belief or attitude is over-emphasized by a culture (cf. 1970*a*). A study of Mohave infanticide (1948) recorded the tradition that before the accidental discovery of agriculture, the Mohave ate their children; this tradition does not prove, of course, that they actually did so in early times. I only learned from a paper by Dell Hymes (1961) that my paper on Mohave voice and speech mannerisms (1949) dealt with a neglected problem and that my paper on Mohave profanity (1951*b*) was of importance to linguists. I have also shown the Mohave equate feminine bleeding at puberty, defloration and childbirth (1950). Contrary to current theory, the latency period was shown to be a product of culture, not paleopsychologically determined. This section does not mention Mohave papers incorporated in books (e.g., 1961*a*, 1970*a*, 1972*a*) and, as noted, makes no mention of many other papers dealing with the Mohave. I continue to hope for a chance to publish in book form all my papers on the Mohave, both published and unpublished, for they constitute a corpus of knowledge, especially on "primitive" sexuality.

PARAPSYCHOLOGY

The study of so-called parapsychological phenomena now appears to gain recognition as a legitimate branch of anthropological endeavor and will, no doubt, soon claim to be a branch of psychological anthropology. Some material issued by a newly organized group of parapsychological anthropologists views me as a forerunner because I formerly did some work on this subject (1953*a* and also some articles). But this prospectus fails to stress that my attitude toward parapsychology was and is utterly skeptical. Specifically, I have stated that two seemingly "paired" occurrences (e.g., a prophetic dream and its "realization") cannot be juxtaposed logically until an *intelligible nexus* is established between the two. Moreover, the presence of anagrams in the names of persons allegedly belonging to "Ruth Simmons'" earlier life as "Bridey

Murphy'' and her hypnotist's name suggest that not memories of reincarnation but neurotic fantasies are the root of this "record" (1956c). As to seemingly parapsychological occurrences in psychoanalytic sessions, they should, in the analytic frame of reference, be viewed solely as "red herring" resistances. Their parapsychological "dimension" (if any) does not concern the analyst *qua* therapist.

I note, *in fine*, that before Freud devised the "primary death instinct" (which many classical analysts, myself included, find unnecessary) both he and other analysts were skeptical of parapsychology. After the introduction of that speculative concept many analysts became persuaded of the reality of such phenomena. I hold this change in outlook to be part of a disturbing trend: the increasing contamination of scientific psychoanalysis by a questionable kind of philosophy.

In short, precisely because my work on allegedly parapsychological occurrences was and continues to be skeptical, I cannot concur with the well meant allegation that I am a forerunner of parapsychological anthropology.

CLINICAL PAPERS

Though numerous, my clinical papers cannot be discussed here for lack of space. I simply note that they differ from the usual psychoanalytic-anthropological papers in stressing not the contributions of psychoanalysis to the understanding of anthropological data but the exact opposite: the usefulness of anthropological knowledge in the interpretation of clinical data. I also did some pioneering work (1944, 1949b) on the therapeutic fitness of the kind of society that comes into being in psychiatric hospitals.

PERSPECTIVES FOR THE FUTURE

I was about sixteen when, fairly soon after the great Berzelius predicted no one would ever be able to produce an organic substance synthetically, I learned a French chemist did achieve just that. This left an indelible impression on me. Nearer to our time, the debate over the *possibility* of producing a nuclear bomb once more demonstrated the dangers of prophecy in science—a danger I do not care to court.

I can, however, appraise what has been achieved not as a culmination, but as a point of departure and to highlight certain recurrent changes of attitudes toward that which has been—or seems to have been—established so far. Before I do so, I would simply say that, in the long run, H. Ling Roth's *The Aborigines of Tasmania* (2nd edition, Halifax 1899) has a better chance of surviving than the most brilliant theoretical work, for it contains *induplicable* data, which, since the Tasmanians are extinct, cannot be superseded by anything better.

By contrast, even the best theoretical work, though irreplaceable as the propulsor of science, is soon superseded by newer (though *not always* "better") theories and ceases to interest anyone except the historian of scientific ideas. Otherwise expressed, every theoretical work ceases, after a while, to function *primarily* as both an interpretative summary of what is known and as an impetus for further research and becomes simply a raw datum for *another* discipline: the history of scientific ideas.

The theoretician must reconcile himself to the fact that his work is but one of Sisyphus' many near-successes in rolling a stone to the summit of a hill.

My field data and clinical records thus have a better chance of survival (as bricks that can be used over and over again by theoreticians in the field of the sciences of man) than has my theoretical work, which like *any* theoretical work is, in the long run, self-abolishing. In fact, the better (more stimulating) it is, the more self-abolishing it is bound to be, for stimulating interpretations always incite the formulation of newer (and *perhaps* better) interpretations.

Another aspect of this problem may also be considered. Periodically even the validity of theories held to be absolutely fundamental tends to be questioned. The debate between F. G. Donnan and Sir James Jeans over whether the second law of thermodynamics applies also to living beings—a debate which, in the opinion of many (myself included) proved Donnan to be right in asserting that nothing escaped the sway of this law—reminds one that, given sufficient genius (or sufficient obstinacy and prejudice) everything *can* be questioned. (See Devereux 1953a, p. 420 for references on this controversy.)

Broadly speaking, periods of obsessive confidence seem to alternate with periods of compulsive questioning. It is hardly necessary to indicate to which of these two types of epochs ours belongs. But even this distinction is, as my use of the word "compulsive" indicates, not sufficiently refined, for man is an ambivalent creature. As I pointed out over thirty-five years ago (1970a, chapter 3, first published in 1940): man affirms on one level what he denies on another level; compare the two logically absolutely incompatible beliefs of the Mohave, concerning twins (summarized in 1961a, pp. 348ff.), whose interrelatedness only the theory of ambivalence is able to discern.

Nor is that all! In periods of obsessive confidence (with *necessarily fragmentary* knowledge and in conclusions drawn from it) man is automatically led to evolve mutually incompatible tenets and then obliges himself to "believe" both of them at the same time (1970*a*, chapter 10), which, predictably, causes much discomfort and in the long run, leads to the collapse of both incompatible articles of faith.

Conversely, in periods of compulsive doubt, skepticism itself becomes a creed no one may question: criticism and doubt turn into a kind of religion, as harsh, violent and irrational as any "revealed" religion ever was or can be.

On the whole, whatever *is* tends to be criticized and negated *in terms of itself* (1970*a*, chapter 1). Thus, the affirmation that *all* reality is an illusion *(maya)* presupposes, it would seem, the existence of the sensorium whose sole function is that of deceiving the "soul." Even Descartes' rationalism had to postulate that God would *not* deceive us with illusory sense impressions.

In short, man's quest for absolute and lasting certainties (always on the basis of *necessarily* still incomplete knowledge) seems to culminate invariably in a doubt which exceeds in intensity what most men can tolerate. Few men can recite with conviction Moses Maimonides' prayer: "Oh Lord, teach my tongue today to say: 'I do not know'!" And even *this* prayer presupposes the certainty of the existence of God! As to the straightforward admission: "I do not know, but can bear the uncertainty"—it is beyond the powers of nearly all of us.

Hence, the great problem in science, quite as much as in daily life, is both to live with what *seems* to be sure knowledge (for the time being) and to tolerate what, today, seems to be dubious. This task is doubly arduous in the sciences of man, for in these disciplines "countertransference" type distortion is maximal, as is correspondingly maximal the personal, biased involvement of the student of man with the object of his study. It is this finding which led me to suggest that our most productive data are our distortions of facts, and our most effective approach the analysis both of our distortions of facts and of our "countertransference" induced need to distort them (1967*a*). This methodological (*not* substantive) position implies, of course, that "phenomena" *do* exist and *are* perceived, though always in a distorted manner, and that the "partition" between object and observer is created *de novo* at every instant. This additional clause does *not* postulate the true and mutually distinct existence of either the object (phenomenon) "without," or of the observer ("within"), though, to use an expression of Henri Poincaré, it may well be "convenient" *(commode) to operate* as if they actually existed and were distinct. By contrast, the "existence" of a partition between the two is *not* postulated *even in this manner*—i.e., as a "convenience." The "putting in place" of a partition (of any kind) is simply viewed as an operation—be that operation real or as fictitious as that which underlies Medea's "debate" with her "thymos" in Euripides' *Medea*. In terms of the psychoanalytic frame of reference, that "debate" is a strife between two psychic instances, one of which *(thymos = animus,* passion, etc.) is treated as though it were *external* to the self, i.e., as, roughly speaking, ego-alien. In the end Medea's *thymos* carries the day—she does kill her children to punish her unfaithful husband, but in so doing, her *thymos* ceases to seem external. In retrospect, it simply appears to instance what I have called the (subjective) feeling of "drivenness" (1956a).

Nothing in the preceding paragraph postulates the existence of a *"thymos"* or of a "self"; as to the "partition" between the two, rigorously speaking, it is a purely operational device which permits the *thymos* to be now excluded from and now included in what is (rightly or wrongly) felt to be the self ("within"). Also, though my conviction that the psychoanalytic frame of reference and *modus operandi* are, at present, the most efficient interpretative means we possess need hardly be reiterated, it is well to recall that in writing this passage (vv. 1019–80) Euripides was *not* using the psychoanalytic frame of reference. He was simply describing, in a manner both traditional and poetic, a mode of reaction discernible by anyone endowed with a modicum of psychological perceptiveness. I therefore simply indicate that, *as of 1975,* Medea's debate with herself can be conveniently viewed as a debate between two psychic instances or between two endogenous impulses, one of which (the *thymos*) is projected "outside" what Medea *feels* to be her real self.

It seems probable that, for some time to come, psychological anthropology—and even all sciences of man—will have to face the inside/outside (object/observer) problem which has preoccupied me scientifically since 1931 and will have to come to terms with the distortions resulting from it. No matter how many new techniques we devise, it is unlikely that, in the foreseeable future, data will come to us as aseptically packaged as did, in the 1930s, certain food products proudly labelled "untouched by human hands." For even the contents of such *hypothetically* uncontaminated fact-packages end up in *someone's* (contaminated) mind. Kronecker's dictum, "God created the integers; man created all the rest" is well worth pondering here, for man took the "aseptic" integers and from them derived the "dogma" of the Holy

Trinity: $1 + 1 + 1 = 1$. The dogmas of those whose Truths come out of man-programmed (contaminated) computers are, for the time being, not much different, for they, too, end up in "contaminated" human minds, which interpret these Truths in their own way.

I see no escape, in the foreseeable future, from this predicament, save only by completely abolishing the profession of the "student of man" and storing the results of processed *hypothetically* uncontaminated data in locked files. And even this leaves unresolved the problem of collecting data aseptically, i.e., in such a manner that "the observed" is totally unaware of being observed and does not even observe himself —which is *also* a constraint *sui generis* (1972a, *Argument*).

I cannot bring myself, even now, to ignore how wrong Berzelius' prophecy was and therefore dare not affirm that no way of collecting and processing "aseptic" data will ever be discovered. I simply consider such a discovery most unlikely. But if my prevision should turn out errone-ous, it is likely it will be disproven only by someone who takes into account what I wrote on this matter. After all, no one attempted to build a "perpetuum mobile" *before* physicists declared the "per-petuum mobile" to be impossible; no one tried to square the circle *before* geometricians said it could not be done. (The fact that no "perpetuum mobile" has, as yet, been built, and that no one has, so far, squared the circle, is, in principle, quite irrelevant in this context). In short, especially those who seek to gather and to process data asep-tically, will have to take my conclusions into account, *before* they can attempt to transcend them. For the time being, it is likely that the next steps in the quest for *more* aseptic data, and methods of processing data, will have to pass through the stage of a more consistent enquiry into the distortion or contamination (sepsis) of the data in collecting and process-ing them. In fact, it is probably that our most "aseptic" data will, at least to begin with, concern the *distortion* of data. This is another way of saying that our most important and productive data are, for the time being, those which result from the study of the manner in which we distort data (1967a).

PERSONAL COMMENTARY

The editors have asked me to conclude with a balance sheet of my life's work. I cannot do so without also taking into account the eight filing cabinet drawers full of manuscripts, only some of which contain unpublished Hopi, Sedang, etc. field notes and clinical data.

As a *fieldworker*, I regret that a lack of grants and publishing opportunities prevented me from publishing *all* of my Mohave material, not to mention 99 percent of my Sedang data. I feel the same regret with respect to masses of *clinical* data, including the near-verbatim record of a complete psychoanalysis, and eighty recorded psychoanalytic sessions with a Plains Indian woman.

As regards *epistemology* and *methodology,* things are much more satisfactory: most of what I have done is published. Also, should I have further ideas in these disciplines, I think I can *now* count upon being able to publish them.

As regards *substantive* high-level *theory,* as exemplified by (1972, especially chapter 1), only part of my work is published. I could probably publish the rest, as well as quantities of middle-level *theory* papers. There are in my files many such manuscripts—anthropological, sociological, psychiatric and psychoanalytical. However, I could prepare them for publication only if I had some technical and clerical assistance. Unfortunately I do not seem to have mastered the technique of getting grants, for in the last forty years, I totalled only $4000 in grants for my own work: an average of $100 per year.

What I regret most is that, despite large masses of data accumulated over the past forty-three years, I was never in a position to write the *Treatise on Ethnopsychiatry,* which I had planned to write ever since 1935. But at least what would have been most of the key *theoretical* chapters of that work were published (1951*a*, 1961*a*, 1970*a*). Even that *Treatise* could still be written, were I assisted by a research and clerical team, over a period of three to four years; but my one attempt to raise the money was unsuccessful.

All things considered, my most recent interest, ancient Greece, led proportionally to the most publications in terms of the totality of my relevant written output, published *and* unpublished—perhaps because the hellenists' reception of my Greek work was so spontaneous and hospitable. As of now, it seems likely that I will be led to devote the rest of my life primarily to this field of enquiry simply because, unlike my work in other fields, it can be done without major grants.

Finally, I am less than certain I will be able to bring to fruition, without substantial grants and assistance, an enquiry having important biological-evolutionary implications into the extensive overlap of fantasy, belief, and reality—an enquiry of which (if ever completed) it would be possible to say *finis coronat opus.* With one exception, the few scientists with whom I have discussed my working hypothesis, were most encouraging. But this project which, unless I am much mistaken, would surpass in importance all but my epistemological and methodological work, cannot be carried out without substantial assistance, which, judging by past experience, I am not likely to get.

Considering all things—even the years of actual starvation, the lifelong insecurity of employment, no retirement income, six vacations in forty-three years, work seven days a week year in and year out, and, finally, thirty-five years in outer limbo, I deem myself fortunate on two capital scores: I have made no compromises and I have done work that passionately interested me. The title of the late Professor Roger Bastide's review ''A Puritan of Thought'' (1972*a*), is all I need in the way of an epitaph.

CONCLUDING SUMMARY

I was, so far as I know, the first scientist to have made ethno-psychiatry the *primary* forms of my research: its theory as well as its practice. But, in the early 1930s, ethnopsychiatric data were scarce, methods for processing them highly inadequate, a suitable theoretical framework for their analysis inexistent and the use for a nonreductionistic epistemology for handling key problems (culture/psyche, outside/inside, individual/group) not even dimly felt. Psychological/psychoanalytic and sociocultural reductionism, culturology, cultural relativism, etc. were not yet seen to be obstacles to, rather than means of, solving crucial problems. Everything had to be done from scratch.

Epistemology

1. Sociocultural vs. psychological/psychoanalytic explanations stand in a (Heisenberg-Bohr type of) complementarity relationship to each other. Each phenomenon needs to be explained completely in two ways (''double discourse''). The partition between outside/inside (culture/psyche) was not a ''given'': it resulted from the research method adopted. The partition came into being at the point where the observed was permitted to say—where the observer was willing to hear him say, ''And this I perceive.''

2. No device can filter out the observer's distortions of what happens (countertransference). Hence, the scientifically most relevant and exploitable datum is the self-scrutiny of the observer: insight into his manner of distorting the phenomena he observes.

3. The statements of the observer *and* of his informants must be analyzed in terms of Bertrand Russell's theory of mathematical types. The (Cretan) Epimenides' statement that all Cretans are liars *can*, in terms of such an analysis, be true.

4. The notion of a ''typical Mohave (or Frenchman, or . . .)'' presupposes saying X has all the qualities of a Mohave (etc.) in a way in which ''all the qualities'' is *not* viewed as a totality in itself (B. Russell).

5. Rules for switching from a sociological to a psychological explanation (or vice versa) must be defined.

6. No explanation (or experiment) may be so exhaustive as to explain away (or destroy) the phenomenon it explains (N. Bohr's *Abtötungsprinzip*). What is left after a fact is *over*-explained psychologically, is a purely sociological residue—and vice versa, of course.

Ethnopsychiatry

"Normal" is a psychological, "adjusted" a sociological label. A normal person may be maladjusted; an adjusted person may be abnormal (e.g., in a Hitlerian or Stalinian society). The ethnic unconscious contains material repressed by all members of a given culture; the idiosyncratic unconscious contains material repressed as a result of culturally atypical personal experiences. Culture evolves standardized defenses against routine stresses, provides prefabricated symptoms and even global patterns (syndromes) of "insane" conduct, related to Lintonian "patterns of misconduct." It also provides "signal symptoms," which indicate that one is "mad" and *not* e.g., criminal, feeble-minded, etc. Types of social structure (e.g., complex vs. simple, network vs. pyramid) can, despite differences of content, produce similar "type" disorders and can cause fragile persons to develop its symptoms. Schizophrenia is a *type* psychosis of all complex and/or rapidly and brutally changing societies; it is also one of the (inculcated) *ethnic* psychoses of the Western world. All symptoms (*qua* compromise solutions) are, of necessity, socially negativistic: deviant and provocative. The vicissitudes of cultural material in psychological disorders are of crucial importance: Are they recognized as being of "external" origin? Are they experienced as they are *supposed* to be experienced? (For example, for a neurotic woman coitus may be an "oral" nursing and *not* a "genital" experience.)

Psychiatry qua therapy (*iaomai,* to heal; *iatros,* the healer) is of three types:

1. *Intracultural:* patient and therapist belong to the same culture.

2. *Intercultural:* the two belong to different cultures but (a) the therapist knows the patient's culture and (b) uses cultural "levers" therapeutically, but must use them in a *self-abolishing* manner: the cured patient should be able to *stay* well without continuing to rely on those levers; and (c) *Metacultural* (ex*transcultural*[2]): the therapist does not know the patient's particular culture, but understands "culture"

2. I devised this term, but ceased using it after it came to denote (abusively) ethnopsychiatry as a whole. I note that I used "trans-" in the "beyond" sense (trans-alpine, trans-danubian).

(per se) as a general human characteristic. The possibility of metacultural diagnosis and therapy (especially psychoanalysis) proves that ethnopsychiatry can dispense with cultural relativism.

A true *recovery* can be achieved only through insight. Folk psychotherapy can only lead to more or less precarious *remissions*, punctuated by relapses. However the *study* of ethnopsychiatry, *qua folk* "science," is also indispensable for the development of a scientific ethnopsychiatry.

The outer boundaries ("reach") of ethnopsychiatry have not yet been fixed. Thus, I was able to show that ethnopsychiatry can even help one amend a badly transmitted passage of Aeschylus, previously considered to be hopelessly corrupt ("locus desperatus").

Culture and personality studies are, in addition to their inherent value, important preliminary approaches to ethnopsychiatric work. They provide clues to the culture-specific structure of the ego (Róheim) and hierarchical patterning of the defense mechanism.

Psychological/psychoanalytic interpretations of culture or of society are logically fallacious: they cannot attain their intended objective. (On this point the difference between Róheim's views and my own is absolute.) They can, however, yield valuable if unintended by-products: clues to the subjective (cultural as well as idiosyncratic) manner in which members of a given culture *experience* the world and themselves.

REFERENCES CITED

Bastide, R.
    1972   Un puritain de la pensée. *La Quinzaine Litteraire* 150:21–22, 16–31.
Besancon, A.
    1971   Review of Devereux (1970*a*). *La Quinzaine Litteraire* 31 janvier.
Bohr, N.
    1937   Causality and Complementarity. *Philosophy of Science* 4:289–98.
Caudill, W.
    1951   Review of Reality and Dream: Psychotherapy of a Plains Indian, by G. Devereux. *American Anthropologist* 53(4):565–67.
Devereux, G.
    1937   Institutionalized Homosexuality of the Mohave Indians. *Human Biology* 9:498–527.
    1939   The Social and Cultural Implications of Incest Among the Mohave Indians. *Psychoanalytic Quarterly* 8:510–33.
    1941   Mohave Beliefs Concerning Twins. *American Anthropologist* 43:573–92.

1944   The Social Structure of a Schizophrenia Ward and Its Therapeutic Fitness. *Journal of Clinical Psychopathology* 6:231–65.

1948   Mohave Indian Infanticide. *Psychoanalytic Review* 35:126–39.

1949a   The Social Structure of the Hospital as a Factor in Total Therapy. *American Journal of Orthopsychiatry* 19:492–500.

1949b   Mohave Voice and Speech Mannerisms. *Word* 5:268–72.

1950   The Psychology of Feminine Genital Bleeding: An Analysis of Mohave Indian Puberty and Menstrual Rites. *International Journal of Psycho-Analysis* 31:237–57.

1951a   *Reality and Dream: The Psychotherapy of a Plains Indian,* (Preface by Karl Menninger and Robert H. Lowie). New York: International Universities Press. (Second augmented ed. Preface by Margaret Mead. Anchor Books and New York University Press, 1969.)

1951b   Mohave Indian Verbal and Motor Profanity. In *Psychoanalysis and the Social Sciences,* ed. Geza Roheim, v. 3. New York.

1951c   The Primal Scene and Juvenile Heterosexuality in Mohave Society. In *Psychoanalysis and Culture,* Roheim Festschrift. New York.

1953a   *Psychoanalysis and the Occult,* (An anthology, edited by G. Devereux, and containing two chapters by him). New York: International Universities Press.

1953b   Why Oedipus Killed Laius: A Note on the Complementary Oedipus Complex. *International Journal of Psycho-Analysis* 34:132–41.

1955a   *A Study of Abortion in Primitive Societies.* New York: Julian Press (2nd ed. International Universities Press, 1976).

1956a   *Therapeutic Education.* New York: Harper.

1956b   (Devereux, ed.), Ralph Linton: *Culture and Mental Disorder.* Springfield, Ill. (Thomas).

1956c   Bridey Murphy, A Psychoanalytic View. *Tomorrow* 4(4):15–23.

1959   The Nature of the Bizarre. *Journal of the Hillside Hospital* 8:266–78.

1961   Mohave Ethnopsychiatry and Suicide. *Smithsonian Institution, Bureau of American Ethnology, Bulletin No.* 175, Washington, D.C. (Augmented edition 1969).

1967   *From Anxiety to Method in the Behavioral Sciences,* Preface by Weston La Barre. Paris and The Hague: Mouton and Cie.

1970   *Essais d'Ethnopsychiatrie Generale,* Preface by Roger Bastide. Paris: Gallimard. (2nd ed. 1973, 3rd ed. 1977).

1972   *Ethnopsychoanalyse Complementariste.* Paris: Flammarion.

1975   *Tragedie et Poesie Grecques.* Paris: Flammarion.

1976a   *Dreams in Greek Tragedy.* Oxford and Berkeley: Blackwell and University of California Press.

1976b   Augmented edition of Devereux (1955a).

Freud, S.
1957   *Mourning and Melancholia.* Standard Edition XIV. London.

Gebhard, P. H. et al.
1958   *Pregnancy, Birth and Abortion.* New York.

Hymes, D. H.
   1961   Linguistic Aspects of Cross-Cultural Personality Study. In *Studying Personality Cross-Culturally*, ed. B. Kaplan. New York: Harper and Row.
Kaplan, B.
   1961   *Studying Personality Cross-Culturally*. New York: Harper and Row.
Lévi-Strauss, C.
   1949   *Les Structures Elementaires de la Parente*. Paris: Presses Universitaires de France.
Linton, R.
   1956   *Culture and Mental Disorders*, ed. G. Devereux. Springfield, Ill.: Thomas.
Loewenstein, R. M.
   1947   The Historical and Cultural Roots of Antisemitism. *Psychoanalysis and the Social Sciences*, ed. Geza Roheim, 1:313–56. Also in *The Yearbook of Psychoanalysis*, ed. S. Lorand (1948) 4:226–62.
Menninger, K. A., and Devereux, G.
   1950   *A Guide to Psychiatric Books*. New York: Grune and Stratton.
Pickthal, M.
   1930   *The Glorious Koran*, translation (Surate 109, The Unbelievers *Al Kâfirûn*). New York: n.p.
Price-Williams, D.
   1968   Review of *Anxiety to Method*, by George Devereux. *Man* 82:105–07.
Psychoanalytic Study of Society, The.
   n.d.   Annual volume, edited by Warner Muensterberger and Aaron H. Esman. New York: International Universities Press.
Smelser, N. J., and Smelser, W. T., eds.
   1963   *Personality and Social Systems*. New York: John Wiley.
Spiro, M.
   1969   Review of Anxiety to Method. *American Anthropologist* 71:95–97
Weidman, H. H. and Wittkower, E. D.
   1973   Magical Thought and the Integration of the Psychoanalytic and Anthropological Systems. In *Psychopathologie Africaine* 9:17–39.
Wulff, E.
   1974   Einleitung (to the German edition of Devereux 1970.) Frankfurt: Suhrkamp.
Yearbook of Psychoanalysis, The.
   n.d.   Edited by Sándor Lorand. New York: International Universities Press.

Part II

Theodore Schwartz
Robert B. Edgerton
Erika Bourguignon
Theodore D. Graves
Nancy B. Graves
Victor Turner
Douglass Price-Williams
Michael Cole

Introduction to Part II
GEORGE SPINDLER

The authors of the papers included in Part II are not all "newcomers" to anthropology. Three of the eight could well have been included in Part I agewise and in terms of years of academic experience. These three, Bourguignon, Turner, and Price-Williams, are placed in Part II rather than Part I because their interests are congruent with models of research and interpretation that have only recently emerged as parts of psychological anthropology. Four of the remaining five received their Ph.D.'s after 1960 and were therefore socialized into the discipline after culture and personality had presumably died and been buried. In contrast, all the workers in Part I were socialized, before 1960, into the "somewhat inchoate" psychodynamic learning theory model.

Many of the issues raised by the papers in Part II have been anticipated in the discussion of those in Part I. We can retain with profit the four pivotal problem areas that were developed and applied in that discussion: reductionism; cultural over-determinism; the distribution of culture and personality; and the "Devereux effect." Many subsets of these four problem areas were touched upon and others will emerge in the introduction to Part II. Certain considerations that could be placed in this introduction will be reserved for the concluding remarks.

The Chapters

The first chapter in Part II, on the distributive locus of culture, by Theodore Schwartz, has had a decisive influence in the phrasing of the discussion in the introduction to Part I. Problems in the distribution of culture were dealt with in various ways in most of the papers. Most of the studies reported in Part II are more concerned with the distribution of phenomena within populations than with measures of central tendency distinguishing populations.

It is important to keep in mind that Schwartz is including both commonality and diversity in his distributive model, but that culture is not simply that which is shared nor personality that which is idiosyncratic. The assignment of commonality and diversity has dogged much

409

anthropological thinking about culture and personality. Schwartz mentions the influence of Devereux and Spiro in the development of his model, and then analyzes the difference between his model and Anthony Wallace's ("The Organization of Diversity" and "The Replication of Uniformity"). He sees Wallace as dissolving culture in equivalence structures and taking an extreme position in reaction to theories of cultural uniformity. Significantly, in saying that "a culture has its distributive existence as the set of personalities of the members of a population," and that "psychological processes define not merely the possibility but the content of culture . . .", Schwartz's thought is related to that of Kroeber, who said, in effect, that the ultimate reality of culture is psychological. Presumably, the new model will make it unnecessary to continue to act as if this were not so.

The problem with Schwartz's formulation for most readers is that he does not apply it to a specific culture in this paper, though it grew out of his research in the Admiralty Islands. Until this is done, it remains an abstraction. In thinking about his model in terms of Louise Spindler's and my field work, I can see that parts of cultural systems vary enormously in the extent to which there may be overlap, or lack of it, of "idioverses" (individual cognitive, evaluative, and affective mappings of the structure of events and classes of events) with each other. In sectors where there is minimal overlap of idioverses, we might anticipate quite different kinds and degrees of communication, emotional commitment, and relationships between declared norms and behavior, than when there is extensive overlap. The identification of such different areas of culture may be one of the more important tasks for the psychological anthropologist. I remain impressed, for example, by the virtual identity (though of course I did not conceptualize it in terms of idioverse overlap) of cognitive-perceptual structure, ritual, and ideology among the Menomini Peyotists (G. and L. Spindler 1971).

In any event, distributions of phenomena are a particularly significant problem in psychological anthropology but riddled with paradoxes. One of the paradoxes is that we frequently refer to the *individual* as our focus but more often than not ignore individual variation in favor of modes, means, or ideal types. The journal *Ethos* is described by its editors as "a new quarterly journal directed to the interface area between culture, society, and the individual," but 70 percent of the articles published in the first three years of its existence do not use the individual as the unit of analysis (Cone 1976, p. 197).

Robert Edgerton's chapter on deviance relates closely to Schwartz's concerns. We anthropologists have been so involved with norms and tendencies that we could not give major attention to deviance or deviant behavior. We have tended to regard deviants as dangerous sources of misinformation, sample skewers, or simply minority misfits to be ignored. Only in culture change situations do we begin to focus on deviant behavior—within the framework of individuation as a concomitant of social disorganization and the deterioration of cultural norms. Schwartz's concept of idioverse includes the deviant cognitively and emotionally as well as socially in the total culture. The deviant cannot be "outside" of the culture and must be considered if the conception of the culture is to be complete. Presumably the area of overlap among the idioverses of deviants and between them and nondeviants is smaller than "normal" or "usual" but here we would have to be very careful to study the possibility that our sample of deviants may express a "systematic deviation" (Lemert 1951). The Menomini Peyotists, for example, were a systematic deviation within the Menomini sample as a whole. They were like each other but different from everyone else. The problem becomes, once again, one of identifying different sectors of culture and personality relationships within culture systems. A distributive model of culture, and of personalities, is essential. All deviant, even severely retarded, individuals are part of the population that constitutes the "distributive existence" of the culture.

Chapter 14 on spirit possession and altered states of consciousness by Erika Bourguignon, also relates closely to the Schwartz and Edgerton concerns. Spirit possession and trance states were hardly a respectable subject of inquiry in the 1940s, partly because such states were regarded as manifestations of deviant behavior and anthropological concern was with norms and modes. Of course the trance state and the individual idioverse of the trancer are a part of the culture and must be studied. The bias went further. The generalized negative Western attitude toward possession and trance phenomena prevented researchers from seeing their importance—another example of the way in which a personal-cultural relationship (the Western anthropologist in another culture) can distort observations and interpretation. Bourguignon directly addresses the problems of distribution and determinism. "We no longer ask—what is the Haitian modal personality like and how does it develop so that we may account for the phenomenon of ritual possession? Instead, the question is: What is the Haitian behavioral environment like so that ritual possession makes sense?" There is a shift from emphasis on predispositions, inherited from previous socialization, that the individual brings into the social situation and that determine individual behavior in those situations as they trigger the predispositions, to an interactionist view of individuals making sense in situations that are structurally possible in a given cultural system setting. This shift is notable in much of Hallowell's work—his concept of self in the behavioral environment anticipates this thinking and Bourguignon acknowledges his influence. It is carried to its logical extreme in the current work of some ethnomethodologists who would probably be happier if both culture and personality were to simply disappear (for a brief and useful bibliography of ethnomethodology, see McDermott and Wertz 1976). Bourguignon moves toward an ethnomethodological stance, and Hallowell did too, but attention to the behavioral environment does not make one an ethnomethodologist. It does, however, lead one to quite a different position than does linear cultural determinism and is one kind of answer to the problem of over-determinism.

The chapter by Theodore and Nancy Graves on evolving strategies in the study of culture change, like those preceding, uses a model that forces attention to diversity. The Graves are interested in intragroup differences and overt behaviors, such as drinking behaviors. They are not so concerned with modal differences between groups. They depend heavily upon quantification and look for uniformities in the ways in which social psychological principles work themselves out in different cultural contexts. In their use of statistics they join the majority, but not overwhelming majority, of authors contributing to *Ethos* since 1973. Twenty-nine of fifty contributors used quantified data to test hypotheses or support inferences or conclusions (Cone 1976, p. 197). Quantification is not new to psychological anthropology. Six of the eleven "veterans" included in Part I have used statistical treatments in major contributions, many of them in the early forties and fifties. To quantify or not to quantify is probably not a live issue today. Most researchers will quantify if the data are quantifiable and if the range of phenomena or variables being studied makes qualitative analysis inadequate. The *sine qua non* of anthropology, however, is participant observation in a natural history setting. The Graves' use of traditional anthropological field methods expanded rather than contracted during the period of their research. The reader will note similar trends in the work of Price-Williams and Cole.

The Graves are frankly anti-cultural determinism. "Recourse to cultural explanations only serves to conceal our ignorance of underlying processes." They conceive of themselves as doing cross-cultural psychology. There may be some disciplinary identity problems in this stance. The Graves use a complex of variables such as achievement motivation, role regulation, group reaffirmation, revitalization, economic stress, arrest rates, and drunkenness. There is anthropological holism and eclecticism here. In any event, their methodology is ingenious and complex.

The Graves incorporate explicit psychological material and citations in their work. So do other anthropologists who do psychological anthropology, but by no means all. About twenty percent who have published articles in *Ethos* did not, and many who do so cite only one or two pieces. Whether the ultimate goal should be a clear interdisciplinarianism is still open to question, however. There may be incompatibilities between psychology and anthropology that make real collaboration of ideas and people unlikely unless one (usually the anthropologist) gives up more identity than the other.

For many anthropologists, the Graves' conclusions, so hard wrought out of so much careful work and ingenious methodology, don't warrant the effort. The conclusion drawn from a substantial research effort, "those migrants (Navajo) with the greatest psychological motivation to get drunk tend to seek out social situations in peer groups in which heavy drinking is normative, and when in those groups are most likely to fulfill the social expectations," is not likely to stir anthropologists to great bursts of enthusiasm. Navajo who want to drink join groups which do and while in them drink—is a conclusion we might want to start with, then join a drinking group to find out what really happens, then eventually work our way back to families of origin, selective factors in migration, rebuffs and frustrations in the city, etc., as the Graves actually do (without joining the drinking group, as far as I know). However, we might find our starting assumption to be quite wrong. Heavy drinkers may drink in solitude. Groupness may assuage feelings of anomie that may in turn reduce drinking and drunkenness, and so on. The road to scientific credibility is not an easy one and verification of what *seems* to be obvious is probably necessary. It is, however, somewhat contrary to the ethos (no pun intended) of anthropology.

Victor Turner's "Encounter with Freud," Chapter 16, may or may not be psychological anthropology. It is the most deviant paper in this volume and will prove to be a mind-stretcher for readers familiar with neither symbolic anthropology nor Freud. The paper challenges us to re-examine our position on reductionism. Whether Turner is doing psychological anthropology or not, his interest in symbols is shared with the psychoanalytic greats, with Freud foremost, whose thinking has provided the major structure of reference for psychocultural analysis, from Róheim to Kardiner to LeVine. But Turner, though he uses concepts such as repression, displacement, multireferentiality, contamination, and transference, does not feel it is theoretically admissible "to explain social facts, such as ritual symbols, directly by the concepts of depth psychology." He is concerned with collective process, the "metasocial commentary," not with individual psychological processes. He uses psychoanalytic concepts in a parallel fashion, as metaphors, as a style of thinking.

It seems to me that what Turner describes does depend upon individual psychological process, though I do not think, for his purposes, that analytic involvement with these processes is essential. I do not see, though, how the multireferentiality of the Blood Tree, for example (blood spilling, red meat, rich feeding, menstrual blood, blood at circumcision, etc.) becomes "a general and ambiguous potency" that is then deflected to the more abstract values and norms of matrimony, inducing the individual to feel the awesome power of his social obligations without individual psychological processing. Nor do I think Turner thinks it does. Many of us might contend that if we knew how this process, which Turner leaves at the collective level, occurs in the "minds" (perceived, cognited, affectively reinforced) of the ritual participants we would understand Ndembu ritual only a little or perhaps not at all better, but we would understand ritual and symbolism in panhuman terms much better. That is, excepting in metaphoric terms, Turner's analysis is culture-bound. This is precisely the purpose of psychologizing—to make it possible to move the culturally particular to the psychological, human nature generalizable level. At the same time, many of us as anthropologists would be compelled to confess that the collective representations, systems analysis in which Turner engages is highly satisfying, and that attention to "depth psychology" (or rather, to individual psychological processing) seems largely irrelevant to this analysis. It could even distract from the insights about Ndembu ritual symbols in relationship to Ndembu social structure that Turner so tellingly derives from his application of Freudian-derived metaphors. We must rest the case as moot; it depends upon purposes. An ultimate psychological anthropology, however, should encompass both purposes —to understand collective systems *and* individual psychological processing. Turner's analysis does, however, introduce some cautions we should heed. The symbols in all their multireferentiality are not activated by individuals as such but as actors in culturally defined situations and interactional sequences that reinforce certain dimensions of social structure ranging from formal social institutions like matrimony to processes like conflict. As anthropologists we ignore or de-emphasize this level of analysis at our peril.

The last two chapters of Part II are both on the cross-cultural study of cognition. The authors, Douglass Price-Williams and Michael Cole, are psychologists by training who became interested in the cross-cultural study of cognition after their professional careers had started. They have both now had intensive ethnographic experience. For this reason they are particularly sensitive to the differences that separate a psychological and an anthropological view. As Price-Williams says, "Both disciplines have as ultimate explanatory models, conceptual schemes that pass one another by."

Both are interested in studying the *process* of thinking rather than the results. Both have had to struggle with the fact that most culturally appropriate problems have culturally defined solutions. People (potential subjects) vary in the spreed and accuracy with which they arrive at culturally defined solutions. Psychology defines thinking as the process of arriving at a new (not already available in the culture) combination of previously learned elements. To study thinking, then, the investigator must interfere with the naturally occurring situation in some way—he must experiment. He cannot simply do ethnography. Or can he? This is the problem that Price-Williams and Cole face.

Both Cole and Price-Williams have devised and run many experiments designed to reveal the process of thinking, or cognitive development through various age levels. Both have faced squarely the fact that their experiments must use culturally appropriate categories and yet call for culturally unanticipated solutions—in the sense that the specific solution of the problem is not available in the culture known to the respondent. Price-Williams used kin terms, Cole used rice, among other culturally relevant items. Both arrived at interesting but equivocal results. Both have serious doubts about cross-cultural comparisons and experimental methods. Neither is willing to give up such methods. Both have turned to exacting ethnographic procedures, including ethnoscientific ones. An ethnography of cognitive activities, they hope, may make it possible to create experimental situations with opportunities for the display of cognitive skills already understood in their natural settings.

Readers will, of course, find many refinements of the above outline in the two papers. They deserve a careful reading. We know from these papers that psychology and anthropology are not about to go marching off into the sunset, arm in arm. Price-Williams and Cole challenge the cross-cultural, experimental, comparative approach (and support it). And their work raises questions about some of the pivots around which we anthropologists are reorganizing our thinking as we try to formulate a workable and productive psychological anthropology. Cultural over-determinism has become one of our pivotal problems. We all seem ready to confess our errors and face a brave new future with an open mind about human nature and its biocultural antecedents. I think we are right in doing so, and yet I am uneasy about some potential consequences. Price-Williams and Cole have found that cultures create such total contexts for thinking and learning to think that it is almost impossible to construct valid experiments that rise above this context. Human nature apparently cannot be studied except in its cultural manifestations, by social scientists at least. Perhaps we had better not discard all of our cultural determinism and culture relativism just yet. Our growing understanding of the interaction of cultural, social, psychological, techno-environmental, and biological factors has already caused us to revise substantially our concepts of determinism, and this revision is just beginning. We will soon be able to place cultural factors in a more accurate perspective, but this will not mean discarding them.

The reader is invited to examine the papers included in Part II in the light of those in Part I and the introductory discussions for each part. The distributive locus of culture, and of personality, deviants and individuals and diversity in all forms, differences within populations rather than between them, are matters of greater interest in Part II than in I, but these concerns emerge at various points in Part I. The questioning of cultural determinism and extreme cultural relativism begun in Part I is reinforced by the papers in Part II. The bothersome dichotomy—culture and personality—had mostly been done away with in Part I and little or no trace of it lingers in Part II. Tendencies toward anthropological holism and natural historicism persist in Part II, tempered by more attention to selected, discrete variables and experimental or neo-experimental research designs. There is more interest in cognitive processes in Part II. In general there is continuity in many sectors though there is a retreat, in Part II, from the grand models governing much of the earlier work.

REFERENCES CITED

Cone, C. A.
   1976   Steps Toward an Ecology of Ethos. *Reviews in Anthropology* 3:187–98.
Hallowell, A. I.
   1959   Behavioral Evolution and the Emergence of the Self. In *Evolution and Anthropology: A Centennial Appraisal,* ed. B. Meggers, pp. 36–60. Washington: Anthropological Society of Washington.
Lemert, E. M.
   1951   *Social Pathology.* New York: McGraw-Hill.
McDermott, R. and Wertz, M.
   1976   Doing the Social Order: Some Ethnographic Advances from Communicational Analysis and Ethnomethodology. *Reviews in Anthropology* 3:160–74.
Spindler, G. and Spindler, L.
   1971   *Dreamers Without Power: The Menomini Indians.* New York: Holt, Rinehart and Winston.
Spiro, M.
   1951   Culture and Personality: The Natural History of a False Dichotomy. *Psychiatry* 14:19–46.

The Author

THEODORE (TED) SCHWARTZ was born in south Philadelphia in 1928, the fifth son of Jewish immigrants from Russia and Roumania. He grew up on the business interstices of an ethnic mosaic, where he learned life was not to be contained within any single culture. He says he endured a perfunctory religious initiation as his last religious act at thirteen, only to find later that the ethos though not the faith of his parents' culture had been absorbed, and he has spent much of his professional career trying to understand what other people believe. He was a history major at Temple University, drawn to the study of religious movements.

In the senior year his first anthropology course with Jacob Gruber led to graduate study at the University of Pennsylvania. He went with the intention of becoming a physical anthropologist, but a course with A. I. Hallowell led him to specialize in psychological anthropology, though he was almost equally influenced by work in linguistics. After two years of preparation for research in Africa he was chosen by Margaret Mead as field assistant for her restudy of Manus (Melanesia) in 1953. There his dissertation research on religious and political movements "just happened."

He has pursued a longitudinal study of the Manus and of the peoples of the Admiralty Islands through five field trips of some five years' total duration over the past twenty-two years. In between he worked at the American Museum of Natural History, spent three years in the study of a Mexican village directed by Erich Fromm, two years of post-doctoral study in Paris where, he says, he did not become a structuralist, and taught at Michigan, Chicago, Hawaii, University of California at Los Angeles, and for the past five years at the University of California, San Diego.

His most recent research has been a study of cognitive acculturation. He points out that much of his work remains in draft or moving slowly toward publication. He is widely recognized for his work on cults in Melanesia. He has done much personality and cognitive testing and, although observation and interview remain basic anthropological methods, he believes the problem of measurement is crucial. All its difficulties must still be dealt with. He was one of the organizers of the journal *Ethos,* which now serves the field of psychological anthropology.

This Chapter

In this chapter Theodore Schwartz provides a model that attempts to resolve the tension between the extremes of heterogeneity and nonsharing proposed by some psychological anthropologists and the extreme of sharing and homogeneity espoused by early exponents of modal personality and similar concepts. He dispenses with *a priori* ascriptions of homogeneity but makes no *a priori* assumption of heterogeneity. He assumes there will always be both.

His essential concept is the "idioverse"—the total set of implicit constructs of each individual in a cultural system. The individualized texture of a culture is at the level of the idioverse. The idioverse derives from the experience of the individual in all the events making up his life history but it also consists of new formations based on manipulation, combination, or transformation of constructs. Schwartz recognizes that variation and change, as well as stability, are intrinsic to the nature of culture.

Some readers may be inclined to see this model as arguing against sharing and commonality within a cultural system. This is not Schwartz's intention. The structure of commonality is created from all of the intersects among idioverses of the members of a society. Both the idioverses and the intersects are constituents of the culture. A degree of commonality, at one level, makes possible a degree of human communication at other levels.

The model helps to resolve the bind of assigning commonality to culture and personality to individuals, and avoids the charge of reductionism from a cultural to a psychological level that has been a bugaboo to anthropologists ever since culture and personality emerged as a field.

This chapter concludes with a discussion of the similarities and differences between his model and those of others.

G.D.S.

12 Where Is the Culture? Personality as the Distributive Locus of Culture

THEODORE SCHWARTZ

The notion that anthropologists deal with relatively homogeneous cultures—abstracting an essential homogeneity from the background noise of insignificant diversity—has greatly influenced our approach to the study of cultures. Views of culture based on uniformity have been subject to a number of incisive critiques, particularly those of Devereux (1945), Spiro (1951), and Wallace (1961, 1970). The question, however, becomes this: if culture is *not* necessarily shared uniformly, what and where is it? And how does it relate to social structure and personality? For some time, our definitions of culture have centered on the shared-ness of rules, beliefs, and practices among members of a society. If practices varied, they could be explained by a welter of contingencies. The notion of homogeneity could be preserved by assuming that the rules, at least, were invariant even if people deviated from them in differing degrees and circumstances. True, obvious status differences such as sex and age were sometimes considered. But for many other aspects of culture, mention of even this rudimentary differentiation was often absent from ethnographic accounts.

When I was just out of graduate school I found myself doing field work among the Manus people of the Admiralty Islands of Melanesia.[1] Armed with the notion that there is *a* culture to be discovered, I confronted my informants with the sorts of questions that had been handed down to me. To my confusion, I encountered such diversity of opinion that I asked myself, "Where is the culture?" Had I been misled by overly systematized ethnographies, on which I had been raised as a student? Or was it that the Manus somehow represented an

1. From 1953 to 1954 I took part in Margaret Mead's restudy of the Manus, and continued field work among them between 1963 and 1966, and again in 1967, 1973 and 1975.

abnormal situation? The conspicuous individuality of informants, their characteristic styles, their stubbornly individualized viewpoints, their lengthy discussions both in response to my questions and in terms of their own problems of action, *their constant litigation of culture*—were all these things the effects, perhaps, of acculturation? The Manus, after all, had been confronted with the life styles of Asians, Europeans, Australians, and Americans. If that were the case, then the precontact situation may well have corresponded to the Durkheimian notion of uniform collective consciousness and solidarity based on likeness.[2] But the more I have studied the Manus, the more I have come to doubt that such homogeneity has ever characterized their culture. Even in Margaret Mead's, and including Reo Fortune's 1928 studies of the then much less acculturated horizon of Manus culture, it is possible to look past the generalizations and see in the fine descriptive work the same strong and distinctive personalities, the same diversity of approaches, the same multitude of small innovations and individual styles competing in the shaping of events.

I now believe that even the most minimal community would reveal a comparable distinctiveness of personality and cultural variation which, *when viewed against the scale of the culture and by the concerns of its members,* cannot be considered trivial. The cultures of relatively small-scale societies were much more complex than I had expected. To produce a highly filtered and homogenized ethnography would mean discarding the bulk of my observations—a great loss of information in a dubious leap of abstraction. What I began to perceive, during that initial period of field work (1953–54), was the need for a model or a conceptualization of culture that was adequate for the complexity of the culture I was observing. The implication, of course, was that if existing models did not fit even small-scale societies, then our concept of culture was grossly inadequate for application to the obviously diverse, stratified, regionally differentiated, ethnically complex, pluralistic, national, and industrial societies. A view of culture either as homogeneous or as including only those features that met some threshold value of commonality, or some central tendency of a given magnitude, also presented considerable problems for attempts to reintegrate culture with social structure, and with personality in the individual. Once these aspects were separated analytically, it would be difficult to rediscover the unity they presumably have in behavior and experience.

One could perhaps find some personal trait that led me to value the

2. Durkheim 1893 (translation in 1933 and discussed in Schwartz 1972 from which the present paper is, in part, adapted).

diversity of views and practices of the Melanesian villagers with whom I lived. I had grown up in an ethnically and acculturatively heterogeneous neighborhood. What I saw in the Admiralty Islands seemed altogether natural, once I had relaxed my trained expectations. I had intended to write a dissertation on the languages and kinship systems of the Admiralty Islands, and I did collect the necessary data. But I found myself in the thick of events that I could not ignore. The Paliau Movement (named after its leader) and the related cargo cults were among the most dramatic and widely recurrent events of the Melanesian contact culture, and they became the focus of my work. They required reconstruction, observation, and elicitation around past and current events in which thousands of persons were involved. The diversity of accounts about the role of Paliau alone tempted me at one time to write my monograph in the form of a series of gospels about the life and works of Paliau according to each of a number of major participants in the story. But the more I learned, the more the events of those years took on an individualized texture of the many who had cooperatively and competitively given form to those events. It is difficult enough to produce an historical account, let alone to arrive at the underlying culture-in-process that was passing through different states as well as undergoing more fundamental change even as it was being documented. And with each return to the field, I found my informants having not only a different present but a different past.

Over the years, my continuing longitudinal study helped to clarify the distinction between state shifts (from one to another state of a culture, each having certain characteristics potential in that culture),[3] change in the culture itself, and phase shifts (marking changes in the characteristics of the process of change; Schwartz 1962). One form of error, often unavoidable without longitudinal study, is the failure to see that some feature one attributes to a culture is state- or phase-relative. Thus, for example, the relationship between cult and movement (the latter more secular, political, culture wide, and programmatically, temporally extended than a cult) changed from one phase to another, and much that I had thought defunct in Manus culture was found efflorescent ten years later as expectations about imminent achievement of parity with European standards of living had diminished.

As Manus culture underwent marked change, the flow of population through time was punctuated—segmented historically and perceptually by the differing events, experiences, and situations of successive

3. F. Gearing's concept of "cultural stance" in ethnohistorical study of the Cherokee is similar (Gearing 1962).

age cohorts. As in all rapidly changing cultures, we have to deal with a time-stratified culture. Generation becomes not merely a status in a repetitive cycle, but a cultural differential.[4] Longitudinal study points up the problem: When has something become a part of a culture? Still more difficult, when is something such as a word or a rite no longer a part of a culture—when it has not been used for the past five hours, or the past five or fifty years? We cannot be satisfied with an arbitrary answer any more than with some arbitrary degree of prevalence of its use across individuals within the society. We require a model that takes both flowthrough and distribution into account.

The question of delimiting a culture spatially and demographically is equally problematic, although perhaps more familiar. The Manus people are rather easily bounded ecologically, linguistically, and in other cultural respects. The same cannot be said for their neighbors in the Admiralty Island Archipelago, who show more complex cultural and linguistic gradations. However, the problem remains, even for the Manus, for theirs is a culture specialized in fishing and trade, interlaced in exchange relations with all other peoples of the Archipelago. From my contacts with other Admiralty Island peoples in 1953 and 1954, I felt that there was an underlying similarity of institutions even though native perceptions of cultural differences were focused on certain key or emblematic traits. Manus culture seemed to me not understandable in itself; in some ways it had to be seen as part of a single interactive areal culture encompassing the whole of the Admiralty Islands.[5] I have spent some years constructing an areal ethnography of the Admiralty Islands, including what would conventionally be considered psychological variables among the cultural dimensions on which the many local groups may be compared. I have continued to the present my initial search for "the culture" and what it is becoming in space, in time, and in its distribution across individuals, groups, and populations. The remainder of this paper will treat only distributive models of culture in relation to personality. No matter how we segment a population in space, time, or social groups, the problem remains of the distribution of culture within and between the segments.

DISTRIBUTIVE MODELS OF CULTURE

I have come to view culture as embodied in a set of constructs or representations about behavioral events and classes of events. That set of

4. See Schwartz, 1975*b*, for further discussion of time-stratified cultures and generational relations.
5. I have discussed aspects of the structure and process of this areal culture in Schwartz, 1963; and Schwartz, 1975*a*.

constructs is formed or internalized by the members of a society, externalized in the structuring of events, or stored externally as artifacts or messages that are readable (that is, capable of being internalized). By "internalized" I do not mean internalization of "*the* culture." "Internalization" refers to the continuous process in which individuals form, modify and store derivatives or representations of events. "Internal" refers to physical, bodily events, processes and structures resulting from interactions within environmental events. Further "internal" events may transform such structures through recombination, synthesis, and in other ways, so that they need not remain simple copies of external reality and may, in turn within the constraints of that reality, affect the individual's perceptions of it. Our internal representations are subject to the corrective impact of that reality to the extent they have reference to it. Whether dealing with event constructs or fantasies, one posits the objectivity of the subjective and pursues the interactions between external and internal reality.

It should be unnecessary to offer this explanation of the term "internalization" but one might be taken as suggesting the individual swallows his culture whole—the distributive view of culture is to the contrary as will be seen. Or, one might be seen as having taken sides with the "internal" in a forced choice between mentation and situation —a choice between inseparable aspects of a single process, which I reject. Or, one might be taken for an "idealist" in some polemical survival of the anachronistic opposition between idealism and materialism applied to culture because one claims relevance to on-going behavior for states, processes and structures of a human organism derived from its previous participations in events (its life historical experience) in interaction with an environment that includes in its physical presence other "learned" persons. I suppose I tend to be a dichotoclast.

The distribution of a culture among the members of a society transcends the limitations of the individual in the storage, creation, and use of the cultural mass. *A distributive model of culture most take into account both diversity and commonality.* It is diversity that increases the cultural inventory, but it is commonality that assures a degree of communicability and coordination.

A distributive model of culture is one that is based on the distribution of a culture among the members of a society (or over some field of persons, however bounded). Given that the relations among the members of the society are socially structured, a distributive model of culture seeks to indicate the mapping of a cultural system upon a social system. The social structure itself, however, is a cultural artifact, having a distributive and variable cultural base. Its substance is the relations among persons and groups. This substance is variously perceived and shaped, partitioned, labeled and manipulated like any artifact by the many participants of a society in accordance with their prior experience and adaptive needs in a given environment.

A distributive model of culture offers several advantages. It avoids the *a priori* assumption of homogeneity or of some degree of homogeneity, arbitrarily chosen, in the content of a culture without requiring a corrective dissolution of culture into distantly receding idiosyncrasies against which we may, at best, project a loose coordination. It indicates an approach to describing and studying the distribution of culture among the members of a society and it provides a useful basis for articulating culture with social structure and personality.

In the evolution of systems, the relation between parts and wholes changes at the human level, but not just in terms of the specialization and interdependence already characteristic of organic systems. More profoundly, the parts—the human actors in a social system—form or internalize representations of the whole as well as of the subsystems in which the individuals were participants. Individuals store representations of past states of the system, each according to his own history of participations. And because the relation among parts (individuals or groups) is in some degree determined and oriented in terms of these stored representations which are in turn subject to modification in further events, the system is an open or evolving one.

In contrast to the relative isolation of the stored genetic materials of organic systems, the set of constructs of the enculturated individual is not isolated. It is subject to continuing communication with the structures of all events in which the individual takes part. In place of genotype and phenotype, there are implicit constructs and artifacts. An artifact is any thing or event to which form is given in the process of behavior, whether this form be transient (such as a gesture, a facial expression, or an utterance) or relatively permanent (such as a monument).

CONSTRUCTS AND THE "IDIOVERSE"

I initially defined the total set of implicit constructs of each individual in a cultural system as his "idioverse,"[6] which I then conceived of as a sector of his personality. The idioverse may be said to be the

6. This term was coined, I believe, by the psychologist Saul Rosenzweig, mentioned in a 1953 lecture by Jules Wishner, University of Pennsylvania psychologist. I have been using it in the above sense since 1958 (Mead and Schwartz).

individual's "portion" of his culture. At the level of the idioverse is the individualized texture of a culture. It is the distributive locus of culture, its social unit.

The constructs comprising the idioverse are derived from the experience of the individual in all the events making up his life history. The idioverse consists, further, of new formations based on manipulation, combination, or transformation of such constructs. The representational processes that generate and reapply these constructs are construals of experience both of specifics and of classes of events, objects, persons, relations, and other domains. Some constructs or representations are also directly inculcated (with varying effectiveness in domains in which a society "seeks or requires" a higher level of commonality) as "correct" labels, symbols, rules, propositions, and standardized event constructs. Rather than being bound to the replication of reality, constructs may image its contrary; they may also project goal-states and events not yet experienced but representable by transformation of the construct-store at hand. Variation and change are both intrinsic to the nature of culture as well as reflective of environmental change, providing the basis for internal diversity, adaptation, and cultural differentiation.

The constructs making up the idioverse are simultaneously cognitive, evaluative, and affective mappings of the structure of events and classes of events, both past and possible, real and hypothetical. Constructs vary in form and in articulation, depending on the domains they represent and on their place in a hierarchy of specificity-generality of representations.

In construct formation, the cognitive may seem to have priority in representing the form of a behavioral event and its articulation with other events. But the form is embodied also in the affective and evaluative internal and external response to the referent event. It may be of considerable heuristic value to assert that there is no such thing as "pure cognition." At the very least, cognitive process is motivated. The demonstrability and behavioral force of a construct depends largely on responses to the crossing of gradients in the structure of behavior. Such crossings—that is, transgressions of construct lines—are manifested in subjective responses such as awareness, discomfort, anxiety, shame, and anger; they may show up in external responses by others to the behavior in the attention it arouses, the sanctions it may elicit, or in its perception as familiar or unfamiliar.

Such a construct may be envisioned as a frame that defines limits in one direction on the form of behavior or of events, and that defines in another direction the limits on the environments or situations in which

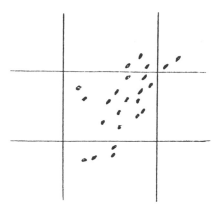

Figure 1.

the behavior may properly occur. The horizontal lines in Figure 1 represent the limits on the form of the behavior or event. The vertical lines represent its situational limits. Each dot represents the occurrence of a specific behavioral event over this field, which is partitioned or framed by a construct. The behavior-determining or motivational valence of such a construct has to do with a degree or strength of its constraint on the referent behavior. Deviation is represented by a distance of each occurrence from the boundary gradients of the frame; within the frame, there is free variation. Deviation distance and the behavior-determining or motivational valence of the frame determines the strength of the aroused internal or external reactions to the behavior, or to the perception of the behavior as familiar or unfamiliar. Similarly, we may speak of the mapping of consciousness over a given phenomenal or behavioral field. Consciousness is mapped onto constructs as a variable component of constructs along with their cognitive, affective, and evaluative components.

To illustrate this conceptual sketch of a construct, we may use the culturally defined behavior, "sitting." If we look around a college classroom, it is likely that during the lecture period (the situational, or vertical lines) the students will be sitting; the instructor may be sitting, standing, or perhaps walking back and forth in front of the room. The professor's range of permissible, expected behaviors is broader than that of the student, extending over several related frames of the postural-action domain, each of which has a certain range of free variation. We do not have to look very closely to see that each student is behaving quite differently at some level of physical or anatomical specification. And yet, even though no two behaviors are physically alike, all the students are "sitting." Cultural sameness is a matter of formal, not physical, identity. As long as sitting behavior of the students is within the bounds of free variation, a person entering the room would notice nothing exceptional. He would not think, "Everyone is sitting." Unless the behavior were discrepant in form or situation of occurrence, he would probably not be in any way conscious of their behavior.

The construct lines should be thought of as more or less steep gradients. For each participant in the classroom event, the gradients may be drawn at somewhat different positions on the field of possible behaviors and situations. A slight transgression—for example, someone sitting on their seat in the lotus position—might make an observer aware of a difference; he might even experience some slight anxiety or discomfort and may raise an eyebrow or edge away as a minor sanction. A greater deviation—for example, if it were the professor sitting this way on a laboratory demonstration table and swaying rhythmically as he lectured on chemistry—would prompt everyone's recognition that his behavior in that situation, his status in that class of events, would be highly discrepant with respect to the constructs of all other participants. More extreme sanctions might be provoked or, eventually, constructs might be redrawn to allow for acceptance of the behavior.

I can only suggest here the many extensions of this schema which may be useful. We may imagine some cultures or sectors of cultures of narrow mesh, with narrowly drawn constructs having sharp gradients and high behavior-determining or motivational valences; we may assume a continuum from this to wide-mesh cultures. We could explore the variable mapping of constructs in terms of consciousness, affect, and value. We could examine events as a process of communication among individuals in terms of their respective constructs and the structure of the event itself. Individuals enter events with preconstructs. They compete and cooperate in the shaping of that event. And they may or may not modify their postconstructs in terms of the structure of that event. The events may drift across the behavioral field partitioned by the constructs of the members of a culture until many or most events appear discrepant in comparison with the older constructs. This condition may persist, with attempts to bring events back into line; constructs may be updated; or the culture may become generationally or temporally stratified. In short, it should be evident that representations of experience— whether as internalized constructs or as external artifacts distributed across time, space, and individuals, may be considered the stuff of which cultures are constituted. A theory of representations must have a central place in a theory of culture.

THE STRUCTURE OF COMMONALITY

If culture is not a shared or common set of constructs held by all members of a society, how should it be delimited? Between the extremes of total homogeneity and total heterogeneity we may speak of a *"structure of commonality"* which is neither one nor the other. That structure consists of all of the intersects among idioverses—among all pairs, all triads, etc.—all subsets of the total set of idioverses of the members of a society. Although the structure of commonality thus defined serves as a useful theoretical limit, containing all shared constructs, within it there is the *"social structure of commonality"* comprising the intersects among the idioverses of sets of individuals having some common social function, attribute, identity, or accorded significance. We would expect the intersects for such status groups (the "cells" of the social structure of commonality) to contain the relative peaks of commonality to be found among the cells of the overall structure of commonality. Such peaks reflect a degree of common experience among the members of a social category or status group, as well as some of the specializations or socially functional standardizations that operate for a given status or profile of statuses.

"CULTURE" DEFINED IN TERMS OF THE IDIOVERSE

Having dispensed with the *a priori* assumption of a given degree of homogeneity in a culture, we could identify "culture" distributively with the structure of commonality but this would seem to me not to go far enough. There is reason to include in the culture *all* of the content of each idioverse; not only that which lies in some intersect among idioverses, but also that which lies in the differences among idioverses (Figure 2).

I include in the culture all of the constructs—all of the derivations of experience and transformations of these available to the members of a society. This inclusiveness is important to the adequacy of the culture concept to deal with change, innovation, creativity, and the internal productivity of new content and goals within a cultural system. The distribution of the content of a culture expands that culture only to the extent that there exists the possibility of communication and access to that which is not already shared. Without including the areas of idioverses that lie outside the set of intersects, much that is exactly like that which is included would be arbitrarily left out. There are many obvious kinds of constructs confined to single idioverses which should not be

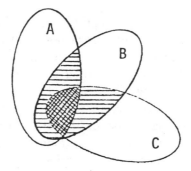

Figure 2. The ovals represent the idioverses (the set of all constructs) of three individuals. The crosshatched area is the intersect of all three; in other words, it represents those constructs the individuals have in common in the sense of formal identity. Culture defined in terms of commonality alone would be confined to this crosshatched area. The lined areas are the intersects of pairs of idioverses. These would be a part of the structure of commonality. If culture were defined as the structure of commonality, it would be confined to the lined and crosshatched areas. The clear areas within the ovals are the (symmetrical) differences between the three idioverses. The model presented here argues for the inclusion of the differences (the idioversal constructs which, at a given level of contrast, are not shared) in the culture. In terms of set theory, the culture is defined as the (weighted) union of idioverses rather than as the set of all intersects or the intersect of all idioverses.

excluded from the culture; for example, the knowledge of a genealogical expert in Manus. His knowledge was available for the structuring of events, and when he died, without transmitting this knowledge to a protégé, the culture was importantly altered. But his views (or constructs) on many other things less obviously specialized were also deleted from the input to events. The idioverse of each individual is a significant portion of a culture, contributing both to the size and the weighting (frequency of occurrence of constructs) of the union of idioverses.

Without this inclusive view, each act of communication would produce a now-you-see-it-now-you-don't crossing of the line bounding the culture as something passes from one idioverse to the intersect of more than one idioverse. Innovations would keep appearing unaccountably as they leap into culture. Communication, aside from internal processing within the individual, implies imparting new information, forming or changing constructs. It requires involvement of the disjoint portions (not held in common) of the idioverses of individuals. The rest is ritual or the exchange of tokens or symbols of commonality, which while of great importance in culture is not taken here as wholly comprising culture to the exclusion of communication. A degree of commonality at one level makes possible a degree of communication about difference at another. *Both* are part of culture.

As the personnel of an event give form to that event, *all* the constructs of their respective idioverses potentially enter into the orientation of behavior in that event. The inclusion of the differences among idioverses brings into this model of a culture all constructs that are *available* for the structuring of events. A further result of this inclusive distributive model of culture is the interesting possibility that it offers for an overall conceptualization of the articulation of culture, social structure, and personality. For these reasons, I define "a culture" as the set of idioverses of the members of a society, including, but not wholly comprised by, the structure and social structure of commonality. It includes all the experientially derived and transformed constructs held by any member of that society.[7]

PERSONALITY IN RELATION TO CULTURE

This model of culture has implications for a unified model of the relation of personality and culture. *Culture is no more that which is shared by all members of a society than personality is confined to that which is unique to the individual.* "Personality" is defined here as the total set of experiential derivatives of an individual. It includes those derivatives or constructs which are unique to him or held in common with various subsets of individuals; it includes the possibility of some experiential derivatives (or constructs) that may be held in common with all other members of that society. Further, no one culture defines all the commonality of human experience; the personality of the individual includes experiential residues of events and situations that may be extremely prevalent or common to members of certain types of societies. These may derive, for example, from recurrent biological or social relations. Thus, the personality of the individual takes part in a hierarchy of commonalities, ranging from the unique to the universal.

Under this formulation, the concepts of "idioverse" and of "personality" overlap considerably. It would be possible at this point to differentiate them further or to seek to make them coincide. In the manner of current tripartite models of culture, social structure, and personality, the motivational and dynamic aspects of personality could

7. I am using the term "society" here without critical examination because of space limitations. Generally, a society is an identified population, interdependent and intercommunicating at some level. It may be complexly subdivided and may itself be a subdivision of a larger social integration. Its identity and structure is itself to a large extent cultural. (Culture aspects of social identities are discussed in Schwartz, 1963 and 1975a.)

be separated from the cognitive aspects of the idioverse.[8] I choose the other course, experimentally, of assimilating "personality" and "idioverse" by defining the personality as the individual's total set of experiential derivatives conceived of as a set of representations or constructs that, as defined for the idioverse, represent the form and situation of behavioral events. The constructs have cognitive, affective, and evaluative components, variably summing to the behavior-determining or motivational potential of the construct. In terms of their accessibility to awareness, personality constructs occur in the conscious, the preconscious, and the unconscious, or they may have components from all of these levels.

Without attempting a comprehensive translation of personality into idioversal constructs, I will take the personality of the individual as including at least four types of constructs. The first is a set of self-reflexive constructs. The second is a set of constructs of broad behavioral generality, closely associated with significant others in their origin in the process of socialization. The third is the set of basal constructs of great generality, underlying ways of responding, acting, experiencing, and of constructing experience, that we might consider an affective and cognitive character structure. The fourth is the large set of constructs representing the knowledge, beliefs, and the norms and expectations of events. These four sets of constructs overlap, but they may be grouped in this way to indicate their partial correspondence to self, superego, character, and the remainder of the stored residues of experience that were taken as comprising the idioverse.

The personality, as the idioverse previously defined, accumulates some degree of inertia given the increasing commitment of basal constructs in the enculturation process. But it exists in constant communication with the structure of the events in which it participates and in the structuring of which it competes and cooperates with other personalities. It provides the individual's behavioral orientation in the very perception and construal of events. It exists in a kind of respiration of internalization and externalization, exchanging preconstructs for postconstructs and construct for action in entering and leaving events.

The result of this identification of the idioverse and personality is a unified rather than a dual or tripartite theory of culture and personality, which are seen as differing not in substance or content but in their place

8. See Talcott Parsons, 1951, as a basic source of the tripartite view; and Melford Spiro, 1972, for a cogent recent argument for the analytic utility of this view (see especially footnote 5, p. 589).

or level in a distributive, hierarchic structure. *A set of personalities constitutes the distributive locus of a culture. A personality is the individual's version and portion of his culture. A culture consists of all of the personalities of the individuals constituting a society or subsociety, however bounded.*[9] The reader should review the previous sections on the idioverse in relation to culture and the structure of commonality. Substituting "personality" for "idioverse," all statements remain applicable and are important to this model of personality as the distributive locus of culture.

A description of the personality as a distributive unit of a culture does not amount to the microcosmic viewpoint,[7][10] which considers the personality as a microcosm of the culture as a whole, somehow reduced and internalized by each individual. Nor is it a view of the culture in the Benedictian sense as personality writ large. Any one personality is not a culture. But that personality with all others of a society interacting in events does constitute a culture. A given personality is not necessarily representative in a statistical sense, nor is the approximation to some central tendency the aspect of culture stressed by a distributive model. Rather, this model emphasizes the whole array of personalities, the constructs they bring to and derive from events, and their structuring of events in construct-oriented behavior. Centrality (or typicality) would not necessarily be predictive of (it may even be negatively correlated with) the contribution of a given personality to the structuring of events. It is essential, then, to emphasize that although individual personalities and their cognitive-evaluative-affective constructs of experience are the constituents of culture, they may be discrepant and conflicted among (and within) themselves or with central tendencies or configurations in the overall population of personalities comprising a culture or subculture. Similarly, the constructs of the individual will vary in the adequacy with which individuals anticipate and conduct the course of events. The model of culture as a set of personalities does not preclude conflict; rather, the inclusion of the differences as well as the similarities among personalities in the culture makes social coordination a central research

9. While for present purposes I define a culture as a population of personalities, I must add, "and their artifacts," keeping in mind that in the process of cultural evolution externally stored information is an increasingly large part of the total mass of a culture in comparison with the internal storage of experience and information distributed among the members of a population. This external part of the culture is prosthetic—an extension of man and raises many questions such as access, control, readability which cannot be discussed here. It may be better to regard the artifactual realm as part of the cultural environment capable of use and intermittent internalization by individuals.

10. See Wallace 1970, p. 123*ff.*

problem implied by this model.[11] Differences may lead to conflict or complementarity. The perception of commonality or difference are themselves construals which, at times, may mask their opposite (Schwartz 1975*a*).

The microcosmic analogy within certain limits is not without some value. Both the configurational approach of Ruth Benedict, Margaret Mead, Gregory Bateson (and myself at times: Schwartz 1973) and the cultural deductive work of Abraham Kardiner and, extended to cross-cultural research, John Whiting, contribute greatly to our understanding of culture and personality in spite of its vulnerability for their audacious derivations of patterns attributed to whole cultures. In a system consisting of human beings, the parts have many ways of transcending the particular. Individuals may, for example, form constructs of the whole, just as the personality may contain self-reflexive constructs construing some image of the self. So also we would expect personalities to have a view of their social and cultural milieu. All of its constructs involving multi-personal events would contain expectations about the behavior of others. And these constructs would range from highly specific expectations about particular individuals or groups to expectations geared to classes of individuals in classes of situations. In short, the personality contains constructs that are its part of the culture's self-ethnography, as well as constructs of expected behavior and characteristics of all other groups with which the individual's group is in contact.

The constructs of the individual personality must include some internalization of the expectations of others. These expectations are taken into account in the choice among alternative constructs in events. There must also be the capacity for role taking, for seeing an event to some extent as the other may see it, and (accurately or erroneously) to make inferences about the motivations and interests of others. As A. Irving Hallowell, George Devereux, and others have pointed out, the individual in any culture must make cultural and personological inferences of at least some minimal degree of accuracy in order to interact effectively and to maintain some state of relatively secure expectation in his social environment. At all times, he is both consciously and unconsciously processing behavioral data in building his own distributive ethnography.

11. These remarks are a partial response to the important criticism of Spiro (personal communication) that a unified model such as this or his earlier one (Spiro, 1951) of personality, social structure and culture would be less useful than the tripartite model in dealing with conflict and social control. I cannot represent his criticism adequately (but see Spiro 1961) in a paper in which I do not take up the question of social structure to any extent.

OTHER DISTRIBUTIVE MODELS OF CULTURE

I cannot attempt in this paper an inventory or history of distributive models of culture. My own model was first developed briefly in Mead and Schwartz (1958), later in my 1962 monograph, and again in an article with Margaret Mead, "Micro and Macro Cultural Models for Cultural Evolution." The model was developed further in my paper, "Beyond Cybernetics" (1968). There, the idioverse was seen as a component of personality; this paper attempts to equate the two.

In my own anthropological lineage a distributive view of culture appeared intermittently and usually implicitly in the work of many in the field of culture and personality studies. Personality itself often tended to be seen in its standardized aspects, with the variation taken either as insignificant or as deviant. The ethnographies to which culture and personality theories made reference often stopped at describing basic themes or configurations of the culture taken as if homogeneous.

Culture and personality theorists invoked the individual in critical response to the superorganic view of culture, which often chose metaphors that would lead one to imagine culture as floating somehow disembodied in the noösphere or, at best, carried by human beings as a conductor might carry an electric current containing information. Psychological anthropologists were at pains to assert that culture inhered in the internalization of experience by individuals. A. I. Hallowell could object to such a notion as "culture contact" with "Cultures don't contact, people do." Without an explicit distributive model of culture, however, such statements do not go beyond the obvious. Leslie White would dismiss the relevance of psychology in explanation of the variation of cultures with his conundrum, "A constant cannot explain a variable." But he was not concerned with subvariation within a culture taken as a kind of species. Psychology, of course, is a constant if one is referring to the "psychic unity" of mankind—the basic capacities that underlie our use of culture. But if one is concerned—as so much of modern psychology is—with the effect of the experience of individuals shaping their further experience and behavior; if one accords importance to the cognitive orientations and affective responses people bring to the events in which they participate, and if learning, perception, and personality formation are psychological matters, then these psychological processes define not merely the possibility but the content of culture, given that they are adaptive as well to external circumstances.

George Devereux (1945) and Melford Spiro (1951) offered explicit distributive models for culture and personality which were particularly influential for me and which should be consulted for their continuing importance. Spiro accounted for individual and small group variation in culture through the process of cultural transmission, in which the cultural "heredity" of the individual must inevitably diverge from the cultural "heritage" available in previous generation. Spiro offered a partial model, similar to my own in many ways, for the expected internal diversity of a culture and for personality and culture as closely related abstractions from the same behavioral data (see also Spiro 1972).

The most widely known and most well elaborated distributive model of culture presently in use is that of Anthony Wallace. For this reason I discuss his model critically below, stressing points of difference to clarify his model and my own while leaving the extensive similarities as a tacit offering to the *Zeitgeist*. A more recent distributive model of culture is that of Ward Goodenough (1971).[12] Early workers in the field of psychological anthropology undertook to characterize whole populations in psychological or personality terms. Formulations such as those of Abraham Kardiner (1939, 1945) seemed unsatisfactory because they assumed a relatively homogeneous central or basic personality structure for a population, even though this could not be demonstrated at the time.[13] Anthony Wallace (1952) developed further Cora DuBois' (1944) notion of a modal personality structure and attempted empirically to show the distribution of a set of scores on a psychological test administered to a sample of Tuscarora Indians. From these distributions he defined, statistically, a modal group of individuals; he then described in a synthetic way the personality characteristics of this modal group.

The percentage of people (37 percent) who fell within the modal range on the twenty-one Rorschach test variables has become one of the magic numbers of anthropology cited in many texts. The question is whether this 37 percent indicates much or little commonality in the distribution of personality traits in this population. Generally, it seems to be taken as indicating that there is surprisingly less commonality than might be supposed in basic personality theory. Actually, the number is meaningless as a statistic estimating the amount of commonality. The 37

12. Goodenough's model of culture is extensively similar to my own. He labels "propriocept" an entity that closely resembles the idioverse or Wallace's "mazeway." Goodenough tends to define the culture in terms of that which is shared, albeit complexly and distributively, while what I have defined as the culture (including the total set of personalities, both their intersects and symmetrical differences), he terms the "cultural pool"—in other words, all cultural constructs that are available potentially to members of a society. In that article he does not undertake the extension to personality.

13. In other respects, however, the work of Kardiner and his anthropological associates was epochal, applying a flexible psychoanalytic-cultural theory to the analysis of a series of specific ethnographic descriptions.

percent would be extremely high if the twenty-one variables were independent. The chance of falling within the modal range on each of twenty-one independent variables would be very small indeed, but because the interdependence of the variables is not analyzed, it does not lead to any meaningful assessment of centrality or commonality.[14]

Wallace went on to formulate a general distributive model of culture based on a notion he called the "mazeway" of the individual that is similar in some ways to the idioverse. The implication he drew from the Tuscarora study was that commonality is and need be much less in an adequately integrated society than we might have expected. Wallace argues that virtually no shared constructs are needed in order for the behavior of individuals to be coordinated with that of others (1961, 1970). They need not have the same representations of situations. They need only have a representation that leads them to behave in some appropriate way at the right time while others are behaving under the same stimulus in appropriate but diverse ways. Each has a construct orienting his own behavior, but he need not have one that represents the behavior of others. All that is required, Wallace argues, are equivalence structures—in other words, that people behave conjointly in different but appropriate ways to common situational stimuli.

Wallace's reasoning leads not only to the recognition of diversity but to the virtual elimination of commonality in culture. In its place it leaves equivalence structures of persons holding different but functionally coordinated constructs. I believe this may have been a useful antidote to more homogeneous views of culture, but it is an overdose that leads to a symmetrical and opposite malady. The model I have drawn above assumes both commonality and difference. The differences may be functionally integrated (equivalent) or conflictful or irrelevant (neutral) at a given time or event.

Wallace concludes that because it is not necessary for actors to have the same construct for a joint event, then cognitive sharedness is not a functional prerequisite of culture. This excludes a middle ground where much of culture may be found. Although it is easily demonstrated that participants in an event need not have constructs that are identical in their totality at a given level of specification, this does not exclude the probable case that sharedness and formally identical constructs may occur extensively and may have functional importance, or that some

---

14. Other statistical, methodological, and psychological problems largely invalidate the Tuscarora analysis (Thomas Hay n.d., and an independent reanalysis of the Tuscarora by the present author is in process). The study has nevertheless led to Wallace's widely appreciated thinking on the distributive relation of culture and personality.

level and kinds of commonality may be a requisite of cultural and personal integration and individual adjustment.

Wallace further argues that all the members of a society need not share a single construct, although "it may happen in some peculiarly simple society" (1970, p. 33). He asserts that two or more parties may indeed share a common cognitive map, but that this would be wasteful because the common map would have to be larger than their individual maps, which show the event only in their own perspective. The argument from economy is a dubious one; nonredundant constructs that are blind to the overall event and that involve no "role-taking" or sharedness affect a relatively minor economy compared to the vastly greater economy of distribution and specialization of culture over statuses and over persons in terms of experiential differentiation. Here, as Durkheim, Compte, Spencer, and many others have argued, is the economy on which much of cultural growth is built (along with that of external storage and implementation). The economy of nonredundant, individually minimal constructs sacrifices the gains of a functionally adequate level of redundancy and reduplications of overlapping individual networks that serve so importantly in social organization.

Wallace gives an example involving parents, a child who puts his baby tooth under his pillow, and the good fairy who leaves a dime in its place (1970, pp. 28–33). Each (with the possible exception of the good fairy) supposedly has a distinct and minimal construct of the situation. The event is, however, wrongly and too simply analyzed; the imagined constructs are minimal. The child does not experimentally discover that if he leaves his tooth under the pillow the tooth is replaced by a dime and then invent the good fairy explanation. A construct is inculcated, probably along with situational cues indicating less than complete seriousness. On the other hand, where Wallace, for his own purposes, speaks of the child later pretending to still believe the good fairy makes the replacement, he provides a good example of a kind of sharedness that we may take as a counterinstance to his vision of a coordinate, self-sufficient cognitive isolation. The child here has a remarkable and yet not unusual insight into the parent's constructs and motives in the situation, and he plays along. There is much of this in ritual (and in much of culture generally)—a sharedness that may be seen as a kind of benevolent collusion.

Wallace goes on to argue that because each man's cognitive maps may be about as complex as he can handle, then even a two-man event, summing the constructs of both, produces a social structure of a complexity beyond the grasp of either of its participants. The notion that constructs would typically be at the limit of the individual's ability to handle cognitive complexity is a dubious one. Refutation would require showing that individuals use greater than minimally nonredundant event constructs that map more than their own act sequence and the minimally necessary contingencies. In any case, it could be shown that a given construct is a part of a hierarchy of constructs at different levels of specification (or abstraction). The summation of two or more constructs could take place and could be represented at the level of the constructs in question, or it could be represented at a higher level, a more general one. But while one recognizes that there are possible limits to the unit representation at a given level of specificity, the prevalence of high degrees of redundancy in human communication argues against taking assumptions of economy as the criterion excluding some significant structure of commonality among the members of any given society.

Every theory has its world view. (Someone other than me will have to discern mine.) That which underlies Wallace's extreme dissolution of culture to equivalence structures may be indicated in his seeing his adversaries as "advocates of togetherness." And in the following, "It may appear to be a bleak prospect to consider that human beings characteristically engage in a kind of silent trade with all their fellow men, rarely or never actually achieving cognitive communality. Indeed, one may suspect that the social sciences have nourished the idea of cognitive sharing for so long, just because the world may seem rather a lonely place if the wistful dream of mutual identification is abandoned."

Wallace takes an extreme position in a reaction to the theories of cultural uniformity, but it makes as little sense to depict the distribution of culture among the members of a society as totally heterogeneous and unique in each individual as it did to argue for complete homogeneity. We must dispense with the *a priori* assumption of homogeneity. But, similarly, we are not served by an *a priori* assumption of heterogeneity. The model of the distributive structure of culture presented in this paper assigns a place in culture to the complex structure of commonality and difference, and to the hierarchic structure of commonality in which the personality participates, ranging from the idiosyncratic to the universal.

CONCLUDING REMARKS

The model I have described in this paper has at least the following features:

1. A culture has its distributive existence as the set of personalities of the members of a population.

2. A culture is neither homogeneous nor heterogeneous; rather, it has a complex structure of commonality and difference.

3. Personality and culture are in the relation of part to whole.

4. Personalities are formed in and are dependent upon continuous communicative interaction with a community of personalities in events.

5. The personality of an individual is the more or less organized accumulation of experiential derivatives of events. These derivatives are sometimes termed "representations" or "constructs." These constitute a complex hierarchy of levels of specificity or generality with respect to events or classes of events and other phenomenal domains. Many of the conventionally understood functions of the personality can be seen as having a place in sectors of this hierarchic structure, from base-level characterological constructs of great behavioral generality to the organization of the individual's knowledge, beliefs, and behavioral prescriptions.

6. Although a culture of even a "simple" society is highly complex and inexhaustible, both in the magnitude of its detailed content and its productivity, it can be studied and sampled in many ways, much as a geologist might construct a good model of the structure of the earth's crust from a study of a series of cores.

7. Personalities and the cultures they constitute are real and must not be confused with the ethnographies that we construct from our probes. This confusion of the culture with the ethnography occurs often, as when "culture" and "personality" are defined as two levels of abstraction either from the same or from different data.

REFERENCES CITED

Devereux, G.
  1945   The Logical Foundations of Culture and Personality Studies. *Transactions of the New York Academy of Sciences,* series 2, 7:110–30.
DuBois, C.
  1944   *The People of Alor.* Minneapolis: University of Minnesota Press.
Durkheim, E.
  1893   *De la division du travail social: Etude sur l'organisation des Sociétés Supérieures.* Paris: Félix Alcan.
  1933   (translation) *The Division of Labor in Society.* New York: MacMillan Co.
Fortune, R. F.
  1935   *Manus Religion.* Philadelphia: American Philosophical Society.

Gearing, F.
   1962   Priests and Warriors. *American Anthropological Association Memoir No. 93.*
Goodenough, W. H.
   1971   Culture, Language, and Society. *Addison-Wesley Modular Publications:* 1–48.
Hay, T.
   n.d.   Personality and Probability. The Modal Personality of the Tuscarora Revisited. *Ethos,* in press.
Kardiner, A.
   1939   *The Individual and His Society.* New York: Columbia University Press.
   1945   *The Psychological Frontiers of Society.* New York: Columbia University Press.
Mead, M.
   1931   *Growing Up in New Guinea: A Comparative Study of Primitive Education.* London: George Routledge and Sons, Ltd.
   1956   *New Lives for Old: Cultural Transformation—Manus, 1928–1953.* New York: William Morrow and Co.
   1964   *Continuities in Cultural Evolution.* New Haven: Yale University Press.
Mead, M. and Schwartz, T.
   1958   The Cult as Condensed Social Process. *Transactions of The Fifth Conference on Group Processes.* New York: Josiah Macy, Jr., Foundation.
Parsons, T.
   1951   *The Social System.* New York: The Free Press of Glencoe.
Schwartz, T.
   1962   The Paliau Movement in The Admiralty Islands, 1946–1954. *Anthropological Papers of the American Museum of Natural History* 49:207–421.
   1963   Systems of Areal Integration: Some Considerations Based on The Admiralty Islands of Northern Melanesia. *Anthropological Forum* I:56–97.
   1968   Beyond Cybernetics: Constructs, Expectations and Goals in Human Adaptation. *Wenner-Gren Symposium No. 40, The Effects of Conscious Purpose on Human Adaptation,* Burg Wartenstein.
   1972   Distributive Models of Culture in Relation to Societal Scale. *Wenner-Gren Symposium No. 55, Scale and Social Organization,* Burg Wartenstein.
   1973   Cult and Context: The Paranoid Ethos in Melanesia. *Ethos* I:153–74.
   1975a   Cultural Totemism: Ethnic Identity Primitive and Modern. In *Ethnic Identity: Cultural Continuities and Change,* eds. G. DeVos and L. Romanucci-Ross, pp. 106–31. Palo Alto, California: Mayfield Publishing Co.
   1975b   Relations Among Generations in Time-Stratified Cultures. *Ethos: Special Issue Dedicated to Margaret Mead* (in press, summer 1975.)
   1975c   Cargo Cult: A Melanesian Type-Response to Culture Contact. In *Responses to Change,* ed. G. DeVos. New York: Van Nostrand, in press.
   1975d   Societal Scale: Ratios and Relations. In *Societal Scale and Social Organization,* ed. F. Barth (in preparation 1975).
Schwartz, T. and Mead, M.
   1961   Micro- and Macro-cultural Models for Cultural Evolution. *Anthropological Linguistics* 3:1–7. Reprinted in M. Mead, *Continuities in Cultural Evolution.*

Spiro, M. E.
  1951 Culture and Personality: The Natural History of False Dichotomy. *Psychiatry*
        14:19–46.
  1961 An Overview and a Suggested Reorientation. In *Psychological Anthropology*,
        ed. Francis L. K. Hsu. Illinois: Dorsey Press. (2nd ed., 1972, Cambridge,
        Mass.: Schenkman Publishing Co.)
Wallace, A.
  1970 *Culture and Personality*. New York: Random House. (First published in
        1961.)

The Author

ROBERT B. EDGERTON, Professor in Residence, Department of Psychiatry and Anthropology, University of California at Los Angeles, was born in Maywood, Illinois. After primary and secondary schooling in California, he attended several universities as an undergraduate,  taking his graduate training in anthropology at UCLA where he received the Ph.D. in 1960. He has taught at UCLA since 1962, holding appointments in the Departments of Psychiatry and Anthropology. His initial field research was with the Menomini Indians of Wisconsin followed by research in East Africa, Hawaii, and various parts of the urban United States. He has published widely on various forms of deviant behavior, including mental retardation, intersexuality, tattooing, psychosis, mental illness, drinking behavior, and violence. He has also published on sexual behavior among chimpanzees, methods in psychological anthropology, folk psychiatry, cultural and ecological factors in the expression of personality characteristics, the use of the Rorschach, and the study of values. He says of himself:

My major professional interests include many that remain central to anthropology—cultural adaptation, ecology, methodology—as well as some that I believe ought to be, such as the study of human nature. But I have also pursued subjects like mental illness and mental retardation that occupy the borderland between anthropology and other disciplines. The study of deviant behavior is an effort to integrate these kinds of interests in a way that has theoretical and practical value, not only for anthropology, but for other disciplines as well. For me, the fundamental challenge for anthropology is that of developing more general theory, while at the same time contributing as much as possible to the solution of human problems. I believe that this dual focus must become a commitment, not merely a shibboleth, if anthropology is to survive as a viable field of study.

442

This Chapter

Robert Edgerton attacks the *tabula rasa* concept of human nature, as does Melford Spiro most explicitly and others by implication, and the excesses of the cultural internalization model. He traces the emergence of his interest in deviance in a series of his research projects and sites. He wonders why in his first Menomini research, and even later, in the cultural ecology project in East Africa, he did not take the problems of deviance more seriously. He searches for adequate definitions of deviancy and calls for more attention to deviant persons and deviant acts and describes approaches that would be useful in their study. He laments the lack of knowledge about deviance and deviants in other societies. He ends with the possibility that "aspects of human nature—genetically encoded potentials for behavior that we all share—may underlie man's propensity for deviance."

Though Edgerton's attention to deviants is exceptional in this volume he shares with other contributors a rejection of the over-socialized model with which we once all worked, calls attention to the individuated reactions of persons to their total environment and to themselves, and posits universal tendencies in human nature.

As Edgerton is treating deviance in this chapter it includes a very wide range of individuation and nonconformity. Deviance includes everything, then, from the behavior of a severely retarded person to diversity in private life and in private space. What is often called deviant behavior is really conformity —that is, it is formed in a search for approval from a group of peers, or models —groups and peers or models that are divergent from those "establishment norms" governing whatever social context an individual's behavior is being judged deviant in. It is not only a universal human tendency to search for individual self-expression—man also searches for approval and social-emotional support. Deviation can only exist because society and its norms do. On the other hand, society may be said to exist because man exhibits constant tendencies toward individuation, self-assertion and self-gratification as well as a search for approval. As Edgerton points out, this is not a new problem. Plato, Rousseau, Locke, Hobbes, and more recently, Durkheim and Parsons and many others, have engaged with it. In this chapter Edgerton brings a wide range of experience and sharp conceptualization to bear upon the problem, and gives special attention to forms of deviation that are not necessarily a search for approval.

G.D.S.

13 The Study of Deviance—
Marginal Man
or Everyman?

ROBERT B. EDGERTON

A Pygmy steals from a respected member of his band; an Eskimo murders a man after lending his wife to him; a Sirionó man inflicts painful wounds on the breasts of women during sexual intercourse; an East African woman who is forced to marry an older man hangs herself. These are acts of what we have come to call "deviance"—the troublesome violation of a socially accepted rule. There are people in all societies who engage in wrongdoing, and sometimes cause serious trouble by doing so. Some people do so repeatedly. Although not all human beings are guilty of serious or repeated wrongdoing, it is inconceivable that any man or woman could live a lifetime without being guilty of misbehavior, and children, of course, misbehave by the very nature of things. The study of deviance, then, has to do with wrongdoing, with its causes and its consequences.[1]

Deviance, or deviant behavior as it is often called, is an important focus of study in such fields as psychology, psychiatry, and sociology. In these fields, deviance is a major clinical and practical concern relating to such matters as mental illness, delinquency, sexual abnormality or collective violence. These fields have also generated various theories about deviance ranging from its role in human development to its role in the maintenance or destruction of social organization. Deviance has not been accorded similar attention by anthropology; even psychological anthropology which has borrowed so freely from psychology, psychiatry, and sociology has not given much attention to deviance.

In what follows, I shall discuss the reasons why psychological anthropology has made deviance only a tangential focus of study—"marginal men" on the margins of our interest. I shall also try to indicate how our basic understandings of human behavior might change if we were to alter our view of deviant people from, as it were, freaks in a side show, to the principal performers in the everyday dramas of life. I shall

1. I gratefully acknowledge support received from NICHD Grant No. HD–04612.

try to accomplish these goals by chronicling my own research interests and experiences from the mid-1950s, when I began training as a graduate student in anthropology, to the present day.

SOME HISTORICAL NOTES ON THE CONCEPT OF DEVIANCE IN ANTHROPOLOGY

I entered UCLA as a graduate student of anthropology in the mid-1950s. Although anthropology students in those days were required to study all four fields of discipline—cultural anthropology, archaeology, linguistics, and physical anthropology—we were also expected to specialize, and even as an undergraduate, I had decided that my major interests lay in what was then known as "culture and personality." One of my major interests in culture and personality was deviant behavior, which I then thought of in terms of categories such as theft, homicide, witchcraft, and mental illness.

At that time, anthropology at UCLA was a joint department with sociology, and I soon learned that while anthropology had no great interest in deviance, sociology did. It seemed to me, as it did to sociologist Dennis Wrong who wrote about the matter in 1961, that this interest by sociologists during the 1950s was oddly one-sided, amounting to a "conventional wisdom" which brooked no opposition. This almost dogmatic position which Wrong (1961) termed the "oversocialized view of man," asserted that human beings typically conform to the rules of their culture because over the course of their socialization they "internalize" their culture's ideas of right and wrong, and because they seek the esteem of their fellowmen. These two fundamental principles, it was said, accounted for the presence of social order. Given this assumption, the fundamental question was not why social order existed, but why in spite of the force of socialization, some people nevertheless misbehaved?

There is a long history to this conventional position which cannot be recounted adequately here (Edgerton 1973), but, in brief, the Hobbsian, Paulist, and Freudian view that man is naturally given to self-serving behavior and hence, sometimes, to deviance came to be rejected in favor of a contrary position that may have begun with Locke, was given great power by Durkheim, and was formalized by the sociologist Talcott Parsons. In Durkheim's view (1895), human beings want to behave correctly and receive positive satisfaction from conforming; virtue, literally, is its own reward. Yet Durkheim acknowledged that deviance was inevitable, because as Sartre (1964) put it years later, "To give oneself laws and to create the possibility of disobeying them come to the same thing.'' The idea that society—not man's animal instincts—was the source of deviance became almost axiomatic after Durkheim.

In American sociology, perhaps the most important theory relating to the problem of deviance and order was developed by Parsons. Parsons admitted that external force was an important means of maintaining social order, but he placed it in a secondary position to Locke's emphasis on shared values as a source of conformity. He also invoked "social equilibrium" as an important concept. Parsons believed that individuals in a social system *do* share values and that people tend to act in accordance with them. The resulting patterns of behavior have a structure which is in equilibrium—a delicate and self-correcting balance. In Parson's formulation, equilibrium was maintained by two phenomena. First, and most important, is socialization, the process by which children learn to do, and *want to do,* what is required and expected by others. The basic mechanism in socialization is *the desire for approval.* The results of the process are often unconscious so that people "internalize" values and motives, thus reaffirming Durkheim's insight that people *feel* rewarded when they behave properly. Second, should socialization not suffice to keep people in line, there is social control—both external, as Hobbes had in mind when he conceived the Leviathan, and internal as Freud had it when he saw guilt as a basic factor in controlling man and allowing the development of "civilization."

Parsons' so-called functionalist theory ruled sociology for over three decades before it came under serious attack. It also influenced many anthropologists (it was the dominant theoretical position when I was a graduate student). Thus, until quite recently American sociology, and social science in general, saw deviance not as a product of man's animal nature, but as the result of a disturbance in social equilibrium. Consistent with the idea that society and not man was the source of deviance, sociologists in the 1950s had developed a number of theories about how disturbances in a society's equilibrium could lead to deviant behavior. Perhaps the best known was Robert Merton's famous "anomie" theory about how disjunctions between people's goals and their means of attaining them led to wrongdoing (Cohen 1966).

Anthropology in the 1950s had no equivalent interest. To illustrate, *Anthropology Today* (Kroeber 1953) was a compendium of the field at that time, and it did not even index the word "deviance," even though it did contain advice that fieldworkers should avoid "recognized deviants" as informants because they can become a "public relations liability" (Paul 1953, p. 444). This advice is not necessarily bad, by the way, but the point is that anthropological interest in deviance at that time can hardly be said to have assumed importance.

The prevailing attitude in anthropology during the 1950s can be exemplified, and only slightly exaggerated, by Ruth Benedict's article, "Anthropology and the Abnormal":

The deviants, whatever the type of behavior the culture has institutionalized, will remain few in number, and there seems no more difficulty in moulding the vast malleable majority to the "normality" of what we consider an aberrant trait, such as delusions of reference, than to the normality of such accepted behavior patterns as acquisitiveness. The small proportion of the number of deviants in any culture is not a function of the sure instinct with which that society has built itself upon the fundamental sanities, but of the universal fact that, happily, the majority of mankind quite readily take any shape that is presented to them. [1934, p. 196]

Although Benedict's more general "configurationist" point of view was heavily criticized and often discarded by the 1950s, her view of deviance survived, at least implicitly. Since a number of her ideas on deviance were important in the 1950s, and some persist today, it is worthwhile to specify them here.

First is the so-called *tabula rasa* assumption that almost all infants are sufficiently malleable to fit easily into the demands of any viable culture. This view did not deny the presence of a genetic core of "human nature" but said instead that the core was minimal in comparison to the infant's capacity for malleability, for learning. Given this assumption, one obviously could not posit a genetic core that would lead all humans to deviance. Neither could one argue that many persons would become deviants due to their individual temperament. The assumption of *tabula rasa* still influences some anthropologists, although others now credit "human nature" and "temperament" as being potentially important biological constraints upon unlimited human malleability (Edgerton 1973).

Second, the interest of most anthropologists was directed to the process of institutionalization wherein individuals, however diverse their temperaments, were in fact "molded" into accepted members of their society. Such a perspective does not deny that deviants may exist, but it focuses attention almost exclusively upon the sociocultural processes that give shape to people's personalities, values or attitudes.

Third, not only was anthropological attention focused primarily upon the processes of institutionalization, when attention was turned to individuals, it turned to "typical" ones, to the majority or the modal group that was thought to represent the outcome of some form of institutional process (Singer 1961).

Fourth, this institutional perspective created a dichotomy between the majority who were said to conform and a small minority who were said to deviate (LeVine 1973; Edgerton 1973). Thus the fact that many people, if not all, commit deviant acts was obscured by the idea that deviant persons are those who have become socially recognized as flagrant or chronic rule violators. If one wished to study the *process* of rule violation, of disputes and their adjudication, as a result of which some persons might or might not become "deviant," one had to turn to "primitive law." In the mid-1950s, such a processual view of rule violations, their antecedents and their consequences, was not very well developed in anthropology (Pospisil 1972).

Finally, it was implicitly assumed it was "natural" for a social system to contain only a few deviant persons, and that the presence of a larger number of deviants indicates disturbance of the sociocultural equilibrium. The idea that "natural" or so-called folk societies which are small, homogeneous, nonliterate, isolated and possessed of a sense of community also lack deviance was brought into anthropological prominence by Robert Redfield, but the contrast between the good and noble "folk" life and the evil of cities is an ancient one, present in the works of Aristophanes, Tacitus, and the Old Testament (Baroja 1963). It became well-known in Europe in the nineteenth century with the works of Tönnies and others, and it has continued to influence modern anthropology (e.g., Henry 1958; Goodman 1967). Despite criticism of this conception from various sources (Edgerton 1973), the idea that deviance is almost entirely a product of disequilibrium or disorganization (which is most often seen in cities or rapidly changing societies) remains so deeply entrenched that it is still possible to find social scientists who *define* social disorganization by the presence of a high rate of deviance (Kaplan 1971).

As well as I can remember, these were the prevailing assumptions that underlay the way we thought about deviance in the 1950s. To be sure, we did learn something about deviant persons (in addition to the admonition to avoid them as informants). We read about people who stole, murdered, committed incest, became witches or innovators. Most of all we studied the mentally ill, but we did not, as I can recall, think of them as "deviants." We saw them instead as casualties of social or cultural stress, or, that is, disequilibrium. We had no concerted theory of deviance as a process or a phenomenon; indeed, I cannot recall any anthropologist at that time who discussed "deviance" as an important concept or issue.

At this time there was only one actual textbook in culture and personality, John Honigmann's *Culture and Personality* (1954). Probably more influential was a collection of readings, *Personality in Nature, Society and Culture* (1953), the second edition of which was edited by Clyde Kluckhohn, Henry A. Murray, and David M. Schneider. Also available were two or three similar but less well-received collections of articles. All of these materials reflect the influence of the five basic assumptions I have mentioned, but they also indicate how central was psychological anthropology's concern with personality development, and how important were projective techniques as the approved means of testing these theories. One searches these volumes almost completely in vain for any interest in such currently important aspects of psychological anthropology as psychobiology, social learning theory, cognition, perception or labeling.

This was a time of intense neo-positivism in anthropology, and because culture and personality had come under severe attack for its vacuous and tautological conceptual structure, and its "unscientific" methods (Lindesmith and Strauss 1950), we scorned the lax, "humanistic" approaches of our elders and learned (mostly from sociologists and psychologists) the currently approved "rigorous" and "operationalized" methods of hypothesis construction, sampling, data collection, and statistical analysis. Because our interests were psychological we learned about testing, and because only projective tests had any apparent promise for cross-cultural research, we learned most of all about projective tests; for example, I spent a year studying the Rorschach technique with Bruno Klopfer. We then struggled to make projective testing more scientific, i.e., more reliable and valid.

EARLY RESEARCH—THE PROCESS OF INSTITUTIONALIZATION

I completed my graduate courses and examinations in 1958 without having a clear-cut dissertation project in mind. I was best prepared to do projective testing, and Walter Goldschmidt, who had guided me while sustaining my interest as he did so, suggested that I build upon the earlier work of George and Louise Spindler with the Menomini. I agreed, and so did the Spindlers, who graciously gave me assistance and advice.

In visiting the Menomini, a people who were already well-studied and whom I proposed to visit only to add to what the Spindlers had already done, I foreclosed many research options. Nevertheless, I was anything but reluctant. Projective testing was in vogue and I thought I knew something about how to do it. Curiously, or perhaps not so curiously, it never occurred to me to focus upon deviance. This was especially curious when one considers that by 1959 projective testing in anthropology had produced a veritable landslide of evidence pointing to widespread diversity and even deviance in personality.

For example, Cora DuBois, who went to the Island of Alor in Indonesia in 1938, returned with ample evidence of diversity and deviance among the Alorese in her various projective test materials (DuBois 1944). However, subsequent, and somewhat Procrustean, analysis by the psychoanalyst Abram Kardiner (1945) emphasized commonalities, not differences, and it was these commonalities that found their way into our literature. Nevertheless, in 1952, A.F.C. Wallace published his Rorschach research among the Tuscarora Indians. Wallace's work seemed to show great diversity in Rorschach response patterns. Furthermore, and even more significantly, Wallace (1952) reported that these Rorschach profiles bore no necessary relationships to actual behavior. A year later, Gladwin and Sarason (1953) published *Truk: Man in Paradise,* in which they reported that their projective test data (as interpreted by the psychologist Sarason) did not regularly agree with the ethnographic data (as understood by the anthropologist Gladwin). But both authors agreed that the differences in Trukese personality were at least as important as the similarities. In 1954, Bert Kaplan published *A Study of Rorschach Responses in Four Cultures* (Zuni, Navaho, Mormon and Spanish American) in which he reached the following conclusion:

That great variability exists does not argue against the influence of culture on personality; it means merely that cultural influences do not necessarily create uniformity in a group. All individuals interact with their cultures. However human beings are not passive recipients of their culture. They accept, reject, or rebel against the cultural forces to which they are oriented. In many cultures, including our own, there exists a pattern of outward conformity and inner rebellion and deviation. It is probably correct to say that individuals seem a good deal more similar than they really are. [1954, p. 32]

If the implications of these studies and others like them were not sufficient, when I turned to the work of the Spindlers concerning the Menomini (G. Spindler 1955; L. and G. Spindler 1958; L. Spindler 1958), I found further evidence of deviance and diversity. The Spindlers showed that groups of Menomini at different levels of acculturation differed markedly in personality patterns and furthermore, that some of these Menomini groups could be thought of as deviant either in terms of traditional Menomini values and personality or in their contemporary adaptation to the sociocultural conditions of reservation life. Nevertheless, I read the Spindler's work as an example, and a most persuasive one, of the processes of institutionalization at work in such a way that even relatively minor differences in acculturation could be seen to have substantial impact upon modal personality patterns. Only much later in reading *Dreamers Without Power* (G. and L. Spindler 1971) did I realize that the Spindlers were also interested in the impact of individuals upon their social and cultural world.

Thus, with Goldschmidt's encouragement and assistance, I set out to determine whether Menomini values, like their patterns of personality, were equally predictable in terms of an acculturative process. We developed a picture test to elicit value judgments and found that the picture test did indeed evoke the values we had predicted on the basis of the Spindlers' prior work (Edgerton 1960; Goldschmidt and Edgerton 1961). This was a gratifying finding, not only because it seemed to show that this sort of picture technique could accurately elicit values, but because it added to our knowledge of the process of institutionalization.

Despite the fact that some Menomini produced highly discrepant value responses, that some of the pictures themselves were designed to evoke idiosyncratic or deviant responses, and that deviant behavior in the form of drunken violence and sexuality was common in some parts of the reservation, I made no effort to study deviance among the Menomini. In part I avoided the issue so as not to enter a sensitive domain for research, but most of all I did so because my research problem focused upon the process of institutionalization.

After a year or so of research with mentally retarded people—whom I also studied as products of an institutional process that shaped their behavior and their personalities—I accepted Goldschmidt's invitation to join his *Culture and Ecology in East Africa* project. The project, which was an outgrowth of Goldschmidt's long-standing interest in cultural evolution (Goldschmidt 1959), was an effort to determine how various aspects of culture adapted to changing ecological circumstances. Specifically, the project proposed to study how certain economic changes having to do with cattle herding on the one hand and farming on the other, led to concomitant alterations in institutional behavior, in values, attitudes, and personality. Four tribes in East Africa (the Sebei of Uganda, the Kamba and Pokot of Kenya, and the Hehe of Tanzania) were chosen for study because each contained some communities in which people lived primarily by farming and others in which their livelihood was based on pastoralism. The research design called for an ethnographer to work in each of the four societies, dividing his time between a typical family community and a pastoral one. At the same time a geographer would visit all eight communities in the four societies to study the cultural and physical geography especially as it related to the technological and economic use of the environment. My role in the project was to divide my time among the eight communities, studying personality, values, and attitudes (Goldschmidt 1965). The goal, once again, was to better our understanding of the processes by which individuals, their institutions and their culture, adapt to changing ecological conditions.

Since my research problem was primarily one of achieving cross-cultural equivalence in the measurement of personality, values, and attitudes, and since both time and manpower were limited, I chose not to rely on formal observation (I simply could not expect to carry out systematic observation of relevant behaviors in eight separate communities in the time available) and instead developed a battery of interviews and projective tests I hoped could be made equivalently meaningful in all the communities.

With the help of all my colleagues, and careful pretesting after arriving in Africa in the summer of 1961, I managed to interview and test at least thirty men and thirty women in each of the eight communities, over five hundred people in all, before leaving the field in the fall of 1962. Subsequent analysis of the data collected by these procedures did show consistent differences between farmers and herders in the four societies (Edgerton 1965; 1971). Many of these differences were of the sort originally predicted, thus giving support to Goldschmidt's theories about the ways in which ecological circumstances call forth adaptive responses in people and their institutions. At this level of micro-evolutionary or ecological theory, the project was well-conceived, and I believe my research procedures were appropriately designed and carried out, adding a useful component to the larger project.

This was a project concerned with the processes by which changes in economic and ecologic circumstances shaped groups of people. Neither deviance nor diversity played a central part in our thinking. Indeed, some of our research procedures were intended to minimize the "noise" these factors might produce as we searched for modal patterns of adaptive response to the ecology. Needless to say, we were aware that both deviance and diversity would be present, and as I shall later indicate we did look at such matters, but our essential concern was the discovery of regular, shared patterns of adaptation. In our search for such patterns, for example, we employed a kind of probability sampling within the eight communities (Edgerton 1971), but we intentionally excluded obvious deviants by restricting our sampling universe to married men and their wives. We did so because such persons were the most respected and responsible members of their communities and their behaviors, values, etc., were most likely to be typical. An unmarried adult in those societies was almost by definition a deviant and such a person would not, we reasoned, be a typical product of the process of cultural adaptation we were attempting to study. In fact, there were very few such people whom we excluded (certainly less than five percent of the adult population) so the statistical effect of their exclusion was slight. The principle, however, is worth noting.

Another procedure was more significant. As I constructed the interview battery I not only had to select questions and picture stimuli that could be understood in all eight communities, I tried to select (with a few exceptions such as the Rorschach) stimuli that would evoke culturally shared responses, not idiosyncratic ones. Thus I did not ask, "How do you personally feel about a poor man?" I asked, "How do people (here in this community) feel about a poor man?" I was asking primarily about shared beliefs and values because we were seeking to discover patterns (of similarity or difference) within or between communities. We were interested in how diversity was patterned, not in diversity *per se*. Wallace's (1961) discussion of the "organization of diversity" would have been extremely helpful had it been published only a year earlier. To be sure, I received much personal opinion and idiosyncratic response in the course of the interview, but I was not attempting to elicit such material.

When it came to the various analyses of these data, I did of course, use statistical procedures that took variations in response fully into account, but with a few exceptions I did not concentrate upon the diversity in the responses, because I did not feel (then or now) that the existing variation in response was significant for the problem we were studying, with one exception. The Sebei response pattern was almost twice as variable as that of the other three tribes; this finding may relate to Goldschmidt's contention that the Sebei lack commitment to their culture (Goldschmidt n.d.). I might also add that I have only recently begun an analysis of those men and women whose response pattern was highly divergent from the typical pattern in their community.

As I shall indicate shortly, I did collect data on deviance in each community, but these studies were done on the side as it were, after the major work for which the project was organized had been carried out, and I did not conceive of them as having any important relationship to the problem of institutional cultural adaptation. I should note here that Goldschmidt himself has used data from this project to make a contribution relevant to deviance; for example, *Kambuya's Cattle* (1969) is a valuable account of the individual manipulation of culture for personal self-interest, and *Sebei Law* (1967) records the normative side of Sebei culture. This same theme of individual motivation in responding to and breaching the norms and values of his culture was one that Goldschmidt emphasized quite early (1956), along with aspects of human nature, and has continued to pursue. While this influence was not entirely lost upon me, it took longer to emerge than it might have.

My participation in the *Culture and Ecology* project was not my last work on the process of institutionalization. In 1965, for example, a psychiatrist, Marvin Karno, and I initiated a large-scale survey of attitudes about mental illness. Using a complicated probability sampling design, we interviewed almost seven hundred people, Anglo-American and Chicano, in three neighborhoods of East Los Angeles (Karno and Edgerton 1969). Our long interview schedule was focused upon attitudes and beliefs about mental illness and its treatment, but it also contained questions about criminality, drug usage, gang violence, and the like. The research was directly linked to the goal of providing psychiatric services for the large Mexican-American population of East Los Angeles. The interview was an initial step to provide knowledge of existing beliefs and practices, knowledge which was later to prove valuable when Karno did establish a Spanish-speaking psychiatric clinic in this part of the city. This research was quite sensitive to diversity since we were concerned not only with contrasts between the Chicano and Anglo neighborhoods, but with the degree of consensus within each. One of our major findings was the great degree of diversity within the Chicano community which was related, at least in large measure, to acculturation. There were also some individuals whose responses were highly atypical, but we made no special study of these people as potential ''deviants.''

I see nothing wrong with the fundamental character of this sort of research. Research which attempts to determine whether or to what degree groups of people have adapted their behavior, their beliefs, or their feelings to social and cultural circumstances is important, and it will continue to be. Such studies tell us a great deal about conformity to institutional process; that they usually tell us very little about deviance is another matter.

STUDIES OF DEVIANT PERSONS

Consistent with my interest in the process of institutionalization, I began as early as 1960 to study certain kinds of deviant persons as *products* of that process. Sometimes these persons were seen as casualties of the process, when that process went wrong, but at other times they were simply anomalous persons for whom the system could not make a place. Either way, these studies (all of which were conducted early in the 1960s, although some were not published for several years) dealt with deviant persons, not with the process of deviance—i.e., with the process in which a role is violated, consequences occur, and someone may or may not become known as a deviant.

Several of my studies of mentally retarded persons took this form. The mildly retarded can become deviant as "casualties" of the system, when for reasons of social deprivation, cultural difference, and the like, they become labeled as incompetent, even though they might be fully competent under different social or cultural conditions. For example, such has often been the fate of Blacks, Chicanos, or the poor whites of Appalachia. But the retarded can also simply be anomalous when, as in cases of severe retardation, their organic impairment makes them manifestly incapable of competent membership in their society. I looked at both kinds of persons.

For example, I examined those retarded persons in a large state hospital who inflicted tattoos on themselves, and I found reason to believe that they like others in many parts of the world, did so as a means of clarifying their identity or creating a more favorable one (Edgerton and Dingman 1963). These were people, I thought, whom life had deprived of a satisfying identity and who in response, had attempted to give themselves a better one by the social or symbolic significance of their tattoos. Since the act of tattooing was disapproved by parents, friends, and hospital officials, the act was patently deviant. I also studied a clique of relatively intelligent, highly delinquent patients who had formed themselves into an "elite" group which maintained its prestige vis-à-vis other patients by violating the hospital's rules (Edgerton 1963). I saw this deviant behavior as a response to the stigma of retardation by people who were attempting to deny the reality of the label of mental retardation by claiming the status of normal teenage delinquents and thereby elevating themselves above other patients in the hospital for whom they indicated the retarded label might be appropriate.

I also reported on the life circumstances and adaptive strategies of some fifty mildy retarded persons who had been discharged from this same hospital. In *The Cloak of Competence* (1967) I concluded that those persons were overwhelmed by the stigma of their labeled retardation and by the experience of hospitalization and that as a consequence their lives were singularly devoted to denying the legitimacy of this label and passing as normal people. In all these studies, then, I saw the mildly retarded as casualties of a larger sociocultural system that had—correctly or not—identified them as "incompetent," and I chronicled their efforts as individuals to cope with their circumstances.

With psychologist Craig MacAndrew, I later looked at more severely retarded people. In one instance (MacAndrew and Edgerton 1966) we reported in detail upon the sensitive and enduring friendship established by two severely retarded men. We thought their friendship was remarkable and poignant, but also that it was a symbiotic response (one man was blind, and the other was cerebral palsied) to their organically induced impairment as well as to the circumstances of their lonely hospital existence. We also described a hospital ward that housed almost one hundred men, none of whom had an I.Q. over 20 (MacAndrew and Edgerton 1964). Most of these males (men seems an inappropriate term) were grotesquely disfigured. Few could speak, but instead howled, screeched, and cried in an awful cacophony. Their behavior was no less alarming: some jumped, climbed, slapped their arms, twirled rags, or masturbated; others rocked stereotypically; a few slept or stared vacantly. We described these profoundly retarded human beings as problems for society, as indeed they and 100,000 others like them continue to be, but we also concluded that these human beings were undeniably human, not only in terms of their emotions, but in terms of their moral character as well. This realization made the problem they represented even more distressing. How should society respond to such organically deviant persons?

My African research from 1961 to 1962 also produced studies that emphasized deviant persons. For example, the Culture and Ecology interview schedule contained several questions about mental illness. When the answers to this interview were combined with direct observation, further ethnographic interviewing, and work with native specialists, I was able to assemble a report about the similarities and differences among the four tribes with regard to their ideas about the causes, symptoms and treatment of psychotics (Edgerton 1966). Although I looked upon the manifestations of psychosis in these societies primarily as products of social and cultural conditions in East Africa (similar to the way my colleagues and I later looked at the disordered sexual behavior of caged chimpanzees as a product of their isolation and confinement [Killar, Beckwith, and Edgerton 1968]), I also noted similarities between the symptomatology seen in East Africa and that seen in Western mental hospitals (suggesting the possibility of an organic substrate in psychosis) and I noted that the process by which people came to be recognized as psychotic was a complex negotiation with moral and legal implications. I was to return to this idea more directly in a few years.

There were other studies of deviant persons, as for example, when I found that the Pokot of Kenya were well aware of the existence of intersexed persons and animals. I explored further and found that several such persons were known to be living among the Pokot, two of them quite nearby. I reported the circumstances of these intersexed persons' lives, emphasizing the obvious dilemma they faced by being ambiguously sexed persons in a society that stresses sexuality and requires that both males and females be circumcised before they may marry and achieve adulthood (Edgerton 1964). Despite their obvious inability to fulfill normal sexual roles or to achieve unambiguous sexual identity, both persons were able to survive by virtue of hard and unrelenting work which benefitted others. In the conclusion of this article, I began to move away from the emphasis on deviant persons toward a concern with the process of deviance:

A number of infrequently occurring phenomena—intersexuality, blindness, deafness, epilepsy, and mental retardation, to name a few which usually fall outside the view and notebook of anthropologists, have potential for suggesting and confirming hypotheses about cultural structures and processes. To return to the original presumption of this essay, it is suggested that people everywhere make assumptions about the nature of normality. In some instances, these assumptions become so basic that people are only minimally aware that they hold them at all—cultural reality simply *is*.

Intersexuality has much to recommend it as a topic for study for it contravenes one such assumption, that of a natural and normal world in which there are, and ought to be, biological males and biological females. Infants with the genitalia of both sexes challenge both this assumption and the culturally defined sex roles that emanate from it. [1964, pp. 1297–98]

STUDIES OF DEVIANCE AS A PROCESS

At the same time that I was writing about deviant persons, I was also writing about the process by which people break rules and suffer the consequences, sometimes including recognition as a deviant person. But it was only as I rummaged through my past research interests in preparing this essay that I realized I was not fully aware of the importance of the distinction between deviant *persons* and deviant *acts* until probably around 1966, that is after much of the work I am about to discuss had been done. This disclosure is embarrassing if one considers all the good reasons why I should have known better much earlier. I had, for example, read Machiavelli avidly as an undergraduate, and had been impressed by his elegant discussions of men struggling against chance and circumstance in an effort to accomplish something desirable by managing appearances for their own self-interest. Machiavelli's *Prince* foreshadowed Goffman's many works on the presentation of self (e.g., Machiavelli said that everyone could see what you appear to be, but few could understand what you really feel you are). Erving Goffman's major writings began to appear in 1959, and symbolic interactionism expanded with him, but careful readers of G. H. Mead would have known far earlier what I apparently did not adequately know, even after Goffman. Consider, too, that the Chicago School of Social Deviance, which followed in Mead's heritage, had spent the early 1960s actively creating an awareness of deviance as a property that is conferred upon an individual by others who disapprove of his actions or beliefs. The growth of ethnomethodology with Harold Garfinkel and Aaron Cicourel also made matters clear, as did Kai Erickson's (1966) significant study of deviance among the Puritans, in which he argued that deviance may actually be necessary for the maintenance of social order. All of this, available by 1966 and before, made it obvious that in order to understand anything of importance about wrongdoing, it was necessary to study the *process* by which people commit deviant acts. To study only labeled deviants as the end product of such a process is to miss almost everything that is significant about rule violation.

Perhaps I might seek solace in the fact that the first explicit recognition of this important distinction that I am aware of seeing in anthropology was written by Robert LeVine in his *Culture, Behavior, and Personality* (1973), but, then, I suppose that since so few anthropologists have explicitly concerned themselves with deviance at all, this is not a particularly compelling excuse. Here I might note that the modern field of psychological anthropology reached a kind of apogee in 1961 when four major books appeared: Kaplan's *Studying Personality Cross-Culturally* (1961), Hsu's *Psychological Anthropology* (1961), Wallace's *Culture and Personality* (1961), and Cohen's *Social Structure and Personality* (1961). However, none of these books gave the concept of deviance better than passing mention (Cohen's book gave it the fullest treatment) and more recent books have done very little better. For example, none has made the distinction between deviant persons and deviant acts. Indeed, psychological anthropology has still not displayed any concerted interest in deviance, and it certainly has done little enough to clarify the distinction between deviant persons and the process of rule violation.

As I look back now at what I wrote then about the process of deviance, it seems to me that two themes have recurred: (1) rule violation and deviant status can have advantages as well as disadvantages, and (2) rule violation often creates serious trouble which people attempt to minimize through a process of negotiation.

The first point, that deviant acts can confer advantages, is a commonplace one. To illustrate briefly, in studying the retarded in large hospitals, I noted that some employees were responsible for maintaining a system in which patients regularly washed staff member's cars for a minimal charge (Edgerton, Tarjan, and Dingman 1961). Staff members produced a rhetoric which attempted to construe this activity as therapeutic, but it was clear (as was sometimes admitted in unguarded moments) that many staff members maintained the system not to carry out their therapeutic mandate, but to obtain a cheap car washing service; a motive that could only be described as deviant. Other patients in this hospital systematically violated the hospital's rules concerning violence and sexual behavior not merely, I argued, to gratify their basic urges, or to give vent to their frustrations, but to maintain their sense of self-esteem as quasi-normal persons in the face of a massive institutional onslaught to define them as subnormal and incompetent. By violating the hospital's rules, they became recognized by themselves and the staff as delinquents with at least some claim to normal respect and accountability, not as incompetents in need of custodial care (Edgerton and Sabagh 1962; Edgerton and Dingman 1964).

The second point is neither as self-evident nor as straightforward as the first. By saying that the outcome of a deviant act is determined not primarily by recourse to jural principles—to the "law," or to what is "right"—but by a negotiated settlement that seeks to balance the costs and benefits of participants while minimizing the potential for serious trouble, was a far more complex and problematic assertion, especially in the early 1960s. Although somewhat similar ideas had been expressed by Gluckman, Bohannon, Leach, Pospisil, Goffman, Becker, Lemert, and others, the process itself had seldom been studied (for an exception see Pospisil 1958), thus its generality was not known.

In a number of papers based on East African materials collected from 1961 to 1962, I attempted to look at aspects of this process of negotiating the outcome of deviant acts. First, E. V. Winans and I (1964) wrote about a kind of "moral magic," called *litego,* among the Hehe of Southern Tanzania. We noted that when a dispute occurred, one line of recourse was juridical appeal through the system of chiefs and courts, but another, equally approved option involved recourse to what we called magical justice. Where the Azande, as described by Evans-Pritchard (1937), were obliged to take their complaints to court when clear evidence of wrongdoing existed, the Hehe could licitly choose to invoke magical retribution. We attempted to sort out some of the issues involved in this dual system of justice, showing, we believed, that the existence of a system of magical justice lessened the likelihood of serious consequences. Because the wrongdoer in this system was obliged to confess, apologize, and pay compensation we concluded that "grievances, feuds or bad feelings are less likely to follow" (Winans and Edgerton 1964, p. 764).

In the same year, I wrote (with Francis Conant) about *kilapat,* a Pokot practice by which aggrieved women shamed their errant husbands (Edgerton and Conant 1964). In this socially approved practice a Pokot woman who has been seriously mistreated by her husband (e.g., insulted, ignored, beaten) can join with other women to "shame" him. These women literally seize the unfortunate husband in his sleep, tie him securely, beat him painfully, urinate and defecate upon him, all the while maintaining a stream of abusive and humiliating songs. Finally, the women propose even more severe beatings, but the wife intercedes saying that her husband has suffered enough and that even though he has truly been a rotter, he deserves another chance. The wife, then, initiates the punitive process, but she also terminates it. There is marked antagonism between Pokot husbands and wives, but women have few means of jural recourse, lacking effective access to kin-based or political power. Instead they can nag, gossip, or flee, none of which is a powerful threat; they can also, however, take more severe countermeasures by engaging in sorcery, poisoning, or suicide. All of these latter actions are greatly feared by men and, should they occur, bring about very serious consequences. We saw *kilapat* as a middle-range solution for women, one that effectively controlled serious misconduct by husbands without invoking even more serious actions by wives. It was a recognition of this fact, we believed, that led Pokot men to accept *kilapat* as a legitimate practice.

I also wrote about a Hehe traditional doctor, whom I called a "psychiatrist" since he specialized in the treatment of mental illness. This man, Abedi, was widely known and respected for his therapeutic skills which, it turned out, involved the use of a psychoactive pharmacopoeia as well as suggestion and appeals to faith. In addition to his therapeutic skills, however, Abedi's diagnostic sensitivity played a vital role in reducing the potential for serious conflict. This was so because everyone knew that illness, including mental illness, could be the result of witchcraft. When the presence of such evil is confirmed, counter-measures must be taken and the result can be an escalation of the conflict. Abedi's role mitigates this potential for serious conflict.

When a patient, who is often in an acutely psychotic state, is brought to Abedi, he begins to divine, rubbing a small wooden cylinder diagonally along a water-slick groove in a wooden board—his *bao*.

As the water in the groove dries up, the counter moves less easily and at some point it will stick. This is taken as an affirmative answer to the last question addressed to the *bao*. As long as the counter moves freely, the answers to questions addressed to it are usually taken to be negative. In any case of illness, Abedi asks five preliminary questions: Did the patient commit adultery? Did he steal? Did he borrow money and refuse to repay it? Did he quarrel with someone? Did he actually have a fight with someone? In some instances, the answer to all the questions is negative. This indicates that the patient has become ill for no good reason and hence the cause is natural. Or, it means the effective counter magic must be made against the evil person who has per-formed magic or witchcraft against the patient without cause. This Abedi determines by further questions. He then asks specific questions about his ability to cure the patient, alternating "yes" and "no" questions until the *bao* answers. Finally he asks about the effectiveness of various medicines until the *bao* selects for him the medicine favored by God.

Throughout the investigations and supplications Abedi takes great care, for both he and his patient realize that the treatment of illness is dangerous, involving as it does not merely natural phenomena but such critical matters as moral magic, witchcraft, spirits, and the like. All realize that a faulty diagnosis endangers the doctor as well as the patient. [1971a, pp. 264–65]

In my experience with Abedi, he avoided diagnosing witchcraft unless the evidence of an ongoing feud was too obvious to ignore. Even when he divined the cause as witchcraft, he usually concluded that it was being perpetrated by someone far away, often so far up a distant mountain range that no personal or clan retribution could result. His peacemaking efforts were not simply a product of good citizenship; as mentioned, a native doctor who diagnoses witchcraft becomes vul-nerable to potential retribution and is himself endangered. There-fore it was the role of the native doctor more than the wisdom of Abedi that served to mitigate conflict and bring about a peaceable solution to the unsettling occurrence of illness.

I also wrote about what I called "disillusionment" in culture contact (Edgerton 1965) attempting to specify the factors that I had seen lead to conflict between "Europeans," including anthropologists, and the culturally different peoples whom they encounter. In this paper, I wrote not about the negotiated resolution of conflict, but about its development:

The process of disillusionment as visualized here may be regarded as simply one variant of a more general form of interpersonal conflict. This conflict develops from unsuccessful attempts to establish trust between two persons or, more accurately, persons from two different categories. It has these essential features: (1) there is a differential in rights, privileges, prestige, and power, (2) the status superior has a typical biography involving the use of his prestige and power to punish, discomfit, or discredit a status inferior, (3) there are mutually derogatory stereotypes which ascribe improper, irresponsible, or hostile conduct to both the status superior and inferior, (4) as a consequence, both parties are mistrustful of the other, (5) the status superior offers to suspend the established relationships and behave as a friend, although not necessarily as a status equal, (6) the status inferior must probe to determine to what extent he can trust the superior, (7) because of basic mistrust and status inequality, this probing will be indirect and devious. With these features operative, the probability of failure, disillusionment, and heightened mistrust is great. [1965, pp. 241–42]

I did not write this article with the general process of deviance in mind, but it seems to me that aspects of the process by which this kind of conflict is engendered are also relevant to many kinds of conflict situations that involve deviant acts.

There were other papers like these but my point of view about the process of deviance is best seen in a paper that appeared in 1969, although it was originally written in 1966—"On the 'Recognition' of Mental Illness" (Edgerton 1969). In this article which clearly reflects the influence of the contemporary ideas of sociologists like Goffman, Becker, and Lemert who were studying the process by which some people came to be labeled as deviants, and particularly the work on mental illness by the psychiatrist Thomas Szasz (1963) and anthropologist George Devereux (1963), I attempted to understand how it was that people came to be recognized as mentally ill. At the time that I wrote, I was unaware of the similar work of the sociologist Thomas Scheff (1966).

I examined the processes by which various East Africans came to be known as mentally ill and I compared what I saw to the diagnostic routine in modern psychiatry. I concluded that in both places (and elsewhere in the world where I could locate evidence) the recognition of mental illness was a social process with both moral and jural components because mental illness is a status that involves rights and responsibilities, not only of the person found to be mentally ill, but of those who must interact with him as well. Hence the status of mental illness is agreed upon by a negotiation that revolves around a person's entitlement to this status, one which almost always involves a reduction in rights and responsibilities. I found, with the exception of a few particularly chronic and severe cases, that the perceptions of a potentially mentally ill person, the labels that can be applied to such a person, and the actions that follow from such labeling are all, in principle, negotiable. In East Africa, as in modern America, the cardinal issue to be negotiated is whether a person who is thought guilty of wrongdoing should be held fully responsible for this act, or should be seen as mentally ill and hence lacking intent to offend, and therefore usually not fully punishable as a consequence. In Africa where corporate responsibility of clansmen was often involved, this matter could be especially important as clansmen sought to avoid the payment of compensation. Another issue was the effect of the label on close kinsmen. Since the label can be stigmatizing, carrying with it a loss of rights as well as responsibilities, negotiations by parents and kin (especially where no major wrongdoing was involved) had the goal of avoiding the imposition of the label.

I concluded that however much modern psychiatry was a science and however scientific were psychiatrist's efforts to diagnose, the recognition of mental illness by lay persons and professionals alike is always a social transaction with moral and jural features, and that the outcome of this transaction is essentially negotiable should involved parties wish it to be.

In the same year, Craig MacAndrew and I published *Drunken Comportment* (1969), although once again many of the basic ideas in the book had been worked out many years earlier, particularly on MacAndrew's part. The book attempted to explain why it is that people so often misbehave when they are drunk, violating commonly accepted and enforced rules, especially those concerning aggression and sexual behavior. We reviewed the world's literature on drunkenness and discovered a number of interesting patterns. For example, there were several societies in which people drank astonishing amounts of alcohol but never violated any rules having to do with sexuality or aggression. Furthermore, even when drunkenness was accompanied by rule violation, these violations were patterned—they occurred within limits such that one could readily predict what kinds of mayhem or debauchery would and would not occur. We concluded that one could not possibly account for such findings, as was conventionally done, simply by announcing that alcohol's toxic properties had a disinhibiting effect upon man's cortex. Instead we looked for a social explanation and found that when drunken misconduct occurred in a society, that society defined drunkenness as a time of reduced responsibility, or "time out," as we called it. Drunkenness, then, was an excuse (complete or partial) for conduct that would otherwise be unacceptable.

We examined drunken misconduct in many of the world's societies and concluded that while people were clearly socialized to believe that alcohol produced specific effects (for example many Americans have been socialized to the belief that alcohol releases our inhibitions about sexuality and aggression) and we act quite unconsciously to fulfill those beliefs, that some people also take advantage of situations in which drunken misconduct is excused by seeming to be drunker than they "really" are, or by misbehaving long before alcohol could have had a toxic effect on their inhibitions. Such persons are deviants twice over. Not only are they drunken brawlers (or seducers), they are false claimants to the excuse. Finally, we suggested that periods of "time out," such as drunkenness, may serve societies well because where misconduct is punished at most times, but excused on certain occasions (drunken ones), people tend to save up their misconduct for those times when it is excusable and hence serious conflict and lasting bad feeling can be lessened. People who do not hold a "drunk" responsible for what he says or does, must expect to see drunks doing and saying improper things, but people may nevertheless retain the option of avoiding occasions or places where drunkenness is likely to occur, and hence may avoid impropriety or at least make its occurrence more predictable and manageable. This book with its focus on the relationship between responsibility and deviance, reinforced and clarified my earlier ideas about the process of deviance.

DEVIANCE AND PROBLEM OF ORDER

In all my studies thus far mentioned, whether they dealt with deviant persons or deviant acts, no attention was given to the concept of deviance itself nor to its implications for the problem of order. In 1970, during a year's leave, I began systematically to review the theoretical literature on deviance and the problem of order. I also read over one hundred ethnographies representing societies at all points on the continuum from folk to urban. I found, as I expected, that rule violations, serious and slight, were a part of life in all societies. Marvin Harris recently reported a similar conclusion:

Every human society known to anthropologists, no matter how simple the technology and sparse the population, has its share of interpersonal strife, aggression, and crime. Murder, for example, is reported from even the smallest and simplest hunting and gathering groups. [1971, p. 369]

I might add to Harris's comments that not just murderers, but conspicuously deviant persons of all sorts are found in these small and simple societies, just like the large and complex ones (Edgerton 1973). Indeed, so compelling is the ethnographic evidence, that I concluded my review by saying:

Perhaps the best that we can say about the folk-urban continuum as an explanation of deviance is that it often fails to find support either from the study of small and isolated societies or from large urban ones. We are left with this observation: troublesome behavior is frequent and varied in the world's small and simple societies, so frequent and so varied, in fact, that there is no reason to believe that deviance is wholly or even largely a product of urban living. An explanation of human deviance must be sought in less simplistic terms.

What must shape the nature of our inquiry is this: *deviance occurs in all societies.* It occurs in the small as well as the large, the simple as well as the complex. Deviance may take different forms and frequencies from one society to another, but deviance is ubiquitous. What David Matza has said of Western society appears to be true for any society: ". . . deviant phenomena are common and natural. They are a normal and inevitable part of social life, as is their denunciation, regulation, and prohibition (1969, p. 13)." If deviance is an ever-present fact of human existence, as it appears to be, how might we explain it? [1973, p. 25]

In reviewing the existing panoply of explanations for deviance I found plausibility for all of them, not only the popular ones involving social, cultural, and psychological factors, but man's temperament and his biogenetic composition as well. What is more, I argued that there may well be aspects of human nature which could underlie man's seemingly universal propensity for deviance (Edgerton 1973). But I also noted that our knowledge of the process of rule violation and its resolution was very shallow. Even the best available accounts as, for example, Colin Turnbull's report of the "Crime of Cephu" among the Bambuti pygmies (1961) leave far too many questions unanswered.

Therefore I began a program of research in Los Angeles to provide greater detail about this process. I have added some comparative material to this program by continuing work in Hawaii, and by a brief trip to Kenya in 1972. In discussing this research and the perspective it takes, I shall mention some of the nagging questions about "deviance" that such an approach helps to remove. For example, I have spoken of deviance as rule violation that leads to trouble. A definition like this one is widely used by social scientists, but even at this basic level of definition there are serious disagreements (McHugh 1970; Schur 1971). Does it matter, for example, whose rule is being violated? Can it be one man's rule or must it be widely shared? Is one man's rule less "legitimate" than a rule that is shared? Should we speak of "deviance" at all unless the person who violates a rule intended to do so? To be considered deviant, must rule violation discredit the violator? Should "deviant" be used to refer only to persons who are not merely discredited because of their rule violations, but remain so for long periods of time? All these issues are relevant conceptually, but it should be noted that they refer to *our* concept—"deviance." People whose rule violations we may choose to call "deviance" may use a different term for those violations, or they may use none at all. In seeking peoples' own perspective on rule violators, we must study their behavior, their discussions, and their arguments. We must also wait to see what transpires weeks and months after the original violation. We cannot study deviance in this manner by using interviews or psychological tests; we must rely instead on naturalistic procedures that permit us to observe events and their consequences over long periods of time without, by our presence, altering either the initial event or its outcome.

In taking such a perspective it is important to note that behavior can often vary greatly without violating any rule or calling forth any punitive action. All societies provide for acceptable variation in many areas of behavior. Diversity is not simply an inevitable fact of life, it can have positive social value as well (Wallace 1961). We know when the limits of acceptable variation have been exceeded because the result is "trouble" in the form of complaints, disputes, accusations, recriminations, and the like. Trouble, whether it sets an entire community against one man or merely brings two individuals into conflict, calls our attention to the rule violation itself, to its antecedents and its consequences. As such it is a valuable focus for our attention. Before the trouble that may result from rule violation can be resolved, the participants often call for an *account* to determine which consequences should follow. An account is a person's explanation of why he acted as he did, and, therefore what should be done about his actions.

Each step in the process of a troublesome rule violation calls for detailed consideration. First, we have the person who committed the misdeed. We must understand how he is constrained in his behavior by such factors as his beliefs, his understanding of the situation, his conception of himself and others, his personality, his physical attributes, and a host of similar factors. As a person goes through any given day, he must be aware of his society's rules (that is, the expectations that other people have regarding appropriate behavior), his own expectations about the behavior of others, and a generalized set of understandings about what is right, proper, allowable, etc. Not all men see all rules in the same way, however. Even in the simplest of societies not everyone understands all the rules, and some people, children or the senile, for example, may "know" relatively little about the rules. Many rules, in fact, are not completely clear to begin with, and their legitimacy is not always agreed upon by all. Moreover, almost every rule is contingent upon a person's status, what the situation might be, and the intent of the persons involved.

It is little wonder then, that people sometimes act in ways that offend others, with troublesome consequences. Before turning to these consequences, we should note that the person who violates a rule can become a "troublemaker" by his own accusation as well as by the accusation of others. People everywhere sometimes blame and punish themselves for what they see as wrongdoing. The result may be shame, guilt, despair, even suicide, or it may be a determination to improve. More often, however, it would appear that others do the accusing, and this accusation, as I mentioned, often calls for an account—an explanation of the troublesome rule violation. The study of such accounts has produced a small literature of high quality, beginning perhaps with Max Weber and Kenneth Burke, pursued by C. Wright Mills (1940), and advanced by British scholars such as Austin (1961), Peters (1958), and Hart (1960). A recent review has been provided by Scott and Lyman (1968). The study of "trouble cases" in anthropology derives from a different background, and makes different assumptions, but is nevertheless similar and useful (Nader 1965; Beals and Siegel 1966).

In general, accounts can *exacerbate* the trouble, *excuse* or *justify* it. There are also tactics for avoiding accounts provided in an awareness of the potential consequences of the trouble that is at issue. Accounts explain the troublemaker's motives—his fury, compulsion, forgetfulness, courage, insanity, provocation, illness, fear, negligence, confusion, etc. Accounts explain why the act occurred as it did and, therefore, they indicate what should be done. For example, if a plea for justification is made and is successful, the presumed troublemaker may be rewarded or praised. If the plea is rejected, negative sanctions may be imposed. These may include labeling the troublemaker as a special kind of person (e.g., murderer, rapist, liar) who is as a result vile, dangerous, repellent, or the like. Because the stakes are often high, accounts can be serious matters, but because the outcome is so seldom predetermined, the process of an account is sensitive to the suasive influence of privilege or circumstance; it is usually more a negotiation than a mechanical or impartial application of justice. It is here, perhaps, that Mary Douglas's writings about the importance of anomaly and ambiguity in preliterate societies are most significant (Douglas 1966), as the deviant process is shot through with both anomalous and ambiguous phenomena.

The research I am currently carrying out involves the collection of a large number of carefully observed episodes in which rule violations are recorded in their fullest possible context from beginning to apparent end, however long that may take to come about. This emphasis upon the duration of deviant acts is important for too often we conceive of trouble as dying out when its more visible properties melt away. Such appearances of early resolution can be deceiving as we all know if we reflect upon our capacities to remember past grievances and act accordingly. For example, in Kenya in 1972, I found that a dispute that I had witnessed among the Kamba in 1961 was still very much alive, even though a man whose wrongdoing then had led him to be called an "irresponsible child," was eleven years later seen to be a more or less innocent victim of an old woman's wrath. In time, I hope that such a longitudinal way of studying deviance will add to our understanding of how people get into and out of trouble.

THE YEARS AHEAD

I have contended that much of anthropology's failure to better comprehend the many aspects of deviance is a product of our partition into two kinds of studies—studies of deviant persons, and studies of deviant acts. As I wrote earlier:

We need to know why some men become deviants, while others, who also break rules, do not. Indeed, we need to know why men break rules in the first place, and why some rules but not others, why some times and not others, and why the consequences of rule violation are so variable. We also need to know why societies differ in the kind, frequency, and seriousness of deviance, and what purpose is served by labeling some of their members as deviants. [1973, p. 34]

What is called for is not necessarily a new paradigm with regard to deviance; even an integration of the existing paradigms would be a positive step. What matters is that both deviant persons and deviant acts receive equal attention, and that the causes of deviance be sought in both the sociocultural environment and in man himself. Were we successfully to achieve such an integration, we would improve our present understandings in a number of ways.

First, such a perspective would be helpful in the study of any individual society. Were we systematically to collect and analyze rule violations and the accounts that accompany them in any given society, we would not only improve our understanding of processes of deviance, we would also better our understanding of many of that society's most fundamental features. For example, through the study of accounts given by people in trouble, we might better understand sources of social strain and the prerogatives of privilege and power. Accounts also provide evidence about a society's most basic norms and values—constitutive rules, as Garfinkel has called them—the violation of which threatens that society's viability. A recent book, *Zapotec Deviance,* by anthropologist Henry Selby (1974), is a promising and provocative example of how an intensive study of the process of deviance (in this case primarily witchcraft) can yield an understanding of these most fundamental norms and values in a small Indian community in the Valley of Oaxaca. We need more concerted studies like Selby's, and like those now being undertaken by students of legal anthropology, if we are to achieve a more rounded view of the deviant process. Currently, even the best of the existing ethnographic literature rarely provides more than a tantalizing glimpse of this process. Instead, we read about one deviant act in detail, but learn of no others; or we see such an act from only one point of view; or only the court process is known; or the process is lost sight of long before its natural life has run its course.

In addition to the need for an accumulation of knowledge about the deviant process in particular societies, there is an obvious need for comparative studies of deviance in societies of many different kinds. Our existing generalizations about deviance are clearly ethnocentric. They are based almost entirely upon the work of sociologists, usually Americans, whose research has been confined to technologically advanced, urbanized Western societies, principally in the United States. As a result, the generality of the many tempting findings of these studies cannot be determined. We simply know too little about deviant processes in other, non-Western societies to permit generalization. I have argued that there is no compelling evidence to support the idea that there is more deviance in urban than in folk societies (Edgerton 1973), but this is an assertion based upon my reading of inadequate ethnographic evidence; it is not a scientific proof. When we attempt to examine hypotheses about the form a society takes and the amount or kind of deviance within it, we find that our existing evidence is wholly inadequate. For example, I believe that hunting and gathering societies have a different pattern of deviance than that found among peasant farmers or nomadic pastoralists or urban slum dwellers, but the evidence necessary actually to test my ideas does not exist. Another example can be taken from the sociologist Kai Erikson's study, *The Wayward Puritans* (1966). Working from surviving records of seventeenth century Massachusetts, Erikson concluded that deviance helps a society to define its boundaries and that the occurrence of deviance therefore serves a positive social and cultural function. This is an important hypothesis but it is not yet one that we can test by examining the literature about very many—if any—small non-Western societies.

More important still is our inability to test any proposition about the relative adequacy of a society. Our relativistic tradition in anthropology has been slow to yield to the idea that there could be such a thing as a deviant society, one that is contrary to human nature and therefore fails adequately to provide for man's basic needs. Yet the idea of a deviant society is central to the alienation tradition in sociology and other fields (Etzioni 1968) and it poses a challenge for anthropological theory. Because we know so little about human nature—or basic human needs—and because our knowledge of the rates and kinds of deviance in the world's societies is so inadequate, we cannot say whether, much less how, any society has failed to meet the needs of its members. Nevertheless, a glance at any urban newspaper's stories of rising rates of homicide, suicide, rape and other violent crimes should suffice to suggest that the question is relevant not only for theory, but for questions of survival in the modern world.

Better comparative research concerning deviance is essential not only for our understanding of society and culture, but also for our understanding of man as an organism. Any viable human science must conclude that human behavior is always a product of an *interaction* between a human organism and its environment. While it is probably correct to say that most forms of deviant behavior are more clearly a product of one's environment than they are one's biology, it does not follow that one's biology is altogether irrelevant. The capacity of any human being to adapt to his environment—that is, to learn what others expect of him and to respond appropriately to these expectations—is necessarily at least in part a function of one's biology. As a growing body of research now indicates, certain individuals may commit deviant acts not only because of social, cultural, and psychological influences, but because they are biologically predisposed to deviance by their genetic composition, their exposure to pre- and perinatal stress, by poor nutrition, or by the diseases, toxins or injuries life brings them.

One example, of many possible, can be taken from the research of Thomas, Chess and Birch (1968), who studied the temperament of children in relationship to their subsequent deviant behavior. Their work suggests that infants are born with markedly varying patterns of temperament (e.g., irregularity, mood, persistence, distractibility, etc.) and that these patterns are difficult to change. If societies choose to regard some temperaments as good—e.g., positive mood, easy adaptability and regularity—while others are seen as bad, we have a perfect example of biology as the source of deviant behavior. It is important to note that this formulation differs from Benedict's in two important ways: first, not a few children, but many, can be expected to have temperaments that do not fit the ideal patterns, and second, these children cannot easily be molded to fit that ideal pattern.

More fundamental still is the possibility that aspects of human nature—genetically encoded potentials for behavior that we all share—may underlie man's propensity for deviance. The issues here are complex; indeed the concept of human nature itself is unacceptable to some serious scholars (Geertz 1965). Nevertheless, I have suggested elsewhere that certain aspects of human nature can be identified and may well predispose humans toward deviance (Edgerton 1973). The most obvious of these is man's "instinct" for self-preservation, perhaps better construed as his "flight/fight" mechanism in which he responds to threat first with flight, only secondarily does he fight. The presence of such a "mechanism" or "instinct," should one exist, could help to account for man's pursuit of his own self-interest, security or survival even at the cost of deviance. Another, less obvious source of deviance, might be man's intolerance for boredom, an aspect of human nature that Ralph Linton (1936) thought was at the heart of culture itself. I have suggested that this same intolerance for boredom could compel humans to seek new experience, variety, or adventure, with rule violation a likely outcome (Edgerton 1973, p. 32). Such speculation may or may not prove to be correct, but the principle—that man's basic animal nature may impel him toward deviance—remains. This possibility is exemplified by the existence of an Azande trickster named Ture, about whom E. E. Evans-Pritchard has said the following:

The animals act and talk like persons because people are animals behind the masks social convention makes them wear. What Ture does is the opposite of all that is moral; and it is all of us who are Ture. He is really ourselves. [1967, p. 30]

REFERENCES CITED

Austin, J. L.
   1961 *Philosophical Papers*. London: Oxford University Press.

Baroja, J. C.
  1963   The City and the Country: Reflexions on some Ancient Commonplaces. In *Mediterranean Countrymen*, ed. J. Pitt-Rivers, pp. 27–40. Paris: Mouton.
Beals, A. R. and Siegel, B. J.
  1966   *Divisiveness and Social Conflict. An Anthropological Approach.* Stanford: Stanford University Press.
Benedict R.
  1934   *Patterns of Culture.* Boston: Houghton Mifflin.
Cohen, A. K.
  1966   *Deviance and Control.* Englewood Cliffs, New Jersey.
Cohen, Y.
  1961   *Social Structure and Personality: A Casebook.* New York: Holt, Rinehart and Winston.
Devereux, G.
  1963   Primitive Psychiatric Diagnosis: A General Theory of the Diagnostic Process. In *Man's Image in Medicine and Anthropology*, ed. I. Galdston. New York: Universities Press.
Douglas, M.
  1966   *Purity and Danger: An Analysis of Concepts of Pollution and Taboo.* London: Routledge and Kegan Paul.
DuBois, C.
  1944   *The People of Alor.* Minneapolis: University of Minnesota Press.
Durkheim, E.
  1895   *Les regles de la methode sociologique.* Paris.
Edgerton, R. B.
  1960   *A Picture Test of Values.* Ph.D. dissertation. University of California, Los Angeles.
  1963   A Patient Elite: Ethnography in Hospital for the Mentally Retarded. *American Journal of Mental Deficiencies* 68:372–85.
  1964   Pokot Intersexuality: An East African Example of the Resolution of Sexual Incongruity. *American Anthropologist* 66:1288–99.
  1965   Some Dimensions of Disillusionment in Culture Contact. *Southwest Journal of Anthropology* 21:231–43.
  1966   Conceptions of Psychosis in Four East African Societies. *American Anthropologist* 68:408–25.
  1967   *The Cloak of Competence.* Berkeley and Los Angeles: University of California Press.
  1969   On the "Recognition" of Mental Illness. In *Changing Perspective in Mental Illness*, ed. S. Plog and R. B. Edgerton, pp. 49–72. New York: Holt, Rinehart and Winston.
  1971   *The Individual in Cultural Adaptation: A Study of Four East African Societies.* Los Angeles: University of California Press.
  1971a A Traditional African Psychiatrist. *Southwestern Journal of Anthropology* 27:259–78.
  1973   Deviant Behavior and Cultural Theory. *Addison-Wesley Module in Anthropology No.* 37. Reading, Massachusetts.

Edgerton, R. B. and Conant, F. P.
   1964   Kilapat: The "Shaming Party" Among the Pokot of East Africa. *Southwest Journal of Anthropology* 20:404–18.

Edgerton, R. B. and Dingman, H. F.
   1963   Tattooing and Identity. *International Journal of Social Psychiatry* 9:143–53.

   1964   Good Reasons for Bad Supervision: "Dating" in a Hospital for the Mentally Retarded. *Psychiatric Quarterly Supplement* 38:221–33.

Edgerton, R. B. and Sabagh, G.
   1962   From Mortification to Aggrandizement: Changing Self-Concepts in the Careers of the Mentally Retarded. *Psychiatry* 25:263–72.

Edgerton, R. B., Tarjan, G. and Dingman, H. F.
   1961   Free Enterprise in a Captive Society. *American Journal of Mental Deficiencies* 66:35–41.

Erikson, K.
   1966   *Wayward Puritans. A Study in the Sociology of Deviance.* New York: Wiley.

Evans-Pritchard, E. E.
   1937   *Witchcraft, Oracles and Magic Among the Azande.* Oxford: Clarendon Press.

   1967   *The Zande Trickster.* Oxford: Clarendon Press.

Geertz, C.
   1965   The Impact of the Concept of Culture on the Concept of Man. In *New Views of the Nature of Man*, ed. J. Platt, pp. 93–118. Chicago: University of Chicago Press.

Gladwin, T. and Sarason, S.
   1953   Truk: Man in Paradise. *Viking Fund Publications in Anthropology No. 20.* New York.

Goldschmidt, W.
   1956   Culture and Behavior. *Proceedings of the International Congress of Ethnological and Anthropological Sciences, Philadelphia.*

   1959   *Man's Way, A Preface to the Understanding of Human Society.* New York: Holt, Rinehart and Winston.

   1965   Theory and Strategy in the Study of Cultural Adaptability. *American Anthropologist* 67:402–08.

   1967   *Sebei Law.* Berkeley: University of California Press.

   1969   *Kambuya's Cattle: The Legacy of an African Herdsman.* Berkeley: University of California Press.

   1971   Epilogue: The Relation of Intrapsychic Events to Ecological Adaptation. In R. Edgerton (1971) *The Individual in Cultural Adaptation.* Berkeley: University of California Press.

   n.d.   *The Sebei.* Berkeley: University of California Press, forthcoming.

Goldschmidt, W. and Edgerton, R. B.
   1961   A Picture Technique for the Study of Values. *American Anthropologist* 63:26–47.

Goodman, M. E.
   1967   *The Individual and Culture.* Homewood, Ill.: Dorsey.

Harris, M.
   1971   *Culture, Man, and Nature: An Introduction to General Anthropology.* New York: Thomas Y. Crowell.

Hart, H. L. A.
   1960   The Ascription of Responsibility and Rights. In *Logic and Language,* ed. A. Flew, pp. 145–66. Oxford: Basil Blackwell.
Henry, J.
   1958   The Personal Community and its Invariant Properties. *American Anthropologist* 60:827–31.
Honigmann, J.
   1954   *Culture and Personality.* New York: Harper and Bros.
Hsu, F. L. K.
   1961   *Psychological Anthropology.* Homewood, Ill.: Dorsey.
Kaplan, B.
   1954   A Study of Rorschach Responses in Four Cultures. *Papers of the Peabody Museum of American Archeology and Ethnology, Harvard University* 42, no. 2. Cambridge, Massachusetts.
Kaplan, B., ed.
   1961   *Studying Personality Cross-Culturally.* Evanston, Ill.: Row, Peterson, and Co.
Kaplan, B. H.
   1971   *Psychiatric Disorder and the Urban Environment.* New York: Behavioral Publications.
Kardiner, A.
   1945   *The Psychological Frontiers of Society.* New York: Columbia University Press.
Karno, M. and Edgerton, R. B.
   1969   The Perception of Mental Illness in a Mexican-American Community. *Archives General Psychiatry* 20:233–38.
Killar, E. J., Beckwith, W. C., and Edgerton, R. B.
   1968   Sexual Behavior of the ARL Colony Chimpanzees. *Journal of Nervous and Mental Diseases* 147:444–59.
Kluckhohn, C., Murray, H. A. and Schneider, D. M.
   1953   *Personality in Nature, Society, and Culture,* 2nd ed. New York: A. A. Knopf.
Kroeber, A. R., ed.
   1953   *Anthropology Today. An Encyclopedic Inventory.* Chicago: University of Chicago Press.
LeVine, R. A.
   1973   *Culture, Behavior, and Personality.* Chicago: Aldine.
Lindesmith, A. R. and Strauss, A. L.
   1950   A Critique of Culture-Personality Writings. *American Sociological Review* 15:587–600.
Linton, R.
   1936   *The Study of Man.* New York: Appleton-Century-Crofts.
MacAndrew, C. and Edgerton, R. B.
   1964   A Procedure of Interrogating Non-Professional Ward Employees. *American Journal of Mental Deficiencies* 69:347–53.
   1966   On the Possibility of Friendship. *American Journal of Mental Deficiencies* 70:612–21.
   1969   *Drunken Comportment: A Social Explanation.* Chicago: Aldine; London: T. Nelson and Sons.

Matza, D.
    1969   *Becoming Deviant.* Englewood Cliffs, New Jersey: Prentice Hall.
McHugh, P.
    1970   A Common-Sense Conception of Deviance. In *Deviance and Respectability.*
            The Social Construction of Moral Meanings, ed. J. D. Douglas, pp. 61–88.
            New York: Basic Books.
Mills, C. W.
    1940   Situated Action and the Vocabulary of Motives. *American Sociological Review*
            6:904–13.
Nader, L., ed.
    1965   The Ethnography of Law. *American Anthropologist* 67, no. 6, part 2 (special
            publication).
Paul, B.
    1953   Interview Techniques and Field Relationships. In *Anthropology Today,* ed.
            A. R. Kroeber, pp. 430–51. Chicago: University of Chicago Press.
Peters, R. S.
    1958   *The Concept of Motivation.* London: Routledge and Kegan Paul.
Pospisil, L.
    1958   Social Change and Primitive Law: Consequences of a Papuan Legal Case.
            American Anthropologist 60:832–37.
    1972   The Ethnology of Law. *Addison-Wesley Module in Anthropology No. 12.*
            Reading, Massachusetts.
Sartre, J. P.
    1964   *Saint Genet.* New York: New American Library.
Scheff, T.
    1966   *Being Mentally Ill.* Chicago: Aldine.
Schur, E. M.
    1971   *Labeling Deviant Behavior. Its Sociological Consequences.* New York: Harper
            and Row.
Scott, M. B. and Lyman, S. M.
    1968   Accounts. *American Sociological Review* 33:46–61.
Selby, H.
    1974   *Zapotec Deviance.* Austin, Texas: University of Texas Press.
Singer, M.
    1961   A Survey of Culture and Personality Theory and Research. In *Studying Per-*
            sonality Cross-Culturally, ed. Bert Kaplan, pp. 9–90. New York: Harper and
            Row.
Spindler, G.
    1955   Sociocultural and Psychological Processes in Menomini Indian Acculturation.
            University of California Publications in Culture and Society, vol. 5. Berkeley:
            University of California Press.
Spindler, G. and Spindler, L.
    1958   Male and Female Adaptations in Culture Change. *American Anthropologist*
            60:217–33.
    1971   *Dreamers Without Power. The Menomini Indians.* New York: Holt, Rinehart
            and Winston.

Spindler, L.

1958   Sixty-one Rorschachs and Fifteen Expressive Autobiographic Interviews of Menomini Indian Women. In *Microcard Publications of Primary Records in Culture and Personality,* vol. 2, no. 10, ed. B. Kaplan. Madison: University of Wisconsin Press.

Szasz, T.

1963   *Law, Liberty and Psychiatry.* New York: MacMillan.

Thomas, A., Chess, S. and Birch, H.

1968   *Temperament and Behavior Disorders in Children.* New York: Holt, Rinehart and Winston.

Turnbull, C. M.

1961   *The Forest People.* New York: Simon and Schuster.

Wallace, A. F. C.

1952   The Modal Personality Structure of the Tuscarora Indians as Revealed by the Rorschach Test. *Bulletin, Bureau of American Ethnology No.* 150.

1961   *Culture and Personality.* New York: Random House.

Winans, R. B. and Edgerton, R. B.

1964   Hehe Magical Justice. *American Anthropologist* 66:745–64.

Wrong, D.

1961   The Oversocialized Conception of Man in Modern Sociology. *American Sociological Review* 26:183–93.

The Author

ERIKA BOURGUIGNON was born in Vienna, Austria, and came to the United States in 1939. She received her early education in Vienna, in Tel-Aviv and in Switzerland. She has a B.A. from Queens College, New York, where she took her first course in culture and personality from Hortense Powdermaker. In her senior year, she also took a course on "moot problems in anthropological theory" then taught by Claude Lévi-Strauss at the New School. After a semester of graduate work at the University of Connecticut, she went on to Northwestern for her Ph.D. in anthropology. There she studied under A. I. Hallowell and M. J. Herskovits, whose influences on her later work are reflected in this paper. In preparation for field work, she obtained training in Rorschach Test Analysis, attending the Rorschach Summer Institute in two successive years. Her field work in Haiti introduced her to possession trance and the research problems associated with that subject. Some of these problems were pursued by her, later, in a large scale, comparative study, carried out during the years 1963 through 1968 under a grant from the National Institute of Mental Health. She directed this project at the Ohio State University, where she has been teaching since 1949. Among its major results is the volume *Religion, Altered States of Consciousness, and Social Change* (Ohio State University Press, 1973), edited by Professor Bourguignon and including contributions by research associates and former students. The comparative work on hundreds of societies involved in this project required an examination of hologeistic methods and approaches. This examination resulted, in part, in *Diversity and Homogeneity in World Societies* (HRAF Press, 1973), a volume based on the data of Murdock's Ethnographic Atlas and prepared in collaboration with Dr. Lenora Greenbaum.

In Professor Bourguignon's view, altered states of consciousness should be of particular interest to anthropologists because they represent points of juncture between various dimensions of human existence: the biopsychological and the sociocultural, the individual and the social, the ecological and the historical, the ritual, the mythical and the experiential. The work undertaken so far represents only an initial approach to this vast subject, producing evermore new questions as new approaches of investigation are developed.

Professor Bourguignon is currently chairman of the Department of Anthropology at the Ohio State University. She is married to the Belgian artist and painter Paul-Henri Bourguignon.

This Chapter

As Erika Bourguignon points out in this chapter, altered states of consciousness are now a popular and respectable subject of inquiry, but in 1947 when field research was just beginning, trance states experienced by possessed persons were regarded as mental illness, hypnotic phenomena, or outright simulation, and not to be taken seriously as culture relevant phenomena. This paper traces the development of one of the most significant contributions to the present state of the subject of inquiry.

Professor Bourguignon found very early in her research in Haiti that *Vodoun* had to be considered in a much larger context than simply as a sign of neurotic adaptation or psychopathology—that is, within the context of a world view and the structure of a total society. She began to turn to questions of identity, of personal identity and culturally sanctioned discontinuity. She found continuity of motivation in disassociated individuals in spite of apparent the "uniqueness of every culture" argument, which offered no chance for systematic theory building, Bourguignon turned to both the cross-cultural files and to systematic comparisons of selective societies. She and her coworkers examined more than twenty-two hundred ethnographies over a period of five years in a number of languages and instituted a series of statistical studies using a representative sample of 488 societies from the world ethnographic atlas. Field studies of selected societies were then begun, ranging from tent revivalism in Columbus, Ohio, to the Umbanda cult in Sao Paulo, Brazil.

Her work is a witness to both the unity and diversity of human nature. Altered states of consciousness play a significant role in the overwhelming majority of human societies but they are patterned within a variety of cultural contexts. Her studies shed light on our universal human nature and how this raw material is utilized in building culture. Her work is both substantively and methodologically significant, for she uses a disciplined cross-cultural approach, combines both emic and etic strategies (grouping native concepts of disassociated states into an etic classification), and has developed in depth studies of individual societies—all on a topic that might have been thought too exotic for even a single case study in the 1950s.

G.D.S.

14 Spirit Possession and Altered States of Consciousness: The Evolution of an Inquiry

ERIKA BOURGUIGNON

The review of the history of one's own research presents an interesting challenge: on the one hand, it provides an opportunity to reflect on what was done and how, and why. Also, in conducting such a review, one may hope to discover some new dimensions of the research problem. On the other hand, it is quite obvious that we can have only a limited, and probably distorted, view of our own intellectual histories in the context of the wider history of our discipline and of the world in which we live.

Some comments on this larger context are in order at the outset of this review. The subject of the research to be discussed involves segments of the field now commonly called "altered states of consciousness" (ASC) as well as reference to beliefs in what is spoken of as "possession" by spirit entities. These subjects seem very timely indeed as this is being written. Yet when the original field research in Haiti was begun in 1947 nothing could have been more exotic. Surely, in modern Western industrial societies people did not believe in such things! That exorcism was still "on the books" as a ritual of the major denominations could only be due to institutional conservatism and cultural lag. As for the "trance" state that supposedly "possessed" persons experienced, that was certainly either mental illness, perhaps hysteria, or at best, a somnambulistic or hypnotic phenomenon, if not outright simulation. I recall that much later, in the early 1960s I mentioned my research interests to a colleague, a political scientist. He was clearly disappointed to learn I was spending my time on subjects of such limited antiquarian interest when so many burning problems of practical importance needed to be attended to.

In the pages that follow I shall attempt to show how my own research interests have grown from more circumscribed beginnings, how they were influenced by developments within anthropology as well as by new questions that arose in the pursuit of answers to the first formulations of the problem. At the same time, the research interacted with developments in the wider society. Finally, I wish to show how this apparently "esoteric" research may be said to have bearings on our understanding of a series of what are generally conceded to be "significant concerns."

POSSESSION IN HAITIAN *VODOUN*

In 1947, relatively little anthropological field work had been carried out in Haiti. There were numerous popular accounts, many dating from the period of the American occupation of that country (1915–34), full of sensational revelations concerning "voodoo." There was, however, one major exception to this. In 1937, M. J. Herskovits published his *Life in a Haitian Valley*, a study of the village of Mirebalais, placed in the larger setting of Haitian history and society. The importance of this work for later Haitian history, as well as for Afro-American studies, can scarcely be exaggerated. (For a discussion of the significance of Herskovits' work, see Whitten and Szwed, 1970.) Having studied Afro-Americans in Suriname both among the Bush Negroes and the city people of Paramaribo, and having carried on field work in West Africa, particularly in Dahomey, Herskovits (Herskovits and Herskovits 1933; Herskovits 1938)[1] was struck by the continuity Haitian culture showed with ancestral African patterns in family form, economic organization and, in particular, in religion.

He sought to redress the balance against the sensationalists, to show the values of African traditions in the life of the Haitian peasantry. And in doing so, he gained the respect and gratitude of Haitian intellectuals, who were to lay the ground work of their own ideology of cultural identity. He saw Haitian culture, including religion, as the result of acculturation,[2] as a partial amalgam of European and African elements.

1. Dates of publication do not accurately reflect dates of research. The field work in Dahomey was carried out in 1931, that in Haiti in 1934.
2. Herskovits evolved a theory of acculturation beginning its elaboration in the 1930s, a theory in the development of which his several African and Afro-American studies represented so many milestones. He saw Haitian culture not as a true amalgam, but as a situation in which people tended to be pulled between the two poles, the African and the European, and he formulated the concept of "socialized ambivalence" to describe this state of affairs. I have pursued this subject elsewhere (Bourguignon 1969).

This was most strikingly true in religion, where Catholic saints were identified with African gods (Herskovits 1937*b*).

The element in Haitian religion which had attracted most sensational notice was that of spirit possession. During *vodoun* [3] rituals, some of the faithful impersonate various spirits. That is to say, it is believed that their actions and words are no longer their own but those of spirits (saints, African gods) that take over their bodies. Afterwards, they have no memory of the events. A Haitian psychiatrist, J. C. Dorsainvil (1931), had argued that possession was the result of neurotic strains in Haitian heredity. Herskovits emphatically came down on the side of cultural relativism: "in terms of the patterns of Haitian religion, possession is not abnormal, but normal; it is set in its cultural mold as are all other phases of conventional living. That it gives release from psychic tensions does not alter the case. . . ." (Herskovits 1937*a,* p. 147). The point is forcefully elaborated some years later: "The very definition of what is normal or abnormal is relative to the cultural frame of reference . . . when we look beneath behavior to meaning, such conclusions [of psychopathology] become untenable. . . . The [possession behaviors] are *culturally* patterned, and often induced by learning and discipline" (Herskovits 1948, pp. 66–67, emphasis in original). And again:

The terminology of psychopathology has been readily applied to these states of possession. Such designations as hysteria, autohypnosis, compulsion, have come to rest easily on the tongue. . . . the connotation they carry of psychic instability, emotional imbalance, departure from normality recommends the use of other words that do not invite such a distortion of cultural reality. For in these Negro societies the interpretation given behavior under possession—the meaning this experience holds for the people—falls entirely in the realm of understandable, predictable, *normal* behavior [ibid., emphasis in original.]

As Herskovits points out, the interpretation of possession in terms of psychopathology is rejected by him "in the light of the principles of cultural relativism" (ibid, p. 371).[4]

3. Herskovits writes *vodun* both for Haiti and for Dahomey, where the word means "deity." This Dahomean word is also the etymological source of the U.S. term *voodoo,* which refers primarily to magic, however. Consistent with the present standardized spelling of Haitian créole, the form *vodoun* is used in this paper.

4. For a discussion of cultural relativism in the work of Herskovits, see Simpson 1973, pp. 96–100, as well as Herskovits' own posthumous book, *Cultural Relativism* (1973).

Much of the literature of culture and personality has been concerned with the question of whether psychopathology is to be defined in cultural terms, as *deviancy* and whether any supracultural concept of mental health can validly be established. We shall have occasion to return to this point below. For a review of some of these issues see Bourguignon 1973, pp. 1095–96; J. G. Kennedy 1973.

In spite of such insistence on cultural normality, Herskovits was aware of the limitations of our understanding of the phenomena in question. In the context of his discussion of possession in Haiti, he commented on the difficulty of dealing with the subject:

Scientifically, the phenomenon of possession in Negro cultures, at least, is as yet unsatisfactorily explained, largely because of the almost complete absence of adequate reports on the background and incidence of specific cases. [1937a, p. 147]

As a student at Northwestern, I went to Haiti in 1947[5] to carry on research within the larger framework of Afro-American studies pursued by Professor Herskovits, his associates and his students. Mine was to be a broad ethnographic study in areas of the country not previously investigated. However, having worked closely also under the direction of Professor A. I. Hallowell, I wished to bring my training in culture and personality to bear on problems of spirit possession.

In my thinking about that puzzling phenomenon, I found myself concerned with the cultural patterning of this behavior and with the role of culture in the definitions of the normal and the abnormal. Hallowell (1938) had proposed, on the basis of Ojibwa data, that neurotic anxiety and realistic fear are not different categories, as suggested by the psychoanalytic literature. Rather, he had argued for an interpretation which sees anxiety and fear as the ends of a continuum, along which we may find culturally patterned intermediary terms. What is realistic reaction to danger will depend on the cultural perception of dangers, not on the evaluation of a situation by an outsider. Could giving up one's identity to that of a ''possessing'' spirit and the acting out of that spirit role also be seen in these terms? If ''possession behavior'' is cultural behavior rather than idiosyncratic deviancy, then—culture being learned—possession behavior must be learned. How then, is it learned? What are the features of Haitian modal personality structure which make such learning not only possible but appropriate?

Answers to these and related questions were to be obtained through observations of possession behavior, life history materials, including dreams, the collection of projective test protocols—particularly the Rorschach—as well as observations and other information on the enculturation of Haitian children.[6]

5. My field research in Haiti was supported by grants from the Carnegie Corporation of New York and the Graduate School of Northwestern University.
6. The term *enculturation* was coined by Herskovits (1948, pp. 38ff.) to refer to the total process by which an individual ''gains competence in his culture.'' *Socialization*, defined as the process by which ''an individual is integrated into his society,'' is seen merely as a part of enculturation.

Although I was concerned with these ideas, I should like to stress that the approach to field work emphatically encouraged by Professor Herskovits was not that of problem oriented research, of hypothesis testing. Indeed, such focused research was said to limit the attention of the ethnographer to selected aspects of culture, and to lead to the neglect of others, not foreseen in the hypothesis. In this sense, ethnographic research was to be totally open-ended and the ordering of data was to be done after the field work had been completed. It should be noted, in this connection, that in his chapter on field work in *Man and His Works* (1948) there is no reference to hypotheses and their testing, nor is there reference to the work of those who employed such an approach.

Learning a foreign culture through participation in another society is quite another matter than gaining acquaintance with unfamiliar ways of life through the reading of anthropological reports. The anthropologist seeks to put order into his data, if only by devoting different chapters to each of the various aspects of culture, what Clark Wissler called "the universal table of contents" of anthropological monographs: economics, family organization, religion, etc. Furthermore, an attempt is generally made to find some coherence in the observational materials, to look for threads and trends that interrelate given actions and attitudes. It is expected that behavior is not random, that no people live in a chaotic world and that it behooves the anthropologist to find the underlying order, whether that order be referred to as patterns, themes, motifs, modal personality structure or social structure.

The actual experience of life in a society, of interaction with individuals, presents cultural data pell-mell. Possession, I came to see, had to be understood not only within the specific confines of the ritual settings wherein for the most part it occurred, but rather within the larger *vodoun* world view and, indeed, within the structure of the total society. What, then, was the cultural universe of the lower class Haitian? For one thing, I found Haiti to be a highly stratified society, and even in relatively remote rural areas there was awareness of this stratification and its impact on peoples' lives. However, I began my work in the capital city, and there the evidence of the stratified world was everywhere. *Vodoun* was denied or belittled by the élite, at least in public. For the lower class *vodouists,* however, the reality of the stratified society was built into the *vodoun* universe; it was reflected by the hierarchical arrangement of the spirits, which mirrored even the racial and linguistic distinctions in the population. Secondly, the *vodoun* world view presented a framework within which all kinds of experiences, all kinds of aspects of the world were given meaning. For example, if I, as a foreigner, wanted to learn about *vodoun,* it had to be that its rituals were practiced in my country, and that I came to receive training I could put to use on my return.

I soon discovered a number of things concerning possession I had not fully understood from my pre-field work studies. For one thing, the transformations in actions, expressions, attitudes of possessed individuals were indeed drastic and often dramatic. The learning involved in the acquisition of possession behavior would, I thought, have to be of two kinds: on the one hand, individuals would have to acquire knowledge of the behavior appropriate to possessed persons. Yet this conscious learning alone would not be enough to produce the behavior, for then it would merely be skilled play acting. On the other hand, since this behavior was so very widespread, there would have to be the development of a special modal personality type, a personality having the capacity of entering into possession states.[7]

I noted that the concept of possession—in Haitian parlance, being "mounted" by a spirit—had a broader range of applications than expected. And in my field notes I began to distinguish between what I thought of as a supracultural, medical—or psychiatric—definition of "possession" and the way in which the Haitians conceived of the state of being "mounted." I thought in the former sense possession might be defined as temporary loss of consciousness, followed by amnesia, sometimes accompanied by violent convulsive movements and sometimes by complete alteration of the personality, lasting from a few moments, to— reputedly—a week or even ten days. Such behavior might occur at ceremonies and might be considered appropriate there, if the spirits had been invited. If not, it might be considered ill-mannered on the part of the spirit. Possession might occur spontaneously outside of ritual settings, such as in children's games or in crisis situations. Yet being "mounted" might also refer to speaking in one's sleep. In cultural terms, the two are equivalent—in psychiatric terms they clearly are not. On the other hand, there might be situations in which a break in consciousness occurs, yet either because the individual is alone or the situation or the associated behavior is inappropriate, such a break is not referred to as possession. Hallucination would be one such example, as would be drunkenness or certain delusional states. Furthermore, there are a variety of circumstances in which possession states are culturally appropriate, and where the behavior is most likely to be imitative rather than genuine; an example of this is found in the supposed manifesta-

7. Although the majority of possessed persons are indeed women, claims that the behavior does not occur among men (e.g., E. Douyon 1965) are quite unfounded.

tions of the spirits of death *(Guedé)* in Haitian market places on Hallo-
ween. And, finally, there are other types of possessions, illnesses interpreted as due to spirits of the dead "sent on" an individual by sorcerers.
Such possessions by the dead are not linked to impersonations or unconsciousness (Bourguignon 1965, 1970*a*).

Looking at the culture of the Haitian masses as the result of the
acculturation of transplanted Africans, I saw much that gave evidence of
that African past, many examples of what Herskovits had termed retentions and syncretisms. Among these retentions, on the psychological
level, I thought, was the "continued capacity for spirit possession,"
suggesting a continuity of personality structure with their African ancestors even greater than the continuity of cultural content (Bourguignon
1951). Note I implied here that spirit possession behavior represented a
"capacity" rather than a type of pathology or a defect, and also, that I
thought of this capacity as a feature of personality structure.

Yet, I did not address myself in my analysis directly to the matter
of personality structure. Rather, I was preoccupied with questions of
cognition, with the structuring of the behavioral environment in which
the behavior took place and in terms of which it "made sense." Thus, I
noted that ritual possession behavior involved impersonation and dis-
guise, external and internal transformations of a person's essence. These
themes play important roles in a variety of areas of Haitian life. *Vodoun*
spirit possession had to be seen, therefore, in a larger context. And so I
proceeded to consider this context from a number of vantage points:
analyzing informants' talk about dreams (Bourguignon 1954), about
the ever-favorite subjects of magic, cannibalism, and zombies (Bourguignon 1959), or their responses to unstructured psychological tests,
such as the Rorschach (Bourguignon and Nett 1955; Bourguignon 1956,
1969). And so the pieces gradually began to fall into place. For example,
disguises appear frequently in the Rorschach protocols of adults and of
children, as do a variety of transformed beings: werewolves, demons,
zombies, etc. The same appears to be the case in dreams. Many of these
themes of transformation are related to anxiety about the dangers of the
world in which one lives. A second theme—most clearly expressed in
regard to werewolves, zombies, cannibalism as well as the Afro-Catholic
spirits—has to do with eating, feeding (the spirits) and being eaten.
And a third theme is that of the totally hierarchical universe. The spirits,
the political and economic society, the family, the cult groups all are
organized in a hierarchical fashion. There are no equals, only superiors
and inferiors. Transformation and instability of personal form and
identity, oral anxiety and oral dependence, and the sado-masochism of

hierarchical organization appear to be crucial elements in the total Haitian behavioral environment and in the Haitian personality as well. "Fear of witchcraft, magic, evil spirits, etc. is to be understood as displacement of aggression. . . . Whiting and Child [1953] found fear of others correlated with socialization anxiety in aggression training. Both propositions fit the Haitian data" (Bourguignon 1959, p. 43). The aggression is often, perhaps primarily, oral aggression, and Whiting and Child (1953) also find fear of others correlated with oral socialization anxiety. How does all of this help us to understand possession behavior?

To begin with, let us be clear about what it is we are dealing with. "Possession behavior" is really a culture-bound term, and unless the anthropologist wishes to view the phenomenon only from the perspective of the Haitians (or of others with similar beliefs and behaviors) it is better to use a more neutral term. From a psychological perspective, the behavior is best considered as "dissociation." In M. J. Field's words (1960, p. 19) this is defined as a "mental mechanism whereby a split-off part of the personality temporarily possesses the entire field of consciousness and behavior." The elements of personality that make up the various spirit roles, or "personalities," represent such split-off parts of the personality. These are felt to be alien to the individual's personal identity and often act in ways not acceptable for that identity. It should be noted, however, that for Field, as for myself, the term dissociation is neutral with regard to any implications of pathology.

A. I. Hallowell, in his important papers on "The Self and its Behavioral Environment" (1955a, b) notes that self-awareness is a generic human trait, which is a cultural and social product, and considers how personal identity is maintained within the context of a culturally constituted behavioral environment. Applying such a framework to my Haitian data brought them sharply into focus (Bourguignon 1965). In the Haitian context, we needed to consider not only continuity of personal identity but also the culturally sanctioned discontinuity of that identity. Ritual dissociation, interpreted as spirit possession, represented such discontinuity. By means of it, the individual may temporarily but repeatedly change his—or more often, her—identity, changing his position in the hierarchical universe. That behavior, that discontinuity, is culturally and ritually sanctioned and rewarded, as well as subject to certain norms. One of the principal rewards consists in the fact that the dissociated individual, playing the role of spirits, has a considerably enlarged scope of action. This may not be used only for immediate impulse gratification and for compensations for the frustrations of everyday life, or to deal with the problems of others. More importantly, this enlarged scope of action provides the individual a means of dealing with his own situation in the real world of everyday life. One of the most striking findings to come from the examination of my data (and which I believe to be supported by data since collected by others) concerns the continuity of motivation of dissociated individuals, in spite of the break in consciousness and the discontinuity of personal identity. Ritual dissociations are notably self-serving and self-enhancing. The very self whose continuity is denied by the cultural dogma embodied in possession belief and by the psychological experience of dissociation is served through this discontinuity. This suggests that the loss of continuity is in fact a valuable asset to the individual in dealing with his life situation, rather than damaging and hence pathological. I have, therefore, suggested that ritual dissociation might best be understood as a "dissociation in the service of the self" whose ends are served. And I concluded by arguing that ritualized dissociation

provides the self with an alternate set of roles . . . in which unfulfilled desires, "unrealistic" in the context of the workaday world, get a second chance at fulfillment, a fulfillment which is surely not merely vicarious because the glory goes to the possessing spirit, rather than to the "horse" [i.e., the possessed person]. . . . In a world of poverty, disease and frustration, ritual possession, rather than destroying the integrity of the self, provides increased scope for fulfillment. [Bourguignon 1965, p. 57]

Given the Haitian data, we may admit that ritual dissociation is of practical utility to the individual's adjustment. Yet we shall also have to ask why such a devious means of dealing with problems of living is required of the Haitian. Just what is the world like in which such indirect actions are necessary? The answer appears to be that it is, indeed, a world perceived as hostile in which the individual is anxious and powerless. Only the spirits appear to have the power to effect the required changes. And so the individual—partly in fantasy and partly through the acceptance of a collective fantasy by his peers—may become powerful by impersonating the spirits.

This overall picture of the behavioral environment of the Haitian masses has emerged gradually through the separate analyses of several subsets of data. The question studied changed in the course of the investigation. We no longer ask: what is Haitian modal personality like and how does it develop so that we may account for the phenomenon of ritual possession? Instead, the question is: what is the Haitian behavioral environment like so that ritual possession makes sense? How is this behavior learned and rewarded, and, moreover, of what do the rewards consist?

In the development of the research summarized here, the terminology used to describe the phenomenon under consideration has changed, reflecting a somewhat more sophisticated understanding, distinguishing the analytic level from that of the participant. We have moved from a purely descriptive level, asserting that "possession behavior is normal" because it is culturally sanctioned and ritualized, to an understanding of it as part of a world view in which the natural, the social and the personal are brought into a coherent whole.

THE CROSS-CULTURAL STUDY OF DISSOCIATIONAL STATES, 1963–68

During the 1950s a number of things happened that led me, eventually, to undertake a much broader and quite differently conceived study of possession beliefs and associated behaviors.[8] My interests in the general subject were maintained by the publication of a number of significant studies on Haiti and on related Afro-American and African cultures. For example, A. Métraux (1955, 1959) emphasized the importance of the histrionic and theatrical elements in Haitian possession behavior, as M. Leiris (1958) did for the zar cult of Ethiopia. Messing (1958), on the other hand, noted the group therapy aspects of the zar cult. This pointed up a major difference between Haitian *vodoun*, the other Afro-American cults and the West African forms from which they derived and the historically unrelated zar cult: zar possession involved the element of illness and therapy. Where in Haiti, for example, illness might be interpreted as *sent* by spirits and cult initiation might be one of several possible therapeutic measures, in the zar cult illness, itself, was seen as a form of possession. Inducing dissociation, causing the patient to impersonate the possessing spirit, was a way of coming to terms with it. In spite, then, of some remarkable similarities between zar possession and Afro-American possession, there were important differences to be observed as well. Clearly, we were dealing here with a different type of cultural structuring of the possession trance phenomenon and one needed to be cautious in generalizing from one to the other.

During this period, one of our graduate students, Frances Mischel (now Henry), became interested in possession in the course of a study of a Black Pentecostal Church in Columbus and went on to investigate this type of behavior in the context of the Shango cult of Trinidad. In a paper resulting from this research (W. and F. Mischel 1958), the behav-

8. This study was supported in whole by P.H.S. Research Grant MH–07463 from the National Institute of Mental Health.

ior was analyzed in the light of social learning theory suggesting that possession behavior provided important prestige satisfactions for people who did not receive such recognition in everyday life.

In quite a different vein, the British psychiatrist W. Sargant (1957) proposed a theory based on Pavlovian psychology to account for the striking similarities he noted between "brain washing" (a subject then much in the news as a result of the experiences of American POWs in Chinese prisons during the Korean War), sudden religious conversion (including possession) and shock treatment in psychiatry. In the same year, P. Verger (1957) published an outstanding photographic study which documented in astonishing detail the continuity of West African ritual and numerous details of possession behavior to be found in the Afro-American cults of Brazil. That book also contained a chapter on the psychological aspects of the initiation process.

These studies, among others, added to our knowledge of possession behavior, or better, of dissociation culturally interpreted as possession by spirits. (We eventually came to refer to this as "possession trance," and this term will generally be used in what follows.) Yet, while these various studies added descriptive information, each presented its own interpretation of this material. This, it seemed to me, was not different from what was to be observed in other areas of anthropological research. The argument that cultures were unique entities, and the consequences for cultural relativism that flowed from it, seemed to encourage a tendency for *ad hoc* interpretation. The result was that no systematic theory building, at least in the area of interest to me, was possible. For instance, social learning and histrionics might well be complementary interpretations of the same body of data, not competing ones, yet group therapy was surely something different. And just how was brainwashing like possession? And in all of this the question of possible psycho-biological, physiological mechanisms in the dissociation process remained unresolved, and, indeed, essentially unattacked, except by Sargant who was little interested in cultural differences. It seemed all very well to say that possession trance is learned, and that reinforcement plays a role in this learning process. But what happens in the organism as part of consciousness is tuned out? We did not even know, it seemed, how much similarity there was on the simple observational level in physiological as well as psychological changes in dissociated individuals. How did cultural factors influence differences in observable behavior? Dissociation was, of course, not limited to societies where it was tied to a belief in possession. But what effect did such a belief have on the behavior? Consequently, it seemed to me that we were dealing with a species-wide capacity. The behavior it made possible is sometimes but not always culturally patterned and interpreted as spirit possession. This, in turn, is sometimes evaluated positively and encouraged, sometimes evaluated negatively and treated with exorcistic ritual, that is, the actor is, in effect, punished. Both this negative form and the type of dissociation behavior not interpreted as possession are treated as pathological behavior. If so, we were in fact concerned with the question of the range of human variability within the limits of a universal human nature. And if indeed that was the case, it seemed surprising that thirty years of culture and personality research appeared to have neglected the subject.[9]

Concern with the limitations imposed on anthropology by focusing on cultural uniqueness and by unstandardized reporting was increasingly being expressed by anthropologists of various persuasions, and something was being done about it. The work of G. P. Murdock and his associates at the Human Relations Area Files was of major importance in this regard. This organization was launched in 1949 as the successor of the Cross-Cultural Survey. Its *Outline of Cultural Materials* (Murdock et al. 1961), updated several times, became a major instrument of increased standardization in field research, as well as in the organization of data in the HRAF. In 1954 an *Outline of World Cultures* (Murdock 1954) was published, presenting what was believed to be a representative sample of world cultures, organized into major regions. In 1957, Murdock published his World Ethnographic Sample (WES) including data on 565 societies (Murdock 1957). It divided the world into six major ethnographic regions, each of these in turn subdivided into ten minor regions, with data on approximately ten societies for each of these regions. The coded data dealt with major aspects of subsistence economy, social organization and political organization. The WES, and its successor, the *Ethnographic Atlas* (Murdock 1962–67, 1967) were destined to revolutionize anthropology in significant respects.

However, while these developments were underway, a number of anthropologists sought means of making broad generalizations through comparisons and through the formal testing of hypotheses on selected societies. The work of F. Eggan (1954) and S. F. Nadel (1952) offered

9. A partial explanation of this, I now believe, is to be found in the selection of regions where American culture and personality research was carried out. For example, during the heyday of culture and personality research, the African societies where these phenomena were so very evident had largely been the domain of British functionalist anthropologists.

such approaches by means of the controlled comparison of specific features of a small number of societies. Whiting and Child (1953), however, used a statistical approach to the testing of psychological hypotheses on what seemed then a relatively large sample of societies. And although I, like many others, reacted to this pioneering work with initial scepticism, it increasingly became clear that, whatever the limitations of that first study, and indeed of the whole cross-cultural approach, it did offer some hope of bringing order into the masses of data anthropologists had accumulated in the course of nearly a century of research.

In 1962, as a result of these and related considerations, I undertook, in collaboration with a physical anthropologist, Louanna Pettay, and a psychiatrist, the late Adolf Haas, to submit to the National Institute of Mental Health a proposal for a coordinated cross-cultural research effort dealing with dissociational states and linked beliefs. Although our initial plan was for a two-year, library-based study, we eventually received support for five years of work, including several field investigations.

However, before moving on to a discussion of our project, we must stop for a moment to consider some other matters. In addition to the changing trends in anthropology sketched above, there were several developments in the broader society that came to be relevant to our research. They presaged the drug culture of the sixties, a growing concern with religious experimentation and renewal, as well as the veritable explosion of interest in the occult of the early seventies. Among these was the dramatic growth in the use of psychoactive drugs, tranquilizers, and psychic energizers, that revolutionized psychiatric practice during the 1950s in this country and abroad; this in turn stimulated a great research interest in the relationship between drugs and behavior (e.g., Uhr and Miller 1960). In 1963, the International Federation for Internal Freedom (IFIF) began to publish the *Psychedelic Review* to encourage exploration of what was being termed "consciousness-expansion" through the use of such psychoactive substances as LSD-25, psilocybin and others. The use of these substances was thus tied to an ideology, a conception of mind and consciousness, which may well be termed religious. On the other hand, in about 1958, there were the first beginnings of speaking in tongues (glossolalia) within the Episcopal church. This type of behavior had long been found among Pentecostalists, but was alien to the established denominations. Bishop Pike, then of the California Diocese of the Episcopal Church, established a commission to investigate the theological and psychological aspects of this behavior (Diocese of California 1963). And although we were then only marginally interested in these developments on the American scene, they clearly came to form a backdrop of our cross-cultural research and to point up its relevancy to an understanding of our own culture.

Aims and Problems

In our research proposal we noted that, although dissociational states were generally discussed in a clinical context in Western society, in many other societies such states were both institutionalized and culturally rewarded. And in spite of the existence of many descriptive studies of these behaviors in specific societies, no theory with transcultural implications had as yet been formulated, nor were the data assembled in a manner that permitted the formulation of such a theory. Yet, we felt, the ethnographic descriptions accumulating in our libraries might be of considerable relevance in the construction of such a theory. Furthermore, they might be useful in the context of a growing interest in the effect of drugs on behavior, in hypnosis and brainwashing. And although we thought it premature to formulate hypotheses for testing, we suggested that the sociocultural correlates of culturally institutionalized dissociational states interpreted as spirit possession could be expected to differ from those of states involving hallucinations. Specifically, we implied that hallucination and so-called possession states—in contrast to much that had been said (and continues to be said)—involved significantly different kinds of behavior. Before we could undertake to formulate hypotheses for testing, however, we needed to know a great deal about the beliefs and behaviors in question. Although we asserted that dissociation represents a widely distributed human phenomenon, we did not know how widespread it was in fact, and we, therefore, proposed to map its worldwide distribution.

In beginning our study with a broad exploratory investigation of the descriptive ethnographic literature we found ourselves confronted with a series of problems typical of such an enterprise. The first of these concerned some aspects of the literature that were linked to the particular nature of our study: some of the difficulties we encountered with the ethnographic sources seemed to have a basis in the culture of the observers (Bourguignon and Pettay 1964). Dissociational states were often referred to as "trance" or as "spirit possession." Those who spoke of trance might not elaborate on the cultural explanation and those who spoke of spirit possession might not adequately describe the observable behavior. Yet the terms were often used indiscriminately and inter-changeably.[10] The fact that concepts of possession have deep roots in the heritage of the Western society, in the Greek tradition no less than in the Judeo-Christian sources, has influenced both the perception and the language of the observer. And this is true of the anthropologist as well as of the missionary and the explorer. However, yet another factor has influenced anthropological reporting of these phenomena. In the late 1800s, under the sway of a unilineal evolutionary theory, Tylor and his contemporaries saw spirit possession beliefs as a primitive trait, charac-teristic of "savages." Reports of travellers and missionaries were often heavily concerned with exotic materials, with the "backwardness" and "irrationality" of primitives. As modern anthropology came to lay stress on a relativistic view of the peoples it studied as well as on showing the adaptive qualities of diverse cultures, the exotic and sensational was de-emphasized in descriptive ethnographies and in more popular writ-ings as well. Instead, stress was often placed on the more "genuine" or harmonious traditional ways of primitives in contrast to the "spurious" and destructive ways of modern Western societies. Also, for a period of time, studies of religion went into a decline and came to be neglected in anthropological analyses.

In sum, the materials we had to deal with were scattered and unsys-tematic. The reporting was influenced by at least two kinds of bias, and the data had to be teased out of the descriptive literature. To do so, we developed systematic outlines to help us in locating relevant informa-tion, outlines that went through several revisions over the period of our study.[11] On the whole, we had overestimated the quality of the ethno-graphic literature as it related to the types of information we sought to extract from the sources. In the course of five years, we inspected more than twenty-two hundred ethnographic sources in a number of lan-guages. Yet more than one fourth of these sources turned out not to yield any relevant information. The work of collecting and analyzing data required an extensive effort in bibliographic research, translation, excerpting and coding. It required the development of coding outlines, and of a system of files and records, of ethnographic maps and other research aids. Our statistical studies required sampling procedures. And each activity involved numerous decisions that would affect the direction

10. This pattern has continued as is shown in a recent book by Sargant entitled *The Mind Possessed* (1974), who speaks of "religious and non-religious possession."

11. I have discussed the final version of the outline in greater detail elsewhere (Bourguignon 1974*a*); it is included in the Final Report of the project (Bourguignon 1968*a*).

of our research and thus the nature of our findings. Most importantly, a group of research associates had to be assembled, who came to form a team. Several of its members have gone on to make major contributions on their own.

The Outlines

Consistent with our view that it was necessary to distinguish as carefully as possible between belief and behavior, we developed two outlines. One of these dealt with possession belief, the other with the behaviors we referred to as "trance." This term was found to be most common in the literature, where the descriptions, however, were often such that we could not be quite certain that reference was indeed being made to dissociation. (Today, I prefer ASC as a general term.)

We did not have a preconceived theory to test or a ready made typology to order the data; rather, we wished for a classification and for hypotheses to emerge from the data. Nonetheless, we were aware that the very act of inclusion or exclusion of items in our outlines was an act of theoretical choice which would necessarily affect the building of typologies and the formulation of hypotheses to be tested. We attempted to guard against premature delimitation of our field by including open-ended questions and by revising the outlines several times during the life of the study. We were, in effect, saying, however, that trance behavior and/or possession belief could be isolated from the rest of the culture for purposes of comparative analysis. This caused us to combine a series of native concepts under a common heading of "possession." If these combinations are in fact nonsensical, then the analysis should not be expected to yield meaningful results. We shall return to this point presently.

We defined "belief in possession" to mean that some aspect of an individual's behavior or of his capacities and aptitudes is interpreted by himself and/or by other members of his society as the behavior of another entity—a spirit, a ghost or other personality, or of a "power" having volition. This entity is believed to be in him or to act through him. The individual is its "vehicle"—it rides him as a mount (horse, camel, mule) or as a canoe, or fills him as a sack or a vessel. Such a spirit may transform the behavior and consciousness of the individual for a shorter or longer period of time, or it may be present permanently—or for periods of extended duration—in a latent form and modify consciousness only on specific occasions; or again, it may be present permanently, without producing modifications in overt behavior and/or consciousness. Rather, the possessing spirit or power may lend capacities of a special kind, for good as in curing, or for evil, as in certain kinds of witchcraft. Or again, the alterations undergone by the individual are those of illness. In the case of behavioral modifications involving changes of consciousness, we speak of possession trance (PT). This may involve impersonation, as in Haitian ritual possession trance, or it may involve primarily mediumistic activity, that is, alterations in verbal behavior. It may even involve changes in language, as in glossolalia. On the other hand, where alterations of capacity are involved, rather than those of consciousness and behavior, we deal with a separate form of possession belief (P). We found that in a given society either, both or neither may exist; we referred to this classification as possession types. Where both P and PT exist, a variety of relations between these two types of belief are possible. For example, the Shilluk king experiences possession trance when he accedes to his position; he is then possessed by the spirit of the first king (Lienhardt 1954). Although the altered state of consciousness (PT) is temporary, he remains possessed (P) by the spirit for the rest of his life. On the other hand, the Ethiopian woman (Leiris 1957; Messing 1958) who is diagnosed as possessed by a zar spirit shows evidence of this possession (P) through illness. She experiences possession trance (PT) only during the initiation rite and at other rites of the group which she joins. In still other cases, P and PT may exist independently of each other in different sectors of a society.

This classification arises entirely from the descriptive ethnographic literature. It could not have been anticipated by any theoretical scheme. However, it should be emphasized that the categories are not emic, for then we would, in fact, have a different set for each culture. Rather, we constructed categories by grouping reported concepts which seemed to us to be akin in important respects. However, within each category there are a great many possible variations: for example, PT may or may not be intentionally induced, and methods of induction, too, are diverse. PT and P may both be valued either positively or negatively, etc.

We defined "trance" to mean any altered state of consciousness, modifying, in varying degree any of the following: memory, sensory modalities, sense of identity, perception, etc. In the literature, there might be reference to a variety of clinical entities: dissociation, fugue, loss of consciousness, physiological collapse, obsessive ideas, and/or compulsive actions, hallucinations (Bourguignon 1968*b*, *c*). Where such alterations are culturally interpreted as due to possession we term this possession trance (PT); where it is not so interpreted, we speak of trance (T). T might be interpreted naturalistically, for example, as due to fever or drugs or in supernaturalistic terms, as due to soul loss or spiritual journeys. In our comparative study we focused on the fact that such states did not merely exist in a given society but were institutionalized and ritualized in a religious context.

In our outlines we sought to identify the cultural context of the behavior, as well as its personnel. We sought to identify as much as possible of the observable features of physiological change in the induction of the behavior, in its course and in its termination. We sought to discover methods of induction and termination and the subjective aspects of the experience as well. This involved great quantities of information present only in incomplete form even in the most detailed references. However, the outlines also proved to be invaluable as guides to field research.

As in the case of possession belief, we found that a society might have either PT or T or both or neither. We referred to these as trance types. Since a given society might also have P, our classification of beliefs and behaviors (P, PT, T) leads to a total of eight possible types of societies:

1. T–O–O: Societies that had trance (T), but no possession belief, either linked to it or apart from it.

2. O–P–O: Societies having a possession belief (P), but no form of trance.

3. O–O–PT: Societies with a possession belief linked to trance (or, if one prefers, trance behavior interpreted as possession) (PT), but no other trance behavior and no other possession belief.

4. T–P–PT: Societies with two forms of trance behavior: one linked to a possession belief (PT) and one explained in some other manner (T), and also having a possession belief (P) referring to some manifestations other than trance.

5. T–P–O: Societies with T (as in a visionary trance), and P (as an explanation for illness), but no possession trance (PT).

6. O–P–PT: Societies having possession trance (PT) and a separate possession belief (P), but no other trance behavior.

7. T–O–PT: Societies having both trance (T) and possession trance (PT) but no other possession belief.

8. O–O–O: And finally, there are some societies that, as far as we were able to determine, have no forms of possession belief and have not institutionalized forms of trance (or ASC) *in a religious* context.[12] We have identified only relatively few such societies for, since observers

12. Of course, they may have institutionalized some type of ASC in a secular context, for example, a pattern of using opium or hashish, or alcohol to produce such a state. We were not concerned with these.

rarely make statements about the absence of beliefs and behaviors, it is usually difficult to decide whether one deals with a true absence or only with a lack of reporting.

Note that this is a typology of societies, not of beliefs, states or institutions. Indeed, a given society might have several forms of T, or several forms of PT. At the level of this classification, we were only concerned with the institutionalized presence or absence of T, P, and PT. In other contexts, however, the more detailed information was, of course, of importance. Before, however, considering more of our findings, we need to consider the problem of selecting societies for study.

Selecting Societies to be Studied

We were keenly aware of the fact that the worldwide distribution of ritualized forms of altered states of consciousness, institutionalized in a religious context, was unknown, as was the distribution of the various cultural theories used to account for them. We, therefore, wished to cast as wide a net to gather information on these subjects as we could. In fact, in the five years of the study, we examined the literature on over 1200 cultural and subcultural units. Of these, 488 constitute a representative sample of the 863 societies coded for a series of dimensions in the *Ethnographic Atlas* (Murdock 1967); these were used by us for a series of statistical studies. The societies included in the *Ethnographic Atlas,* it will be remembered, are not a sample of societies but constitute the total universe of societies studied by anthropologists. (See Bourguignon and Greenbaum 1973 for a detailed discussion of the *Atlas.*[13])

Since the *Ethnographic Atlas* includes primarily societies studied by anthropologists, European and Overseas European societies are underrepresented and illustrated by village communities. These societies presented a particular problem for us. To cite the United States as an example: in dealing with institutionalized forms of altered states of consciousness and possession beliefs, we know that they exist in a series of subcultural units, but at the same time, whether we refer to Pentecostal glossolalia, to demonic possession and exorcism, or to drug cults, it is clear that the "normative" or "official" culture tends to deny respectability to such beliefs and practices. A single coding for the United States would, therefore, be inappropriate. We avoided the problem by omitting the United States from our statistical sample, although

13. Prior to the *Summary,* the *Atlas* included a total of 1132 societies. Of these we had coded 569. For a more detailed discussion of our sampling procedures, see Bourguignon 1968*a,* 1973 and Greenbaum 1970.

we considered certain aspects of these matters in other contexts (Kimball 1966; Bourguignon 1970*b*, 1973*a*, 1976*a*). European village studies, such as those of Wylie (1957) or Pitt-Rivers (1954) make no reference to the belief in demonic possession and the possibility of exorcism within the Catholic Church. Yet there is other evidence (e.g., Bouteiller 1950; Lhermitte 1963) which would suggest that these and related beliefs and practices may still be found to play a role in European folk life. Islam, as well as Christianity, involved the same kind of difficulty for our attempt to derive codes from ethnographic studies of specific communities. Although general accounts of the area speak of possession illness, brotherhoods seeking ecstatic trance, and possession trance cults with wide distributions throughout the area, authors of community studies often limit themselves to noting that "the religion of the people is Islam."

The ethnographic literature presented two additional problems: acculturation and crisis movements. With regard to the former, we collected data on various levels of acculturation of given groups, as these were available. Some of these were used in intensive studies of single areas (Gussler 1973; Leonard 1973). However, for purposes of our statistical sample, we attempted to use the sources employed as a basis for the codings of the *Ethnographic Atlas,* or, when these did not prove to provide the information we required, we sought to locate others referring to the same community and date of observation. (Needless to say, this requirement caused us to eliminate a number of societies from the statistical sample.)

With regard to crisis movements (La Barre 1970, 1971) we proceeded in a similar manner. We collected descriptive materials, but for purposes of the statistical sample, we sought to deal with what might be considered a "stable" traditional society (and not an "atypical" crisis period) as represented by the date of observation given by the *Atlas.* Crisis movements frequently include altered states, visions, etc. I have reviewed some of these materials elsewhere (Bourguignon 1974*b*).

Thus, the work of the project involved the gathering of data on a statistical sample, as well as information on a sizable number of other societies, cults and movements. Finally, it included the collection of field data.

The broad survey work made it possible to propose to a 1966 Conference on Trance and Possession States a typology of both trance behavior and associated beliefs and of possession beliefs and associated behaviors, as well as to review their distributions (Bourguignon 1968*c*).

Beliefs associated with trance behavior were divided into "naturalistic" and "supernaturalistic" explanations. The latter in turn were classed into two groups: possession beliefs and nonpossession beliefs. Both of these included some types evaluated positively and others negatively. The positive ones would be sought intentionally, such as mystic states, in the case of nonpossession, or mediumistic states in the case of possession. In the naturalistic context, negative would mean pathological, as for instance, in fever deliriums caused by somatic illness, while positive would equal nonpathological, as exemplified by hypnosis. Some categories might be indeterminate and their evaluation would then be situational. For example, in nonpossession trance, the concept of soul absence would be positively evaluated when it refers to the shaman's spirit journey and negatively if it referred to illness caused by such an absence. Here, the shaman's voyage could be part of the therapy. In the case of possession trance, impersonation of a spirit presence might be positive, as in our Haitian example, or negative, as in European (or Indian) possession by evil spirits. In the interesting East African case of the zar spirits, mentioned earlier, a negative illness possession could be transformed into a positive theatrical or therapeutic possession trance, by accommodation with the spirit. Positive and negative here are emic evaluations, answers to the questions: is possession trance intentionally induced? Is the spirit invited? Driven out? Feared?

A similar division into positive and negative poles is found in the analysis of possession beliefs and associated behaviors. The behavior belongs either in the category of "trance" or "nontrance." Thus, as noted, where possession belief is linked to trance behavior, we may deal with either desired, positive or undesired, negative spirit impersonation, or presence of powers. Where nontrance behavior is involved, there may also be positively evaluated power acquisition or negatively evaluated acquisition of a witchcraft agent or of illness.

At a later date, I pursued the matter of classification more intensively for a more limited region, using illness as a criterion for grouping African possession cults into a West African and an East African type (Bourguignon 1974d, [originally published in 1968]).

A different sort of exploration involved a study of the relationship between trance, possession and divination in sub-Saharan Africa (Bourguignon 1968b). This paper explored some structural relationships between mediumistic and other types of divination in Africa and also noted the frequent predominance of women in African possession trance cults. The suggestion is offered that this predominance involves two sets of factors: the status of women and the social uses of possession trance cults in particular societies. Three kinds of situations are specifically referred to: predominance of women in possession trance cults represents a balancing element (for example, a situation in which the pronouncements of female mediums are interpreted by male political leaders) or an element of revolt (or, in terms used by Lewis [1966, 1971] reaction to "social deprivation") or, finally, particularly in Islamic societies, an element of conservatism. Yet in reconsidering these, it appears that in fact each involves a type of balancing mechanism. The important role of women in Afro-American spirit possession trance cults was considered in a later paper (Bourguignon 1975).

One final exploratory study may be mentioned here: a review of the relationship of trance and possession trance to dance, ecstatic and curative, and of all of these to social change (Bourguignon 1968*d*).[14]

Before we move on to consider our statistical studies, reference should be made to the field studies carried out by several members of the project team. Anne Leonard, a member of our research team, went to Micronesia during 1965–66, where she studied possession trance behavior in Palau (Leonard 1973). The study was largely concerned with the effects of acculturation on traditional beliefs and practices involving altered states, but it had the additional importance for us of testing our outlines in the field.

During the same period of time, Linda Kimball studied an evangelistic tent revival in Columbus. Her interest was particularly drawn to the motor behavior of the evangelist to which she attempted to apply the linguistic approach of generative grammar (Kimball 1966).

In 1966, also, Jeannette Henney conducted a study of the Shakers, or Spiritual Baptists, on the previously unstudied West Indian island of St. Vincent (Henney 1973, 1974). Here two forms of altered states were found to have been institutionalized: (1) possession trance, conceptualized as manifestations of the Holy Spirit, which occurs in public, collective situations. In this context, there is speaking in tongues. The collective possession trance behavior is at times characterized by a "choral" phase, in spite of the considerable individual differentiation of motor behavior. (2) Trance, in the form of visionary experiences, which occurs during retreats, termed "mourning." Of particular interest is the detailed similarity drawn by Henney between this ritual and the hallucination-producing sensory deprivation experiments. Henney

14. It should be noted that while these several studies, as well as our Final Report, all bear the same date, they were completed at different times over a period of four years.

also collected data on another group, calling itself "Streams of Power," founded by a Dutch evangelist. These people also used dissociation, primarily in the form of glossolalia.

During 1966–67, Esther Pressel conducted a study of the Umbanda cult in Sao Paulo, Brazil (Pressel 1973, 1974). Umbanda is a highly syncretic religion, appealing largely to the Brazilian middle class, which combines elements of Catholicism, African possession trance cults, spiritism and certain putative American Indian elements. This represented a first anthropological analysis of this growing movement. Pressel's data are rich in materials on the learning of possession trance behavior by individuals. She also reviews the symbolic meaning of the cult ideology within Brazilian culture.

When Henney returned from the field with tape recordings of glossolalia, I suggested to another member of our team, F. D. Goodman, who had been trained as a linguist, that she might develop an approach to their analysis. Goodman found striking common features in intonational patterns in these utterances, as well as in samples of glossolalia from three other cultural settings. She proposed that these features might be due to their being connected with the characteristic neuropsychological features of trance (Goodman 1969). On the basis of these tentative findings, she sought to conduct research among non-Indo-European speakers who practiced glossolalia. She found such people among Maya Pentecostalists; there she has conducted a continuing study from 1969 to the present. Although this field study was not part of the project, it grew directly out of it, and its findings are of considerable interest (Goodman 1972, 1973, 1974). First of all, the Maya study confirmed Goodman's view of glossolalia as ecstatic vocalization, sharing fundamental patterns regardless of the native language of the subjects. She also noted a characteristic pattern of attenuation over time in the experience of trancers. Secondly, in Goodman's first period in the village a movement she terms "a trance-based upheaval" began in the Pentecostal congregation. This has since run its course, and she was able to observe it at various stages of its growth and decline (Goodman 1974).

Aspects of these focused field studies have been presented together with results of our statistical studies as well as two detailed studies of possession trance in Africa (Bourguignon, ed. 1973). The studies have a good deal of unity in orientation, yet they reflect the difference of the settings and some differences in the interest of the investigators. Such coordinated research permits focusing on the relationship between on the one hand altered states of consciousness as institutionalized in a variety of religious settings and on the other, various kinds of social change. These relations are complex, both on the societal and on the individual level. Our review suggests a good many problems for further testing.

Statistical Studies

We began by asking two questions: how widespread are altered states of consciousness, institutionalized in a religious context, among the 488 sample societies? And how widespread are possession beliefs?

The answer to the first of these questions is that they are virtually universal: 90 percent of our worldwide sample of societies have institutionalized forms of T and/or PT (Bourguignon 1973a, Table 1, pp. 10ff.).[15] However, there are important differences among the six major world areas, so that the frequencies range from 97 percent in North America to 80 percent in the Circum-Mediterranean area. The clear implication seems to be that most societies have found it adaptive to institutionalize one or more forms of the universal human capacity for altered states, to utilize it, or at least, to bring this potentially dangerous force under social control. ASCs are ritualized and as I have noted elsewhere, "the rituals employing ASCs are dramatic two-way communications that make the will and the actions of spirits immediately evident to human participants" (Bourguignon 1974c, p. 13).

The 10 percent of non-ASC societies represents the exception. Indeed, it is likely that better reporting (and further analysis of the literature) would in fact reduce that percentage.

With regard to possession belief (P and/or PT) the situation is somewhat different. On a worldwide basis, 74 percent of our sample societies have some form of possession belief. Here the incidence varies from a high of 88 percent in the Insular Pacific to a low of 52 percent in the societies of native North America (Bourguignon 1973a, Table 2, pp. 17ff.).

The lower incidence of possession belief points to the fact that such beliefs are, indeed, human inventions, cultural artifacts, and as such are not universal. Note that in this respect the Americas differ significantly from the rest of the world: almost half of the societies of North America and more than a third of those of South America do not have a possession belief.

If we consider the distributions of trance types (T, PT, both or

15. To compare the distribution of societies having T and/or PT with those lacking such patterns, we group types 1, 3, 4, 5, 6, 7 and contrast them with types 1 and 8. To arrive at a distribution of societies having P and/or PT we group types 2, 3, 4, 5, 6, 7 and contrast them with types 1 and 8.

neither)[16] and of possession types (P, PT, both or neither) the situation becomes somewhat more complex (Bourguignon 1968, 1973*a*, 1976*b*). Of our 488 societies, as we noted earlier, 10 percent have neither T nor PT. For the other types, we get the following rank order: T, 35 percent; PT, 28 percent; T and PT, 24 percent. Again, the major ethnographic regions vary drastically from this average.

For possession types we find that possession belief is absent in 26 percent of the societies; the other types are ranked as follows: P and PT, 35 percent; PT, 22 percent; and P, 16 percent. Again, the individual regions differ greatly from these averages.

How are we to account for these differences? Clearly diffusion must be considered an important factor here. Yet the question of functional relations needs to be investigated. From preliminary explorations we arrived at the hypothesis that PT is more likely to be institutionalized in traditional societies of higher complexity. This was expected to be true in contrast to both T societies and P societies. We proceeded to test these two hypotheses separately.[17]

We compared our trance types (T, T/PT, PT) with respect to sixteen variables drawn from the *Ethnographic Atlas*. On a worldwide basis, we found twelve of these to show statistically significant differences at or below the .05 level of probability as measured by chi-squares. The PT group of societies is indeed consistently more complex with regard to such variables as population size and size of local group, stratification, slavery, sedentary settlement patterns, hierarchy of jurisdictional levels, marriage with compensation, extended families and polygynous marriages. Three other patterns also distinguish our groups, although their relation to complexity is less evident: unilineal kin groups, duolateral cousin marriage and the segregation of adolescent boys. T societies are consistently characterized by lesser complexity and T/PT societies generally are intermediary (Bourguignon 1973, p. 20).[18]

16. To establish trance types we combine 1 and 5 into T, 2 and 6 into PT, 3 and 7 into T/PT and 2 and 8 into O/O. To establish possession types we group 2 and 5 into P, 3 and 7 into PT, 4 and 6 into P/PT and 1 and 8 into O/O. Because of the small number of O/O societies we have omitted them in our correlational studies.

17. For purposes of these tests we used the data coded in the *Ethnographic Atlas* in revised form. For a detailed discussion of these revisions and of our rationale for them, see Bourguignon and Greenbaum 1973. This source contains detailed coding information.

18. When we made the same calculations for each of the six regions individually, we found we did not get the same results. The problem of regional differences with regard to correlations among variables (and not only uniqueness of distributions) will require much further work by comparativists (see Bourguignon and Greenbaum 1973, pp. 84–87).

More recently, I have tested for the variable of subsistence economy and found that where agriculture accounts for 46 percent or more of a society's subsistence, PT, alone or with T, is significantly more likely to be present than in societies with less dependence on agriculture. This difference is statistically significant below the .001 level of probability. The converse is also true, with T alone more likely among societies with a heavy dependence on hunting, fishing and gathering (Bourguignon 1974c). These general findings were confirmed in a later reanalysis of our data (Bourguignon and Evascu 1977). Using ordinally scaled data, we correlated our trance types with four variables: stratification, jurisdictional hierarchy, percentage of dependence on economic production (that is, contrasting foraging societies with those depending to a more or less greater extent on agriculture and/or animal husbandry), and percentage of dependence on agriculture. For our 488 societies, we obtained high correlations between trance type and all four variables, but also evidence to suggest the influence of diffusion (or "Galton's problem"). When we drew a sample of 84 societies and controlled for diffusion, the correlations of trance type with our four variables remained equally high. However, as we had found in our earlier work, when our samples were divided into regional subsamples, there was wide variation among them, and the hypothesis concerning relations among variables was not confirmed for the individual regions. Such regional variations have also been found by researchers dealing with a number of other variables.

Interpretations of Results

Why should one expect an association between PT and relative complexity (agriculture, stratification, greater population size, etc.) and between T and relative simplicity (a hunting, gathering and fishing economy, lack of stratification, small population, etc.)?

We may begin by noting that societies of greater complexity are more highly differentiated and offer a larger number of roles. This differentiation of major activities is represented symbolically by major gods (or spirits) (Swanson 1964). Possession trancers reflect this complexity by impersonating the spirits and possession trance rituals thus may be thought of as expressions of a society's model of its own social structure. Furthermore, such rituals often occur within structured cult groups. These groups are themselves a feature of complex societies, including specialized and ranked positions. The structure of these groups, too, is reflected in the possession trance rituals. By playing various spirit roles an individual may find ways of coming to terms with alien or dangerous aspects of his society or of his society's relations with other groups or forces in the environment. As suggested earlier with regard to Haiti, possession trance may increase the individual's range of personal options, a suggestion which is confirmed by several of our field studies. Another suggestion for which we found support is one by I. Lewis (1971) arguing that possession trance is often linked to social deprivation. Such deprivation is, incidentally, itself a feature of more highly differentiated societies. (On the other hand, we did not find support for his claim that possession trance of the socially deprived constitutes a means for utilizing supernatural sanctions against the powerful. Nor did we find his distinction between "central morality religions" and "amoral peripheral spirit cults" applicable.)

Greenbaum (1973*a, b*), focusing specifically on sub-Saharan Africa, similarly found a high association between fixed status distinctions (stratification, slavery)—a characteristic of complexity—and the presence of PT. To account for this association, she sought an intermediary variable, suggesting that such complex societies are more likely to be rigid than simpler ones, and furthermore that in rigid societies PT, here redefined as mediumistic spirit possession, offered individuals elbow room in the decision making process. A detailed descriptive study of a sample of fourteen societies strongly supported this suggestion.

Additional light on the relationship between PT and complexity may be shed by comparing ideal-typical PT and T (see Bourguignon 1974*c* for a more detailed discussion). Whereas PT involves the active acting out of spirit roles, T involves direct contact with spirits. PT is followed by amnesia, T by memory; in PT the actor is the passive vehicle of the spirits who deal directly with an audience, in T the active seeker for spirit contact goes on a spirit journey but is likely to be physically passive; PT is generally induced through suggestion, dance, hyperventilation, group atmosphere, drumming, etc.; T through drugs, sensory deprivation, mortification, hypoglycemia, etc.; PT more typically involves women, T men; PT is a performance, T an experience; PT is public, T is intrapersonal, often secret. PT is a social phenomenon and a product of social interaction, its results may affect the group. In T the individual may acquire power, a spirit helper, and it primarily concerns the trancer himself. Where PT involves obedience to spirits and submission to their will, to the point of total abolition of the individual's personality during the period of possession trance, T emphasizes the theme of independence of human helpers, self-reliance by acquiring spirit power, achievement. These contrasts, as I have pointed out elsewhere (Bourguignon 1974*c*) suggest differences in the ideal typical personality of the possession trancer and the trancer. And differences in personality suggest differences in socialization.

By following through on these ideas we come to the development of a model of culturally patterned ASCs (Bourguignon 1974c). So far, we have found a relationship between one type of ASC, namely T, with a subsistence economy of hunting, gathering and fishing, and also with absence of stratification, and of slavery, with small populations, lack of differentiation of levels of jurisdictional hierarchy. These societal characteristics are also clearly related to such a subsistence economy. On the other hand, we have found another type of ASC, namely PT, to be associated with a different kind of subsistence economy, a high dependence on agriculture (and also a relatively high dependence on pastoralism). PT is also linked to stratification, slavery, larger populations, several levels of jurisdictional hierarchy, etc. And these are linked to each other and to the agricultural subsistence base. The model suggests that the intervening variable between characteristic forms of spirit beliefs on the one hand and economy, social structure and ASCs on the other is to be found in socialization. This leads to the resulting personality type, and, additionally is mediated by characteristic types of stresses. The stresses may derive from ecological factors (Gussler 1973; Foulks 1972) or from acculturative situations, as in many crisis cults and revitalization movements (La Barre 1970, 1971; Wallace 1956).

Barry, Child and Bacon (1967) related types of economy to adult role behavior and to child training. They confirmed that low accumulation societies (typically, hunting and fishing) socialize for assertion, independence and self reliance. On the other hand, high accumulation societies (agriculture and/or pastoralism) socialize for obedience and compliance. They also found that women are consistently socialized to a higher degree for compliance and men for assertion regardless of the subsistence economy.

Both of these findings fit into our distinction between PT and T societies. Note also that men are more likely to seek T and women to experience PT (Bourguignon 1972).

. . . an ecological adaptation in which adult economic role behavior requires compliance leads to socialization for compliance, producing adults who demand compliance in familial and political situations and who at the same time believe in spirits (ancestors or departed chiefs or other powerful beings) who demand compliance. These spirits can be dealt with through impersonations during ASC (possession trances) which dramatize the requirement for compliance made by these powerful beings. Yet, through the fact that, after all, humans play the roles of these impersonated entities, the ASC allow those in possession trance to act out their own needs for assertion, and they present them with an opportunity to manipulate others and their own real life situations as well.

On the other hand, an ecological adaptation demanding assertion, independence, self-reliance in the economic life of its adults, requires socialization directed to these ends. Social organizations of independent assertive adults, with few accumulated resources, will reach only a low level of complexity and limited social and economic cooperation, with little delegation of authority to a higher human power. Spirits, under such conditions, are perceived as having limited powers and can be induced to share some of this power by expressions of normally unadmitted dependency and powerlessness. Such spirit allies will then help the seeker in overcoming other dangerous entities, increasing his own powers. [Bourguignon 1974c, p. 24]

Our findings for possession types, comparing societies having PT, P or both, are on the whole consistent with those regarding trance types. Societies having possession belief only (P) are more likely than PT societies to depend heavily (46 percent or more) on a combination of hunting, gathering and fishing for their subsistence; they are less likely to have class stratification, or to have slavery; they are more likely to be nomadic or semi-nomadic in settlement pattern, not to have a jurisdictional hierarchy above the local level, to have a small estimated total population and a small local population. These differences were found to be significant below the .001 level of probability. Also, P societies were less likely than PT societies to have male genital mutilation (significant below the .01 level). All of these societal dimensions are related to the subsistence economy (Bourguignon 1976b).

Although P and PT both involve a belief in spirits in general and in possession by spirits in particular, the differences between these resemble in important ways the differences between T and PT that we have just reviewed. Consequently the model we have constructed for altered states may also be applied to possession beliefs. Whereas in PT, as we have seen, impersonation and the discontinuity of the self play an important role, this is not the case in P. Here, rather, there is not an alteration of consciousness but of capacities, either enhancing or diminishing the powers of the self. And such an alteration may be permanent. These differences with regard to the self concept bring us back to the differences in child training discussed previously: PT as noted involves compliance, obedience, dependence. On the other hand, those who acquire power of spirits or of forces through possession—whether the power of the curer or the witch—acquire such powers as their own. Their selves are enhanced—or diminished—they are not displaced. Such an alteration of capacities involves the intimate relationship between a human individual and a spirit or power entity. Often enough such power is acquired through a visionary trance experience.

Much work remains to be done; we have not answered all the questions with which we began—indeed, we have a good many new ones now. This seems to be typical of much scientific research, not only that of the anthropologist: questions are transformed, not answered in a direct manner. Yet, we can now make a number of assertions with some degree of confidence. A concern with altered states of consciousness, particularly within a religious context, is neither antiquarian and esoteric nor faddish. Rather, it sheds a light on our universal human nature and on how this raw material is utilized in the building of cultures. We have found that such states play and have played a significant role in the overwhelming majority of human societies; their antiquity must be very great as evidenced by the "dead man" in the Upper Paleolithic cave paintings at Lascaux. This vast antiquity and near-universality alone would justify the anthropologist's interest. Our large scale comparative research has shown these states to be a psychobiological phenomenon patterned within a variety of cultural contexts, a witness to both the unity and the diversity of human nature. They and their associated belief systems have great relevance to studies of social and individual and ecological stress, to culture change and the position of women, to psychopathology, medical anthropology, drugs and a variety of other subjects. Members of our research team have turned to such varied subjects as glossolalia, sex and trance, nutrition, psychobiology, decision making processes and refinements of cross-cultural methodology. New graduate students have turned to subjects of related interest: Kenneth McGuire is currently completing a study of an American Catholic charismatic community; Patricia Lerch is planning a study of women's roles in Brazilian cults.

Since we began our study in 1962, a large number of descriptive ethnographies has been published dealing with altered states of consciousness, particularly hallucinatory trance states (e.g., Furst 1972; Harner 1972; Dobkin de Rios 1972; Castaneda 1968, 1971, 1972) as has a number of remarkable large scale studies with direct bearing on the subject (Wasson 1968; La Barre 1970). Rather fewer studies have been directed to the description of possession trance (but note, e.g., Beattie and Middleton 1969; J. Monfougas-Nicolas 1972; S. and R. Leacock 1972), and there have been fewer generalizing studies (Zaretsky 1967; Lewis 1971; Walker 1972). The literature dealing with drugs, in particular, has received a large audience (J. White 1972; C. T. Tart 1972). In some respects, it would appear we began our study too early: at present, there are larger numbers of fuller descriptive materials available to satisfy more of the needs of our outlines. Specifically, excellent materials are not available (for example, the book on the Hausa cited above by Monfougas-Nicolas) on previously inadequately covered groups. A similar comment may be made concerning statistical cross-cultural studies, which have developed greater sophistication in recent years. At the same time, as altered states and possession beliefs have made spectacular gains in our own society, our work has gained in relevance: in what is clearly a crisis situation, many in the Western world have responded in old and familiar ways by attempting to manipulate their relationship to reality by seeking such altered states, whether as an escape from the pressures of daily life or by searching for supernatural assistance (however that supernatural may be conceptualized, in mystical or in demonic terms) through drugs, meditation, religious rituals and charismatic groups or through the manipulations of the occult. R. Bastide (1972) has pointed to the great growth of possession trance cults in Africa in recent years. La Barre (1970, 1971) has shown how crisis cults result from the stresses of acculturation. Our own society is undergoing such crises as well, and though a revitalization movement has not taken shape, the turning to altered states surely is a symptom of the stresses Western society confronts. In this connection, it should be noted that the possession trance cults of traditional societies have sprad to industrialized societies, whether it be Cuban *santería* and Haitian *vodoun* in the United States, or *vodoun* and various Indo-Chinese cults in France. Thus, the comparative perspective of anthropologists sheds light on the peculiarities of their own society.

REFERENCES CITED

Barry, H., Child, I. L., and Bacon, M. K.
  1967 Relation of Child Training to Subsistence Economy. In *Cross-Cultural Approaches: Readings in Comparative Research*, ed. C. S. Ford. New Haven: HRAF Press.

Bastide, R.
  1972 Preface. In J. Monfougas-Nicolas: *Ambivalence et culte de possession*. Paris: Editions Anthropos.

Beattie, J. and Middleton, J., eds.
  1969 *Spirit Mediumship and Society in Africa*. New York: Africana Publishing Corporation.

Bourguignon, E.

1951   Syncretism and Ambivalence: An Ethnohistorical Study. Ph.D. dissertation, Northwestern University.

1954   Dreams and Dream Interpretation in Haiti. *American Anthropologist* 56: 262–68.

1956   Rorschachs of Seventy-five Haitian Children, Aged 7–15, and Forty-two Haitian Adults. In *Microcard Publications of Primary Records in Culture and Personality* 1, ed. B. Kaplan.

1959   The Persistence of Folk Belief: Some Notes on Cannibalism and Zombies in Haiti. *Journal of American Folklore* 72:36–46.

1965   The Self, the Behavioral Environment and the Theory of Spirit Possession. In *Context and Meaning in Cultural Anthropology In Honor of A. I. Hallowell*, ed. M. E. Spiro. New York: Free Press.

1968a   *Final Report, Cross-Cultural Study of Dissociational States.* The Ohio State University Research Foundation.

1968b   Divination, Transe et Posession en Afrique Transsaharienne. In *La Divination*, eds. A. Caquot et M. Leibovici. Paris: Presses Universitaires de France.

1968c   World Distribution and Patterns of Possession States. In *Trance and Possession States*, ed. R. Prince. Montreal: R. M. Bucke Memorial Society.

1968d   Trance Dance. *Dance Perspectives* 35. Dance Perspectives Foundation, New York.

1969   Haiti et l'ambivalence socielisée: Une reconsidération. *Journal de la Société des Américanistes* 58:173–205.

1970a   Ritual Dissociation and Possession Belief in Caribbean Negro Religion. In *Afro-American Anthropology: Contemporary Perspectives*, eds. N. E. Whitten Jr. and J. F. Szwed. New York: Free Press.

1970b   An Anthropologist's Reflections on Hallucinogenic Drugs. Paper read at Centennial Symposium on the Relevance of the Social Sciences, College of Social and Behavioral Sciences, The Ohio State University.

1973a   Introduction: A Framework for the Comparative Study of Altered States of Consciousness: An Assessment of Some Comparisons and Implications; Epilogue: Some Notes on Contemporary Americans and the Irrational. In *Religion, Altered States of Consciousness and Social Change*, ed. E. Bourguignon. Columbus: The Ohio State University Press.

1973b   Psychological Anthropology. In *Handbook of Social and Cultural Anthropology*, ed. J. J. Honigmann. Chicago: Rand McNally.

1974a   Foreword. In F. D. Goodman, J. J. Henney, E. Pressel: *Trance, Healing, and Hallucination: Three Field Studies in Religious Experience.* New York: Wiley.

1974b   Cross-Cultural Perspectives on the Religious Uses of Altered States of Consciousness. In *Pragmatic Religions: Contemporary Religious Movements in America*, eds. I. I. Zaretsky and M. P. Leone. Princeton: Princeton University Press.

1974c   Culture and the Varieties of Consciousness. *An Addison-Wesley Module in Anthropology* 47. Reading, Mass.: Addison-Wesley Publishing Co.

1974*d* Illness and Possession: Elements for a comparative study. *R. E. Bucke Memorial Society Newsletter Review* (Montreal), pp. 31–46. (Originally published in 1968.)

1975   Importante Papel de las mujeres en los cultos afroamericanos. *Montalbán* 4:432–38.

1976*a* *Possession.* San Francisco: Chandler and Sharp, forthcoming.

n.d.   Hallucinatory (Drug-Induced) Trance versus Possession Trance: Male and Female Forms of Altered States? Manuscript in preparation.

1976*b* Spirit Possession Beliefs and Social Structure, IX International Congress of Anthropological and Ethnological Sciences. In *World Anthropology.* The Hague: Mouton, forthcoming.

Bourguignon, E., ed.

1973   *Religion, Altered States of Consciousness and Social Change.* Columbus: The Ohio State University Press.

Bourguignon, E. and Evascu, T. L.

1977   Altered States of Consciousness within a General Evolutionary Perspective: A Holocultural Analysis. In *Behavior Science Research,* forthcoming.

Bourguignon, E. and Greenbaum, L.

1973   *Diversity and Homogeneity in World Societies.* New Haven: HRAF Press.

Bourguignon, E. and Nett, E. W.

1955   Rorschach Populars in a Sample of Haitian Protocols. *Journal of Projective Techniques* 19:117–24.

Bourguignon, E. and Pettay, L.

1964   Spirit Possession, Trance and Cross-Cultural Research. In Symposium on New Approaches to the Study of Religion. *Proceedings of the 1964 Annual Spring Meeting of the American Ethnological Society,* ed. J. Helm, pp. 38–49.

Bouteiller, M.

1950   *Chamanisme et guérison magique.* Paris: Presses Universitaires de France.

Castaneda, C.

1968   *The Teachings of Don Juan: A Yaqui Way of Knowledge.* Berkeley and Los Angeles: University of California Press.

1971   *A Separate Reality.* New York: Simon and Schuster.

1972   *Journey to Ixtlan.* New York: Simon and Schuster.

Diocese of California of the Episcopal Church in America, Division of Pastoral Services, Study Commission on Glossolalia.

1963   *Preliminary Report.*

Dobkin de Rios, M.

1972   *Visionary Vine.* San Francisco: Chandler Publishing Co.

Dorsainvil, J. C.

1931   *Vodou et névrose.* Haiti: Port-au-Prince.

Douyon, E.

1965   La Crise de possession dans le vaudou Haitien (abstract of Ph.D. dissertation, University of Montreal). *Transcultural Psychiatric Research* 2:155–59.

Eggan, F.
 1954   Social Anthropology and the Method of Controlled Comparison. *American Anthropologist* 56:743–63.
Field, M. J.
 1960   *Search for Security*. Evanston, Ill.: Northwestern University Press.
Foulks, E. F.
 1972   The Arctic Hysterias of the North Alaskan Eskimo. *Anthropological Studies No.* 10. Washington, D.C.: American Anthropological Association.
Furst, P. T., ed.
 1972   *Flesh of the Gods: The Ritual Use of Hallucinogens*. New York: Praeger.
Goodman, F. D.
 1969   Phonetic Analysis of Glossolalia in Four Cultural Settings. *Journal for the Scientific Study of Religion* 8:227–39.
 1972   *Speaking in Tongues*. Chicago: University of Chicago Press.
 1973   The Apostolics of Yucatán: A Case Study of a Religious Movement. In *Religion, Altered States of Consciousness and Social Change*, ed. E. Bourguignon. Columbus: The Ohio State University Press.
 1974   Disturbances in the Apostolic Church: A Trance-Based Upheaval in Yucatan. In F. D. Goodman, J. H. Henney, Esther Pressel: *Trance, Healing and Hallucination: Three Field Studies in Religious Experience*. New York: Wiley.
Greenbaum, L.
 1970   Evaluation of a Stratified versus an Unstratified Universe of Cultures in Comparative Research. *Behavior Science Notes* 5:251–90.
 1973a Societal Correlates of Possession Trance in Sub-Saharan Africa. In *Religion, Altered States of Consciousness and Social Change*, ed. E. Bourguignon. Columbus: The Ohio State University Press.
 1973b Possession Trance in Sub-Saharan Africa: A Descriptive Analysis of Fourteen Societies. In *Religion, Altered States of Consciousness and Social change*, ed. E. Bourguignon. Columbus: The Ohio State University Press.
Gussler, J.
 1973   Social Change, Ecology, and Spirit Possession among the South African Nguni. In *Religion, Altered States of Consciousness and Social Change*, ed. E. Bourguignon. Columbus: The Ohio State University Press.
Hallowell, A. I.
 1938   Fear and Anxiety as Cultural and Individual Variables in Primitive Society. *Journal of Social Psychology* 9:25–47.
 1955a The Self and Its Behavioral Environment. In *Culture and Experience*. Philadelphia: University of Pennsylvania Press.
 1955b The Ojibwa Self and its Behavioral Environment. In *Culture and Experience*. Philadelphia: University of Pennsylvania Press.
Harner, M. J., ed.
 1973   *Hallucinogens and Shamanism*. London: Oxford University Press.
Henney, J. H.
 1973   The Shakers of St. Vincent: A Stable Religion. In *Religion, Altered States of*

Consciousness and Social Change, ed. E. Bourguignon. Columbus: The Ohio State University Press.

1974 Spirit-Possession Belief and Trance Behavior in Two Fundamentalist Groups in St. Vincent. In F. D. Goodman, J. H. Henney, Esther Pressel: *Trance, Healing and Hallucination: Three Field Studies in Religious Experience.* New York: Wiley.

Herskovits, M. J.

1937*a* *Life in a Haitian Valley.* New York: A. Knopf.

1937*b* African Gods and Catholic Saints in New World Negro Belief. *American Anthropologist* 39:635–43.

1938 *Dahomey: An Ancient West African Kingdom.* New York: J. J. Augustin.

1948 *Man and His World.* New York: A. Knopf.

1966 *The Negro in the New World,* ed. F. S. Herskovits. Indiana: Indiana University Press.

1973 *Cultural Relativism,* ed. F. S. Herskovits. New York: Random House.

Herskovits, M. J. and Herskovits, F. S.

1933 Outline of Dahomean Religious Beliefs. *Memoir No. 41 of the American Anthropological Association.* Wisconsin: Menasha.

Kennedy, J. G.

1973 Cultural Psychiatry. In *Handbook of Social and Cultural Anthropology,* ed. J. J. Honigmann. Chicago: Rand McNally.

Kimball, L. A.

1966 An Application of Generative Grammar to Non-Verbal Behavior: A Preliminary Study. M.A. thesis, Ohio State University.

La Barre, W.

1970 *The Ghost Dance: The Origins of Religion.* Garden City, New York: Doubleday.

1971 Material for a History of Studies of Crisis Cults: A Bibliographic Essay. *Current Anthropology* 12:3–44.

Leacock, S. and Leacock, R.

1972 *Spirits of the Deep: Drums, Mediums and Trance in a Brazilian City.* Garden City, New York: Doubleday Natural History Press.

Leiris, M.

1958 La possession et ses aspects théatraux ches les Ethiopiens de Gondar. *L'Homme* 1. Paris: Plon.

Leonard, A. P.

1973 Spirit Mediums in Palau: Transformations in a Traditional System. In *Religion, Altered States of Consciousness and Social Change,* ed. E. Bourguignon. Columbus: Ohio State University Press.

Lewis, I. M.

1966 Spirit Possession and Deprivation Cults. *Man* 1:307–29.

1971 *Ecstatic Religion.* Baltimore: Penguin.

Lhermitte, J.

1963 *True and False Possession.* New York: Hawthorne Books.

Lienhardt, G.
    1954   The Shilluk of the Upper Nile. In *African Worlds*, ed. D. Forde. London: International African Institute.

McGuire, K.
    1976   *People, Prayer and Promise: An Anthropological Analysis of a Catholic Charismatic Covenant Community*. Ann Arbor, Michigan: University Microfilms.

Messing, S.
    1958   Group Therapy and Social Status in the Zar Cult. In *Culture and Mental Health*, ed. M. K. Opler. New York: MacMillan.

Métraux, A.
    1955   La comédie rituelle dans la possession. *Diogène* 11.

    1959   *Voodoo in Haiti*. New York: Oxford University Press.

Mischel, W. and Mischel, F. O.
    1958   Psychological Aspects of Spirit Possession. *American Anthropologist* 60: 249–60.

Monfougas-Nicolas, J.
    1972   *Ambivalence et culte de possession*. Paris: Editions Anthropos.

Murdock, G. P.
    1954   *Outline of World Cultures*, 3rd rev. ed. New Haven: HRAF Press.

    1957   World Ethnographic Sample. *American Anthropologist* 59:664–87.

    1962   Ethnographic Atlas. *Ethnology* 1–6.

    1967   *Ethnographic Atlas: A Summary*. Pittsburgh: University of Pittsburgh Press.

Murdock, G. P., Ford, C. S., Hudson, A. E., Kennedy, R., Simmons, L. W., and Whiting, J. W. M.
    1961   *Outline of Cultural Materials*, 4th rev. ed. New Haven: HRAF Press.

Nadel, S. F.
    1952   Witchcraft in Four African Societies: An Essay in Comparison. *American Anthropologist* 54:18–29.

Pitt-Rivers, J. A.
    1954   *People of the Sierra*. New York: Criterion Books.

Pressel, E.
    1973   Umbanda in Sao Paulo: Religious Innovation in a Developing Society. In *Religion, Altered States of Consciousness and Social Change*, ed. E. Bourguignon. Columbus: Ohio State University Press.

    1974   Umbanda Trance and Possession in Sao Paulo, Brazil. In F. D. Goodman, J. H. Henney, Esther Pressel: *Trance, Healing and Hallucination: Three Field Studies in Religious Experience*. New York: Wiley.

    1963   *Psychedelic Review*, Volume 1.

Sargant, W.
    1957   *Battle for the Mind*. London: Pan Books.

    1974   *The Mind Possessed: A Physiology of Possession, Mysticism and Faith Healing*. Philadelphia and New York: Lippincott.

Simpson, G. E.
    1973   *Melville J. Herskovits*. New York: Columbia University Press.

Swanson, G. L.
  1964 *Birth of the Gods.* Ann Arbor: Ann Arbor Paperbacks, University of Michigan
        Press.
Tart, C. T., ed.
  1972 *Altered States of Consciousness.* Garden City, New York: Doubleday Anchor
        Books.
Uhr, L. and Miller, J. G.
  1960 *Drugs and Behavior.* New York: Wiley.
Verger, P.
  1957 Notes sur le culte des orisa et vodun. *Memoir d'IFAN no.* 51. Dakar.
Walker, S. S.
  1972 *Ceremonial Spirit Possession in Africa and Afro-America.* Leiden: Brill.
Wallace, A. F. C.
  1956 Revitalization Movements. *American Anthropologist* 58:264–81.
Wasson, R. G.
  1968 *Soma: Divine Mushroom of Immortality.* New York: Harcourt Brace and
        World; The Hague: Mouton.
White, J., ed.
  1972 *The Highest State of Consciousness.* New York: Anchor Books.
Whiting, J. W. M. and Child, I. L.
  1953 *Child Training and Personality.* New Haven: Yale University Press.
Whitten, N. E. Jr. and Szwed, J. F.
  1970 Introduction. In *Afro-American Anthropology: Contemporary Perspectives.*
        Glencoe, Illinois: Free Press.
Wylie, L.
  1957 *Village in the Vaucluse.* Cambridge, Mass.: Harvard University Press.
Zaretsky, I. I.
  1967 *Bibliography on Spirit Mediumship and Spirit Possession in Africa.* Evanston,
        Ill.: Northwestern University Press.

The Authors

NANCY BEATRICE GRAVES, born in Baton Rouge, Louisiana, received her advanced education at the University of California in Los Angeles (B.A. in fine arts and social science 1958) and at the University of Colorado where she finished her Ph.D. in anthropology and psychology in 1970. She has had field research experience with Spanish and Anglo-Americans in Colorado, in Mexico, with Mexican-Americans in Los Angeles, with the Baganda in rural and urban Uganda, and with Polynesian and European New Zealanders. Her psychological training was developmental and behavioral in emphasis, with early experience in ethology. Her first university post was in the Psychiatry Department at UCLA and she holds membership in the Society for Research in Child Development as well as her fellowship in the American Anthropological Association.

Theodore Deumaine Graves was born in Concord, Massachusetts, did his B.A. at Earlham College in Richmond, Indiana, his M.A. at the University of Colorado in anthropology, psychology and sociology, and his Ph.D. in 1962 at the University of Pennsylvania in anthropology. He is presently a Research Fellow at the Department of Anthropology, University of Auckland, New Zealand, and has been professor of anthropology at UCLA. His psychological training was in clinical, personality, and social psychology. His first university level research and teaching appointments were in the Psychology Department of the University of Colorado and he has continuing membership in the American Psychological Association in addition to his fellow standing in the American Anthropological Association. Both Ted and Nancy Graves have been primary school teachers, Ted in a tuberculosis hospital for Navajo Indians. Though they have received broad interdisciplinary training as graduate students and have pursued interdisciplinary careers, their primary professional identification is as anthropologists. They have team-taught courses in research methods, urban anthropology, and interethnic relations in culture change. They have also conducted much of their research together in the American Southwest, Mexico, East Africa and recently in the South Pacific where they serve as codirectors of the South Pacific Research Institute. They have published

516

substantially on acculturation, urbanization, migration, and the implications for personal adjustment.

This Chapter

Unlike most of the contributors to this volume, the Graves are strongly anti-Freudian and employ an essentially psychological research strategy. They try to stay within the psychological explanatory model because "recourse to cultural explanations only serves to conceal our ignorance of underlying processes." Like Robert Edgerton, Melford Spiro, and others represented in this book, the Graves are suspicious of normative regulation: "the typical cultural patterns of appropriate behavior cannot explain the substantial range of intragroup variability in observed behavior."

They are not interested in modal characteristics distinguishing groups from each other but in intragroup differences in overt behaviors, and not in psychological or personality features as such. They try, for example, to understand how acculturation is related to social disorganization, using drinking behavior as an index, and the effect of drinking behaviors on economic access. Like the Spindlers and others they construct indices and instruments which are appropriate for a particular context. They are more concerned than most anthropologists about validation of their instruments. One of their major aims is to develop a single theoretical model of deviant behavior and its social psychological determinants which would be applicable cross-ethnically and presumably cross-culturally. Nancy Graves in particular is working towards a theory linking maternal expectations and behavior based upon research in the American Southwest and with the Baganda.

Their paper discusses their earlier collaborative research, their separate projects in the Southwest and with the Baganda in Kampala, and then their further collaborative work in the South Pacific with Cook Island migrants to Auckland.

G.D.S.

15 Evolving Strategies in the Study of Culture Change

THEODORE D. GRAVES
AND NANCY B. GRAVES

Anthropologists who received their training after World War II were apt to be caught up in problems of culture contact and culture change. Of necessity this forced us to recognize the importance of within-group *diversity* in our analysis. Members of all culture groups vary in the degree to which their behavior conforms to normative expectations. But where they are in contact with alternative norms and behavioral role models, this diversity is undoubtedly increased and cannot be ignored. Rather than bemoaning the loss of the relatively isolated and homogeneous ethnic community, many of us who began our professional careers during this period seized upon variability and change for the research opportunities they presented. Consequently, although identifying and explaining group differences in modal personality has continued to be seen by some scholars as the defining feature of "psychological anthropology" (LeVine 1973), an interest in within-group variation in personality and perception, its experiential origins and behavioral consequences, is now becoming more characteristic of research in this field. Our own investigations over the past fifteen years reflect this trend.

Because we have devoted considerable time and effort over the years to the cross-cultural measurement of personality attributes, we feel a particular kinship with other psychological anthropologists. But our interest in psychological variables is an instrumental one. In almost all our research *within-group differences in overt behavior* have served as the focus of investigation: drinking behavior, child rearing behavior, and various adaptive strategies in urban migration and cross-ethnic interaction. Psychological factors are only one among several types of explanatory variables with which we work. Of at least equal importance are characteristics of the physical and social settings within which an

518

actor finds himself, and the ways in which normative expectations are brought to bear through the social pressures and constraints to which he is subjected. Indeed, our most fascinating empirical results have been found in the interaction between cultural, structural, and psychological determinants.

The goal of our research has been to identify potentially universal principles of human behavior, and to show the varying ways these manifest themselves within different cultural contexts. All psychological measurement is based on an inference from some form of observable behavior—whether verbal responses to a questionnaire or performance on some test or "natural experiment." Since the determinants of this behavior are complex and multidimensional, it is obvious that no two culture groups are likely to display identical response distributions. Using the same psychological measuring instrument in different settings, therefore, it is easy to demonstrate cultural differences, and therefore to infer differences in underlying personality. More difficult, but of greater scientific value, we feel, is to show that for two or more groups, variation in some inferred psychological attribute—regardless of how it is measured within each—is consistently related to variation in a second attribute when other contextual influences are controlled. *It is not the variables themselves which are to be compared cross-culturally, but the relationship between variables.*

A corollary of this stance is that it is no longer necessary to seek universally applicable and "culture-free" personality measures, such as the Rorschach was once believed to be. This effort has proved a will-o'-the-wisp. Rather, it becomes quite reasonable to measure the same underlying psychological attribute quite differently within different cultural settings and therefore to construct indices which are appropriate for the particular context within which they are to be used. When working cross-culturally, however, each measure requires at least the same attention to its validation as would be expected for any new psychological test used in our own society. This makes cross-cultural research in the psychological domain particularly costly, and results in which we can have confidence are not quickly come by.

Our interest in the determinants of overt behavior has influenced the type of psychological attributes which we are prepared to devote the time to measuring. Although historically psychological anthropologists have been strongly influenced by Freudian theory, they have been hard put to demonstrate any reliable relationship between their theoretical constructs and overt behavior. This may, perhaps, simply be a matter of poor measurement (LeVine 1973), an argument open to empirical demonstration. We have preferred, however, to work with more cognitive variables—beliefs and expectations—which in relation to behavior occupy a fairly proximal position. As with other personality attributes, they are conceived of as the residues of past experience which influence an actor's perception of new situations and thereby his behavioral response. But they are not irrevocably laid down in infancy and childhood, though experiential roots may be found there. Rather, they too are continually changing with changes in circumstances. This makes them particularly attractive to the applied social scientist. And as long as they prove empirically rewarding, we will doubtlessly continue our efforts to measure them reliably.

The three research projects discussed in this chapter were all conducted under the auspices of the University of Colorado's interdisciplinary Institute of Behavioral Science. This center, with the many opportunities it provided for scholarly cross-fertilization, was a congenial and stimulating setting for our work. Becuase we have received training in a variety of fields, we have found it relatively easy and comfortable to work closely with scholars from other disciplines who bring to their analyses of human behavior a diversity of theoretical models, concepts, measures, and research strategies. This background has been important in shaping the particular professional roles we have come to play.

TED GRAVES—THE TRI-ETHNIC RESEARCH PROJECT

In 1959 I began dissertation field work as part of an interdisciplinary research team.[1] For the next three years I lived and worked in a rural reservation community in the American Southwest. Almost half the population of about three thousand were Anglo-Americans like myself, a third were Spanish-Americans, and a fifth were members of a single American Indian tribe. The purpose of the project was to explain intergroup differences in behavior, particularly rates of drinking and drunkenness and other forms of "social deviance." Casual observation suggested that rates of deviant behavior, particularly drunkenness, were far higher among the Indians than among either Anglos or Spanish, and this was a source of concern, not only to the dominant Anglo community, but to the Indians themselves.

The project staff was divided into two teams: one under the leadership of an anthropologist (Professor Omer C. Stewart) and one

1. Support for this work was provided by a five-year grant from the National Institute of Mental Health (3M-9156).

under a psychologist (Professor Richard Jessor). As the only anthropologist on a team otherwise composed of sociologists and social psychologists, my job was not to provide an ethnography of the community (the task of the other team), but to draw on my anthropological training and experience living in the field to help make our fairly structured and systematic hypothesis-testing research appropriate to the particular setting in which it was being conducted.

The aim of this team's work, as described in our book *Society, Personality and Deviant Behavior* (Jessor, Graves, Hanson, and Jessor 1968), was to develop a single theoretical model of deviant behavior and its sociopsychological determinants which would be equally applicable to all three ethnic groups, and which could be tested within each through the use of the same research instruments.

At the time we began developing our explanatory model, the most influential sociological theory of deviant behavior had been formulated by Robert Merton in his paper "Social Structure and Anomie" (1949). Briefly, his thesis was that our society encourages all its members to strive for a relatively uniform set of personal goals, but that some individuals have less objective access to these goals than others. Consequently, they are forced to turn to socially unacceptable means for achieving these goals, adopt more readily available but less socially valued goals, seek to overthrow the social order so that it will prove more rewarding to them, or ritually perform their approved social roles without hope of reward, often lapsing into alcohol or other drug-induced retreatism. All of these responses are in some sense "socially deviant."

This sociocultural analysis, however, seemed inadequate to us: not all persons in disfavored structural positions display deviant or retreatist behavior. Psychological factors must also be considered. A person must actually *value* goals which his structural position prevents him from achieving, and he must also come to *perceive* his position as a limiting one. Julian Rotter's concept of "low freedom of movement," a generalized expectation that many available pathways to achieving one's goals are closed or inadequate, seemed a natural parallel at the psychological level to Merton's concept of means-goals disjunctions at the structural level. Rotter's "social learning theory" (1954) was therefore adopted as a useful framework for analyzing the psychological motivations for engaging in deviant behavior.[2]

2. Rotter had been the Jessors' major professor at Ohio State, and I had also studied under him at the University of Pennsylvania. In addition, my major professor at Penn,

Our theory continued to grow, and its full dimensions are well beyond the scope of this retrospect. But the most important additional factors considered were various social and psychological *controls*. Thus though an individual might experience various pressures which could motivate him to get drunk (or engage in other socially deviant acts), he may also be mapped into social control structures, or have developed internalized psychological controls which constrain the overt display of such behavior.

In order to test the adequacy of this model, our next task was to develop numerous specific and cross-culturally applicable measures of each theoretical concept, as well as of the behavior we wanted to predict. My dissertation, for example, was devoted in large part to the construction and validation of several measures of "future time perspective" (T. Graves 1962). What I wanted was an indication of how far into the future a person tends to think, or how much of the future is maintained as part of his current psychological "life space." My assumption was that the more a person looks to the future, the less likely it is that he will engage in deviant behavior which may be immediately gratifying, but which may have long-term negative consequences for him. Subjects were therefore asked to "look ahead for a minute, and then tell me five things which you think you will do or think might happen to you." After these were recorded, subjects were asked to go back and estimate how far into the future each of these events might occur. These estimates varied from a few minutes to a full lifetime; for each subject I have found it convenient and empirically satisfactory to use the median future event recorded as a summary of the full "life space sample."[3] When the distribution of scores for the Anglo, Spanish, and Indian samples was plotted, there were clear ethnic differences among them, with Anglos as a group having the most extended time perspective scores, Spanish intermediate, and Indians the shortest, as one might anticipate from ethnographic accounts. But there was also a large measure of overlap among these three distributions, thus helping to remind us of the intragroup diversity with which we were also dealing (Figure 1).

Using our best validated measures of structural or psychological

---

and my disssertation supervisor, was Anthony F. C. Wallace, whose theories of revitalization movements and schizophrenia were also based on a poor fit between personal goals and culturally provided means for their attainment.

3. See T. Graves 1974 for a convenient discussion of the construction and validation of this measure.

FIGURE 1

A Schematic Distribution of Time Perspective Scores
in a Tri-Ethnic Community

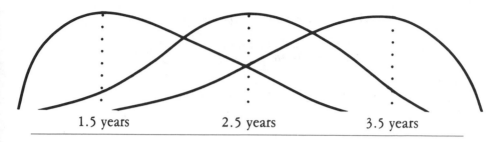

| 1.5 years | 2.5 years | 3.5 years |

pressures for engaging in deviant behavior and structural or psychological controls against its display, we next constructed multivariate "predictions" of deviance rates. At this point our model was essentially additive: each predictor variable was assumed to have a theoretically independent role to play, the probability that any particular person would be classified as "deviant" increasing with each additional factor that he had working against him.

Various combinations of predictors, whether drawn exclusively from among our psychological or from among our sociological measures, provided substantial—and comparable—levels of empirical success. Combining both types of variables within a social-psychological or "field-theoretical" analysis (Yinger 1965), however, did even better. These analyses were replicated within both a high school student and an adult sample, among both men and women, and within all three ethnic groups, using a variety of behavioral criterion measures. Thus, we felt reasonably confident our findings were not the result of particular measures used or particular populations studied. As an illustration, Table 1 presents a summary of findings for a four variable social-psychological analysis, for each group in the adult population.

In assessing these results, the reader should note the following. First, two indices of objective pressures and constraints bearing on these people, and two parallel measures of their subjective counterparts accounted for the vast majority of all variation in deviant behavior to be found within this community. Among those with objective access to the rewards of the dominant society who were also mapped into a system of strong social controls, who felt themselves able to achieve their personal goals in life, and who held nonpermissive attitudes toward engaging in

TABLE 1
SOCIAL-PSYCHOLOGICAL DETERMINANTS OF DEVIANT BEHAVIOR
IN A TRI-ETHNIC COMMUNITY

Field Pattern*	Percent in each group classified as "deviant"					
	Total N=204	Males N=100	Females N=104	Anglos N=91	Spanish N=58	Indians N=55
Optimal	7	0	9	0	0	67
1 Departure	19	25	15	19	14	67
2 Departures	54	56	50	29	44	81
3 Departures	55	50	59	64	32	75
4 Departures	84	93	25	100	60	92

*Field variables used: Socioeconomic status, Access to illegitimate means, Personal disjunctions, and Attitudes toward deviance.
(Jessor, Graves, Hanson and Jessor 1968, tables 11.11 and 11.12, p. 360.)

socially deviant behavior, almost no one could be identified as having engaged in a significant degree of deviant behavior during the last few years. By contrast, among those with the opposite set of characteristics, almost everyone did. Those with intermediate patterns of social-psychological characteristics fell in between.

Almost all the empirical exceptions to this analysis are to be found among women, among Spanish, and among Indians. Only four women in our sample experienced the full range of pressures toward deviance of those in the "four departure" pattern, and three of these were not found to have engaged in any significant deviant acts. Similarly, only five Spanish-Americans fell in this pattern, and only three of these were classified as "deviant." For both groups, therefore, there are probably controls against the overt display of deviant behavior which our theory and measurement did not include. Among Indians, by contrast, few enjoyed a position in the more benign "optimal" and "one departure" patterns, and of the six who did, two-thirds were classified as deviants anyway. This suggests that among Indians there were probably additional pressures to engage in deviant behavior which our theory and measurement did not tap. It should be emphasized that the number of predictive failures involved here is small: five out of forty-seven people falling into the two extreme categories. Nevertheless, the distribution of these failures points, I think, toward the areas of greatest weakness in the Anglo male-generated theory and the set of uniform measures with which we were working.

More important than our empirical failures (which are relatively minor), however, is that in trying to apply theory and measurement uniformly to three quite distinct ethnic groups, we were forced to employ explanatory variables at a fairly high level of abstraction. This makes the analysis appear somewhat sterile and remote from the lives of the people we studied. It might have been better if we had devoted more time and space to showing *how* Anglos, Spanish and Indians were the same or differed in the kinds of goals towards which they strove, in the kinds of means they saw available—and unavailable—for their attainment, in the kinds of social controls to which they were subjected, and so forth. This would have helped the reader see the way in which a uniform set of social-psychological principles work themselves out within different cultural contexts—something which I believe should be the ultimate aim of cross-cultural psychology.

A first step in this direction was taken in my paper "Acculturation, Access and Alcohol in a Tri-Ethnic Community" (1967a). "Acculturation" had not been included as a variable in our original theoretical scheme because it would not be applicable to all three groups. But in the course of working over our data, I had been struck by the fact that various indices of what seemed like an orientation towards the dominant Western cultural tradition were consistently associated with *higher* rates of drinking and deviant behavior within the Spanish sample, while within the Indian sample these same indices were associated with *lower* rates of these same behaviors.

This seeming empirical paradox led to a secondary analysis of our tri-ethnic data which has served as a paradigm for my subsequent work. Here Spanish and Indians were compared to demonstrate (1) the ways in which they were alike, i.e., the same lawful relationships between behavior and its determinants were found, and (2) the ways in which they were different, i.e., variations in cultural context led to differences in the ways these laws displayed themselves in rates of overt behavior. A second departure from the earlier tri-ethnic approach was that my theory was no longer couched in simple additive terms, but instead examined the *interaction* between structural and psychological variables. This, too, has been a continuing theme in my subsequent work.

At the time of this research there had been a long-standing debate within anthropology, particularly involving psychological anthropologists, as to whether or not rapid culture change inevitably increased social and psychological disorganization. A better question, I felt, was "under what conditions is acculturation accompanied by symptoms of social and psychological disorganization, and under what conditions is it not?" (1967, p. 306). Hallowell (1951) for example, had found some of the best and some of the worst adjusted Indians within the more acculturated subgroups. This question was more in harmony with my own emphasis on the determinants of intragroup variation in response to culture contact.

In searching for an answer, the theoretical paradigm developed for the Tri-Ethnic project as a whole served as a guide, but its basic concepts were reinterpreted in terms relevant to the peculiar situation of acculturating minority groups. For example, situations in which individuals hold valued goals which they feel unable to achieve through the normal pathways society provides, we had hypothesized, should generate feelings of frustration and alienation which lead to experimenting with "illegitimate means" (deviant behavior) and/or retreatism, such as getting drunk. This principle, we believed, should be universally applicable, although the particular goals held by different individuals and groups may vary, as well as the socially acceptable means for their attainment.

Acculturating groups, however, are peculiarly vulnerable to this type of "means-goals disjunction." Initially traditional goals may be retained—such as the status provided through skill as a warrior or hunter—but the traditional means for their attainment may be made ineffective through the intervention of a dominant Western group, by, for example, banning intertribal warfare or clearing the forests and fencing the grasslands. Then, through continued exposure to alternative ways of life, some individuals may come to adopt new, nontraditional goals for which traditional (or even nontraditional) pathways available in their society are inappropriate or inadequate. Typically, this involves a desire for material comforts and labor-saving benefits of Western technology and industrial society—radios, sewing machines, electricity, and so forth—which a subsistence economy or a marginal economic position within the total society cannot provide. Theoretically, this should lead to socially deviant behavior, particularly the heavy use of alcohol.

This proposition was then tested with our samples of both Spanish and Indian adults. Those Spanish and Indians who were identified as high in their degree of acculturation (using either years of formal education or a seven item "acculturation index" involving voluntary adoption of Western cultural behavior) were assumed to be orienting toward Western material goals more than their less acculturated neighbors. It was therefore hypothesized that the kinds of jobs they had, and thus their access to these material goals, should affect their feelings of

FIGURE 2
THE EFFECT ON DEVIANT BEHAVIOR
OF THE INTERACTION BETWEEN ACCULTURATION AND ECONOMIC ACCESS
WITHIN A TRI-ETHNIC COMMUNITY

	SPANISH PATTERN		INDIAN PATTERN	
	high economic access	low economic access	high economic access	low economic access
high acculturation	LOW deviance rate	HIGH deviance rate	LOW deviance rate	HIGH deviance rate
low acculturation	LOW deviance rate	LOW deviance rate	HIGH deviance rate	HIGH deviance rate

personal disjunction and alienation, and therefore their drinking behavior. Those with relatively good, steady jobs should feel less psychological pressure to drink heavily than those with marginal, part time employment. By contrast, less acculturated individuals who were not as oriented toward Western goals should be less influenced in their behavior by the kinds of jobs they had.

This was exactly what we found. In a series of tables using alternative measures of acculturation and drinking behavior, a consistent pattern emerged, which is summarized in Figure 2. Acculturating individuals were responding to new pressures and opportunities in roughly the same way, regardless of their ethnic affiliation. Similarly, less acculturated individuals within both ethnic groups were essentially unaffected in their drinking by the kinds of jobs they had. This analysis of overt behavior had an exact parallel for three psychological measures of their subjective feelings as well.

The two unacculturated groups differed sharply, however, in the general level of deviance and drinking they displayed. The culturally traditional Indians exhibited far more drunkenness and social problem behavior than did the culturally traditional Spanish. This was the source of our empirical paradox when we had been looking at the behavioral correlates of acculturation alone.

To explain these gross behavioral differences, I turned next to the control structures which each group experienced. Here differences in Spanish and Indian cultures became significant. Tradition-oriented Spanish-Americans in our community were found on our measures to be generally subject to the strong social and psychological controls which have been reported ethnographically throughout the Southwest, and which we would expect in a settled agricultural group. Of particular importance were the influences of church and family, which had apparently been strongly internalized. By contrast, tradition-oriented members of our Indian sample generally reported weak social and psychological controls on our measures, and a reluctance to intervene in the lives of others, also noted in the ethnographic literature among similar tribal groups from a semi-nomadic hunting-and-gathering background. Exposure to Western society, furthermore, has had quite different effects on these two ethnic groups. Among our Spanish-American subjects, acculturation resulted in a general weakening of traditional controls, whereas acculturating Indians were being mapped into new, nontraditional social control structures, and were becoming less permissive in their attitudes towards drinking and deviance. Thus our apparent empirical paradox was explained.

I should add one footnote to this work. Nothing in the tri-ethnic paradigm assures that *drunkenness* will be a behavioral consequence of the social-psychological pressures we were analyzing, though alcohol's ready availability and its narcotizing effects—easily discoverable by all drinkers—make it a natural candidate. (This is why, of course, we included global measures of behavioral deviance in areas other than drunkenness.) Our most effective critics, therefore, have argued that our theoretical scheme will ''work'' only within culture groups where getting drunk is seen as an *appropriate* way of coping with psychological problems. Thus they hope to reassert the causal primacy of cultural norms. This could serve to explain why Indians appear to drink more under pressure than other groups we have studied, and why women generally drink less. The argument has been given empirical support by the Jessors' own subsequent research on drinking behavior in Italy, using the tri-ethnic paradigm (Jessor et al. 1970).

Without denying the cogency of this argument, I am reluctant to include it in my formulation until alternative avenues have been more fully explored. Recourse to cultural explanations only serves to conceal our ignorance of underlying processes. We still need to know, for example, why some culture groups have found drunkenness such a satisfying way of coping with psychological pressures, while other groups have not. My subsequent research among Navajo Indian migrants to Denver sheds at least some light on this problem.

TED GRAVES—THE NAVAJO URBAN RELOCATION RESEARCH PROJECT

In 1963, when the Tri-Ethnic research funds were running out (but —typically—the analysis of our data was far from complete) I obtained funds to conduct research under my own direction on the adjustment problems of Navajo Indian migrants to Denver, Colorado.[4] American Indians have been leaving their reservations in search of better economic opportunities since before the turn of the century. This migration was given added impetus after World War II by a government-sponsored urban "relocation" program designed to promote Indian assimilation and solve their economic problems (Officer 1971). Because of its proximity to their reservation, roughly one-third of the Indians who came to Denver under this program were Navajos, and they constitute the largest single tribe of Indians in the city. I had worked periodically with Navajos over the previous decade, learned rudiments of the language while a primary school teacher for Navajo children, travelled extensively on their reservation, and was familiar with the relevant anthropological literature on this group. This background served as the source of my own predisposition to undertake their study.

The Navajo Urban Relocation Research Project was intended to serve in part as a training laboratory for anthropology graduate students. I therefore deliberately designed it to provide maximum research flexibility, so that all of us involved could explore how best to go about studying a significant social problem within a cross-cultural field setting. I also hoped to build on our tri-ethnic findings, while avoiding some of its methodological limitations.

In the Tri-Ethnic project I had experienced and observed two contrasting approaches to field research. While the anthropological team collected everything they could about everything that went on in the community, the social-psychological team followed a fairly rigid hypothesis-testing approach. The contrast which this experience provided confirmed my commitment to "theory-guided research" (Graves

4. Initial support for this research was provided by the University of Colorado Council on Research and Creative Work, followed by a three year grant from the National Institute of Mental Health (1R 11 MH–1942–01, 02, 03). A special fellowship from NIMH (1–FO3–MH–43, 794–01) provided freedom to conduct further analyses in 1970–71, and is gratefully acknowledged.

1966). But this approach also has its liabilities, which had become keenly obvious to me as well. In the Tri-Ethnic project our commitment to testing an *a priori* theory of Western origin within three ethnic groups in a uniform manner prevented us from adequately exploring other factors which might have been particularly relevant for the two minority groups, or from developing new concepts grounded in the setting under investigation. For my own project, I sought greater research flexibility.

But then how to avoid the theoretical anarchy into which projects of this kind might degenerate? The social scientist who decides to collect everything and let the data speak for themselves does not thereby avoid theoretical commitments. Faced with the infinite variety of data that *could* be collected, he is forced to make choices. The basis for these choices generally turns out to be his implicit theories about which factors are likely to prove important and which are not. But there is no reason to assume that data based on implicit theory are any more likely to prove fruitful than data based on explicit theory. A good deal of experience suggests just the opposite.

We therefore decided to confront the theoretical question as directly as possible, by specifying certain theoretical predispositions in advance. At the same time, however, we wished to avoid dedication to one particular theory which might blind us to negative data, or to the role of variables not specified by that theory. Our solution was to construct a series of alternative models of the adaptation process, which could then be tested simultaneously (Graves 1966). Each of these models directed our attention to a different set of potentially relevant factors in Navajo adaptation to city life. And each implied different criteria of urban adjustment as well. For example, one model was grounded in decision theory, in which each migrant's personal values and expectations were examined in order to understand why some decided to remain in the city while others quickly returned home (Graves and VanArsdale 1966). By contrast, an alternative model looked at migration as a process of shifting reference groups and social relationships. Those working within this framework wanted to know how quickly a migrant made non-Navajo friendships and cut his social and emotional ties with the reservation, and the influence of peer groups on a migrant's behavior in the city (Snyder 1968, 1971, 1973). Economic determinism provided the basis for a third model, and led others to examine economic factors in a migrant's decision to move to the city (Weinstein 1973), his position within the Denver opportunity structure (Weppner 1968, 1971, 1972), and elements in his background and training which might affect his urban wages (Graves and Lave 1972). Yet another analyzed migrant adjustment within the framework of a psychophysiological "stress" model (Alfred 1965; T. Graves and N. Graves 1974*a*), which required data on such things as a migrant's medical history, psychosomatic symptoms, and blood pressure.

One dividend of this strategy has been that when viewing the same phenomenon through alternative theoretical lenses, we became keenly aware of the distortions which each introduced. Although any one model provides a limited perspective, each offers insight into just those aspects of the phenomenon which the others neglect. It is as if we were viewing a complex sculpture from several vantage points. My task, still uncompleted, has been to pursue systematic linkages between models, and to construct a more comprehensive theory of migrant adaptation, firmly grounded in our empirical results (T. Graves, in preparation).

To avoid the pitfalls of *post hoc* explanation, which such an open strategy invites, a convergent approach to measurement and data collection was also adopted. Our main instrument was a lengthy formal interview of about two hours duration, which included factual material on the migrant's training, experiences, and job history both before and after migration, recreational activities and health record in the city, as well as various psychometric and sociometric procedures specifically designed for this study. Between 1963 and 1966 this interview was administered to 135 Navajo migrants in Denver and 124 former migrants on the reservation, randomly selected to represent the total migrant population, as well as matched comparison sample of 115 young Navajo men still living on the reservation. Small samples of migrant wives and urban whites who worked side by side with the Navajos in similar jobs were also interviewed.[5] Comparison data from interviews with 139 Spanish-American migrants were also made available to us.[6]

In addition to the data contained in these interviews, ratings were collected from virtually all Denver employers hiring Navajo Indian workers, the day by day records kept by the Bureau of Indian Affairs on each sponsored migrant during his first few months in the city were abstracted, as were police records for the migrant and all comparison

5. Each subject was paid five dollars for his time. Besides myself, the interviewers included twelve male anthropology graduate students, while four female students were employed to interview migrant wives.

6. The Spanish-American sample was part of a parallel study of migrant adaptation being conducted within this group by other social scientists at the Institute of Behavioral Science. I want to thank the project director, Professor Robert C. Hanson, and Dr. Gabino Rendon (1968), who did much of the interviewing, for having graciously made these data available to us for comparative purposes.

samples. These formal data were supplemented by participant observation and intensive case studies (McSwain 1965; Ziegler 1967; McCracken 1968). Thus a wealth of both qualitative and quantitative information has been available to draw on.

Given the difficulties and ambiguities inherent in field research—the many threats to the validity of your empirical findings (Campbell and Stanley 1966)—I would strongly urge this type of methodology on anyone undertaking psychological research cross-culturally. As in the Tri-Ethnic study, we frequently have alternative and operationally distinct measures of major concepts, or supporting evidence from other sources. As a result, our confidence in the conclusions now emerging is grounded not in the vagaries of statistical significance, but in the consistency of a highly complex *pattern of convergent evidence* (Kaplan 1964; Morrison and Henkel 1970).

Since several preliminary reports from this research are now readily available (T. Graves 1970, 1973, 1974), I will detail only two analyses which clearly build on and extend the insights from the earlier Tri-Ethnic study. Both also illustrate my intellectual fascination with the behavioral consequences of an *interaction* between psychological predispositions and objective circumstances.

Many of the problems and rewards of cross-cultural research within the psychological domain can be found in our work with achievement motivation. As I had learned on the Tri-Ethnic project, developing and validating cross-cultural measures of some personality predisposition requires an inordinate effort: in this case one of my students devoted the better part of two years and most of his subsequent Ph.D. dissertation to the task (Michener 1971). The measure of need-achievement he devised was modelled on the TAT test of this variable employed by McClelland and his associates within our own society (McClelland et al. 1958), but reconstructed to fit the particular cross-cultural setting in which it was to be used. Briefly, we contrived a series of more than a dozen situations familiar to Navajo migrants within which achievement themes might be expected to emerge. A Navajo artist was then commissioned to draw stimulus pictures representing these situations, and after pretesting, six were selected for final use. In the order of presentation, these included a picture of a young man speaking with an employer, a young man seated in a classroom, a young man watching a piece of Navajo jewelry receive a prize, a Navajo family boarding a bus, a young man speaking to an assembly of Indians, and a young man counting a handful of paper money.

In all the pictures, the main character was an Indian with whom the respondent could easily identify. Subjects were asked to make up a story

for each picture presented. These were tape-recorded and later transcribed for scoring. A scoring manual was prepared from preliminary
data, with scoring criteria refined through use and statistical analysis.
Three scorers were trained, and all protocols were independently scored
by each, with disagreements resolved through subsequent discussion.

This psychological test can be thought of as a more direct measure
of an Indian's acceptance of Western goals of status and material
advancement than the acculturation and education indices used in the
Tri-Ethnic study. In the Navajo research, furthermore, we had far more
refined measures of economic achievement as well. It is interesting to
note, therefore, that *essentially the same pattern of results emerged.*
Placed in a two-by-two table comparable to that presented in Figure 2,
this pattern can be summarized as follows:

FIGURE 3

THE EFFECT ON DEVIANT BEHAVIOR OF THE
INTERACTION BETWEEN ACHIEVEMENT MOTIVATION AND ECONOMIC
ACCESS AMONG NAVAJO INDIAN MIGRANTS TO DENVER, COLORADO

	high economic access	low economic access
high need-achievement	LOW arrest rate	HIGH arrest rate
low need-achievement	LOW arrest rate	INTER-MEDIATE arrest rate

This is a good example of what I like to refer to as "sloppy replication," which at this stage in our science seems to me more informative—
and less boring—than more strict replication. Where strict replication
may only duplicate the mistakes and artifacts of the original study,
sloppy replication is more likely to result from some underlying theoretical relationship. In the present case, for example, all of our Navajo
migrant subjects can probably be considered to have at least a moderately strong orientation towards economic achievement, since this is
their major motivation for leaving the reservation. So we are looking

essentially at people like the acculturated Spanish and Indians who would fall within the top half of Figure 2. Yet even within this group, the effect of poor jobs is variable, increasing as the migrant's orientation towards these material goals increases. For those Navajos with the greatest desire to "get ahead," the frustration of poor opportunities takes a severe toll. Those receiving low wages were being arrested (almost always for drunkenness and drinking related offenses) at a rate of close to two times per man-year in the city, well over four times the arrest rate of those with similar high levels of achievement motivation but better jobs (Graves 1974). This same pattern was repeated regardless of our measure of economic position in Denver. And since it confirms a pattern found in a rural setting, within another Indian tribal group and their Spanish neighbors, using entirely different measures of all variables both dependent and independent, we feel particularly confident in its stability, and therefore in its theoretical significance.

Finally, this study is yielding some fascinating results with respect to the interaction between psychological predispositions and social expectations. Anthropologists are fond of evoking normative pressures as major determinants of social behavior. In the case of Indian drunkenness, they will argue it is mainly a product of social norms in which periodic binge drinking is the expected pattern (MacAndrew and Edgerton 1969). Certainly our observations and interviews confirm this as "typical" among Navajos: Well over 50 percent of our Navajo migrant population joined a peer drinking party in Denver at least once a week, usually Friday and Saturday evenings when they had their pay checks in hand. But we also know that many migrants do *not* go out and drink with their friends every weekend, and many others do *not* get uncontrollably drunk at every sitting. Typical cultural patterns of appropriate behavior cannot explain this substantial range of intragroup variability in observed behavior.

A more adequate explanation requires us to go beyond the description of a cultural norm to an analysis of how it is maintained, and what function it serves for those conforming to it. Through participant observation we have been able to document the social pressures to get drunk placed on a migrant by his peers. These pressures were very much like those I had repeatedly observed among Indians (and to a lesser degree among the other two ethnic groups as well) in our tri-ethnic community. But the *a priori* theoretical model we were testing there had neglected to include peer pressures as possible determinants. Among Navajo migrants, being mapped sociometrically into peer groups where these social pressures would be experienced was associated with higher arrest rates even when other determinants were controlled. Similar peer pressures, therefore, were doubtless a factor in the high deviance and drunkenness found by the Tri-Ethnic staff among even those Indians who were not in marginal economic positions and did not reveal strong psychological pressures to get drunk.

Nevertheless, in the Navajo project, our systematic data were also able to show that *those migrants with the greatest psychological motivation to get drunk tend to seek out social situations and peer groups in which heavy drinking is normative, and when in those groups and situations are most likely to fulfill these social expectations* (T. Graves, in preparation). Peer drinking groups thereby serve as a remarkably appropriate social invention for meeting the psychological needs of many core participants. It is this fit between social and psychological forces, I would argue, which gives rise to and maintains a stable cultural norm.

As in the case of any evolutionary adaptation, the issue of which factors have causal primacy probably cannot be answered unequivocally. Undoubtedly norms of drunkenness contribute to Indian difficulties in economic adjustment, and therefore to their feelings of frustration and alienation as well. And historically drunken excesses appear to have become a normal Indian pattern of behavior since early exposure to alcohol. But it is also significant that traditional Indian culture was crumbling at the same time that alcohol was introduced, and that the frustrations of military defeat, white deception, and reservation confinement, in which traditional goals, and even minimal self-respect could no longer be achieved, provided an appropriate psychological context for the development of such norms.

Regardless of which came first, culture, situation, or personality, the important thing is that all three must be considered. Personality predispositions, formed in response to earlier situations, lag behind the changes in objective circumstances which inevitably accompany culture contact. Shared social norms are even slower to follow. Consequently, we would rarely expect to find a one-to-one relationship between these three types of variables. Since there is a demonstrable effect of each on human behavior, however, this results in the fascinating interactions between these factors which I have discovered in my data over the years.

NANCY GRAVES—URBAN MIGRATION, ACCULTURATION, AND CHILD REARING

In 1964 I began work as an anthropology graduate student with a background in primary and preschool teaching and an interest in interpersonal interaction. At the University of Colorado's Institute of Behavioral Science three major studies of acculturation situations were near completion or well underway: the Tri-Ethnic Project, the Navajo Project, and a study of Spanish-American male migrants to Denver by Drs. Robert Hanson and Ozzie Simmons. Since I spoke Spanish well, I also decided to work with Spanish Americans, the largest minority group in the city, and in the fall of 1965 I began visiting migrant families. I chose to focus on child rearing because mother-child interaction was easy to observe and a topic to which I related well, having three small children of my own.[7]

During this early period of participant observation and discussions with mothers about city life, I tried to develop a model of change which might be appropriate to these migrants. I was influenced both by theories of change processes (acculturation, modernization, urbanization) and by child development-socialization theory. From the vantage point of the 1970s, it seems to me that most of these theories shared at that time certain naive assumptions. Change, whether for children or adults, was seen as learning knowledge or traits from a donor, or cultural transmitter. This process was voluntary, in the sense that the material transmitted could be adopted or rejected. Finally, the traits were passed to the receiver relatively intact, with only accidents accounting for transformation of the elements.

In acculturation studies these basic assumptions took the form of an assimilation model whereby "donor" cultures presented traits which could be accepted or rejected by "receiver" cultures. Psychological acculturation studies (e.g., T. Graves 1967*b*) focused on the acquisition of norms, beliefs, and values from other groups. This adoption process was mediated through "cultural brokers" or "reference groups" (Hughes 1957; Chance 1960; Berreman 1964) from whom adopters could learn new psychological or behavioral traits.

Modernization and urbanization processes were seen by most change theorists as undifferentiated from each other and essentially similar in form to acculturation (Beals 1951). Inkeles' (1966) studies in six countries of the adoption of "modern man" traits (general value-orientations such as personal control over one's fate) by urban migrants reflected this global assimilation viewpoint.

Socialization theories, whether concerned with impulse control, learning of cultural precepts, or role training, usually focused on the parent as a transmitter of information to the adopting child. LeVine (1973) has elaborated this approach in his most recent book, proposing that personality traits selected by cultural pressures are duplicated in the

7. This research was made possible by the financial support of the National Institutes of Mental Health in a predoctoral fellowship (5 F1 MH–30, 956 BEH–B) and a field research grant in 1967–68 (1 TO1 MH 11236).

second generation through deliberate parental socialization. He also suggests that unplanned parental acts are simply accidental "slippage between environmental information and subsequent performance" (1973, pp. 105–106). Theories of child rearing under conditions of social change also employed concepts of parental mediators as transmitters of information about the changed environment to the children (Inkeles 1955; LeVine et al. 1967).

Thus as I developed my model for urban migrant child rearing I drew upon these basic concepts for elements which I sought to incorporate: (1) a group which could transmit new psychological traits to migrant mothers, (2) a series of psychological attributes indicating migrant assimilation, and (3) a mechanism for explaining the way in which these psychological attributes could influence maternal child rearing *behavior* so as to reflect her attempts to transmit the requirements of the new environment to her child (parental mediation of change to the second generation).

I had two major models I wished to test in the field. The first was an *Assimilation Model* predicting the direction of voluntary change among migrants. The concept of "acculturation" which Ted had only been able to measure crudely in his re-analysis of the Tri-Ethnic data could now be broken into component parts. When this was done the model ran as follows. Those mothers who had the most *exposure* to members of another culture, who chose them as their reference group for psychological *identification*, and who had more *access* to the goals of the other culture were expected to *adopt* the most norms, value orientations, and behavior relating to child rearing from that group. Urban mothers were hypothesized to be more likely to have high exposure, identification and access than rural mothers in a traditional setting.

The second model was a *Parental Mediation Model*. Rotter's social learning theory (1954) provided a good basis for understanding the mechanism by which maternal psychological attributes might influence choice of child rearing techniques. In the Rotter paradigm, the probability for the occurrence of a given behavior was dependent upon both *expectations* that the behavior would be rewarded and *values* attached to that reward. These cognitive variables seemed more likely to predict actual interaction between a mother and her child than the in depth personality variables frequently posed as determinants of child rearing. Furthermore, Rotter's concept of "internal control," a *generalized expectancy* that reward is contingent on one's own behavior rather than on external agents, was very similar to Inkeles' descriptions of the value-orientations of modern man.

The internal control concept, however, had most frequently been used in experimental situations in which a single actor was involved. In order to apply it to an interpersonal situation such as child rearing, I needed to modify it to reflect maternal perceptions of the second party to the interaction, the child himself. In my theory, maternal *expectations* of success in raising the type of child she valued (the reward) was therefore broken into two aspects: *Mother Efficacy* and *Child Potential*. Mother Efficacy concerned the degree to which a mother felt she was a capable and important influence upon whether the child turned out the way she wanted. This was an analogue to Rotter's internal control—a generalized expectancy for maternal success over the many situations arising in child rearing. Child Potential dealt with the degree to which a mother believed her child was capable of being influenced, molded, or taught—a generalized expectancy across the many different capabilities one might find in a preschool child. Mothers with low Mother Efficacy were conceived as generally expecting that *other* persons, agencies, or even chance events would be more influential or capable than they. Those with low Child Potential would expect children either to have intractable, inborn traits or to be too young (at ages three to six) to be trained to a prescribed pattern of the parent's choice.

The way in which internal control is related to behavior had been tested in a number of psychological experiments (Rotter, Liverant and Crowne 1961; Blackman 1962; Holden and Rotter 1962). These indicated that a task where a person believes the outcome is determined by his own actions will command more effort than one seen as dependent upon chance. I therefore predicted that high expectations of success in child rearing goals should be related to maternal behavior which reflected efforts to teach the child to become in the future the kind of person she preferred (future-oriented methods). On the other hand, low maternal expectations should lead to acts merely containing the child in the present or responding to mood (immediate-reactive methods).

This Parental Mediation Model not only provided a bridge between assimilation of Anglo psychological and behavioral traits, but it tested a general problem in socialization: the nature of the relationship between maternal attitudes and behavior. Regardless of the origin of expectations, whether adopted during culture contact or arisen from other sources, they should bear a lawful relation to certain kinds of child rearing.

Spanish-Americans seemed a particularly appropriate group with whom to test these models. "Fatalism" (a cultural value orientation which corresponded to expectations of "external control" in the Rotter paradigm) had long been claimed as a characteristic of Spanish-American and Mexican cultures as contrasted with Anglos (Kluckhohn and Strodtbeck 1961; Saunders 1954; Madsen 1964). The Tri-Ethnic project had supported this contrast, finding Spanish lower than Anglos on their measure of internal control (Jessor et al. 1968). Spanish were also said to be less future-oriented than Anglos (Kluckhohn and Strodtbeck 1961; Madsen 1964), a comparison again supported by Ted's use of the future-time perspective measure in the tri-ethnic setting (Graves 1962). Furthermore, in her two samples of these value orientations over a fifteen-year period, Florence Kluckhohn had found both these value-orientations shifting in an Anglo direction.[8]

I chose three groups to study in testing my change hypotheses: Urban lower-income Anglos—a potential new reference group in the city for Spanish lower-income mothers; Urban Spanish-Americans—the migrant group possibly assimilating Anglo traits; and Rural Spanish-Americans—a traditional group remaining behind in the area from which the Urban Spanish had migrated. I expected to find a continuum of norms, values, expectations and related behavior such that the Urban Anglos would be the least fatalistic group (highest in Mother Efficacy-Child Potential) and the most future-oriented in their child rearing, while the Rural Spanish would be the most fatalistic, with fewest Anglo norms and values and displaying the least amount of future-oriented child rearing. The Urban Spanish, if they had come to identify with Anglos by virtue of their increased exposure to this new reference group and access to Anglo material goals in the city, should fall somewhere in between in expectations, choice of Anglo norms, and future-oriented behavior. However, within the Spanish group as a whole, high expectations should be related to high use of teaching, future-oriented behavior.

Not being a member of a large team, I chose a three stage sampling technique which would provide a variety of kinds of data, a modicum of representativeness, and yet be possible for one researcher to handle. A survey interview was developed for the first and largest sample of sixty-six Spanish families. This structured interview included demographic data, two norm scales contrasting Spanish and Anglo norms of family life and child rearing, an identification scale (using personal preferences for voluntary activities considered more than mere accommodation to urban conditions, e.g., choice of language to speak at home, family meals, etc.), and an exposure scale indicating both type and amount of contact with Anglos. I controlled for socioeconomic status by choosing

8. Later Ted found similar evidence for psychological shifts related to acculturation in a cross-sectional analysis of the Tri-Ethnic data (T. Graves 1967b).

all lower-income families: an increase in access was assumed for Spanish moving to the city, which provided better job opportunities and more modern goods than were available to Spanish in the country.

Next, twenty Urban and Rural Spanish mothers who reflected in demographic characteristics the range and average of the larger sample were chosen for intensive study. A sample of ten Anglo families from the same neighborhoods as the Urban Spanish was chosen for comparison. The mothers in the three subsamples were visitied over a period of weeks or months and systematic observations made of their interaction with their preschool children. Each mother was observed for a minimum of three hours and over 1300 maternal actions were recorded per group. After observations were completed, the mothers were given an extensive, open-ended tape-recorded interview covering their child rearing values, expectations and methods. Fathers of these families were interviewed whenever possible.

Last of all, a third sample was drawn from the two Spanish groups for case studies which included a deeper analysis of their friendship networks, influences on their child rearing, and, where relevant, urban experiences.

I will describe the use and analysis of one of these multiple methods, the systematic observation technique, as I feel it contributed the most to my ultimate understanding. Although the majority of socialization studies have relied on parental reports of child rearing methods, I preferred a comparison of interview data with observation of actual interaction to discover, if possible, sources of distortion in retrospective reports (Yarrow, Campbell and Burton 1970; Freeberg and Payne 1967). Many psychologists were requesting more use of measures of overt behavior for the study of socialization (Wright 1960; Caldwell 1964), and I surveyed existing observation schemes. In the end, I developed one of my own which was relevant to the problem I wished to study, and which was at a level of inference less abstract than categories used in the Six Cultures Study (Whiting et al. 1953) yet less concrete than the ethological descriptions of Barker and Wright (1954).

This observation system consisted of a set of twenty-six content categories, each of which could be expressed in either a verbal or non-verbal mode and with positive, neutral, or negative emotional tone. Each category was applicable to either mother or child, and the combination of content, mode, and tone made possible the recording of over 300 logically possible acts. The code was recorded as a series of initiations and responses occurring in sequential order.

The concept of future-oriented behavior was operationalized as the use of actions aimed at teaching the child or giving him information for future guidance (e.g., instruction, explanation, teaching information and suggestion). Immediate-reactive behavior was indexed by actions aimed at simply controlling the child through parental power-assertion (e.g., command, threat). These two sets of categories reflected *instrumental* child rearing: what the mother did to get the child to do what she wanted. Other categories measured the *affective* dimension of child rearing, reflecting maternal warmth or coldness in both content and emotional tone. Additional categories were added to cover the major dimensions of maternal and child behavior discussed in socialization literature.

The categories were admittedly etic in origin—I had neither the time nor assistants who could help me develop emic ones. The fact that they were precoded made rescoring difficult, although I kept a descriptive record of the context of the acts whenever possible alongside the codes. However, the succinct code made possible the gathering of a great deal of information which otherwise would have been missed and was a great improvement over less systematic observation.[9] I was able to develop, with a fellow student, a high degree of reliability for these categories. In each case I visited the home a number of times, sometimes bringing my children with me, before recording interaction; and mothers expected that the behavior of their child was the object of study. They cooperated by following household routines to make the situation as normal as possible for the child.

In analyzing these data the twenty-six content categories were combined into larger syndromes, and individuals were given scores on the proportion of his or her total acts which represented a particular category or syndrome. This was done for mode and emotional tone as well. Because of the wealth of data, computer programs were developed to compile, test, and discover typical sequences of acts.[10]

The empirical results of this first study (N. Graves 1971; N. Graves n.d.) were quite disconcerting and forced me to reconceptualize my initial assimilation model. At first glance, Urban Spanish mothers could be said to be "assimilating" as I had expected. Spanish in the city

9. Some of these problems can be overcome by more sophisticated equipment. Now that small cassette tape recorders are available, I whisper into one of these—following a structured outline for descriptive details of context. These records are then transcribed and can be post-coded in a number of different ways. Another method we have developed is the two-stage process of open-ended and structured observations described in the concluding section of this paper.

10. Grateful appreciation is due the staff I worked with in the Mental Retardation Center of the Neuropsychiatric Institute of the University of California at Los Angeles for help in analyzing these data. Funds for this assistance were obtained from the California State Department of Mental Hygiene and Mental Retardation Center Grant HD–04612.

identified more highly with an Anglo reference group than did their country cousins, and they had a history of more extensive and intensive contact with Anglos (presumably providing an opportunity to learn their ways). As for economic access, almost all had come to find jobs for the father, and the mothers uniformly appreciated the modern conveniences of city life. However, these experiences and an increasing shift of reference group were *not* affecting their child rearing in the way the theory had predicted.

To begin with, Urban Spanish mothers were not adopting Anglo norms of family life and child rearing faster than Rural Spanish. In fact, my data suggested just the opposite; that the city was inhibiting the rate of norm adoption. The amount of identification and contact required to produce a given level of norm adoption was greater for mothers living in the city than for those in the country. Nor did norm adoption lead to much assimilation of Anglo-like expectations or behavior. Adoption of norms was not correlated with high expectations for success in child rearing and was only slightly or not at all related to child rearing behavior.

Most importantly, Urban Spanish mothers had *lower* expectations than did Rural Spanish mothers of being able to control the course of child rearing and achieve the type of child they valued: the more contact a Spanish mother had with Anglos, and the more highly she identified with them, the lower were her scores on Mother Efficacy and Child Potential. These expectations were reflected in child rearing behavior: the Urban Spanish mothers were using more immediate-reactive and fewer future-oriented methods than the Rural Spanish mothers. This was not due to imitation of a lower-class Anglo model. Anglo mothers in the same neighborhoods had higher expectations of success than either Urban or Rural Spanish, and were observed to use far more future-oriented methods than did either group. Thus the voluntary adoption predicted for the instrumental aspect of child rearing was not taking place despite some psychological assimilation in the form of a change in reference group.

I was also impressed by the differences between Rural and Urban Spanish in the affective aspect of maternal behavior, an area of child rearing likely to be involuntary and subconscious. Urban Spanish were far less warm, more cold, with their children. The more exposure to and identification with Anglos a Spanish mother had, the more likely she was to be cold and hostile with her children instead of warm and loving, and this tendency to be emotionally distant increased with the amount of time she had lived in the city.

The Parental Mediation Model, however, had stood up well. Consistently, those Spanish mothers with the highest Mother Efficacy and Child Potential were most likely to use future-oriented techniques and were lower in their use of power-assertive, immediate-reactive methods. Here were the germs of a theoretical reconceptualization. If change of reference group was leading to *lowered* feelings of control, at least two inferences could be made. First, the expectations measured were not simply value-orientations to be learned and adopted but probabilistic assessments of the objective situation and its rewards for the Urban Spanish. If low expectations had been traditional, Rural Spanish should have been more fatalistic, but they were more like Anglos than Urban Spanish. And Anglo-identifiers tended to become more fatalistic, not less.

Second, it was likely that the limited economic access found by moving to the city was not enough to allow Urban Spanish mothers to believe they would be assimilated into their chosen Anglo reference group. This inference was supported by material from the exposure measure, the father interviews, and the case studies. While many Urban Spanish had worked with or been in school with Anglos, none had Anglo friends who invited them to their homes. It appeared that the more one had peripheral but not intimate contact with Anglos, and yearned to be like them, the more rejected one felt when denied *social access* to their group.

However, there was an alternative explanation that was equally compelling. The constraints of city life (crowding, danger for small children, etc.) might account for the lowered expectations and high use of power-assertive techniques as well as the involuntary emotional reactions observed. The length of time a Spanish mother had been in the city was at least as highly correlated with these child rearing variables as were the acculturation variables of identification and exposure. It now seemed crucial to separate theoretically the change processes of urbanization and acculturation in order to determine the influences of each upon child rearing. In practical terms, however, these processes were inextricably mixed for the Spanish, who had no opportunity to migrate to an all Spanish American city.

At this point (1967) Ted and I were given an opportunity to go to East Africa, and it seemed a perfect chance for me to test both the generality of the Parental Mediation Model within another culture and to straighten out the combined influences of urbanization and acculturation upon the Spanish. I now developed a model of individual responses to acculturation encompassing two major dimensions: Voluntary-Involuntary and Adoptive-Reactive (see Figure 4). Assimilation,

FIGURE 4
ALTERNATIVE RESPONSES TO ACCULTURATION SITUATIONS

ADOPTIVE

Voluntary Adoption

  Assimilation
   Exposure
   Identifcation
   Access
   Adoption

Involuntary Adoption

  Accommodation
   Instrumental adaptation
   Superficial adoption
   Role segmentation
   Situational personality

VOLUNTARY————————————————————INVOLUNTARY

Voluntary Reaction

  Reaffirmation of
   own culture group
  Revitalization or
   nativistic
   movements
  Isolating mechanisms

Involuntary Reaction

  Psychological withdrawal,
   low expectations, apathy,
   retreatism, alienation, or
   hostility
  Value and belief conflicts
  Role shifts
  Anti-social behavior

REACTIVE

under this model, was seen as only one type of adaptive response to a culture contact situation, i.e., Voluntary-Adoption. These responses are not mutually exclusive categories; a person in an acculturative situation can simultaneously or sequentially display alternative types of response. The lowered expectation and disturbed emotional relations I had observed among Spanish mothers could be classed as involuntary reactions to minority group status. A Voluntary-Reactive response was also taking place in the form of a revitalization movement among people of Spanish heritage calling themselves Chicanos, but at the time of my research, this had not taken hold among the families I visited.

I also reconceptualized urbanization and modernization along these same dimensions, and devised ways to separate all three change processes conceptually and operationally (N. Graves n.d., Chapter 4). My proposed research strategy was as follows: if an urbanizing but unacculturating African group could be found I could attempt to discover whether rural-urban shifts in child rearing among them were similar in *type, magnitude,* and *extent* to those found among Spanish Americans. To the degree that rural-urban differences were *similar* to those of the Spanish, *urbanization* could be surmised as the cause. To the degree that there were *differences* between the Spanish and African shifts in attitudes and behavior, those differences might be ascribed, at least in part, to the minority group status and lack of social access of the Spanish in an *acculturation* situation.

The Baganda of Uganda, East Africa, were finally chosen for this comparative study.[11] Baganda families were migrating to Kampala, a city similar in size to Denver, and various aspects of their urbanization had already been studied (Gutkind 1956, 1962; Southall and Gutkind 1956; Southall 1967). Most importantly for my theory, Baganda were the major culture group in the Kampala region, and at that time had long been dominant in national affairs. Writers had commented on the Baganda sense of pride in their own cultural traditions, and pointed out their ability to absorb modern influences without sacrificing the values or psychological characteristics associated with Baganda culture (Fallers and Musoke 1964; Doob 1957). In short, the Baganda did not seem likely to be undergoing any of the voluntary or involuntary aspects of acculturation with respect to the Anglo-Europeans resident in Kampala, and they usually looked down on other African groups, who were forced to "Ganda-ize" (Gutkind 1956).

In Kampala I chose a section of the city, Katwe, which was mainly Baganda and which had predominantly lower-income families. In a preliminary survey I discovered that most of the families with preschool children came from the Masaka district, about one hundred miles southwest of the city. I then found a village around fourteen miles from Masaka in which to work as well. With the help of staff and students from Makerere Institute of Social Research I developed measures which were comparable in concept, but not identical in content, to the scales used in the American study.[12] For this study I was able to find assistants to help with the observations who taught me the nuances of maternal behavior and emotions, and who helped translate the verbal content of the mothers' behavior. The same sampling procedures and organization of measures were used as in America, and the study in Uganda lasted approximately one year.

When the results were analyzed, I found that as suspected the

11. The Makerere Institute of Social Research provided working facilities and authorization for my research in Uganda, and I am thankful for the considerable help given me by its faculty and staff.

12. All verbal measures were back-translated twice for accuracy.

Baganda lower-income mothers had almost no exposure to Anglos and did not identify with them at all. Rural and Urban Baganda were no different in their norms of child rearing, but they differed strongly in the type of child they valued, in their expectations of success in getting such a child, and in their use of future-oriented techniques. In general, the more urban experience a Baganda mother had, the less control she felt and the fewer future-oriented, teaching methods she employed with her children. Thus, when I compared the Baganda and Spanish data I was able to make the generalization that urban living for first generation migrants was associated with a lowering of expectations for successful child rearing results, and a concomitant lessening of efforts to influence the child in a desired direction by deliberately teaching him. Both Baganda and Spanish mothers complained of crowded city conditions indoors and out, of physical dangers and bad social influences, and of urban "pleasures" which lured the fathers away from home. They were left alone to cope with the household and small children more often than in the country setting, and this may have lent to a "harassment" syndrome, since for both groups the effect on child rearing was more strong the more preschool children the mother had in the home.

Nevertheless, despite these similarities, the theory linking maternal expectations and behavior worked itself out differently for the two culture groups. The Urban Baganda mainly had low expectations of being able to follow through in their personal influence on the child (Mother Efficacy), while the Urban Spanish mainly lowered their estimations of what preschool children were capable of learning and doing (Child Potential). This is explicable on the basis of the material from the open-ended interviews and case studies from the two cultures. Baganda mothers were in an extremely insecure economic position in the city, whereas in the country they had been the main providers for the family. Kampala mothers complained that husbands could leave on a whim and get a new wife; there were many unattached women in the city. The mothers had no recourse to welfare funds, and the new wife would bring up the children, who by law belonged to the father.

Both urban groups lowered their expectations concerning the degree of domestic help a child was capable of performing compared to rural mothers.[13] But for the Baganda this drop was partially compensated for by high expectations of academic success and high estimates of children's receptivity to training, while Spanish mothers had no such compensating expectations for their children. Urban Baganda children had more opportunities for formal schooling than they would in the

13. Clignet (1967) found the same result among two West African tribes.

country, and though their mothers had only three years of education on the average, they often taught their children the rudiments of reading since the first years of school were conducted in Luganda. Urban Spanish, however, although averaging eleven years of school, felt insecure about their children's learning abilities and they seldom sought to teach them academic things. In the interview they emphasized the importance of education even less than the Rural Spanish. Schooling, usually under conditions where speaking Spanish was forbidden, had been for them an exercise in personal failure and deprivation. The more years of school Spanish mothers had, the lower their expectations of success for themselves and their children, while the opposite effect was found for the Baganda, for whom education was a key to modern opportunities rather than an acculturation experience.

The major point I wish to make by explicating this example at some length is that efforts to reflect the interactive nature of a psychological variable (expectations) by measuring two aspects of a single concept (locus of control) paid off by supporting a general principle of relationships between attitudes and behavior. If I had measured only one type of expectations with respect to child rearing, either Mother Efficacy or Child Potential, I would not have adequately understood the situation among these two groups of urban mothers nor would I have had a good case for cross-cultural validation of the Parental Mediation Model.

I also would not have found such a validation if I had only used reports of child rearing behavior. In the Spanish case, reported and observed future-oriented methods both correlated with expected results in the same way (i.e., mothers who had high expectations for themselves and their children also tended to report many future-oriented methods as well as to use them). But the Baganda show *no* relationship between what they said they did with their children, and what I observed directly. Consequently, the relationship between Mother Efficacy and reported methods was zero, and the correlation between reports and Child Potential was opposite to the direction predicted.

Despite the Baganda and Spanish similarities in direction of rural to urban changes, my suspicion that the acculturation situation played a role in influencing Urban Spanish child rearing did not go unsupported. On every measure indicating involuntary reactions to change except Mother Efficacy, the Spanish showed shifts of greater magnitude and extent than did the Baganda. First, Urban Baganda, while decreasing future-oriented methods to a lesser extent than did Urban Spanish, showed only a slight tendency to increase their power-assertive techniques with time spent in the city. Not only did Urban Spanish use considerably more power-assertion than Rural Spanish, they began to evaluate obedience more highly, yet expected that their children would be less capable of obeying them than did country Spanish mothers. (In fact, Urban Spanish children were observed to be *more* compliant, on the average, than Rural Spanish children!)

Urban migration showed no consistent effect on Baganda affectional relations with their children. In general, Baganda mothers showed rather neutral emotional tone, though some few were especially harsh or loving in each setting. Urban Spanish, on the other hand, seemed more irritable or upset with their children than Rural Spanish, who were more relaxed and tolerant.

In addition, time spent in the city had a direct effect on both instrumental and affective behavior, independent of feelings of control, that was much larger for the Spanish than for the Baganda. All of this evidence indicates, I feel, a deprivating effect of culture contact beyond the pressures of urban living common to both groups.

My model had evolved from one emphasizing the voluntary, deliberate aspects of child training to one in which involuntary but *non-random* reactions predominated. The importance of non-deliberate socialization was early apparent from the observations of mother-child interaction since even among Urban Anglos future-oriented, teaching behavior accounted for only 20 percent of their actions, while for the Urban Spanish this dropped to 7 percent. This unplanned component is of significance not only for child rearing but for other responses to culture contact and change: drinking and drunkenness for example. Involuntary reactions are nevertheless adaptations to realistic assessments of measurable aspects of the contact situation and need to be given greater attention in our theories of change processes.

TED AND NANCY GRAVES—MIGRATION
AND CHANGE IN THE SOUTH PACIFIC

Reviewing the progress of our research, we see ourselves outgrowing a series of theoretical and methodological shells. With each successive study new concepts have been added, and old ones differentiated. Simple unilinear models have given way to more complex ones, containing interaction effects and feedback loops (T. and N. Graves *1974a*). And there has been a steady shift away from the theory testing format which guided our earlier research towards strategies which include more opportunities for theoretical serendipity. Our goal is a better mix of inductive and deductive processes, of qualitative and quantitative data.

As we strive today to build a joint approach to research based on the results of earlier studies and the confluence of our particular styles, we have attempted to select a setting where relatively neglected factors can be given greater research attention. Our field of study is again an acculturating, modernizing and urbanizing group from a non-Western tradition: Cook Island migrants to Auckland, New Zealand.[14] In our previous research the economic and social marginality of our subjects seemed over-determining. In New Zealand, with its strong ethic against racial discrimination and its many opportunities for unskilled labor, we hope to have found a contact situation where economic and social access for migrants is more variable. Then other factors in the adjustment process can assume greater prominence.

Migration involves adaptive changes within three distinct groups: the migrants themselves, the host community they are entering, and the home communities from which they come (N. Graves and T. Graves 1974). In our previous work we have devoted most of our attention to the migrants themselves. But adaptations going on within the host community interlock with and affect migrant adaptations. At the conclusion of her study, for example, Nancy keenly felt a lack of adequate data on the mechanisms of social rejection by the Anglo reference group in their effects on migrant expectations and aspirations. We began our present program of research therefore, with a study of white New Zealanders (Pakeha), their attitudes toward various migrant groups, especially Polynesians (T. Graves and N. Graves, forthcoming), and the behavior they exhibit in various settings where contact with Polynesians normally takes place (N. Graves and T. Graves 1973). Presently we are conducting field work in one of the Cook Islands where out-migration is proceeding apace, to document its effects on the home community.

In our previous research a good deal of time was devoted to participant observation and the collection of in depth case studies. But the purpose of this work was not to suggest new theoretical direction, although that sometimes occurred. Rather, as Ted liked to say at that time, it was "to put flesh on the bones of our statistical analyses" and to provide a sounder basis for their interpretation. In retrospect, this seems a too limited use of these traditional anthropological field methods. The problem with qualitative techniques such as these is that they do not clearly indicate what the next step in the research should be. What is needed is some framework for the use of both qualitative and quantitative techniques for systematic theory-generating (Glaser and Strauss 1967). In our current studies we are attempting to formulate such a

14. We wish to thank the Royal Society of New Zealand for their support of our current research.

framework. We began by sampling widely a range of cross-ethnic contact situations, using unstructured narrative descriptions, in order to discover potentially significant theoretical categories. Their relevance and appropriateness is then being tested using more systematic procedures within a limited range of contrasting situations. This is followed by a return to more open-ended data collection aimed at discovering possible antecedents and consequences of each new concept, in order to begin mapping these into a system of theoretical relationships. Finally, this emergent theory will have to be tested through a return to more structured data gathering.

As one example, over one hundred students were trained to observe in a wide range of urban situations and write narrative reports including features of physical setting, context, and interpersonal behavior. One finding was that Pakeha and Polynesians appeared to differ in their preference for an individual versus a group style of interaction. Systematic observational measures of this style were then developed and applied within school settings selected to represent wide variation in ethnic mix (N. Graves and T. Graves, forthcoming). We are presently exploring the antecedents of this behavioral style in the experience of Polynesians in an island community, and will later examine its consequences in the European-dominated urban setting with respect to migrant choices among adaptive strategies such as kin-dependency.

In the course of investigating adaptation to contact and change, our awareness of what is yet to be explained has grown. This could lead to intellectual paralysis, a cry for help as the scholar sinks beneath the weight of his increasingly complex models. Our own adaptive strategy is to choose areas for intensive study which represent major gaps in our knowledge rather than simply to replicate previous measures and models in our present research.

REFERENCES CITED

Alfred, B. M.
    1965   Acculturative Stress among Navajo Migrants to Denver, Colorado. Ph.D. dissertation, University of Colorado.
Barker, R. G. and Wright, H. F.
    1954   *Midwest and its Children.* Evanston, Illinois: Row Peterson.
Beals, R. L.
    1951   Urbanism, Urbanization and Acculturation. *American Anthropologist* 53: 1–10.

Berreman, G. D.
  1964   Aleut Reference Group Alienation, Mobility, and Acculturation. *American Anthropologist* 66:231–50.

Blackman, S.
  1962   Some Factors Affecting the Perception of Events as Chance Determined. *Journal of Psychology* 54:197–202.

Caldwell, B. M.
  1964   The Effects of Infant Care. In *Review of Child Development Research*, vol. 1, pp. 9–88. New York: Russell Sage Foundation.

Campbell, D. T. and Stanley, J. C.
  1966   *Experimental and Quasi-Experimental Designs for Research.* Chicago: Rand McNally.

Chance, N. A.
  1960   Culture Change and Integration: An Eskimo Example. *American Anthropologist* 62:1028–44.

Clignet, R.
  1967   Environmental Change, Types of Descent and Child Rearing Practices. In *The City in Modern Africa*, ed. H. Miner, pp. 257–96. New York: Praeger.

Doob, L. W.
  1957   An Introduction to the Psychology of Acculturation. *Journal of Social Psychiatry* 45:143–60.

Fallers, L. A. and Musoke, S.B.K.
  1964   Social Mobility, Traditional and Modern. In *The King's Men*, ed. L. A. Fallers, pp. 158–210. London and New York: Oxford University Press.

Freeberg, N. E. and Payne, D. T.
  1967   Parental Influence on Cognitive Development in Early Childhood: A Review. *Child Development* 38:65–87.

Glaser, B. G. and Strauss, A. L.
  1967   *The Discovery of Grounded Theory: Strategies for Qualitative Research.* Chicago: Aldine Publishing Co.

Graves, N. B.
  1971   City, Country, and Child Rearing: A Tri-Cultural Study of Mother-Child Relationships in Varying Environments. Doctoral thesis, Department of Anthropology, University of Colorado, Boulder, Colorado. University Microfilms.

  n.d.   *City, Country and Child Rearing: Cross-National Observations of Mother-Child Interaction.* Westport, Connecticut: Redgrave Publishing Co., forthcoming.

Graves, N. B. and Graves, T. D.
  1973   Culture Shock in Auckland: Pakeha Responses to Polynesian Immigrants. Paper read for the Dean's Lecture, Auckland Medical School.

  1974   Adaptive Strategies in Urban Migration. In *Annual Review of Anthropology*, ed. B. Siegel. Palo Alto: Annual Reviews Inc.

  n.d.   Inclusive versus Exclusive Behavior in New Zealand School Settings: Polynesian-Pakeha Contrasts in Adaptation. Research report to the Royal Society of New Zealand, submitted for publication.

Graves, T. D.
  1962   Time Perspective and the Deferred Gratification Pattern in a Tri-Ethnic

Community. Ph.D. dissertation, University of Pennsylvania, Dissertation Abstracts, vol. 23, p. 1161.

1966   Alternative Models for the Study of Urban Migration. *Human Organization* 25:295–99. Reprinted in *The Sociology of the North American Indians,* ed. J. H. Marsh. Toronto: McClelland and Stewart.

1967a   Acculturation, Access and Alcohol in a Tri-Ethnic Community. *American Anthropologist* 69:306–21.

1967b   Psychological Acculturation in a Tri-Ethnic Community. *Southwestern Journal of Anthropology* 23:337–50.

1970   The Personal Adjustment of Navajo Indian Migrants to Denver, Colorado. *American Anthropologist* 72:35–54. Reprinted in *Native Americans Today: Sociological Perspectives,* eds. H. M. Bahr, B.A. Chadwick, and R.C. Day. New York: Harper and Row, 1972, pp. 440–66.

1973   The Navajo Urban Migrant and his Psychological Situation. *Ethos* 1:321–42.

1974   Urban Indian Personality and the "Culture of Poverty." *American Ethnologist* 1:65–86.

n.d.   *There But For Grace: A Social-Psychological Study of Urban Indian Drunkenness,* forthcoming.

Graves, T. D. and Graves, N. B.

1974a   Social-Psychological Factors in Urban Migrant Adaptation. *Proceedings: Conference on Migration and Related Social and Health Problems in New Zealand and the Pacific.* Sponsored by the Wellington Postgraduate Medical Society and the Epidemiology Unit, Wellington Hospital, Wellington, New Zealand.

1974b   As Others See Us: Inter-Ethnic Perceptions in New Zealand. *Proceedings: Lecture Series on Race Relations and Attitudes in New Zealand in Relation to Foreign Policy.* Wellington: New Zealand Institute of International Affairs.

Graves, T. D. and Lave, C. A.

1972   Determinants of Urban Migrant Indian Wages. *Human Organization* 31:47–62.

Graves, T. D. and VanArsdale, M.

1966   Values, Expectations and Relocation: The Navajo Indian Migrant to Denver. *Human Organization* 25:300–07.

Gutkind, P. C. W.

1956   Town Life in Buganda. *Uganda Journal* 20:37–46.

1962   African Urban Family Life. *Cahiers d'Etudes Africaines* 3:149–217.

Holden, K. B. and Rotter, J. B.

1962   A Nonverbal Measure of Extinction in Skill and Chance Situations. *Journal of Experimental Psychology* 63:519–20.

Hughes, C. C.

1957   Reference Group Concepts in the Study of a Changing Eskimo Culture. In *Cultural Stability and Cultural Change,* ed. V. F. Ray, pp. 7–14. American Ethnological Society.

Inkeles, A.

1955   Social Change and Social Character: The Role of Parental Mediation. *Journal of Social Issues* 11:12–23.

1966   The Modernization of Man. In *Modernization*, ed. M. Weiner. New York: Basic Books.

Jessor, R., Graves, T. D., Hanson, R. C., and Jessor, S. L.
1968   *Society, Personality, and Deviant Behavior: A Study of a Tri-Ethnic Community*. New York: Holt, Rinehart and Winston.

1970   Perceived Opportunity, Alienation and Drinking Behavior among Italian and American Youth. *Journal of Personality and Social Psychology* 15:215–22.

Kaplan, A.
1964   *The Conduct of Inquiry: Methodology for Behavioral Science*. San Francisco: Chandler Publishing Company.

Kluckhohn, F. R. and Strodtbeck, F. O.
1961   *Variations in Value Orientations*. Evanston, Illinois: Row, Peterson and Co.

LeVine, R. A.
1973   *Culture, Behavior, and Personality: An Introduction to the Comparative Study of Psychological Adaptation*. Chicago: Aldine Publishing Co.

MacAndrew, C. and Edgerton, R.
1969   *Drunken Comportment: A Social Explanation*. Chicago: Aldine Publishing Co.

McClelland, D. C. et al.
1958   A Scoring Manual for the Achievement Motive. In *Motives in Fantasy, Action, and Society*, ed. J. W. Atkinson. Princeton, New Jersey: D. Van Nostrand.

McCracken, R. D.
1968   Urban Migration and the Changing Structure of Navajo Social Relations. Ph.D. dissertation, University of Colorado, University Microfilms.

McSwain, R.
1965   The Role of Wives in the Urban Adjustment of Navajo Migrant Families to Denver, Colorado. Masters thesis, University of Hawaii.

Madsen, W.
1964   *The Mexican-American of South Texas*. New York: Holt, Rinehart, and Winston.

Merton, R. K.
1949   Social Structure and Anomie. In *Social Theory and Social Structure*. Glencoe: The Free Press.

Michener, B. P.
1971   The Development, Validation and Applications of a Test for Need-Achievement Motivation among American Indian High School Students. Ph.D. dissertation, University of Colorado, University Microfilms.

Morrison, D. E. and Henkel, R. E., eds.
1970   *The Significance Test Controversy: A Reader*. Chicago: Aldine Publishing Co.

Officer, J. E.
1971   The American Indian and Federal Policy. In *The American Indian in Urban Society*, eds. J. O. Waddell and O. M. Watson, pp. 9–65. Boston: Little Brown.

Rendón, G., Jr.
1968   Prediction of Adjustment Outcomes of Rural Migrants to the City. Ph.D. dissertation, University of Colorado, University Microfilms.

Rotter, J. B.
   1954   *Social Learning and Clinical Psychology.* Englewood Cliffs, New Jersey: Prentice Hall.

Rotter, J. B., Liverant, S., and Crowne, D. P.
   1961   The Growth and Extinction of Expectancies in Chance Controlled and Skilled Tests. *Journal of Psychology* 52:161–77.

Saunders, L.
   1954   *Cultural Differences and Medical Care: The Case of the Spanish-Speaking People of the Southwest.* New York: Russell Sage Foundation.

Snyder, P. Z.
   1968   Social Assimilation and Adjustment of Navajo Migrants to Denver, Colorado. Ph.D. dissertation, University of Colorado, University Microfilms.

   1971   The Social Environment of the Urban Indian. In *The American Indian in Urban Society,* eds. J. O. Waddell and O. M. Watson. Boston: Little, Brown, and Company.

   1973   Social Interaction Patterns and Relative Urban Success: The Denver Navajo. *Urban Anthropology* 2:1–24.

Southall, A. W.
   1967   Kampala-Mengo. In *The City in Modern Africa,* ed. H. Miner, pp. 297–332. New York: Praeger.

Southall, A. W. and Gutkind, P. C. W.
   1956   Townsmen in the Making. *Kampala: East Africa Institute of Social Research, East African Studies No. 9.*

Weinstein, R.
   1973   *Native Americans in Rural and Urban Poverty.* Austin: Center for the Study of Human Resources, University of Texas.

Weppner, R. S.
   1968   The Economic Absorption of Navajo Indian Migrants to Denver, Colorado. Ph.D. dissertation, University of Colorado, University Microfilms.

   1971   Urban Economic Opportunities: The Example of Denver. In *The American Indian in Urban Society,* eds. J. O. Waddell and O. M. Watson. Boston: Little, Brown and Co.

   1972   Socioeconomic Barriers to Assimilation of Navajo Migrant Workers. *Human Organization* 31(3):303–14.

Whiting, J. et al.
   1953   *Field Manual for the Cross-Cultural Study of Child Rearing.* New York: Social Science Research Council.

Wright, H. F.
   1960   Observational Child Study. In *Handbook of Research Methods in Child Development,* ed. Paul H. Mussen, pp. 71–139. New York: John Wiley and Sons.

Yarrow, M. R.
   1963   Problems of Methods in Parent-Child Research. *Child Development* 34:215–26.

Yinger, J. M.
  1965   *Toward a Field Theory of Behavior.* New York: McGraw-Hill.
Ziegler, S.
  1967   An Urban Dilemma: The Case of Tyler Begay. Unpublished research report, Navajo Urban Relocation Research, University of Colorado.

The Author

VICTOR TURNER, born in Glasgow, Scotland, is Professor of Social Thought and Anthropology at the University of Chicago, having taught previously in England at Manchester University. Earlier he was research officer at the Rhodes-Livingstone Institute in Northern Rhodesia (now Zambia) where he did field work for almost two and one-half years among the Ndembu, a Lunda-speaking people. In addition to membership in the Royal Anthropological Institute (Rivers Memorial Medal, 1965) and the Association of Social Anthropologists of the Commonwealth, he is also a member of the American Academy of Arts and Sciences, the American Anthropological Association, and the International African Institute and was a Fellow of the Center for Advanced Study of the Behavioral Sciences and of the Society for the Humanities. His books include *Schism and Continuity in an African Society* (1957), *The Forest of Symbols* (1967), *The Drums of Affliction* (1968), *The Ritual Process* (1969), *Dramas, Fields, and Metaphors: Essays in Comparative Symbology* (1974), and *Revelation and Divination in Ndembu Ritual* (1975).

Turner's earlier investigation of social structures and processes in preliterate societies has yielded place to the comparative investigation of the semiotics both of cultural action genres (life-crisis, seasonal and therapeutic rituals; carnivals, charivaris, festivals and spectacles; pilgrimages; revolutionary scenarios), and literary and artistic genres (epic, romance, drama, poetry, the novel, iconography, architectural forms, etc.), in preindustrial, industrializing and post-industrial societies of varying scale and complexity. He is particularly interested in liminal or marginal phenomena, and in working collaboratively at the interface of disciplines: anthropology, depth psychology, semiotics, social history, sociology, and literary criticism.

This Chapter

For Victor Turner a flat description of ritual does not express its transformative capacity, the spontaneity present in most ritual, the responsiveness to present circumstances or its competence to interpret current situations and provide viable ways of coping with contemporary problems. He warns that our own culture misconstrues the nature of ritual because it is so deeply influenced by the Protestant Reformation which condemned Catholic ritual as empty "formalism" and by cultural Darwinism which regards ritual as "survivals" from the past. He points out that each type of ritual has its own idiosyncratic pattern in symbolic forms and actions that cannot be explained either by abstract structural principles or by factional or personal conflicts and that arrays of nonverbal symbols exceed verbal accounts by ten times in his field data—only a fraction of which could be related to social structure as the regular British functionalist rationalism would believe that it could. For Turner there are "hundreds, even thousands" of distinguishable symbolic objects and actions in rituals that seem to have little or nothing to do with social structure.

These insights are a result of his two and one-half years of field work with the Ndembu of Northwestern Zambia, but it was not until his re-encounter with Freud that the present style of his symbolic analysis began to emerge. He rediscovered Freud after "twenty years of latency." This re-encounter opened his eyes, as he puts it, to the fact that certain important kinds of symbols in ritual are multireferent—that is they have a "large number of significations." This recognition brought him then to the pursuit of multivocality, polarity, sublimation, the repression and situational suppression of meaning, and to the metasocial commentary characteristic of many rituals. In these analyses, he uses, metaphorically and analogically, the Freudian concepts of sublimation, repression and the unconscious, defense mechanisms and projections and the central recognition of multireferentiality. It is not that he takes Freud whole but rather derives a style of thinking from the Freudian pursuit of insight.

These are remarkable discoveries for a man who was trained within the framework of British functionalist rationalism. The emergence and development of his style of symbolic analysis is the schematic basis for this chapter. It also contains some descriptive data he has never published before.

G.D.S.

16　Encounter with Freud: The Making of a Comparative Symbologist

VICTOR TURNER

PROBLEMS IN THE ANALYSIS OF RITUAL SYMBOLS

Each human culture has its own form and style, and these insist upon being recognized by the anthropological fieldworker. The Ndembu of Northwestern Zambia, among whom I did about two and one-half years' fieldwork, from 1950 to 1954, invested much time, energy and wealth in the performance of various kinds of ritual. I had entered the field as an orthodox British structural-functionalist, motivated by my mentors to collect data on social organization. But the genius of the culture gently nudged me towards the description and analysis of ritual behavior. At first, of course, I thought that I had adequate conceptual instruments for this task in the repertoire inherited from Comte and Feuerbach via Durkheim, Radcliffe-Brown, and Malinowski; the rich legacy of confluent positivism, materialism, and rationalism. In effect, these scholars held that ritual symbols and processes "reflected" or "expressed" social structure, and that social structure was a more or less distinctive arrangement of mutually dependent institutions, and the institutional organization of social positions and/or actors which they imply. But I was immediately confronted with the difficulty that many of the hundreds, even thousands of distinguishable symbolic objects and actions I found in ritual performances seemed on the face of it to have little, if anything, directly to do with components of social structure as defined above. And it was no use ignoring this aggregate of individual symbols and declaring that at any rate the "implicit aim" or "latent function" of ritual was "to promote or restore social cohesion" and "to reanimate the sentiments of solidarity on which the collective life depends"—if I may paraphrase and coalesce dicta on ritual by the distinguished ancestors I have just cited. The specificity of each symbol and their shifting combinations and permutations in performative ensembles presented a challenge I could scarcely avoid.

A PERFORMANCE OF HUNTING RITUAL

Let me give an example here of an extremely simple Ndembu ritual performance. It is not uncommon to see an Ndembu hunter standing before a forked tree branch known as *chishing'a*, peeled of bark, planted in the earth, its extremities sharpened, and adorned with small portions of meat (on the tips or in the crotches). If you listen you will hear him upbraiding a dead hunter kinsman whom he believes to be somehow present in the *chishing'a*, which we may perhaps translate as a "shrine," for failing to bring him animals to kill, or even for positively driving them from his path. There is no question here of a public collective ceremony; just a private individual apparently talking to himself before a mutilated tree outside his village. But when we begin to learn the cultural vocabulary and to grasp its "syntactical rules," we shall find that we are in the presence of quite an elaborate system of beliefs and practices.[1] Moreover, we will discover that the curious monologue we have intruded upon is really only a phase or episode in a sequence of ritual activities, some of which involve a few cocelebrants and fellow hunters of our irate friend, and others a large concourse of persons of both sexes and all ages, only a few of them hunters. Furthermore, we shall note that these ritual episodes are intermittent, broken by tracts of non-ritualized time, in which a hunter goes off into the uninhabited woodlands and plains in search of game, and his fellow villagers pursue their ordinary avocations. But let us, for the sake of analytical parsimony, focus on the simple episode first mentioned. It is this kind of behavior which induced me in an earlier work (*Forest of Symbols*, 1967, p. 19) to follow a well-worn anthropological tradition and define ritual as "prescribed formal behavior for occasions not given over to technological routine, having reference to mystical beings or powers." Prescription and formality are to be found in the manner in which the shrine is constructed and in the hortatory style of address to the shade of the deceased. The hunter is not employing the technological routine of his craft, and he is addressing an entity whom he believes to "exist" although not as ordinary living men exist—for the

---

1. For an analysis of *chishing'a* symbolism, see my *Forest of Symbols*, pp. 285–98, Cornell University Press, 1967.

addressee is dead though sentient, invisible though potent. But my formulation, I have come to see, is anything but adequate. It is a flat description of ritual action as it appears to an alien observer and says nothing about what ritual means to a native actor. Nor does it capture the transformative capacity of ritual, its competency, from the actor's standpoint, to raise him from a lower to a higher level of knowledge, understanding, or social being. Nor does it correctly characterize the component of spontaneity present in most ritual, its responsiveness to present circumstance and its competence to interpret the current situation and provide viable ways of coping with contemporary problems. Probably our own culture has misconstrued the nature of ritual because it has been influenced, on the one hand, by the Protestant Reformation which condemned Catholic ritual as mere empty "formalism," and, on the other, by cultural Darwinism, which regarded ritual as a "survival" of formerly functional behavior patterns, which have become irrelevant to present circumstances. If anthropology has taught us anything, it is to be wary of taking anything for granted, especially the axiomatic values of our own particular cultural heritage. If man is to make a metalanguage, he must have exhaustive knowledge of all the languages—and by language I mean nonverbal as well as verbal means of communication, for men everywhere exploit the total sensorium for their communicative codes. Sight, smell, touch, taste, and kinetic experience are exploited for their symbolic wealth, as well as hearing (for speech demands an ear, without which tongue and palate would be "lodged with us useless").

This digression is necessary to prepare us for the particularities of the "simple" ritual act I described above, for we are dealing with a sequence of symbolic actions framed by a subsystem of symbols which is itself encompassed by a more inclusive system. In the first place, no Ndembu can lay claim to being a hunter outside a context of cult membership. Practical performance may be a necessary, but it is not a sufficient, condition of entry into "huntsmanship." But an anthropologist cannot know this until he has achieved sufficient linguistic proficiency to ask members of the culture about the what, why, and wherefore of the witnessed ritual acts. This was my first "narcissistic wound" (to use Freud's telling phrase). For one of the implicit rules of my training had been that native behavior was to be explained by Western theory. The possibility that there were indigenous taxonomies and even "metalanguages" was not then taken very seriously. But some anthropologists, in Central Africa, notably Godfrey Wilson, Monica Wilson, and Audrey Richards, had, in fact, strongly counselled anthropological neophytes to take seriously "the inside view" provided by native informants of their own culture. Even before I spent six months at the University of Cape Town, discussing my data with Monica Wilson herself, I had read her articles urging ethnographers to collect native interpretations of the symbols in their own rituals. I therefore began to enquire of Ndembu who were patently interested in what they were doing in ritual situations and prepared to talk about it, how they interpreted the objects, gestures, actions, and relationships between persons and things, manifested in ritual contexts. There was enough agreement between informants whom I considered intelligent to suggest that their explanations were not merely idiosyncratic (like responses to a Rorschach test), but were, within specifiable limits, collectively transmitted and held. I could now make much more sense out of the hunter's monologue before the hunter's shrine.

SHRINES AND CULTS

To begin with, the shrines were revealed to be of different kinds and I came across them in different locales set in different types of terrain. Some were in the village at a little distance from the hunter's hut and were often elaborate and quasi-permanent ("quasi" because villages moved about every five years under the exigencies of "slash-and-burn" or "swidden" cultivation). Others were set on large termite hills (often fifteen feet high), others near crossroads. I found that these differences were associated with different types of ritual processes within the generic hunters' cult. This cult is divided into main branches: the Bow-Hunters' Cult *(Wubinda)* and the Gun-Hunters' Cult *(Wuyang'a)*. The first branch has deep ancestry, the second, Ndembu say, was introduced by Ovimbundu slave traders from the Angola coast in the latter half of the nineteenth century, who brought muzzle-loading guns to trade for slaves (to be sold to the Portuguese who used them in plantation labor well after the international interdiction on this traffic). The Bow-Hunters' Cult was an assemblage of five rites: *Mukala, Chitampakasa, Kalombu, Mundeli,* and *Ntambu.* The Gun-Hunters' Cult was a graded series of four rites, each of which indicated the attainment of a certain degree of proficiency both in killing animals and in esoteric knowledge of the cult mysteries. The Bow-Hunters' Cult was dominated by the idiom of affliction. It was concerned with the native explanation of misfortune in the chase. Each of the named rites referred to a different kind of hunter's problem: the absence of game from part of the forest where they would normally be expected *(Chitampakasa);* the sudden bolting of a herd of antelope before the hunter could get within range *(Mukala);* the mysterious missing of one's aim *(Ntambu),* etc. Again, each connoted a different malignant manifestation of a deceased hunter ancestor: *Mukala* appears in dreams, is short in stature, wears a dress of skins or leaves, manifests himself by whistling in the bush or as a marsh-light misleading hunters into swamps, and rides the leading animal of a herd away from the hunters; *Ntambu* is a hunter-ancestor in the form of a lion (manifested in dreams), etc. Here I wish to pay attention to a solitary hunter who is addressing a spirit whom he believes to be afflicting him in the mode or form of *Mundeli.* I should mention that when I was in the field the Bow-Hunters' Cult and the Gun-Hunters' Cult had become interdigitated in a single ritual subsystem of the total ritual system. The pervasive idiom of Ndembu rituals of affliction dominated this subsystem. A hunter advanced in prestige through the system not merely through slaying game but also by experiencing misfortune, believed to have been brought on by a specific named ancestor. Between every stage of advancement in the Gun-Hunters' Cult *(Wuyang'a)* lay a period of failure at his avocation. The hunter went into the bush *(mwisang'a)* but was unsuccessful. Continued failure made him seek recourse to a diviner. The diviner prescribed the performance of one of the five rites of the Bow-Hunters' Cult, in no set order, but dependent on the verdict of the diviner's apparatus. If the rite was successful the hunter would kill again. If he killed well he could proceed in the Gun-Hunters' Cult—and every able hunter managed by hook or by crook, by purchase or inheritance to acquire one of the ancient muzzle-loaders, often Tower muskets, which ranked as guns. But progress in the dual system was an alternation of success and failure; the Gun-Hunter Cult registered success, the Bow-Hunter Cult mastered failure. The spirits of dead hunters were regarded as the dynamic of the Bow-Hunters' Cult; they punished breach of taboos laid on hunters, they rewarded their recognition by the living in the form of ritual performance. The Gun-Hunters' Cult was more a matter of moving from one stage of prowess to another.

I found it necessary to know all this (and more) to make sense of a hunter's earnest address to an Invisible. In these frames the seemingly random speech became a meaningful communication. Even if it was not overheard it was meaningful for the hunter, for it related him in his own eyes to an ordered universe and explained for him his losses and gains in his chosen avocation. Two elements composed his performance; a harangue to the hunter-spirit and a sequence of symbolic acts. Let us examine the acts first, for they frame the speech, bracket it within the accepted system of Ndembu ritual.

The hunter I am discussing was not standing just anywhere. He was standing near a stream at some distance from his home village. Furthermore he was standing in a cleared space. A forked branch has been inserted there; from it two peeled wands of the *mukula* species are placed horizontally. Sometimes they merely reach the stream; sometimes, when they cross it, they are called "the bridge of the ancestral shade" *(chawu chamukishi)*. During my field work I came to understand that every detail in a ritual setting was important, everything "meant" something, or as Ndembu said, "went into" something. If you wanted to ask the meaning of an object or act, you usually asked, *"Chaya mudihi?" "What does it go into?"* We might say, "What is its place in the scheme of things?" In time I came to learn the significance of the cleared space, the forked branch, the *mukula* sticks, the stream, and other details.

In the first place, the clearing itself has symbolic value; it is not just what it seems to be, a site cleared with a hoe for convenience in performing ritual. As in many other instances in Ndembu culture the name of the clearing is itself a symbol and can be connected by informants with other terms in a folk-etymological subsystem. Ndembu declare that *mukombela*, a "clearing for ritual purposes" is connected with (1) *kukomba,* "to sweep or clear dirt or rubbish away from a selected place"—and all acts of prayer performed before a tree of any species planted in memory of an ancestral shade or some other type of spirit begin with "aspersion;" an officiant uses a broom made of the leaves of three species of trees to sweep the shrine-tree's base; (2) one of the species so employed is *mukombukombu* which is also said to be derived from *kukomba;* (3) *kukombela* (from *kukomba*) refers to the act of praying to or invoking ancestral shades—it is the verbal equivalent of the action of sweeping clean—through prayer you "make your liver white" *(muchima to-o)* as Ndembu put it, indicating that there is no grudge, malice, or impediment in the relationship between the living and the dead, no remembered slight or injury, and that the living are in harmony with one another. The ideas of sweeping, confessing, cleansing, prayer, right relationship between living and dead and among the living, and whiteness are closely connected in Ndembu thought as I have shown in several books (*The Drums of Affliction* 1968; *The Ritual Process* 1969).

The *mukombela* is, then, a cleared space for ritual activity, notably prayer and invocation. It is used in many kinds of ritual. But what does it mean in *Mundeli*, for the behavior we are witnessing pertains to the earliest stages of this rite of the Bow-Hunters' Cult? Here let us pay attention to what Ndembu hunters have told me. One explains *mukombela* thus: "*Mukombela* is made to please the spirit of *Mundeli*, for *Mundeli* is of the water." I ask, "Why of the water?" The hunter answers, "Because *Mundeli* came with the Ovimbundu people from Angola. When these people first saw Europeans *(ayindeli)*, they thought that they had come out of the water (the sea) for they were pale, like drowned persons with bleached skins. The Mbundu word for ancestral shade *(Mukishi)* is *ondele;* they called Europeans by this word because they were white like spirits *(akishi)*." The Ndembu term for a living European is *Chindeli*, but the radical *-ndeli* is retained in the cult term *Mundeli*. One of my informants told me what induces a hunter to begin the sequence of ritual phases making up *Mundeli:* "The hunter has been unlucky and killed no animals for a long time. He then dreams he sees a European *(Chindeli)* near the water or sitting in a little ritual hut *(katala*—often made to serve as an intermittent residence for the shades of the dead). The European tells him, 'From now on I am not going to give you an animal because you have erred *(wunaluwi)* with regard to me.'" My informant meant that the hunter had broken one of the taboos laid on initiated hunters. He continued: "When the hunter wakes up he goes to a diviner who shakes his basket (containing symbolic divinatory objects, including figurines) and says: 'You erred. It was either because you let a woman eat some parts of the lungs and intestines of your kill (portions reserved for the hunter himself and forbidden to non-hunters), or you failed to give some portions to your relatives. They complained about it. This *Mundeli* shade does not like people (specifically a group of kinsfolk) quarreling and grumbling about meat. That is why he is denying you meat. What you must do is to cut two *mukula* branches and remove their outer bark coverings and put up a *muchanka* (one name for the forked-branch shrine) for *Mundeli.*'" The same informant explained to me that in the pre-European past *mukombela* (the ritual clearing) also designated "a big path or road cleared with hoes." He said that the *mukula* sticks placed parallel to one another running from the stream to the *muchanka* was also a "path" *(njila)* from the watery abode of *Mundeli* to the forked-branch shrine, regarded as a temporary abode for hunters' shades. The whole clearing was described by my informant as "the eating place of the spirit." Offerings of meat are indeed made to hunter-shades on such shrines, impaled on their tips (compared with the tines of antelopes' horns) or placed at the juncture of branches. Blood of a new kill may be poured out at their bases or over their branches as a libation. Honey-beer *(kasolu)* is the "sacramental" drink of both Hunting Cults and is also poured before forked-branch shrines *(nyichanka* or *yishing'a)* as a libation to the hunter-shades. Hunters and hunter-shades in the more complex public ceremonies of the cults are believed to commune together in meals of sacred inner-meat (lungs, intestines, heart, liver, etc., where blood is rich and plentiful) and honey-"wine." For Ndembu hunters are associated with the richest, most nourishing, and most intoxicating viands and beverages—hence the most coveted and quarreled over. Correspondingly, hunter-shades are both the most beneficent and the most punitive, in Ndembu belief, super-superegos!

Mukula wood is used for the "path" from the watery habitat of the hunter-shade "in *Mundeli,"* because *mukula* is a "symbol" *(chinjiki-jilu*—literally the "blaze" cut by a hunter with his axe or knife on trees to find his way home after pursuing an animal into unknown bush) for "blood" or "meat." Ndembu explain this from the fact that *mukula* bark regularly cracks and exudes a red coagulative gum. This is declared to *be* "blood" *(mashi)* or "meat" *(mbiji,* typically "bloody" meat). They have many rites stressing blood (human and animal) and all represent blood by *mukula* symbolism (even when green leaves or brownish root scrapings of the "Blood Tree" are used they have by metonymy the symbolic value, "blood"). The rites range from boys' circumcision *(Mukanda),* to a rite to cure women's menstrual disorders (*Nkula*—where both menstrual blood and "maternal blood" are represented by *mukula* symbols), and other gynecological rites, to antiwitch-craft rites (witches are necrophagous), and to rites of the Hunters' Cults (where *mukula* dominantly represents the animals' flesh and blood which nourish human beings and make for good "maternal blood," blood which in the pregnant woman coagulates round the foetus and makes a "strong" baby and a good placenta). By using *mukula* branches to frame a "path," the hunter embodies in symbolic action his petition to the deceased hunter-ancestor to emerge from the water and bring meat along that path to his shrine, and *a fortiori* to the villagers dependent on him. Clearly these symbols embody a wish and are a shorthand for a sequence of desired events.

The explanation given me by my informant that the hunter was afflicted by a deceased kinsman who "came out in *Mundeli,"* that is, manifested himself in the form of *Mundeli* as a European dream-appearance and as an inimical influence on his hunting, because the shade was offended by taboo-breaking or the quarreling of kin, is far too abstract and stereotyped. Let me cite what I have actually overheard from a hunter addressing an afflicting shade. I checked over his harangue with him, and invited my two best informants Muchona and Windson Kashinakaji to comment on it. We move, as you will see, from generalities to particularities of social relationships.

PRAYER

Praying is a complicated matter for Ndembu. Not only is there a verbal statement with set and free components, but there is also nonverbal behavior. The petitioner takes some powdered white clay *(mpemba)* from a pouch, moistens his right thumb, places it in the powder, then anoints first his stomach just above the navel and then his orbits just beside the eyes. Sometimes he may also anoint his arms and legs at the main joints. Whiteness, most fully expressed by white clay, represents the good things of life, both moral and pleasurable, ranging from piety to the ancestors to milk and semen. As informants say, *"Mpemba* is placed above the navel *(mukovu)* because the stomach *(ivumu—* which also means 'womb' and 'matrilineage') is where life *(wumi)* is, and where food goes. When it is put beside the eyes it makes people see well, all things are clearly visible *(mwakumwena chachiwahi yuma yejima)."* As a general statement this means that a person thus anointed will see matters as they really are *(chalala)* and will not be deceived by appearances. When one seriously communes with the ancestors one must be absolutely honest and pure, and one will be given the gift of clarity of eye and heart. But in the Hunters' Cults the use of *mpemba* has more professional benefits: "The shade helps the hunter by pointing out to him where the animals are. The shade gives him the good luck to see animals well, and to track them and shoot them properly." These desirable things are represented by the *mpemba* eye anointings. Seeing animals in the obscurity of the forest is a species of the thematic genus "revelation" which I learned was a pervasive theme of Ndembu ritual. To bring matters into the open, either as nonverbal symbolic construction or as explicit statements, is the way to undo the harm concealment *(kusweka),* whether conscious and malicious or unconscious and thoughtless, is believed to cause to persons, to interpersonal relationships, and to entire social groups. Thus, when one prays to a shade it is not enough to make a general confession or to admit inadvertent taboo-breaking. One must specify just what was the secret grudge or problem in the relationship between the living and the dead. It is this covered-up matter which is believed to be affecting not only the quality of the social life but even the biological state of living members of the society, and their environmental conditions. Thus a plague might be affecting the health of the invoker's group, or the forest near his village may be mysteriously deprived of its usual quota of game animals. Particulars must be stated if the general welfare, and not merely that of the person offering prayer alone, is to improve. This is my excuse for presenting the actual text of a prayer made at the beginning of a *Mundeli* ritual sequence by a hunter, Kusaloka. It also throws into relief my problems of how to define, describe, and then interpret Ndembu ritual action.

Kusaloka's name is one of a limited set conferred on hunters initiated into the Gun-Hunters' Cult, that is, on proven hunters. It is the first word in a sonorous phrase which it metonymously represents: *Kusaloka mutondu wakedilang'a mutondu wawanjing'a namayang'a-yang'a,* ''sleeping restlessly, a tree which produces fruits all the time, the tree of *njing'a* birds [which eat ripe fruits] and for trumpeter hornbills.'' Kills of game are often compared to fruits in the hunters' cults, and an active hunter will be always in the forest, ''restless *(kusaloka)* until he produces through killing many carcasses, as a tree produces fruits for noisy birds'' (representing Ndembu villagers). I heard Kusaloka pray to his deceased hunter-kinsman Sakateng'a as follows:

> *Sakateng'a twadisumbwili hamwaka ambanda. Ifuku*
> Sakateng'a, we exchanged women in marriage long ago. Today
> *dalelu mumbanda wanyinkeli wafwili Nyamukola.*
> the woman you gave me, Nyamukola, died. (He means ''recently.'')
> *Mwanyinkeli nyilong'a, ami nafweteli kud' enu. Mandumi*
> You gave me cases at law. I paid you in full. Your mother's
> *yenu nawa cheng'i wansema'mi. Ami Kusaloka nenzi dehi,*
> brother, moreover, begat me. I, Kusaloka, have come already,
> *kanda mutiya kutamaku.*
> do not feel ill-disposed (towards me).

A PRAYER IN ITS SOCIAL CONTEXT

The prayer goes on to detail how Kusaloka had married into the same village from which his father had acquired a wife. This was the village of the deceased hunter Sakateng'a who was now afflicting Kusaloka with bad luck. Sakateng'a had been Kusaloka's cross-cousin, the child of Kusaloka's father's sister. Among Ndembu, cross-cousins of the same sex joke with one another and marriage between those of opposite sex is encouraged, though it is an Ndembu joke that when joking partners marry they cease to joke! Particularly encouraged is the exchange of sisters between male cross-cousins. Normally this type of marriage does not entail the payment of bridewealth since reciprocity is built into the sister-exchange itself. When a married person dies the surviving spouse and his or her close kin are expected to pay the family and close matrilineal kin of the deceased a sum of money called *mpepi.* Quite often this is waived when there has been sister-exchange, but sometimes the kin of the deceased put pressure on the widow's or widower's kin to pay up. I have discussed *mpepi* technically in *Schism and Continuity in an African Society* (pp. 263–65, 267–74) and refer the reader to that account for further information. It is sufficient to mention here that Sakateng'a, when he lived, had in fact demanded *mpepi* from Kusaloka when his sister, Kusaloka's wife, died. Kusaloka had then refused to pay the large amount demanded. This was the origin of Sakateng'a's grudge *(chitela)* against Kusaloka, a grudge which survived death, and induced him to "come out of the grave in *Mundeli,*" as Ndembu put it, "to tie up Kusaloka's huntsmanship *(wubinda)."* The prayer by the stream concluded by Kusaloka's saying:

> *Lelu komana ching'a niyi mwisang'a nakuloza mbiji yatata*
> Today indeed I must go into the bush to shoot meat for my
> *yami adi atiyi kuwaha. Eyi Sakateng'a*
> father that he may eat and feel happy. You, O Sakateng'a,
> *walozeleng'a mbiji watwinkeleng'a ni Wuyang'a,*
> used to shoot meat, you used to give us huntsmanship too
> *lelu wutwinki*
> [that is, helped us to kill animals], today you must give us
> *mbiji tutiyi kuwaha ejima wetu tutiyi kuwaha.*
> meat that we may feel good, all of us, that we may feel good.

He is referring to the fact that he is currently living with his stepfather, the hunter Wamukewa, who married his widowed mother— she, incidentally, was also raised in the aggrieved shade's matrilineal village, though she was not a close matrikinswoman of his. He is urging the shade to relent and give him back his "huntsmanship," his power to slay animals. He promises in his prayer to "feed" the shade, to put pieces of meat on the forked-branch shrine and to sprinkle it with the blood of any kill he may be allowed to make by the offended shade.

HOW A SOCIAL-STRUCTURALIST WOULD ANALYZE THE SITUATION

A full contextualization of the prayer text, from which I have made excerpts, would entail writing a fair-sized monograph. When I was in the field, given my British structural-functionalist orientation, I did indeed try to work out the social structural context of most rituals I observed. It was much easier to do this with the help of clues provided in verbal behavior than by an examination of the rich arrays of nonverbal symbols. At each ritual performance I attended I made careful records of all the prayers, invocations, harangues, addresses to the shades or to the congregation; they totalled up to an inventory of the current state of relationships between members of the group centrally concerned in the performance. Some were torn with overt dissension and redolent with ill-feeling *(kutiya kutama),* others were reckoned to contain covertly disruptive tendencies, secret grudges, hidden envy, concealed jealousy. The principle that the hidden, the dark should be revealed *(kusolola* or *kumwekesha)* to the ancestors, as betokened by the white clay used in veneration, motivated people to confess their grudges in public—and thus to render them accessible to remedial ritual action, to the beneficent influences of the powers and virtues elicited from herbs and trees, from slaughtered animals, from mimetic actions of various kinds. The long cherishing of grudges was thought to lead to recourse to witchcraft; confession forestalled this deadly outcome. Verbal behavior, then, revealed the seamy side of Ndembu social life in its primary groups, its families, matrilineages, villages and neighborhoods. But to understand the conflicts in the social system, one had first to grasp it in its regular operation. As a structuralist in the tradition of Radcliffe-Brown, Evans-Pritchard, Fortes, Gluckman, Colson, and Mitchell, I conceived it to be my duty not only to collect full data on the abstract norms of kinship and local organization, but also to take village censuses and genealogies and make plans of huts and gardens. From such information one could infer closeness or distance of current relationships between kin and neighbors.

Thus, to contextualize adequately the conflict-ridden relationship between Kusaloka and the late Sakateng'a I found it theoretically necessary to make a census of the villages in which they normally resided, to collect genealogies from all their inhabitants, to trace the movements of each village over time (Ndembu practiced swidden agriculture and changed residential sites every few years) and of each of their members (since high spatial mobility of individuals and groups was a feature of Ndembu society). I further collected information about the gardens cultivated by village members, their acreage, distribution, type, time under cultivation, crops grown on them, etc. These data gave me information about the contemporary standing and wealth of protagonists in the ritual situation, which as *Mundeli* progressed through its public phases involved more and more of Kusaloka's kin and neighbors, as well as members of the Bow-Hunters' and Gun-Hunters' Cults, unrelated political figures in the neighborhood, and a number of onlookers and bystanders attracted by the meat, beer, and cassava-mush made available to them by Kusaloka and his wives, the fruits of his hunting and their gardening. Such local data had then to be set in a context of information provided by my wider census and genealogical surveys in Mwinilunga District, the Ndembu and Lunda domain then under British overlordship. From statistics based on censuses of seventy villages I discovered that Ndembu villages consisted of cores of closely related male matrilineal kin, their wives and children, and sisters who as a result of frequent divorce had returned to their natal villages bringing their junior children with them. Ndembu married *virilocally,* that is, the wife resides in her husband's village. In a sense, village continuity depended on marital discontinuity, since one's right to reside in a given village was primarily determined by matrilineal affiliation, though one could reside in one's father's village while he was still alive. Villages persisted by recruiting widows, divorcees, and their children. In *Schism and Continuity* (1957), *The Forest of Symbols* (1967), *The Drums of Affliction* (1968), and *The Ritual Process* (1969) I have tried to work out how stresses between matrilineal and patrilateral affiliation, between virilocal marriage and matrilineal succession and inheritance, and other processes and principles, have affected various mundane and ritual processes and institutions in Ndembu society, such as village size, structure, mobility, fissiveness, marital stability, relations between and within genealogical generations, the role of the many cult associations in counterbalancing cleavages in villages, lineages and families, the strong masculine stress on complex circumcision and hunting rites in a system ultimately dependent on women's agricultural and food-processing activities, and the patterning of witchcraft accusations.

Clearly, much of the content of Kusaloka's prayer can be demonstrably related to these and other social structural factors. Thus the relationship between close male cross-cousins is always a tricky one since in it patrilateral and matrilineal affiliation may tug against one another in the important matter of residence—who will one live with, one's father's or mother's matrilineal kin—and the fact that both father and mother are embedded in matrilineal groups emphasizes both the ultimate triumph of this principle and the constant rearguard action of males to delay that triumph through such devices as virilocal marriage (where the wife resides in her husband's village) and rituals celebrating male activities and attributes. The conflict between cross-cousins of the same sex, especially when there has been sister-exchange between them, is complicated by another Ndembu custom, that of positional inheritance. A man may inherit the social status, standing and property of his mother's brother. Thus, if a man's mother's brother, an authority figure among the matrilineal Ndembu, dies and he inherits the dead man's "universe of law" (and also his name, in a complex ceremony, *kuswanika ijina*), he becomes "structurally" his cross-cousin's "father." That is, he ceases to be a joking partner of the same generation and becomes instead an authority figure of the generation immediately senior—since among Ndembu fathers exert more authority than in matrilineal societies without virilocal marriage. When one resides in one's father's village, the father belongs to the first ascending genealogical generation, and shares in the authority held by that set. In the case before us, Sakateng'a had succeeded to the position of Kusaloka's father, and this had cancelled out his previous institutionalized cross-cousin "joking" equality. I should feed into this information the further structural point that when Sakateng'a died, Kusaloka had formally inherited not only his muzzle-loader but also one of his front upper incisors (known as *ihamba*), which he retained as a hunting "fetish," carefully concealed in a shoulder-slung cloth pouch when he hunted and hung on the forked-branch shrine before Kusaloka's hut when not in active employment. An *ihamba* concretely signifies, and actively demonstrates through its power to kill, that one has a deceased hunter kinsman as one's guardian or tutelary shade, to help one in the chase. Thus Kusaloka was subordinate to Sakateng'a, both when he lived and after his death, in several asymmetrical dyadic relationships. When Kusaloka mysteriously lost his luck at hunting, it was perhaps only natural that the diviner, after eliciting enough information, should diagnose the afflicting agency as his aggrieved "structural father" and tutelary in the hunting cult. Diviners are always alert to stresses and strains in extant social relations and understand just where the major problem areas are located in the social field.

THE INTRACTABILITY OF KEY SYMBOLS
TO STRUCTURAL-FUNCTIONALIST ANALYSIS

My own problem in the field was that while it was possible to make a perfectly satisfactory analysis of the verbal behavior even of a solitary individual in terms of the "surface structures" of Ndembu society, it was less easy to see how, if at all, the nonverbal symbols related to social structure at any level. The open discussion of social conflict was all very illuminating—it revealed discrepancies between norms and principles of social organization and conflict between an individual's self-interest (refusal to pay *mpepi*) and his social obligations (piety to the dead, fair and customary division of slain animals among kin, etc.). But problems and quarrels of these and similar kinds characterize *all* ritual performances, regardless of their stated purposes. They are the content, the *business* if you like, transacted by the ritual actors; they do not constitute the ritual itself, the frames and bracketings within which the verbal behavior is stimulated and encouraged to flow, the significant *form* of the ritual. Everyone has overt or hidden grudges, everyone quarrels, everyone is envious of others' success, and these propensities are themselves framed in a specific social order, find their ends and means in its prizes, institutions, beliefs, favored goals of action, etc. But each type of ritual has its own idiosyncratic clustering and series of symbolic forms and actions. These patterns cannot be directly explained either by abstract structural principles or by factional or personal conflicts conducted with cognizance of those principles. Even the individual symbolic objects and actions cannot be explained as epiphenomena of social structural processes.

Thus, even in the simple performance of *Mundeli's* first phase, I found it hard to pinpoint social bases for such symbols as the clearing, the shrine-tree, the "red" *mukula* road or bridge, the white clay smeared by the eyes and above the navel, the belief that hunter-ancestors would take the form of Europeans and emerge from water in dreams. And, in any case, why did the Ndembu only make public their "structural" disputes with one another at sacred times and in sacred spaces?

I followed the advice of other Central Africanists, notably Monica Wilson, and wherever possible obtained native explanations of the symbols. The outcome was that I had a heap of "exegetic" material to go with each set of observations I made. This only compounded the problem of how to analyze the specific symbols of each kind of ritual, and of each performance of *that* kind. Ultimately, I had something approaching a comprehensive account of all the kinds of rituals used by Ndembu (at least in the early 1950s, together with not a few elders' accounts of rituals no longer performed). I had, additionally, a set of observations and exegeses of variant forms of each ritual type. Scanning my field data I find that arrays of nonverbal symbols exceed accounts of verbal behavior explicitly related to ritual occasions about ten times. And only a limited amount of nonverbal symbols can be directly connected with components and attributes of the "social structure" as this emerged from my analysis both of quantitative data and informants' accounts.

THE DISCOVERY OF FREUD

In the field, then, I was at a loss how to proceed further. I did not relish jettisoning so much painfully collected information (many sleepless nights I had, watching and recording ritual-in-action, even dancing ritual as best I could!). It was at this point, about two years into my field work (mid-1953) that I rediscovered (after about twenty years' latency period!) Freud's *Interpretation of Dreams*. As all now know, this great paradigmatic work is concerned in large measure with dream symbols and their interpretation. I was also concerned with symbols, but with *cultural* symbols, an aggregate transmitted from generation to generation by precept, teaching, and example, but not—at least for all practical purposes—psychogenic in origin. They referred to the shared experiences of Ndembu and even, in numerous cases, of all West-Central Bantu-speaking peoples, to the activities of the family, the village, the gardens, and to the common stock of knowledge possessed by hunters as they tracked, snared, butchered, and divided up the meat of game. Yet these sociocultural symbols had at least one important property in common with dream symbols as Freud conceptualized these. They were "multivocal," that is, susceptible of many meanings, or to be more precise, a single sensorily perceptible vehicle (the "outward form") can "carry" a whole range of significations, not just a single meaning. Thus, *mukula* wood (or leaves and roots) stands not only for the meat and blood of slaughtered game—its dominant signification in the hunting cults—but also for various categories of human "blood." In the circumcision ritual, *Mukanda*, informants declared that it represented the blood of the circumcised novices and its hoped-for coagulation after the operation; in the women's *Nkula* ritual it represented both menstrual blood and maternal blood *(mashi amama)* used to feed the foetus and "shown" during childbirth—it also stood for the coagulation of these kinds of blood which the ritual is expected to produce and thus prevent its "running away" uselessly in protracted menstruation or hemorrhage; in other ritual contexts *mukula*, often connected with other red symbols such as powdered red clay *(mukundu* or *ng'ula)*, stands for the patient's or novice's matrilineage.

Freud, more than anyone else, opened my eyes to the simple fact—monotonously confirmed by the explanations of my Ndembu informants—that multireferentiality was a central characteristic of certain kinds of symbols. I had hitherto regarded it as a blemish on my field technique, or, at best, a freak of Ndembu culture that so many of the symbols given special attention in Ndembu ritual seemed to be poly-semous or multivocal. But Freud's analysis of dream symbols in his Central European clinical experience gave me my first clue to the aggre-gative capacity of certain culturally crafted and defined sensory percep-tible "forms" (or, as one would now say, "vehicles"). To them could be attached a large number of significations ("denotations," "conno-tations," "senses," "meanings," "designations," "conceptions"). These vehicles, together with the significations given them by Ndembu, I called "dominant" symbols. "Dominance," however, was relative; a symbol might be dominant in a single episode of a complex ritual, in several episodes, in the whole symbolic sequence, in hunters' cults, in gynecological cults, in life-crisis rites, or in the entire field of Ndembu ritual—where it might be considered a "master" symbol. *Mukula,* the Blood Tree, was one such master symbol; *Mudyi,* the Milk Tree, was another; *Musoli,* the Revelatory Tree, yet another, as my various writ-ings on Ndembu ritual abundantly document.

MULTIVOCALITY, POLARITY, AND SUBLIMATION

In my preliminary formulation I described a class of "instru-mental" symbols, which is "univocal" in representative capacity, hav-ing only one meaning, and largely employed to further the ritual action or reinforce the situationally dominant reference of a dominant symbol. At first, following Sapir, I called these univocal vehicles "signs," reserv-ing the term "symbols" for those objects, activities, ritualized utter-ances, relationships, roles, etc. which were multivocal. I found, how-ever, that the significations assigned by Ndembu to such multivocal symbols were ordered into a system. Here Freud's notion of *sublimation* provided a useful theoretical aid. By it, Freud meant "an unconscious process by which a sexual impulse, or its energy, is deflected, so as to express itself in some non-sexual, and socially acceptable activity" (J. Drever 1952, p. 281). Now when I set down the total array of informa-tion given me by informants about such dominant symbols as the Blood Tree, the Milk Tree, etc., I found that it was possible to array them in two contrasting clusters. *Mukula,* the Blood Tree, for example, as we have seen, represents various kinds of "blood" (e.g., hunting, maternal blood, menstrual blood, circumcision). These I called the "physiological pole" of meaning. But *mukula* also represents "matriliny," a principle of social organization, and I found it also to be associated with sentiments of solidarity, reciprocity, loyalty, together with the obligation to perpetuate the matrilineage and those entailed in the relationships between particular categories of matrilineal kin belonging to the *ivumu,* the "womb-group," descended lineally from a specific woman through female links. This semantic "pole" I called the "normative" or "ideological pole" of meaning. Here, of course, it was not a question of "unconscious sexual impulses," since Ndembu were quite explicit about the sexual referents of the Blood Tree—they had hardly begun to experience the sexual repressions concomitant with the spread of the Protestant Ethic! But the concept of sublimation enabled me to picture the process of Ndembu ritual as involving perhaps a "deflection" of impulses, and of their "energy." These impulses, in a culture where ritual was "a going concern," were regularly aroused by the appearance of the Blood Tree under the stimulating circumstances of drumming, dancing, singing, wearing unusual dress and body-painting, etc., an appearance which reinforced previous similar experiences in other rituals. The impulses were deflected on to the abstract notions which formed the "normative" pole of the Blood Tree's "semantic field," as its total ambience of meaning may be termed.

But it should be stressed that a major difference exists between the sublimation process going on within an individual and this process of sociocultural "sublimation." For the latter is directed to a collectivity, rather than arising within an unconscious "psyche." Thus it is characterized by "average," generalized, typical, "habitual," universalized, "gross" features, rather than possessing the uniqueness of an individual's development. What may be hypothecated as "happening" within the individuals participating wholeheartedly in an Ndembu ritual in which the Blood Tree plays a dominant symbolic role is that the specific affects attached to the ideas or idea-complexes represented by this symbol at the physiological pole—the joys and hazards of hunting with its blood-spilling, red meat, and afterwards rich feeding; the terror of polluting menstrual blood inimical to the "blood of hunting;" the triumph of giving birth with its attendant flow of blood; the celebration of male initiation through "the blood of circumcision"—these mixed feelings of pleasure and unpleasure, of happiness and anxiety, are, as it were, averaged out into a single ambiguous quantum of generalized affect. This general, ambiguous potency, succinctly manifested as the Blood Tree, is then deflected to the more abstract values and norms of matriliny—central articulating principle of residential and jural structures—making the obligatory desirable, as I wrote in an early article, inducing the individual to feel the awesome power of his social obligations instead of regarding them as either remote or a nuisance.

I was, in these respects, not basing my analysis directly on Freud's system, but rather using certain of his concepts analogously and metaphorically, as a means of gaining some initial purchase on a set of data hitherto unanalyzed in any depth and detail by my structuralist-functionalist colleagues. One might say that what was required here was "something more like" Freud's approach than their approach. Freud's intellectual cutting tools were better honed to slice up the beast I was intent on carving, ritual seen as a sequence and field of symbol-vehicles and their significations, than those bequeathed to me by the social anthropologists. All symbols have something in common, and intrapsychic and interpsychic symbols, formed in the processes of human interaction and transaction, have a great deal in common. This was the general logic of my approach at the time. I still think that it is theoretically inadmissible to explain social facts, such as ritual symbols, directly by the concepts of depth psychology. But one can learn a great deal from the way a master thinker and craftsman works with data, especially when he is working in an adjacent field of problems.

REPRESSION AND SITUATIONAL SUPPRESSION OF MEANING

Freud opened up for me far more than multivocality and cultural sublimation. He showed me how to formulate the relationship between behavior manifesting actual extant social relationships and the traditional forms and symbols of Ndembu religious culture. It was in the study of this relationship that I began to understand the connections between "conscious" and "unconscious" behavior in Ndembu culture. In a paper read to the Association of Social Anthropologists of the Commonwealth in London, March 1958 (published in *The Forest of Symbols,* pp. 19–47), I showed how in the girls' puberty ritual, *Nkang'a,* the dominant symbol, the Milk Tree, was the center for ritual and symbolic action throughout the first phase, the Rite of Separation, of this protracted performance, and how in each successive episode different facets of its total meaning were revealed. What was more interesting, however, was that the behavior of the participants at each episode mimed conflict; conflict which contrasted with the native interpretation of the Milk Tree's meaning during that episode. Thus, Ndembu stressed the harmonious, integrative aspects of the Milk Tree's meaning when talking about it in abstraction from ritual activity; but in that activity the tree could rather be seen as a catalyst of conflict. In exegesis, the Milk Tree, typically multivocal, at different times in the ritual, stood for: breasts, breast milk, the mother-child relationship, the novice's own matrilineage, matriliny, womanhood in general, married womanhood, childbearing, and even for Ndembuhood, matriliny being the part taken for the whole "metonymously." Yet mimetic behavior of groups circling around or confronting the Milk Tree clearly indicated: hostility between men and women as categories; conflict between the novice's matrilineal kin and her husband's matrilineal kin; between the novice and her mother; between her mother and the adult women who are ritually incorporating her daughter into their married ranks and removing her from "mother's knee" (Ndembu use the same idiom as ourselves here); and between the novice's matrilineal village and all other villages, in effect, between matriliny and virilocality (the principle of removing a bride to her husband's village). Thus, for every verbal statement of social solidarity there is, in effect, an "action statement" of social conflict. Tribal unity is contradicted by the female / male mimed opposition, lineage unity by the clash between novice's mother and other lineage women, family unity by the mother / daughter opposition, marital unity by the contradiction between matriliny and virilocality—which we saw above was a prime source of turbulence in Ndembu culture.

RITUAL EPISODES AS "METASOCIAL COMMENTARY"

One must of course be wary of the use of "unconscious" here. Ndembu are perfectly aware, outside the context of the Girls' Puberty Ritual, that there are tensions between the categories and personae mentioned above. But one feature of ritual situations is that they "make visible" (to use terms employed by Ndembu themselves, *kusolola* or *kumwekesha*) only one aspect, norm or principle of a cultural or social structural schema at a time. There is, in fact, situational suppression (rather than "repression" where painful emotions are thrust out of the consciousness) of all that may impugn the purity or legitimacy of the norm or principle being represented. To abstract is to suppress or at least thrust out from attention the other properties of the data from which certain common features are being abstracted. When such data make up the total load of rules governing social interaction in a given cultural milieu, it is impossible totally to exclude them in holding up a single rule or harmoniously interconnected set of rules for special ritual attention. Thus women interconnected by matriliny find themselves divided by village affiliation or by loyalty to their husbands or by age group or by some other recognized principle. Such division cannot be publicly admitted in ritual which expresses and extols matriliny, or even one of the dyadic relationships (mother's brother/sister's son, mother/daughter, mother's mother's brother/sister's daughter's daughter) composing a matrilineal lineage of restricted span. Another way of putting it would be to say that not only each kind of ritual but also each phase and episode of a ritual constitutes a *discourse* or "metasocial commentary" (Geertz 1972) on Ndembu culture as viewed from a given sociocultural perspective. Such a commentary may be explicit or implicit, verbal or nonverbal, direct or indirect. In the case of the Girls' Puberty Ritual, "discourse" is upon the full range of consequences of matrilineal organization for Ndembu social life. These are partly harmonious, partly disharmonious. Material symbols, such as the Milk Tree, postulate matriliny as a harmonious frame for social behavior; kinetic and mimetic behavior "comment" upon the struggles between social groups and roles which are the result of dissonance between matriliny and other principles, "commentary" here being in the sense of actions speaking louder than words. Some of the notions I have just advanced have been influenced by fairly recent anthropological thought (Gregory Bateson, Clifford Geertz, Erving Goffman, Roberto da Matta, Barbara Babcock, Terence Turner, etc.), stressing that ritual language is often a language "about" nonritual social processes rather than a direct expression or reflection of it, as the functionalists supposed it to be. It is a metalanguage with its own special grammar and vocabulary for scrutinizing the assumptions and principles which in nonritual (mundane, secular, everyday, or profane) contexts are apparently axiomatic. This critical function of ritual is still incompletely recognized by investigators who continue to see ritual either as a distorted reflection of "reality" (i.e., "empirical" or "pragmatic" reality) or as an obsessional defense mechanism of culture against culturally defined illicit impulses and emotions. But the "critique" is not, as in industrial societies, individualized; it is, as it were, expressed, like proverbs, in formulas of collective wisdom, in this case, *acted-out* formulas. From the point of view of those enacting a given ritual episode, implicit comment on conflict within supposed harmony may be, if not "unconscious" in the strict Freudian sense, at least temporarily thrust outside the field of personal awareness (preconscious?), but from the pansocietal viewpoint its cultural embodiment in symbolic action indicates it to be part of a collective consciousness, a well from which groups and individuals may draw, if they so need or wish.

Metasocial commentary may be verbally quite explicit within the frame constructed by symbolic action and topographically laid out in patternings of symbolic objects. I have mentioned above how in the first phase of the *Mundeli* ritual of the Bow-Hunters' Cult, the hunter's monologue or prayer to his deceased hunter-kinsman was rich with reference to personal conflicts between the two of them in the latter's lifetime, with the inference that his grudge *(chitela)* continued beyond the grave. I mentioned how the fact that hunter and shade were cross-cousins made their relationship both more intimate and more fraught with conflict than the ordinary run of kin relationships, in view of the tension between matriliny and virilocality metasocially commented upon also in such rituals as *Nkang'a* and *Nkula*. The additional fact that both were fellows in the Hunting Cult further amplified both their comradeship and their competitiveness. In essaying to understand situations of this sort, Freud's view of ambivalence as the alternation, even at times coexistence, of the opposite feelings of love and hate, was helpful.

PROJECTION, PRAYER, AND ANCESTORS

Still focusing on the "framing" of hunting ritual, Freud's notion of "projection" gave me clues to an understanding of the beliefs about ancestral powers to harm the living if the latter transgressed social and cultural norms. In *Mundeli* specifically, ancestral shades, in the guise of aggressive and politically omnipotent Europeans, white and not black, or "anti-black" in color, deny Ndembu hunters the fruits of their skills because they—or their close kin—have transgressed values set on sharing meat, the most valuable food, or breaking taboos of the hunting cults, those concerned with the procurement of this rich nourishment. Aliens here represent moral imperatives, or rather are the sanctions against breaking such commands—male aliens particularly. For Freud, all this would be "suspicious." One would have to look, in his view, very much closer to home. Thus a theory that projects bad luck in the very economic pursuit which produces the most happiness in the village and in its families and sibling groups on to the ultimate image of stranger-hood must be taken with more than a grain of salt (to use one of our own culture's more "tasty" metaphors!). For Freud, "projection" tends to mean the attributing *unconsciously* (and in this Ndembu instance I think we have an authentic instance of the panhuman "unconscious" at work) to other people (here *dead* or *ancient* people, at any rate, in principle if not in practice, not known, named, or intimately connected people), usually as a defense against unpleasurable feelings in ourselves, such as the feeling of guilt or of feelings of inferiority (peculiarly the unsuccessful hunter's predicaments), of thoughts, feelings and acts towards us, by means of which we justify or legitimate ourselves in our own eyes. Thus, the hunter Kusaloka, in the case we have been considering, seems to have "projected" on to the image of *Mundeli*, the deadly white European spirit, in which his own chronologically older cross-cousin was involved or "masked," his own feelings of guilt at having distributed the meat of his kills inequitably. Several informants told me that Kusaloka, like most hunters, was "unfair" in his division of his kills. He kept much of the meat for himself, gave more than their share of joints to his "mistresses" *(andowa),* and did not report his successes to those of his matrilineal and patrilateral kin who should have had good portions. But when he "projected" on to an intimately connected cross-cousin—for his own father had also married into Sakateng'a's village—clothed in antique (Portuguese) European supernatural power *(Mundeli)* the responsibility for his own temporary loss of success at hunting he must have publicly cleared himself (in Ndembu evaluative terms) of "guilt," by claiming merely that the shade had been affronted by the behavior of his (Kusaloka's) kin, particularly his female kin—who had probably broken a taboo laid on all who wish to eat a hunter's kill, by consuming portions reserved to members of the cult. Thus Kusaloka's selfishness was not at issue, only the transgressions of others. In this way, too, the tensions that must have existed—and much other evidence available attests to this—between villages connected by a sequence of sister-exchanges, producing complicated relations between cross-cousins (where mother's brothers become fathers-in-law and father's sisters become mothers-in-law, and joking cross-cousins serious spouses), must have been ritually mitigated by "projection." While I was in the field I was also struck by the congruence between the Ndembu theory of "revealing" or "producing to view" *(kusolola),* and the Freudian notion that cure of neurosis depends essentially upon educing from the patient a conscious understanding of the events and conditions which, too painful to endure in infancy and replicated in maturity, have been repressed into the unconscious, charging it with the affects of culturally defined "dangerous" wishes and impulses. Both Ndembu ritual and Freudian analysis rest upon the assumption that what is known, consciously articulated, and confessed before a legitimate public authority, individual or collective, has been defused of its inwardly believed power to harm. When the unknown, invisible, nameless agency has been "produced to view" the assumption is not only that it has now become aseptic, deprived of capacity for ill, but also that the very energies which, unconsciously, debilitated the patient, when conscious actually empower him to help himself and his kin and friends. What distinguishes the Freudian approach, based as it is on the Western European scientific attitude (with its emphasis on controlled comparison, experiment, testing of hypotheses by rigorously controlled data, and resting on materialist assumptions) from the Ndembu approach is that the latter rests on belief in the reality of invisible as well as visible beings (spirits, shades, witches' familiars, and the like), on the objective power of wishes and thoughts to bless and curse, and on the efficacy of focused social intentions to benefit a patient's total "enterprise." But the principle of "exposing to view" is the same, even if the exposure is in the one case to a legitimate collectivity and in the other to a certificated individual. Confession in both cases cures, but confession in neither instance is an easy spontaneous matter. In each case, the terms of confession which evaluate its honesty and depth are laid down in a cultural subsystem. Among the Ndembu an implicit *weltbild* keys the confession to certain assumptions about the "social, moral, and natural" orders (to use terms familiar from our own cultural history). For psychoanalysis the metaphysical theory that matter is the only reality and that "psychical" processes and phenomena are really *epiphenomena* of matter, holds sway. Yet a curious complicity exists between these apparently disparate systems, even if Ndembu beliefs do not include psychoanalytical theories and psychoanalytical theories were developed in the infancy of anthropological field investigations of tribal ritual, for both assume that the living truth of human social relationships should be manifested if the health both of individuals or groups is to be sustained. Anything short of this internally divides the individual or the group. Where continuous self-revelation is viewed against the backdrop of a cosmology taken to be both an expression and explanation of the nature of things sensibly apprehended, the rituals associated with this process may be termed *religious*. Where self-revelation is confined to the individual psyche and its instrumentalities are claimed to have been derived by inference from clinically controlled data, the process of encouraging self-revelation may be called *therapeutic*. In practice, these distinctions tend to become blurred: Ndembu seek so to restore the morale of hunters that they recover their power to kill skillfully, and of women with reproductive ailments, including frigidity and propensity to miscarry, that they give birth easily to "live and lovely children." And it is not altogether a libel to speak, as many have done, of a "religion" of psychoanalysis. For if religion means something like "ultimate concern," what ultimate concern is greater than full human capacity to function socially and sexually? And if the capacity to relate to other human beings creatively and fully is the "ultimate concern" of a community of dedicated physicians, how can we deny such an intention the name of "religion"? Perhaps what is required is to impart a greater sense of *communitas* to psychoanalytical practices and a much richer knowledge of empirical cause and effect relations to "tribal" rituals. The results might be mutually fructifying, for men are "relational" creatures and cannot be validly studied apart from the network of love and interest in which they are incessantly involved. Each man also possesses the dignity of his unique history and problems. If, then we could give our therapies in the West a "religious" dimension and insist that our religions as well as those in the Third World take into full account the scientific dimension of therapy, we might learn something of practical consequence from the symbolic actions of the preindustrial peoples we have studied.

In conclusion, I consider my encounter with Freud's work, particularly *The Interpretation of Dreams,* to have been decisive in arriving at an independent theoretical position. It was his *style* of thinking and working which gave me encouragement rather than his actual inventory of concepts and hypotheses. None of these could be applied mechanically or literally to the data I had collected. Social and cultural systems and fields are, after all, at the level of observation, quite different from, though interdependent with, psychological relationships. They involve different kinds of sustentative processes, have different developmental cycles. But Freud's implicit emancipation from mechanistic approaches —despite his own attempts under the sway of the *Zeitgeist* to employ "economic models," etc.—and his willingness to take into analytical account from the very outset the ambivalence, plurivalence, contradictoriness, and just "plain cussedness" of human "constructions of reality" made it possible to see not only analogies but also homologies, correspondences in basic types of structures, between the cultural (especially ritual) symbols whose structures, properties, and relationships I was being forced to explain and the private dreams and symptoms with which he, as soul-doctor, dealt.

REFERENCES CITED

Drever, J.
    1952   *A Dictionary of Psychology.* London: Penguin Books.

Freud, S.
  1950   *Interpretation of Dreams.* New York: Random House.
Geertz, C.
  1972   Deep Play: Notes on the Balinese Cockfight. *Daedalus* (Winter): 1–37.
Turner, V.
  1957   *Schism and Continuity in an African Society.* Manchester: Manchester University Press.
  1967   *Forest of Symbols.* Ithaca, New York: Cornell University Press.
  1968   *Drums of Affliction.* Oxford: The Clarendon Press.
  1969   *The Ritual Process.* Chicago: Aldine.

The Author

DOUGLASS PRICE-WIL-
LIAMS was born and raised
in the London area. He was
educated at Uppingham, an
English public school, and
received his Bachelor and
doctoral degrees from the
University of London. During the last two years of
World War II, he was a radio

Photo courtesy of D. R. Sutherland

officer in the British Merchant Navy. His early career included jobs as a local
newspaper reporter and as a schoolmaster in England. He spent two years in
Denmark as a practitioner of body posture. Price-Williams has had a cosmo-
politan career as a teacher and a researcher. He was Lecturer in Psychology for
ten years at the London School of Economics and Professor of Psychology at
Rice University, where he was chairman of the department for five years. He is
now Professor in Residence in the Departments of Psychiatry and Anthropology
at the University of California at Los Angeles. He has also been a visiting
lecturer and scholar at the University of Kansas and at the Social Science
Research Institute in Honolulu.

Recognized as a pioneer in cross-cultural psychology, Price-Williams has
done psychological work with the Tiv and Hausa of Nigeria, with Guatemalan
Indians, with Mexican children in the state of Jalisco, and with Black and
Chicano children in Texas. He has published widely on perceptual processes,
classification, use of intelligence tests, displacement and orality, the psychology
of caste, the philosophy of science, kinship concepts, cognitive style, and
relational thinking in these settings. At present he is directing a research team
on the big island of Hawaii.

This Chapter

Douglass Price-Williams is interested in general thought processes, not in the
products of these processes. This is where he immediately parts company with

584

many anthropologists, as is proper for a psychologist turned to cross-cultural work. However, to study thought processes he immediately went to a true anthropological stance in that he developed procedures using the material familiar to the Tiv, his first subjects, learned their language and lived *in situ*. His initial research into the classification processes and abstractions among Tiv children showed no significant differences between literate and illiterate children—a finding in opposition to the conclusions of most other workers at the time. He found clear evidence in working with Tiv children that nonlinguistic approaches to the study of cognition, like sorting, arranging, choosing, or matching, often reveal mental operations that are not expressed in the language. As a consequence of this even today he is "left with a feeling of lack of closure with respect to the role of language in cognitive analysis." He feels further that "embedded in our traditional tasks of psychology are implicit categories, duly formulated and articulated in our Indo-European language, which may not be at all relevant for other languages."

He points out that anthropologists typically approach cognition from an environmental point of view—stressing institutionalized rules that are products of collective cognitive experience and that form part of the cultural environment in which individuals function. The psychologist on the other hand approaches from the side of the individual organism that is acquiring cultural categories and using them in problem solving. One of the vexing conditions of Douglass Price-Williams' existence is that the two points of view rarely meet.

In his search for functional equivalents, that is, procedures that are culturally relevant but not so bound by cultures as to make the application elsewhere impossible, he has chosen kinship as a useful point of entrée. He uses applications of kinship to egocentric and other-centered relationships. He laments that useful functional equivalents that can make cross-cultural psychological research meaningful are not easy to find. He draws a conclusion that will make many an anthropologist happy, "one is left with the uncomfortable sense that cross-cultural and cross-societal comparisons are gained at the expense of destroying the data that is gathered with a more close-up lens." He recommends a very thorough investigation of the culture to be worked in, including a thorough ethnoscientific analysis, as a way of reducing distortion.

G.D.S.

17 Cognition: Anthropological and Psychological Nexus

DOUGLASS PRICE-WILLIAMS

A retrospective account[1] of one's scholastic enterprises undoubtedly takes on the rationalizing quality of a myth. Hindsight assumes a deterministic perspective: the unfolding series of events are more likely to have been in the nature of a series of accidents. One is reminded of Kierkegaard's dictum that "it is probably true, as philosophers say, that life must be understood backwards. But they forget the other proposition, that it must be lived forwards." In trying to explain my own involvement in what is now called psychological anthropology, I must own that there is some of this mythic quality invoked. In any case, as I started off my career as a psychologist proper, with only an auxiliary knowledge of anthropology, I need to account for my present bridging position of the two disciplines and the nature of my research.

My interest was roused from a reading of the literature on the thought processes of so-called primitive peoples. At that point in time (circa 1957) the literature consisted mainly of two kinds. There were the philosophical books of Lévy-Bruhl (1923, 1926, 1928) which, although empirical material was given, were more in the nature of speculation. Then there was the entire corpus of intelligence tests given to people in underdeveloped societies, which struck me as a nonrewarding enterprise. There were indeed some other studies that did not fall under either of these two headings: they were however, sparse and relatively insignificant. In any case there was hardly anything which bore on the development of thought processes of primitive peoples which would bear severe psychological scrutiny. In deciding to carry out some research which would throw light on this aspect of cognition, and having had

1. This work was supported in part by the Regents of the University of California, and by U.S. H.E.W. grants Nos. HD–04612, HD–00345, MH–10473, and MCH–927, to the Neuropsychiatric Institute, University of California.

good advice from two psychologists who had worked in an intelligent way with different cultural groups (the late Professor Gilmore Lee and Professor Gustav Jahoda), I decided that three criteria would have to be met. The first was that I needed to live with any tribe that I selected for study, in the manner of an anthropologist; perhaps doing some necessary ethnographical work, but primarily to make psychological studies. As a corollary to this first criterion, I should choose a society where an exhaustive ethnographical enquiry had already been carried out so that I could be prepared for the social background of the people before I arrived. The second criterion should be a serious attempt to learn the language and carry out psychological experiments in the vernacular. The third criterion referred to actual psychological experiments. There should be experiments and not just observational or anecdotal material. However, the actual choice of what should be done and the manner in which it should be performed should await considerable acquaintance with both the potential subjects and their way of life. The first criterion —the people chosen—was met by the Tiv people of central Nigeria. Professor Paul Bohannan and his wife had done the original ethnographic work and their publications were easily available. In addition I corresponded with Professor Bohannan well before I set off for Nigeria. The second criterion, language, was met by a prior eighteen month individual tuition with Professor David Arnott of the School of Oriental and African Studies in London. Professor Arnott indeed went further than language tuition. He provided me with a series of contacts that enabled me in advance to select a specific compound in the Tiv area, with all the necessary official backing to get me on my way. The third criterion for the experiment will be discussed in the ensuing section.

CLASSIFICATION

At the time of the initial research there was little to go on for the understanding of classificatory ability among illiterate or low-literate groups. There were of course the contributions of the *Année Sociologique* school which had entered anthropological thought; most notably the essay on primitive classification, originally published in 1905 and now recently translated into English and edited by Rodney Needham (Durkheim and Mauss 1963). However, to a psychologist, this type of effort was not directly relevant as it was tied in with collective representations. On the psychological side, where work on classification had been done with individuals, all that was relevant came through the machinery of intelligence tests or formal tests related to abstract thought. At this point it is necessary to outline the intention of psychologists when they study classification. The concern is less with what is classified or what kind of labels are given to the divisions of the operation, as with the general thought process involved. Indeed, with the study of cognition as a whole, psychologists are interested in the process and not the product. The question then arises as to what kind of parameters should be employed to measure the process. A traditional distinction in psychology has been between abstract and concrete. The distinction dates back to the days of empirical philosophers of the eighteenth century. When the distinction entered into an operational phase in the form of tests and experiments used in psychology, the ability to abstract was used in two ways. One was the observed ability to "shift" from one type of classification to another. The other was the ability to erect a superordinate scheme of classification, a taxonomy, wherein actual concrete objects were arranged into an inclusive set such that there was an ascending hierarchy of terms given to more and more inclusion of the objects. The measures can be made clearer through reference to formal tests. These generally consist of objects already predetermined in their categories of description. Thus there might be a collection of blocks of different sizes (big, small); of different colors (red, green, white); of different shapes (round, rectangular, triangular). The ability to shift in this collection would be for the subject to first collect in three piles the red and the green and the white blocks. Then, on request to classify in a different way, for him to make three piles by shape; and then on a third trial to arrange the blocks by size. Superordinate arrangements are best indicated by describing a task carried out on Australian Aborigine children (De Lacey 1970). There were food and other objects in a basket. Together they constituted a four-tier hierarchy: all objects in the basket, food and other objects, fruit and other food, bananas and oranges. The following questions were then asked of the children. (1) If we put all the fruit in another basket, will this one (indicating an orange) go in? (2) Is a basket of all the bananas more or less than a basket of all the fruit? (3) Is there more fruit or more food? (4) If we eat all the oranges, will there be any fruit left? (5) If we eat all the fruit, will there be any oranges left? In this kind of task, as De Lacey indicates, there is the element of intension, defined as the common character to be seen in a variety of examples, and there is the element of extension, defined as the list of class members. The hierarchical chain of classification from concrete to abstract can be picked up in the ability to comprehend the four-tier arrangement of the collection. In other words to understand that a specific orange is a kind of fruit, that fruit is a kind of food, that food plus objects constitute a collection, that the term "all" means totality. There are many difficulties of interpretation in this kind of task. What is usually recognized as abstraction is the tendency to go beyond the event in its present context and to go beyond the immediately perceptible. How one then proceeded to work out the details of measuring this ability was often a matter of personal decision for the investigator. The principles were plain; the specific measurements were sometimes arbitrary.

At the time of planning the Tiv enterprise, I had read carefully a paper by Gustav Jahoda (1956) in which he had made perfectly clear that it was not only intelligence tests that were culturally inappropriate; he also considered the formal tests for measuring abstraction open to this criticism. This persuaded me to steer clear of such tests and to search for material that would be not only familiar to the Tiv, but also salient. This is to say the material selected would have to be something that the Tiv worked with on a day to day basis. This was not something I could decide upon in advance, but from my reading of Tiv existence I knew they would be familiar with certain kinds of animals. So I brought toy models of these animals with me. I knew also from prior reading, particularly Laura Bohannan's book (1954), that the Tiv were very knowledgeable about plants; indeed, had expected Mrs. Bohannan to learn all the names of these plants. Plants, it seemed to me, could well constitute a collection of experimental examples. How one would actually carry out this experiment and what kinds of instruction to indicate what needed to be done awaited time to become accustomed to the children and to get to the point of Tiv language when this could be done satisfactorily.

The actual experiment has been described in detail elsewhere (Price-Williams 1962). The format proved to be extremely simple. First, a collection of toy animals was displayed in random fashion in front of the children. These were composed of pairs of animals: cocks, hens, snakes, cows and others the Tiv children would recognize. Then there was similarly displayed a collection of plants taken from the vicinity of the compound where I was living. These were plants clearly known by name to the children, such as guinea-corn, millet, benniseed and yams. The instructions given to the children when each collection of animals and then plants was displayed were very simple. The specific wording in Tiv had been tested with bilingual Tiv in advance. The children were asked individually to put into rows those animals (plants) that belonged together. A record was then made of the reason for the basis of the grouping. After the first classification, the children were asked to put those that belonged together again, but in a different way. And to continue in as many different ways as they could. This latter instruction was to find out the "shift" ability, how many ways the children could group. Now the age range of the children ran from approximately six and one-half years through eleven. As there was some difficulty in precisely ascertaining the chronological age of the children—there were, of course, no birth records—the age determination was based on the literate group attending the bush school, that constituted one of the comparison groups. The age groups in school were composed of children of mean age as follows: 6.5, 8, 9.5, and 11 years. On advice from the teachers of this bush primary school adjoining the compound, deviants in age from each class were excluded. If for example it was clear to the teachers that a much older boy attended the class of which the mean age was 6.5, this particular boy was excluded from the sample. In the case of the illiterate sample, those children not attending school, the measurement of age was made from an individual matching of child to child with those of the school group. The selection of the illiterate sample was a tedious and laborious business; and it was recognized that, while the relative age determination was fairly accurate, the absolute age measurement was open to error. Relative age, then, and the comparison between the literate and illiterate samples provide the basis of comparison. The measurement problem was met in two ways. The first was the simpler: one could count the number of "shifts" or bases of classifying the material. Taking this, it was seen that the increase of age correlated with an increased number of shifts, both for literates and illiterates— there being no significant difference between the two groups. The second method of measurement proved to be more complex. To begin with, the recorded list of reasons for classifications for both animals and plants was needed. It was then necessary to quantify the responses in such a way as to place them on a continuum from concrete to abstract. Again the decision was made to follow a very simple procedure. Any answer given in terms of an immediate sensory impression, such as on the basis of color, shape or size (e.g., "it is brown; it is a big plant") was given a zero mark. Also any classificatory response made on the basis of usual context (e.g., "this plant comes from a tree") was given a zero notation. Similarly measured as zero was a response by name: "this is a goat." When there was clear evidence of a movement away from the immediate situation, as for example when there was a division of the material made on the basis of edibility versus nonedibility for the plants and domesticity versus wildness in the case of animals, a mark of two was given. A third kind of response fell between these two extremes. This type of response was exemplified by classifying animals on the basis of numbers of legs. Such a response qualified for sensory immediateness as the legs on the toy animals were clearly visible to the children. On the other hand, there was a reasonable attempt to select an attribute across the manifold of different kinds of animals, and base a class on it. A mark of one was given for these responses. The scoring system is laid out below for convenience.

Score 0. Animal Classifications: name, color, size, situation
       Plant and Leaf Classifications: size, coming from earth or trees (situation)
Score 1. Animal Classifications: number of legs.
       Plant and Leaf Classifications: roots versus non-roots, number of seed-leaves
Score 2. Animal Classifications: domesticity versus wildness.
       Plant and Leaf Classifications: edibility.

The results of the analysis indicated there was a progressively higher score as the children became older. In other words, there was less dependence on the obvious concrete items. As with the "shift" score, there did not seem to be any significant difference between the literate and illiterate groups. The important question arises as to exactly at what age identifiable class systems based on some abstract principle emerge. From the detailed responses (see Price-Williams 1962, Table 6) it appears that the notion of classes comes through clearly by the age of the third school group, which was the criterion for chronological age. This was the age group with the mean of 9.5 years. Below this age group was the school group with the mean age of 8.0 years, and here as was noted in the original article (Price-Williams 1962, p. 60) there did seem a deficiency of the ability to abstract. However, there was a curious exception to this trend. This came from the scores of classifying plants on the basis of edibility. The very youngest group returned a higher percentage on this basis, and the percentages actually declined as the children grew older. Leaving aside the edibility aspect of plants, which was attributed to the high need for food in a subsistent economy, the remainder of the data indicated that sometime between the ages of eight and nine and one-half, the ability to form proper classes among these Tiv children was formed. From the European work of Jean Piaget and his colleagues, we know this ability is formed at the stage Piaget calls "concrete operations" (the term is unfortunate as what is meant is the very reverse of what is usually meant by the term "concrete"). With European children this stage is reached by approximately the age of seven. Comparison between a Western and non-Western group based on this type of experiment and with a measurement system which is not at all standardized has been subsequently criticised by Okonji (1971). However, it was my impression at the time that, compared to European norms, there was a small lag in age for the attainment of this Piagetian stage. What was more important though, was the fact that Tiv children undoubtedly attained this stage. Finding no difference between literate and illiterate children proved to be at variance with later research, which will be discussed presently.

FURTHER WORK BY OTHER INVESTIGATORS ON CLASSIFICATION

Within the discipline of experimental psychology it is always hazardous to jump to any conclusion on the basis of one study or one series of experiments. All kinds of variables enter into the total picture which take time to even out. In the experiment described there were at least three main factors to consider: chronological age; formal education; and experimental format, which in turn breaks down into the components of type of instructions, type of materials, and type of task required of the subjects. The complexity for experimental psychology lies in the fact that it is not at all infrequent that a slight deviation in any one of these variables produces different results. When one couples this fact with the understanding that study of other cultures on this same subject of classification entails different linguistic systems, different ecologies and different degrees of formal education, it is truly difficult to make any firm generalizations. Nevertheless, in spite of the recognized variance inevitably operating throughout all such studies, certain invariants do emerge. Certain differences emerge also. To gain some understanding of the difficulties in this type of psychological study, I will describe two subsequent studies that touched on the same problem of classification in two other parts of Africa, both of which could be related to my initial study.

The first was a study by Okonji (1971) who worked with Ibo groups. For his starting point Okonji took up the aspect of using locally familiar materials, which I had thought important in my study. Accordingly, Okonji compared two different groups with material which differed in familiarity for each. The groups he took for this comparison were low income Scottish children in Glasgow and Ibo children living in Ibusa, midwestern Nigeria. All the children went to school and fell into an age range of six through twelve years. Okonji used two sets of materials. One set was composed of plastic toy animals equally familiar

to both Scottish and Ibo groups. The other set consisted of an assortment of objects which, while some of them were readily identifiable by
the Scottish children (such as a bicycle spoke and a needle), contained
in addition many which would be more familiar to the Ibo children
(such as a certain kind of Ibo musical instrument and a type of Ibo
cooking pot). Identification of all the objects by both Scottish and Ibo
groups was ascertained in advance of the actual classification task; the
Ibusa group correctly named all of the objects while the Scottish children
could only name some of them. This labelling by name procedure was
done to confirm the familiarity component of the experiment. The task
with the objects was the one relevant to the present discussion of
familiarity. It should be noted that the procedure was slightly different
from the one I followed in the Tiv experiment. A "key" object was
selected by the experimenter and the children were asked to collect all
the other objects that were like it in one way or another. Like my own
study, Okonji decided to measure the verbal bases of sorting performance by three levels of abstraction. In discussing his results, he divided
his spectrum of ages into three groups: 6–8, 9–10, and 11–12. There was
no difference in abstraction ability with the first two age groups between
the Scottish and the Ibusa samples. With the third group of the highest
age, the Ibo children proved to have an ability for abstraction superior
to the Scottish children. Okonji felt his results indicated the influence
of familiarity with experimental material. He reasoned this way. By the
age of 11–12 the effect of formal schooling with Ibo children is maximal.
Even at the earliest age of the experimental subjects (6–8) the Scottish
children in contrast have already had some familiarity with the kind of
task presented. As there was no difference in this experiment between
the two groups for the first two age groups, and as in the third group the
Ibo children were actually superior, Okonji concluded that familiarity
with the items bore fruit. The phenomenon of "shifting" was tested in
Okonji's research with the animal material. His procedure here was
identical to mine. He simply displayed an assortment of toy animals and
requested the children to put together those that "went together or
were like one another" (1971, p. 42). Having done this, the children
were asked to sort the animals any other way. They continued this
procedure until they ran out of different ways of classifying. On this
aspect of the research Okonji found that both cultural groups made
fewer shifts than the Tiv children, but there was no difference between
the two groups in doing this. Okonji, in discussing his results in general,
made an important point in elucidating the nature of familiarity of
materials involved in this kind of classificatory task:

It is interesting to note that while greater familiarity gave the Ibusa *S* an edge over the Glasgow *S* in the use of superordinate concepts in the verbalization of the bases of their grouping, it did not give them any advantage in their coordination of the "intension" of their groupings with their "extension." This is quite surprising; it was thought that being more familiar with the objects, the Ibusa children could more easily pick out all the objects that belonged to the groups formed. Perhaps all that familiarity does to aid classification is to facilitate in a given context the availability of appropriating verbal templates and provide some visual cues for defining classes. [1971, pp. 47–48]

The second study to be considered raises a point which I will consider further in the following section on ethnoscience. This study was a multiple research carried out on children in Senegal, Alaska and Mexico (Bruner, Olver and Greenfield 1966). The procedures need not concern us. What is important in these studies was the universal finding that formal schooling did make a substantial difference in classificatory ability or equivalence grouping. Now, it is a difficult job to ascertain the impact of degrees of formal schooling in different parts of the world, and it may be that in the Tiv example the bush primary schooling was not sufficiently impactful to make a difference. I had, at the very time of reporting my original results, speculated along these lines (1962, p. 59). The authors of the Senegal-Alaska-Mexico study considered a different type of explanation for the variance between their results and mine (Greenfield, Reich and Olver 1966, p. 297). The point they raised, which I think is valid, is that of the factor of a contrast set. In the case of the Senegalese (Wolof) data, the factor of a different contrast set was very evident. As these authors pointed out, in the Tiv experiment edible plants were placed in their appropriate context by being placed in an array of different kinds of plants. In the Wolof experiment "things to eat" were contrasted with a clock, for instance. As the authors say: "In order to make a functional grouping in this situation, one would have to define the concept more in terms of a higher-order similarity than in opposition to a category on the same level of similarity."

The question of context, then, and particularly what is contrasted with the item chosen for comparison, seemed to be important. As this is a feature which had been given particular attention by ethnoscientists in their consideration of taxonomies, a discussion of this point and its possible relationship to experimental psychology is in order.

THE ETHNOSCIENCE APPROACH

The methods and analyses of cognitive anthropology have recently been well presented in a comprehensive book (Tyler 1969). The intention of ethnoscience is to represent classificatory domains in terms of the societies' own style. This style may or may not be congruent with the manner to which we in the Western mode of thought are accustomed. A meso-American classification of plant life, for example, may be arranged in a manner which contrasts with out accustomed Linnaean system. As Tyler explains it, there are basically two steps involved (Tyler 1969, pp. 12–13). The first is that of eliciting the information about the type of classification required. This is done by utilizing the "sentence frames derived from the language of the people being studied (Tyler 1969, p. 12)." Technically, this approach is known as "controlled eliciting." Tyler gives an example from our own culture, imagining a situation in which an alien to American culture wishes to find out how a particular animal is classified in the English language:

Q. What is this?
A. This is a sow.
Q. Is that a sow, too?
A. No, that's a boar.
Q. Is a boar a kind of sow?
A. No, a boar is a kind of livestock.
Q. Is a sow a kind of livestock?
A. Yes.
Q. How many kinds of livestock are there?
A. There are pigs, horses, mules, sheep, goats, and others. [Tyler 1969, p. 12]

The second step is that of "formal analysis." This means arranging the classificatory system of the respondents in a way which relates the various units mentioned in a consistent and complete form. With the above example from the English language, an alien ethnographer would be able to construct a taxonomy in which it could be seen that livestock was a superordinate item which included a number of animals with quite different names. Further enquiry would reveal specific criteria that would be relevant for a complete taxonomic system. For example the question of sex could be asked, thus indicating a difference between sows and boars.

It is not the intention here to explain the entire world of cognitive anthropology. The reader can be referred to the book by Tyler with its comprehensive bibliography. What is necessary to discuss is the relevance or nonrelevance of the approach used by the experimental psychologist. There are at least three aspects to consider. The first aspect concerns the very definition of what constitutes thinking. This point has been well outlined by Michael Cole (1974) in adjudicating naturally occurring behavior as a source of evidence about thinking processes. He cites the paradigm of a man looking at black clouds on the horizon and predicting it will rain. The problem is: did this man make an inference, or did he simply remember the association from an earlier experience? Cole goes on to say it is impossible to tell the difference without a great deal more knowledge. Consequently, Cole concludes that the logic of an inference obtained from a natural occurring situation is ambiguous. We cannot tell, in other words, whether the person is really "thinking" or merely reiterating what he has been told or overheard from others. Cole continues to make the important observation that such a difficulty has led psychologists to define thinking as a new combination of previously learned elements. It follows naturally that without interfering with the naturally occurring situation in some way—that is to say, without experimentation—one cannot find out anything about a person's thought processes. As the approach of ethnoscience depends largely, if not exclusively, on naturally occurring sentence frames, on what people are actually saying in their customary terms and style, any inference to jump from this to conclusions about their thought processes arouses hazards of interpretation. The difficulty has been appreciated by cognitive anthropologists themselves. The opposing schools of formalists and psychological realists clash on this issue. The first school states that all that ethnoscience tells us is what native groups say about their own ways of classification. The proponents of this school are largely operationalists. They do not go beyond the linguistic evidence. The other school maintains that the obtained evidence indicates the working of the mind. The different positions are well discussed in two papers by Anthony Wallace and Robbins Burling, reprinted in the Tyler book (Wallace 1965; Burling 1964). From a psychological point of view one would be forced to say that the purely linguistic evidence is a necessary requisite for any considerations about cognitive processes, but it is not sufficient. This immediately leads to the second aspect to be discussed, which indicates that a nonlinguistic approach to the study of cognition, like sorting or arranging or choosing or matching, while sometimes merely expressing that which is embedded in the language, often reveals mental operations that are *not* expressed in the language. Evidence of this can be found in my original article on Tiv classification. I had best quote a passage from the original article at this point:

. . . there was little reference to the formal system of classification reported by ethnographers. For example, the term for a domestic animal is *"ilev."* Of the responses noted as domesticity versus wildness of animals, very few children actually used the term *"ilev."* The distinction was eked out by circuitous descriptions of animals that one found in the compound and which could be left to roam about on their own, which did not attack one and the like. It was clear here that the category of "domestic animal" was uppermost although the actual term was not used. The findings reported, therefore, are not fully determined by the existing linguistic classification. It was also noted that linguistic terms could be constructed if, in fact, there was no corresponding term in the language. For example, there is no Tiv term for "triangle." When . . . this figure was drawn, it was labelled a "three cornered square." Actually, there is really no term for square either, but a drawing of a square proper or a rectangle was called after the native term for that shaped hut—"*gondo.*" A three-cornered "*gondo*" was merely an extension, constructed to fill a lacuna in their own language. [Price-Williams 1962, p. 59]

The relationship of language to thought in the study of non-Western groups nevertheless presents a problem for psychologists. One notices even with sophisticated cultural psychologists like Michael Cole and his colleagues (Cole et al. 1971) that the factor of language in experiments with indigenous groups remains ambiguous. For example they note that there is an emphasis in American classification tasks on color and form. They recognize that such stimuli are lacking as meaningful among the Kpelle of Liberia. All the same they persisted in carrying out classification tasks with these stimuli among Kpelle children, despite their awareness that language differences may play a role. As such experiments were not of the usual type performed by Cole and his colleagues—which they themselves recognized—it is pertinent to quote their reasons for introducing such tests:

. . . we realize that by adopting traditional psychological methods for the study of concept learning, we are exposing ourselves to a series of difficulties in the interpretation of data. It is our belief that if we are careful in the way that we evaluate exactly what it is our subjects do when we present them with a classification task and if we restrict ourselves to inferences warranted from the data, artificially constructed experimental tasks can be useful in cross-cultural research. [1971, p. 146]

One is left with a feeling of lack of closure with respect to the role of language in cognitive analysis. The big question of whether language determines thought or is only a means of expression for thought is a debate in its own right, and has been given serious attention by psychologists (see Brown 1958, chapter 7, for good coverage of the problem). The problem for cross-cultural psychology is a little different: it is to what extent does one embrace language as evidence on cognition, in any particular case. This is a question which, as far as my own thinking goes, is still unanswered. One can only indicate certain interim judgments. One judgment is that the analysis of language by itself does not carry the psychologist to the extent that he wishes in his study of thinking. Another judgment is less emphatic. While agreeing partly with the decision of Cole and his colleagues that one can use artificially constructed experimental tasks with caution, one is still left with the misgiving that one is imposing an external classificatory system on a group. In my own opinion, expressed in more detail elsewhere (Price-Williams 1974), the problem of the choice of categories in cross-cultural experimentation is very fundamental. The problem extends beyond descriptive categories into that of explanatory categories. I have argued that there are implicit categories embedded in our traditional tasks of psychology, duly formulated and articulated in our Indo-European languages, which may not be at all relevant for other languages. It is not a matter of translation, and I am not necessarily arguing a Whorfian position of linguistic determinism. It is simply that most of our experimental tasks imply divisions of such dichotomies as abstract-concrete, rhetoric-logic, fact-metaphor; and that such divisions are not at all salient in many other cultures. I am left with the conviction that, in cross-cultural experiments on cognition particularly and perhaps in some other fields, we need to find some approach that is not wholly dependent upon the indigenous language, yet at the same time does not violate the rules that generate language production. The solution remains a conceptual and a methodological enigma. If one cannot find the answer, there is always the satisfaction that one has at least formulated the problem.

The third aspect of ethnoscience which needs relating to experimental psychology, is the point Greenfield brought up, that was cited previously. Actually even before this chapter of Greenfield was published, I encountered an incident in research with children in Guatemala, which made me wonder about contrast sets and their relevance to the kind of work that psychologists do. I have often used this example in conference presentations; I give the example now from a book I have recently completed:

I was working with (a Guatemalan child) on Riley Gardner's object assembly test, and the child had put together, under one group, the electric light bulb and the candle. On interrogation, he stated convincingly enough that the reason why he had put these two objects together was because they both gave light. Then, almost as an afterthought, he said he wanted to place them apart, singly. I asked him why, and he said that one gave light from the ceiling and the other gave light from the table or floor. What appeared to be happening here was that suddenly this child shifted his contrast set. [Price-Williams, 1975*b*]

Now contrast sets have been given serious attention by ethnoscientists. The particular example which convinced me that the notion was important was an article written by Frake (1961) which has been quoted extensively in the ethnoscience literature, and which I myself have held up as a guide for caution in psychological work on classification. I might add at this point that I would agree with Roger Keesing (1972) that the early promise of ethnoscience, represented by work such as that of Frake, has not been fulfilled in its subsequent development. Frake's domain was that of skin disease; he examined the notions of this complaint among the Subanun of the island of Mindanao in the Philippines. In his article there is a taxonomic chart showing the various terms used by Subanun for skin diseases. At the highest superordinate level there is the term which simply means "skin disease." This is broken down at the next level into three distinctions: inflammation, sore and ringworm. The middle term—sore—again divides into two other types of complaints: distal ulcer and proximal ulcer. At the lowest level of the taxonomy are fourteen individual terms covering the range of skin complaints. For convenience, I reproduce the table from Frake's article (Table 1). Frake indicates that a given category contrasts with another category only at that level where the pair share a horizontal boundary. Thus a deep distal ulcer contrasts with a shallow distal ulcer; a proximal ulcer contrasts with a distal ulcer; skin disease itself contrasts with wound. The whole scheme depends on the context of the situation and speakers involved. The point which strikes the psychologist interested in classification is that there is a deliberate flexibility in the system, and that alternative responses depend primarily on the kind of question asked. These criteria seemed to me to present difficulties to the psychologist who investigates another cultural group armed with a ready-made taxonomy. The objection to my Tiv work on classification made by Greenfield and my own experience with the Guatemalan child led me to have doubts as to what exactly is going on internally in a subject we are studying. One just does not know the various mental sets that are operating; or, to put the problem in another way, we do not know what contrast set is operating at the given time of doing an experiment. In traditional psychology with the cultural groups with whom we share a common language and set of expectancies (that is, Americans and Europeans), the problem perhaps may not arise—although the same difficulty may also be present with minority groups. The problem becomes maximal in dealing with those societies in which there is no extensive written language or where it may even be completely absent. It

Table 1

samad 'wound'			
muka 'skin disease'			
	menjebag 'inflammation'	bugu 'rash'	
		nuka 'eruption'	
		baḡid 'inflamed quasi bite'	
		bekukay 'ulcerated inflammation'	
		menjebag 'inflamed wound'	
	beldut 'sore'	telemaw 'distal ulcer'	telemaw glai 'shallow distal ulcer'
			telemaw bliqun 'deep distal ulcer'
		baga? 'proximal ulcer'	baga? 'shallow proximal ulcer'
			beguɨk 'deep proximal ulcer'
		beldut 'simple sore'	
		selimbunut 'spreading sore'	
	buni 'ringworm'	buyayag 'exposed ringworm'	
		buni 'hidden ringworm'	
	bugais 'spreading itch'		

Source: "Levels of Contrast in 'Skin Disease' Terminology." Frake 1961, p. 196, Figure 1.

is in these societies, where oral communication is dominant, that context becomes important. It struck me that it was hazardous to infer a cognitive process completely from evidence gained from a single method and from a somewhat artificially constructed experiment. The material that Frake presented also convinced me that one could not judge a society's level of thought, as exemplified through a study of a sample of individuals, by just choosing one domain. Frake made a further point in that same article which, once more, I have been fond of quoting, and will do so once again:

If the botanical taxonomy of tribe A has more levels of contrast than that of tribe B, it means that the members of tribe A communicate botanical information in a wider variety of sociocultural settings. *It does not mean that people in tribe A have greater powers of "abstract thinking."* As a matter of fact it says nothing about general differences in cognition, for when it comes to fish, tribe B may reveal the greater number of levels of contrast. [italics mine; 1961, p. 122]

The conclusions I came to as a result of my reading and of my own experience at this point in time amount to the following. As expressed previously one could not remain at the purely linguistic level; one needed to experiment. Whatever one experimented with, the materials involved at least needed to be salient in the society studied. Further, the target scheme studied needed to be functional for the society in question. And lastly, somehow, one needed to choose a domain which got over the difficulty of being completely idiosyncratic for that society so that equivalent studies could be done in other societies. These considerations led me to a study in collaboration with Professor Robert LeVine of the University of Chicago which will now be discussed.

PSYCHOLOGICAL STUDY OF KINSHIP CONCEPTS

A domain which fulfilled most of these requirements was kinship. This domain had the added advantage of not only being given copious attention by traditional ethnography; it had also been given close analysis by ethnoscience. Furthermore, although the well-known Swiss psychologist Jean Piaget had analyzed children's ideas about family relationships in European nuclear families (Piaget 1928), there had really been no attempt to extend this approach to the kinship relationships of a radically different kinship system, as exemplified in our case by the Hausa of Northern Nigeria. What LeVine and I had in mind by attempting such a study was to find a rapprochement between anthropological and psychological approaches to the study of cognition. As we wrote in the published article:

The word cognition, however, is given different meanings by different investigators. Anthropologists typically approach cognition from the environmental side, emphasizing the institutionalized rules that are products of collective cognitive experience and form parts of the cultural environment in which individuals function. Psychologists, on the other hand, typically make their approach from the side of the individual organism, emphasizing the mental capacities that enable individuals not only to acquire cultural categories but also to use them in adaptive activities such as problem-solving. Rarely do the two approaches meet. [LeVine and Price-Williams 1974, p. 25]

In studying kinship concepts from the point of view of psychological growth, one is moving from the psychology and logic of classes to the psychology and logic of relations. More specifically it involves two distinct psychological processes: the ability to handle relational concepts and the ability to comprehend a decentered perspective. These two processes are distinct, but the crucial psychological question is the shifting from an egocentric perspective to a relativistic one. This transference means acquiring the ability to take the role of others and is a basic ingredient in the understanding of social concepts.

To explain these processes we need to outline the main methods and results of the study. For a fuller exposition the reader is referred to the original article and to an affiliated research report on the question of the same children's grasp of left and right orientation (Price-Williams and LeVine 1974). Our sample was fifty-three Hausa-speaking children aged four through eleven, living in a specific central ward of a market town in northwestern Nigeria. It should be noted that this particular research was part of a much larger investigation (under the supervision of Professor LeVine), wherein a good deal of ethnographic work had been conducted and also in which other kinds of psychological work had been conducted. It should also be mentioned that the actual inquiries of the kinship research were carried out by native Hausa speakers, university students who were trainees in child development research. The inquiries were handled in as informal a situation as possible; the sessions were conducted near the child's home and with his siblings present. One further preliminary point needs to be added. Hausa kinship terminology had been well analyzed in a previous publication by Smith (1955, pp. 41–48). This enabled our interviewers to frame the questions on kin relationships in a relevant and comprehensible manner. We found no discrepancy between Smith's account of kin terminology and that of the locality in which we were operating. Hausa kinship terminology does introduce certain difficulties in the formulation of questions which would be comparable to studies such as those of Piaget. Again it is necessary to quote from the original article:

. . . the sibling terms used in the domestic group for both reference and address are *wa* (elder brother), *ya* (elder sister), *kane* (younger brother) and *kanwa* (younger sister). These are the terms with which children are most familiar. Unlike the English and French terms for brother and sister, they are not symmetrical and therefore cannot be used to indicate the child's development of the capacity to understand the logical concept of symmetrical relations. There are Hausa terms that have the literal meanings, "son of mother" *(danuwa)* and "daughter of mother" *('yaruwa)*, and designate brotherhood and sisterhood in the abstract, but these are infinitely extendible terms for same-generation collateral kin (except cross-cousins) and even for persons of the same community in certain social contexts. Thus these general terms could hardly be used to frame a question like, "How many brothers do you have?" It is possible in Hausa to specify a "real" brother *(danuwa sosai)*, but as Smith (1955, p. 41) points out this normally requires the further specification of having the same mother and father, same father and different mothers (as in the polygynous context), or same mother and different fathers (as in the context of a divorced and remarried woman). While Piaget's questions could have been framed in this descriptive terminology, it would have involved not only a departure from our preference for using terms of maximum familiarity, but also the questionable taste, according to Hausa norms, of inquiring about parents' marital relationships and marital histories. Furthermore, the complexity of descriptive specification, involving three different types of siblingship, is a far cry from the simple questions Piaget used. (1974, p. 27).

Psychologists usually regard questions and instructions equivalent to the instruments used by the "hard" sciences. The cross-cultural psychologist is in a more hazardous position than his colleagues in other subdisciplines, as he is forced to adjust his instructions in order that they are understood in a relevant and appropriate manner by his subjects. Instructions and formulation of questions are not, therefore, in this case analogous to a telescope or microscope that are equivalently manipulated by whosoever has the expertise to use them. In turn, this gives rise to serious problems of inference when comparing different cultures. As with more straightforward psychological enquiries (see Berry 1969 for a discussion of the problem of methodological equivalence), one has to settle for functional equivalence as distinct from literal equivalence. Our research with the Hausa very clearly expresses the difficulties of comparing this investigation with that of Piaget. As a matter of fact, I have since done research with Hawaiians on this same subject, and once again it was found inappropriate to phrase questions with these islanders in the same manner as we did with the Hausa. In the final section, I will return to this problem of method as it has obvious ramifications for both disciplines of cross-cultural psychology and psychological anthropology.

Each child was asked five questions about kin relationships. As a beginning the child was asked merely who lived in his compound. This question elicited several names. When the child stopped generating names, the interviewer asked him (her): "Who else?" This constituted a division of the first question, as it was thought proper to separate a spontaneous list of names from an elicited list. On the second question item the Huasa interviewer would go down the list of names that the child had spoken and asked the question, "Who is?" The child could answer in any way he chose. I may add here that the response was not always that of a kin description—the child could refer to a person by occupation or even in some idiosyncratic way. With the third question the relationship concept was directly tapped. With the first two questions, kin terminology could arise, but it was not asked. If kin terms had not been already produced in these first two items, the question was then asked of any person referred to other than by kin: "How is he (she) related to you?" We already had the adult census material for this group, so we could check the responses against this information. The fourth question was the other key psychological concept of decentration. Going over the child's list again, pairs of adjacent names on the list were selected, and the question asked: "How is this one related to that one?" In this case, of course, the child is required to put himself in the role of another person. To put this in concrete terms, the difference between the third and the fourth questions was this: with the third question, a child might be given the name of one of his father's fathers and asked how is X related to you? With the fourth question both the child's father and X were paired, and the question asked, how is X related to your father? The fifth and final question was one of definition. The child was asked to define three kin terms which he had formerly used. I will focus here on the responses and analyses to the third and fourth questions as these entail the crucial psychological processes in which we are interested. There were actually two analyses made of the answer to the third question which probes the child's capacity to grasp kin relationships to his or her self. The first analysis was just a simple frequency count, which one could then relate to the ages of the children. When this was done, we found a fairly linear trend, with the youngest children giving kin terms for only about fifty percent of the people that they named in the compound, while the oldest children gave kin terms for nearly all the people mentioned. As a small number of kin terms could have been used consistently by these children and thus would artificially boost the final count expressed as a bad percent measurement, we made another analysis whereby the measurement was made of *different* ego-centered kin terms. When the analysis was done in this manner the correlation with age was higher than in the previous case. The fourth question, to repeat, now gets at the ability to place oneself in another's place. With this we found that the younger children had indeed very little ability to apply kin terms in other centered relationships; after the age of seven or older there was more proficiency in this. These are the two main results that correspond to the two psychological processes. The reader is requested to inspect the article in order to follow our reasoning that the results indicated something truly conceptual and not just a matter of increasing vocabulary (LeVine and Price-Williams 1974). In addition to these two measures, there were the responses to the definition question at the end. We made partial correlations, with age control, of all the measures; we had correlations also with quite another domain of cognitive enquiry—the ability to reverse left-right orientations with hands and with dolls. A substantial finding from all these intercorrelations was that the ability to apply kin terms to ego-centered and other-centered relationships are correlated with each other and with one test of left-right reversibility, all with holding age constant. This, particularly, gave LeVine and me confidence that we were tapping true conceptual ability and not just an artifact of vocabulary.

As a footnote to this research among the Hausa, I may give just a fleeting reference to a similar approach among Hawaiian children. As pointed out earlier, formulation of the questions could not be done in the precise manner worked out with the Hausa study. It just did not make sense to express the questions in this way with Hawaiian children. Nevertheless, my colleagues and I (Price-Williams et al. 1974) followed the same type of procedure and we were searching for the same type of psychological processes. We observed that these children spent a good deal of time talking about family relationships, and it seemed with them, as it had with Hausa, that this type of question was highly relevant and salient. Actually, continuation of the first steps of this research are still in progress and we cannot communicate the final analysis yet. One finding has already emerged, however, which can be indicated. Namely, while the results for both ego-centeredness and for other-centeredness are positively correlated with age, we found that household size was a more significant factor. This finding, if supported by further analysis and by other research, would be significant, as it indicates strongly the role of experience. It is variables like this which enrich the enquiry of the psychologist; at the same time they complicate his life, for their very diversity makes it difficult to make generalizations.

SPECULATIONS

A reassessment of one's own previous data collection is really inadequate in tracking one's scholastic development. Even when placed in the
framework of theory that dictated the empirical work, there is still
something missing. The missing elements are more in the nature of
speculations, which prompt searching in this or that direction in the first
place. This kind of speculation somehow gets eliminated in the usual
journal article or book, as the background gives way to the focus on
techniques and findings. Speculation, though, is continually being
generated; it operates at the present moment as it always has done in the
past. With the kind of chapter that is now being presented, it behooves
the writer to present his ideas on the present state of the art and related
matters in a pristine manner that will undoubtedly lack subsequent
refinement.

In doing so, I will advance two ideas which I have recently given
preliminary consideration. The first idea is concerned with the whole
question of method. Cross-cultural psychology can be conceived as
involving two problems: adjusting traditional psychological inquiry to
an individual culture, and comparing psychological findings between
cultures. The second problem should logically be predicated on the
success of the first problem, but the field has been noted for a relative
ignoring of the first problem altogether, thus resulting in spurious
comparison between cultures. We have already seen with the kinship
example that a strict enforcement of similar method on two different
cultures is not possible. One primary speculation is the dark suspicion
that it may not be possible at all to make meaningful comparisons
between cultures owing to the difficulty of standardizing the measuring
devices. One might label this a cultural uncertainty principle, on the
grounds that adapting a psychological method from one culture to
another thereby distorts the method to the extent that consequent
results are incomparable. I would prefer to emphasize at this point that
this is a suspicion for me, and not a certainty. I am dealing in speculations, not confirmations. I do find the possibility to be a concern. If one
adopts the viewpoint that functional equivalence is all that is required,
then there may not be so severe a concern. But I think there is a real
difficulty here; it is not trivial and it should not be glossed over. The
difficulty, in my own case, has been sufficient to direct my thoughts, as I
shall presently indicate. It might be thought that the difficulty, if
indeed it is that, is less worrisome for the psychological anthropologist
than it is for the cross-cultural psychologist. This is because the discipline of psychology is more committed than is anthropology to an

"abstractive, hypothesis-testing orientation" (Campbell and Naroll 1972) on a universalistic basis. All the same, a related if not exactly similar problem, has emerged in the arena of psychological anthropology. My attention was drawn to an article written by Shweder (1973). Shweder made a general point that the indices used for a cross-societal study relating egoism to nurturance correlated negatively with one another; whereas the very same indices used for a single society did not so correlate. The difficulty may be simply one of scale. One is still left with an uncomfortable sense that cross-cultural and cross-societal comparisons are gained at the expense of distorting the data that is gathered with a more close-up lens.

At the very moment of writing, then, I am left with methodological and logical quandaries. Recently I have tried to grapple with these quandaries in two directions. The first direction I have already indicated in this chapter; it is that of questioning the very conceptual basis of our experimental tasks and psychological tests. This questioning, of course, is only a very preliminary step. It indicates essentially what one should not do; it does not necessarily indicate what one should do. The defense or rationalization of this approach is that of the necessity of clearing away the weeds on the field before resowing. The nature of the seeds, to pursue the analogy, that then need to be sown is still not clear. My judgment at the present time is that any experimental step has to be preceded with a very exact examination of the culture to be investigated. An ethnoscience approach is advocated, with the important qualification that the categories to be discovered thereby are only accepted as a basis for more experimental intervention. In other words, the resultant divisions of a domain uncovered by componential analysis, tree analysis, and other related methods, would then serve as a basis for experimental designs that follow the format of traditional psychology to a certain extent. The qualification helps to introduce a related point. This entails a direct focus on method. I first formulated the notion of a graduating steps design in a talk at Harvard in 1967; only recently has it been formulated in written form (Price-Williams 1975b). Essentially the idea is that of introducing a set of experiments which are structured in the following manner. We begin with pure observation of some domain we wish to study; then little by little there is an interference with this domain by altering the context in which it is usually practiced, altering the materials which are usually associated with it, altering finally the task itself to the extent that the final experiment of the series is totally unfamiliar to the individual. The point of the innovation is to enable us to judge how individuals from other cultures are able to transfer their problem-solving abilities from a totally familiar experience to a totally unfamiliar experience. The innovation is aimed at eliminating the disadvantages of the experimental method that injures the very phenomenon it is inspecting, and reinforcing the obvious advantages of experimentation which constitute a way of revealing attributes not on the surface.

This first idea I have presented is aimed exclusively at empirical research. The second idea I wish to discuss is more philosophical, though it may lead eventually to pragmatic studies. It concerns the old question of so-called primitive mentality. We started off this chapter with only a passing reference to this notion that Lévy-Bruhl developed. It was glossed over at the beginning as indeed, at the chronological start of my speculations in this field, the conception was dismissed as being mistaken. While still considering Lévy-Bruhl was mistaken in his main thesis—that so-called primitive man had a different type of reasoning from educated man—there are aspects of the viewpoint that need re-evaluation. A particular facet of Lévy-Bruhl's thesis is the domain of the mystical; the chief character of which links the individual to "things" by a process he labelled "participation mystique." Lévy-Bruhl's error was to generalize this mode of thought to all of the "primitive" person's ratiocinations. In this, of course, he was mistaken, as many have pointed out. Nevertheless many scholars, such as Evans-Pritchard (1971), Lienhardt (1956) and Horton (1973) have presented expositions that re-evaluate the "primitive mentality" thesis. The main point to be kept in mind is that, if there is a truly different mode of thought operating, it is not peculiar to traditional peoples. Recently I wrote a somewhat cynical article that presented the thesis that contemporary analysis of "altered states of consciousness" would seem primitive to those traditional groups that have been living with this mode of cognition for centuries (Price-Williams 1975a). Expanding on this view (Price-Williams 1975b) I made a link with the Lévy-Bruhl position, that what really was at stake here were attempts to fuse affective components of behavior with intellectual components. And far from being a "primitive" way of knowledge, these attempts by traditional peoples were really quite sophisticated. Our failure to understand them is a consequent of the Western world's rejection of this realm of experience. Recently, we are witnessing a reversal of attitude on the part of a segment of the educated population on this type of experience, now labelled "altered states of consciousness." When Lévy-Bruhl was writing his books the educated Western world was still in the high throes of

extreme nineteenth century rationalism. Lévy-Bruhl's style and nomenclature indicated the culture in which he was embedded. There was very
little relevant literature from which Lévy-Bruhl could draw to make
his points in a more appropriate manner. The conceptual machinery of
psychoanalytic thought and that of Jungian analytic machinery might
possibly have helped him out. Freudian theses ran into trouble with
anthropologists from the very beginning. One of the big errors with this
school of thought, in my opinion, was that the various expositors who
alluded to anthropological material made the mistake of imposing
Western content of primary process material onto non-Western minds.
There might have been a quite different result if the *mechanism* of
primary process thinking has been accepted and the *content* drawn from
the indigenous society. Be that as it may, one can look at "participation
mystique" from the perspective of fusing different elements of experience into a category of cognition that has quite functional social and
interpersonal attributes. There would seem to be no reason why we
should regard this component of "primitive man" as in any way
different from attempts by educated people to deal with mystical,
religious and communion with nature experiences. This seems a fruitful
way of interpreting the Lévy-Bruhl position, and lacks its usual disdain-
ful perspective.

My treatment has been with the nexus of two disciplines. One is
obliged to conclude with some thoughts as to the necessity of coming to
grips with both anthropology and psychology. This is not at all easy. A
study of cognition is helped but not solved by the mere collaboration of
exponents from each of the two disciplines. We have in fact noted that
the very term "cognition" is understood differently by anthropology
and psychology. There are also radical differences in attitude by each of
the disciplines towards the aims of the other. The psychologist never
gets beyond the "ethnographic" aspect of the anthropologist. He does
not understand that it is in the purview of the anthropologist to "enter
the mind" of the people he studies. On the other hand, the anthropologist never gets beyond the product component of thought. He does
not understand the concern of the psychologist for process, nor the
worry the psychologist has for drawing conclusions by way of unim-
peachable methods. Both disciplines have as their ultimate explanatory
models, conceptual schemes that pass by one another. If there is to be a
true integration of disciplines, it may have to start at the level of
undergraduate instruction. Only out of the crucible of early exposure to
these disciplines is there likely to be forged fresh orientations.

610   DOUGLASS PRICE–WILLIAMS

REFERENCES CITED

Berry, J. W.
  1969   On Cross-Cultural Comparability. *International Journal of Psychology* 4:119–28.

Bohannan, Laura (under the pseudonym of E. Smith-Bowen)
  1954   *Return to Laughter.* London: Gollancz.

Brown, R.
  1958   *Words and Things.* Glencoe, Illinois: Free Press.

Bruner, J. S., Olver, R. R., and Greenfield, P. M.
  1966   *Studies in Cognitive Growth.* New York: John Wiley and Sons, Inc.

Burling, R.
  1964   Cognition and Componential Analysis: God's Truth or Hocus-Pocus? *American Anthropologist* 66:20–28.

Campbell, D. T. and Naroll, R.
  1972   The Mutual Methodological Relevance of Anthropology and Psychology. In *Psychological Anthropology,* ed. F. L. K. Hsu. Cambridge, Mass.: Schenkman Publishing Co., Inc.

Cole, Michael
  1974   Towards An Ethnographic Psychology. In *Cross-Cultural Perspectives On Learning,* vol. I. Beverly Hills, Calif.: Sage Publications, Inc.

Cole, Michael, Gay, J., Glick, J. A., and Sharp, D. W.
  1971   *The Cultural Context of Learning and Thinking.* New York: Basic Books, Inc.

De Lacey, P. R.
  1970   A Cross-Cultural Study of Classificatory Ability in Australia. *Journal of Cross-Cultural Psychology* 1:293–304.

Durkheim, E. and Mauss, M.
  1963   *Primitive Classification,* ed. and trans. R. Needham. Chicago: University of Chicago Press.

Evans-Pritchard, E. E.
  1971   Introduction. In *The Soul of the Primitive,* by L. Lévy-Bruhl. Chicago: Henry Regnery Co., Gateway Edition.

Frake, C.
  1961   The Diagnosis of Disease Among the Subanun of Mindanao. *American Anthropologist* 63:113–32.

Greenfield, P. M., Reich, L. C., and Olver, R. R.
  1966   On Culture and Equivalence II. In *Studies in Cognitive Growth,* eds. J. S. Bruner et al. New York: John Wiley and Sons, Inc.

Horton, R.
  1973   Lévy-Bruhl, Durkheim and the Scientific Revolution. In *Modes of Thought,* eds. R. Horton and R. Finnegan, pp. 249–305. London: Faber and Faber.

Jahoda, G.
  1956   Assessment of Abstract Behavior in a Non-Western Culture. *Journal of Abnormal and Social Psychology* 53:237–43.

Keesing, R. M.
  1972   Paradigms Lost: The New Ethnography and the New Linguistics. *South-western Journal of Anthropology* 28:299–327.

LeVine, R. A. and Price-Williams, D. R.
  1974   Children's Kinship Concepts: Cognitive Development and Early Experience Among the Hausa. *Ethnology* 13:25–44.

Lévy-Bruhl, L.
  1923   *Primitive Mentality*. New York: MacMillan Co.
  1926   *How Natives Think*. London: G. Allen and Unwin.
  1928   *The Soul of the Primitive*. New York: MacMillan Co.

Lienhardt, G.
  1956   Modes of Thought. In *The Institutions of Primitive Society: A Series of Broadcast Talks,* pp. 95–107. Oxford: Basil Blackwell.

Okonji, O. M.
  1971   A Cross-Cultural Study of the Effects of Familiarity on Classificatory Behavior. *Journal of Cross-Cultural Psychology* 2:39–49.

Piaget, J.
  1928   *Judgment and Reasoning in the Child*. London: Routledge and Kegan Paul.

Price-Williams, D. R.
  1962   Abstract and Concrete Modes of Classification in a Primitive Society. *British Journal of Educational Psychology* 32:50–61.
  1974   Psychological Experiment and Anthropology: The Problem of Categories. *Ethos* 2:95–114.
  1975a Primitive Mentality—Civilized Style. In *Cross-Cultural Perspectives On Learning,* vol. I, eds. R. Brislin, S. Bochner and W. Lonner. Beverly Hills, Calif.: Sage Publications, Inc.
  1975b *Explorations in Cross-Cultural Psychology*. San Francisco: Chandler and Sharp.

Price-Williams, D. R., Hammond, O. W., Walker, M., Edgerton, C., and Newton, F.
  1974   Kinship Concepts and Relational Thinking Among Rural Hawaiian Children. *Proceedings of Conference of American Psychological Association* (Abstract).

Price-Williams, D. R. and LeVine, R. A.
  1974   Left-Right Orientation Among Hausa Children: A Methodological Note. *Journal of Cross-Cultural Psychology,* 5:356–363.

Shweder, R. A.
  1973   The Between and Within of Cross-Cultural Research. *Ethos* 1:531–45.

Smith, M. G.
  1955   *The Economy of Hausa Communities of Zaria*. London.

Tyler, S. A., ed.
  1969   *Cognitive Anthropology*. New York: Holt, Rinehart and Winston.

Wallace, A. F. C.
  1965   The Problem of the Psychological Validity of Componential Analyses. *American Anthropologist* 67:229–48.

The Author

MICHAEL COLE, Professor of Ethnographic Psychology at the Rockefeller University, New York, is one of the major contributors to an emerging cross-cultural psychology concerned particularly with cognitive studies. He heads the laboratory of comparative human cognition at Rockefeller. His time is divided between comparative research in New York City and research on the intellectual consequences of literacy conducted among the Vai people of Liberia.

He began his work in social science at Oberlin College in 1955. In 1957 he moved to UCLA where he majored in psychology and took his only course in anthropology. He went to Indiana University to do graduate work in mathematical psychology. While at Indiana, he became interested in Soviet psychology. When he received the Ph.D. in 1962 in psychology and Russian area studies, he went to Moscow where he studied with Alexander Luria and was first exposed to cross-cultural research.

Since 1964 he has become increasingly more involved in the study of cultural influences on the development of intellectual activity described in this article.

This Chapter

Professor Cole says this article is quite different from anything that he has written before. "I have tried to write a making article, not a picture of a well-wrought product." He wrote it while "setting up shop" in Monrovia for his most recent project.

The paper shows neatly how the intellectual climate of the times and certain assumptions built into Western culture influenced what Michael Cole

612

and his close colleague John Gay and their coworkers and fellow observers saw and thought about as they tried to understand the learning difficulties Liberian children had with Western mathematical learning. Their work began during the period of the discovery of the "disadvantaged" child and of great excitement about the relationship between language and thought. The major results of their early work were published in 1967 in *The New Mathematics and the Old Culture,* published in the education and culture series created and edited by George and Louise Spindler.

As ethnoscience developed in anthropology, it became useful to Gay and Cole and their associates in their further work as they attempted to map all of the basic linguistic categories in Kpelle language and culture. Their work has proceeded over the past decade with a sensible and creative mix of inductive and deductive experiments. Michael Cole reinforces what Douglass Price-Williams says when he points out that cross-cultural psychologists are interested in the *process* of cognition, not in its *results* "as anthropologists are."

This chapter is a behind-the-scenes look at how a group of innovative, determined researchers studying cognitive development in a non-Western culture puzzled their way through to some tentative but highly suggestive conclusions about cognitive development. They discovered, among other things, how important to performance familiarity with the components in an experiment is. Partly as a result of this the researchers came to question seriously their initial assumption that differences between subjects with and without formal schooling could be measured.

Michael Cole ends with questions about experimental procedure—whether they tap psychological process reliably enough to be useful. He says, "We must develop new techniques in order to study everyday cognitive activities." He has suffered a "loss of certainty" about "the most trusted tool" of the psychologist, the experiment. The fact that experiments are not to be trusted may not be news to most anthropologists, to be sure, but when Cole points out that there is not much in published ethnography to help him in his concerns either, we have a mutual problem.

G.D.S.

18 Ethnographic Psychology of Cognition—So Far

MICHAEL COLE

It is with considerable reluctance that I undertake an autobiographical account of my part in the making of psychological anthropology.

There is more than ritual modesty behind my reluctance. First, I have been doing work relevant to this broad, if fuzzily defined topic for only a decade. My formal training as an anthropologist has been negligible. And whatever it is I have been doing must be understood in the "present progressive" tense. Readers will have to decide for themselves if what I am making fits their idea of psychological anthropology.

Second, I am by nature, a person who likes to work with other people. I have been particularly fortunate in having encountered many creative and unusual people who have shaped the ideas that currently guide our work. I am who I meet. So this will be the story of a collective effort, expressed at present through me, but which could be expressed in a similar form by many of the people who will figure in my narrative.

Like many psychologists who have engaged in cross-cultural work, my own introduction to this general enterprise was fortuitous. In the winter of 1963 I was a research associate and lecturer at Stanford University, attached to the Institute for Mathematical Studies in the Social Sciences. Trained in the subdiscipline called mathematical learning theory, I was completing my training under William Estes, with whom I had received my degree the previous year.

At this same period the director of the Institute, Pat Suppes, was involved in a "new mathematics" project, intended to improve mathematics education in the English-speaking countries of Africa. A small part of the overall project was devoted to a pilot study of the indigenous mathematical knowledge of one of the projects target groups in an effort to better orient the writing of future curriculum materials. The focus of this pilot study was the country of Liberia, and particularly members of the Kpelle tribe who inhabit a relatively large part of the north central area of this small, West African country.

The choice of the Kpelle was *not* fortuitous. When the group with whom Suppes was working held curriculum workshops at Entebbe,

Uganda, one of the participants was John Gay, who was then teaching mathematics at Cuttington College in the heart of Kpelle Country.

A former mathematician who had chosen to work as a missionary, John had taught and observed in nearby village schools as well as at the College. He believed that the curriculum innovations suggested at Entebbe were inadequate. He suggested that a broad study of Kpelle mathematical knowledge would be more helpful in understanding the difficulties his pupils encountered in learning mathematics.

Suppes and the group of scholars who were associated with the broader curriculum project (including Jerome Bruner and Ted Martin) sought an expert who could come to Liberia to work with John. But they were unsuccessful in finding anyone who was both willing to undertake the task and who had the needed background in mathematics, linguistics, anthropology and educational psychology. So they decided instead to send a series of consultants, each of whom would tutor John in their own specialty. I was chosen as the psychology tutor.

At the time Suppes suggested that I visit John, I was uncertain of Liberia's geographical location. I was busily engaged in trying to construct a mathematical model to account for the choice behavior of college students who had to predict which of three lights on a board would light up when I gave the ready signal. As I said earlier, my involvement in psychological anthropology was somewhat fortuitous!

I got off the plane in Liberia with no more information about my task than I have described so far. However, my lack of sophistication as an anthropologist and my general ignorance about the Kpelle did not mean that I arrived in Liberia a mental *tabula rasa*. As a recent Ph.D. trained in the traditions of American learning theory, I came bearing an invisible cargo of assumptions about human nature and human cognitive process.

Like most of my colleagues, I was an environmentalist. I was willing to grant individual differences in all sorts of human attributes, including some loosely labelled "intelligence," but I did not believe that any one social or ethnic group was likely to be endowed with any more of that stuff than another. More important, I was convinced that the psychological processes people develop are very much a function of their early experiences; lacking certain experiences, various psychological processes are unlikely to develop, or at least, to develop fully. But given a proper environment, everyone is likely to mature into a fully competent adult.

As an experimental psychologist, I knew a good deal about the experimental method. I could properly design and execute a wide variety of experiments, collect the data in tables and analyze those tables of numbers by a variety of statistical techniques. I knew, because I had been taught well, that psychological experiments are essential tools for understanding something called a psychological (in my case, cognitive) process. Depending upon the kind of process I wanted to study, I could use any one of several tests or experimental procedures, each of which had a special diagnostic function.

Subjects' ability to classify or think abstractly could be studied by a variety of classification and discrimination learning techniques. Using various transfer-of-learning procedures I could assess the degree to which learning was mediated by internal, representational responses. I could use the free recall of potentially categorizable lists of words to determine if people were learning by rote. The list of techniques is extendable, and we have extended it in the past decade.

When I first arrived in Liberia, I spent a good deal of time travelling around the countryside asking about the source of the mathematics difficulties which had prompted my trip. The answers I got from people who spent time around children (teachers, doctors, American mothers who had observed African children playing with their offspring) were consistent with expectations I had brought with me.

The list of things the tribal children could not do, or did badly, was very long indeed. They could not tell the difference between a triangle and a circle because they experienced severe perceptual problems. This made the tribal child's task almost hopeless when it came to dealing with something like a child's jigsaw puzzle, explaining why "Africans don't know how to classify" and, of course, the well-known proclivity of African school children to learn by rote came in for a lot of discussion. Almost everyone had a favorite deficit in the child's experience which, if rectified, would greatly benefit the educational products of Liberian schools. A physics teacher suggested that AID buy tinkertoys for every child in Liberia.

The collection of assumptions I brought to Liberia as a result of my graduate education and the diagnoses of my hosts concerning the learning difficulties of Liberian students were very much a part of the times. This was the era America "discovered" the disadvantaged child. In language very much like that applied to Kpelle children in Liberia, American scholars and educators offered explanations for the school difficulties of American minority groups and the poor in the presumably inadequate learning environment of their homes.

John Gay and I also sought the source of school difficulties in the child's home background. But it turned out, in retrospect, that we approached this problem with added assumptions that really were not a part of my psychological training and were not shared (or at least not taken into consideration) by the educators and psychologists with whom we talked. First, we assumed that although Kpelle children lacked particular kinds of experiences that our own children routinely encounter, they were by no means lacking in learning experiences. In fact, we explicitly began with the assumption that "we must know more about the indigenous mathematics so that we can build effective bridges to the new mathematics that we are trying to introduce" (Gay and Cole 1967). This assumption led us into an exploration of such questions as the way that numbers, geometrical forms and logical operations are expressed in the Kpelle language. We also investigated situations in which the Kpelle use measurement, engage in arguments, and organize situations for the education of their children.

Our second, somewhat unprofessional assumption was that people would be skilled at tasks they had to engage in often. This statement may appear patently obvious or trivial, but its consequences are neither. Eventually it led me to reformulate the problem of the relation between experience and the development of cognitive processes, as I shall attempt to make clear presently. In the 1960s, it led us to discover that Kpelle people are masters at measuring rice. For this area of their experience, they have a highly developed vocabulary and a system of measurements that is completely consistent. When measuring distance or lengths, however, the vocabulary is less detailed, and we discovered that very often non-interchangeable units of length depended upon the kind of object or distance being measured.

It is natural enough that our initial effort would contain both conceptual and factual errors. Scanning our early work I can see more examples of both than I care to admit. Many generalizations about the Kpelle came to be modified as John Gay got deeper into the language and the culture (see, for example, Gay 1973). Our heavy emphasis on the close relationship between vocabulary and learning ability, although a part of the times, also led us into error. For example, our initial linguistic analysis suggested that the various senses of "or" in English were represented by a single concept in Kpelle. When we found no difference in learning conjunctive ("and") and disjunctive ("or") conceptual rules, we thought we had simultaneously bolstered our view of the relation between language and logic while upsetting a widely held generalization in American psychology that conjunctive rules are inherently easier to learn. (Upsetting well-established generalizations is an especially attractive outcome for newcomers in science.)

Subsequent linguistic analysis by John Gay, assisted by William Welmers, revealed that the Kpelle language does indeed make distinctions corresponding to those made in English. Subsequent experimental analysis (Ciborowski and Cole 1973) demonstrated that idiosyncratic experimental procedures were the source of the unusual equivalence in rates of learning conjunctive and disjunctive concepts. So much for that discovery.

Despite these and other shortcomings, I have come to believe that the odd mixture of "scientific" and common sense approaches represented in *The New Mathematics and an Old Culture* (Gay and Cole 1967) carried the seeds of the work which has followed. In particular, it led us to emphasize the content-and-situation-specific nature of cognitive processes and the consequent need to finally link experimental techniques with careful ethnographic observation in the study of culture and cognition.

But in the winter of 1965, when John Gay and I wrote our first monograph, we were only dimly aware of the directions this work would lead us. That winter John was on leave at Stanford increasing his exposure to anthropology and psychology. I was a second-year faculty member at Yale University where I was having a difficult time deciding whether to pursue the work among the Kpelle, or to follow a more standard line of research on animal conditioning. It was to be several years before I made this decision in favor of the cross-cultural research. Two developmental psychologists at Yale, Joseph Glick and William Kessen, were influential by supporting my initial uncertain steps in that direction.

During the 1965–66 academic year, Kessen, Glick and I shared a small grant which supported further analysis of some of our Kpelle data and new research studies in New Haven. I sought contact with developmental psychologists for a simple, but to me compelling, reason. If we assumed Kpelle children are not born possessing markedly different ways of thinking from American children, the differences we were observing between adults in the two cultures must have appeared some time during the child's development; differences should increase with increasing age. I had never taken so much as an introductory course in child development, so I was extremely lucky to find two interested colleagues to point the way.

Soon I began to see the possibility that Kpelle-land might offer even better opportunities to study the impact of experience on cognitive development than I had originally thought. In the United States and Europe, which are the main sources of theories of cognitive development, virtually all normal children begin to attend school between the ages of five and seven years. The five to seven year age range is also exactly the period in which major changes take place in the basic composition and structure of children's cognitive processes according to all the books I was reading. What could be producing changes so uniform that Jean Piaget and American behaviorists would agree that qualitative changes were taking place while disagreeing in their accounts of what these changes were, and what was producing them? In our early work, John Gay and I had seen several instances where children who had attended school for a few years performed differently from children who had not attended school. Since formal schooling was a recent innovation in Kpelle-land in the mid 1960s, and most children lived far from available schools, we hit on the idea of conducting developmental studies that compared people at different ages who had, or had not, attended school. The work among the Kpelle would unravel the mysteries of cognitive development!

So, in the spring of 1966, John Gay, Joe Glick and I wrote a proposal to study the development of learning and problem solving processes among the Kpelle. In our proposal we drew heavily on our earlier decision to make close contact with objects and events people knew and dealt with in their everyday lives. We added a clearer idea of studying contrasting experiences within Kpelle society (especially formal schooling) and a better range of tasks to sample different cognitive processes.

John returned to Cuttington College at the end of the academic year. At the same time, I left New Haven in a move that profoundly influenced the shape of our work in the coming years. Although Yale provided an excellent academic environment for many purposes, I did not find it a particularly hospitable place for a junior person whose work was spilling over into unanticipated areas of his own discipline and on into other disciplines as well. I was learning a little about cognitive development, but I could see that anthropology and linguistics were going to be necessary tools if I was going to continue to do cross-cultural work.

When I was offered a job at the University of California at Irvine, it appeared a perfect place to go. This new campus had a school of social sciences that was not organized into disciplinarily defined departments. Its young faculty included scholars whose specialties were exactly what I needed to learn about. And its teaching program was organized to permit faculty a wide range of options in what and how they taught.

At Irvine I met Duane Metzger and Volney Stefflre, both of whom taught me a great deal about anthropological linguistics and formal eliciting techniques. Allowed to teach what I pleased, I constructed a class in cognitive development (the first I had attended myself). I pursued my interest in cross-cultural work in a class taught jointly with an anthropologist, an economist and a political scientist. Perhaps we were inflicting our ignorance on our students, but in its early years our faculty at Irvine learned a lot from each other.

My experiences at Irvine soon made themselves felt; the National Science Foundation announced that it would support our work among the Kpelle. In the winter of 1966, Joe Glick and I flew to Liberia, where John Gay had gathered and begun to train a small band of researchers. We knew that in order to lay the groundwork for the learning and problem solving studies to follow, we needed a firm grip on the basic semantic categories in the Kpelle language. We also needed more information on indigenous problem solving and the ways in which schools influence children.

Our first work concentrated on the language. With the help of John Kellemu, a college educated Kpelle man, John Gay began to elicit information about basic categories in Kpelle. Inspired by the general view current in the branch of anthropology called ethnoscience, John aspired to mapping all of Kpelle culture via a mapping of its basic, linguistic categories. The methods we finally used were a characteristically motley assemblage of techniques from linguistic anthropology. The formal eliciting procedure developed by Metzger was used, but a number of the sessions were conducted with a group of elders in a manner consistent with Kpelle practice, but unlocatable in any methods book. At one point, thanks to John Gay's vision of a giant culture chart, the fruits of this work (summarized in chapter 3 of *The Cultural Context of Learning and Thinking*) filled a long wall of the house near Cuttington College that served as project headquarters.

For subdomains of the Kpelle taxonomy of things (Seng), we cross-checked the results of our elicitation using Volney Stefflre's idea that items which can be used in the same way in normal sentences are likely to go together "in people's heads." We reasoned that if our formally elicited categories were not imposed by us, the categories should reappear using this different technique, in which subjects were free to reach their judgments based on the appropriateness of entire sentences, rather than inquiries about individual words. Happily for us, the results of the two techniques coincided rather well.

It was at this time that we began the first of our studies of free recall. We had become familiar with the American psychological literature showing that adults asked to memorize a long list of words consisting of prominent categories typically "clustered" their recall; although presented in a haphazard order, a list consisting of the names of tools, vehicles, clothing and food will generally be recalled category by category.

Lacking experience with the technique, we did some pilot work using prominent Kpelle categories and items that were both common and portable. We developed a reasonable set of instructions (ones that retained their meaning when translated back and forth between Kpelle and English while communicating the basic idea of what the rememberer was supposed to do). We also worked out procedures for other pilot studies, some designed to follow up on the work that had gone before, some designed to begin tracing the ways in which the "Seng chart" was reflected in tasks that required some kind of classification activity.

It is in the nature of scientific publications that the researchers try to present their work in a coherent fashion, stating hypotheses and proceeding to bring relevant data to bear on them. *The Cultural Context of Learning and Thinking,* which represents a summary of our work between 1966 and 1970, is written more or less in this fashion. In it my colleagues and I lay out our understanding of the material we had collected, *taken as a whole.*

I emphasize the last phrase because our text neglects to detail all of the false (and often amusing) misadventures that made up the actual doing of the work. Yet, if we are talking about the doing of science, not merely the results of the doing, mistakes can be as informative as successful tests of hypotheses. Our chapter on memory, for example, concludes with a generalization that still makes good sense to me: uneducated tribal adults perform poorly in recall tasks that require spontaneous application of retrieval strategies to unstructured, isolated materials (words or objects), but they can recall perfectly well when the task is structured to elicit appropriate retrieval activity. But this neat conclusion was reached in an office building in New York, not a small village in Liberia.

The very first study, begun while Glick and I were making our first trip together, turned out to be something of a fiasco. The young man who was responsible for data gathering was the son of a prominent Mandingo man. Our recall list did not include the word "cow," but "cow" kept turning up, sometimes repeatedly in people's recall. A little detective work indicated that the boy's father was renowned for the cows he owned. There were more serious shortcomings in these initial efforts. For example, we almost overlooked a really major phenomenon because our plan was to present each person a list of items to be remembered only once. Here a study conducted in the United States by Donald Sharp played a key role.

Don had worked with me while an undergraduate at Yale. He came to Irvine late in the winter of 1966 to enter graduate school and immediately became a part of our research group. He was present when the results of our earliest free recall study arrived from Liberia. Don and I decided to conduct a study of free recall with children in nearby schools with the special purpose of finding out the rate of development of recall when objects or spoken words were used as stimuli. Our eventual objective was a study of memory for concrete (object) versus abstract (word) stimuli among the Kpelle. But we had no basis for comparison because no work on the topic had yet appeared in the American literature. Don suggested we give each child several opportunities to learn the list on the assumption we would obtain a more stable picture of the effect of stimulus differences if we had several recall samples from each subject. The outcome of this first study and two which followed it are described in Cole, Frankel and Sharp (1971). For this present discussion, the major outcome was to point up the fact that important differences between age groups were concentrated largely in the extent to which they improved their performance over repeated trials of the same list. A single recall trial was an insensitive indicator of group differences in free recall. This simple procedural change was extremely important because when we returned to Liberia in the summer to take up this line of study, we found little difference in performance between schooled and unschooled subjects on the first recall trial but on later trials group differences did occur because subjects with more than six years of education improved their performance with practice, while uneducated subjects did not.

Another important point in our recall work came when we began to cast around for memory tasks that would dramatically improve the performance of our uneducated subjects. We spent a good deal of time looking for children's games that required remembering. We tried evoking a realistic context, such as actually sending someone into the village store to "buy a list of items." We played with functionally related items. We invented folk stories. We piled items on chairs.

Some of these techniques worked in the sense that recall improved markedly. But many things remained unclear. One set of unresolved problems concerned inconsistencies between tasks. On some occasions recall was enhanced only if categories were associated with physically separated chairs, but in one study, recall improved if only a single chair was used. Was it something about how the physical conditions influenced the time and emphasis that the experiments allotted each item? Detailed observation of different experimenters and procedures didn't resolve the matter.

Also unresolved was the issue of improvement with practice on the same list. Unnoticed because of our success in pinning down some of the conditions which controlled recall among the educated and uneducated Kpelle groups was the fact that the procedures which augmented overall recall acted primarily on the first trial. We have not yet, in any of our work with traditional Kpelle people, observed a pattern of learning over repeated trials where everyone eventually masters the entire list.

Despite these and many other unresolved issues, our alloted time and money were finally used up. During the 1968–69 academic year, John Gay was a visiting faculty member at Irvine. His absence from the scene in Liberia was compensated by the presence of three Irvine graduate students—Don Sharp, Tom Ciborowski and David Lancy, all of whom eventually wrote doctoral dissertations on aspects of their work among the Kpelle. These men added substantively to the research and helped us fill in gaps we had left behind.

At Irvine, John and I worked at weaving together different strands of the research. We were joined in the summer by Joe Glick. For some time we were really uncertain what form our eventual write up of the work should take. The unevenness of progress on different subtopics was evident. The work on free recall, while incomplete, was much further along than studies of syllogistic reasoning and concept formation. We had minutely detailed information on a variety of semantic domains (different kinds of snakes, mats, vines), but we had succeeded in completing only a few studies linking knowledge of these domains to learning skills.

We finally decided on the mixed strategy of writing a monograph synthesizing whatever insights we had gained, to be supplemented by specialized reports. But what was the synthesis lurking in the moldy boxes of data sheets? In part it was empirical. We could group our tasks according to the niches they occupy in modern cognitive psychology or anthropology, and look at how performance differed according to subjects' ages and educational backgrounds. This approach would be consistent with our explicit aim of providing evidence on the role of formal schooling in promoting intellectual development. But none of us felt comfortable with a bare empirical summary. Our idea of the enterprise we were engaged in was changing at least as rapidly as new facts were accumulating.

As reported in *The Cultural Context of Learning and Thinking* (p. 223 ff.) formal schooling in varying amounts affected different kinds of tasks differently. But the pattern of results was not easy to summarize. While we did, indeed, find that educated and noneducated subjects performed differently on a variety of tasks, we were most forcefully struck by the fact that the uneducated subjects performed differently on different versions of tasks we considered logically equivalent.

Two examples will suffice: In one set of studies we were interested in the way small children would learn to select the "correct" block from a pair that differed according to one of its attributes. Two different tasks were presented to two different groups of young children. For one group the blocks varied in brightness; the children learned to choose the darker of two gray blocks. For the other group the blocks varied in size; the children learned to choose the larger one.

Once the task had been mastered (e.g., the child constantly chose the larger or the darker of the two blocks) he was presented with a new pair of blocks. For the group who had learned to discriminate brightnesses, the blocks were two different shades of gray, both *darker* than he had seen before. For the group presented a larger and smaller block, both blocks in the new pair were *larger* than he had seen before.

The issue was: what choice would the child make when presented two blocks he had not seen before? Would he choose the block that was correct according to the *relations* that distinguished the blocks he had been trained on (e.g., "larger," "darker")? Would he choose the block most similar in color or size to the originally correct block? We asked these questions because extensive research in the U.S.A. up to that time had demonstrated that between four and seven years of age, the choices children make on this kind of task shift markedly. Older children tend to make their choices on the basis of relations like larger and darker; younger children tend to select the block most similar to the originally correct one.

According to developmental theories (which disagree on the details, c.f. Bryant 1973) this age-related shift in the choice responses reflects a parallel shift in the basic mechanisms of learning at the different age levels. Consider the quandary this line of reasoning placed us in when we discovered that results for the two forms of the experiment did not coincide. The children asked to learn to choose blocks differing in size almost all selected the larger block on the test trial. But the children asked to learn to choose blocks differing in brightness chose the darker block less than half the time on the test trial. According to the logic of developmental, psychological theory, our Kpelle subjects were in different stages of development, characterized by different rules of learning at the same time!

We encountered a similar problem when we imported a device intended to assess children's ability to make inductive inferences. Again it was the case that age-related changes in performance in the United

States had given rise to theories postulating the development of new capacities as children grew older. In this case, the subject's task was somewhat more complex than the one I have just described. A box with three panels, each covered by a flap, is placed in front of the subject who is seated at a table. The flaps can be lifted one at a time or all together to display the panels singly, or as a unit. The task was presented as follows. First, the subject was taught that pushing the button on the left hand panel would give him a marble. Then he was taught that pushing the button on the right hand panel would give him a ball bearing. Next, the two side panels were closed and the center panel opened. It contained a small tray at the bottom, a slot, and a window through which a piece of candy could be seen. The subject was handed a ball bearing and a marble and told that one of them, if dropped in the slot, would make the candy fall down into the tray. Rarely did anyone require more than a few practice trials to master each of the component tasks. Once this phase of the problem had been reached, all three panels were exposed simultaneously. The subject was told that now his job was to get the candy, which he could keep and eat. This inference task (devised by Tracy and Howard Kendler, who generously gave us the apparatus to use) has several features which make it attractive as a way of analyzing inferences. It specifies the "premises" (the way to get the ball bearing and the marble) from which the "solution" (get the candy) must be reached. It ensures that the subject knows each component of the problem well, but because of its uniqueness, guards against the possibility that the subject could simply remember what to do from some previous experience unknown to us. Our earliest studies with the "inference box" (as we called it) were conducted at our project house near Cuttington College. We had no trouble finding subjects; when the local children learned there was candy to be had we soon had a small throng at the door. We carried the box from house to house when working with older people.

Our first study of inferential behavior using this apparatus indicated that schooling was associated with improved performance. But this result interested us less than the fact that the uneducated subjects, even people in their teens, experienced real difficulty in coming to a solution. Only three out of twenty uneducated teenagers spontaneously pressed the button on the correct side panel and proceeded to drop the appropriate object in the slot. While most could be coaxed step by step to get the candy, there was no evidence of inference playing a role. The difficulties experienced by our older subjects puzzled us. There are only so many things one can do with two buttons, two small round objects and a slot! We were extremely reluctant to come to the conclusion that the ability to make inferences doesn't develop without formal schooling. We had encountered far too much behavior that seemed to require far more difficult reasoning in dealing with these people on an everyday basis to believe in the existence of such a radical deficit. But what was the source of the difficulty? Subjects had learned the component parts of the problem. They seemed to enjoy themselves. Where did the confusion come from? We decided to begin by looking for some form of the task that involved objects Kpelle people would often use. John Gay hit on the idea of keys and locks. We could paint two keys to different doors and arrange it so that only one would open a locked box with candy inside. To simulate the first step in the process we placed a red key in one, distinctively marked matchbox and a black key in another matchbox. Now the subject's initial tasks were to learn which matchbox contained which key and which key opened the locked box. In this version of the problem ninety percent of our subjects, including young children, solved the task. The majority reached for the correct matchbox and solved the problem right away.

Again we encounter an anomaly if we try to interpret performance within the framework of a generalized theory of cognitive development. The same groups of subjects, presented with two forms of the same task, perform ''at different levels.'' In the case of the inference experiment, we were able to carry our work a little further than in the "two block" studies I described earlier. In particular, we were able to establish the component subtask that was the root of the problem especially for the uneducated subjects. In this case, we began our detective work with the matchbox-key-lock version of the problem. Was it just the subjects' familiarity with these objects that facilitated performance? Or, perhaps the important change involved the fact that all of our subjects had learned that keys go in locks long before they ever encountered our strange games. What we needed were familiar objects, but a completely arbitrary relation between the component parts of the problem. To accomplish this goal we resorted to a technological artifice suggested by David Lancy; we cut a slit in the locked box and attached an old fashioned camera shutter button to the lid of the box. When a subject slipped the correct key through the slit in the locked box, we pushed the button that allowed the lid to flip open. Performance was as good or better with this arrangement as it was when the key-lock relation had some operative significance! It appeared that mere familiarity was crucial.

Further work more closely specified the stage in the process at which familiarity exerted its effect. We rigged various combinations of components using both the inference box and our ''Kpelle inference apparatus'' and conducted a rather elaborate study with both Kpelle and American school children. Many interesting observations came out of this study (see Cole, Gay, Glick and Sharp 1971, Appendix K). But for present purposes the key result was to show that unfamiliar objects used in the *early* stages of the problem solving process were critical for impeding performance—if keys from match boxes were dropped into the inference box to get a candy, the solution rate was as good as for the key-lock procedure itself.

Findings such as these pushed us well beyond the limits of our initial enquiry. We had begun *assuming* we could interpret the intellectual consequences of attending school in terms of prevailing psychological theories of cognitive development. As time progressed and contradictions mounted, we were pushed to reject this line of interpretation. But what could we replace it with?

During the 1969–1970 academic year, which I spent at Rockefeller University as a visitor of my former teacher, William Estes, I searched widely in the psychological and anthropological literature for a theoretical framework that would encompass the range of facts we were attempting to cope with. I learned a great deal from my library excursions, but I couldn't find any existing framework to bridge the conceptual and empirical distance between cognitive psychology and cognitive anthropology, nor to resolve the paradoxes I saw in the data.

Our writing and research in recent years represents a continuing search for such a framework (Cole 1975; Cole and Scribner 1975; Scribner and Cole 1973).

By the end of the year (and the last chapter of *The Cultural Context of Learning and Thinking*) we had reached a guiding formulation that rested on a distinction between "having" an ability and knowing how and when to apply it. In 1971 we phrased this distinction as follows:

Cultural differences in cognition reside more in the situations to which particular cognitive processes are applied than in the existence of a process in one cultural group and its absence in another. [Cole et al. 1971, p. 233]

I still believe this statement to be true, but its acceptance should not obscure many unresolved issues. First, it should be noticed that our statement is neatly hedged to allow for the possibility that there exist specific cognitive deficits arising from the absence of specifiable experiences. Our methodological critique of current experimental and inferential practices is not a denial that there may be cultural differences in the *existence* of cognitive process. In fact, when we identify formal schooling as an important and perhaps necessary condition for inducing people to actively organize disjointed information for purposes of remembering it later, we are specifying just such a "lack of prior experience produces cognitive deficit" relationship. It should also be clear that demonstrating that a noneducated Kpelle person has the capacity to organize material for recall or to form new, artificial concepts is not a claim that there are no important differences in cognition. Kpelle children often fail to remember well in school; they may not make "obvious" inferences about the cause of hookworm; they do not readily generalize from $2 + 2 = 4$ and $4 + 4 = 8$ to $2 + 2 + 4 = 8$. These difficulties may all arise from a failure to apply existing capacities effectively to the problem at hand. But the difficulties are none the less real, and they are often the source of great personal suffering.

Although I have become acutely conscious of the ambiguities plaguing cross-cultural studies of intellectual activity, I have by no means decided to chuck the whole enterprise. Rather, in close collaboration with Sylvia Scribner, I have been attempting to formulate methods of comparative research and theory that deal explicitly with the ambiguities and limitations of current research practices.

It has long been the tradition in cross-cultural research, psychological as well as anthropological, to view cultural variations as "natural experiments" providing for unique tests of hypotheses about human societies and human nature. Our attempts to separate the influence of formal education and maturation using the scarcity of educational facilities in Kpelle-land were squarely in this tradition. When there has been debate among psychologists about the interpretation of such work, it has usually focused on the problem of adequately specifying *the* crucial cultural variables (differences in upbringing, environment, education, language) at work. For example, educated and noneducated Kpelle people may differ in many respects other than their exposure to formal education. Especially above grades 2–3, there are undoubtedly strong selective factors at work, rendering comparisons involving high school students risky. Careful consideration of this research problem was pioneered by Campbell (1961) and we have struggled with it as best as we could. However, this use of "culture as an independent variable" approach itself rests on a strong assumption, not generally shared by anthropologists, which we have also come to doubt. This is the assumption, mentioned earlier in this paper, that psychological experiments "tap," "measure" or "assess" specific cognitive processes. The burden of all the work I have been describing urges on us great skepticism when someone fails to perform a task designed to "assess process x." All too often the inference—lack of performance implies lack of process—has been uncritically accepted.

But if we cannot assume experiments are a true reflection of the process we set out to study, what is the point in experimentation? Despite my skepticism about particular ways of drawing inferences from experiments I do not want to suggest that experiments are irrelevant to cross-cultural cognitive research. After all, the behavior we observe is *not* random. Tests often do distinguish systematically between populations. But now we are led to look deeper into tests and experiments themselves. What sort of things are they? What sorts of activities do they demand of subjects? Where else are such demands encountered? If we want to pursue the generalization that noneducated Kpelle will face memory difficulties if they are required to engage spontaneously in structuring to-be-remembered material, we must ask if such situations ever arise in everyday Kpelle life. Further, do they ever arise in the United States outside of school?

Suppose we imagine the task facing a non-literate Kpelle wife who must make a long trip to market. Does she systematically check her larder before she sets off? Does she commit the needed items to memory before leaving? Or does she wait until she reaches the market to "be reminded" of what she needs? Our psychological analysis emphasizes the difference between actively rehearsing to-be-recalled materials and using ready-made recall cues. Which activity does going to market require of the Kpelle housewife?

Many more questions such as these need to be asked for a great variety of cognitive tasks. We need, in effect, an ethnography of cognitive activities, where the nature of each activity is probed by a variety of observations, including experimentally contrived ones.

Relatively early in our thinking we were led to remark that experiments might most usefully be treated as special occasions for the manifestation of cognitive skills. Now I believe that the use of the term skills here may tempt us into misleading inferences, carried over from European-based psychological theory as if the meaning remained intact. Rather, I prefer to speak of experiments as specially contrived occasions for engaging in specified intellectual activities in which many skills may play a role.

At present I would like to believe that both the cognitive anthropologist and the cognitive psychologist are dealing with the same subject matter—intellectual activity. Research using naturalistic observation, formal elicitation and experimentation are all pieces of a single enterprise which seeks to analyze how the varieties of this activity are shaped and organized by the features of the particular situations in which they occur.

For the psychologist this position poses the need to develop new techniques in order to study everyday cognitive activities and their relation to the special activities he designs. It also means the loss of certainty about his most trusted tool, the experiment.

Traditional anthropological analysis provides no easy answer for these problems. There is precious little in the anthropological literature to guide anyone convinced that real life situations as well as experiments must be included in a science of culture and cognition. Neither analysis of belief systems nor sophisticated contrastive analyses of folk taxonomies are likely to carry as far. What we need is ethnography that analyzes cognition as specific sets of activities engaged in on specificable occasions. Whether the resulting research is called anthropology or psychology will then not depend upon objects or methods of observation, but on the theoretical objectives of the researcher. The psychologist will look to the effect of different organizations of activities of individual behavior. The ethnographer will concentrate on the ways larger social factors (economic activities, religion, family structure) organize different intellectual activities.

The research Sylvia Scribner and I are now pursuing, which I call the ethnographic psychology of cognition, aspires to subsume both psychological and ethnographic concerns in a search for the social, experimental determinants of individual cognitive activity.

Better scholars have failed in such an enterprise, so success seems unlikely. But this is my own life's work, in the making.

REFERENCES CITED

Bryant, P.
  1974   *Perception and Understanding in Young Children: An Experimental Approach*. New York: Basic Books.
Campbell, D.
  1961   The Mutual Methodological Relevance of Anthropology and Psychology. In *Psychological Anthropology*, ed. F. L. K. Hsu, pp. 333–52. Homewood, Illinois: Dorsey Press.
Ciborowski, T. and Cole, M.
  1973   A Developmental and Cross-Cultural Study of the Influences of Rule Structure and Problem Composition on the Learning of Conceptual Classifications. *Journal of Experimental Child Psychology* 15:193–215.
Cole, M.
  1975   An Ethnographic Psychology of Cognition. In *Cross-Cultural Perspectives on Learning*. Beverly Hills: Sage Publishers.

Cole, M., Frankel, F. and Sharp, D. W.
   1971   The Development of Free Recall Learning in Children. *Developmental Psychology* 4(2):109–23.
Cole, M., Gay, J., Glick, J. A. and Sharp, D.W.
   1971   *The Cultural Context of Learning and Thinking*. New York: Basic Books.
Cole, M. and Scribner, S.
   1975   Theorizing about Socialization of Cognition. *Ethos* 3(2):249–68.
Gay, J., and Cole, M.
   1967   *The New Mathematics and an Old Culture*. New York: Holt, Rinehart.
Gay, J.
   1973   *Red Dust on Green Leaves*. Thompson, Connecticut: Inter-Culture Associates.
Scribner, S. and Cole, M.
   1973   Cognitive Consequences of Formal and Informal Education. *Science* 182: 553–59.

Concluding Remarks

GEORGE SPINDLER

I do not have in mind a neat set of conclusions, nor do I think anyone reading the volume should arrive at such. I have tried to explore ideas and implications raised by the papers in a fairly free manner in the introductions to Part I and Part II, and these serve some of the functions usually served by concluding chapters. Doubtless alert readers have arrived at relationships and have drawn inferences that have not occurred to me.

This book is titled *The Making of Psychological Anthropology*. The term "psychological anthropology" is itself fairly new. Probably its use in the title of Francis Hsu's edited text (first edition 1961) can be thought of as marking the watershed between culture and personality and psychological anthropology. Such nomenclature implies a strong potential or real relationship between psychology and anthropology. What is the state of this relationship?

In 1953 M. Brewster Smith, a psychologist, said "the boundary dividing these disciplines (anthropology, psychology, and sociology) from one another is by no means sharp, stable, or justified on obviously rational grounds" (Smith 1953, p. 32). He goes on to say that they are academic specializations that emerged late in the nineteenth century, and that it would be hard to "give satisfactory conceptual definitions that would unmistakably distinguish the three disciplines for the uninitiated," and yet "practically no one who is professionally involved in them has any doubt about whether he is a psychologist, an anthropologist, or a sociologist" (ibid., p. 32). He ends his discussion with cautious optimism to the effect that the emergence of "a comprehensive structure is possible if we will give explicit attention to the problems of articulation in framing working concepts and hypotheses" (ibid, p. 66).

Nearly a quarter of a century later nothing much seems to have changed. The three disciplines have continued to develop separately their lore, their criteria of credibility, their values, and their models of theory and methodology. A few individuals cross over from one discipline to another in their interests and research, but there has been no general synthesis leading to a new comprehensive structure. A sampling of recent introductory psychology texts by this editor shows very little use of anthropological data or concepts, and citations are limited to a very few anthropologists—usually Margaret Mead and one or two others. A similar analysis of introductory anthropology texts reveals a slightly different situation in that there is usually a chapter on personality and culture or the individual and culture, but almost no psychologists are cited. Citations are reserved almost exclusively for anthropologists who have written in these areas. Introductory textbooks may be the last to change, but if there had been any substantial disciplinary interpenetration one would expect it to show up in such texts.

Robert Edgerton, in a review of two recent works in cross-cultural psychology, considers the relationships between this field and psychological anthropology, an interaction that one would think likely to be sympathetic and productive (Edgerton 1974). He points out that both fields want to discover general truths about human nature and that though psychologists tend to be more etic and nomothetic in approach, and anthropologists more emic and idiographic, the differences are a matter of degree. Both subdisciplines agree that "success in their enterprise calls for etic comparison based upon emic equivalents" (ibid., p. 62). He points to some "emerging convergence" between the fields, best exemplified in the work of Michael Cole and his associates. He concludes that the reason why cross-cultural psychology and psychological anthropology have not converged more rapidly is because of basic differences in research paradigms and background assumptions centering on the issue of experimental methodology. Most cross-cultural psychologists remain committed to experimental procedures as their ultimate means of verification. Most anthropologists are fundamentally opposed to experimental procedures. Experimenter and experimental effects seem, from an anthropological point of view, to distort results unacceptably, given the fact the experimental procedures are carried from the West to the non-West.

Edgerton sums up his analysis of anthropological rejection of experimental methods and their assumptions:

At heart anthropologists are naturalists whose commitment is to the phenomena themselves. Anthropologists have always believed that human phenomena can best be understood by procedures that are primarily sensitive to context, be it situational, social, or cultural. Our methods are primarily unobtrusive, non-reactive ones; we observe, we participate, we learn, hopefully we understand. We rarely experiment, and then only under special conditions. This is our unspoken paradigm and it is directly at odds with the discovery of truth by experimentation which, at least as many anthropologists see it, ignores context and creates reactions. [ibid., p. 64]

There is ample evidence in the papers in this volume that Edgerton is essentially correct in his assessment of the anthropological *Zeitgeist* and the reasons for anthropological rejection and suspicion of the research paradigms of cross-cultural psychology. He is also correct when he argues that we must reconcile two apparently unreconcilable paradigms —experimentalism and naturalism—if there is to be much meaningful convergence. Again, of the current work, that of Price-Williams and Cole and his associates represents the longest steps taken in this direction. They have come to question the experimental method and have turned increasingly toward ethnography. And there are anthropologists who do essentially cross-cultural psychology, including cross-cultural social psychology.

There are some straws in the wind that suggest that psychologists may be taking anthropological paradigms seriously. I have already mentioned the presidential address of Donald T. Campbell to the American Psychological Association meetings in 1975. The major thrust of the address is that psychology should take the validity of moral structures and problem solutions represented in existing society more seriously, for they are more time and trouble tested than any theories about behavior that psychologists or psychiatrists have devised. The paper is complex and ranges widely over an enormous variety of material. I find it instructive and very enjoyable. I particularly enjoy such sentences as "Alexander (1975) adds the hypothesis that biological evolution has selected human beings so as to repress from conscious awareness the ruthless selfishness of their own behavior, so as to produce a more sincere hypocrisy" (Campbell 1975, p. 1112). The point, however, is that Campbell cites a great deal of anthropological literature, most of it admittedly by evolutionists and not psychological anthropologists, but raises questions that are a far cry from conventional, tough-minded, agentic, to - be - answered - experimentally - and - nomothetically, type of questions that are more usually the style of respectable psychologists. They are not exactly anthropological questions. But most of the questions he raises can only be studied effectively using anthropological approaches (in combination with others) and he has rediscovered a kind of cultural relativism.

The Distinguished Scientific Award Address, at the meetings of the American Psychological Association in New Orleans, in September 1974 by Lee J. Cronbach, is even more direct evidence of significant movement from within psychology that may make some form of convergence between the two disciplines more likely. Cronbach, highly respected as a tough-minded academic psychologist, expresses pessimism about the predominant norms and strategies currently employed in the quest for nomothetic theory (Cronbach 1974, p. 116). He berates psychologists for not taking into account important variables in natural settings and cites as an example emerging evidence that social class moderates instructional effects so that the lower-class child responds better to "didactic teaching, with explicit requirements and close-coupled rewards." The problem-oriented, ego-motivated supportive methods of teaching, long advocated by educational psychologists, benefit only the middle-class child (Cronbach 1974, p. 121). He points out that even the animal experimenter is not immune to such interactions, and goes on to say, "The experimental strategy dominant in psychology since 1950 has only limited ability to detect interactions" (ibid., p. 123), and states that "the time has come to exorcise the null hypothesis," and calls for descriptions that "encourage us to think constructively about results" (ibid., p. 124). He emphasizes that "generalizations decay" due to changes in the natural settings in which they were originally established. And finally he calls for "intensive local observation" going beyond discipline to an "open-eyed, open-minded, appreciation of the surprises nature deposits in the investigative net. I suspect that if the psychologist were to read more widely in histroy, ethnology, and the centuries of humanistic writings on man and society, he would be better prepared for this part of his work" (ibid., p. 125).

Two psychologists, however distinguished, do not constitute a movement, but it seems likely that what they have said constitutes both an index of something going on in psychology and influential statements that will reinforce this kind of movement and give it legitimacy. It is possible that with movement of this kind in psychology, and the traditional eclecticism of anthropologists and their growing concern with credibility in research and the analysis of results, there might actually be a productive convergence.

We should recognize that the trend noted above supports not all, but some of what we anthropologists have been doing all along. Our naturalistic, emic, participant, nonobtrusive strategy has produced much that is good and useful. We should not forsake it in favor of strategies that psychologists are just beginning to question. Most of us have also realized we must combine idiographic and nomothetic methods to answer many of our questions. We can do much better than we have in examining psychological concepts and research results, and incorporating them into our work. Whether this will result in some kind of renaissance in psychological anthropology or the emergence of a new kind of field we cannot know. We can be sure that psychologizing in anthropology will not stop, for the psychological processes are at the core of the human adaptation whether we are dealing with relatively stable cultural systems or with (more frequently the case) changing systems and changing conditions of existence. As we look back over the papers in this volume it appears we have not done too badly. We have tried various approaches. Some have been productive. We have learned from our mistakes. We have been naive about theory. We are becoming more sophisticated. We aren't about to forget we are anthropologists, but we are becoming aware that others have something to say that we should know about. And our world view may be finding its way into the other moiety.

REFERENCES CITED

Campbell, D. T.
    1975   On the Conflicts Between Biological and Social Evolution and Between Psychology and Moral Tradition. *American Psychologist* 30:1103–26.
Cronbach, L. J.
    1975   Beyond the Two Disciplines of Scientific Psychology. *American Psychologist* 30:116–26.
Edgerton, R. B.
    1974   Cross-Cultural Psychology and Psychological Anthropology: One Paradigm or Two? *Reviews in Anthropology* 1:52–64.
Hsu, F., ed.
    1961   *Psychological Anthropology: Approaches to Culture and Personality*. Homewood, Ill.: Dorsey Press.
Smith, M. B.
    1954   Anthropology and Psychology. In *For a Science of Social Man*, ed. J. Gillin, pp. 32–66. New York: The MacMillan Co.

Index of Authors

General Index

Abel Limited Free Design Test, 92

Abnormal and normal behavior, 155–156; cultural relativism of, 481–482; and deviance, 447; distinguished from adaptation, 375, 403

Abortion, 369–370

Abstract thought, and tests for classificatory ability, 587–594, 597, 616, 620–627

Acculturation, 498; among the Blood Indians, 189–191, 192, 193; and child rearing among Spanish Americans, 535–548; controlled comparisons of, 188–191; among the Dakota Indians, 73; development of psychological approach to, 11, 176–178; in Haitian culture and religion, 480–481, 485; Instrumental Activities Inventory and theoretical model as a technique in study of, 191–194; of Japanese-Americans, 226; "levels" of, 179; among the Manus, 420; among the Menomini Indians, 178–181, 185–192, 450–451; and migration in New Zealand, 549–550; model of using Voluntary-Involuntary and Adoptive-Reactive dimensions, 543–544, 547, 548; and personality among the Wisconsin Chippewa, 67, 68–74; related to economic access and drinking behavior, 525–535 *passim;* related to social and psychological disorganization, 517, 525–529; Rorschach techniques used in study of, 178–188, 190, 195, 197; and urbanization, 176–177, 193–195, 530–548 *passim. See also* Adaptation; Psychocultural change and urbanization

Acculturative adaptation: alternative models in study of, 530–531; psychological and sociocultural processes in, 178–187; social interaction as variable in study of, 187–188

Achievement motivation: and culture and personality among Japanese-Americans, 221–226; and economic access among the Navaho Indians, 532–534

Adaptation, 1, 388; elicited by ecological circumstances, 451–454; by the Japanese to change, 219–256; general adaptation syndrome, 208; and normal and abnormal behavior, 375, 403

Admiralty Islands, 101–102, 410, 417, 421, 422

Affect: and culture, 157–158; as intimacy, 162; vs. role, 156–157, 164

Africa: ecological conditions and adaptation in, 451–454; mathematical education in, 614–615, 616, 628; possession trance cults in, 499–500

Agamemnon, 161

Age: and the ability for abstract thought, 590–592, 593; and changes in responses to tests, 624–625; and consistent changes in behavior, 56

Aggression: and cultural determinism, 338–343; and dependency as a characteristic, 368; as a function of historically specific cultural determinants, 339; group differences in, 358; internalization of and suicide, 254–255; as an invariant psychological characteristic, 352; psychological theory of, 339–340; training for, 48

Agricultural subsistence, and possession trances, 504, 506–507

Ainu, the, 240

Alcohol. *See* Drinking behavior

Algonkian Indians, 80, 83, 84, 212

Alienation: and deviancy, 238–240; and suicide, 249, 251

Alorese: child training and personality among, 154; diversity and deviance among, 450; personality generalizations about, 65

Altered states of consciousness (ASC), 2, 479–511; anthropological interest in, 477, 508; contemporary analysis of as primitive, 608; model of culturally patterned, 506; ritualized, 502; as a term, 494; universal human capacity for, 502; visionary revelations during, 206. *See also* Spirit possession; Trance states

Amae, defined, 252

American Anthropological Association, 121, 214, 268, 282, 285, 336, 366

American Anthropologist, 166, 385

American Historical School, 42

American Museum of Natural History, 101